Mastering

Excel 2003 Programming
with VBA

Mastering™
Excel 2003 Programming with VBA

Steven M. Hansen

SYBEX®

San Francisco   London

Associate Publisher: Joel Fugazzotto

Acquisitions Editor: Tom Cirtin

Developmental Editor: Brianne Agatep

Production Editor: Susan Berge

Technical Editor: Acey Bunch

Copyeditor: Rebecca C. Rider

Compositor: Jeff Wilson, Happenstance Type-O-Rama

Proofreaders: Laurie O'Connell, Amy J. Rasmussen, Nancy Riddiough

Indexer: Ted Laux

Book Designer: Maureen Forys, Happenstance Type-O-Rama

Cover Designer: Design Site

Cover Illustrator: Tania Kac, Design Site

Library of Congress Card Number: 2003115586

ISBN: 0-7821-4281-8

Manufactured in the United States of America

10 9 8 7 6 5 4 3 2 1

005.54
H

Dedicated to my
mom to whom I am
indebted for instilling
in me a hefty dose of
curiosity, patience,
and independence

Acknowledgments

WRITING A BOOK OF this type is an interesting activity. As you may suspect, it is also very solitary. Thankfully, though, you don't have to read the raw manuscript. Many people contributed their special talents to translate my thoughts into the cohesive whole you are holding.

My development editor, Brianne Agatep, kept me focused, fed my ego with praise, and managed the entire project. Brianne, you are tops on my list. Thank you for all of your hard work and encouragement.

The production editor handles the schedule for the project and makes sure everything runs smoothly. My production editor was Susan Berge. Susan did a wonderful job of keeping everything moving according to schedule.

My technical editor was Acey Bunch. Acey had a tough job—he not only had to read each chapter to check it for technical accuracy, he also tested all of the listings to see if they all worked as they should. Acey went above and beyond by performing all his required duties and providing me with many useful comments and suggestions.

In my opinion, the copy editor, Rebecca Rider, had the toughest job. She had to make sure each chapter lived up to the grammatical standards of my publisher. You should see all of the edits she made! Thank you, Rebecca, for making me look like I know how to put together a sentence.

I must extend a special thanks to the acquisitions editor, Tom Cirtin, for his help in getting me involved with this book and all of the constructive feedback he provided throughout the project.

Thanks as well to the rest of the staff at Sybex including Amy Romanoff who was responsible for the cover copy; the folks at Happenstance Type-O-Rama who laid out the book; proofreaders Laurie O'Connell, Amy J. Rasmussen, and Nancy Riddiough; and indexer Ted Laux.

I would also like to thank my former colleagues Chris Kunicki and Charles Maxson. Chris and Charles run the OfficeZealot.com website—a useful site for VBA/Microsoft Office developers. Chris and Charles gave me several ideas and provided some useful information about XML and Smart Document functionality.

No one knows how much work it is to write a book (especially on top of your "regular" job) better than the close friends and family of an author. The process of writing this book had a profound impact on those closest to me. I mean, does a five-year-old really understand why you suddenly can't play with him as much as you used to? Cole, it tore at my heart to leave the house to go write on the weekends rather than play with you.

Do you know how movie stars and producers always emphasize their thanks to their spouses when they receive an award for their hard work? I now understand and appreciate this practice. Any significant undertaking is hard work, but all of the satisfaction of completing it goes to the person doing the work, not the person who has to stay at home and take up the slack of the "I'm too busy" spouse. Therefore, I would like to end by extending a heartfelt thank you to my wife Kelly for managing without me while I was writing. You put your needs on hold through this whole process to care for our newborn daughter Kennedy and our son Cole without much help from me. Thank you with all of my heart.

Contents at a Glance

Contents

Introduction

Do you enjoy helping people? Are you seeking the warm satisfaction associated with creating value? If you learn how to develop applications based in Excel, you will be a happier person because you'll have the opportunity to help people and create value by creating applications that allow people to work *much* more efficiently.

I was talking to an Excel guru the other day. We were reflecting on what we have enjoyed most about our consulting careers. We both agreed that the most satisfying aspect of our career is the fulfillment we experience after solving some problem and witnessing the genuine satisfaction and elation a client expresses in the result.

Because so many people spend their whole day working with Excel and because it is so easy to program in Excel using Visual Basic for Applications (VBA), you still have a lot of opportunity to develop useful applications that create value. This book will teach you how to develop such applications based in Excel using VBA and, according to the preceding logic, lead you to happiness.

Philosophy

There are many approaches to presenting technical information. One approach is to write a voluminous tome of dry, factual information and leave it up to the reader to figure out how to apply the information or decipher the useful content from the not-so-useful content. You may have come across these types of books before. They are much like the information in help files, except rearranged.

At the other extreme, you can write to the dummies. That is, you can write a book that can be read without much mental activity on the part of the reader. In order to write a book like this, you must stick to trivial content and trivial examples. It is then up to the reader to figure out how to make the mental leap from the trivial examples presented in the book to the complexities presented by real-world problems. From my own observations, it seems as though most people don't make the leap (they buy another book instead). I've always thought that in order to learn, you have to exercise the brain. No pain, no gain, right?

Hopefully I've achieved something of a middle ground with this book. I did not cover every nook and cranny associated with Excel development. Nor did I hesitate to get in deep on the topics that are critical to developing Excel applications. I picked the topics that have been most important to my development experience and presented the necessary facts about them along with illustrations of useful ways to apply them. Finally, I hope that I've sprinkled this book with just enough good-natured reflection and commentary to make this a more colorful read than other programming books. If this book were a television, I would like to think of it as an HDTV.

Finally, I've attempted to inject a significant amount of real-world examples in this book. In order to become proficient in Excel development, you'll need to develop your own collection of generic procedures or building blocks. By building on your prebuilt foundation, so to speak, you can churn out applications with less effort and in a shorter amount of time. In order to help you acquire your own foundation of generic routines, I present many useful procedures that illustrate the topic at hand. I use many of these procedures in nearly every application I build.

Who Are You?

This book was written to two primary audiences: Excel power users who want to learn how to program, and programmers who want to learn about the Excel object model. That said, anyone who wants to acquire Excel VBA development skills will find useful information in this book. I should also add that this book was written with a corporate audience in mind. If you aren't part of that audience, fear not, you won't have any trouble understanding the material, you'll just find that many of the examples are business oriented.

Excel power users are people who use Excel on a daily basis for their job, are comfortable using it, and are fairly knowledgeable about Excel's functionality. If you are part of this group of readers, you may be interested in acquiring some Excel development skills so that you can automate aspects of your job. I recommend that this group read this book cover to cover, paying particular attention to the first two parts (through Chapter 10).

Programmers bring a different perspective to the table. Programmers can span the spectrum in terms of programming skill and general knowledge of Excel. If you do not have experience with Visual Basic, I would recommend that you read the first two parts (Chapters 1–10) and then those chapters applicable to your situation. If you have a fair amount of experience with Visual Basic, I'd advise you to focus primarily on the second part (Chapters 5–10), which deals with the Excel object model, and then read the chapters applicable to your situation.

Regardless of your background, everyone should pay particular attention to Part 2, which covers the Excel object model. These chapters are critical to developing any useful Excel development skills.

The remaining sections of the book are organized by high-level task with the exception of Part 3, which focuses on slightly more advanced topics such as developing classes and best practices. If you need to integrate Excel with other applications or use data from an external data source, you'll find coverage of this material in Part 4. Finally, the book ends with Part 5, which covers user interface development.

Version Differences Are Not Critical

I developed the examples in this book using Excel 2003. For the most part, however, you can apply the material presented to previous versions of Excel back to Excel 97. If you are working with an older version of Excel, you may occasionally see a reference to an object in this book that is not available in your version. Generally, if you're familiar with the incremental functionality offered by each version of Excel, you'll already have a good idea of what type of programmatic differences there are between versions. These differences are minor in the grand scheme of things. In fact, I still approach projects the same way today as I did with Excel 97. For that matter, you could also use many of the procedures in this book with Excel 5.0. In fact, I wrote some of the procedures presented in this book using Excel 5.0 in 1996.

However, two chapters contain information specific to Excel 2003: the chapter concerning Excel XML functionality (Chapter 17) and the chapter covering the development of Smart Documents (Chapter 21). As far as I'm concerned, XML functionality and Smart Document technology are the two most exciting improvements in Excel 2003.

Website Extras

All of the examples presented in this book are available on the web at www.dakotatechgroup.com/ExcelVBA. In addition to the example workbooks, I'll post any updates, corrections, and other useful information related to this book. You can also obtain the example workbooks from Sybex's website (www.sybex.com).

Your Feedback Is Important

Before I move on, I'd like to say that your feedback is important to me. Although I might not be able to respond to all of your comments and questions, I guarantee that I'll read them all. Please feel free to e-mail your questions and comments to me at ExcelVBA@dakotatechgroup.com.

I hope you enjoy reading this book as much as I enjoyed writing it. Well, as much as it is possible to enjoy reading a technical book anyway. Happy reading....

Part 1

Introduction to Excel Development

Chapter 1

Excel as a Development Platform

I OFTEN FIND MYSELF explaining what it means when I say I am an Excel developer. People have heard of Java developers, C/C++ developers, Visual Basic developers, web developers, and many other various technologies that people develop in, but an Excel developer?

This chapter introduces you to what it means to be an Excel developer and why Microsoft Excel makes such an interesting and useful development platform for many types of applications.

Who Develops in Excel?

When I was younger, I remember wanting to be many different things: a dolphin trainer, a professional hockey player, and a pilot, to name a few. I also went through a phase when I thought it would be cool to be a programmer (except as a kid I wanted to develop games, not boring business programs). Then I grew up and my priorities changed. In fact, in my first "real" career job, I was a financial analyst. At no point in my life did I plan on becoming an Excel developer; it just happened. The factors that drove me to become one are interesting and, I believe, quite common in the corporate world.

First, most analysts, and many other "knowledge workers" for that matter, live and breathe spreadsheets. I was no different in that regard. I figured the better I understood all of the features and functions available in Excel, the better I would become at my job as it would enable me to analyze data more efficiently and with fewer mistakes.

Second, the analytical process tends to be a very tedious affair. Generally, you need to pull data from disparate systems and organize it in a way that provides meaning. Then repeat, and repeat, and repeat as reporting cycles dictate. You have daily tasks, weekly tasks, monthly tasks, and so on. You need to work quickly *and* accurately—two characteristics that are generally diametrically opposed. The greater the pressure to finish something, the easier it is to make mistakes. I felt that I spent more time collecting and formatting data then I did analyzing or thinking critically about the results. To me, this didn't seem right. There had to be a better way.

Third, I had a manager who recognized my interests and understood the potential productivity gains that could be had via analytical automation—that is, automating the analytical process. This manager understood that though it takes a little more time upfront to build solutions rather than just spreadsheets, the time could be easily recouped with each reporting cycle.

Finally, I had a genuine interest in technology in general. I enjoyed learning about the different ways I could employ technology to make my life easier. I found that employing technology to make my job less tedious had immediate rewards that served to reinforce my interest.

The result of all of these factors was that after a few years as a financial analyst, I came to realize that my true calling was as a developer and not just any developer. I was an Excel developer, a developer specializing in developing analytical applications.

What Is an Excel Application?

First of all, I should define what I mean by an Excel application. By Excel application, I mean a spreadsheet that you have developed using Excel and VBA for use by yourself or other users. VBA stands for Visual Basic for Applications, which is essentially Visual Basic that has been modified to run within other host applications such as Excel or Microsoft Word. Excel applications contain VBA code that may perform one or more of the following tasks:

Automate tedious processes.   Many times, once you create a useful spreadsheet, in order to maintain it, you need to perform a set of tasks in a specific order on a frequent basis. Often, you can automate such simple tasks using Excel's macro recorder. For more complex tasks you need to write VBA code.

Enhance the user experience.   The experience and comfort level of people using Excel varies widely. One way to spread the wealth of a useful spreadsheet is to incorporate a user interface into the workbook that can serve to guide the less experienced users and help the more experienced users work more efficiently.

Hide the underlying complexity of a spreadsheet.   One of the quickest ways to limit the usefulness of an otherwise excellent spreadsheet is to expose people to numerous worksheets containing an expanse of calculations or data. You can use VBA to manage the layout and display of a workbook so that users don't get lost in your otherwise brilliant work.

Integrate with another application or database.   Most corporate data is locked in other applications or databases. By enabling Excel to integrate with these sources of data, you can empower users to analyze this data with much greater efficiency.

Prevent the modification of certain aspects of a spreadsheet.   Once you have laboriously created your spreadsheet, you are apt to have sections that others could modify to their own detriment. To prevent this from occurring, you can use various techniques to allow others to interact with the workbook only in the ways that you intended.

Some Excel applications contain very little code. These applications are models that are thoughtfully and consciously designed for the task at hand by applying sound design methodologies to the design of a spreadsheet. Although you'll find a sprinkling of advice regarding general design methodologies throughout this book, I focus more on teaching you how to use VBA rather than how to design efficient spreadsheets.

A Short Survey of Excel Applications

Over the course of my career, I have had the opportunity to observe hundreds of ways that various corporations use Excel. I am continually amazed at their creativity. Many times Excel is used appropriately; however, some applications in Excel are clearly the result of a developer (or otherwise) who did not know how to solve the problem using other technology better suited for the task at hand. In these cases, though I personally would not have chosen Excel as my canvas, I am often impressed that Excel solved the problem. To this I attribute the imagination of the creator and the broad *and* deep capabilities of Excel.

I have seen or developed Excel applications that are used for a diverse range of activities. Some of the uses that I have seen or developed include these:

Investment research publication   A blue-chip investment bank used Excel to pull data from a back-end database, assemble the data in a meaningful manner, and create a printer-ready, 100+ page document that included financial data and statistics, reports, a Table of Contents, and an index.

Sales quote generation   A manufacturing company used Excel to create a sophisticated sales quote application. This application incorporated the detailed specifications required by their customers and produced a set of reports that specified costs, engineering specifications, and a quote for the client.

Budget/forecast models   Nearly every firm I have had the opportunity to work with uses Excel in some shape/form in their budget or forecast process. These models have ranged from simple one-worksheet models to very complex workbooks that integrate with various other applications.

Complex financial analysis   Excel is so well suited for financial analysis that it is no surprise that firms use it to perform many of their most complex analysis tasks. A standout example in this category would be an extremely complex financial model that estimates the gain associated with various portfolios of asset-backed securities. Here's another example: if you're familiar with the concept of Economic Value Added (EVA) and Market Value Added (MVA) developed by Stern Stewart, you may be interested to know that Stern Stewart's own EVA application is an amazingly sophisticated example that is developed using Excel.

Sales commission models   A financial services company developed an Excel application that used detailed sales data to determine the commission earned by each sales representative.

Financial proposal generators   A large financial services company used Excel, in conjunction with Microsoft Access and Microsoft Word, to develop an application that would allow advisors to assemble a "custom" financial profile of a client along with recommendations that fit the client's risk tolerance and financial objectives.

Many times I view Excel as the Swiss Army knife of the software world—maybe it is not the best tool for all purposes, but it is adequate for most and flat out excellent for many. As much as I admire the versatility of Excel, I must point out one thing, which I can say without hesitation: Excel is miserable as a word processor. Oddly enough, some have tried to prove me wrong on this one, but they've failed sensationally.

Why Use Excel?

Many people with only a superficial knowledge of Excel ask the question, "Why develop an application using Excel?" I say "superficial" because in my own experience, many people claim to be familiar with Excel, but on further qualification or observation, they do not *know* Excel. Because they don't know Excel, they may have a hard time envisioning what kind of application could possibly be built. It would be like someone who knows of only 16 colors trying to envision how to produce a work of art. Artists know how to blend colors to create a full palette that they can use to create amazing masterpieces.

This does not mean that you must be an Excel guru to start developing with Excel. However, I would strongly suggest that you continue to expand your knowledge of Excel's capabilities in general. You'll find that as your knowledge of Excel grows, your development skills will benefit, and vice versa.

So, why use Excel as a development platform? Here is a short list.

- ◆ You can build on the functionality of Excel rather than starting from scratch.
- ◆ Excel is already installed on nearly every corporate PC.
- ◆ Excel applications are easy to distribute.
- ◆ Your users already have some degree of experience using Excel.
- ◆ Excel applications can be developed very rapidly.
- ◆ VBA is relatively easy to learn.

Let's investigate these reasons in a little more depth.

Extend a Great Product

When you use Excel as a development platform, your application has access to all of Excel's functionality and then some, and this is all without you having to write a single line of code. That means you already have a way to gather input and display output, *and* you have a sophisticated calculation engine all without doing a single thing. If you write an application using Visual Basic, Java, or some other language, you need to consider how to handle these aspects and code them from scratch.

Two huge benefits arise from not having to start from scratch. First, when you start from scratch you have to write a lot more code and more code means a longer development cycle. Second, by using Excel's native capabilities, you get to use the proven performance and reliability of Excel; this means that you can reap the benefit of countless man-hours of development and testing from Microsoft, as well as testing and use by millions of users around the world. Contrast that against starting from scratch where the code you write may be exposed to maybe dozens or maybe even hundreds of development and testing hours.

Millions of Potential Users

You are probably not targeting every Excel user worldwide for your application, but if you are, you have a potential market numbering in the millions. Some compatibility issues exist between different versions of Excel, but in general, all your customer needs to run the application you develop is a copy of Excel. Think about it; unless you're a government worker in Munich (the government there recently adopted Linux as its operating system, and will therefore, presumably not be using Microsoft Excel), your business and nearly every other business of decent size uses Excel to some extent.

File ➤ Send To...

Not every Excel application can be distributed by simply sending the file to the intended user, but many can. You'll find that you have numerous options available for distributing your Excel application, and most are as simple as clicking File ➤ Send To to send the file to the intended recipient. Contrast that to installing traditional applications.

As you may know, installing traditional applications can be problematic on multiple levels. First, you must create a setup program just to install your application. You have to be sure that any dependent files are installed on the system and if they aren't, you have to install them too. Often, these dependent files are shared files known as dynamic link libraries, or DLLs. Managing DLLs on a system is frustrating at best. What happens is that many applications are dependent on a specific version of a DLL. When a new application is installed, occasionally the new application overwrites an older version of a DLL with a new version, breaking other applications that depend on the old version. When software that has run flawlessly in the past suddenly stops working, suspect number one is the last software package that you installed.

The second problem is that many organizations have strict, sometimes draconian, policies regarding the installation of new programs or the modification of any programs already installed on the computer. Often these policies are for good reason. However, for smaller, departmental type applications, these policies mean that more work is involved in dotting all the i's and crossing all the t's than it takes to develop and test the application.

Sadly, I have worked with many departments that are not pleased with the "customer service" they receive from their own IT departments and are loathe to do anything that places them in a position of being increasingly reliant on IT. By developing an application using Microsoft Excel or one of the other Microsoft Office products, you can fly under the radar, so to speak. Occasionally this tactic is used by project sponsors to develop a proof of concept and demonstrate the potential value of solving a particular problem. Once others see the potential, you'll find that it is much easier to obtain the necessary approvals to develop a traditional application.

Exploit the Knowledge Base

Although proficiency levels vary widely, most corporate employees have some experience with Excel. Why not exploit that familiarity rather than force them to learn something entirely new?

In my opinion, one of the big drawbacks in the corporate rush to put every application on their intranet is that, so far, web applications offer little in terms of interaction with the data they present. Web applications are great for disseminating data, but lousy at aiding the analytical process. Unless the application designers dream up every conceivable way that someone would want to look at the data, inevitably people will need to export, copy/paste, or manually rekey the data into another application. Which application do you think they will put this data in? So if one of the objectives of your application is to facilitate analysis, why not deliver the application using a medium that your users understand and use for analysis in the first place?

Rapid Development. Really.

Just about every development tool these days promises rapid development. Excel can truly deliver it. One reason, as I talked about already, is that you are building on top of Excel with all of Excel's functionality already there for your use. You do not have to worry about writing code for input, output, to support printing, and so on.

Another reason is that the code you write will be using Visual Basic. Visual Basic was originally developed specifically for rapid application development. It is a proven language in this regard.

It's Not Rocket Science...

Finally, developing applications using Excel is not rocket science. If you are familiar with *either* Excel *or* a programming language, especially Visual Basic, you will be successful, provided you have a genuine interest in acquiring the skill.

If you have a good background using Excel, then you won't have to work so hard to understand the Excel object model, which is just a fancy term for the way that you refer to various Excel objects programmatically. You should focus initially on the basics of learning VBA.

If you have a background with another programming language, you'll find VBA very easy to pick up. You'll need to spend more time becoming familiar with the Excel object model.

Stop When You See Red

Sometimes Excel is not an appropriate solution. Well, at least it's not appropriate as the only component of your solution. Many times, I see Excel used as a database. There is a fine line when it comes to using Excel as a database. Using the term database to describe the use of Excel in this manner is, in all fairness, an injustice to real database products. A better way to think of Excel's capabilities in this regard is that it functions as a list manager.

If your list is small, maybe a couple thousand rows at most, Excel may be adequate for your needs. However, I would urge you to consider using a database to handle the storage of your data. You can still use Excel to analyze and display your data; you'll learn techniques to do this later in the book.

If your list is larger, you really should use a database. Microsoft Access is a good choice because it is probably already installed on your computer if you have Excel, and it contains many features that help beginners learn the basics of using a database.

Making the call as to when to use a database comes with experience. Generally however, when you find yourself writing a lot of code to manage or otherwise work with a list in Excel, a big red light should come on in your head. You should stop immediately and do the following three things. First, import all of your data into a table in Access. Second, investigate the capabilities of Microsoft Query for bringing necessary data from your database into Excel for analytical or reporting purposes. Third, check out Chapter 16 to learn how to programmatically retrieve data from a database and use the data in your spreadsheet.

By combining Access (or another database product) and Excel, you will significantly expand your capabilities to develop capable and sophisticated systems that can handle large amounts of data.

With time, the following statement will become clear, but anytime you are writing a lot of code to deal with one particular facet of an application, red flags should appear in your mind. You'll know it when this happens to you—your code will seem awkward and complex. This is not right. Stop, take a breather, and reevaluate. Evaluate three things: your design, the technology you used to develop a solution, and the application of the technology you choose. One or more of these is wrong. You may find some advice regarding your problem in Chapter 13.

A Reflection on the Learning Curve

I believe that learning how to develop in Excel using VBA is easy. That said, you'll notice a dramatic improvement in your ability to churn out applications efficiently as you progress. When I first started learning VBA in Excel 5.0, I had a significant amount of experience with Excel. In fact, I was the Excel guru at work. Back then, the development environment wasn't nearly as friendly and hospitable to beginners as it is now. You actually had to memorize the Excel object model—you didn't have IntelliSense to show you applicable properties and methods (we'll discuss IntelliSense in the next chapter). Anyway, developing an average application might have taken 3 months or more once I got past the initial learning stage. These days, the average application takes 2 or 3 weeks. Many smaller applications can be completed in less than a week, simple utilities can be completed in as little as 15 to 30 minutes, and user-defined functions can be coded in a matter of minutes.

In my experience, many people are interested in developing proficiency with VBA but never really commit to it. Therefore, they never get to the point where they are able to start applying it. It can be difficult to commit to at first. You've got a million things to do and not enough time to do it all. Who's got time to learn something new? Believe me, though; learning VBA will yield huge dividends to you. Once you develop a little proficiency, you'll be able to automate various tasks that you perform manually now. The timesavings by automating these tasks can be orders of magnitude. Tasks that take hours of manual effort can be reduced to minutes and completed with the click of a mouse. Many of the repetitive tasks that knowledge workers perform can also be automated by creating simple utilities.

As you progress, not only will you become much more efficient at using Excel's object model, but you'll develop a critical mass of code that you can reuse later in other applications. This book will get you off to a great start by providing you with many generic routines that you're apt to find useful in nearly every application you write.

Summary

Many people do not realize that they can develop applications in Excel or understand why they would want to. The next time you tell someone that you develop in Excel, look them straight in the eye and tell them that you create a significant amount of value by creating Excel applications. Excel applications have tremendous potential to help people work more efficiently and they provide ways to manipulate and therefore internalize data in ways that would be impossible or difficult to do otherwise. Before they give you a rebuttal, mention that your applications are completed in less time than it takes to design an application using traditional methods and technologies. Finally, be sure to tell them how much fun you have doing it. When your web developer friend chuckles at this, smile and tell her that just last week you finished in application that enabled users to actually *analyze* the data obtained from a web application rather than merely view it.

Well, hopefully you are now even more motivated to start learning how to develop Excel applications using VBA, so let's dig in and get going. Your first task is to take an inventory of the development environment, the Visual Basic Editor.

Chapter 2

Getting to Know Your Environment

BEFORE YOU CAN START writing any serious code, you need to learn your way around the development environment. In this chapter, you'll examine the various aspects and features of the Visual Basic Editor (VBE). The VBE includes many features that do an excellent job of easing beginning developers into programming and helping experienced developers become more productive.

Personally, I have always disliked these kinds of chapters because I am always so eager to get on to the good stuff. If you have felt the same with other books, I hope you'll find this a little different. I am fairly confident that you'll find a few nuggets here that will make you glad you took the time to read it.

NOTE   *While exploring the VBE, you may come across functionality related to developing User Forms and debugging. I'll cover the features related to these topics separately. In Chapter 4, I'll cover functionality related to debugging, and I'll cover functionality related to forms in Chapter 20.*

One Exceptional Editor

The VBE is an excellent editor in the context in which it is used. It has just enough features to help your project along, but not so many that you feel overwhelmed. The quickest way to display the VBE is to press ALT+F11. For those of you with a strong affinity for your mouse, choose Tools ➢ Macros ➢ Visual Basic Editor from the Excel menu. Figure 2.1 shows a picture of the VBE.

In Figure 2.1, you can see three windows that are docked to the outer boundary of the main window: the Project window, the Properties window, and the Immediate window. You can toggle these windows on if they are not visible using either the View menu or their shortcut keys. As you can see in Figure 2.2, you can display other items using the View menu. The Locals, Watch, and Call Stack windows are typically used for debugging and I'll cover them in the next chapter. The Microsoft Excel menu item just takes you back to Excel.

FIGURE 2.1
The VBE

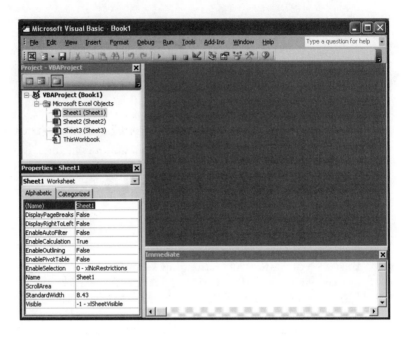

FIGURE 2.2
Use the View menu
to open various VBE
windows.

Note that you can't close the windows using the View menu. To close one, you must click the X icon in its upper-right corner.

Also, these windows can float in other locations if you desire. To move a window, simply click the window's title bar and then drag and drop it in the location of your choosing. To dock a window to one of the borders, just drag its title bar to that border. On the other hand, if the docking functionality drives you nuts, you can turn it off by right-clicking in the window and unchecking the Dockable item in the context menu. Alternatively, go to Tools ➤ Options and choose the Docking tab to change the docking capabilities of the various windows of the VBE.

Finally, the VBE remembers the last position of a window, so once you arrange them to your liking, you don't need to rearrange them every time you use the VBE or close and reopen the windows.

Now that you know how to display the various windows of the VBE, let's explore some of them in a little more detail.

Navigating Projects with the Project Explorer Window

The Project window (aka Project Explorer), shown in Figure 2.1, doesn't look like it has much to offer. This is because I only have one workbook open and have yet to insert any forms, modules, or class modules. Figure 2.3 shows a more realistic example of the Project Explorer.

In Figure 2.3, three workbooks are open. The Project Explorer considers each to be a separate project. All of the projects in this figure have the default project name of VBAProject followed by the name of the workbook in parentheses. You can change the name of a project by selecting the project in the Project Explorer and then changing the name associated with the selected project in the Properties window.

By default, the Project Explorer groups like objects together in folders. Depending on the project, you may have up to four kinds of objects associated with a project.

Microsoft Excel objects Each worksheet in a workbook is considered an Excel object. Also an object called ThisWorkbook represents the workbook as a whole. Because a workbook must have at least one worksheet, you'll always find at least two items in this folder, one worksheet object and the ThisWorkbook object.

FIGURE 2.3

A busy Project Explorer

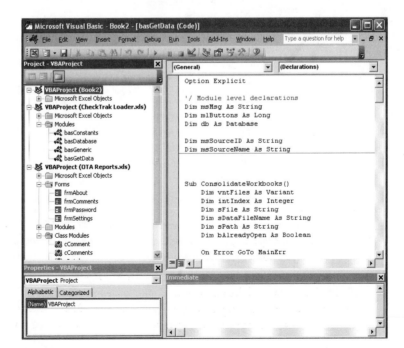

Forms   Forms represent user forms that can be added to a project. We will discuss user forms in detail in Chapter 20.

Modules   A module is a container for the procedures you write. When you start writing code, you'll begin by inserting a module into the project.

Class modules   Class modules are a special kind of module that allows you to develop your own custom objects. I'll discuss this in great detail in Chapter 11.

You can also view the various objects in a project without the folders, as shown in the following graphic, by clicking the tool button in the Project Explorer toolbar. The ToolTip for this icon is Toggle Folders.

The Project Explorer toolbar also includes two other tool buttons: one labeled View Code (the button on the left) and another labeled View Object (the button on the right).

All four kinds of objects associated with a project have a VBA code window associated with them. You can view the code window associated with an object by selecting the object in the Project Explorer and clicking the View Code button. Microsoft Excel Objects and Forms also have a viewable object associated with them. If you select a worksheet object and click View Object, for example, you'll be transported back to the main Excel window, which will have the appropriate worksheet displayed. Forms are slightly different. Forms have a visual design window associated with them. This window is what is displayed when you use View Object on a form object.

NOTE   As with just about anything, when it comes to performing various tasks in the VBE, you can achieve the same result in more than one way. For example, you can also view code by performing one of the following three actions: (1) right-clicking the object to display the context menu and choosing View Code, (2) selecting the object and choosing the View ➤ Code menu item, or (3) selecting the object and pressing F7. I'll present the various flavors of using the context menu, the main menu, or shortcut keys throughout the book. Shortcut keys are my favorite because they are extremely efficient when compared to other methods.

DON'T MISS THIS OVERLOOKED TIP

Now that I have your attention, you have got to know one other thing about the Project Explorer that many people overlook; this can be a real timesaver. As you start developing a critical mass of code, you'll occasionally want to transfer forms, modules, or class modules between projects. You can perform this action very quickly using the Project Explorer. Simply open the workbook that contains the object you want to transfer and any workbooks that you want to transfer the object to, and then drag and drop the object into the project that you want to transfer it to. This doesn't remove the object from the original project; it just copies it into the destination project. Though it would be nice, you can't transfer worksheets between workbooks in this manner.

TIP   *You can drag and drop forms, modules, and class modules between projects.*

The Versatile Properties Window

The Properties window is mainly used for Microsoft Excel Objects and Forms. The Properties window is context specific—this means that, depending on what you have selected either in the Project Explorer or while designing a form, the Properties window displays a number of properties (you can think of these properties as settings or characteristics) associated with the object that you can examine and edit. If you are not sure what a particular property is, select the property in the Properties window and press F1 to view documentation related to the property.

YOU CAN'T DO THIS USING THE NORMAL EXCEL USER INTERFACE

In Chapter 1, I mentioned that you can use VBA code to do things that you can't perform through the normal Excel interface. I am excited to tell you about one trick that you can pull off with the Properties window without knowing how to do it using VBA code. Well, its not really a trick, but it is a very useful functionality that hardly anyone knows about outside of the Excel development community.

Have you ever wanted to hide a worksheet? I mean really hide it? I'm talking so hidden that it doesn't appear when you select Format ➢ Sheet ➢ Unhide. You can make a worksheet this hidden using the Properties window. Select the worksheet you want to hide, and in the Properties window, change the Visible property to 2 - xlSheetVeryHidden.

This has to be one of my favorite defined constant names (a constant is just a human-readable name that has been given to a literal value to help make code easier for homo sapiens to decipher). Do you suppose that someday we might have an option for xlSheetVeryVeryHidden? Maybe one that you can only read and set programmatically? That would be nice too!

Anyway, once hidden in this manner, the only way to unhide the worksheet is either programmatically or by changing the Visible property back to -1 - xlSheetVisible using the Properties window.

Capabilities of the Immediate Window

Using the Immediate window you can perform three primary tasks. First, you can use it to display useful output during the development process. Second, it can inspect the state of objects and variables while your code is in Break mode. Third, you can use the immediate code to execute statements. I'll be covering the first two tasks in Chapter 4. For now you'll just see how to use the Immediate window to execute statements.

If the Immediate window is not already visible, you can display it by selecting View ➢ Immediate Window. To execute statements, type a question mark (?) followed by the statement you wish to execute and press Enter.

As you can see, you can do everything from evaluating math statements to calling functions and exploring object properties. As you'll see later, this feature is particularly useful for experimenting with functions.

TIP   When the Immediate window gets rather cluttered with output and you're ready to start fresh again, place the cursor in the Immediate Window, press CTRL+A, and then press the Delete key to quickly clear the window.

Managing Your Modules

As you build a project, you'll need to add and remove modules, class modules, and user forms. For the purposes of this chapter, I'll use the term component to refer to either a module, a class module, or a user form. You already saw that it is very easy to transfer existing components from one project to another. As you'd expect, adding and removing components from your project is a trivial process.

Adding New Components to Your Project

Once you're ready to start coding, the first thing you'll need to do is add a component. For most of the examples in this book, you'll need to insert a module. To add a module to your project, select Insert ➢ Module. If you have more than one workbook open, be sure you have the appropriate project selected in the Project Explorer first.

It is a good idea to name each component as you add it—especially forms and class modules—because chances are, other code you write will need to refer to these by name. If you change the name of a component later, any code that you've written that refers to the object by name will no longer function.

To name a component after you add it, select it in the Project Explorer (it will be selected for you by default right after you add it) and use the Properties window to change the value associated with the Name property. For modules, it is generally a good idea to give the module a name that indicates what kind of functionality the procedures in the module provide. If your module contains functionality to display an income statement, for example, you might want to name it IncomeStatement. The names that you use must begin with a letter and can't use spaces.

NOTE *It used to be and, for some, still is the custom to use a convention that indicated what kind of component the object was/is. For example, modules were/are prefixed with something like "bas" (this is the file extension of Visual Basic files) such as basIncomeStatement. I grew accustomed to this practice and, because old habits die hard, still practice it today (I'm on a 12-step program to quit, however). I must admit that I can't think of one benefit that this practice provides me. If you're in the habit of prefixing calls to procedures located in other modules using the form Your-OtherModuleName.SomeProcedure, then I suppose you may benefit marginally from knowing that YourOtherModuleName is a module and not a class module, form, or other object. I haven't seen many people use this form of referring to procedures in other modules, however.*

NOTE *Forms have traditionally been prefixed with frm such as frmLogin. Because forms are commonly referred to by name in other parts of your application, you may find this naming pattern beneficial.*

Removing Components from Your Project

Removing a component from your project is nearly as easy as right-clicking the object in the Project Explorer and choosing Remove *YourComponentName*. This process has a built-in safety/annoyance feature that asks you if you want to export the component before removing it. This is kind of a silly question because the menu item immediately above the Remove item is Export File. As if you couldn't find the Export File feature! Anyway, it does help prevent accidental deletion when you select the Remove item unintentionally.

Importing and Exporting Components

Though moving components between Excel projects is very easy, you can also import and export components. One reason you might want to do this is that it allows you to reuse generic components in other applications using Visual Basic or VBA. Maybe you have some generic routines in a module that communicate with a database, for example. You could use Export to save the module to a file and then in, say, Microsoft Word, you could open up the VBE and import it into your Word application.

To Export a component, right-click the component in the Project Explorer and choose Export File, then navigate to the folder where you want to store the file and supply a filename.

To Import a component, right-click the project or any item associated with the project in the Project Explorer, choose Import File, navigate to the folder where the component is stored, select the file, and click Open. If learning how to program is this easy, you'll have it nailed in no time, right?

Optimizing Your Editor

I often wonder why so many people do not take advantage of some of the useful features of the Visual Basic Editor. For example, one feature that I hardly see anyone use is syntax highlighting. Syntax highlighting allows you to change the background color or font color based on the type of function or object that the various syntax elements represent. Syntax highlighting is enabled by default; however, the default settings do not convey nearly as much information as you could convey by tweaking the settings a little further. Other than syntax highlighting, you can also customize the editor by changing fonts and font sizes and toggling a number of editor options on or off.

Give Syntax Highlighting a Try

To change the syntax highlighting settings, select Tools ➢ Options and then choose the Editor Format tab. The Editor Format tab is displayed in Figure 2.4.

NOTE   *In the next chapter, I'll begin covering information that will give this section more context. For now, just realize that this feature exists and that it can be very helpful in your development and maintenance efforts.*

For each item in the Code Colors list box, you can set the foreground color (the color of the font), the background color, and the indicator color. The indicator color is not applicable to every item on the list. As you change the settings, the picture in the Sample box changes to show you what your settings would look like.

As you can see, the Editor Format tab is also the place to change the font and font size. These settings are applicable to all kinds of syntax elements. However, note that you can't set a different font or font size for each item in the Code Colors list box.

I'll touch on this subject again in Chapter 13, and by then, you'll have written enough code to be able to experiment with the settings and better appreciate why this feature can be so useful. If for nothing else, you can use this feature to add a little color to your life.

FIGURE 2.4
Use the Editor
Format tab to
change the syntax
highlighting settings.

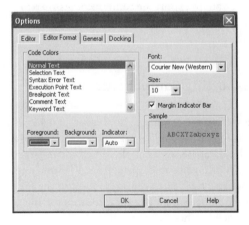

Turn On All of the Code Settings

The Code Settings on the Editor tab should all be turned on, especially because you are learning (see Figure 2.5). However, you could argue that Require Variable Declaration should be left off because it allows beginners to begin developing without an ounce of knowledge regarding how to use variables While this is true, if Require Variable Declaration is left off, subtle yet serious errors may be introduced that beginning developers are presumably not well equipped to correct or diagnose yet. Because it only takes one ounce of understanding to explicitly declare variables, I believe you are far better off using this feature, and therefore you are able to avoid the most common and frustrating errors that plague beginners who do not explicitly declare variables. You'll see an example of this problem in the next chapter.

Generally the only thing I ever turn off is the Auto Syntax Check option when I am working with a large block of text or code that I know needs editing and I do not want to be bothered with notifications of syntax errors. I'll cover what these functions actually do later in the chapter.

If you are working with other developers, you'll want to be sure that everyone is using the same tab width; otherwise you'll wind up with some terribly aligned code.

Regarding the Window Settings, the Drag-and-Drop Text Editing feature allows you to select segments of text and drag and drop it where you want it. You may find that this feature gets in your way occasionally, causing you to accidentally drag and drop stuff you didn't mean to move.

TIP *Rather than Drag-and-Drop Text Editing, I would recommend that you use CTRL+C to copy (CTRL+X to cut) the text selection and CTRL+V to paste it where you want it. After awhile, this will seem like second nature to you and you'll be able to work much faster than you could using Drag-and-Drop Text Editing.*

The Procedure Separator is applicable only if you use Default to Full Module View option. The Default to Full Module View option shows all of the procedures in a module, class module, user form, or Excel object in the same window. If you have Procedure Separator turned on, each procedure is separated by a thin line.

FIGURE 2.5

All of the Code Settings on the Editor tab will be helpful, especially when you are learning.

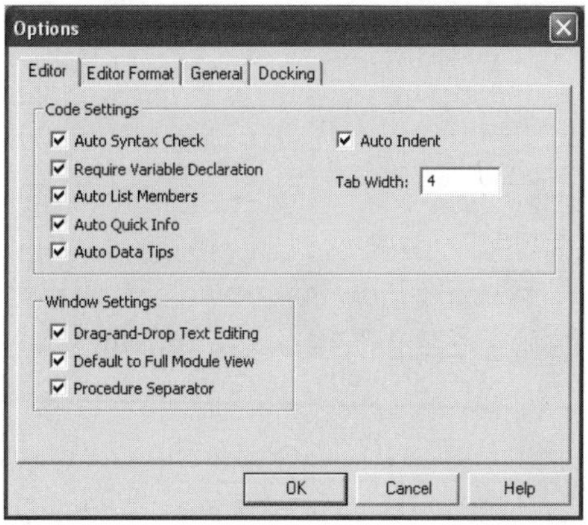

If you turn off the Default to Full Module View option, procedures in a given component are only displayed one at a time unless you use the split bar (discussed later in the chapter). If you change this option, it does not apply to any open code windows; it only applies to code windows opened after the setting is changed. You choose which procedure is displayed by selecting the procedure from a drop-down list.

I prefer to use the Default to Full Module View option. To me, it visually reinforces the concept that all of the procedures in a given component are related in some way. Also, I believe it is quicker in that you have another way to move to different procedures. You can scroll, select procedures from the drop-down list, or navigate using the keyboard. Additionally, because it is possible to view more than one procedure at a time this way, you won't find yourself flipping back and forth between the procedures as much (provided that the procedures you are looking at are physically close together in the module).

NOTE *The General tab of the Options dialog box contains various miscellaneous settings. I'll discuss these settings when I cover the functionality related to each setting later in the book.*

Helpful Editor Features

As I alluded to in the discussion of Code Settings earlier, the VBE contains numerous settings that facilitate both learning and efficient development. Forgive me if this section reads like a sales pitch, but here is a quick description of the features present in the VBE to aid developers.

Auto Syntax Check   As you enter your code, the VBE checks to make sure that the code you enter adheres to the syntax requirements of Visual Basic for Applications (VBA). In the following picture (Figure 2.6), I have mistakenly entered Debug.Prinf rather than Debug.Print. When I hit Enter, the Auto Syntax Check feature catches this error and tells me what the problem is.

FIGURE 2.6
Auto Syntax Check notifies you of syntax errors as you enter your code.

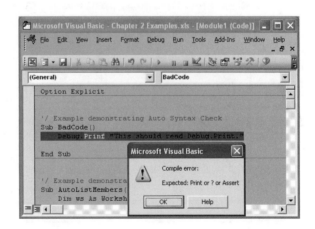

Auto List Members   This is probably my favorite feature. I think that if I was stuck on the proverbial island with an editor that has only one feature, I would choose Auto List Members (see Figure 2.7). The neat thing about this feature is that it benefits advanced developers as much as it does beginners. So what is it? Auto List Members is aware of each object's properties and methods. For example, it knows that a worksheet object has a Name property, a Delete method, a Visible property, and all of the other worksheet properties and methods. After you declare a variable specifically as a worksheet object, when you use that variable, the Auto List Members displays a list of all of the properties and methods of that variable as you type.

This helps beginners by not forcing them to memorize the entire object model in order to start being productive. It helps everyone, including advanced developers, by requiring much fewer keystrokes to code an application. This is because Auto List Members pares down the list as you type. As soon as the list is narrowed down to the property or method you are looking for, you can press the spacebar and Auto List Members enters the rest of the code for you. For example, if you need to enter the following code:

```
Debug.Print ws.Name
```

and ws has been declared as a worksheet object, you only need to enter this:

```
Debug.P <spacebar> ws.N <enter>
```

Auto Quick Info   Auto Quick Info (see Figure 2.8) displays information about functions and function parameters. This is very helpful because many functions contain numerous parameters. Without Auto Quick Info, you'd need to memorize or look up the parameter names, order of parameters, and each parameter's data type.

FIGURE 2.7

The Auto List Members feature displays relevant choices as you enter your code.

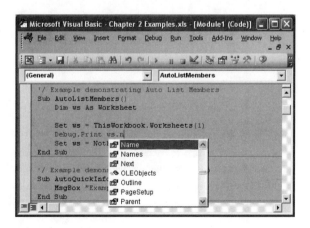

FIGURE 2.8
The Auto Quick Info feature displays function information as you supply parameters to a function.

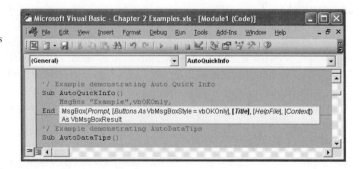

Auto Data Tips   This feature is applicable only in Break mode. Break mode doesn't refer to the time when you go get coffee or talk to your colleagues around the water cooler. Break mode is a special mode you'll use when you develop applications in which you can execute code one or more lines at a time. Often developers use Break mode when they are debugging applications; I'll cover it in Chapter 4. Anyway, the Auto Data Tips feature displays the value of variables as you hover the cursor over the variable name (see Figure 2.9).

FIGURE 2.9
The Auto Data Tips feature shows you the value of variables when you hover over the variable in Break mode.

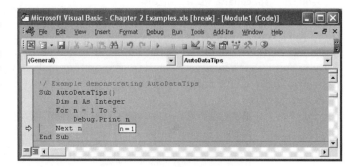

Understated Features of the Code Window

The code window will be your primary focus when you are programming with VBA. I've already discussed numerous ways in which you can customize this window. Now you'll look at it and I'll discuss the different ways in which you might work with it. An example of the code window is shown in Figure 2.10.

The drop-down list at the upper left is known as the Object list. This list contains any objects associated with the code window. For a standard module, (General) is the only item. However, a User Form will have an entry for each control or element on the form. The drop-down list at the upper right is known as the Procedure list. It lists all of the procedures associated with the object selected in the Object list. As you select different elements in each list, the code window displays the appropriate procedure.

FIGURE 2.10

The code window looks rather sparse initially, but its subtle features can help facilitate the development process.

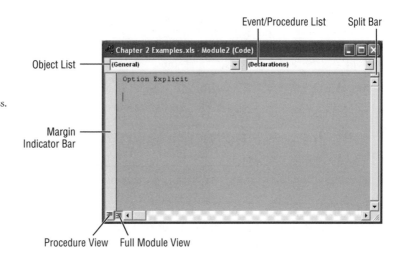

The code window also has a split bar (see Figure 2.11). You can drag the split bar down the window to create two independent views. Just drag and drop the split bar to where you want the split to appear. If I were a betting man, I would bet that in the initial stages of your development as a programmer, as soon as you start writing any procedures of significance, these procedures will be very long, perhaps requiring two or three windows to display a procedure in its entirety. As you go through this stage, you may find that the split bar is a convenient way to view a critical piece of the procedure while you are working on a related critical piece as opposed to scrolling up and down repeatedly.

The split bar also allows you to view two procedures at once if you are not using the Procedure view (described momentarily). You can use the Page Up/Page Down keys to toggle among the various procedures in your module.

FIGURE 2.11

The split bar can save you time by eliminating the need to scroll back and forth in a long procedure.

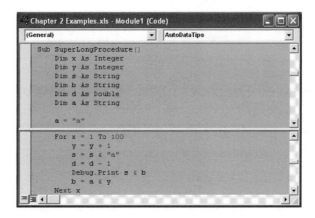

In the "Turn On All of the Code Settings" section, we discussed the use of the Default to Full Module View option. You can easily toggle between full module view and procedure view by clicking the appropriate icon in the lower-left corner of the code window. By using the split bar in conjunction with the Procedure view, you can see more than one procedure at a time using this feature. If you use the split bar with the Procedure view, the drop-down list box selections apply to whatever pane the cursor is in.

Object Inspection Using the Object Browser

When you develop in Excel with VBA, your programmatic interaction with Excel consists of manipulating or using Excel's various objects. Excel has many, many objects available for you to manipulate. Without any other information, you can probably surmise that a worksheet object represents worksheets and a workbook object represents workbooks. One way you can see what other objects are available is to use the Object Browser. An example of the Object Browser is shown in Figure 2.12. To display the Object Browser, press F2 or select View ➢ Object Browser.

You can use the Object Browser to view information for all object libraries, a specific object library, or your own project. By information, I mean a list of all the objects in the library, and for each object, a list of the object's members. An object library is a set of objects that are related in some way. For example, an object library for Excel contains all of the objects in Excel. An example of this is shown in Figure 2.13.

If you look on the right side of the window in Figure 2.13, you can see all of the members of the Worksheet object. The flying cube icons signify that the member is a method, the lightning bolt indicates that the member is an event, and the index card denotes the member as a property. I'll discuss the meaning of these terms later in the book.

If you want to know more information about either the object or one of its members, select the item and either press F1 or click the question mark icon. This will open up the Help topic associated with the object.

FIGURE 2.12

Using the Object Browser is a great way to take inventory of the various objects available for programmatic manipulation.

FIGURE 2.13
By changing the library to Excel, you can view all of the objects in the Excel object library. As you can see, sure enough, there is a Worksheet object.

FIGURE 2.14
You can use the Object Browser to quickly take inventory of your own project.

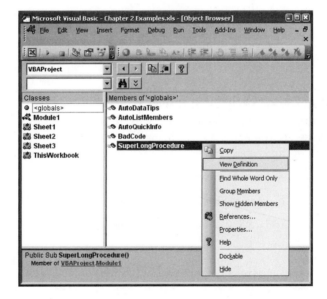

In addition to providing a way to view the Excel object model, the Object Browser also has the capability to provide you with information regarding your own project. If you are working on a large project, the Object Browser can be a convenient way to get a quick overview of all of the components of a project. Further, if you want to investigate a particular procedure in more detail, you can right-click it and choose View Definition. This quickly transfers you to where the procedure is located. Figure 2.14 shows an example of how you can use the Object Browser to view the items in a project.

FIGURE 2.15
The Object Browser
can be handy for
locating objects
of interest.

Locating Objects with the Object Browser

You can also use the Object Browser to search through object libraries for the text of your choosing. For example, suppose you were interested in any object or object member that had something to do with calculation in the Excel object library. To quickly generate a list of applicable items, follow these steps:

1. Open the Object Browser.

2. Choose Excel in the Library/Project drop-down list.

3. Enter **calculate** in the Search Text drop-down list.

4. Click the Binocular icon. You should see results similar to those shown in Figure 2.15.

From here, you can mentally narrow down the list of items that are applicable to your task and F1 them to quickly view the documentation for the item. You know how Google has also become a verb? To F1 it is the same kind of thing—it is short for "press F1 for help."

Obtaining Help Has Never Been So Easy

You've now seen that you can use a simple keystroke to obtain detailed help and documentation about an item directly from the Object Browser. As you develop your application, you can highlight any keyword, statement, or object, and also obtain help just by pressing F1. The VBA help files are quite detailed and contain lots of examples. That said, I won't spend any time here detailing how to use the help system other than to point out a few things. Figure 2.16 shows the help page for the Worksheet object.

FIGURE 2.16
You'll appreciate the quality documentation and help files that are a keystroke away.

Many objects show some sort of hierarchy similar to what you see in Figure 2.16. Though it might not immediately be apparent, the rectangles that say "Multiple objects" are clickable. When you click one, you can either quickly view ancestors or descendents of the object as demonstrated in Figure 2.17.

WARNING *The VBA help files are not installed by default when you install Excel. You may need to locate your installation disks the first time you try to display help for VBA-related information.*

Finally, as you are learning the Excel object model, something I'll spend most of the book covering, the help page shown in Figure 2.18 may be of use to you. You can find it immediately below the Microsoft Excel Visual Basic Reference item on the Contents tab.

By clicking the small triangle to the right of some of the objects, you'll be taken to a detailed object model associated with the given object.

Finally, many times you can strike it rich when you're looking for help by using the Ask a Question feature. You may have noticed this little feature in Microsoft Office applications. It hangs out in the upper-right corner of the window. If you haven't used it before it probably reads "Type a question for help." You don't need to type a question; a simple phrase that captures the essence of what you want to do does the trick. For example, type **loop through a range**. In this case, a help topic discusses this very procedure. Some other phrase examples are "hide worksheet," "save a workbook," "print a chart," and "if then else." Many times this feature gets you pointed in the right direction.

FIGURE 2.17
Click the objects in the Help files to see their ancestors or descendents.

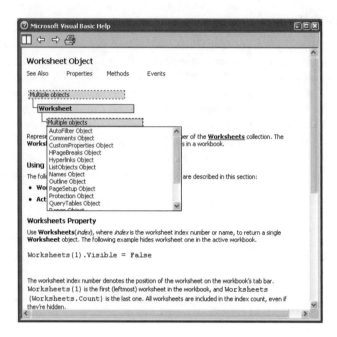

FIGURE 2.18
The Excel Object Model Help Page not only provides a visual representation of the Excel object model, but it also provides a click-through to the documentation associated with each object.

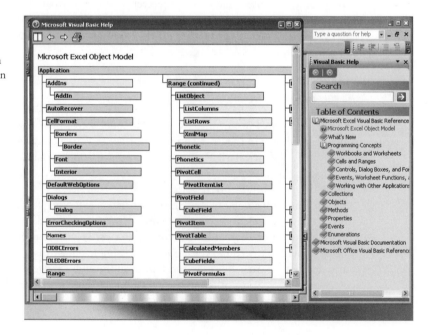

Securing Your Project

Often, your project contains settings or code that you do not want your end users to see. Or, maybe you have made a worksheet very hidden, as described earlier, and do not want someone to easily stumble across it. You can lock your project with a password so that it can't be viewed without the password. To do this, you need to display the Project Properties dialog box (see Figure 2.19). The name given to this is a little confusing because Project Properties *can't* be viewed in the Properties window. If you haven't named your project, you can view this dialog box by selecting Tools ➤ VBAProject Properties. If you have named your project, substitute the name of your project for VBAProject.

To lock your project, select the Protection tab (see Figure 2.20) and check Lock Project for Viewing. Finally, enter a password that either you won't forget or you'll write down somewhere.

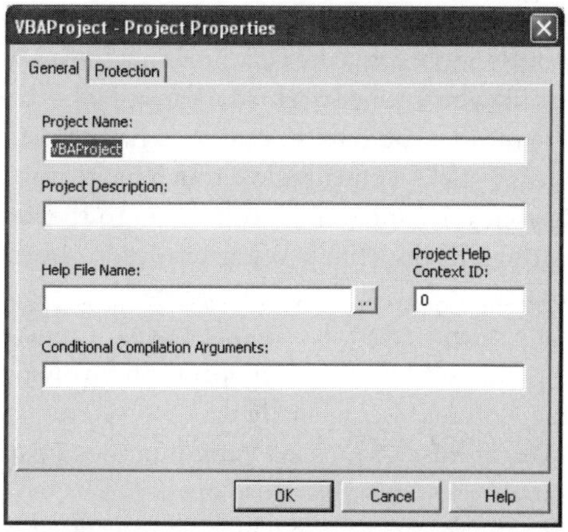

FIGURE 2.19

Don't confuse the Project Properties dialog box with the Properties window in the VBE.

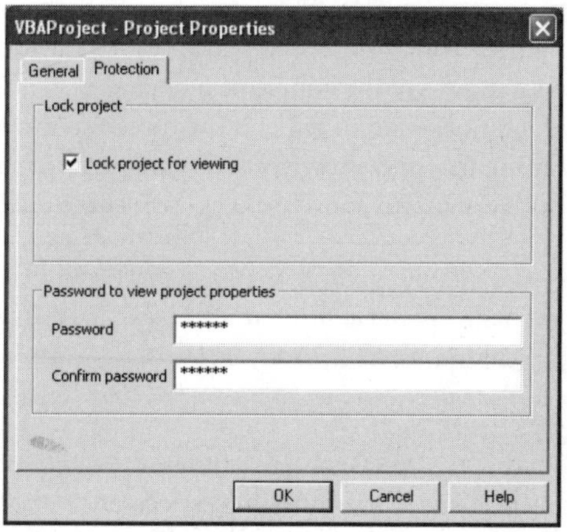

FIGURE 2.20

Use the Protection tab to lock your project so that it can't be viewed without a password.

TIP   *Create a passwords file in Excel to hold all of the passwords associated with your projects. You can lock this file with a password and place it in a secure folder. Of course, you'll need to remember the password, but that's just one password rather than many. Until I started using something like this, on a few occasions, I came dangerously close to forgetting a few passwords on important projects that I hadn't viewed for awhile.*

NOTE   *Although no native way exists to recover a lost password, third party products are available that you can use to recover passwords—Google "recover Excel password" to find out about some of these.*

Quick Code Navigation

I am a big proponent of using shortcut keys. Some people may not think that using shortcut keys is worth the effort of remembering them. After all, how much time are you really saving? Well, programming involves a lot of keyboard input, which means that both your hands need to be on the keyboard. When you use the mouse, you have to remove a hand (assuming you're not using an exceptionally pokey pointing stick or equally slow touch pad), grab the mouse, navigate to the menu/toolbar/scrollbar, make your selection, return your hand to the keyboard, and finally reorient your hand so that your index finger is over the J. When you use a shortcut key, this whole sequence is replaced by one keystroke.

I haven't conducted any scientific studies on this, but how much time does a keystroke take? Less than a tenth of a second perhaps. How about an operation involving the mouse? Consider that if you have to do some scrolling, you may occasionally take 5 to 10 seconds. For more simple mouse operations, I'd guess that it takes at least a couple of seconds between your last keystroke before the mouse operation and the first keystroke after the mouse operation.

Recently, a Microsoft commercial aired in which a guy walks around the company telling everyone "We just saved a nickel." He finally tells some bigwig this, adding that they are saving a nickel on every transaction. The bigwig knows that the company happens to process five million transactions per month, so that means big savings. Using shortcut keys is the same kind of thing. Each one is only a small second or two in time savings, but when you spend all day doing this kind of thing, it all adds up to a substantial time savings over the course of a day.

Therefore, although I am not going to tell you the three ways to perform every action in the VBE (menus, toolbars, context menus) and show you every menu item and toolbar button, I am going to provide you with a list of very useful shortcut keys (see Table 2.1).

TIP   *You can choose from a few different strategies to learn shortcut keys. One strategy is the sink or swim method. Unplug your mouse for a day. This is difficult at first, but you really can use Windows without a mouse, and after you get to know the shortcut keys, you can use it quite efficiently. Print out all of the shortcut keys and put them by your monitor. The second method is to commit yourself to learning a few each day. Start with Cut (CTRL+X), Copy (CTRL+C), and Paste (CTRL+V).*

This list is not a definitive list; rather it is a good selection of shortcut keys to get you started. You can obtain a complete list via your help files. See the Shortcuts section under the Visual Basic User Interface Help.

TABLE 2.1: USEFUL SHORTCUT KEYS

DESCRIPTION	SHORTCUT
Cut the selected text to the clipboard.	CTRL+X
Copy the selected text to the clipboard.	CTRL+C
Paste the contents of the clipboard.	CTRL+V
Move one word to the right.	CTRL+ →
Move one word to the left.	CTRL+ ←
Select one word right.	CTRL+SHIFT+ →
Select one word left.	CTRL+SHIFT+ ←
Next procedure.	CTRL+ ↓
Previous procedure.	CTRL+ ↑
Beginning of module.	CTRL+HOME
End of module.	CTRL+END
Move to beginning of line.	HOME
Move to end of line.	END
Undo.	CTRL+Z
Delete current line.	CTRL+Y
Delete to end of word.	CTRL+DELETE
View Definition.	SHIFT+F2
Go to last position.	CTRL+SHIFT+F2

Two of the items in this table probably need a little more clarification. The View Definition shortcut key is very helpful when your projects start getting a little more complex. With View Definition, you can select a procedure name and press SHIFT+F2 to be taken to that procedure. To return to where you were or to go to your last position press CTRL+SHIFT+F2.

Summary

The VBE is a useful, concise editor with just enough features to aid both the beginning and advanced developer. Until your projects become more complex and you start using forms, the Project Explorer and the Properties window will not reveal their true usefulness, although you did see that by using the Properties window, you can make worksheets very hidden so that they don't appear when a user selects Format ➤ Sheet ➤ Unhide.

Help abounds throughout the VBE and the help files are very thorough. Often, the only thing you need to do is select the word or item you are wondering about and press F1. That said, thanks to features such as Auto List Members and Auto Quick Info, developers don't need to refer to the help files nearly as much as they used to.

Because much of the work in developing is keyboard oriented, it helps to learn the shortcut keys that allow you to navigate through your code and perform various editing activities such as cut/copy/paste.

I'm sure you are anxious to start learning some useful Excel development skills. However, you have two more pieces of the foundation to complete before you get into the real Excel-oriented features. In Chapter 3, you'll learn the basics of the VBA language. This will allow you to give the VBE a test drive as you experiment with some of the example code listings. After that, you'll learn about the debugging features of the VBE and how you can put them to good use to troubleshoot your applications. After all, while you are learning, you can expect to have a lot of things go wrong. With some debugging skills, you can learn from your mistakes without sustaining too much frustration.

Chapter 3

Getting Started with VBA

FIRST OF ALL, LET'S make sure you're in the right frame of mind. Programming with VBA is easy and everything you need to know to begin programming with VBA is in this chapter. By programming with VBA, your efficiency as an Excel developer improves in three ways:

◆ By increasing your familiarity with the code manipulation of common Excel objects

◆ By improving your mental model of programming

◆ By increasing your understanding of the rules

This chapter introduces you to the rules or syntax of VBA programming and provides you with an initial mental model that you can use to help frame your programming tasks.

NOTE   If you're totally new to programming, you may find it advantageous to read this chapter twice. The reason is that it is difficult to explain and demonstrate certain concepts without referring to other concepts that I've not covered yet. The second time you read the chapter, you'll have the advantage of having been exposed to all of the concepts; things that didn't make sense the first time around will be clearer.

Thinking Like a Computer

Imagine the most mentally incompetent person you know. Now picture someone 10 times more inept. This is your new imaginary friend. You should cut your new friend a little slack and assume that he has two redeeming traits: he is excellent at following directions and he can follow these directions at amazing speeds. Oh, one more thing, your friend will do anything you say without question—provided he understands you, of course. That imaginary friend is your computer.

The problem with your friend is that he has an extremely limited vocabulary, so you can't simply say "take out the trash" or "wash my car." Instead, you must instruct him how to perform each task in great detail. The only assumption you can make is that your friend has no clue about anything other than the few dozen words he understands.

Fortunately, Microsoft has already taught your friend how to use and perform many tasks associated with Microsoft Excel and other objects within your computer. As a result, you don't have to go into quite as much detail as I may have led you to believe. In later chapters, you'll explore your friend's competencies in this regard.

For now though, your task for is to develop some skill at communicating with your new friend. Let's work through an example.

Consider the list of names shown in Figure 3.1. How would you instruct your friend to make any name that begins with an "A" appear in bold font?

FIGURE 3.1

A simple list

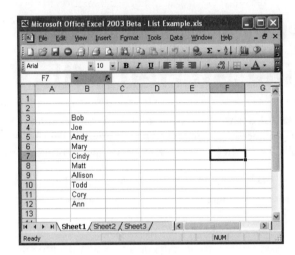

In order to perform this task, your friend needs to know the following information:

◆ Where does the list begin?

◆ Where does the list end?

◆ How should I navigate the items on the list?

◆ What is the distinguishing characteristic of the items that need to be modified?

◆ How do I modify the items?

Instead of just saying, "Make any name that begins with an 'A,' bold," your instruction needs to be something similar to the following:

1. Open the workbook List Example.xls located in the folder C:\Examples.

2. Work with the worksheet named Sheet1.

3. Starting with cell B3 and continuing until an empty cell is found,

   1. Check the first letter of the value in the current cell.

   2. If the value is "A", make the cell bold. Otherwise leave the cell alone.

   3. Move down one cell.

You could describe how to complete this task in many other ways. For now, all that matters is that you can describe how to complete various tasks in great detail. The result of this exercise is called pseudo-code or p-code. It can also be called an algorithm.

Though by choosing one algorithm over another you'll experience performance and maintenance implications, usually you'll find that you can come up with multiple solutions to the task at hand. This is one of the reasons that many programmers consider their work to be as much an art as it is science. In any event, being able to clearly describe a solution to a given problem is half the battle, and as you can see, you don't need to know anything about the programming details to perform this. Later in the chapter, you'll translate this p-code into actual working code.

VBA Building Blocks

In the previous chapter, you learned how to insert an empty module into a VBA project. A module is a container for your code and discrete sections of code are called procedures. For simple projects, you may only have a single module containing one or more procedures. As your projects become more complex, you'll have many modules. One of the benefits of using multiple modules is that it allows you to group related procedures together.

For the purposes of this discussion, you'll also become familiar with two types of procedures: subroutines and functions. Modules, subroutines and functions are the building blocks of a VBA project.

Modules—A Home for Your Code

A module is your canvas, so to speak. Modules serve to contain related procedures, provide a mechanism for declaring variables shared by all module procedures, and provide you with the ability to hide private procedures from procedures located in other modules. Until you start to understand the subtle reasons for using multiple modules, you may question why you would want to use more than one.

The main reason for using more than one module is to improve the maintainability and reusability of your code. One strategy is to use modules to segment your subroutines and functions by the type of functionality they provide. For example, you may have one module that contains code that interacts with a database, one module that is responsible for formatting data for output, and another module that contains all of the code that handles interaction with the end user. The benefit of segmenting your code in this manner is that if something goes wrong or needs to be modified, it is easy to know where to go to make the modification.

Another reason to use modules is that by doing so you can easily manage the visibility of your subroutines and functions. I'll cover this subject in more detail later in the book. For now, suffice it to say that sometimes you'll write a subroutine based on certain assumptions and this subroutine won't work unless the assumptions are correct. Therefore, you want to ensure that only a handful of other subroutines have the ability to call or execute this one. By using separate modules, you'll be able to create private procedures that can only be called by other procedures in the same module.

You can customize the behavior of modules in four ways:

Option Explicit   When you use Option Explicit, you must declare every variable in all of the procedures in the module; otherwise a syntax error occurs and the code won't compile. I highly recommend that you use this option as it can eliminate subtle (and not so subtle) bugs in your code—for example, those that occur when you misspell a variable name. If you misspell a variable that you've used previously without Option Explicit turned on, VBA simply gives you a new variable to use, which likely doesn't contain the correct value. You can automatically include this statement in every new module by turning on the Require Variable Declaration option. From the Visual Basic Editor (VBE), select Tools ➢ Options and check the Require Variable Declaration setting on the Editor tab.

Option Private Module   This option marks the code in the module as private so that it can't be seen by users in the Macros dialog box. It also prevents a module's contents from being referenced by external projects. Subroutines in a private module won't appear in Excel when you choose Tools ➢ Macro ➢ Macros. They'll still be available to other modules within the same project provided the procedures in the private module weren't individually declared as Private.

Option Compare {Binary | Text | Database}   The Option Compare statement specifies the string comparison method (Binary, Text, or Database) for a module. The default text comparison method is Binary. With binary comparison, "AAA" < "aaa". With text comparison, "AAA" = "aaa".

Option Base {0 | 1}   The Option Base statement specifies the first index number of an array. If this option is not specified, it defaults to 0.

To use these options, just enter the option and its setting at the top of the module to which it should apply. For example, to require variable declarations and mark a module as private, you'd enter the following at the top of the module:

```
Option Explicit
Option Private Module
```

Actually, you can use two types of modules: standard modules and class modules. You'll use class modules to create your own objects later in the book. Until we get to class modules, you can use standard modules for all of the examples.

NOTE   *Class modules are covered in Chapter 12.*

Procedures

A procedure is a collection of statements that performs one or more given tasks. As I mentioned earlier, you'll come across two types of procedures: subroutines and functions. The main difference between the two is that functions can return a value to the process that uses them. Subroutines, however, do not explicitly return a value.

SUBROUTINES

A subroutine is the smallest element of a program that can be executed. The general syntax of a sub routine is as follows:

```
[Private|Public|Friend][Static] Sub SubRoutineName ( (parameters) )
    [statements]
End Sub
```

Private   The private keyword is optional. A private subroutine can only be executed by other subroutines or functions in the same module.

Public   The public keyword is optional. A public subroutine can be called by any other subroutine, function, or class module. Sub routines are public by default.

Friend   This keyword only applies to class modules and I'll cover it later in the book (Chapter 12).

Static   A static subroutine remembers the values of its local variables between calls.

Parameters   You can declare one or more parameters for use by the subroutine. When you specify a parameter, any procedure that calls or executes the subroutine must supply a value for any required parameters. You'll see some example procedures that use parameters later in the chapter beginning with Listing 3.3.

For now, here is the easiest way to declare a new subroutine:

```
Sub MyFirstSubRoutine()

End Sub
```

These statements declare a new public subroutine that can be referred to by the name MyFirstSubRoutine. You can make this your first complete, self-sufficient subroutine by adding one line of text:

```
Sub MyFirstSubRoutine()
    MsgBox "This is my first subroutine"
End Sub
```

If you haven't already done so, give it a try:

1. Open a new Excel workbook.

2. Press Alt+F11 to view the VBE.

3. Choose Insert ➢ Module.

4. Enter the code just shown.

5. Run the code by placing the cursor on any one of the three lines of code and pressing F5.

As you are learning, most of the code you write will be inside subroutines. However, the more quickly you start incorporating functions, the better, because functions provide one critical benefit you won't find in subroutines—they allow you to return a value.

Conceivably, you could write all of your procedures as functions, but unless you really need to return a value from a procedure, the extra couple of steps you need to complete to do so just take a little more time without providing any real value in return.

THE MSGBOX FUNCTION

The MsgBox function is a useful function on a number of different levels. You can use MsgBox to display information to an end user, to gather Yes/No/Cancel input, and to help debug your code by providing you with a glimpse of the values contained in your variables as your code runs. However, as you become more proficient with the various debugging facilities and techniques, you'll use MsgBox much less often for debugging purposes. Here is the syntax for MsgBox:

```
MsgBox(prompt[, buttons] [, title] [, helpfile, context])
```

The prompt parameter is the text that you want displayed, whereas the buttons parameter controls what buttons are displayed. If you don't provide a value for buttons, the default is 0 (OK Only). The title is the text displayed in the title bar of the dialog box. If you don't provide a value for the title parameter, it will default to Microsoft Excel. The remaining parameters are only applicable if your application includes custom developed help files.

```
This function can be used to display a simple message such as the following:
```

```
MsgBox "This is a useful function."
```

Alternatively, you can use the function to capture input such as this:

```
Response = MsgBox("Continue processing?", vbYesNo)

If Response = vbYes Then

    MsgBox "You chose yes."

Else

    MsgBox "You chose no."

End If
```

Once completed, subroutines can be called or executed by other subroutines simply by placing the name of the subroutine at the desired location in the calling subroutine. Alternatively, you could use the Call statement, but Call is not required and I've never thought of a compelling reason to use it. As an example, both of the following statements would have the effect of calling a subroutine named MyFirstSubRoutine.

```
Sub CallAnotherRoutine
    Call MyFirstSubRoutine      'Execute MyFirstSubRoutine
    MyFirstSubRoutine           'Execute MyFirstSubRoutine
    ' Call a subroutine with two parameters
    TwoParameterSubRoutine x,y
End Sub
```

If you call a subroutine that has parameters, simply list the parameters after the subroutine separating multiple parameters with comments.

TIP   You can place comments anywhere in your code by preceding your comment with a '. Comments help you document general high-level operations, explain tricky or complex blocks of statements, document the required parameters of subroutines and functions, describe the output or purpose of a procedure, and many other things. Comments can either occur on their own line or at the end of a statement.

FUNCTIONS

Functions go a step further than subroutines in that they allow you to return a value to the procedure that called the function. Functions are also used to create user-defined functions that are used like normal Excel functions such as SUM(), PMT(), and so on.

When you declare a function, you should also specify the return value's data type. If you do not specify a data type, the function will return a variant. The general syntax of a function is as follows:

```
[Private|Public|Friend][Static] Function FunctionName ( (parameters) ) [As Type]
    [statements]
    FunctionName = FunctionResult
End Function
```

Notice the following differences between the function syntax and that of a subroutine declaration. First, you use the Function keyword rather than the Sub keyword. Likewise you end with End Function rather than End Sub. Second, [As Type] is where you specify the return value's data type. Though the brackets indicate that supplying a data type for the return value is optional, I would recommend getting in the habit of always specifying the data type, even if you desire a variant. Doing so makes your code easier to read and clearly expresses your intentions. The final difference is that somewhere inside your function you must assign a return value to the name you used for your function.

As an example, the following function returns yesterday's date:

```
Function Yesterday() As Date
    Yesterday = Now - 1
End Function
```

This function uses the Now() function, which returns the system date and subtracts one day to yield yesterday's date. Try it out:

1. Open a new Excel workbook.

2. Press Alt+F11 to view the VBE.

3. Choose Insert ➤ Module.

4. Enter the code for the Yesterday function shown previously.

5. Press Alt+F11 to return to Excel.

6. Choose Insert ➤ Function.

7. Select the User Defined category.

8. Select the Yesterday function and click OK.

9. Select OK to accept the value.

10. You may need to format the cell as a date. If so, select the cell and choose Format ➤ Cell, choose the Date category, and click OK.

Of course, you could also simply type in the formula =**Yesterday()** in any cell and achieve the same result. Any public function that you write in a module that doesn't contain the Option Private Module statement will appear in the User Defined category as was just demonstrated.

Variables Are the Elements You Interact With

Your code consists of variables, operators and statements. Variables are the nuts and bolts of an application. Conceptually, variables represent the items or objects that your code works on. For example, a variable can represent a number that you need to perform math on, a text string that you need to edit, a worksheet, a workbook, and so on. You can programmatically manipulate anything in Excel that you interact with in normal use. To interact with these items

◆ Create a variable of the appropriate object or data type.

◆ Assign an initial value to the variable.

◆ Perform operations or execute statements to modify or interact with the variable.

VBA makes it very easy to start programming without first having a fundamental understanding of the concept of declaring and using variables. Unlike many other programming languages, you can use a variable simply by using a variable name in your code (provided that you're not using the Option Explicit statement). This is known as implicit variable declaration. For example, consider the following simple subroutine that displays an informational message box.

```
Sub DisplayMessage(Message)
    InfoButtons = vbOKOnly + vbInformation
    MsgBox Prompt:=Message, Buttons:=InfoButtons
End Sub
```

In this example InfoButtons is a variable that contains a value that instructs the MsgBox function which buttons and icon to display. You didn't need to do anything special to begin using this variable other than come up with a name.

In most other programming languages, you'd first need to declare the variable. Conceptually you can think of it as declaring your intention to use the variable. Internally, when your program runs, the computer reserves a chunk of memory that your program can refer to by the name you gave it. When you declare a variable, you also need to state to what kind of data type the variable refers. Among other things, this allows the computer to determine how much memory it needs to set aside because different data types require different amounts of memory for their storage.

At first, you may think that using variables without having to declare them is a gift. Those programmers at Microsoft sure are good to us to give us this functionality. I mean, why declare variables if you don't have to, right? Unfortunately, a drawback to this exists. Although it helps ease people into programming, it also allows you to shoot yourself in the foot because it allows you to introduce visually subtle, yet programmatically significant errors into your programs. The people who tend not to explicitly declare variables are usually beginners who may not yet have the debugging proficiency to easily identify the source of their problem. The following example easily illustrates the issue at hand.

```
Sub ImplicitVariablePitfall()
    DomesticInvestments = InputBox("Enter domestic investment amount")
    ForeignInvestments = InputBox("Enter foreign investment amount")
    TotalInvestment = DomesticInvestments + ForiegnInvestments
    MsgBox "The total investment = " & TotalInvestment
End Sub
```

Enter this code into an empty module that doesn't specify Option Explicit and run it a couple of times. You should notice that no matter what you input for the foreign investment amount, the total investment amount always equals what you entered for the domestic amount. The reason is that there is a spelling error in the TotalInvestment calculation. The "ei" in ForeignInvestments has been transposed. As a result, a new variable (with an initial default value of 0) is used in this calculation rather than the variable you intended to use. Unlike this short example, many beginners tend to write very lengthy procedures that make this type of error much more difficult to locate.

Now, enter the statement **Option Explicit** at the top of the module. If you run the procedure now, you'll get a "Variable Not Defined" compile error and the first offending statement will be highlighted. In order to remedy the situation, you need to rewrite the procedure as follows:

```
Sub ImplicitVariablePitfall()
    Dim DomesticInvestments
    Dim ForeignInvestments
    Dim TotalInvestment
    DomesticInvestments = InputBox("Enter domestic investment amount")
    ForeignInvestments = InputBox("Enter foreign investment amount")
    TotalInvestment = DomesticInvestments + ForiegnInvestments
    MsgBox "The total investment = " & TotalInvestment
End Sub
```

If you attempt to run this code (the spelling error is still present) a compile error occurs and the misspelled variable is highlighted. The result is that you find out about these kinds of errors in the development process rather than in a meeting where your boss is presenting errant numbers due to your faulty program. I'll dive a little deeper into declaring variables later in this chapter.

Developing their conceptual model of variables is one of the first hurdles for many beginning programmers. The easiest way to get started with variables is to start with the basic types. First, you need to be aware of the different kinds of data types that are available.

Data Types

When you declare or create a variable, it is best to think about what kind of data the variable will hold and then create a variable of the appropriate data type. You can think of a variable as a container that can hold a value. Variables can be declared specifically to hold certain kinds of values or data types. If you declare a variable as capable of storing Integer values, that variable would be referred to as an Integer variable. If you are not sure what kind of data the variable will hold, you can declare the variable as a Variant. A Variant is a special kind of variable that can represent anything. I'll get into the details of a Variant later in this section. Table 3.1 lists the basic data types.

TABLE 3.1: DATA TYPES

DATA TYPE	RANGE OF VALUES	MEMORY USAGE
Boolean	True or False.	2 bytes
Byte	0–255.	1 byte
Currency	−922,337,203,685,477.5808 to 922,337,203,685,477.5807.	8 bytes
Date	1 January 100 to 31 December 9999 and times from 0:00:00 to 23:59:59.	8 bytes
Decimal	With no decimal places, the largest possible value is +/− 79,228,162,514,264,337,593,543,950,335. With 28 decimal places, the largest value is +/− 7.9228162514264337593543950335.	12 bytes
Double	−1.79769313486231 to −4.94065645841247E-324 for negative values and from 4.94065645841247E-324 to 1.79769313486232E308 for positive values.	8 bytes
Integer	−32,768 to 32,767.	2 bytes
Long	−2,147,483,648 to 2,147,483,647.	4 bytes
Object	Can have any object reference assigned to it.	4 bytes
Single	−3.402823E38 to −1.401298E-45 for negative values and from 1.401298E-45 to 3.402823E38 for positive values.	4 bytes
String	A variable-length string can contain up to approximately 2 billion (2^31) characters. You can also declare fixed-length strings up to about 64,000 characters.	Varies
User Defined	User-defined data types can contain one or more other data types, an array, or a previously defined user-defined type.	Varies
Variant	Varies—see section on variants later in this section.	Varies

Until you are confident with the subtleties of when to use one data type over another, I'd suggest that you focus on the following data types:

Boolean Booleans are used frequently to help implement logic in your programs. You may use them in If…Then statements, Do…While statements, and as a return type for functions. For example, in Chapter 7, you'll implement a function named WorksheetExists that returns a Boolean. This function tests to see whether or not a given worksheet name exists in a workbook.

Integer Integer variables are probably the most frequently used data type. You'll use integer variables in conjunction with For…Next statements, to refer to elements within an array or collection and to help navigate around a worksheet.

Long   Occasionally an integer just isn't big enough and you'll need to use its big brother, the Long.

String   Strings are one of the contenders for the most frequently used data type. You'll use strings to store the names of worksheets, workbooks, and named ranges among other things.

Currency, Date, and Double   Occasionally, you'll also have a need for Currency, Date, and Double. Usually you'll need to use these data types when you are either implementing a function that calculates values or to store data found on a worksheet.

Before I go on to discuss the Variant data type, it is worth mentioning again that you should declare variables as precisely as possible rather than always declaring them as Variants. Declaring variables using specific data types helps to eliminate programming errors and is more efficient from a system resources standpoint.

VARIANT VARIABLES

A Variant is a flexible data type that can represent any kind of value except a fixed-length string. Beginning with Excel XP or 2002, Variants even support user-defined types. Additionally, a Variant can represent the special values Empty, Error, Nothing, and Null.

If you declare a variable (see the next section "Declaring Variables") without specifying a data type, the variable is given a Variant data type by default. Likewise, if you use a variable without first declaring it, the variable is given a Variant data type.

You can test for the underlying data type of a Variant by using the VarType function. Table 3.2 shows the return values of VarType for various data types.

VarType(_varname_**)**

You may use this function to test a Variant before passing it to another procedure or block of code that assumes the variant is of a particular subtype. For example, if you have a block of code that expects to operate on an integer, you could use the VarType function.

```
If VarType(MyVariantVariable) = vbInteger Then
    ' some code specific to integers goes here
End If
```

Another useful function for determining the underlying data type of a Variant is the TypeName function.

TypeName(_varname_**)**

TypeName returns a string that indicates the underlying data type. You could use the TypeName function in a similar manner as the VarType function just mentioned.

```
If TypeName(MyVariantVariable) = "Integer" Then
    ' some code specific to integers goes here
End If
```

As mentioned earlier in the section, variants can also represent the following special values.

TABLE 3.2: DETERMINING UNDERLYING DATA TYPES

UNDERLYING DATA TYPE	TYPENAME RETURNS	VARTYPE RETURNS (DEFINED CONSTANT)
Boolean	Boolean	11 (vbBoolean)
Byte	Byte	17 (vbByte)
Currency	Currency	17 (vbByte)
Date	Date	7 (vbDate)
Decimal	Decimal	14 (vbDecimal)
Double	Double	5 (vbDouble)
Empty	Empty	0 (vbEmpty)
Error	Error	10 (vbError)
Integer	Integer	2 (vbInteger)
Long	Long	3 (vbLong)
Null	Null	1 (vbNull)
Object	Object	9 (vbObject)
Single	Single	4 (vbSingle)
String	String	8 (vbString)

Empty   This value indicates that a variant variable has been declared but no initial value has been assigned to it yet. An Empty variable is represented as zero (0) in a numeric context or a zero-length string ("") in a string context.

Error   The Error value is used to indicate that an application-defined error has occurred in a procedure. This is a different kind of error from regular errors in that you, the application developer, define the error. This allows you to take some alternative action based on the error value. You create Error values by converting real numbers to error values using the CVErr function.

Nothing   Nothing is actually a keyword you use to disassociate a variable from the object to which the variable referred. In this context, a variant variable that has been set to Nothing is sort of in limbo. It doesn't refer to anything, but the variable name still exists in memory.

Null   Null indicates that a variable contains no valid data. To be Null, a variable must be explicitly set to Null or have participated in an operation in which one of the expressions contains Null. Do not confuse Null with Empty. Because Null values must be explicitly set, Null indicates that the variable *intentionally* contains no valid data. This is a subtle but important distinction.

Before we move on, you should be aware of one more important thing that Variants can do. Variants can also hold arrays. I'll discuss this important functionality in the upcoming section "Basic Array Usage." Generally the only place I use variants in an application is to hold arrays or to read data from a worksheet. In other situations, I'd advise you to use a variable of the appropriate data type.

Doing so is more efficient from a memory and processing standpoint, helps eliminate programming errors, and is much cleaner from a readability/maintainability standpoint.

Declaring Variables

Once you have decided the appropriate data type for a variable, declaring it is easy. The basic syntax for declaring a variable is as follows:

```
Dim VariableName [As DataType]
```

Here are some examples:

```
Dim RowCount As Integer
Dim WorksheetName As String
Dim CellValue As Variant
Dim Salary As Currency
```

Note that if you don't specify a data type, the variable is given a Variant data type. Consequently, CellValue could also be declared simply as

```
Dim CellValue
```

However, when programming, a general rule of thumb is to write your code in a way that clearly expresses your intention. By explicitly declaring CellValue as a variant, it is clear that you intended CellValue to be a variant. If you do not explicitly declare CellValue as a variant, your code could have two possible explanations. The first explanation is that you intended the variable to be a variant and, knowing that the default data type is Variant, you chose not to explicitly state the data type. The second explanation is that you mistakenly forgot to state the data type and perhaps intended CellValue to be of a different data type.

You can also declare multiple variables on one line. Indeed, if you have experience in other programming languages, you may be used to declaring variables in this manner. You need to be aware of one gotcha to this practice. Consider the following declaration:

```
Dim RowNumber, ColumnNumber As Integer
```

In some other languages, this type of declaration is a legal way to declare multiple variables of the same data type. In VBA, however, the result is that RowNumber is given a Variant data type whereas ColumnNumber is an Integer as intended. The correct way to declare the two variables on one line is as follows:

```
Dim RowNumber As Integer, Dim ColumnNumber As Integer
```

You aren't limited to just declaring variables of one given data type on one line. It is perfectly legal to declare variables with different data types in this manner.

Though it is legal to declare multiple variables on one line, I'd recommend that you employ this tactic infrequently, if at all, as I believe it makes it harder to keep track of your variable declarations.

Variable Scope and Lifetime

Variables have both a scope and a lifetime. Understanding the concepts of scope and lifetime are often critical to writing code that works as you expect.

VARIABLE NAMING CONVENTIONS

It is common practice to use naming conventions to add meaning to your variable names. One convention, of course, is to not use any convention at all. Another convention is to append a one- to three-letter prefix to your variable names to help remind you of the variable's data type. Some programmers also may prefix their module level variables with an "m" and their global variables with a "g" in addition to the data type prefix.

I have tried many different conventions over the years and have settled on the following. For the most common data types, I use a single letter to denote the data type. For the less common basic data types, I use two letters. Finally, I prefer to prefix module level variables with an "m".

```
Dim nMyInteger As Integer

Dim mnMyModuleLevelInteger As Integer

Dim sMyString As String

Dim lMyLong As Long

Dim vMyVariant As Variant

Dim cMyDollar As Currency


Dim dtMyDate As Date

Dim dbMyDouble As Double

Dim sgMySingle As Single
```

Naming conventions are really a personal preference. I recommend that you find something that works for you and then use it consistently. In some cases, your company may already have conventions that you are required to use, in which case you may not have any choice.

VARIABLE SCOPE

Variable scope refers to the breadth of a variable's visibility and is determined by the location of the variable's declaration or the use of the Public or Private keywords. You have three possibilities when you are determining a variable's scope: procedural scope, module scope, and global scope.

Variables declared within a procedure are local to the procedure only and are referred to as procedural-level variables. You can only access procedural-level variables with code that resides in the procedure in which the variable was declared.

Variables can also be declared at the top of a module as either module-level variables or global variables. If you declare a variable at the top of a module, the variable is a private or module-level variable by default. This means that only code that resides in the same module that contains the variable declaration can access or use the variable. If you replace Dim with Public, you can create a global variable. Global variables can be used by any code in the same project. Consider the following three variable declarations placed at the top of a module.

```
Dim msMessage As String       ' A module level variable
Private msMessage2 As String  ' A module level variable
Public gsMessage As String    ' A global variable
```

The first two declarations perform the same task. They declare module-level variables. The second declaration, using the Private keyword, is preferred in that it explicitly makes your intentions clear. The third declaration creates a global variable. Note that the variable names are prefixed with an "m" if the variable is a module-level variable and a "g" if it is a global variable. This convention is a matter of personal preference. I like the fact that, if used consistently, when you see the variable being used in a procedure, the "m" or "g" prefix gives you a clue as to where to look to find the variable's declaration.

VARIABLE LIFETIME

The lifetime of a variable refers to the period of time from which the variable is available for use in your code to the period of time in which the variable is removed from your computer's memory.

For procedural-level variables, the variable exists from the moment the procedure begins executing until the Exit/End statement is executed. The next time the procedure executes, a brand new set of variables are created. That is, the value of each variable is not preserved between runs. This rule has two exceptions: the first is for *subroutines* declared using the Static statement, the second is for *variables* declared using the Static statement. In each of these two exceptions, the lifetime of a variable begins the first time that procedure is executed and ends when the workbook that contains the procedure is closed. You can use the following two procedures to experiment with static variables. The first routine uses the Static keyword in the procedure declaration. The second routine uses the Static keyword in the declaration of the procedure level variable.

```
Static Sub TestStaticRoutine()
    Dim x As Integer

    MsgBox "X = " & x
    x = x + 1
End Sub

Sub TestStaticRoutine2()
    Static y As Integer

    MsgBox "Y = " & y
    y = y + 1
End Sub
```

To experiment with these, perform the following steps.

1. Copy the code above into a module.

2. Put the cursor in the procedure you'd like to run and press F5 to execute the code.

3. Rerun each procedure a few times and you'll see the applicable variable increment with each run.

4. Save and close the workbook.

5. Reopen the workbook and then rerun the procedures.

For module-level variables, the variable exists from the moment the workbook containing your code opens until the workbook is closed. The value of a module-level variable behaves something like a static variable in the sense that once a value is given to it, the value remains in place until you change it or close the workbook.

Constants

Constants are used in much the same way as a variable except that, as their name indicates, a constant's value doesn't change unless you explicitly and physically change the value of the constant in your source code.

Constants are private by default. When declared within a procedure, they are always private and can't be seen by code outside the procedure. When declared at the module level however, constants can be declared as public and, therefore, can be seen by procedures located in other modules. Here are some sample constant declarations.

```
' Declare public module level constants
Public Const APP_NAME As String = "My Excel Application"
Public Const APP_VERSION As String = "1.0.0"

' Declare private, module level constant
Private Const FTE_HOURS_WEEK = 40

' Declare private, module level constant
' If not specified, constants are private by default
Const SECONDS_PER_MINUTE = 60
```

Naming constants using all capitals is a widely used naming convention. Note that if you don't specify a type for the constant using the As statement, VBA chooses a type that is appropriate to the value specified for the constant.

Constants can make your code easier to read and modify and are recommended in instances where you find yourself hard coding, or physically entering literal values throughout your code.

Operators

Operators are elements of a programming language you can use to either make comparisons or change the value of program elements in some way. One of the primary uses of elements is to perform mathematical operations. For mathematical operations, using these operators is similar to how you'd use them to express any basic equation. Therefore, I won't spend a lot of time covering operators as they apply to mathematical operations. Table 3.3 lists all of the operators available to you.

TABLE 3.3: VBA OPERATORS

OPERATOR	DESCRIPTION
&	Used to join two or more strings together to form a single string.
*	Used to perform multiplication.

TABLE 3.3: VBA OPERATORS *(continued)*

OPERATOR	DESCRIPTION
+	Addition operator.
−	Subtraction operator.
/	Floating-point division operator.
\	Integer division operator.
^	Used to raise a number to the power of an exponent.
=	Assignment operator. Used to assign a value to a variable or property.
AddressOf	Used to pass the address of a procedure to API procedures requiring function pointer.
And	Checks two expressions to see if both expressions are true.
Comparison Operators	The various combinations of =, <, and > used to compare expressions.
Eqv	Performs a logical equivalence on two expressions.
Imp	Performs a logical implication on two expressions.
Is	Used to compare object references.
Like	Used to compare strings.
Mod	Used to find the remainder resulting from the division of two numbers.
Not	Performs logical negation.
Or	Checks two expressions to see if one or both are true.
Xor	Checks two expressions to see if one and only one expression is true.

Other than the mathematical operators, you'll usually find yourself using the comparison operators alone or in conjunction with And, Is, Not, and Or to implement logic in order to determine when to terminate loops, or as part of an If...Then statement. Looping and If...Then statements are covered in the next section.

Directing Your Program with Statements

Statements are the workhorses of the VBA programming language. Among other things, statements allow you to implement looping and make logical decisions. You already used a few statements earlier when you declared variables, subroutines, and functions. This section deals with the statements that are most useful for implementing logic in your programs.

Implementing Loops

Looping, or executing a section of code repeatedly, is a common need in programming. There are two classes of loops: fixed loops, have a definite, known number of times that they execute, and variable loops generally rely on a logical expression to determine whether looping should continue or not.

FIXED LOOPS: FOR...NEXT

Not only are For...Next loops easy to use, they're also fairly flexible. I show the general structure of a For...Next loop in the following simple procedure. This procedure prints the numbers 1 to 50 in the Immediate window.

```
Sub SimpleForNext()
    Dim n As Integer

    For n = 1 To 50
        Debug.Print n
    Next
End Sub
```

As the following example illustrates, you can also go backward and use increments other than 1. The following procedure prints even numbers in descending order from 50 to 1 to the Immediate window.

```
Sub ReverseForNext()
    Dim n As Integer

    For n = 50 To 1 Step -2
        Debug.Print n
    Next
End Sub
```

DEBUGGING WITH DEBUG.PRINT

Debug.Print is useful during the development process to check various aspects of your code. Debug.Print [output] prints the output to the Immediate window. For example, by sprinkling Debug.Print statements in your code, you can record how a particular variable of interest changes as your program executes. You can print multiple variables at once by separating each variable with a comma as shown in the following example.

```
Sub IllustrateDebug()

    Dim x As Integer

    Dim y As Integer


    Debug.Print "-X-", "-Y-"

    For x = 1 To 10

        For y = 10 To 1 Step -1

            Debug.Print x, y

        Next

    Next

End Sub
```

Often you'll use For...Next to loop through various workbook and worksheet objects such as worksheets, rows, columns, open workbooks, and so on. Listing 3.1 presents one way to loop through all of the worksheets in a workbook.

LISTING 3.1: LOOPING THROUGH WORKSHEETS IN A WORKBOOK

```
Sub WorksheetLoop()
    Dim nIndex As Integer

    For nIndex = 1 To ThisWorkbook.Worksheets.Count
        Debug.Print ThisWorkbook.Worksheets(nIndex).Name
    Next
End Sub
```

In Listing 3.1, I simply declared an integer variable named nIndex and used a For...Next loop to work my way through each worksheet, printing the name of each worksheet as I went. I'll cover the details of ThisWorkbook later in Chapter 5, but it is probably apparent what I'm doing with it here. ThisWorkbook is just a shorthand way to refer to the workbook that contains the code.

For...Each Variation

Often the items that you need to loop through are objects in a collection. A collection is a kind of object that contains like objects. For example, the Worksheets collection contains all of the worksheet objects in a workbook. VBA provides the statement For...Each specifically to loop through collections. For example, Listing 3.1 could also be written as follows:

```
Sub WorksheetLoop2()
    Dim ws As Worksheet

    For Each ws In ThisWorkbook.Worksheets
        Debug.Print ws.Name
    Next
End Sub
```

This variation can also be useful for looping through the elements in an array as demonstrated here:

```
Sub ArrayLoop()
    Dim avColors As Variant
    Dim vItem As Variant

    avColors = Array("Red", "Green", "Blue")

    For Each vItem In avColors
        Debug.Print vItem
    Next
End Sub
```

This procedure creates an array using the handy Array function that assigns an array to a variant variable. It then loops through the elements in the array using For…Each.

Before I move on to the next topic, I should point out one more thing you can do within a fixed loop. Occasionally, you may need to exit a For…Next loop before completing all of the iterations. To exit a For…Next loop early, you can use the Exit For statement. For example, suppose you are looping through a bunch of cells on a worksheet looking for a cell that exhibits a certain characteristic. Once you find the cell, you don't need to look in the remaining cells. Listing 3.2 demonstrates this functionality.

LISTING 3.2: EXITING A FOR…NEXT LOOP EARLY

```
Sub ExitForExample()
    Dim nLastRow As Integer
    Dim nColumn As Integer
    Dim nRow As Integer
    Dim ws As Worksheet

    Set ws = ThisWorkbook.Worksheets(1)
    nLastRow = 15
    nColumn = 1

    For nRow = 1 To nLastRow
        If ws.Cells(nRow, nColumn).Address = "$A$7" Then
            Debug.Print "Found cell. Exiting for loop."
            Exit For
        Else
            Debug.Print ws.Cells(nRow, nColumn).Address
        End If
    Next

    Set ws = Nothing
End Sub
```

This listing draws on many of the topics we've discussed and some that we've yet to discuss. Let's take a minute to analyze this listing and review what we've discussed. First, notice the empty rows between some of the statements in this listing. These empty rows serve to break the procedure into four logical groupings. The first grouping contains the subroutine declaration and declares the variables the procedure will use. The second grouping initializes any applicable variables. This procedure uses an object variable named *ws* to refer to a worksheet. Notice that object variables are assigned using the Set keyword. The third grouping represents the main body of the procedure—where the logic of the procedure is implemented. The final grouping dereferences any object variables and formally marks the end of the procedure.

To dereference an object variable is to explicitly free the memory associated with the variable. Dereferencing object variables is not technically required, but it is good programming practice. Remember, your goal should be to write code that clearly and explicitly expresses your true intentions.

By explicitly dereferencing an object variable, you indicate that you are through using the object. You'll experience some technical benefits as well, but they are just gravy for now.

VARIABLE LOOPS: DO...LOOP

You can use Do loops to create a repetitive code sequence that repeats until it finds a terminating condition. In fact, a terminating condition isn't even required. A Do...Loop without a terminating condition keeps repeating indefinitely. The Do...Loop has two variations. Here is the general syntax of the first variation:

```
Do [{While | Until} condition]
    ' your code
    [Exit Do]
    ' your code
Loop
```

Using Do...While causes the loop to continue *while* a condition is true. The Do...Until form loops *until* the condition becomes true. Exit Do allows you to exit the Do loop immediately from within the loop.

Here is the general syntax of the second variation:

```
Do
    ' your code
    [Exit Do]
    ' your code
Loop [{While | Until} condition]
```

The difference is that the first variation won't execute the statement block within the Do... Loop if the condition is false to begin with (assuming you're using Do...While). With the second variation, the statement block with the Do...Loop always executes at least once.

Do loops have the potential to hang your application in the form of an endless loop. It almost goes without saying then that you must take great care in ensuring that you choose a terminating condition that is a sure thing.

Implementing Branching with If...Then

Now that you know how to execute repetitive blocks of code, you need to know how to implement branching in your code. Branching is the process of selectively executing certain blocks of code depending on the value of an expression.

You use the If...Then statement to implement branching. The simplest form of the If...Then statement tests a single expression and executes a single statement if the expression is true. An example of a simple If...Then is shown here:

```
If sLetter = "A" Then rg.Font.Bold = True
```

If you need to execute multiple statements when a particular expression is true, then you can use the If...End If variation. Here's an example:

```
If CurrentDate > PaymentDueDate Then
    AmtDue = AmtDue + LateFee
    rgCustomer.Interior.Color = vbRed
End If
```

Another variation on If...Then is the If...Then...Else...End If variation. This form allows you to execute one or more statements if the expression is true and one or more statements if the expression is false. For example, consider the following small block of code. This small fragment provides an example of how you might use If...Then to decide what to do with the response the user provides to a MsgBox function.

```
nResponse = MsgBox("Finished processing. Process another?", vbYesNo)

If nResponse = vbYes Then
    OpenNextFile      ' mythical procedure to open another file
    ProcessNextFile   ' mythical procedure to process another file
Else
    CloseCurrentFile ' mythical procedure to close current file
    ShutdownApp       ' mythical procedure to gracefully end application
End If
```

USING IF...THEN...ELSEIF

Occasionally you'll have more than two different branches that you'll want your code to choose from. One of the solutions in this case is to use If...Then...ElseIf. This variation allows you to choose one of any number of different branches. Listing 3.3 illustrates the use of If...Then...ElseIf.

LISTING 3.3: USING IF...THEN...ELSEIF

```
Sub TestIfThenElseIf()
    IfThenElseIf 5, 4
    IfThenElseIf 7, 0
    IfThenElseIf 13, 4
    IfThenElseIf 12, 12
End Sub

Sub IfThenElseIf(n As Integer, y As Integer)
    If n = 5 Then
        Debug.Print "n = 5"
        ' you could have more statements here
        ' or you could call another procedure
    ElseIf n = 6 Then
        Debug.Print "n = 6"
        ' you could have more statements here
        ' or you could call another procedure
    ElseIf n = 7 Then
        Debug.Print "n = 7"
        ' you could have more statements here
        ' or you could call another procedure
    ElseIf y = 4 Then
        Debug.Print "y = 4"
```

```
            ' you could have more statements here
            ' or you could call another procedure
        Else
            Debug.Print "This is a default action"
            ' you could have more statements here
            ' or you could call another procedure
        End If
    End Sub
```

Running TestIfThenElseIf produces the following output:

```
n = 5
n = 7
y = 4
This is a default action
```

This listing draws on some concepts that were covered earlier in the chapter. The main thing to point out is that parameters are used in the declaration of the IfThenElseIf procedure. Once you declare parameters in the declaration of a procedure, you can use those parameters as you would any other variable in the body of the procedure. Notice in the TestIfThenElseIf procedure that when you call a procedure that uses parameters, you specify the parameters after the procedure name separated by commas.

The If...Then...ElseIf statement in Listing 3.3 highlights the flexibility you are afforded when you use this statement. Specifically, when you are testing the various expressions, nothing prevents you from testing nonrelated variables. For example, the last ElseIf tests the y variable rather than the n variable. This allows you to construct complicated logic. Be careful not to shoot yourself in the foot with this. You'll find it easy to create such complicated logic using this technique, but it's very difficult to debug or modify it later. In such cases, it's usually a better idea to develop a function specifically to test the expressions.

Another option to using If...Then...ElseIf is to consider the Select Case statement, which is covered in the "Choosing Actions with Select Case" section later in the chapter.

NESTING IF...THEN STATEMENTS

You can nest If...Then statements to create any branching structure you need or to check for multiple conditions before you execute a statement. It can be easy to lose your place so to speak when you're using nested If statements, so you'll find that it helps to use indenting to clarify which If...Then block those statements are associated with. Also, I find it helpful to create the entire skeleton of an If...Then...Else statement when I first create it and then go back and add the statements that are part of each branch.

A NOTE ON INDENTING CODE

Indenting your code has the benefit of making your procedures easier to read. The need to indent becomes clear once you start nesting If...Then statements. As with variable naming, how and whether you use indenting is personal preference; however, the style I've used in this book is widely accepted and I'd strongly recommend adopting it.

CHOOSING AN ACTION USING IIF

An alternative to If…Then is the IIF() function. This function behaves just like the IF worksheet function in Excel. The syntax of IIF is as follows:

```
IIf(expr, truepart, falsepart)
```

For example:

```
IIF(1<10, "True. 1 is less than 10", "False. 1 is not less than 10")
```

would return the text "True. 1 is less than 10".

You'll find IIF useful when you are conducting simple calculations and comparisons. The main limitation of IIF versus If…Then is that IIF can't be used to perform branching because you can't execute statements from within IIF().

Thinking Like a Computer Revisited

At the beginning of the chapter, I talked about a simple program that would loop through the items on a worksheet list and highlight any item that begins with 'A' in bold font. You're now familiar enough with the vocabulary of VBA that you can implement this program using terms your computer can understand, as shown in Listing 3.4. The part that I haven't covered yet is how to use Excel's Workbook object and Range object. I'll cover these in Chapters 7 and 8, respectively. However, I think you'll find that using these objects is pretty straightforward for the purposes of this easy exercise.

LISTING 3.4: SIMPLE LIST PROCESSING

```
Sub SimpleListProcessing()
    ' Declare our varibles
    Dim wb As Workbook
    Dim rg As Range

    ' Initialize our variables
    Set wb = Workbooks.Open("C:\Examples\List Example.xls")
    Set rg = wb.Worksheets("Sheet1").Range("B3")

    ' Loop through cells moving down one cell
    ' until an empty cell is found
    Do Until IsEmpty(rg)
        If Left(rg.Value, 1) = "A" Then rg.Font.Bold = True
        Set rg = rg.Offset(1, 0)
    Loop

    ' Dereference object variables
    Set rg = Nothing
    Set wb = Nothing
End Sub
```

As in Listing 3.2, this procedure has four logical sections. Many procedures follow this four-section grouping, but there is no rule or guideline to follow regarding the organization of your procedures. You may find that you prefer to organize your procedures differently. The high-level organization is to declare variables, initialize variables, implement procedure logic, and dereference object variables. This procedure uses two object variables: the Workbook object and the Range object. I'll cover these objects in great detail booking Chapters 6 and 8, respectively. As you'd expect, the Workbook object has an Open method that allows VBA code to open workbooks. Note that this listing assumes that the list example workbook is in the folder C:\Examples. If you try this procedure, be sure to either copy the list example workbook to this location or modify this line appropriately.

Your Do...Loop relies on the IsEmpty function to determine if an empty cell has been reached. Once an empty cell is found, the Do...Loop terminates. Inside the loop, you can use the Left function to return the first character of the value found in the current cell. If the first character is "A", then you use bold font in the cell. To move to the next cell you employ the Offset method of the Range object. Finally, in the last section, you dereference your object variables and formally end the subroutine.

Hopefully what you take away from this is that although you can't just say, "make any cell that begins with the letter 'A' bold," it is fairly straightforward to accomplish this.

Choosing Actions with Select Case

As you saw earlier, one way to check an expression against a range of possible values is by using If...Then...ElseIf as you did in Listing 3.3. This method has the advantage of being able to check expressions containing unrelated variables. Most of the time, however, you only need to check for a range of possible values related to a single variable. For this purpose, Select Case is a better choice. The general syntax of Select Case is as follows:

```
Select Case YourExpression
    [Case expression1]
        [statements1]
    [Case expression2]
        [statements2]
    [Case expressionn]
        [statementsn]
    [Case Else]
        [statementselse]]
End Select
```

When Select Case finds a match to *YourExpression* in one of the expressions following a Case statement, Select Case executes the statement block associated with the Case statement. After it executes the statement block, program control resumes with the statement that follows the End Select statement. Note that if you are coming from a different programming language, this behavior is different from what you may be used to. Select Case doesn't evaluate any other Case statements after a match has been found. The optional Case Else statement acts as a default case and executes any code that you want to run if it doesn't find a match.

Select Case is quite flexible in how it interprets the Case expressions. You can specify individual values or ranges of values and use comparison operators. Listing 3.5 provides an example of this.

LISTING 3.5: SELECT CASE EXAMPLE

```
Sub TestChooseActivity()
    Debug.Print ChooseActivity(25)
    Debug.Print ChooseActivity(34)
    Debug.Print ChooseActivity(35)
    Debug.Print ChooseActivity(65)
    Debug.Print ChooseActivity(66)
    Debug.Print ChooseActivity(75)
    Debug.Print ChooseActivity(95)
End Sub

Function ChooseActivity(Temperature As Integer) As String
    Dim sActivity As String

    Select Case Temperature
        Case Is < 32
            sActivity = "Snowmobiling"
        Case 33, 35 To 45
            sActivity = "Housework"
        Case 34
            sActivity = "Snowball Fight"
        Case 46 To 50, 65, 70 To 72
            sActivity = "Clean the Garage"
        Case 75 To 80
            sActivity = "Golf"
        Case 80 To 100
            sActivity = "Waterski"
        Case Else
            sActivity = "Take a nap."
    End Select

    ChooseActivity = sActivity
End Function
```

Executing TestChooseActivity produces the following results:

```
Snowmobiling
Snowball Fight
Housework
Clean the Garage
Take a nap.
Golf
Waterski
```

Notice in Listing 3.5 that the Case statements use a variety of methods to determine whether there is a match. This listing uses the less than (<) comparison operator, ranges, lists of values, and individual values. This code is also exciting because it demonstrates how you might use a function procedure for something other than a user-defined function. These internal functions demonstrate a much more common use of functions other than as user-defined functions on a worksheet. Although user-defined functions are useful, when I reflect on all of the functions I've coded, I've probably written 50 internal functions for every user-defined function.

Basic Array Usage

An array is a set of indexed elements that have the same data type. An array allows you to declare a single variable with many individual compartments. You declare arrays the same as you would any other variable with the exception that you generally specify the size of an array (the number of elements it can contain) when you declare it. An array whose size is specified in its declaration is said to be a fixed-length array. Alternatively, if you don't specify a size when you declare an array, a dynamic array is created. A dynamic array is an array whose size can be altered at run-time or during the execution of your code. Listing 3.6 contains some sample array declarations.

LISTING 3.6: SAMPLE ARRAY DECLARATIONS

```
' Declare an array of integers with 26 elements
Dim anIntegerArray(25) As Integer

' Declare a two-dimensional long array
' with 10 rows and 15 columns
Dim alLongArray(9, 14) As Long

' Declare a dynamic array of variants
Dim avVariantArray() As Variant
```

By default, the index of an array begins with 0. That is why the array declarations above contain one more element than the number specified in the declaration. If you specify Option Base 1 at the top of your module, then the index of your arrays will begin with 1 rather than 0.

The second array declared in Listing 3.6 contains two dimensions. You can declare arrays with up to 60 dimensions. A word of warning however—multidimensional arrays can quickly sap your system resources, so if you're using more than a few dimensions, you'll want to keep an eye on the number of elements so that you can estimate the total impact on your system. To estimate the memory required by an array, take the product of the number of elements in each dimension times the storage size of the underlying data type. For example, consider the following array:

```
Dim adBigDoubleArray(10, 25, 50, 50) As Double
```

This declares a four-dimensional array containing 11 * 26 * 51 * 51 elements or 743,886 elements. It takes 8 bytes to store a single double variable, so the memory requirement of this array is 743,886 * 8 bytes (5,951,088 bytes).

Specifying the Index Range of an Array

As I mentioned earlier, by default the first element of an array is located at index 0. By using the Option Base 1 statement at the top of your module, you can instruct VBA to begin all arrays at index 1. Another way to specify how your array indexes the elements it contains is by using the To clause in the declaration. A good example of this is an array that holds data specific to the day of the week. For example, suppose you need a variable to hold sales data associated with each day of the week. Listing 3.7 demonstrates how you might do this.

LISTING 3.7: ARRAY USAGE EXAMPLE

```
Sub ArrayExample()
    Dim acWeeklySales(1 To 7) As Currency
    Dim n As Integer
    Dim sDay As String

    acWeeklySales(1) = 55100.44
    acWeeklySales(2) = 43666.43
    acWeeklySales(3) = 67004.11
    acWeeklySales(4) = 87121.29
    acWeeklySales(5) = 76444.94
    acWeeklySales(6) = 98443.84
    acWeeklySales(7) = 87772.37

    For n = 1 To 7
        sDay = Choose(n, "Mon", "Tue", "Wed", "Thu", _
            "Fri", "Sat", "Sun")
        Debug.Print _
        "Sales for " & sDay & " were $" & acWeeklySales(n)
    Next

End Sub
```

Executing ArrayExample produces the following output.

```
Sales for Mon were $55100.44
Sales for Tue were $43666.43
Sales for Wed were $67004.11
Sales for Thu were $87121.29
Sales for Fri were $76444.94
Sales for Sat were $98443.84
Sales for Sun were $87772.37
```

Listing 3.7 uses a seven-element array in which the index range is 1 to 7. This makes it easy to translate each element to the day of the week to which it belongs. To do this, I used the Choose function, which works similarly to the Choose worksheet function in Excel. Choose takes an index number (n) and returns the nth item found in the list supplied to it.

Listing 3.7 also introduces the line continuation character (_). I used it in this example to break up a few lines so that they could fit within the pages of this book. You may find it helpful to break up long lines of code so that you can read them without have to scroll horizontally. Make sure that there is a space between the line continuation character and the last element of code or else you'll get a compile error.

Objects—A Human-Friendly Way to Think of Bits and Bytes

Throughout this book, you'll read about objects. Objects are the items available for you to manipulate in your code. Thank goodness brilliant computer scientists came up with ways to program this way; otherwise we'd all have to learn the Assembly language or some other language that is much "closer" to the computer (no thanks!). Basically objects allow you to think and develop using terms that you'd probably use when you talk to your coworkers. In Chapter 13, you'll learn how to create your own objects. Until then, however, you'll focus on learning how to use all of the objects associated with Excel.

In Excel, there is a Workbook object, a Worksheet object, a Range object (a range could be just one cell), a PivotTable object, and even a Comment object. Any item that you can interact with using Excel's menus is also available to you as an object.

If you are a beginner, one benefit of using objects is that once you get past the initial terminology and use of object variables, it is often very easy to find and manipulate the object that you need to use. For example, you can probably tell what the following lines of code do:

```
Sub ManipulateWorksheet()
    Dim ws As Worksheet

    Set ws = ThisWorkbook.Worksheets(1)

    ws.Unprotect "XLCoder"
    ws.Range("A1").Value = ws.Name
    ws.CheckSpelling
    ws.Calculate
    ws.Protect "XLCoder"

    Set ws = Nothing
End Sub
```

As you can see, the worksheet object contains methods and properties that are named the same way you may think about them.

NOTE   You may also see objects referred to as classes. There is, in fact, a distinction between the two terms. A class defines and implements an object. An object refers to a specific instance of the class. The common analogy is that a class is a cookie cutter, and an object is a cookie. For now, I wouldn't worry about understanding this difference as it is not germane to developing a basic understanding of how to use objects.

Methods and Properties

Objects are conceptually simple enough to understand, but it often takes people awhile to understand the difference between methods and properties. Luckily, it is not critical that you understand the difference and eventually it sinks in and makes perfect sense. In fact, you could just lump them all together and refer to them collectively as members of an object.

In a nutshell, properties are the characteristics that describe an object and methods are the actions that the object can perform. Consider where you live. You could call this a Residence object. A Residence object would have a property called Type, which may indicate that your residence is a house, apartment, or condo. It would also have an Owned property, which would be True if you owned your residence or False if you rented. The list below represents other properties your Residence object might have.

◆ Color

◆ Bedrooms

◆ Bathrooms

◆ Square Feet

◆ Temperature

Methods are actions that an object can perform. For example, your Residence object may have a Cool method that cools the house (using the AirConditioner object) and a Heat method the heats the house (using the Furnace object). Many times, but not always, using an object's method alters one or more of that object's properties. For instance, the Cool and Heat methods would change the Temperature property. If you had a Renovate method, perhaps you could change the Bedrooms and Square Feet properties. Unfortunately the Renovate method would probably require quite a bit of cache, er, I mean cash.

COLLECTION OBJECTS

Collections are objects that exist to serve as containers for objects of a given type. The Residence object has two collection objects: Bedrooms and Bathrooms. Bedrooms is a way to collectively refer to all of the bedrooms in a given residence. Another way to describe this is that the Bedrooms collection is a collection of Bedroom objects.

Collection objects generally have special properties and methods that you can use to manage the collection. Usually there is an Add method, an Item method, and a Remove method. The Item method is used to retrieve a specific object from the collection. You can refer to an object in a collection either by name or number. For example, the following two statements would achieve the same result—initializing a Bedroom variable with a Bedroom retrieved from the Bedrooms collection:

```
Set BedroomVariable = Residence.Bedrooms.Item(1)
Set BedroomVariable = Residence.Bedrooms.Item("JoesRoom")
```

Collection objects always have a Count property that returns the number of items in a collection.

Summary

Believe it or not, you now have a basic toolbox with which to begin furthering your skills as an Excel developer. In the process of learning how to use Excel's object model you'll be continually exposed

---

IDENTITY CONFUSION: AM I A PROPERTY OR A METHOD?

One of the reasons that differentiating between properties and methods is often difficult is that programmers don't always follow the conventions for naming properties and methods. The Count property is a good example. Generally speaking, methods are named using verbs or words that describe action, and properties are named using nouns. Based on the name, you'd expect to see Count classified as a method rather than as a property.

Based on the methods-as-verbs rule, the remedy for this situation would be to classify Count as a method or rename it using a more conventional property name such as Number. Granted, the term *Number* may not be as clear semantically as *Count*. In any event, it is not that big of a deal.

The main point is that developers often depart from existing conventions for one reason or another, and you should be aware of this as you develop your mental model. Remember, models are simulations that simplify the complexities of reality.

---

to the language features presented in this chapter (to better learn how to use your tools) and gradually exposed to additional features as they become relevant to the discussion (to expand your toolbox). Therefore, if you're feeling overwhelmed or confused, don't panic. Through the repetition and practice you'll be exposed to in the following chapters, it will become clear.

In summary, focus on the following points:

- ◆ Organize your procedures in modules according to the functionality that each procedure helps provide.

- ◆ Although it is all right to use subroutines, try to find ways to integrate functions into your application. A function returns a value to the procedure that called it; a subroutine does not.

- ◆ Explicitly declare your variables using an appropriate data type where possible. Usually you'll use Strings, Integers, Longs, Booleans, and Doubles.

- ◆ Implement logic in your procedures using If…Then…Else…End If or the Select Case statement.

- ◆ Implement looping using For…Next or Do…Loop.

Keep the concept of variable scope in mind. Variable scope refers to the breadth of a variable's visibility. A variable can be seen only by statements within a given procedure (a local or procedural level variable), by any statement within the same module (a module level variable), or by any statement in any open project (a global variable). Variable scope is determined by the location of the variables declaration and the use of the Public or Private keywords. It is best if you give a variable the narrowest scope possible.

Before we get into using the Excel object model, you need to acquire one more fundamental skill—debugging. You'll make mistakes no matter what your experience level. By developing sound debugging skills, you'll save yourself countless hours and a great deal of frustration. In the next chapter, you'll examine the various debugging features and explore some debugging techniques.

Chapter 4

Debugging Tactics that Work

YOU HAVE ALREADY READ this next statement multiple times: you will make mistakes. Lots of them. This has nothing to do with skill. Everyone makes mistakes. The difference between the beginning developer and the veteran is that the veteran recognizes, diagnoses, and corrects her mistakes much, much more quickly than a beginner.

In this chapter, I'll get you off to a good start by teaching the debugging tools and features included in the Visual Basic Editor (VBE) and tactics that you can employ to troubleshoot your code when things go wrong.

A Bug Epidemic

Three types of bugs or errors can contribute to an outbreak of errors. One kind is rather mild and more of a nuisance than anything. The other two can be more problematic and often work together to really give you fits.

Syntax Errors Are Your Friend

Syntax errors are errors that occur when your code doesn't adhere to the syntax requirements of VBA. Perhaps no error is your friend, but if you had to pick an error as your friend, this would be a good choice. Syntax errors are relatively benign because they *usually* occur at development time and, as long as you have the Auto Syntax Check feature turned on, *some* can be automatically detected by the VBE as you enter your code.

NOTE *Programmers frequently use the terms* development time *and* run-time *when discussing various programming topics. The term development time refers to the period of time when you are actively developing code. The term runtime refers to the period of time when your code is being executed.*

But wait a minute, why doesn't the Auto Syntax Check feature detect *all* syntax errors? The Auto Syntax Check feature can detect only those syntax errors that it has enough context to detect. Specifically, it can only detect syntax errors that occur within a single statement or line of code. For example, the line

```
Debug.Prinf "This syntax error will be detected"
```

is a syntax error that the Auto Syntax Check feature can detect because it doesn't need any other statements to give this line meaning. This statement is an error because Debug.Print was mistakenly entered as Debug.Prinf. Listing 4.1, by contrast, contains a syntax error that can't be found by Auto Syntax Check.

LISTING 4.1: A SYNTAX ERROR SPANNING MULTIPLE LINES

```
Sub MissingNextStatement()
    Dim n as Integer

    For n = 1 To 5
        MsgBox "n = " & n
End Sub

Sub CallBadProcedure()
    MissingNextStatement
End Sub
```

The problem with Listing 4.1 is that it is missing a Next statement. I classify this as a syntax error because it violates the syntax requirements of VBA. Every For statement should be followed at some point in the same procedure by a Next statement. Auto Syntax Check can never alert you to this error because it checks individual statements only as they are entered. Therefore, it can't check for syntax errors that require other statements to ensure proper procedure formation.

Technically, I would still classify this more difficult form of a syntax error as a development time error. Unfortunately, developers often release applications containing syntax errors and their users stumble into them at run-time. This would lead one to believe that these are run-time errors; however, this is not technically correct. End users should never see these kinds of errors because they are easily detected and corrected at development time. I must admit to being guilty of committing the following sin myself. Just so nobody misses the following important debugging rule, we should put this in lights:

Debugging Rule #1: Always compile your project before distributing your "completed" application. You may need to compile multiple times as the compile process stops when it finds its first error. Keep compiling until you aren't notified of any problems. Compile by selecting Debug ➤ Compile *YourProjectName*.

Debugging Rule #2: Use the auto syntax check option. Occasionally it helps to turn this option off for short periods when you are copying/pasting code into a module that requires some editing. This option is found on the Editor tab of the Options dialog box (Tools ➤ Options).

The reason the error in Listing 4.1 can appear at run-time is that VBA lets you save and distribute applications without compiling them as you would in most other programming languages. When your users run your application and cause something to happen that executes the procedure containing the syntax error, an error occurs. By compiling your application before you distribute it, you force it to be subjected to the VBA compiler; this ensures that all of the code in your project is syntactically correct. You can use Listing 4.1 to experiment with this—just follow these steps:

1. Enter all of the code into an empty module and then save the workbook. Notice that you aren't warned of any errors.

2. Switch to Excel, press Alt+F8, and run the macro CallBadProcedure, which just executes the MissingNextStatement procedure. Bingo. You experience the error that your users would see if you sent the workbook to them without compiling it first. The fun-loving users will love to rib you about the "special functionality" you built into your application.

3. In the VBE select Run ➤ Reset to exit from Break mode.

4. Now you need to fool the compiler into thinking it needs to compile again because when you performed step 2, the compiler compiled the MissingNextStatement procedure on demand. Place the cursor at the end of any line and hit the Space bar. The VBE interprets this as a change to your code and allows you to recompile the project in the following step.

5. Compile the application by selecting Debug ➤ Compile VBAProject.

When you perform step 5, the compiler issues the warning shown next. Remember, the last thing you should do before distributing your work is compile your project to ensure that you don't have any syntax errors in your application.

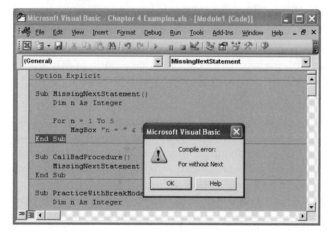

Run-Time Embarrassments

Run-time errors are the most noticeable errors that your end users will encounter. Hopefully you uncover and correct all of these errors in development and testing. Run-time errors occur when your code encounters conditions that either you didn't expect to occur or you didn't think to handle. Examples of run-time errors might include the following:

◆ Dividing by zero

◆ Trying to open a nonexistent workbook

◆ Referring to a nonexistent worksheet

Run-time errors are harder to detect than syntax errors for two reasons. First, the code is flawless from the point of view of the compiler, so it can't automatically detect them. Second, you'll find it hard to envision every possible condition your program might encounter. Even if you could, where do you draw the line between what is likely to happen versus what is not?

This second point gets to the prime strategy for dealing with run-time errors—the best offense is a good defense. In order to prevent run-time errors, you need to consider what types of conditions are likely to occur and write your code to check at run-time for potential problems that would cause a run-time error.

> **Debugging Rule #3: The best offense against buggy programs is good defense.** As an example of what I mean by a good defense, consider a common need in Excel programming—the need to refer to a worksheet by name. Let's say that when you developed your program, you assumed that you'd have a worksheet named Income Statement and throughout your code you had code snippets such as the following:

```
...
Dim ws As Worksheet

Set ws = ThisWorkbook.Worksheets("Income Statement")
...
```

Now, if you haven't taken precautions to prevent your end users from changing the name of the Income Statement worksheet, this code is extremely risky. What happens if the name of the worksheet changes or is deleted? You got it—a run-time error.

In order to deal with situations like this, you need to write code defensively. In this case, you could write a function that makes sure that a worksheet named Income Statement exists before you explicitly refer to it. You could also employ a protection strategy on the Income Statement worksheet so that its name can't be changed. Finally, you could put some error-handling code in your procedure. Because this chapter is aimed more at correcting buggy programs, I'll not get into the details of these strategies at this point. Rest assured, however, once I get into covering the Excel object model in later chapters, I'll provide you with a significant number of code examples that will give you a nice inventory of procedures you can use for defensive programming purposes.

Logical Errors Cause Gray Hair

The third and final classification of errors consists of errors caused by faulty logic. Logical errors have the potential to live unnoticed for a long period of time; this is because your application will, from all outward appearances, appear to work just fine. Logical errors aren't discovered by the compiler at development or compile time and they don't embarrass you by displaying terse run-time errors to your end users. Though most logical errors are found and don't cause serious problems, some logical errors can be extremely difficult to find and have the potential to do great harm depending on what your application is used for.

Let me give you an example. Perhaps you have a reporting routine that performs some calculations. Logical errors in your calculations may be causing your report to be reporting flawed numbers. Unless the numbers are tied out or reconciled against some other source or against manual calculations, no one may ever notice the logical error. Your program will appear to run with nary a hiccup. If your report is used as a primary source of information for important decisions, what would the impact be to the decision making process if the numbers were flawed?

For logical errors, detection is the primary concern. You can't fix anything if you don't know it is broken. Thus we come to rule number four.

Debugging Rule #4: Test. Test. Test.   Although you also want to detect any run-time errors lurking in your program, it is more important to focus on detecting logical errors by comparing the output of critical parts of your program against output that comes from another source or that is manually calculated and validated.

Debugging Weapons in the VBE

Now that you know what kinds of bugs are lurking in your code and how to detect their presence, it's time to talk about the weapons you have at your disposal to assist in their eradication. Most of these weapons can only be used in Break mode, so we'll begin there.

Break Mode: For Fixing Things that Are Broken

The prime time for catching bugs is in Break mode. Break mode is a special mode of operation in the VBE that allows you to execute lines of code one at a time. You can watch your code execute and stop after each line to examine the state and values of your variables.

This can be a big help in eradicating logical errors, because many logical errors stem from a fundamental difference between the way you thought a certain section of code would execute and the way that VBA actually executes it. By watching critical sections of code execute line by line, many times you can quickly see the error of your ways.

You can enter Break mode in multiple ways. Listing 4.2 contains a simple procedure that you can use to experiment with Break mode.

LISTING 4.2: SIMPLE PROCEDURE FOR EXPERIMENTING WITH BREAK MODE

```
Sub PracticeWithBreakMode()
    Dim n As Integer

    For n = 1 To 20
        Debug.Print n
        If n = 5 Then
            Stop
        End If
    Next

    For n = 10 To 1 Step -2
        TrivialSub n
    Next
End Sub

Sub TrivialSub(x As Integer)
    Debug.Print "x = " & x
    Debug.Print "2x = " & x * 2
End Sub
```

This listing just prints some numbers to the immediate window. It does contain a statement you haven't seen yet, however— the Stop statement. You can see this statement in the first For...Next loop when n = 5. When a Stop statement is encountered, VBA suspends program execution and enters break mode. To see what happens when this occurs, follow these steps:

1. Enter the PracticeWithBreakMode procedure and the TrivialSub procedure into a module.

2. Switch back to Excel and Press ALT+F8 to display a list of executable procedures.

3. Run the PracticeWithBreakMode procedure.

If you follow these instructions, you'll probably still have the VBE window open, but minimized, when you execute the procedure. If the VBE window is closed when a Stop statement is encountered, VBA opens the VBE automatically.

WARNING *If you use Stop statements, be sure to remove them before you distribute your application.*

Figure 4.1 displays a screenshot of the PracticeWithBreakMode procedure in Break mode. Note the small arrow in the margin indicator bar. The margin indicator bar is on by default, but you can turn it on or off on the Editor Format tab of the Options dialog box (Tools ➤ Options).

In this figure, you'll also notice that the Stop statement is highlighted (the color of the highlighting is configurable on the Editor Format tab). The highlighting and small arrow in the margin indicator bar indicate the point or the line in your program at which the execution has been suspended. Finally, if you select the Debug menu item, you'll notice that many of the items are enabled.

Once in Break mode, you can execute each line of code individually, step into or over any procedures that the current procedure calls, inspect or change variable values, move the execution point to any valid statement in the current procedure, and even modify certain aspects of your program and then run or rerun them.

FIGURE 4.1
Break mode in the VBE looks only slightly different than normal mode.

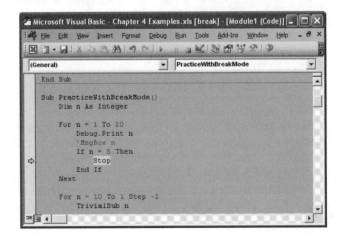

Directing Program Execution in Break Mode

The most common way to execute code in Break mode is to step through it line by line. You can achieve this by pressing F8 or Debug ➤ Step Into.

You'll probably get tired of using the menu item though, so I'd stick with F8. The Step Into method of executing code will go into any procedure that it encounters. For example, in Listing 4.2, the second For…Next loop makes a call to TrivialSub. If you step through this procedure using F8, every time TrivialSub is encountered you'll step through it as well.

Many times you won't want to step through every single procedure. Case in point—after you have stepped through TrivialSub once, is there really any need to step through it the remaining four times? Or you may know that many procedures in your program have been thoroughly tested and proven and are most likely not the source of your problem. In these instances, you'll want to use Step Over—SHIFT+F8 or Debug ➤ Step Over. Step Over runs any procedures called by the current procedure at normal speed, which means that your focus stays on the current procedure. If you experiment with stepping through Listing 4.2 using both F8 and SHIFT+F8, the difference between Step Into and Step Over will become clear.

If you accidentally step into a procedure, you can quickly exit it and return to the previous procedure by pressing CTRL+SHIFT+F8 or Debug ➤ Step Out.

TIP *To execute code in slow motion but without repetitively striking the keys, just hold down F8 or SHIFT+F8.*

While in Break mode, you may want to rapidly advance the code to another statement of interest. Let's say that after you encounter the Stop statement in Listing 4.2, you want to execute all of the code up to the first encounter of TrivialSub. You can accomplish this by placing the cursor on the line containing TrivialSub and selecting Debug ➤ Run to Cursor. When you do this, program execution resumes at normal speed and reenters Break Mode when the line containing the cursor is reached.

Let me tell you about one more way to direct program execution in Break mode. You can also change the execution point by using the Set Next Statement feature. Using Set Next Statement, you can change the execution point to any other valid statement (not comment lines or variable declarations) in the same procedure. Set Next Statement is handy because you can use it to rewind and then rerun sections of interest without starting the program over.

Set Next Statement is a menu item under the Debug menu. Alternatively, you can press CTRL+F9 to set the next statement to the line containing the cursor. Finally, you can drag and drop the execution point indicator in the margin indicator bar as shown in Figure 4.2.

Finally, to exit Break mode and resume normal program execution, press F5 or choose Run ➤ Run Sub/UserForm.

FIGURE 4.2
You can arbitrarily run any statement in a procedure by dragging and dropping the execution point indicator. Releasing the mouse in this picture would move the execution point to the Debug.Print statement.

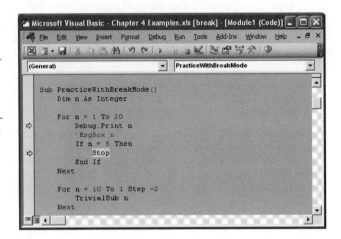

ALTERNATIVE METHODS FOR ENTERING BREAK MODE

Besides using Stop, which though effective, is not the best choice for most situations in which you want to enter Break mode, one of the easiest ways to enter Break mode is to press F8 in the VBE with the cursor inside an executable procedure. An executable procedure is any subroutine in a standard module that does not require any input parameters.

Another way to enter Break mode is by placing Breakpoints in your code. A Breakpoint works similarly to a Stop statement. When you execute a procedure containing a Breakpoint, your code runs normally until it reaches the statement containing the Breakpoint. At this point, Break mode is entered and program execution is suspended. Unlike using the Stop statement, you don't have to add any special statements to your code for this to work, so you don't have to worry about removing them before you distribute the application. Finally, Stop statements are persistent whereas Breakpoints are not. If you close a workbook that contains a Stop statement, the Stop statement is saved just like any other VBA statement. Breakpoints, meanwhile, are only remembered as long as the workbook is open. If you save, close, and then reopen the workbook, any Breakpoints you had before you closed the workbook are forgotten.

You can set Breakpoints in your code by placing the cursor on the line from which you would like to enter Break mode and pressing F9 or Debug ➤ Toggle Breakpoint. Press F9 again to turn the Breakpoint off. You can set any number of Breakpoints in your project. To clear all of the Breakpoints you have set at once, select Debug ➤ Clear All Breakpoints.

Reconnaissance Operations and Tools

When things aren't working right, before you can fix what is wrong, you usually need to gather more information. You can use this to decide on a course of action to correct the error. You can gather information about what is going on with your program in a number of ways including the Debug.Print statement, the MsgBox function, the Immediate Window, the Auto Quick Info option, the Call Stack, and the Locals window.

The Debug.Print statement and MsgBox function perform essentially the same function when you use them for debugging. To use either one of these, you need to embed them into your code at strategic places. You've already seen that Debug.Print prints its output to the immediate window. MsgBox displays its output on a small dialog box. Debug.Print requires you to be in the VBE to see the results while MsgBox shows itself in Excel. You could replace the Debug.Print statements in Listing 4.2 and achieve virtually the same result with one crucial difference—you need to respond to every call to MsgBox by pressing the Enter key.

YOUR PERSONAL FBI (WITHOUT THE SUFFOCATING BUREAUCRACY)

Although Debug.Print and MsgBox are easy to use and handy, they aren't adequate by themselves to perform mass inspection of variables. For Better Investigation of variables you can use the Locals window. I have got to tell you, I love the Locals window. You should learn to love it also. Here is why. The Locals window (see Figure 4.3) allows you to inspect the details associated with every variable that is currently in scope (see "Variable Scope and Lifetime" in Chapter 3). If the variable is an object variable, the Locals window allows you to inspect the values of that object's properties. All you need to do is display the Locals window in Break mode. The Locals window is so invaluable that it deserves a rule.

Debugging Rule #5: Use the Locals window for efficient debugging.   Not only is the Locals window handy for debugging, but using it has the wonderful side effect of increasing your knowledge and familiarity with the Excel object model.

Occasionally you'll have problems with a program because you aren't using or referring to the correct object's property for the task at hand. Or maybe you're in the development process and you're just not sure what property to use. One remedy to this problem is to run your procedure in Break mode with the Locals window displayed. Once you have set a variable to refer to the correct object, you can inspect the values associated with the variable and locate the property containing the value that you are looking for. This can be much faster than trial and error or searching through documentation looking for the appropriate property (though it is not a bad idea to look at the documentation for the property once you've identified it—it might alert you to a potential 'gotcha').

As an example of this technique, take another look at Figure 4.3. The variable *ws* refers to a worksheet object.

WARNING   *Unless you are a glutton for punishment, when inspecting a worksheet object using the Locals window, don't expand the Cells collection. If you do, your computer will work for a long time trying to take inventory on the 16,777,216 cells on a worksheet.*

FIGURE 4.3

The Locals window is great for mass examination of variables.

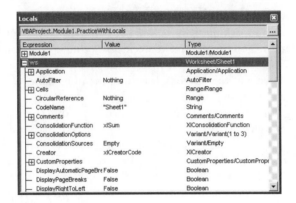

AD HOC INSPECTION TOOLS

For simple ad hoc variable inspection in Break mode, you can use one of two available tools. First, there is the Auto Data Tips feature. I mentioned this feature in Chapter 2 in the "Helpful Editor Features" section. Auto Data Tips shows the value associated with variables when you hover the cursor over the variable in Break mode.

The other tool you can use is the statement evaluation feature of the Immediate window. For example, if you have a variable named x, you could see the value of x by typing ?x in the Immediate window and pressing Enter.

Why would you use these two tools when you can use the Locals window or Debug.Print? Relative to Debug.Print, the advantage of these two tools is that you don't have to plan ahead or add statements to your code to use them.

The Locals window, meanwhile, requires quite a bit of screen real estate to use effectively. I usually only display the Locals window when I really need it. If I only want to examine a few simple variables, it is often faster to just use Auto Data Tips or the Immediate window.

An advantage of using the Immediate window for ad hoc examination is that you can evaluate variables in the context of a function. Perhaps you have a string variable named sFullName that contains the value "Franklin, Benjamin" and you want to know the result of using the variable in an expression such as this.

```
? Trim(Right(sFullName, Len(sFullName) - InStr(1, sFullName, ",")))
Benjamin
```

If your program isn't running correctly and you suspect that it is the result of using a function incorrectly or an expression that isn't logically correct, it is an excellent idea to use the Immediate window to test possible corrections using the variables your procedure uses. The alternative is to change the statement in question and reexecute your program—not nearly as efficient.

A second advantage of using the Immediate window for ad hoc examination is that you can change the value of your variables and then continue program execution. Maybe you have a For...Next loop that contains some sort of error within the body of the loop. If you don't discover or correct the error the first time through the loop, you could start the loop over or focus on a specific loop counter value by resetting the loop counter to another value. Consider the following code fragment.

```
Dim nIndex As Integer

For nIndex = 1 To 10
    ' some statements
Next
```

At any point, you could enter nIndex = 5 in the Immediate window and press Enter to change the value of nIndex to 5.

Zero In on Problem Areas with Watches

Occasionally, your program works as planned most of the time, but it also occasionally bombs out for unknown reasons. Usually this is due to the introduction of unplanned data in your application. One technique you can use to locate the exact spot where your application is encountering problematic data is by using a watch. A watch allows you to instruct the VBE to watch the value of a variable or statement and perform various actions (such as entering Break mode) depending on what happens to the value.

For example, consider Listing 4.3. This listing contains a function named GetMonth that translates a month index into a month name. This listing also houses a simple procedure named Print-Months that calls GetMonth with the values 1 through 13. Of course, no month is associated with the value 13. When it receives invalid numbers, GetMonth returns an empty string.

LISTING 4.3: TESTING THE WATCH FUNCTIONALITY WITH A FUNCTION

```
Sub PrintMonths()
    Dim nMonth As Integer

    For nMonth = 1 To 13
        Debug.Print "The month is: " & GetMonth(nMonth)
    Next
End Sub


' Returns the name of the month associated
' with the MonthIndex.
Function GetMonth(MonthIndex As Integer) As String
    If MonthIndex < 1 Or MonthIndex > 12 Then
        GetMonth = ""
    Else
        GetMonth = Choose(MonthIndex, _
            "January", "February", "March", _
            "April", "May", "June", _
            "July", "August", "September", _
            "October", "November", "December")
    End If
End Function
```

Running PrintMonths produces the following output:

```
The month is: January
The month is: February
The month is: March
The month is: April
The month is: May
The month is: June
The month is: July
The month is: August
The month is: September
The month is: October
The month is: November
The month is: December
The month is:
```

Although the PrintMonths procedure doesn't produce an error, it does produce unwanted content when an invalid month index is encountered. Your task, in this case, is to figure out why/how the number 13 is creeping into your program that only assumes months between 1 and 12 inclusively.

For the purposes of demonstration, it is fairly obvious how 13 is creeping into this procedure. In Listing 4.3, I fixed the For...Next loop to run from 1 to 13. In practice, inputs to your program will come from inputs entered by your end users in forms or worksheets or external sources such as databases or text files. In addition an invalid value may be generated by flawed logic in one of your procedures.

Once you know why and where invalid inputs are encountered, you can develop an appropriate strategy for dealing with them in the future. This is exactly the kind of task that you can use a watch for.

A watch is an expression you define that the VBE observes when your code executes. For the problem mentioned above, you could define a watch on the month number parameter that specifies that when the parameter equals 13, the program should enter Break mode.

USING THE CHOOSE FUNCTION INSTEAD OF SELECT CASE STATEMENTS

Listing 4.3 uses the Choose function to convert a given month number into the month associated with the month number (for example, 3 = March). Converting a number into an instance from an ordered set is a common occurrence. In Chapter 3 you saw that the Select Case statement can be used to perform translations such as this.

```
Choose (index, item₁, item₂, item₃, …,itemn)
```

Index should be a number between 1 and n (where n is the number of choices). The item list is a set of variant expressions containing one of the possible choices. Note that these are variant *expressions*. Whereas in Listing 4.3 I used simple literal values, you could also have a set of expressions such as the following (use your imagination in place of these boring expressions):

```
Choose(3, 2 + 4, 4 * 5, 2 ^ 2)
```

This example produces the value 4 (2^2). The Choose function is also a handy way to perform these sorts of translations. It has the benefit of being very concise and clear. Of course, nothing good is free, and the tradeoff in this case is performance. Unlike Select Case, the Choose function evaluates every item in the list of choices. Thus, the Choose function is best suited for translations with a small, fixed set of elements.

Finally, note that the list of choices to choose from is 1-based unlike the default base of arrays which is 0 (see Listing 4.3). Notice that the first item in the list of months, January, is printed when a month index of 1 is used.

DEFINING A WATCH

Defining a watch involves defining the watch expression and the scope of the watch, and instructing VBA what to do with the watch. Let's set up a watch for Listing 4.3 that suspends program execution (or enters Break mode) when the value of the variable nMonth is 13.

1. Enter Listing 4.3 into a standard module.

2. In the VBE, place the cursor on any line of the PrintMonths procedure and select Debug ➤ Add Watch....

3. Enter the expression **nMonth = 13**.

4. Choose Break When Value Is True.

5. Click OK.

Now that you have defined a watch, experiment with it a little. Run the PrintMonths procedure from the Macros dialog box in Excel (ALT+F8). Also, step through the code once and observe the behavior of the Watch window. Generally the Watch window is used in conjunction with the code window when you are in Break mode.

You can also use watches to observe variables while you're in Break mode, sort of like what you can do using the Locals window except that the only things that appear in the Watch window are things that you explicitly instruct the Watch window to show you. This is in contrast to the Locals window, which shows you everything that is in scope.

If you just want to observe the value of a particular variable, you can quickly add it to the Watch window by selecting the variable or expression and pressing SHIFT+F9 and then clicking Add. This is called a Quick Watch. As an alternative, select the variable or expression and drag it into the Watch window.

Clarify the Muddle with the Call Stack

Initially, you probably won't have much reason to be concerned about a call stack because the procedures you'll write will likely be monolithic in nature with a few procedures. Usually these types of programs have simple relationships between procedures at run-time. As you progress, you'll write smaller, purposeful procedures and build functionality by assembling groups of procedures that collectively perform useful actions.

In assembling groups of procedures, you'll occasionally create a maze of procedural execution with one procedure calling another, which calls another, which calls yet another. As you step through code such as this, it's pretty easy to lose track of where you are in the whole scheme of things. This is where the call stack comes into play.

The call stack is a term for the list of procedures currently in scope according to the order in which they were called beginning with the most recently called procedure. Listing 4.4 demonstrates this concept.

LISTING 4.4: DEMONSTRATING A CALL STACK

```
Sub MainProcedure()
    Procedure1
    Debug.Print "Finishing MainProcedure"
End Sub

Sub Procedure1()
    Procedure2
    Debug.Print "Finishing Procedure1"
End Sub

Sub Procedure2()
    Procedure3
    Debug.Print "Finishing Procedure2"
End Sub

Sub Procedure3()
    Debug.Print "Finishing Procedure3"
End Sub
```

Running MainProcedure produces the following output:

```
Finishing Procedure3
Finishing Procedure2
Finishing Procedure1
Finishing MainProcedure
```

While in Break mode, you can view the call stack at any time by pressing CTRL+L (View ➢ Call Stack…) to display the Call Stack window.

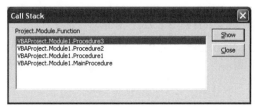

A Simple Debugging Methodology

You labored hard on some procedures, they compile (so no syntax errors), but they don't work correctly. What do you do? How do you go about troubleshooting the problem? This section describes a troubleshooting methodology that works for me.

The first thing I take note of is what kind of error I'm experiencing. If you are not employing an error-handling mechanism (see the next section), this step is easy because, as you'll remember, a run-time error will always display itself clearly while a logical error merely produces errant results. If you are using error handling, the distinction may not be so obvious and you may need to do some sleuthing using the tools described earlier to figure out what exactly is going on.

Correcting Run-Time Errors

Correcting run-time errors is usually a fairly easy process. When the error occurs, VBA gives you the option of debugging the procedure. This allows you to enter Break mode with the statement that is causing the error highlighted.

Your next step is to determine if the run-time error is a result of an input condition that you did not expect (such as referring to a nonexistent worksheet) or a result of using an object in a manner in which it was not designed. For example, object properties can be read/write or read only. If you try to assign a value to a property that is read only, a run-time error occurs.

If the error is a result of an input condition that you didn't expect, your problem is apt to have many solutions to. Basically what you need to do is come up with a defensive mechanism that either prevents the input condition from occurring or devises a way to handle the input condition in your procedure. As I mentioned earlier, when I get into the Excel object model in the coming chapters, I'll show you how to develop a number of procedures that you can use to handle situations that have the potential to generate run-time errors.

Errors that result from the improper use of an object can be more frustrating because there may not be an apparent solution and you'll find yourself resorting to trial and error in conjunction with diving into the help files to see if you can find a reason why an object isn't behaving as you thought it would. As a beginning developer, this type of error will be your nemesis. On the bright side, the battles you fight to overcome these errors will have the wonderful side effect of schooling you on the proper use of the various objects in the Excel object model.

LISTING 4.5: ERROR—YOU CAN'T ASSIGN A VALUE TO A READ-ONLY PROPERTY

```
Sub RTEExample1()
    Dim ws As Worksheet

    Set ws = ThisWorkbook.Worksheets(1)
    ' The following statement is flawed
    ' AutoFilter is a read-only property
    ws.AutoFilter = True
    Set ws = Nothing
End Sub
```

Running this listing produces the following error. Notice that the error doesn't give you any clue that it is a result of an attempt to assign a value to a read-only property.

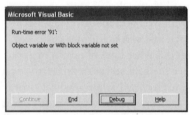

When you see "Run-time error '91': Object Variable or With Block Variable Not Set," this means that you either didn't initialize an object variable correctly with the Set statement, or you're using the object inappropriately.

First, make sure you initialized it correctly. After you validate this, examine the variable using the Locals window in Break mode. Are you using the correct property? Are you attempting to assign a value to a read-only property? If so, you may be able to use a method that allows you to modify the property indirectly. Finally, make sure you are using the correct object. You may need to use a closely related object instead.

Listing 4.6 shows an example of error #91 due to the failure to initialize a variable correctly.

LISTING 4.6: RUN-TIME ERROR RESULTING FROM THE FAILURE TO INITIALIZE A VARIABLE

```
Sub RTEExample2()
    Dim ws As Worksheet

    ' The following statement is flawed
    ' we haven't initialized the
    ' ws variable using the Set
    ' statement.
    Debug.Print ws.Name
End Sub
```

Listing 4.6 produces the exact same error that Listing 4.5 produces. This error always indicates that your problem is the result of using an object incorrectly.

The Locals window is an enormous help in situations like this. For Listing 4.6, if you display the Locals window in Break mode with the execution point at the offending statement, you should be able to identify the problem immediately. Notice in Figure 4.4 that the value of the *ws* object is Nothing. That should immediately tell you that you forgot to initialize the variable, and it rules out, for the time being, the possibility that you are using the object improperly.

FIGURE 4.4

The Locals window can help enormously in determining what is wrong with statements using object variables.

Compare Figure 4.4 with Figure 4.5. In Figure 4.5, you can see all of the worksheet members for the *ws* variable in the Locals window. This means that you have initialized *ws* correctly but are using it inappropriately. If your intent was to turn on the AutoFilter feature, the only way to find the solution in this case is to refer to the documentation or use the Object Browser and search for AutoFilter. Either one of these courses of action would eventually lead you to the solution. To turn on the Auto-Filter, use the AutoFilter method that is a member of the Range object.

Debugging Logical Errors

Logical errors are more difficult to debug mainly because it isn't obvious where the error is occurring. Your first task then is to root out the source of the error. To do this, consider all of the variables that may play a part in the production of erroneous output. Although complex procedures may utilize many different variables, usually, as the author of the program, you'll have a good idea as to the one or two to focus on.

FIGURE 4.5
The Locals Window can validate that you initialized a variable correctly but are not using the object in a manner in which it was intended.

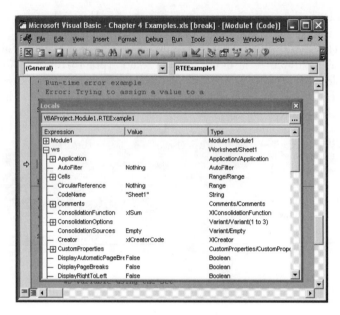

Next, consider whether the error occurs for all inputs or if it only occurs with a few specific inputs. If it occurs for all inputs, it is easier to debug because you can just step through the program in Break mode and observe the variables in question. An even more efficient method is to set a Breakpoint at some point in the procedure in question so you can zip right to the appropriate section in your code without having to step through a bunch of code that is irrelevant to the issue at hand. If the error only occurs for specific inputs, create a Watch that will place you in Break mode when the variable assumes a value that produces an error.

Finally, once you locate the source of the error, you can develop an appropriate solution to the problem like you would with any other error. Ninety percent of the work with logical errors is determining where they are occurring.

Implementing Simple Error Handling

Before I close out this chapter, I want to introduce the error-handling features of VBA. Implementing error handling into your procedures can get complicated really quickly, at least more complicated than you are prepared to handle at this point. However, it is fairly easy to implement basic error handling. In fact, you can implement the most basic error handling into a procedure by including one statement near the beginning of it:

```
On Error Resume Next
```

When an error occurs in a procedure with On Error Resume Next, VBA forgets about it and executes the remaining code as if nothing ever happened. Kind of like an infinite supply of those get out of jail free cards from Monopoly. Before you put this statement in every procedure, you must consider how the remaining code in your procedure will behave if a statement containing an error is ignored. Sometimes On Error Resume Next just delays problems from occurring.

Another benefit to using On Error Resume Next or one of its variations is that when errors occur, you can shield the end user from being dumped into the VBE.

You can use On Error GoTo 0 to disable error handling in a procedure that had previously specified an error-handling mechanism. This allows you to toggle error handling on and off in a procedure as your needs dictate.

Finally, note that On Error Resume Next is disabled if the procedure calls another procedure unless the called procedure also contains On Error Resume Next.

TIP　*Generally it is best to avoid using On Error Resume Next during the development process unless it is specifically needed. That way, when you're developing and testing, you'll be notified of run-time errors and placed into Break mode on the offending line. If you use On Error Resume Next, the procedure will keep executing and you may not know that an error occurred. If you do notice that an error occurred, you won't know which line caused it unless you trace it in some way.*

Another form of the On Error statement follows:

```
On Error GoTo lineLabel
```

This form of error handling allows you to direct any errors to a certain segment of your code that is specifically designed for handling errors. A common skeleton procedure that uses this form of error handling is shown in Listing 4.7.

LISTING 4.7: A GENERIC PROCEDURE SKELETON WITH BASIC ERROR HANDLING

```
Sub GenericProcedure()
    On Error GoTo ErrHandler
    ' procedure statements go here

    Exit Sub
ErrHandler:
    ' error handling statements go here
    ' notify user if desired
    MsgBox "Sorry, but an error has occurred. " & _
            Err.Number & ": " & Err.Description _
            , vbInformation + vbOKOnly, _
            "Oops. An Error has occurred."

    ' and/or make a note in the immediate window
    ' helpful during the development/testing
    ' process
    Debug.Print "ERROR OCCURED IN GenericProcedure..."
    Debug.Print Err.Number & ": " & Err.Description
End Sub
```

As you can see, error-handling code can add quite a bit of code to otherwise simple procedures. You should note three things about this listing. First, the On Error GoTo ErrHandler line means that if an error occurs, the program should go to the line labeled ErrHandler. (You can label lines by entering a label followed by a colon [:].) Second, notice the Exit Sub statement just before the ErrHandler label. During normal, uneventful (no errors) execution of the procedure, the procedure would end at the Exit Sub statement rather than the End Sub statement. Finally, in the error-handling statements, you'll notice statements that refer to Err.Number and Err.Description. Err is a special object that contains information about any error that occurs. When VBA encounters a run-time error it automatically creates an Err object and populates it with information about the error. You can use If…Then statements or Select…Case statements that operate on the Err.Number to decide how to handle an error.

Summary

Debugging an application is certainly not the most glamorous part of the development process, but you can't deny the importance of good debugging skills. Developing good debugging skills can save you a significant amount of time, effort, and frustration.

There are three classifications of errors: syntax errors, run-time errors, and logical errors. Syntax errors arise due to code that doesn't adhere to the syntax requirements of the VBA language. Syntax errors can be detected automatically by the compiler before distributing an application. Run-time errors are the most noticeable errors. Run-time errors occur when your application encounters a condition or set of conditions that it was not designed to handle. Run-time errors are best minimized by incorporating defensive programming into your applications. Logical errors can be the most frustrating errors because they have the potential to lurk in your program unnoticed, possibly producing errant or flawed output. Logical errors are also the most difficult to root out in your code. Unlike with syntax or run-time errors, the VBE can't determine the source of logical errors, so you must invoke more troubleshooting skills to find and fix them.

Thankfully the VBE incorporates a number of features and tools to aid the debugging process. Break mode allows you to execute code one line at a time and inspect variables as you go. You can also set Breakpoints, use the Stop statement, or set Watches to enter Break mode at critical junctures in your code. In addition, you can use Debug.Print and MsgBox to display information about your variables as your program runs. Finally, you can use the Locals window to display a wealth of information about all in scope variables while you're in Break mode.

In the next chapter, you'll finally get into the Excel object model, beginning with the Application object. The Application object contains many useful properties and methods that you'll use in nearly every application you develop.

Part 2

Mastering the Excel Object Model

Chapter 5

Exploring the Application Object

CONGRATULATIONS! YOU HAVE FINALLY arrived at the first chapter that deals directly with one of the key Excel objects, the Application object. It took four chapters to get here, but without those chapters you wouldn't have a foundation to build on.

The Application object is the root object of the Excel object model. This object represents the Excel application as a whole. As such, it has a lot of useful properties and methods. Chances are, you'll use some aspect of the Application object in the majority of the procedures you write. We have a lot of ground to cover, so fill up your coffee or soda, make yourself comfortable, and let's get to it.

A Bird's-Eye View of the Application Object

The Application object has so many useful aspects that it is probably a good idea to quickly summarize. The vast majority of your Excel development tasks will involve performing actions or manipulating lower-level Excel objects, such as ranges and worksheets, along with standard variables that represent the basic data types. Normally you don't spend much time thinking about the Application object. When you do use it though, the functions it performs are often critical to your application. Other times the Application object provides functionality that serves to give your program a professional finish.

If you'll remember from Chapter 3, objects contain members that can be classified as methods or properties (events are also members, but I'll get to them later). You can group the members of the Application object with the following classifications.

Display-oriented members   The Application object has a fairly large collection of members that deal in some way with the display. For example, such members control whether the screen gets updated, what appears in the status bar, the size of the window, and whether or not certain Excel objects are visible.

Excel convenience members   As the root object of the Excel object model, the Application object provides access to any other object in the Excel object model. It also contains a lot of shortcuts that allow you quick access to many relevant Excel objects such as the ActiveCell, ThisWorkbook, and Selection.

File operations   Occasionally you'll need to allow an end user to select a file to open or prompt the user for a place to save a file. The Application object contains members that assist with these activities.

System information If you need to determine information about the environment of the computer on which your application is running, you'll use the Application object. This group of members includes properties such as OperatingSystem, OrganizationName, and UserName.

Other members defy easy classification in one of these categories, so make a mental note that another group of miscellaneous members exists.

The Application object is somewhat unique. You don't need to declare a variable to represent an instance of it. In fact, you don't need to preface some of the Application object's members with the word Application in order to use them. For example, the following two lines perform the same function:

```
Debug.Print Application.ThisWorkbook.Name
Debug.Print ThisWorkbook.Name
```

One thing that is strange is that for other members, you do need to fully qualify the member. The ScreenUpdating property is one such member.

```
' This line works
Application.ScreenUpdating = False
' This one doesn't
ScreenUpdating = False
```

So, if in doubt, fully qualify the member using Application. I usually use the shortened version (without Application) when I'm using the members that begin with Active or This. You'll see examples of this throughout the chapter starting with Listing 5.1.

Display-Oriented Features You Have to Know

Although you could get by if you didn't have access to some of the display-oriented functionality that you can control using the Application object, your custom developed Excel applications would appear much less professional. For example, I use the ScreenUpdating property of the Application object in nearly every Excel application I create in order to make my applications faster and flicker-free.

Gaining Performance and Polish with ScreenUpdating

The ScreenUpdating property is a read/write Boolean property. This means you can set it to be true or false. By default, ScreenUpdating = true, and as your code executes, Excel constantly updates the display as it goes about its actions. If you set ScreenUpdating to false, the screen doesn't update as your procedures run.

It can be very satisfying to watch the screen flicker as your procedures run and your code completes some task in a matter of seconds or minutes that used to take you 10, 20, or 60 minutes or more. After you do this a few times however, you can achieve even more satisfaction by turning ScreenUpdating off at the beginning of your procedure and then turning it back on at the end. Two significant benefits stem from this. First, your code runs considerably faster if ScreenUpdating is turned off. How much faster? Well that depends on how much your procedure performs actions that trigger Excel's need to update the display. Second, your application looks more professional—and we all want to look good, right?

Listing 5.1 demonstrates how to use the ScreenUpdating property and performs a simple test to help quantify the performance impact of turning on/off ScreenUpdating. The first procedure, the subroutine named TimeScreenUpdating, is responsible for calling the function TestScreenUpdating and displaying the result via a message box. TimeScreenUpdating uses the Format function to display the result formatted with only two decimal places. Without the format function, you'd see a bunch of digits after the decimal.

LISTING 5.1: PERFORMANCE IMPLICATIONS OF SCREEN UPDATING

```vba
Sub TimeScreenUpdating()
    Dim dResult As Double

    ' Test with screen updating turned on
    dResult = TestScreenUpdating(True)
    MsgBox Format(dResult, "0.00") & " seconds.", vbOKOnly

    ' Test with screen updating turned off
    dResult = TestScreenUpdating(False)
    MsgBox Format(dResult, "0.00") & " seconds.", vbOKOnly

End Sub

Function TestScreenUpdating(bUpdatingOn As Boolean) As Double
    Dim nRepetition As Integer
    Dim ws As Worksheet
    Dim dStart As Double

    ' Record the start time
    dStart = Timer

    ' Turn screen updating on or off
    Application.ScreenUpdating = bUpdatingOn

    ' Loop through each worksheet
    ' in the workbook 250 times
    For nRepetition = 1 To 250
        For Each ws In ThisWorkbook.Worksheets
            ws.Activate
        Next
    Next

    ' Turn screen updating on
    Application.ScreenUpdating = True

    ' Return elapsed time since procedure started
    TestScreenUpdating = Timer - dStart

    ' Clean up
    Set ws = Nothing

End Function
```

The real workhorse of Listing 5.1 is the function TestScreenUpdating. TestScreenUpdating takes a Boolean (true/false) input parameter named bUpdatingOn and returns a Double (double precision floating point number) that represents the time it took to execute the procedure. To determine the elapsed time, you use the Timer function. Timer returns the fractional number of seconds that have elapsed since midnight.

Next, screen updating is turned on or off depending on the value of the input parameter. To give the procedure something to do, simply loop through all of the worksheets in the workbook 250 times, activating each worksheet as you get to it. This section of code utilizes another property of the application object—ThisWorkbook, which returns a workbook object that represents the workbook in which your code is running.

Finally, the function turns screen updating on and returns the elapsed time by subtracting the start time from the finish time. On my computer, the trial through the worksheets with ScreenUpdating turned on took 6.41 seconds. With ScreenUpdating turned off, the process only took 1.14 seconds.

Keeping End Users Informed with the Status Bar

Another property of the Application bar that I use frequently is the StatusBar property. You can see the status bar in Figure 5.1. Look closely at the bottom-left corner. See the text that reads, "I am the StatusBar. Hear me roar." You may have known right where to look, but many other people don't pay much attention to the status bar. Keep that in mind as you decide what information to display there. If it is critical or important information, you need to present it to the end user using a louder method, such as a message box, because the status bar certainly does not roar.

That said, the status bar is an excellent way to display informational messages to keep the user apprised of what is going on. The great thing about the status bar is that it is nonintrusive to the user and easy to use for the developer. When you display a message in the status bar, the user is not interrupted by having to click an OK button. I prefer to use the status bar to show an update of progress in procedures that process a number of files, rows, or cells. Here's an example in Listing 5.2.

FIGURE 5.1

The status bar is a nice, subtle way to display information to an end user.

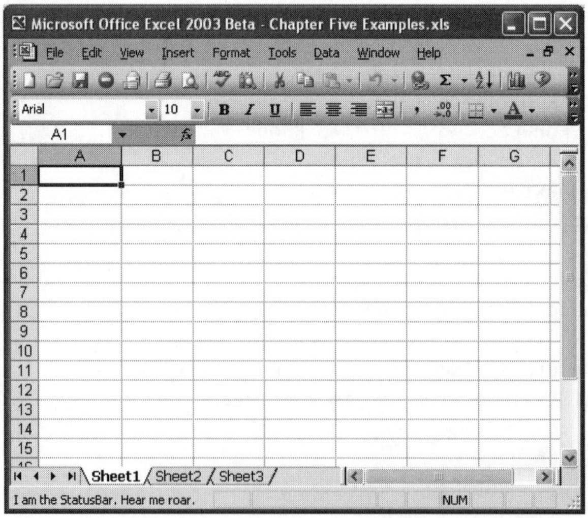

LISTING 5.2: USING THE STATUSBAR PROPERTY TO DISPLAY INFORMATION

```vb
' This subroutine tests the impact of
' using StatusBar to display lots of
' frequent messages.
Sub TimeStatusBar()
    Dim dStart As Double
    Dim dResult As Double
    Dim bDisplayStatusBar As Boolean

    ' Remember original status bar setting
    bDisplayStatusBar = Application.DisplayStatusBar
    ' Turn on the status bar
    Application.DisplayStatusBar = True

    ' Baseline test - no status bar, every row
    ' To isolate how long it takes to
    ' perform mod statement on all rows
    dStart = Timer
    TestStatusBar 1, False
    dResult = Timer - dStart
    MsgBox Format(dResult, "0.00") & " seconds.", vbOKOnly

    ' Time using StatusBar - every row
    dStart = Timer
    TestStatusBar 1, True
    dResult = Timer - dStart
    MsgBox Format(dResult, "0.00") & " seconds.", vbOKOnly

    ' Time using StatusBar - every fifth row
    dStart = Timer
    TestStatusBar 5, True
    dResult = Timer - dStart
    MsgBox Format(dResult, "0.00") & " seconds.", vbOKOnly

    ' Restore the status bar to its original setting
    Application.DisplayStatusBar = bDisplayStatusBar
End Sub


' This subroutine displays a message to the status bar
' (if desired) for each row in a worksheet using the
' interval specified.
Private Sub TestStatusBar(nInterval As Integer, bUseStatusBar As Boolean)
    Dim lRow As Long
    Dim lLastRow As Long
    Dim ws As Worksheet

    ' Using the first worksheet in this workbook
```

```
' No changes will be made to the worksheet.
Set ws = ThisWorkbook.Worksheets(1)

' Every version since Excel 97 has had
' 65,536 rows. Excel 5 had 16,384 rows.
lLastRow = ws.Rows.Count

For lRow = 1 To lLastRow
    ' Test to see if the current row
    ' is the interval specified.
    If lRow Mod nInterval = 0 Then
        If bUseStatusBar Then
            Application.StatusBar = "Processing row: " & lRow & _
            " of " & lLastRow & " rows."
        End If
    End If
Next

Application.StatusBar = False
Set ws = Nothing
End Sub
```

The first order of business when using the status bar is to make sure it is displayed. Users can turn the status bar on/off on the View tab of the Options dialog box (from Microsoft Excel, Tools ➢ Options) or by using the Status Bar item on the View menu. To be courteous and respectful of the user's preferences, you should remember the user's original setting and restore it when you're done. To remember the setting, assign the value given by the DisplayStatusBar property of the Application object to a Boolean variable. Then set the DisplayStatusBar to true so that the status bar is displayed.

Next, you see three similar blocks of statements. Each block performs a test using the status bar and times each test to determine the performance impact of using it. The test, TestStatusBar, consists of a simple loop of, presumably, 65,536 iterations. I had no specific reason for choosing the number of rows in a worksheet other than processing rows may be the type of occasion when you'd use the status bar to display progress information. TestStatusBar updates the message displayed in the status bar at the interval specified by the input parameter nInterval. In order to establish a baseline of how much time it takes to execute the Mod statement that is evaluated in the If...Then statement, I also included a parameter that specifies whether the status bar should be used or not.

Displaying text in the status bar is performed by assigning the text that you want displayed to the Application.StatusBar property as shown here:

```
Application.StatusBar = "Processing row:" & lRow & _
" of " & lLastRow & " rows."
```

The only thing you need to remember is that anything you put in the status bar stays there until you change it or close and reopen Excel. Once you're done with the status bar, the easiest way to clear it and instruct Excel to use it as it normally would is to include the following line:

```
Application.StatusBar = False
```

This method is used at the end of the TestStatusBar procedure.

WARNING   *Any text you display using Application.StatusBar stays there until you change it, unless you restart Excel. Thus, it is important to use Application.StatusBar = False somewhere in your program. It's even better if you devise an error-handling routine that ensures that this line is executed even in the event of a run-time error.*

Finally, the last order of business is to restore the original DisplayStatusBar setting that was in place before you began. To restore the original setting, just assign the setting you remembered in the bDisplayStatusBar variable to the Application.DisplayStatusBar property.

PERFORMANCE IMPLICATIONS OF USING THE STATUS BAR

When you run the code in Listing 5.2, it illustrates the impact of using the status bar. If you don't use the status bar, the TestStatusBar procedure runs in 0.02 seconds. If you do use it and update its text every iteration, the TestStatusBar procedure runs in 5.12 seconds. And if you use an update interval of every 5 iterations, the processing time is reduced to 1.03 seconds.

From this, you can conclude that although using the status bar is useful, it is prudent to choose an updating interval that doesn't impact performance very much and still provides useful information to the user. If you are reading text from a file for example, and you want to let the user know what row you are on, an interval of 10 or 20 is probably a good start. This has hardly any noticeable impact on performance and your process runs so fast that it is doubtful your users will notice any interval at all.

Display-Oriented Features That Are Nice to Know

Although I use the ScreenUpdating and StatusBar properties in nearly every project of significance, I seldom use the remaining display-oriented features. These features deal primarily with manipulating or obtaining information about windows (the user interface element, not the operating system).

The first property I'd like to mention in this section deals with the cursor. In fact, it is referred to as the Cursor property. You can use the Cursor property to change or determine which mouse icon is used in Excel. Listing 5.3 demonstrates the various cursors available.

LISTING 5.3: CURSORS AVAILABLE TO USE WITH THE CURSOR PROPERTY

```
Sub ViewCursors()
    Application.Cursor = xlNorthwestArrow
    MsgBox "Do you like the xlNorthwestArrow? Hover over the worksheet to see it."

    Application.Cursor = xlIBeam
    MsgBox "How about the xlIBeam? Hover over the worksheet to see it."

    Application.Cursor = xlWait
    MsgBox "How about xlWait? Hover over the worksheet to see it."

    Application.Cursor = xlDefault
    MsgBox "Back to the default..."
End Sub
```

As with the status bar, you need to make sure that when you change the cursor you change it back to the default. This can be tricky when errors occur if your error-handling code isn't working correctly. Many times you may switch the cursor to the wait (hourglass) cursor. If you don't change the cursor back to the default, your users may think that the application is hung.

Listing 5.4 demonstrates some of the various window-oriented properties of the Application object. The first property you see in the procedure is WindowState. This property is a read/write property that allows you to determine or change the state of Excel's window. You can set it using the defined constants xlMaximized, xlMinimized, and xlNormal. If you are determining the state of the window, WindowState returns a value that you can use directly or compare against the defined values as shown in the Select Case statement in Listing 5.4.

LISTING 5.4: DEMONSTRATION OF VARIOUS WINDOW-ORIENTED PROPERTIES

```
Sub GetWindowInfo()
    Dim lState As Long
    Dim sInfo As String
    Dim lResponse As Long

    ' Determine window state
    lState = Application.WindowState
    Select Case lState
        Case xlMaximized
            sInfo = "Window is maximized." & vbCrLf
        Case xlMinimized
            sInfo = "Window is minimized." & vbCrLf
        Case xlNormal
            sInfo = "Window is normal." & vbCrLf
    End Select

    ' Prepare message to be displayed
    sInfo = sInfo & "Usable Height = " & _
            Application.UsableHeight & vbCrLf
    sInfo = sInfo & "Usable Width = " & _
            Application.UsableWidth & vbCrLf
    sInfo = sInfo & "Height = " & _
            Application.Height & vbCrLf
    sInfo = sInfo & "Width = " & _
            Application.Width & vbCrLf & vbCrLf
    sInfo = sInfo & "Would you like to minimize it?"

    ' Display message
    lResponse = MsgBox(sInfo, vbYesNo, "Window Info")

    ' Minimize window if user clicked Yes
    If lResponse = vbYes Then
        Application.WindowState = xlMinimized
    End If
End Sub
```

The next four properties used in Listing 5.4 are Height, Width, UsableHeight, and UsableWidth. Height and Width return the height and width of Excel's main application window. Meanwhile UsableHeight and UsableWidth return the maximum height and width that a window can assume within the main application window. Height and Width can only be changed if WindowState = xlNormal. UsableHeight and UsableWidth are read-only. To put all of this information into a single message box, I prepared the message using the defined constant vbCrLF, which places a line-feed character in my text and forces the message box to break the text into multiple lines of text.

Convenient Excel Object Properties

The Application object has a number of properties that conveniently return Excel objects of interest. For example, you often need a way to refer to the currently selected range, the active workbook, or the workbook that the module resides in (this may or may not be equal to the active workbook). The Application object has properties that return objects representing all of these and more. Table 5.1 lists the properties that are useful for returning particular Excel objects.

TABLE 5.1: PROPERTIES RETURNING EXCEL OBJECTS OF INTEREST

PROPERTY	RETURNS	REPRESENTS
ActiveCell	Range	The active cell in the active window.
ActiveChart	Chart	The active chart.
ActivePrinter	String	The name of the active printer.
ActiveSheet	Sheet	The active sheet in the active workbook.
ActiveWindow	Window	The active window.
ActiveWorkbook	Workbook	The workbook in the active window.
Selection	Various	The selected object in the active window. The object returned depends on what is selected. Usually a range is selected so a Range object is returned.
ThisCell	Range	The cell from which a user-defined function is being called.
ThisWorkbook	Workbook	The workbook containing the VBA code.

Many beginners use these properties almost exclusively for some reason, along with the Activate method that activates various objects of interest. Perhaps it is because the macro recorder uses these a lot, and people learn from the code that the macro recorder generates. In any event, the practice of using Activate is inefficient because the Activate method is an unnecessary performance hit since you don't need to activate objects to use them, as you'll see in later chapters. That said, use these properties when you need to, but know that if you're using these properties in conjunction with the Activate method, you are making things tougher on yourself.

Out of all of these properties, I find myself using the ThisWorkbook property the most. You'll see evidence of this throughout the book. The following procedure demonstrates these properties:

```
Sub WhatIsActive()
```

```
        Debug.Print Application.ActiveCell.Address
        Debug.Print Application.ActivePrinter
        Debug.Print Application.ActiveSheet.Name
        Debug.Print Application.ActiveWindow.Caption
        Debug.Print Application.ActiveWorkbook.Name
        Debug.Print Application.Selection.Address
        Debug.Print Application.ThisWorkbook.Name
    End Sub
```

Running this procedure produces the following output (your results may vary):

```
$A$1
HP LaserJet 4000 Series PCL6 on Ne00:
Sheet3
Chapter Five Examples.xls
Chapter Five Examples.xls
$A$1
Chapter Five Examples.xls
```

Common File Operations Simplified

One of the most common file operations is to prompt the user for the name(s) of one or more workbooks to open. The next most common operation is to prompt the user for a filename and folder in which to store a new workbook. The Application object has two methods that make these needs nearly a snap: GetOpenFilename and GetSaveAsFilename.

Obtaining Filenames from a User

You can use the GetOpenFilename method to gather existing filenames from a user. This method displays the common Open file dialog box your users are used to seeing in nearly all Windows applications. The GetOpenFilename method gathers filenames without opening the files. Here is its syntax:

```
Application.GetOpenFilename([FileFilter], [FilterIndex], [Title], _
        [ButtonText], [MultiSelect])
```

FileFilter   This parameter is an optional variant parameter in the format of a string that instructs the Open dialog box to display only files that match the filter supplied. The default is All Files (*.*),*.*.

FilterIndex   This is an optional variant that you can use when multiple filters are supplied as a file filter. The FilterIndex should be a number that specifies which of the parameters is the default filter. By default, the first filter is used.

Title   This is an optional variant that should be a string. Whatever you pass as the Title will be displayed in the title bar of the dialog box. By default, the text Open is displayed.

ButtonText   This optional parameter is applicable to Macintosh computers only.

MultiSelect   This optional parameter specifies whether the user should be able to select multiple files or a single file only. By default, only a single file can be chosen.

Listing 5.5 demonstrates how you might go about obtaining the name of an existing Excel workbook from the end user. The first procedure in the listing, TestGetFile, demonstrates how to use the second procedure, a function named GetExcelFile, and check the result before using it.

You could use the GetOpenFilename without all of this supporting code. However, you'll find that most of the time you need to perform all of these actions together, and that nine times out of ten, you'll want to filter the file list for Excel files only. Wrapping the GetOpenFilename method in a function simplifies your work because it means you only need to specify one parameter—the title of the dialog box. Granted, you really don't need to specify any parameters to GetOpenFilename, as they are all optional. However, using GetOpenFilename isn't nearly as user friendly if you don't specify any parameters, and it is needlessly repetitive to respecify the parameters every time you want to get an open filename. Thus, wrapping GetOpenFilename inside a procedure is a good idea.

LISTING 5.5: OBTAINING A SINGLE WORKBOOK FROM THE USER

```
Sub TestGetFile()
    Dim nIndex As Integer
    Dim sFile As String

    ' Get a batch of Excel files
    sFile = GetExcelFile("Testing GetExcelFile Function")

    ' Make sure dialog wasn't cancelled - in which case
    ' sFile would equal False.
    If sFile = "False" Then
        Debug.Print "No file selected."
        Exit Sub
    End If

    ' OK - we have a valid file
    Debug.Print sFile
End Sub

' Presents user with a GetOpenFileName dialog which allows
' single file selection.
' Returns a single of filename.
Function GetExcelFile(sTitle As String) As String

    Dim sFilter As String
    Dim bMultiSelect As Boolean

    sFilter = "Workbooks (*.xls), *.xls"
    bMultiSelect = False

    GetExcelFile = Application.GetOpenFilename(FileFilter:=sFilter, _
        Title:=sTitle, MultiSelect:=bMultiSelect)
End Function
```

As you can see, the GetExcelFile function is pretty straightforward. It only uses one parameter to specify the title displayed by the Open file dialog box. You've hard coded the filter and clearly specified that you don't want to enable multiple file selection. By *hard coded* I mean that you've assigned a literal value to a variable—sFilter in this case.

In the TestGetFile procedure, you can see that after you use the GetExcelFile function, you need to check to make sure the dialog box was not dismissed without choosing a file. For example, if you press Escape, click Cancel, or close the dialog box by clicking the X in the upper-right corner, Get-ExcelFile returns the value "False", which in turn is the value returned by the GetOpenFilename method (see Figure 5.2). If you find that GetExcelFile returns false, print a message to the Immediate window and exit the subroutine.

FIGURE 5.2
Your users will feel right at home selecting files when you use the GetOpenFilename method. This is the dialog box that is displayed by Listing 5.6.

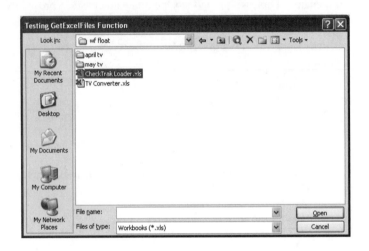

What if you want the user to select one or more files? You may think that one simple way to enable this is to use another parameter in the GetExcelFile function, which you could then pass to the MultiSelect parameter of the GetOpenFilename method. However, a weird thing happens when you set MultiSelect to true. Instead of receiving a variant with a subtype of String, you receive a variant array. This creates subtle differences in how you need to check the value you receive. One way to handle this is to have a separate function that you use when you want to enable multiple file selection. Check out Listing 5.6 for an example.

LISTING 5.6: OBTAINING A BATCH OF WORKBOOKS FROM THE USER

```
Sub TestGetFiles()
    Dim nIndex As Integer
    Dim vFiles As Variant

    ' Get a batch of Excel files
    vFiles = GetExcelFiles("Testing GetExcelFiles Function")

    ' Make sure dialog wasn't cancelled - in which case
```

```
    'vntFiles would equal False and therefore not an array.
    If Not IsArray(vFiles) Then
        Debug.Print "No files selected."
        Exit Sub
    End If


    ' OK - loop through the filenames
    For nIndex = 1 To UBound(vFiles)
        Debug.Print vFiles(nIndex)
    Next nIndex
End Sub


' Presents user with a GetOpenFileName dialog that allows
' multiple file selection.
' Returns an array of filenames.
Function GetExcelFiles(sTitle As String) As Variant
    Dim sFilter As String
    Dim bMultiSelect As Boolean

    sFilter = "Workbooks (*.xls), *.xls"
    bMultiSelect = True

    GetExcelFiles = Application.GetOpenFilename(FileFilter:=sFilter, _
        Title:=sTitle, MultiSelect:=bMultiSelect)
End Function
```

The first thing to notice other than the slight function name change from GetExcelFile (Listing 5.5) to GetExcelFiles (Listing 5.6) is that the return type of GetExcelFiles is a variant rather than a string. This is because GetOpenFilename will return a variant array when you enable multiple file selection. Also, note that you have set the bMultiSelect variable to true. Other than those minor modifications, this is largely the same as GetExcelFile. Figure 5.3 demonstrates the dialog box displayed by Listing 5.6.

FIGURE 5.3

Enabling multiple file selection allows you to select multiple files by holding down either the SHIFT key or the CTRL key.

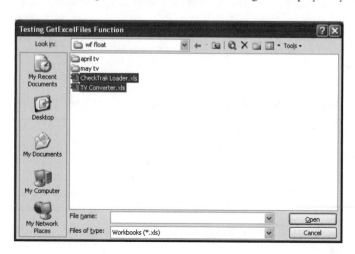

Now for the differences between TestGetFile (Listing 5.5) and TestGetFiles (Listing 5.6). The first difference is that in Listing 5.6, instead of testing the result for the value "False"(as you did in Listing 5.5), you're testing to see whether or not the function returns an array. You can't check for the value "False", because if you use a statement like "If vFiles = False Then" and vFiles is an array, a Type Mismatch run-time error will occur. The second difference is that once you've assured yourself that you got an array (meaning one or more files were selected), you need to loop through the array to print out the full filename of each file selected.

The For...Next statement that loops through the files selected may appear erroneous considering the material concerning arrays that was presented in Chapter 3. Remember that by default, arrays in VBA are zero-based. The For...Next loop in Listing 5.6 starts at 1 rather than 0. What gives? This is one of those quirky programming things. Just when you think you get something, you stumble across something else who ignores convention and casts doubt on your knowledge. Don't worry, the sky isn't falling. The Microsoft programmer that implemented the GetOpenFilename function must have thought that it would be better to return the array as a one-based array instead of zero.

Pick the Perfect Location with GetSaveAsFilename

The yin of GetOpenFilename's yang is the GetSaveAsFilename method. This method presents the user with the familiar looking Save As dialog box found in most Windows applications (see Figure 5.4).

As with GetOpenFilename, GetSaveAsFilename merely allows users to indicate a filename and a location to which to save a file without actually saving it. The syntax of GetSaveAsFilename is shown here:

```
Application.GetSaveAsFilename([InitialFilename], _
    [FileFilter], [FilterIndex], [Title], [ButtonText])
```

The parameters to GetSaveAsFilename are as follows.

InitialFileName   This parameter is an optional variant parameter that should be in the format of a string that suggests a filename. The default is the active workbook's name. You can set this to a zero-length string ("") if you do not want to suggest an initial filename.

FIGURE 5.4
The functionality of the Save As dialog box can be accessed using the GetSaveAsFilename method.

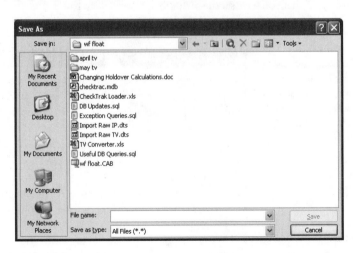

FileFilter   This parameter is an optional variant parameter that should be in the format of a string that instructs the Save As dialog box to display only files that match the filter supplied. The default is "All Files (*.*),*.*".

FilterIndex   This is an optional variant that can be used when multiple filters are supplied as a file filter. The FilterIndex should be a number that specifies which of the parameters is the default filter. By default, the first filter is used.

Title   This is an optional variant that should be a string. Whatever you pass as the Title will be displayed in the title bar of the dialog box. By default, the text Save As is displayed.

ButtonText   This optional parameter is applicable to Macintosh computers only.

The GetSaveAsFilename method can be used simply; Listing 5.7 shows an example.

LISTING 5.7: BASIC USE OF GETSAVEASFILENAME

```
Sub SimpleGetSaveAsFilename()
    Dim sFile As String
    Dim lResponse As Long
    Dim sMsg As String

    Do
        sFile = Application.GetSaveAsFilename
        sMsg = "You chose: " & sFile & ". Keep experimenting?"
        lResponse = MsgBox(sMsg, vbYesNo)
    Loop While lResponse = vbYes
End Sub
```

In Listing 5.7 you have a simple procedure that you can use to experiment with GetSaveAsFilename. Inside a Do...Loop, you assign the return value of GetSaveAsFilename to a string variable named sFile. Then you use the MsgBox function to display the full filename that you provided and ask if you want to keep experimenting. If you click Yes, then the loop terminates. Note that GetSaveAsFilename doesn't actually do anything with the filename you provide.

Although you could use a simple call to GetSaveAsFilename to have the user supply a full name, or filename and path, for a file, it is not very safe to do so because two common conditions could cause a run-time error. The first condition is that a workbook with the given name is already open and you can't save a workbook with the same name as another open workbook. The second condition is that a workbook with the given name already exists at the given location. Excel would prompt the user whether or not they want to save the file anyway in this scenario. The problem is that if the user decides not to save the file, a run-time error occurs. As solving these problems is more related to the Workbook object, I'll cover the details of handling these two scenarios in the next chapter, which covers the Workbook object. For now, I'll lay a little more foundation.

BREAKING DOWN FILENAMES

You frequently need to separate the path component from the actual filename when you're working with files. Both GetOpenFilename and GetSaveAsFilename return full filenames, meaning you get the storage path and the filename. For example, if you had a workbook named MyWorkbook.xls stored in the folder C:\SomeFolder, the full filename would be C:\SomeFolder\MyWorkbook.xls. Listing 5.8 presents a few procedures that work together to isolate the path and filename from a full filename.

NOTE   *This section does not deal directly with the Application object per se. It is more of a value-added section for dealing with the return values of two of the Application object's most frequently used methods.*

LISTING 5.8: BREAKING DOWN FILENAMES INTO PATH AND FILENAME COMPONENTS

```
' A simple procedure for testing the
' BreakdownName procedure
Sub TestBreakdownName()
    Dim sPath As String
    Dim sName As String
    Dim sFileName As String
    Dim sMsg As String

    sFileName = Application.GetSaveAsFilename
    BreakdownName sFileName, sName, sPath
    sMsg = "The file name is: " & sName & vbCrLf
    sMsg = sMsg & "The path is: " & sPath
    MsgBox sMsg, vbOKOnly
End Sub


Function GetShortName(sLongName As String) As String
    Dim sPath As String
    Dim sShortName As String

    BreakdownName sLongName, sShortName, sPath

    GetShortName = sShortName
End Function

Sub BreakdownName(sFullName As String, _
                  ByRef sName As String, _
                  ByRef sPath As String)

    Dim nPos As Integer

    ' Find out where the filename begins
    nPos = FileNamePosition(sFullName)

    If nPos > 0 Then
        sName = Right(sFullName, Len(sFullName) - nPos)
```

```
            sPath = Left(sFullName, nPos - 1)
        Else
            'Invalid sFullName - don't change anything
        End If
    End Sub


' Returns the position or index of the first
' character of the filename given a full name
' A full name consists of a path and a filename
' Ex. FileNamePosition("C:\Testing\Test.txt") = 11
Function FileNamePosition(sFullName As String) As Integer
    Dim bFound As Boolean
    Dim nPosition As Integer

    bFound = False
    nPosition = Len(sFullName)

    Do While bFound = False
        ' Make sure we were not dealt a
        ' zero-length string
        If nPosition = 0 Then Exit Do

        ' We are looking for the first "\"
        ' from the right.
        If Mid(sFullName, nPosition, 1) = "\" Then
            bFound = True
        Else
            ' Working right to left
            nPosition = nPosition - 1
        End If
    Loop

    If bFound = False Then
        FileNamePosition = 0
    Else
        FileNamePosition = nPosition
    End If
End Function
```

In addition to providing you with a useful way to isolate path- and filename components from a full filename, Listing 5.8 includes one brand new concept, which may not be apparent at first glance—output parameters. Take a look at the declaration of the BreakdownName subroutine.

```
Sub BreakdownName(sFullName As String, _
                ByRef sName As String, _
                ByRef sPath As String)
```

See the ByRef keyword in this declaration? This keyword indicates that when/if the Breakdown-Name function modifies these parameters, the procedure that called BreakdownName will see the changes made to the variables.

Listing 5.8 uses a simple procedure to test the BreakdownName procedure. You simply use the Get-SaveAsFilename method to obtain a full filename and pass the filename to the BreakdownName procedure along with two empty variables, sName and sPath. BreakdownName uses the FileNamePosition function to locate the beginning of the filename component. Once you know that, it is simple to break the name down into the path- and filename components using the VBA Left and Right functions. Both Left and Right take a string variable and return the specified number of characters from either the left or the right respectively. In the following screenshots, you can see how I employed the BreakdownName procedure to figure out the path and filename of the file returned from GetSaveAsFilename.

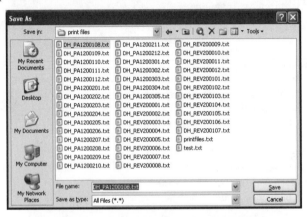

PARAMETERS PASSED BY REFERENCE

ByRef means that the parameter is passed by reference. If you do not use the ByRef keyword when you declare parameters, then the parameters are passed by value. You could explicitly specify this by declaring parameters using ByVal.

Anyway, rather than get into the details of this, it is probably best to just think of parameters in terms of read/write. ByVal parameters are read only from the perspective of the calling procedure. The procedure that is called can change the values of the parameters, but the calling procedure never knows about, or sees the changes.

By reference or ByRef parameters are read/write from the perspective of the calling procedure. Now when the procedure that is called changes the value of a parameter denoted with ByRef, the calling procedure sees the change.

Using ByRef is one way to return or modify more than one value from a function *or* a subroutine.

Occasionally you'll have the full filename of a workbook and only be interested in isolating the workbook name only. Listing 5.8 includes a function for just that purpose, called GetShortName, that serves as a shorthand way to use the BreakdownName procedure.

Inspecting Your Operating Environment

The Application object includes a handful of properties that return information you can use to determine the specifics of the computer your code is running on (see Listing 5.9). You can determine which version of Excel is being used, which operating system is running, as well as memory information such as how much memory the system has and how much of it is in use.

LISTING 5.9: SYSTEM INFORMATION AVAILABLE USING APPLICATION OBJECT PROPERTIES

```
Sub InspectTheEnvironment()
    Debug.Print Application.CalculationVersion
    Debug.Print Application.MemoryFree
    Debug.Print Application.MemoryUsed
    Debug.Print Application.MemoryTotal
    Debug.Print Application.OperatingSystem
    Debug.Print Application.OrganizationName
    Debug.Print Application.UserName
    Debug.Print Application.Version
End Sub
```

This code produces the following output on my computer.

```
114210
1048576
475128
1523704
Windows (32-bit) NT 5.01
Dakota Technology Group, Inc.
Steven M. Hansen
11.0
```

Table 5.2 details some of the system-oriented properties of the Application object.

TABLE 5.2: SYSTEM-ORIENTED PROPERTIES OF THE APPLICATION OBJECT

PROPERTY NAME	VALUE RETURNED
CalculationVersion	Right four digits indicate the version of the calculation engine whereas the digits to the left indicate the major version of Excel.
MemoryFree	Returns the amount of memory in bytes that Excel is allowed to use, not including memory already in use.

TABLE 5.2: SYSTEM-ORIENTED PROPERTIES OF THE APPLICATION OBJECT *(continued)*

PROPERTY NAME	VALUE RETURNED
MemoryUsed	Returns the amount of memory, in bytes, that Excel is currently using.
MemoryTotal	Returns the total amount of memory, in bytes, that Excel can use. It includes memory that is already in use. It is the sum of MemoryFree and MemoryUsed.
OperatingSystem	Returns the name and version of the Operating System.
OrganizationName	Returns the name of the organization to which the product is registered.
UserName	Returns or sets the name of the current user.
Version	Returns the version of Excel that is in use.

Two Useful Bonus Members

You should be familiar with two more members of the Application object. The first one is the Cut-CopyMode property. This property, though not used nearly as frequently as something like Screen-Updating, is handy in certain situations. Have you noticed that when you use Cut or Copy, Excel shows the range that is being cut or copied using moving dashes around the perimeter? Once in a while you'll want to do the same thing using VBA and, after you have performed the copy, you don't want to leave the moving dashes on display (it is not very professional looking). To turn the dashes off, you need to exit CutCopyMode. In the appropriate location in your procedure, insert this line:

```
Application.CutCopyMode = False
```

The second member that is useful to know is the InputBox method. InputBox allows you to capture simple input from your user.

The syntax of InputBox is as follows:

```
InputBox(prompt, [title], [default], [xpos], _
    [ypos], [helpfile], [context])
```

The parameters to InputBox are as follows.

Prompt   This is the only required parameter. It is the text that is displayed that indicates what the user should enter as input.

Title   This is an optional parameter. Any text you supply will be displayed in the title bar of the input box. If omitted, the application name is used.

Default An optional parameter that, if supplied, is used as the default value in the input area of the input box.

Xpos An optional parameter that specifies the distance between the left edge of the input box and the left edge of the window. If omitted the input box is horizontally centered.

Ypos An optional parameter that specifies the distance between the top edge of the input box and the top edge of the window. If omitted the input box is about $1/3$ of the way down the screen.

Helpfile An optional parameter that specifies the help file used to provide context-sensitive help. If this parameter is provided, you must also provide a context parameter.

Context An optional parameter that specifies the help context number of the appropriate help topic. If this parameter is specified, you must also provide the Helpfile parameter.

The following code snippet provides an example of the usage of the InputBox function.

```
Sub SimpleInputBox()
    Dim vInput As Variant

    vInput = InputBox("What is your name?", _
        "Introduction", Application.UserName)
    MsgBox "Hello, " & vInput & ". Nice to meet you.", _
        vbOKOnly, "Introduction"
End Sub
```

The following screenshot shows an example of this simple procedure.

Summary

The Application object contains many members. As the root object of the Excel object model, many of the members are Excel objects that I'll cover later in the book. However, many members are specific to the Application object. This chapter looked at the most commonly used Application properties and methods that pertain to working with the display, returning convenient Excel objects, handling common file operations, and gathering information about the system environment.

Two properties of the Application object control aspects of the display that are very common and nearly indispensable when you are trying to develop a polished, professional-looking Excel application. The ScreenUpdating property allows you to control when the screen is updated so that your application runs faster and doesn't flash spasmodically as it runs. The StatusBar property provides an easy, subtle, and nonintrusive way to display status information and messages to the user.

The Application object contains a number of properties that return Excel objects that represent objects currently in use such as ActiveCell, ActiveSheet, Selection, and ThisWorkbook. You should only use these items to refer to active items when you really need the active item. If you use the Activate method before using one of these properties, you are making your programming chores more difficult and error prone, and as a result, the performance of your application suffers. In coming chapters, you'll see that you don't need to activate objects to work with them.

The methods GetOpenFilename and GetSaveAsFilename provide quick access to the familiar Open and Save As dialog boxes common to nearly all Windows applications. You'll use these methods often, and because of this, it may make sense to wrap these methods into your own procedure that performs other related functionality, such as checking the validity of the result of these methods.

In the coming chapters, I'll tackle the Workbook object and the Worksheet object. In Chapter 6, I'll dive deeper into the topic of opening and saving workbooks using the functionality of GetOpen-Filename and GetSaveAsFilename. Though you can use these methods with one call, you risk run-time errors if you don't incorporate some defensive programming tactics in your code. In addition, I'll cover other common properties and methods associated with the Workbook object.

Chapter 6

Working with the Workbook Object

THE WORKBOOK OBJECT REPRESENTS a single workbook. Though the Workbook object has many properties and methods, you'll use only a handful on a regular basis. In this chapter, you'll examine these common properties and methods along with a few events associated with the Workbook object.

Many objects have a set of actions to which they've been designed to respond. The actions that an object recognizes are known as events. You can write procedures that execute when an object recognizes that a given event has occurred. For example, the Workbook object has an Open event; whenever a workbook is opened, VBA looks for any code associated with the Open event and executes it.

You'll also look at the Workbooks collection object, known as the Workbooks object. The Workbooks object represents all of the Workbook objects that are open in Excel.

Finally, I'll put together all of the concepts you've learned so far to create a set of procedures that you'll find useful for any process in which you need to apply processing to one or more workbooks.

Walk before You Run: Opening and Closing Workbooks

Before you can do anything with a Workbook object, you need to have a Workbook object on which to work. Because this is a VBA book, you might as well open and close your workbooks programmatically. In order to open and close workbooks, you need to use the Workbooks object. It represents all of the open workbooks in Excel and has methods that can open a new workbook, open an existing workbook, or close a workbook.

Like all collection objects, the Workbooks object has an Item property that you can use to access a specific item in the collection and a Count property that returns the number of objects in the collection.

The easiest way to obtain a workbook to play with programmatically is to just add a new workbook. You can achieve this using the Add method. The syntax for the Add method is as follows:

```
Workbooks.Add (template)
```

The template parameter is optional and can be a string specifying the name of an existing workbook that will be used as a template. Alternatively, template can be a constant that specifies that a new workbook should be created with one worksheet of a specific type. You can choose from four types:

xlWBAChart, xlWBAExcel4IntlMacroSheet, xlWBAExcel4MacroSheet, and xlWBATWorksheet. These represent a chart sheet, two flavors of macro sheets, and a standard worksheet, respectively. Finally, if you don't specify a template, Excel just creates an empty, standard workbook.

If you want to open an existing workbook, use the Open method of the Workbooks object. The syntax of Open looks rather daunting because there are so many parameters (16 of them!). Thankfully, all of them except for the first one are optional.

```
Workbooks.Open(Filename, [UpdateLinks], [ReadOnly], _
    [Format], [Password], [WriteResPassword], _
    [IgnoreReadOnlyRecommended], [Origin], [Delimiter], _
    [Editable], [Notify], [Converter], [AddToMru], [Local], _
    [CorruptLoad])
```

Because I'd like this book to be packed with useful and practical content rather than replicate Excel's help files, I'll not go into the details of every parameter here. Most of the time, you'll use the Open method with its only required parameter—the FileName. Occasionally, I'll also use the UpdateLinks and ReadOnly parameters. You can set ReadOnly to true to open the workbook in read-only mode. By default this parameter is false (read-write mode). If the workbook you're opening contains links, you may want to use the UpdateLinks parameter with one of the values shown in Table 6.1.

TABLE 6.1: VALID UPDATELINKS VALUES

VALUE	UPDATELINKS BEHAVIOR
0	Links are not updated.
1	External links are updated but not remote links.
2	Remote links are updated but not external links.
3	Both remote and external links are updated.

You can close workbooks using the Close method of either the Workbooks object or the Workbook object. The difference is that the Close method on the Workbooks object closes all open workbooks whereas the Close method on the Workbook object closes just that workbook.

Listing 6.1 incorporates many of the skills you've learned so far into a set of procedures that you can use to process a batch of workbooks. This is a fairly lengthy listing because it is a fairly robust set of procedures that you can use in real-life situations.

LISTING 6.1: A ROBUST, BATCH WORKBOOK PROCESSING FRAMEWORK

```
Sub ProcessFileBatch()
    Dim nIndex As Integer
    Dim vFiles As Variant
    Dim wb As Workbook
    Dim bAlreadyOpen As Boolean

    On Error GoTo ErrHandler
```

```vba
    ' Get a batch of Excel files
    vFiles = GetExcelFiles("Select Workbooks for Processing")

    ' Make sure the dialog wasn't cancelled - in which case
    ' vFiles would equal False and therefore wouldn't be an array.
    If Not IsArray(vFiles) Then
        Debug.Print "No files selected."
        Exit Sub
    End If

    Application.ScreenUpdating = False

    ' OK - loop through the filenames
    For nIndex = 1 To UBound(vFiles)

        If IsWorkbookOpen(CStr(vFiles(nIndex))) Then
            Set wb = Workbooks(GetShortName(CStr(vFiles(nIndex))))
            Debug.Print "Workbook already open: " & wb.Name
            bAlreadyOpen = True
        Else
            Set wb = Workbooks.Open(CStr(vFiles(nIndex)), False)
            Debug.Print "Opened workbook: " & wb.Name
            bAlreadyOpen = False
        End If

        Application.StatusBar = "Processing workbook: " & wb.Name

        ' Code to process the file goes here
        Debug.Print "If we wanted to do something to the " & _
            "workbook, we would do it here."

        ' Close workbook unless it was already open
        If Not bAlreadyOpen Then
            Debug.Print "Closing workbook: " & wb.Name
            wb.Close True
        End If
    Next nIndex

    ' Clean up
    Set wb = Nothing

ErrHandler:
    Application.StatusBar = False
    Application.ScreenUpdating = True
End Sub
```

PROCEDURAL PROGRAMMING

Procedural programming is a programming paradigm in which a program is constructed of small procedures that are linked together to perform a given task. One school of thought regarding procedural programming is that procedures have one and only one exit point. In Listing 6.1, the use of the Exit statement in the event that an array is not returned would violate this guideline.

The alternative is to embed nearly the entire remaining block of statements inside a giant If…Then statement. I used to follow this practice so that my procedures would adhere to the one and only one exit point guideline. However, it seems to me that it is more difficult to follow and maintain procedures that use many nested If…Then statements than it is to check for a terminating condition and use an Exit statement if a terminating condition is found. For example, Listing 6.1 could be rewritten to follow the one and only one exit point guideline as shown here (many lines omitted for brevity):

```
Sub ProcessFileBatch()

    …

    …

    ' Make sure the dialog wasn't cancelled - in which case
    ' vFiles would equal False and therefore wouldn't be an array.
    If Not IsArray(vFiles) Then
        Debug.Print "No files selected."
    Else

        Application.ScreenUpdating = False

        ' OK - loop through the filenames
        For nIndex = 1 To UBound(vFiles)

            …

            …

        Next nIndex
    End If

    …

ErrHandler:
    Application.StatusBar = False
    Application.ScreenUpdating = True
End Sub
```

Omitting lines for brevity's sake doesn't help illustrate the main problem created by long nested If…Then statements or Loops—they are much harder to read. This is especially true when you need to check for multiple terminating conditions, because this creates deeply nested structures that are nearly impossible to read.

Prior to analyzing this procedure, I've a couple of thoughts I'd like to share. First, before you can use this procedure, you'll need to add a few more procedures you haven't seen yet. I'll get to them after we analyze this listing. Second, this procedure is a good example of a long procedure. I generally don't like to see procedures of this length or longer. Usually such procedures can be factored, or broken into smaller, discrete procedures that work together. The benefit of using smaller procedures is that they are usually easier to understand and therefore easier to debug and maintain. Further, smaller procedures generally offer greater potential for reuse. In this case, the procedure is reasonably factored and logically laid out to the point that I am comfortable with it.

OK, so let's take a look at this procedure. First, after you declare the variables, notice the On Error statement. This statement directs program execution to the ErrHandler label near the end of the procedure in the event of an error. Any time you are opening or saving files, the probability that an error will occur increases, so it is a good idea to use some sort of error handling. Because you'll be using the status bar and turning screen updating off, you need to be certain that these properties will be reset to their original settings no matter what. You need to use error handling here, if for no other reason than to guarantee that these properties get reset. You may add additional error-handling code here as your needs dictate.

After error handling is turned on, this procedure calls the GetExcelFiles function that was listed in Chapter 5 (Listing 5.6) to obtain a batch of files from the user. Next, you need to check the result of GetExcelFiles to make sure it's an array. If it isn't, the user didn't select any files. If files weren't selected, there is no point in continuing the procedure, so you use the Exit statement to end the routine.

The next order of business is to construct a loop that will loop through every filename returned from the GetExcelFiles function. As we discussed in the last chapter, the GetOpenFilename method used within the GetExcelFiles function returns a one-based array rather than a zero-based array, which is the conventional way to work with arrays.

Inside the loop, you need to assign the workbook referred to by the filename to a workbook variable (named wb). In order to do this properly, you need to take into account the possibility that the workbook is already open. I've created a function called IsWorkbookOpen that checks to see if a given workbook is open or not. We will take a look at that after I finish this analysis. If the workbook is open, you just need to set a reference to the open workbook (with help from the GetShortName procedure from Listing 5.8); otherwise you need to use the Open method of the Workbooks object.

In order to leave the environment as it was found, the procedure remembers whether or not each workbook was open. That way, after you finish doing work on the workbook, you can close it if it was closed or leave it open if it was originally open.

At this point in the procedure, you have a reference to the desired workbook and could do any processing on the workbook that you desired. Ideally, you'd create a specialized procedure to perform the processing that takes a workbook parameter as input. For example, you could create a procedure such as this:

```
Sub ProcessWorkbook(wb As Workbook)
    ' do some work on the
    ' wb here
End Sub
```

As you loop through the workbooks, you could simply call the ProcessWorkbook routine such as

```
...
' Code to process the file goes here
ProcessWorkbook wb
...
```

After doing any desired processing on the workbook, you need to save any changes and close the workbook if it was originally closed. Then move on to the next workbook.

Finally, after you've looped through all of the workbooks that the user selected, you come to the last couple of lines that reset the status bar and turn on screen updating. The ErrHandler label doesn't have any effect on program execution other than to provide a bookmark, so to speak, that instructs the computer where to go in the event of a run-time error.

Is That Workbook Open?

Remember the discussion regarding defensive programming in Chapter 4? Well, here is a good example of where you need to employ some defensive programming. Many times you'll need to assign a workbook to a workbook variable. Depending on whether the workbook is open or not, you have to do this in different ways. Alternatively, perhaps you've developed an Excel model that consists of multiple workbooks that work in tandem. In either case, you need a way to check if a given workbook is open or not. Listing 6.2 provides an example of a function that you can use to make this determination.

LISTING 6.2: SEEING IF A WORKBOOK IS OPEN

```
' This function checks to see if a given workbook
' is open or not. This function can be used
' using a short name such as MyWorkbook.xls
' or a full name such as C:\Testing\MyWorkbook.xls
Function IsWorkbookOpen(sWorkbook As String) As Boolean
    Dim sName As String
    Dim sPath As String
    Dim sFullName As String

    On Error Resume Next
    IsWorkbookOpen = True

    ' See if we were given a short name or a long name
    If InStr(1, sWorkbook, "\", vbTextCompare) > 0 Then
        ' We have a long name
        ' Need to break it down
        sFullName = sWorkbook
        BreakdownName sFullName, sName, sPath
```

```
        If StrComp(Workbooks(sName).FullName, sWorkbook, 1) <> 0 Then
            IsWorkbookOpen = False
        End If
    Else
        ' We have a short name
        If StrComp(Workbooks(sWorkbook).Name, sWorkbook, 1) <> 0 Then
            IsWorkbookOpen = False
        End If
    End If
End Function
```

This function requires the BreakdownName and FileNamePosition procedures from Chapter 5. The BreakdownName procedure is handy here because it enables you to create a function that doesn't care if it receives a simple workbook name or a full workbook name that includes the path where the file is stored.

This function is sort of tricky in a number of ways, especially because you haven't covered some of the functionality that makes this function work. One of the first things that clues you in to a critical technique that allows this function to work correctly is the On Error Resume Next statement. This function flat out wouldn't work without it. I'll tell you why in a few minutes. After the On Error Resume Next statement, you can see that I set the default return value to true.

Next, you need to check whether the parameter that was provided is in the form of a filename only, or if it contains that storage path and filename. You do that by seeing if it contains a "\" using the InStr function. Because slashes are prohibited within a filename, the only way you can have one is if you received a storage path in addition to the filename. If the sWorkbook parameter does contain the path in addition to the filename, you use the BreakdownName procedure from Listing 5.8 to isolate the actual name of the file from the location in which it is stored.

The trickiest parts of the IsWorkbookOpen function are the two If…Then statements that use the StrComp function. You might be wondering why you need two If…Then statements, one for the case in which we have a full name and one for the case in which we only have a filename. Why not use one If…Then statement to do this for both cases?

The reason you need two statements is that a significant difference exists between using this function with a short name versus a full name. When you use this function with a short name, you aren't considering the possibility that a workbook with the same name exists in multiple folders. This is fine in situations in which you want to check whether it is safe to open a file (you can't have two files open with the same name even if they are stored in separate folders). However, if you need to be sure that a specific file is open, the only way to do this is to provide this function with a full name.

You can see that the two StrComp function calls use different properties of the Workbook object. One uses the FullName property, which consists of a path and a filename, and the other uses the Name property, which only consists of a filename.

Also, notice how the Workbook object is used here—by going through the Workbooks object. The next section dives into this a little deeper. For now, just understand that you can refer to an individual item (in this case a Workbook object) within a collection by specifying its name within parentheses.

Remember the part about the On Error Resume Next statement being so critical to this function? Here is why. If you recall, the Workbooks object is the collection of all *open* workbooks. If you attempt

SCRUTINIZING STRINGS WITH INSTR AND STRCOMP

VBA has a number of built-in functions for working with strings. InStr and StrComp are used to either look for the presence of one string inside another string or to compare two strings for equivalence.

InStr returns a variant (the subtype is long) that indicates the position of the first occurrence of one string inside another. The syntax of InStr is as follows:

```
InStr([start, ]string1, string2[, compare])
```

The start parameter is optional and specifies where InStr should begin searching for string2 within string1. If omitted, the search begins at the first character position. I prefer to explicitly put a 1 there even though it is the default.

The compare parameter is also optional and is used to specify a text comparison (A = a) or a binary comparison (A < a). You can use the defined constants vbTextCompare or vbBinaryCompare. The default if omitted is vbUseCompareOption, which performs a comparison using the setting of the Option Compare statement. If you don't use the Option Compare statement at the top of your modules, the default is to perform a binary comparison.

If either string is null, InStr returns null. If string1 is zero length, then InStr returns 0. If string2 is zero-length, then InStr returns whatever was specified as the start parameter. The only time you receive a number greater than zero is if string2 is found within string1.

Before I move on to StrComp, I suppose I should mention InStr's backward brother InStrRev, which works just like InStr except it starts at the *end* of a string if start is omitted and works right to left.

StrComp, meanwhile, is used to test for string equivalence. The syntax of StrComp is as follows:

```
StrComp(string1, string2[, compare])
```

The optional compare parameter is used in the same manner as it was for InStr. If string1<string2 then StrComp returns -1. If string1=string2 then StrComp returns 0. Finally, if string1>string2 then StrComp returns 1. The only exception to these return values is in the event that either string1 or string2 is null, in which case StrComp also returns null.

---

to access a Workbook object through the Workbooks object by referring to it by name and the workbook is not open, a run-time error occurs. Because we specified On Error Resume Next, when an error occurs, the procedure executes the next line that sets IsWorkbookOpen to false. If the workbook is open, StrComp returns 0, and the function returns the default value (IsWorkbookOpen = True) that you set at the beginning of the procedure.

Specifying Specific Collection Objects

Say "specifying specific" three times as fast as you can. If you can do that, you can understand this section. You need to build on your understanding of collection objects and their relationship to the objects they contain. In particular, you need to come to grips with the different ways to work with individual items within a collection.

As I mentioned earlier in the chapter, all collection objects have an Item property that you can use to refer to individual items within the collection. For the vast majority of collections, the Item property is the default property. This means that you can access the property without specifying it. The following example demonstrates the various ways you could refer to an item within a collection. This example uses the Worksheets collection object.

```
Sub ReferringToItems()
    ' Refer to a worksheet by index number
    Debug.Print ThisWorkbook.Worksheets(1).Name
    ' once again, but with feeling
    Debug.Print ThisWorkbook.Worksheets.Item(1).Name

    ' Refer to a worksheet by name
    Debug.Print ThisWorkbook.Worksheets("Sheet1").Name
    ' and again using Item...
    Debug.Print ThisWorkbook.Worksheets.Item("Sheet1").Name
End Sub
```

Each line in this procedure refers to the same item within the Worksheets object. You can refer to an item by its position or index within the collection or by using its name.

Now you are probably thinking, "Steve, you have told me three times already that it is best to be explicit." It is. That is still good advice. Referring to individual items within a collection is such a common occurrence within your procedures, and using the default Item property without specifying it is such a frequently used and understood practice that, in this instance, it is OK to ignore this guideline.

NOTE   *Understanding how to refer to individual items within a collection object is crucial to using the Excel object model. You'll see this technique used throughout the rest of the book.*

Untangle Links Programmatically (Part I)

As a former financial analyst (before I learned more efficient ways to analyze data), I used to build elaborate virtual ecosystems of linked Excel models. Inevitably, I'd need to make some sort of change to a particular workbook, and the change would "break" dependencies I had created in other workbooks that linked to the workbook I making the change in. Maintaining this structure was a living nightmare. One of the tools that would've been helpful in those days was one that would automatically examine the dependencies in workbooks.

Believe it or not, it's not very difficult to build such a tool. As you continue through the book, one of the utilities you'll examine will be a Link Rebuilder—a utility you can use to examine workbook links.

One of the reasons that this utility isn't very difficult is that there are some handy methods and properties associated with the Workbook object that return useful information about links. These methods and properties are listed in Table 6.2.

One critical piece of the Link Rebuilder utility is functionality that can, given a workbook, determine all of the links in the workbook (if any). From Table 6.2, you can see that the Link-Sources method performs this feat. Listing 6.3 demonstrates a procedure that prints all of the link information.

TABLE 6.2: LINK-ORIENTED MEMBERS OF THE WORKBOOK OBJECT

MEMBER	DESCRIPTION
SaveLinkValues property	Read/write Boolean that specifies whether Excel saves external link values with the workbook.
UpdateLinks property	Read/write property that indicates a workbook's setting for updating embedded OLE links. You can check or set the value returned using the XlUpdateLink constants xlUpdateLinkAlways, xlUpdateLinksNever, and xlUpdateLinksUserSetting. OLE stands for Object Linking and Embedding, an older Microsoft moniker for the technology that enables linking.
BreakLink method	Converts formulas linked to other sources to values.
ChangeLink method	Changes a link from one document to another.
LinkInfo method	Returns the link date and update status.
LinkSources method	Returns an array of links in the workbook including linked documents, editions, or DDE or OLE servers (DDE and OLE are explained in Chapter 14). This method returns Empty if it doesn't find any links.
OpenLinks method	Opens the document to which the link refers.
UpdateLink method	Updates an Excel, DDE, or OLE link.

LISTING 6.3: PROGRAMMATICALLY RETRIEVING LINK SOURCE INFORMATION

```
Sub PrintSimpleLinkInfo(wb As Workbook)
    Dim avLinks As Variant
    Dim nIndex As Integer

    ' get list of Excel-based link sources
    avLinks = wb.LinkSources(xlExcelLinks)
    If Not IsEmpty(avLinks) Then
        ' loop through every link source
        For nIndex = 1 To UBound(avLinks)
            Debug.Print "Link found to '" & avLinks(nIndex) & "'"
        Next nIndex
    Else
        Debug.Print "The workbook '" & wb.Name & _
            "' doesn't have any links."
    End If
End Sub
```

As you can see, the only thing you need to check for when you're using LinkSources is to see if it returns Empty; this signifies that it didn't find any links. Because the only thing this procedure requires to run is a workbook parameter, this procedure would be an ideal candidate to call from the ProcessFileBatch procedure in Listing 6.1. To do this, locate the following line.

```
Debug.Print "If we wanted to do something to the " & _
        "workbook, we would do it here."
```

Replace that line with this line:

```
PrintSimpleLinkInfo wb
```

Give it a whirl. Select a batch of Excel files including one that is linked to another workbook and check out the Immediate window. When I ran it on a batch of workbooks, I received the following output.

```
Opened workbook: Test.xls
Link found to 'C:\Chapter Six Examples.xls'
Closing workbook: Test.xls
Opened workbook: BTR Loader.xls
The workbook 'BTR Loader.xls' doesn't have any links.
Closing workbook: BTR Loader.xls
Opened workbook: Chapter Five Examples.xls
The workbook 'Chapter Five Examples.xls' doesn't have any links.
Closing workbook: Chapter Five Examples.xls
Opened workbook: Mike_Wileman__1-01-2004_BTR.xls
The workbook 'Mike_Wileman__1-01-2004_BTR.xls' doesn't have any links.
Closing workbook: Mike_Wileman__1-01-2004_BTR.xls
Opened workbook: OTA Reports.xls
The workbook 'OTA Reports.xls' doesn't have any links.
Closing workbook: OTA Reports.xls
```

In later chapters, you'll learn how to produce a better looking display such as output to a worksheet. Are you starting to see how useful the ProcessFileBatch procedure is? Creating utilities to operate on workbooks can often be as simple as creating a simple procedure, as we did in Listing 6.3, and calling the procedure from within the ProcessFileBatch procedure.

Let's take this a little further. What if you move a workbook to a new file location and in the process break all of the links in any dependent files? You could manually open each dependent file and change the link source, but what fun would that be? Besides, it is so much easier and faster to create a simple utility to do it (see Listing 6.4).

LISTING 6.4: UPDATING LINKS WITH A NEW FILE LOCATION

```
Sub FixLinks(wb As Workbook, sOldLink As String, sNewLink As String)
    On Error Resume Next
    wb.ChangeLink sOldLink, sNewLink, xlLinkTypeExcelLinks
End Sub
```

If fixing links was the only thing you needed to do to a workbook, you could put the wb.Change-Link statement right in the ProcessFileBatch procedure. You may be tempted to do such a thing; however, be aware of the slight repercussion to doing so. The error-handling mechanism is different and you could have situations that warrant having separate error handling for both procedures.

Chances are that most of the time when FixLinks is called, an error will be generated. This is because you're not bothering to check if the workbook passed to FixLinks even contains any links, much less a link named the same as the sOldLink parameter. You could easily write a procedure that doesn't rely on error checking to do its job—check out Listing 6.5.

LISTING 6.5: UPDATING LINKS WITH A NEW FILE LOCATION—AN ALTERNATIVE PROCEDURE

```
Sub FixLinksII(wb As Workbook, sOldLink As String, sNewLink As String)
    Dim avLinks As Variant
    Dim nIndex As Integer

    ' get a list of link sources
    avLinks = wb.LinkSources(xlExcelLinks)

    ' if there are link sources, see if
    ' there are any named sOldLink
    If Not IsEmpty(avLinks) Then
        For nIndex = 1 To UBound(avLinks)
            If _
            StrComp(avLinks(nIndex), sOldLink, vbTextCompare) = 0 Then
                ' we have a match
                wb.ChangeLink sOldLink, sNewLink, xlLinkTypeExcelLinks
                ' once we find a match we
                ' won't find another, so exit the loop
                Exit For
            End If
        Next
    End If
End Sub
```

So which is better? That depends on what you value. They're both pretty simple. The second is definitely longer, so you might be tempted to rule that one out. Are you wondering which one runs faster or if there is any difference? So was I. I dusted off the testing routines that you used to test screen updating and the status bar from the last chapter and adapted them to test FixLinks and FixLinksII. The results surprised me. I placed my bets on FixLinks assuming that the internal error-handling implementation was speedy and that less code would mean better performance. Not so. FixLinksII ran in nearly half the amount of time as FixLinks. My rapid assumption of less code = faster code ignored the reality that if you use FixLinks against a batch of files and most of the time there aren't even any links, then most of the time FixLinksII only executes two lines of code. One line to get the list of link sources, and another to see if any link sources were found. If no link sources are found, the procedure ends.

Another piece of functionality you'll need should check the status of links in a given workbook. To check the status of a link, use the LinkInfo method. Listing 6.6 presents a function you can use to check the status of a given link.

LISTING 6.6: LINK STATUS CHECKER

```
Function GetLinkStatus(wb As Workbook, sLink As String) As String
    Dim avLinks As Variant
    Dim nIndex As Integer
    Dim sResult As String
    Dim nStatus As Integer

    ' get a list of link sources
    avLinks = wb.LinkSources(xlExcelLinks)

    ' make sure there are links in the workbook
    If IsEmpty(avLinks) Then
        GetLinkStatus = "No links in workbook."
        Exit Function
    End If

    ' default result in case the link is not found
    sResult = "Link not found."

    For nIndex = 1 To UBound(avLinks)
        If _
        StrComp(avLinks(nIndex), sLink, vbTextCompare) = 0 Then
            nStatus = wb.LinkInfo(sLink, xlLinkInfoStatus)
            Select Case nStatus
                Case xlLinkStatusCopiedValues
                    sResult = "Copied values"
                Case xlLinkStatusIndeterminate
                    sResult = "Indeterminate"
                Case xlLinkStatusInvalidName
                    sResult = "Invalid name"
                Case xlLinkStatusMissingFile
                    sResult = "Missing file"
                Case xlLinkStatusMissingSheet
                    sResult = "Missing sheet"
                Case xlLinkStatusNotStarted
                    sResult = "Not started"
                Case xlLinkStatusOK
                    sResult = "OK"
                Case xlLinkStatusOld
                    sResult = "Old"
                Case xlLinkStatusSourceNotCalculated
                    sResult = "Source not calculated"
                Case xlLinkStatusSourceNotOpen
```

```
                    sResult = "Source not open"
                Case xlLinkStatusSourceOpen
                    sResult = "Source open"
                Case Else
                    sResult = "Unknown status code"
            End Select
            Exit For
        End If
    Next
    GetLinkStatus = sResult
End Function
```

The longest part of this function is comparing the status code that LinkInfo returns against a list of possible codes so that you can translate the code into a human-friendly result. Otherwise, this procedure works like the other link oriented procedures—obtain a list of link sources, make sure the list isn't empty, and loop through the link sources returned until you find the one you're after.

Finally, before I wrap up the section on links I want to show you one more procedure, CheckAllLinks, that you can call from your ProcessFileBatch procedure (Listing 6.1). For now, CheckAllLinks outputs its results to the Immediate window (see Listing 6.7). Later in the book, you'll start outputting to Excel worksheets.

LISTING 6.7: CHECKING THE STATUS OF ALL THE LINKS IN A WORKBOOK

```
Sub CheckAllLinks(wb As Workbook)
    Dim avLinks As Variant
    Dim nLinkIndex As Integer
    Dim sMsg As String

    avLinks = wb.LinkSources(xlExcelLinks)

    If IsEmpty(avLinks) Then
        Debug.Print wb.Name & " does not have any links."
    Else
        For nLinkIndex = 1 To UBound(avLinks)
            Debug.Print "Workbook: " & wb.Name
            Debug.Print "Link Source: " & avLinks(nLinkIndex)
            Debug.Print "Status: " & _
                GetLinkStatus(wb, CStr(avLinks(nLinkIndex)))
        Next
    End If
End Sub
```

To call CheckAllLinks from the ProcessFileBatch procedure, locate these statements shown in the ProcessFileBatch procedure:

```
' Code to process the file goes here
```

```
Debug.Print "If we wanted to do something to the " & _
    "workbook, we would do it here."
```

Replace the Debug.Print statement with the following:

```
CheckAllLinks wb
```

All the CheckAllLinks procedure does is call the GetLinkStatus function from Listing 6.6 for each link source found in the workbook. CheckAllLinks produced the following results when I ran it against some of my test files.

```
Opened workbook: Test.xls
Workbook: Test.xls
Link Source: C:

Status: Old
Closing workbook: Test.xls
Opened workbook: NewLinkSource.xls
NewLinkSource.xls does not have any links.
Closing workbook: NewLinkSource.xls
Opened workbook: NewLinkSourceII.xls
NewLinkSourceII.xls does not have any links.
Closing workbook: NewLinkSourceII.xls
```

Hopefully you are starting to see how easy it is to tie procedures together to do useful things. This allows you to break your programming tasks into small and easy-to-understand (and therefore code) pieces. Once you have all of the pieces, it is usually fairly easy to piece them all together.

Plain Vanilla Workbook Properties

As you would expect, the workbook object has a handful of properties that provide basic information about the workbook. You've seen the Name and FullName properties used in other procedures in this chapter. Other basic properties include CodeName, FileFormat, Path, ReadOnly, and Saved. Listing 6.8 provides an example that displays basic workbook properties.

LISTING 6.8: A SIMPLE EXAMPLE OF STANDARD WORKBOOK PROPERTIES

```
Sub TestPrintGeneralWBInfo()
    PrintGeneralWorkbookInfo ThisWorkbook
End Sub

Sub PrintGeneralWorkbookInfo(wb As Workbook)
    Debug.Print "Name: " & wb.Name
    Debug.Print "Full Name: " & wb.FullName
    Debug.Print "Code Name: " & wb.CodeName
    Debug.Print "FileFormat: " & GetFileFormat(wb)
    Debug.Print "Path: " & wb.Path
    If wb.ReadOnly Then
```

```vba
            Debug.Print "The workbook has been opened as read-only."
        Else
            Debug.Print "The workbook is read-write."
        End If
        If wb.Saved Then
            Debug.Print "The workbook does not need to be saved."
        Else
            Debug.Print "The workbook should be saved."
        End If
    End Sub

    Function GetFileFormat(wb As Workbook) As String
        Dim lFormat As Long
        Dim sFormat As String
        lFormat = wb.FileFormat
        Select Case lFormat
            Case xlAddIn: sFormat = "Add-in"
            Case xlCSV: sFormat = "CSV"
            Case xlCSVMac: sFormat = "CSV Mac"
            Case xlCSVMSDOS: sFormat = "CSV MS DOS"
            Case xlCSVWindows: sFormat = "CSV Windows"
            Case xlCurrentPlatformText: sFormat = "Current Platform Text"
            Case xlDBF2: sFormat = "DBF 2"
            Case xlDBF3: sFormat = "DBF 3"
            Case xlDBF4: sFormat = "DBF 4"
            Case xlDIF: sFormat = "DIF"
            Case xlExcel2: sFormat = "Excel 2"
            Case xlExcel2FarEast: sFormat = "Excel 2 Far East"
            Case xlExcel3: sFormat = "Excel 3"
            Case xlExcel4: sFormat = "Excel 4"
            Case xlExcel4Workbook: sFormat = "Excel 4 Workbook"
            Case xlExcel5: sFormat = "Excel 5"
            Case xlExcel7: sFormat = "Excel 7"
            Case xlExcel9795: sFormat = "Excel 97/95"
            Case xlHtml: sFormat = "HTML"
            Case xlIntlAddIn: sFormat = "Int'l AddIn"
            Case xlIntlMacro: sFormat = "Int'l Macro"
            Case xlSYLK: sFormat = "SYLK"
            Case xlTemplate: sFormat = "Template"
            Case xlTextMac: sFormat = "Text Mac"
            Case xlTextMSDOS: sFormat = "Text MS DOS"
            Case xlTextPrinter: sFormat = "Text Printer"
            Case xlTextWindows: sFormat = "Text Windows"
            Case xlUnicodeText: sFormat = "Unicode Text"
            Case xlWebArchive: sFormat = "Web Archive"
            Case xlWJ2WD1: sFormat = "WJ2WD1"
            Case xlWJ3: sFormat = "WJ3"
            Case xlWJ3FJ3: sFormat = "WJ3FJ3"
```

```
        Case xlWK1: sFormat = "WK1"
        Case xlWK1ALL: sFormat = "WK1ALL"
        Case xlWK1FMT: sFormat = "WK1FMT"
        Case xlWK3: sFormat = "WK3"
        Case xlWK3FM3: sFormat = "WK3FM3"
        Case xlWK4: sFormat = "WK4"
        Case xlWKS: sFormat = "WKS"
        Case xlWorkbookNormal: sFormat = "Normal workbook"
        Case xlWorks2FarEast: sFormat = "Works 2 Far East"
        Case xlWQ1: sFormat = "WQ1"
        Case xlXMLSpreadsheet: sFormat = "XML Spreadsheet"
        Case Else: sFormat = "Unknown format code"
    End Select
    GetFileFormat = sFormat
End Function
```

If you didn't care about translating the value returned from the FileFormat property into a more user-friendly value, you could do away with the lengthy GetFileFormat function. Running the TestPrintGeneralWBInfo from Listing 6.8 produces the following output (your output may vary).

```
Name: Chapter Six Examples.xls
Full Name: C:\Chapter Six Examples.xls
Code Name: ThisWorkbook
FileFormat: Normal workbook
Path: C:\
The workbook is read-write.
The workbook should be saved.
```

Respond to User Actions with Events

Are you ready for this? This is your first exposure to working with events in VBA. Events allow you to create powerful applications that are aware of and respond to various actions that occur due to programmatic and/or end user activities. Something about events excites me. I'm not sure if it is the extra dose of control that events provide or what, but working with events definitely adds to the excitement of programming.

Some of that excitement may come from the satisfaction of creating a well-oiled application that is aware of any pertinent action that occurs. When you use events, especially once you start creating User Forms, the difficulty level of creating error-free applications increases substantially with the number of events that you respond to. That said, the events associated with the Workbook object are generally fairly easy to work with.

So what kind of events would be associated with a workbook? Well, think about the kinds of things that happen to them—they get opened, closed, saved, activated, and deactivated. Table 6.3 presents a complete list of the events associated with the Workbook object.

TABLE 6.3: EVENTS ASSOCIATED WITH THE WORKBOOK OBJECT

EVENT	OCCURS WHEN
Activate	The workbook is activated.
AddinInstall	The workbook is installed as an add-in.
AddinUninstall	The workbook is uninstalled as an add-in.
BeforeClose	Before the workbook closes and before the user is asked to save changes.
BeforePrint	Before anything in the workbook is printed.
BeforeSave	Before the workbook is saved.
Deactivate	The workbook is deactivated.
NewSheet	A new sheet is created in the workbook.
Open	The workbook is opened.
PivotTableCloseConnection	After a PivotTable report closes the connection to its data source.
PivotTableOpenConnection	After a PivotTable opens the connection to its data source.
SheetActivate	Any sheet in the workbook is activated.
SheetBeforeDoubleClick	Any sheet in the workbook is double-clicked and before the default double-click action.
SheetBeforeRightClick	Any worksheet in the workbook is right-clicked and before the default right-click action.
SheetCalculate	Any worksheet in the workbook is recalculated or after any changed data is plotted on a chart.
SheetChange	Cells in any worksheet are changed by the user or by an external link.
SheetDeactivate	Any sheet in the workbook is deactivated.
SheetFollowHyperlink	You click any hyperlink in the workbook.
SheetPivotTableUpdate	After the sheet of the PivotTable report has been updated.
SheetSelectionChange	The selection changes on any worksheet (not on chart sheets) in the workbook.
WIndowActivate	Any workbook window is activated.
WindowDeactivate	Any workbook window is deactivated.
WindowResize	Any workbook window is resized.

As you can see, that is quite a list of events to which you can respond. You may be wondering what you need to do to respond to them. It is actually quite easy; just follow these steps:

1. In the VBE, double-click the ThisWorkbook item underneath the Microsoft Excel Objects in the Project Explorer.

2. Next, select the Workbook option in the Objects drop-down list.

3. Finally, choose which event you'd like to add code to from the Procedures/Events drop-down list (see Figure 6.1).

One annoying thing that happens when you choose the Workbook option in the Objects drop-down list is that the VBE automatically adds code for the Open event into the code window. This is handy when, in fact, you want to add code to the Open event procedure; otherwise it is a minor annoyance. Go right ahead and select the event you want anyway. You can leave the Open event code that was added or delete it.

FIGURE 6.1
Adding code to respond to events is as simple as choosing which event you'd like to respond to from a drop-down list.

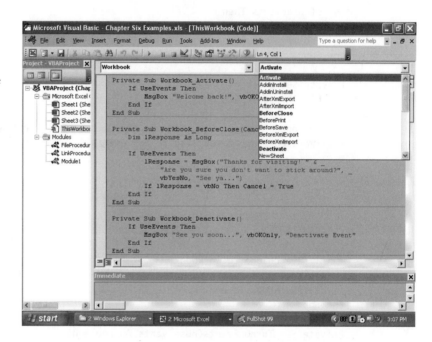

One of the ways that I like to get a handle on all of the events associated with an object and how they behave is to attach a simple call to the MsgBox function to each of the events in which I am interested. Listing 6.9 demonstrates this using various workbook object events.

LISTING 6.9: EXPERIMENTING WITH WORKBOOK OBJECT EVENTS

```
Private Sub Workbook_Activate()
    If UseEvents Then
        MsgBox "Welcome back!", vbOKOnly, "Activate Event"
    End If
End Sub

Private Sub Workbook_BeforeClose(Cancel As Boolean)
    Dim lResponse As Long
```

```
        If UseEvents Then
            lResponse = MsgBox("Thanks for visiting! " & _
                "Are you sure you don't want to stick around?", _
                vbYesNo, "See ya...")
            If lResponse = vbNo Then Cancel = True
        End If
End Sub

Private Sub Workbook_Deactivate()
    If UseEvents Then
        MsgBox "See you soon...", vbOKOnly, "Deactivate Event"
    End If
End Sub

Private Sub Workbook_Open()
    Dim lResponse As Long

    lResponse = MsgBox("Welcome to the Chapter Six Example " & _
    "Workbook! Would you like to use events?", vbYesNo, "Welcome")

    If lResponse = vbYes Then
        TurnOnEvents True
    Else
        TurnOnEvents False
    End If

    ' save change to workbook
    ' so it doesn't bug us later
    ThisWorkbook.Save
End Sub

Private Sub TurnOnEvents(bUseEvents As Boolean)
    On Error Resume Next
    If bUseEvents Then
        ThisWorkbook.Worksheets(1).Range("TestEvents").Value = "YES"
    Else
        ThisWorkbook.Worksheets(1).Range("TestEvents").Value = "NO"
    End If
End Sub

Private Function UseEvents() As Boolean
    On Error Resume Next

    UseEvents = False
    If UCase(ThisWorkbook.Worksheets(1).Range("TestEvents").Value) _
        = "YES" Then
        UseEvents = True
```

```vbnet
        End If
End Function


Private Sub Workbook_SheetActivate(ByVal Sh As Object)
    If UseEvents Then
        MsgBox "Activated " & Sh.Name, vbOKOnly, "SheetActivate Event"
    End If
End Sub


Private Sub Workbook_SheetBeforeDoubleClick(ByVal Sh As Object, _
    ByVal Target As Range, Cancel As Boolean)

    If UseEvents Then
        MsgBox "Ouch! Stop that.", vbOKOnly, "SheetBeforeDoubleClick Event"
    End If
End Sub


Private Sub Workbook_SheetBeforeRightClick(ByVal Sh As Object, _
    ByVal Target As Range, Cancel As Boolean)

    If UseEvents Then
        MsgBox "Right click.", vbOKOnly, "SheetBeforeRightClick Event"
    End If
End Sub


Private Sub Workbook_SheetChange(ByVal Sh As Object, ByVal Target As Range)
    If UseEvents Then
        MsgBox "You changed the range " & Target.Address & _
                " on " & Sh.Name, vbOKOnly, "SheetChange Event"
    End If
End Sub


Private Sub Workbook_SheetDeactivate(ByVal Sh As Object)
    If UseEvents Then
        MsgBox "Leaving " & Sh.Name, vbOKOnly, "SheetDeactivate Event"
    End If
End Sub


Private Sub Workbook_SheetSelectionChange(ByVal Sh As Object, _
    ByVal Target As Range)
    If UseEvents Then
        If Target.Row Mod 2 = 0 Then
            MsgBox "I'm keeping my eyes on you! " & _
                    "You selected the range " & Target.Address & _
                    " on " & Sh.Name, vbOKOnly, _
                    "SheetSelectionChange Event"
        Else
            MsgBox "There is no hiding... " & _
```

```
                              "You selected the range " & Target.Address & _
                              " on " & Sh.Name, vbOKOnly, _
                              "SheetSelectionChange Event"
                    End If
             End If
      End Sub
```

Rather than type all of this in, I'd recommend copying it or downloading it from the website. I included a couple of procedures to enable the ability to turn the events on or off because after you spend a few minutes experimenting with them, they'll drive you nuts. In order for this functionality to work, you need a range named TestEvents on the first worksheet in the workbook. If this range is not present, the code associated with each event will always be executed.

If you are entering this code, be sure to enter it into the ThisWorkbook object. Also, don't change the name of the procedures. You can always spot an event procedure because it must begin with the name of the object that it is associated with, followed by an underscore, followed by the name of the event.

As you experiment with these events, notice that on some occasions, one action will generate more than one event. For example, switching to another worksheet in the workbook generates a sheet deactivate event for the sheet you're leaving followed by a sheet activate event for the sheet you activated.

This is what can make events so tricky to work with. Things really start getting complicated when you're using other objects that also have events. For example, the Worksheet object also has an Activate and Deactivate event. If you attached code to each worksheet object's events, the act of switching between worksheets could then cause four different event procedures to fire (execute). What tends to happen is that you add various event procedures that start to interact with each other in ways that you didn't anticipate. Once this happens to you, you'll appreciate (or learn to appreciate) the debugging skills I talked about in Chapter 4.

Summary

All right, then. So goes the Workbook object. The Workbooks object and the Workbook object are often used to get a reference to other Excel objects of interest such as a worksheet or a range. Workbooks are opened and closed using the Workbooks object. Though you can open a workbook as easily as calling Workbooks.Open and supplying a filename, it is a much better idea to practice a little defensive programming and make sure that the file is not already open.

Speaking of the Workbooks object, this was your first crack at using collection objects. Excel has many collection objects, and you must become familiar with using them and their relationship with the underlying collection object (i.e., the relationship between the Workbooks object and the Workbook object). All collection objects have a property called Item that you can use to refer to a specific object in a collection using either a number that specifies the object's index in the collection, or the name of the object. For most collection objects, the Item property is the default property and you don't need to specify it.

```
Workbooks.Item("Test.xls")
' is equivalent to
Workbooks("Test.xls")
```

The other interesting aspect of this chapter versus the prior five chapters was that you got your first taste of using events. Events are actions that an object knows how to recognize. You can place code inside event procedures to respond to these actions. This gives you an enormous amount of flexibility. This flexibility doesn't come free, however. As you use more and more events in an application, it becomes tricky to manage the interaction that occurs between them because multiple events from multiple objects can be associated with one action.

The Worksheet object is on deck. You'll use the Worksheet object much more than the Workbook object, but not as much as the Range object (which is in the hole). As you learn about the Worksheet and Range objects, you'll finally get to start outputting your results directly on worksheets rather than using the Immediate window and Debug.Print.

Chapter 7

Winning with Worksheets

GENERALLY, THE WORKSHEET OBJECT is your gateway to doing anything useful in Excel. Other than the Range object, it's probably the most common object that you'll use. Unlike the Range object, it's not very difficult to master because it doesn't have nearly as many properties and methods.

Usually, your application will need to make some sort of assumptions about either worksheet names, the order of worksheets in the workbook, or some other identifying feature. Because worksheets can be added, deleted, and renamed, it's important that you program defensively when you're accessing a worksheet to avoid run-time errors. This chapter presents some procedures you can use to avoid the potential pitfalls associated with making assumptions regarding worksheet names.

Whatever you do, don't skip the section of the chapter dealing with worksheet events. Though the Worksheet object is sparse in terms of the number of events it has, it has two events that you can use to implement a wide range of "intelligent" functionality.

Setting the Stage

One of the first things you should learn is that you don't need to activate a worksheet in order to manipulate it programmatically. This inefficient practice is common with beginning Excel developers; I suppose this is the result of them studying code generated by the Macro Recorder. Anyway, this practice leads to slow performing applications. Also, it can cause errors if your code always expects to operate on the active sheet and, for some reason or another, the active sheet changes unexpectedly as your program executes.

The only thing you need to do to manipulate a worksheet is declare a worksheet variable and set it to refer to one of the worksheets in the workbook. The following code declares a worksheet variable named ws and sets it to the worksheet named "Sheet1" in the workbook that contains the VBA code.

```
' Declare a worksheet variable named ws
Dim ws As Worksheet

' Set ws to refer to sheet 1
Set ws = ThisWorkbook.Worksheets("Sheet1")
```

Just as you have a Workbooks object and a Workbook object, you also have a Worksheets object and a Worksheet object. Unlike the Workbooks object, you can't use the Worksheets object without first specifying a Workbook object. The Worksheets object is a property of a Workbook object. The easiest way to get a Workbook object is to use the ThisWorkbook property of the Application object that returns a reference to the workbook containing the executing code.

Alternatively, every Worksheets object has a Workbook object as its parent. In fact, nearly every object has some other object as a parent, and often you can obtain a reference to this parent using the Parent property. Check out Listing 7.1 as an example.

LISTING 7.1: USING THE PARENT PROPERTY TO OBTAIN A REFERENCE TO AN OBJECT'S PARENT OBJECT

```
Sub MeetMySingleParent()
    ' Declare a worksheet variable named ws
    Dim ws As Worksheet

    ' Set ws to refer to sheet 1
    Set ws = ThisWorkbook.Worksheets("Sheet1")

    ' Please meet my parent - Mrs. Workbook
    Debug.Print ws.Parent.Name

    Set ws = Nothing
End Sub
```

TIP Keep the Parent property in mind as you work with the Excel object model. For example, when you write procedures that require parameters that are Excel objects, use a Range object and the Parent property to get the worksheet to which the range belongs, and use the Parent property again to get the Workbook with which the range is associated. This can dramatically reduce the number of parameters that you have to pass between procedures.

Another way to refer to a Worksheet object is using its code name. For example, take a look at the Project Explorer window and Properties window shown in Figure 7.1.

FIGURE 7.1
You can set a worksheet's code name in the VBE and refer to the worksheet in your code via its code name.

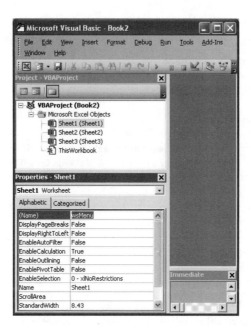

In the Project Explorer window shown next, you can see that after you set the code name, the worksheet appears under Microsoft Excel Objects using its code name with its real name, or the name the user sees, in parentheses.

You can programmatically distinguish between the code name and the real name using the properties CodeName and Name respectively as the following code snippet demonstrates.

```
' prints out name & code name
' assumes a worksheet has been named
' in the VBE as: wsMenu
Sub WhatsMyName()
    On Error Resume Next
    Debug.Print "-----------------------------------------------"
    Debug.Print "The name on my worksheet tab is " & wsMenu.Name & ", "
    Debug.Print "but you can call me " & wsMenu.CodeName & "."
    Debug.Print "-----------------------------------------------"
End Sub


The output of this procedure is:
-----------------------------------------------
The name on my worksheet tab is Test,
but you can call me wsMenu.
-----------------------------------------------
```

So which way should you use to refer to worksheets in code? Each way has its pros and cons, and you'll run across situations that will eliminate one of the methods as an option. For example, often your code operates on workbooks that you have no control over—you can't know or set the worksheet code names ahead of time. On the other hand, it's much more likely that users will change the name of a worksheet rather than the code name of a worksheet (though users can goof with that also unless you have locked the project).

Performance-wise, it's quicker to use the code name. Unless you're setting a reference to a worksheet object thousands of times in a row though (highly unlikely), it really doesn't matter. If you're using the standard way to refer to an item in a collection, such as setting a worksheet variable to refer to a specific worksheet, you usually only do this a few times at most in a given procedure, and the process happens so quickly that you won't experience a relevant performance difference between the two.

Validating Your Worksheets before Using Them

The bottom line regarding which method you use to refer to worksheets is that you don't have a sure-fire way to refer to a worksheet. You need to utilize defensive programming tactics in order to avoid run-time errors due to worksheets that have been renamed or deleted.

In any procedure that refers to a worksheet by name, be sure to check that the worksheet name actually exists in the given workbook. This is easily done using a procedure such as the one shown in Listing 7.2.

LISTING 7.2: ENSURING THE EXISTENCE OF A WORKSHEET NAME BEFORE USING IT

```
' Determines if a given worksheet name exists in a workbook
Function WorksheetExists(wb As Workbook, sName As String) As Boolean
    Dim s As String

    On Error GoTo bWorksheetExistsErr

    s = wb.Worksheets(sName).Name

    WorksheetExists = True
    Exit Function

bWorksheetExistsErr:
    WorksheetExists = False
End Function
```

This function catches the run-time error that would occur in your procedure if you didn't first check the validity of the worksheet name using this function. If it sees that an error occurs, it returns false signifying that the worksheet doesn't exist; otherwise it returns true. The following fragment illustrates how to use this function:

```
...
Dim ws As Worksheet

If Not WorksheetExists(ThisWorkbook, "Sheet1") Then
    MsgBox "Can't find worksheet named Sheet1", vbOKOnly
    Exit Sub
End If

Set ws = ThisWorkbook.Worksheets("Sheet1")
...
```

Alternatively, you can do something like this.

```
Dim ws As Worksheet

If WorksheetExists(ThisWorkbook, "Sheet1") Then
    Set ws = ThisWorkbook.Worksheets("Sheet1")
Else
    Set ws = Nothing
End If

If Not ws Is Nothing Then
    ' do stuff to/with the worksheet
End If
```

What if you need to check for a code name? This is nearly as easy. Listing 7.3 provides an example.

LISTING 7.3: USING A FUNCTION TO CHECK FOR THE EXISTENCE OF A CODE NAME

```
' Determines if a given worksheet name exists in a workbook
' Checks by looking for the code name rather than the name
Function WorksheetCodeNameExists(wb As Workbook, sCodeName As String) As Boolean
    Dim s As String
    Dim ws As Worksheet

    WorksheetCodeNameExists = False
    For Each ws In wb.Worksheets
        If StrComp(ws.CodeName, sCodeName, vbTextCompare) = 0 Then
            WorksheetCodeNameExists = True
            Exit For
        End If
    Next
    Set ws = Nothing
End Function
```

You may be wondering why Listing 7.3 looks so much different than Listing 7.2 considering they both check for the existence of a given name. The reason is that you can't directly check the validity of a code name as you can for a worksheet name.

It's possible to rewrite Listing 7.2 so that it is exactly like Listing 7.3, except that instead of comparing a given name to ws.CodeName, you'd use ws.Name. This isn't quite as fast as Listing 7.2 nor is the performance difference that big of a deal for this function.

Now You See It, Now You Don't

One common need you'll experience when using Excel applications is the need to programmatically hide/unhide worksheets. In Chapter 2, you saw how you to hide a worksheet so that it is very hidden, that is, so hidden it doesn't appear when you choose Format ➢ Sheet ➢ Unhide from the Excel menu. It is also very easy to change this programmatically, as shown in Listing 7.4.

LISTING 7.4: HIDING AND UNHIDING WORKSHEETS

```
'/ Hides the worksheet named sName
Sub HideWorksheet(sName As String, bVeryHidden As Boolean)
    If WorksheetExists(ThisWorkbook, sName) Then
        If bVeryHidden Then
            ThisWorkbook.Worksheets(sName).Visible = xlSheetVeryHidden
        Else
            ThisWorkbook.Worksheets(sName).Visible = xlSheetHidden
        End If
    End If
End Sub
```

```
Sub UnhideWorksheet(sName As String)
    If WorksheetExists(ThisWorkbook, sName) Then
        ThisWorkbook.Worksheets(sName).Visible = xlSheetVisible
    End If
End Sub

Sub UsingHideUnhide()
    Dim lResponse As Long

    ' hide the worksheet
    HideWorksheet "Sheet2", True

    ' show that it is hidden - ask to unhide
    lResponse = MsgBox("The worksheet is very hidden. Unhide?", vbYesNo)

    If lResponse = vbYes Then
        UnhideWorksheet "Sheet2"
    End If
End Sub
```

Listing 7.4 uses the WorksheetExists procedure from Listing 7.2 to make sure that the worksheet name passed using the sName parameter actually exists. Once you verify that the worksheet exists, you can get to the required Worksheet object by referring to a specific item from the Worksheets object associated with the ThisWorkbook object. Finally, you can set the Visible property accordingly. The constant xlSheetVeryHidden hides the worksheet so that it can't be unhidden using Format ➢ Sheet ➢ Unhide. The constant xlSheetHidden hides the sheet normally as if you choose Format ➢ Sheet ➢ Hide from the Excel menu.

Listing 7.4 also lists a procedure called UnhideWorksheet. You may occasionally need this, but if you already have a worksheet variable, you might just unhide the worksheet directly.

An example procedure appears in Listing 7.4 that shows the use of HideWorksheet and Unhide-Worksheet.

Once in awhile, you'll have multiple hidden worksheets and you'll want to ensure that all of them are visible. You can easily unhide them all by looping through each worksheet in the workbook, as shown in Listing 7.5.

LISTING 7.5: UNHIDING EVERY WORKSHEET IN A WORKBOOK.

```
' Unhides all worksheets in the workbook, even very hidden worksheets
Sub UnhideAllWorksheets()
    Dim ws As Worksheet

    For Each ws In ThisWorkbook.Worksheets
        ws.Visible = xlSheetVisible
    Next ws
    Set ws = Nothing
End Sub
```

POLYMORPHISM, WHERE ART THOU?

If you don't know what this means, don't worry, because it isn't available as a programming technique in VBA; if you do, I'm sorry, you can't use it. The HideWorksheet procedure presented in Listing 7.4 would be a wonderful candidate for using polymorphism if it could be used.

What is polymorphism? Polymorphism is the practice of creating multiple versions of a procedure that are named the same but differ in terms of the parameters passed and used by each version of the procedure.

The best way to understand this is via example. The HideWorksheet procedure in Listing 7.4 requires that the name of a worksheet be passed to it using the first parameter, a string named sName. What if you wanted to have another version of the procedure that took a Worksheet object as a parameter instead? You could implement the procedure as follows.

```
' Hides the worksheet

Sub HideWorksheet(ws As Worksheet, bVeryHidden As Boolean)

    If bVeryHidden Then

        ws.Visible = xlSheetVeryHidden

    Else

        ws.Visible = xlSheetHidden

    End If

End Sub
```

If polymorphism was allowed in VBA, you could place this procedure and the procedure from Listing 7.4 in the same module and use either one as your needs dictated. Because polymorphism can't be used, you can't have two procedures with the same name in the same module. For that matter, you can't have two procedures within the same project unless they're in separate modules, and then only one of the procedures can be public.

Because you can't use polymorphism, your only option is to give the procedures different names. For example, you could name one HideWorksheet and the other HideWorksheetName.

Lock Up Your Valuables

If you haven't already, you'll run into many situations that require you to use worksheet protection. When you're developing Excel applications, one of the most common reasons to use worksheet protection is to lock certain sections of the workbook in order to prevent end users from making changes that would break, or in some way negatively affect, the workbook.

Locking up a worksheet presents many challenges. First of all, you need to consider what kind of changes you want to allow end users to make and code appropriately. Thankfully, the Protect method has a number of optional parameters that you can use to allow the end user to make certain kinds of changes. Second, any time you need to make changes to the worksheet programmatically, you must unlock the worksheet, make your changes, and then lock it again. Finally, because you'll need to store the password to the worksheets in your code or elsewhere, you'll then need to lock your project so that the password can't be retrieved simply by looking at the code.

You can use the functions presented in Listing 7.6 and 7.7 to implement the most draconian locking policy—that is, prohibiting any change to the worksheet except changing unlocked cells.

LISTING 7.6: PROTECTING WORKSHEET ASSETS WITH THE PROTECT METHOD

```
Function ProtectWorksheet(ws As Worksheet, sPassword As String) As Boolean
    On Error GoTo ErrHandler
    If Not ws.ProtectContents Then
        ws.Protect sPassword, True, True, True
    End If
    ProtectWorksheet = True
    Exit Function
ErrHandler:
    ProtectWorksheet = False
End Function
```

As you can see, you can use Listing 7.6 to lock down a worksheet. After the ProtectWorksheet function is run on a worksheet, any cells that are locked (all cells are locked by default) can't be changed in any manner by an end user or programmatically until the worksheet is unlocked. ProtectWorksheet is implemented here as a function so that when other routines call it, they can check the result to see if the worksheet really was protected.

Before using the Protect method, ProtectWorksheet checks the ProtectContents property of the Worksheet object. ProtectContents is a read-only Boolean value that you can use to see if a worksheet is protected or not. You don't need to protect the worksheet if it is already protected. Besides, if you try to protect a worksheet that is already protected, nothing happens. You won't get a run-time error, but it doesn't change how the sheet is protected. For example, if you protect the worksheet using the password "Test" and then call the Protect method using a different password, when you check the worksheet, it'll still be protected by the "Test" password.

You could use ProtectWorksheet and the UnprotectWorksheet method (shown in Listing 7.7) without a password by supplying an empty string ("") as the sPassword parameter.

Listing 7.7 shows an example of a procedure you can use to unprotect a worksheet. It also presents a simple procedure that demonstrates how to call these functions from another procedure.

LISTING 7.7: UNPROTECTING WORKSHEET ASSETS WITH THE UNPROTECT METHOD

```
Function UnprotectWorksheet(ws As Worksheet, sPassword As String) As Boolean
    On Error GoTo ErrHandler
    If ws.ProtectContents Then
        ws.Unprotect sPassword
    End If
    UnprotectWorksheet = True
    Exit Function
ErrHandler:
    UnprotectWorksheet = False
```

```
End Function

Sub TestProtection()
    Dim ws As Worksheet

    Set ws = ThisWorkbook.Worksheets(1)

    ' Example of how you might use ProtectWorksheet
    If Not ProtectWorksheet(ws, "TestPassword") Then
        Debug.Print "The worksheet could not be protected."
    Else
        Debug.Print "The worksheet has been protected."
    End If

    ' Example of how you might use Unprotect Worksheet
    If UnprotectWorksheet(ws, "TestPassword") Then
        ' Unprotected - safe to modify the worksheet
        ' contents programmatically now...
        Debug.Print "The worksheet has been unprotected."
    Else
        Debug.Print "The worksheet could not be unprotected."
    End If

    Set ws = Nothing
End Sub
```

Managing Workbook Worksheets

Adding, deleting, copying, and moving worksheets are common tasks you may need to perform programmatically. To add a worksheet, you need to use the Worksheets object; for the other three tasks, the Worksheet or a Worksheets object will suffice.

Adding and Deleting Worksheets

To add a worksheet, you need to start with a Workbook object. Assuming you want to add a worksheet to the workbook represented by ThisWorkbook, the syntax is as follows.

```
ThisWorkbook.Worksheets.Add [Before], [After], [Count], [Type]
```

The parameters for the Add method are explained in the following list.

Before This optional parameter specifies which worksheet the added worksheet(s) should be placed before. *Before* should be a worksheet object. You can't specify the *After* parameter if you specify Before. If neither *Before* nor *After* is specified, the worksheet(s) are added before the active sheet.

After This optional parameter specifies which worksheet the added worksheets(s) should be placed after. *After* should be a worksheet object. You can't specify the *Before* parameter if you specify the *After* parameter.

Count   *Count* is an optional parameter that specifies the number of sheets to add.

Type   This optional parameter specifies which kind of sheet to add. By default, a standard worksheet (xlWorksheet) is added. Use xlWorksheet, xlChart, xlExcel4MacroSheet, or xlExcel4IntlMacroSheet.

This may be a good time to remind you that you can specify parameters in different ways. The following two statements perform identical functions. Note that when you specify parameter names, you don't need to put the parameters in any specific order. If you don't specify names, the parameters must be placed in the order expected by the function (the order displayed by the Auto Quick Info feature in the VBE).

```
' Specify parameters by name
ThisWorkbook.Worksheets.Add Count:=2, _
    Before:=ThisWorkbook.Worksheets(2)
' Specify parameters by order
ThisWorkbook.Worksheets.Add ThisWorkbook.Worksheets(2), , 2
```

Deleting a worksheet can be achieved simply by calling the Delete method. Consider the following simple procedure:

```
Sub TestDelete()
    ' delete the first worksheet in the workbook
    ThisWorkbook.Worksheets(1).Delete
End Sub
```

However, one of the things that can trip you up is that Excel displays a confirmation asking the user if she is sure that she wants to delete the worksheet.

It is easy enough to turn this functionality off though using the DisplayAlerts property of the Application object. Another thing you need to account for is the possibility that the worksheet you want to delete is the only *visible* worksheet in the workbook. If so, this causes a run-time error. For bulletproof applications, you need to develop a procedure or two that handle these issues. Listing 7.8 presents two procedures you need for robust worksheet deletions.

LISTING 7.8: SAFELY DELETING WORKSHEETS USING THE DELETESHEET FUNCTION

```
' deletes the worksheet given in the ws parameter
' If bQuiet then do not display Excel alerts
Function DeleteSheet(ws As Worksheet, bQuiet As Boolean) As Boolean
    Dim bDeleted As Boolean

    On Error GoTo ErrHandler

    bDeleted = False
```

```
        If CountVisibleSheets(ws.Parent) > 1 Then
            ' ok to delete - display alerts?
            If bQuiet Then Application.DisplayAlerts = False

            ' finally! delete the darn thing
            bDeleted = ws.Parent.Worksheets(ws.Name).Delete

        Else
            ' forget it - need at least
            ' one visible sheet in a
            ' workbook. bDeleted is
            ' already false
        End If

ExitPoint:
    ' make sure display alerts is always on
    Application.DisplayAlerts = True
    DeleteSheet = bDeleted
    Exit Function
ErrHandler:
    bDeleted = False
    Resume ExitPoint
End Function


' returns a count of all of the visible sheets
' in the workbook wb
Function CountVisibleSheets(wb As Workbook) As Integer
    Dim nSheetIndex As Integer
    Dim nCount As Integer
    nCount = 0
    For nSheetIndex = 1 To wb.Sheets.Count
        If wb.Sheets(nSheetIndex).Visible = xlSheetVisible Then
            nCount = nCount + 1
        End If
    Next
    CountVisibleSheets = nCount
End Function
```

The DeleteSheet function looks longer than it really is due to all the comments I put in it. So what gives? Why go through all this trouble to delete a worksheet? Two reasons. One, because it really isn't that much trouble. You can reuse this procedure in nearly every project. Two, developers hate run-time errors.

DeleteSheet requires that two parameters be passed to it: first, a worksheet variable named ws that represents the worksheet to be deleted; second, a Boolean variable named bQuiet. If bQuiet is true, then the function won't allow Excel to display the alert that would normally appear when you delete a worksheet.

Inside the DeleteSheet function, you only need one variable—bDeleted, a Boolean variable that keeps track of whether the worksheet was deleted. At the end of the function, the value of this variable is returned as the result of the DeleteSheet function call. Technically, you could even do away with this variable and just assign the result right to the DeleteSheet function. Personally, however, I think it's easier to read when you use a separate variable to keep track of the result as you make your way through the function.

Because you're trying to write a bulletproof procedure, you need to enable error handling in case an unplanned run-time error occurs. This procedure demonstrates an error-handling technique you haven't looked at yet. If an error occurs, then program execution is transferred to the first line following the ErrHandler label.

For the purposes of this procedure, all you need to do is report that the worksheet wasn't deleted. You could simply allow the function to end at this point. However, you should also always make sure to turn DisplayAlerts back on (set it to true). Because this is something you always need to do, even when an error doesn't occur, I've added another label named ExitPoint above the ErrHandler label. Notice the statement Resume ExitPoint in the ErrHandler code. This statement instructs program execution to resume execution at the first line following the ExitPoint label. In the ExitPoint block, you turn DisplayAlerts back on and then return the result of the function. The code between the Exit-Point label and the Exit Function statement is always executed, error or no error.

Okay. Back to the meat of the function. One of the most important things this function does is ensure that the worksheet to be deleted is not the last visible worksheet in the workbook. You must always have at least one visible sheet, worksheet or otherwise, in a workbook. Consequently you need to employ the CountVisibleSheets function. This function just loops through every sheet in the workbook, checking the Visible property and incrementing a count if the sheet is visible. Note that you can't just look at worksheets because that may not produce the intended result. If you have one visible chart sheet and one visible worksheet (two visible sheets total), you can still safely delete the worksheet. If you only considered worksheets in the CountVisibleSheets function, then it would return one visible sheet in this example and the DeleteSheets function would think that it couldn't safely delete the worksheet.

After you've determined it is safe to delete the worksheet you must consider whether you should be quiet about deleting the sheet (suppress the Alert message) or not. If you should be quiet, then you'll just turn alert messages off using the DisplayAlerts property of the Application object.

When you finally get to the statement that actually deletes the worksheet, you may be surprised that this statement is so long. Why not just use ws.Delete? The answer is that you have a distinct advantage when you use the Delete method associated with the Worksheets object rather than the Worksheet object. The advantage is that by using the Worksheets object, you can capture a result code that indicates whether the sheet was actually deleted.

Though the VBA documentation doesn't say so, the Delete method of the Worksheets object actually returns a Boolean result that indicates whether the worksheet was deleted. This is helpful because if you allow the alert to be displayed, the user may choose not to delete the worksheet. The DeleteSheet function captures the value returned by the call to the Delete method.

This doesn't work if you use the Worksheet object because once the worksheet is deleted, the ws variable is toast. Deleting any object also deletes any programmatic information associated with any object variables that referred to the object.

Anyway, because you need to get to the Worksheets object, you first have to get a reference to the workbook using the Parent property.

At this point, execution falls on through the ExitPoint label where it turns DisplayAlerts back on and reports the result of the function to the calling procedure. Clear as mud, right? Hopefully, it's much clearer than that.

Once again, this is another example of the type of defensive programming that you need to implement to avoid run-time errors. All of the extra code beyond the call to the Delete method is defensive. If you don't write specific procedures to handle common tasks such as deleting worksheets, you're either duplicating code in multiple procedures, or you're writing risky code that always assumes the worksheet being deleted isn't the last visible sheet. Unless you lock the workbook and worksheets, you have nothing to prevent users from hiding worksheets, so this isn't a safe assumption.

That said, writing safe procedures doesn't take much effort. Once you write a safe procedure, you can benefit from using it over and over, so you save time in the long run. Also, you can build useful features into these safe procedures, such as the ability to display or not display alerts to the user.

Moving and Copying Worksheets

Moving and copying worksheets is performed easily using the Move and Copy methods. The syntax for each method is identical.

```
YourWorksheetObject.Move [Before], [After]
YourWorksheetObject.Copy [Before], [After]
```

The parameters for the Move and Copy methods are described in the following list.

Before   This optional parameter specifies which worksheet the worksheet(s) should be placed before. *Before* should be a worksheet object. You can't specify the *After* parameter if you specify *Before*. If neither *Before* nor *After* is specified, the worksheet(s) will be placed in a new workbook.

After   This optional parameter specifies which worksheet the worksheets(s) should be placed after. *After* should be a worksheet object. You can't specify *Before* if you specify *After*.

The following snippet shows how you might use these methods. Pretty simple stuff, eh?

```
Sub SimpleWorksheetMovement()
    ' copy the third worksheet to a new book
    ThisWorkbook.Worksheets(3).Copy
    ' copy the third worksheet before the 2nd worksheet
    ThisWorkbook.Worksheets(3).Copy ThisWorkbook.Worksheets(2)
    ' move the second worksheet to end of workbook
    ThisWorkbook.Worksheets(2).Move _
        after:=ThisWorkbook.Worksheets(ThisWorkbook.Worksheets.Count)
End Sub
```

So, what useful things can you do with these methods? It might be nice to be able to alphabetize those long books—you know, the ones with countless worksheet tabs? If you implement a simple sort routine that uses the Move method, this isn't a very hard task. Check out Listing 7.9.

LISTING 7.9: ALPHABETIZING WORKSHEETS IN A WORKBOOK

```
' performs a simple bubble sort to
' sort the worksheets in the workbook
Sub AlphabetizeWorksheets(wb As Workbook)
    Dim bSorted As Boolean
    Dim nSheetsSorted As Integer
    Dim nSheets As Integer
    Dim n As Integer

    nSheets = wb.Worksheets.Count
    nSheetsSorted = 0

    Do While (nSheetsSorted < nSheets) And Not bSorted
        bSorted = True
        nSheetsSorted = nSheetsSorted + 1
        For n = 1 To nSheets - nSheetsSorted
            If StrComp(wb.Worksheets(n).Name, _
                        wb.Worksheets(n + 1).Name, _
                        vbTextCompare) > 0 Then

                ' out of order - swap the sheets
                wb.Worksheets(n + 1).Move _
                    before:=wb.Worksheets(n)
                bSorted = False

            End If
        Next
    Loop
End Sub
```

The most difficult part of this listing is the sorting algorithm. This routine uses a bubble sort algorithm—not the most efficient sorting algorithm in terms of performance, but one of the easier ones to understand. Because I'm not sorting a great number of items, I can live with easier to understand here over fastest performance.

A bubble sort works by comparing pairs of items in a list (in this case, a list of worksheet names). If the first item in the pair is greater than the second item, the items are swapped. If you have four elements in a list, the first two items are compared, then item 2 is compared to item 3, and finally item 3 is compared to item 4. After one pass through all of the items in the list, the last element is the one with the greatest value (A<Z). Because the last item is guaranteed to have the greatest value (it "bubbles" up), you don't need to check it again, so the next time through, you only need to consider the first three items in the list. This process is repeated until all of the items in the list have been considered or the items need no further sorting.

Expounding on Worksheet Events

The Worksheet object doesn't have very many events, but what it lacks in number, it makes up for in terms of usefulness. Table 7.12 lists the events associated with the Worksheet object.

TABLE 7.1: EVENTS ASSOCIATED WITH THE WORKSHEET OBJECT

EVENT	OCCURS WHEN
Activate	The worksheet is activated.
BeforeDoubleClick	The worksheet is double-clicked. Occurs before the default double-click action.
BeforeRightClick	The worksheet is right-clicked. Occurs before the default right-click action.
Calculate	After the worksheet is recalculated.
Change	Cells on the worksheet are changed by the user or an external link.
Deactivate	The worksheet is deactivated.
FollowHyperlink	A hyperlink on a worksheet is clicked.
PivotTableUpdate	Occurs after a PivotTable report is updated on a worksheet.
SelectionChange	The selection changes on a worksheet.

If you compare these events to the events associated with the Workbook object, you see that all of these events also have a related event that occurs in the Workbook object. The difference is that the events in the Workbook object are not sheet specific whereas these are.

For example, if you only cared about changes made to a worksheet named Income Statement, you'd place the appropriate code in the Worksheet Change event associated with the Income Statement worksheet rather than the Sheet Change event associated with the Workbook. Although the Sheet Change event associated with the Workbook object would do the chore, it wouldn't be very efficient because it would also occur any time a change was made on any other worksheet. As a result, you'd always have to see which worksheet the change was being made to. In Figure 7.2, you can see an example of a Worksheet Change event.

Two events in particular pack a strong one-two wallop. The Worksheet Change event and the Worksheet SelectionChange event provide you with a tremendous amount of flexibility to do things like the following:

- Implement your own custom data validation routines.

- Automatically update reports, charts, or other items in a workbook based on an entry made on a worksheet.

- Display user notifications or forms in response to an entry or movement on a worksheet.

- Play practical jokes on your colleagues (OK, I admit that this is not a particularly good idea given all of the rightful paranoia going around about computer viruses, worms, and such).

FIGURE 7.2

Make sure you have the appropriate worksheet selected in the Project Explorer before you select the event to respond to.

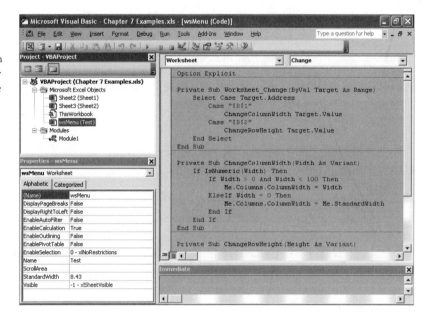

Listing 7.10 shows an example of how you can use the Worksheet Change event to watch specific worksheet cells for changes and then react if the cell is changed to a value of interest.

LISTING 7.10: USING THE CHANGE EVENT TO RESPOND TO WORKSHEET CHANGES

```
Option Explicit

Private Sub Worksheet_Change(ByVal Target As Range)
    Select Case Target.Address
        Case "$B$1"
            ChangeColumnWidth Target.Value
        Case "$B$2"
            ChangeRowHeight Target.Value
    End Select
End Sub

Private Sub ChangeColumnWidth(Width As Variant)
    If IsNumeric(Width) Then
        If Width > 0 And Width < 100 Then
            Me.Columns.ColumnWidth = Width
        ElseIf Width = 0 Then
            Me.Columns.ColumnWidth = Me.StandardWidth
        End If
    End If
End Sub
```

```
Private Sub ChangeRowHeight(Height As Variant)
    If IsNumeric(Height) Then
        If Height > 0 And Height < 100 Then
            Me.Rows.RowHeight = Height
        ElseIf Height = 0 Then
            Me.Rows.RowHeight = Me.StandardHeight
        End If
    End If
End Sub
```

Listing 7.10 changes the width of all of the columns or the height of all of the rows on the worksheet depending on which cell you change. Whenever a change is made to the worksheet, the Worksheet_Change procedure executes. The reason the Change event is so powerful is that Excel passes a reference to the range that is changed. By looking at the address of the range, you can decide what you want to do using a Select Case statement. In the next two chapters, you'll see that you actually have a great number of options when it comes to using the range passed to the event procedure.

In order to keep the Worksheet_Change event procedure small and easy to maintain, it's a good idea to create other procedures that respond to the event. All you do with Worksheet_Change is determine which action to take and then delegate to the appropriate procedure. In Listing 7.10, you call either ChangeColumnWidth or ChangeRowHeight if one of the appropriate cells is changed.

To try this code, follow these steps:

1. In the VBE, select the worksheet you'd like to add the code to in the Project Explorer under Microsoft Excel Objects.

2. Right-click the worksheet and choose View Code.

3. Select Worksheet from the objects drop-down list.

4. Select Change from the Procedures/Events drop-down list.

5. Enter the code for the Worksheet_Change procedure.

6. Enter the code for the ChangeColumnWidth and ChangeRowHeight procedures.

7. Change the values in either cell B1 or B2 to change the column width or row height respectively.

One last comment on Listing 7.10—in the event that 0 (zero) is passed to either ChangeColumnWidth or ChangeRowHeight, the column width or row height will be set to the standard width or height.

Summary

The Worksheet object is used frequently. Many times you'll use it as a gateway to the Range object on which your code needs to operate. Occasionally, you'll need to perform some worksheet-specific tasks such as protecting or unprotecting the worksheet or changing the worksheet's visibility.

The most important thing to keep in mind when you're working with Worksheet objects is that your end user can make changes that have the potential to break things. Worksheets can be renamed, moved, deleted, and otherwise modified. If you don't account for these possibilities, chances are you'll occasionally experience run-time errors. One simple thing you can do to prevent run-time errors is validate worksheet names before you use them in your code.

Finally, the events associated with the Worksheet object can be very useful. Because no events are associated with a Range object, you need to use Worksheet events to watch for events that occur that affect a range of interest. The SelectionChange event and Change event are both useful for this type of activity.

In the next chapter, I'll start the first of two chapters that covering the most important Excel object, the Range object. Not only is the Range object the most important object in terms of manipulating Excel programmatically, but it also has a great deal more properties and methods than any of the other objects we have looked at so far.

Chapter 8

The Most Important Object

THE RANGE OBJECT IS, without a doubt, the most important object to learn if you're going to advance your Excel development skills beyond the beginning level. A range can represent one or more cells on a worksheet. Just about anything useful you do in Excel is done to or with a range.

I must admit, I feel a second wind now that I've gotten to the Range object. Believe it or not, it's sort of difficult to develop quality examples (hopefully you agree that they've been quality) without using a Range object to any great extent. That is why Debug.Print has been the primary output mechanism so far. Although Debug.Print is an extremely useful way to provide a tracing mechanism for you as a developer, it isn't going to win any beauty awards. However, in order to keep your eye on the ball, I didn't want you to get distracted by any aspect of the Range object—and the Range object has a lot to tempt you with.

Because the Range object is so important and has so many properties and methods, this will be the first of two chapters devoted to this object. In this chapter, I'll focus on the fundamentals—referring to a range, moving around a worksheet, and basic input/output. Chapter 9 covers some of the most useful Range methods.

Referring to Ranges

At some point, I read or was told that Eskimos have something like 26 words for snow. Well there aren't 26 different ways to refer to a range, but there are a lot. Table 8.1 lists some of the objects that contain properties that refer to a range.

TABLE 8.1: OBJECTS YOU CAN USE TO OBTAIN A REFERENCE TO A RANGE

OBJECT	PROPERTY
Application	ActiveCell
Application	Range
Application	Selection
Worksheet	Cells

Continued on next page

TABLE 8.1: OBJECTS YOU CAN USE TO OBTAIN A REFERENCE TO A RANGE *(continued)*

OBJECT	PROPERTY
Worksheet	Columns
Worksheet	Range
Worksheet	Rows
Worksheet	UsedRange

As you can see, you have many different ways to obtain a reference to a Range object, and this table doesn't even include the many ways you can refer to a range using the Range object itself.

Listing 8.1 demonstrates how you can use the Application object to obtain a reference to specific ranges.

LISTING 8.1: REFERRING TO RANGES USING THE APPLICATION OBJECT

```
Sub ReferringToRangesI()
    Dim rg As Range

    ' ActiveCell is a range representing the
    ' active cell. There can be one and
    ' only one active cell.
    Debug.Print Application.ActiveCell.Address

    ' Selection refers to a range representing
    ' all of the selected cells. There can be
    ' one or more cells in the range.
    Debug.Print Application.Selection.Address

    ' Application.Range works on the active
    ' worksheet
    ThisWorkbook.Worksheets(1).Activate
    Set rg = Application.Range("D5")
    Debug.Print "Worksheet 1 is active"
    Debug.Print rg.Address
    Debug.Print rg.Parent.Name


    ThisWorkbook.Worksheets(2).Activate
    Set rg = Application.Range("D5")
    Debug.Print "Worksheet 2 is active"
    Debug.Print rg.Address
    Debug.Print rg.Parent.Name

    Set rg = Nothing
End Sub
```

Listing 8.1 uses the Address property of the Range object to print out the address associated with the range. Keep in mind that there is a significant difference between ActiveCell and Selection. If only one cell is selected, they refer to the same thing. However, if you have a group of cells selected, only one of the cells is the ActiveCell whereas all of the cells are the Selection. You'll find this clearly demonstrated in this example if you run it once with a group of cells selected.

This example also illustrates how Application.Range works. When you use the Range property of the Application object, the Range object is associated with the worksheet that is active when the statement executes. Also, notice how you can specify a range address by supplying the A1 style address of the range, such as the one you'd enter in a worksheet formula. You can enter any valid range using this method. For example, all of the following statements refer to valid ranges.

```
Application.Range("A1:C5")
Application.Range("A:A")
Application.Range("3:3")
Application.Range("A1:C5, D6:F10")
```

Cells and Ranges with the Worksheet Object

Most of the time you'll probably use one of the Worksheet object's properties, specifically either the Cells property or the Range property. Let's start with the Cells property because it's probably the easiest to understand. In theory, the Cells property returns a range that represents all of the cells on a worksheet. This is because it's a collection object. Like most collection objects, it has an Item property that allows you to select a specific item in the collection. Also, like most collection objects, the Item property is the default property, so you don't necessarily need to specify it.

Although you'll occasionally need to refer to all of the cells on a worksheet, more often you'll be interested in a specific cell. This is where the Cells property fits in. Unlike most collection objects, the Cells collection object orders its items in a very convenient two-dimensional array. This allows you to easily specify an individual cell by row and column number. Listing 8.2 shows you an example of this.

LISTING 8.2: SPECIFYING INDIVIDUAL CELLS WITH THE CELLS PROPERTY

```
Sub UsingCells()
    Dim rg As Range
    Dim nRow As Integer
    Dim nColumn As Integer
    Dim ws As Worksheet

    Set ws = ThisWorkbook.Worksheets(1)

    For nRow = 1 To 10
        For nColumn = 1 To 10
            Set rg = ws.Cells(nRow, nColumn)
            rg.Value = rg.Address
        Next
    Next
```

```
        Set rg = Nothing
        Set ws = Nothing
    End Sub
```

Listing 8.2 also demonstrates two properties of the Range object: Value and Address. All this listing does is loop through a 10 × 10 block of cells and set the value of each cell equal to the address of the cell, as is shown in Figure 8.1. Your first listing that outputs to a worksheet!

As you can see, the Cells property really lends itself well for use within For…Next statements or Do…Loop statements. By setting up one variable to represent the current row and another to represent the current column, it also makes your code fairly easy to understand.

TIP   *When using the Cells property to work with a worksheet, you may find it helpful to turn on the R1C1 Reference Style option. In Excel, select Tools ➢ Options. On the General tab, check R1C1 Reference Style. The R1C1 reference style uses numbers for columns rather than letters. This is a "sticky" option, which means it comes on whenever the worksheet is opened. Because most people prefer the A1 style, try to remember and turn this option off before you distribute the workbook.*

The Worksheet object's Range property is useful in situations in which you need to operate on a group of cells, though you can also use it with a single cell. The syntax of the Range property is as follows:

```
SomeWorksheetObject.Range( Cell1, [Cell2] )
```

The Cell1 parameter is required and can be a string that represents the address of the range (as was demonstrated with the Application.Range property) or a string that represents a named range on the worksheet. If the Cell2 parameter is used, Cell1 could be a Range object.

The Cell2 parameter is optional and can be a range address, a named range, or a Range object. If you use Cell1 and Cell2 together, you can think of Cell1 as the cell in the upper-left corner of the range and Cell2 as the cell in the bottom-right corner of the range.

Listing 8.3 demonstrates a few different ways in which you can refer to a range using the Range property of the Worksheet object.

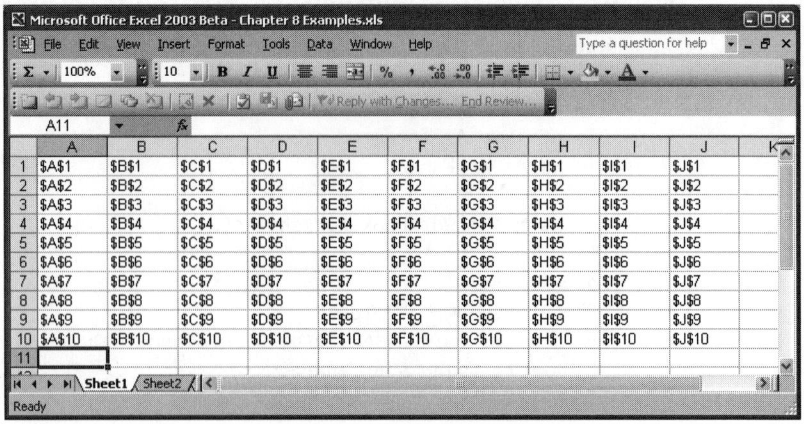

FIGURE 8.1

Use the Value property of the Range object to write a value (or text) to a range.

LISTING 8.3: USING THE RANGE PROPERTY TO REFER TO GROUPS OF CELLS

```
Sub UsingRange()
    Dim ws As Worksheet
    Dim rg As Range

    Set ws = ThisWorkbook.Worksheets(1)

    ' specifying a range using Cells
    ' this range is equivalent to A1:J10
    Set rg = ws.Range(ws.Cells(1, 1), ws.Cells(10, 10))
    ' sets the value of each cell in the
    ' range to 1
    rg.Value = 1

    Set rg = ws.Range("D4", "E5")
    rg.Font.Bold = True

    ws.Range("A1:B2").HorizontalAlignment = xlLeft

    Set rg = Nothing
    Set ws = Nothing
End Sub
```

One important thing to notice in Listing 8.3 is that you don't have to assign values cell by cell. You can assign the same value (or formula, if you're using the Formula property) to a group of cells in one fell swoop. Figure 8.2 shows the output produced by the UsingRange procedure.

FIGURE 8.2

Output produced by the UsingRange procedure from Listing 8.3.

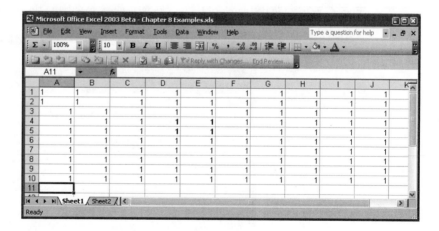

Listing 8.3 demonstrates a couple of formatting-oriented properties of the Range object: the Font Property, which returns a Font object, and the HorizontalAlignment property. Once you set a reference to the range that you need to format, formatting is a snap. Again, the approach is to work with groups of cells collectively rather than by looping through individual cells and applying formatting to each cell individually.

Finally, Listing 8.3 illustrates one technique I find myself using constantly. Consider the following statement from Listing 8.3:

```
Set rg = ws.Range(ws.Cells(1, 1), ws.Cells(10, 10))
```

This statement sets a reference to a range of cells by specifying the top-left cell and the bottom-right cell using the Cells property. Why not just use ws.Range("A1:J10")? The reason is that many times you don't know what the address of the range will be at development time. For example, if you are working with a list of user-entered data, you won't know how many rows the user will enter. You may know the top-left cell, but you'll probably have to dynamically determine (or determine at run-time) the bottom-right cell. This is exactly the kind of situation in which using the Cells property makes sense.

Referring to Named Ranges Can Be Tricky

Named ranges can give you fits. Part of the problem is that many people don't have a basic understanding of, or even realize that there are, two kinds of named ranges in Excel.

Workbook-named ranges are probably the most common type of named range. Workbook-named ranges can be used in formulas throughout the workbook by entering the name of the range as shown in Figure 8.3.

Worksheet-named ranges are named ranges that are specific to a worksheet. You can refer to a worksheet-named range within the same worksheet by entering the name of the range in a formula. On other sheets, however, you must prefix the name of the range with the name of the worksheet. Whereas workbook named ranges must be unique, worksheet named ranges only need be unique to the worksheet in which they are created. As you can see in Figure 8.4, to create a worksheet named range, you include the name of the worksheet when specifying the named range.

FIGURE 8.3

You create workbook-named ranges by entering a name in the Name drop-down and pressing Enter.

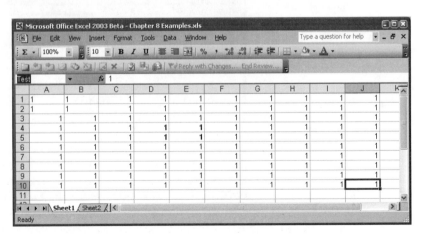

FIGURE 8.4

To create a
worksheet-named
range, you must
specify the name
of the worksheet
in single quotes
followed by an
exclamation point.

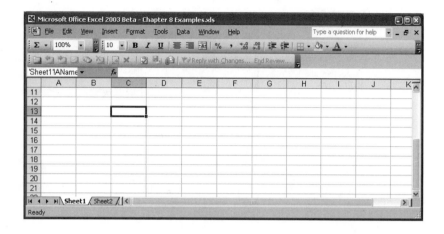

FIGURE 8.5

Worksheet-named
ranges list the name
of the worksheet on
the right-hand side
of the dialog box.

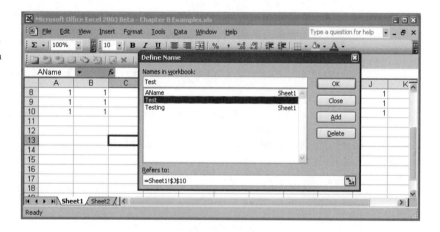

In order to refer to a named range programmatically, you need to know whether the named range is a workbook-named range or a worksheet-named range. Then, to access the named range, you use the Names object associated with the Workbook object for workbook-named ranges or the Worksheet object for worksheet-named ranges. If you didn't set up the named ranges, you can easily inventory all of the defined named ranges by viewing the Define Name dialog box for each worksheet in a given workbook. To view this dialog box, select Insert ➢ Name ➢ Define from the Excel menu.

Using this method of viewing named ranges, you must take into account the fact that only worksheet-named ranges applicable to the current worksheet are displayed. In order to see all of the names in a workbook, you need to visit each worksheet and display this dialog box. In Figure 8.5 you can see that it is easy to distinguish between workbook- and worksheet-named ranges when viewing names in a workbook. Worksheet-named ranges are distinguished by the inclusion of the worksheet name to the right of the named range. In Figure 8.6 I have selected a different worksheet from the one that was active for Figure 8.5. As you can see, both worksheets have a worksheet-named range called Testing.

FIGURE 8.6
Only worksheet-named ranges applicable to the current worksheet are displayed.

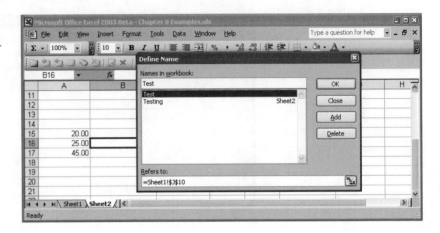

Of course, you can use a much better way to do this programmatically—check out Listing 8.4. Here, the ListWorkbookNames procedure prints out all names in the workbook, including all worksheet-specific names.

LISTING 8.4: USING THE NAMES OBJECT TO LIST ALL NAMED RANGES

```
' Test the ListWorkbookNames procedure
' Outputs to cell A2 on the 2nd worksheet in the workbook
Sub TestListNames()
    ListWorkbookNames ThisWorkbook, ThisWorkbook.Worksheets(2).Range("a2")
End Sub

Sub ListWorkbookNames(wb As Workbook, rgListStart As Range)
    Dim nm As Name

    For Each nm In wb.Names
        ' print out the name of the range
        rgListStart.Value = nm.Name
        ' print out what the range refers to
        ' the ' is required so that Excel doesn't
        ' consider it as a formula
        rgListStart.Offset(0, 1).Value = "'" & nm.RefersTo
        ' set rgListStart to refer to the cell
        ' the next row down.
        Set rgListStart = rgListStart.Offset(1, 0)
    Next
End Sub
```

FIGURE 8.7

The output of the ListWorkbook-Names procedure lists all names, even those that are worksheet specific.

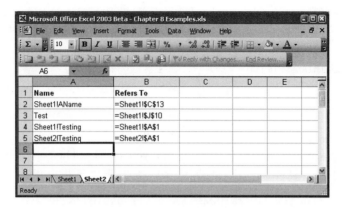

On my test workbook, this procedure produces the output shown in Figure 8.7. Notice that every name in the workbook is listed. Well, I guess you'll have to take my word on that unless you open up the example workbook for this chapter. Anyway, the worksheet-specific names include the worksheet name as part of the name.

The ListWorkbookNames procedure works by looping through each name in the Names collection associated with the workbook passed to the procedure. Inside the loop, you print out the name in the cell referred to by the rgListStart variable. Then use the RefersTo property to display what the name refers to. Using the Offset property, print the value of the RefersTo property one cell to the right of rgListStart. Finally, adjust rgListStart to refer to the cell immediately below itself. Later in the chapter, you'll dig into the Offset property a little more.

You might think that you could return the value in a named range by using a statement such as the following:

```
' this statement doesn't work
vRangeValue = ThisWorkbook.Names("TestName").Value
```

Although this does produce a value, it doesn't give you the value you might expect. Rather than giving you the value that currently occupies the cell referred to by TestName, it gives you the RefersTo value of the range name. In other words, ThisWorkbook.Names(x).Value is equivalent to ThisWorkbook.Names(x).RefersTo. So how do you get the actual value of the cell? To do this, you need to use the RefersToRange property. RefersToRange returns an actual Range object (with its address equal to that given by the RefersTo property) that can be used like any other Range object.

Now that I've spent a good deal of time talking about the Names and Name objects, I should explain the other way in which you can refer to a named range. Basically, you can refer to these ranges much like any other range. For example, if you had a named range called "Testing" on a worksheet named "Sheet2", you could refer to this range with a statement such as the following:

```
ThisWorkbook.Worksheets("Sheet2").Range("Testing")
```

I hear you. Why did I give you such an elaborate explanation on named ranges if you can refer to them so easily? Remember the difference between workbook-named ranges and worksheet-named ranges? Well, forget all of that if you use this method. The only way to refer to a workbook-named range in this manner is to also have a reference to the worksheet on which the name is defined. For example, say you have a workbook-named range called "Test" that is defined on "Sheet1". You cannot reference the Test named range from Sheet2. You can only reference Test from the worksheet object that it is defined on as shown in the following code snippet.

```
' This is legal
ThisWorkbook.Worksheets("Sheet1").Range("Test")
' This is not
ThisWorkbook.Worksheets("Sheet2").Range("Test")
```

I am not sure that all of this detail will make a lot of sense right now, or if it does, you may not grasp why I spend so much time on it. If you use named ranges and refer to them programmatically, however, I'd bet that at some point, the subtleties of using named ranges will cause you some grief.

SAFETY FIRST: VALIDATE NAMED RANGES BEFORE USING THEM

Much like using worksheet names in your code, it's a good idea to validate any range names in your code before you actually use them. Unless you have prevented them from doing so, end users can rename or delete named ranges. Listing 8.5 provides a function that you can use to validate names.

LISTING 8.5: VALIDATING NAMES USING THE RANGENAMEEXISTS PROCEDURE

```
' Checks for the existence of a named range on a worksheet
Function RangeNameExists(ws As Worksheet, sName As String) As Boolean
    Dim s As String

    On Error GoTo ErrHandler

    s = ws.Range(sName).Address

    RangeNameExists = True
    Exit Function

ErrHandler:
    RangeNameExists = False
End Function

Sub ValidateNamedRangeExample()
    If RangeNameExists(ThisWorkbook.Worksheets(1), "Test") Then
        MsgBox "The name exists, it refers to: " & _
            ThisWorkbook.Names("Test").RefersTo, _
            vbOKOnly
    Else
        MsgBox "The name does not exist", vbOKOnly
    End If

    If RangeNameExists(ThisWorkbook.Worksheets(1), "djfs") Then
        MsgBox "The name exists, it refers to: " & _
            ThisWorkbook.Worksheets(1).Names("djfs").RefersTo, _
```

```
        vbOKOnly
    Else
        MsgBox "The name does not exist", vbOKOnly
    End If
End Sub
```

RangeNameExists returns a Boolean value that is true if the range name exists, false otherwise. You may recognize the basic structure of this procedure from the chapter covering the Worksheet object. It's nearly identical to the procedure you use to test for the existence of a worksheet. This procedure relies on error handling to catch the error that occurs if the name doesn't exist and returns the appropriate value.

One catch with RangeNameExists is that it's set up to validate worksheet-named ranges. It also works on workbook-named ranges, provided you supply the worksheet on which the named range is defined. The ValidateNamedRangeExample procedure just demonstrates how you might call Range-NameExists from another procedure.

Finding My Way

Do you know that tune? It's a song from Rush's debut, self-titled album *Rush* (July 1974), first track. Good tune, though I appreciate the deeper lyrics that Neil Peart brought to the band with their second album. Anyway, when it comes to working with worksheets, finding your way is a constant theme.

Though most of the time you'll know the *general* structure of a workbook and worksheet ahead of time, you usually need to feel your way around to get where you are going. Even with highly structured worksheets, it's difficult to predict and account for all of the possible ways end users may use or modify your worksheets.

I certainly don't want to offend anyone with a vision disability by pretending that it's anywhere close to what it is like to be without vision, but that is how I think about navigating worksheets in Excel programmatically when I'm working with documents in which I only have a knowledge of the general structure.

The general technique I use is to feel my way around the document, examining ranges for certain identifying characteristics. These identifying characteristics vary depending on your needs. You may want to look at values; for example, you might contemplate the following questions: Is the cell numeric? Is it within a given range? Or you may consider formatting characteristics; location in the worksheet; location relative to another known range, or a defined name; or the presence of a comment.

Some common tasks you'll need to perform include these:

- Moving from cell to cell on a worksheet
- Finding the last row in a given column
- Determining the last used row for all columns
- Detecting the last column for a given row
- Determining the last column for all rows
- Locating the first empty cell in a column or row

You can apply many different techniques for moving around a worksheet. I'll present a few here that I've used successfully for many different purposes. The two primary ways to move about a worksheet are using the Cells property of the Worksheet object and the Offset property of the Range object. I've already talked about the Cells property earlier in the chapter (see Listing 8.2), so let's take a look at the Offset property.

Offset Is for Relative Navigation

You can use the Offset property of the Range object to refer to ranges on a worksheet based on, or relative to, another range. This property provides you with a great deal of flexibility for moving around a worksheet.

One thing that you can do with Offset is process a structured list. By structured list, I mean a list of items on a worksheet in which you know the order or structure of the columns ahead of time. Consider the list of items shown in Figure 8.8.

One way you could process this list is by setting a reference to the first column of the first row in the list. Then you could loop through the list, advancing your reference down a row, and terminating the loop when you reach an empty row (assuming you know that there won't be any empty rows within the boundaries of your list). As you loop through the list, you could investigate columns of interest by using the Offset property.

Listing 8.6 demonstrates how you could filter this list. You'll have to bear with me and pretend that Excel doesn't have any native filtering functionality (which we'll examine in the next chapter). Anyway, Listing 8.6 uses the Offset property to process the list shown in Figure 8.8 so that it hides any rows that contain cars from the 20th century. Further, this process highlights the mileage column if the car has less than 40,000 miles.

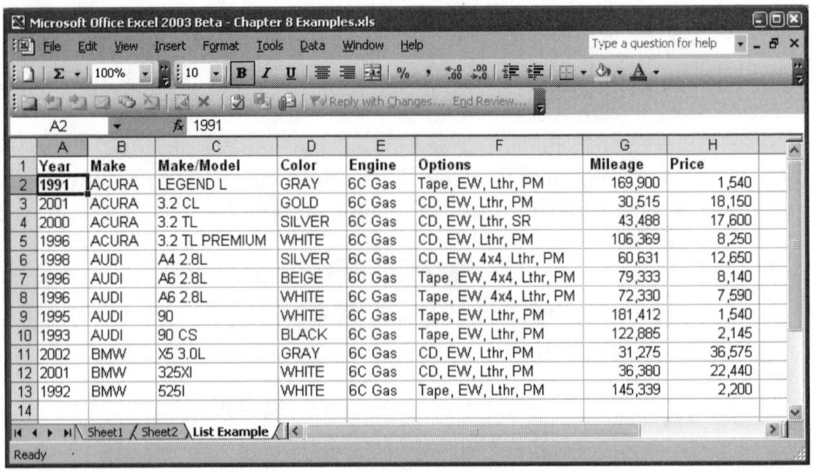

FIGURE 8.8

A simple worksheet list

	A	B	C	D	E	F	G	H
1	Year	Make	Make/Model	Color	Engine	Options	Mileage	Price
2	1991	ACURA	LEGEND L	GRAY	6C Gas	Tape, EW, Lthr, PM	169,900	1,540
3	2001	ACURA	3.2 CL	GOLD	6C Gas	CD, EW, Lthr, PM	30,515	18,150
4	2000	ACURA	3.2 TL	SILVER	6C Gas	CD, EW, Lthr, SR	43,488	17,600
5	1996	ACURA	3.2 TL PREMIUM	WHITE	6C Gas	CD, EW, Lthr, PM	106,369	8,250
6	1998	AUDI	A4 2.8L	SILVER	6C Gas	CD, EW, 4x4, Lthr, PM	60,631	12,650
7	1996	AUDI	A6 2.8L	BEIGE	6C Gas	Tape, EW, 4x4, Lthr, PM	79,333	8,140
8	1996	AUDI	A6 2.8L	WHITE	6C Gas	Tape, EW, 4x4, Lthr, PM	72,330	7,590
9	1995	AUDI	90	WHITE	6C Gas	Tape, EW, Lthr, PM	181,412	1,540
10	1993	AUDI	90 CS	BLACK	6C Gas	Tape, EW, Lthr, PM	122,885	2,145
11	2002	BMW	X5 3.0L	GRAY	6C Gas	CD, EW, Lthr, PM	31,275	36,575
12	2001	BMW	325XI	WHITE	6C Gas	CD, EW, Lthr, PM	36,380	22,440
13	1992	BMW	525I	WHITE	6C Gas	Tape, EW, Lthr, PM	145,339	2,200
14								

LISTING 8.6: LIST PROCESSING WITH THE OFFSET PROPERTY

```vba
Sub ListExample()
    FilterYear 2000
End Sub

Sub Reset()
    With ThisWorkbook.Worksheets("List Example")
        .Rows.Hidden = False
        .Rows.Font.Bold = False
        .Rows(1).Font.Bold = True
    End With
End Sub

Sub FilterYear(nYear As Integer)
    Dim rg As Range
    Dim nMileageOffset As Integer

    ' 1st row is column header so start
    ' with 2nd row
    Set rg = ThisWorkbook.Worksheets("List Example").Range("A2")
    nMileageOffset = 6

    ' go until we bump into first
    ' empty cell
    Do Until IsEmpty(rg)

        If rg.Value < nYear Then
            rg.EntireRow.Hidden = True
        Else
            ' check milage
            If rg.Offset(0, nMileageOffset).Value < 40000 Then
                rg.Offset(0, nMileageOffset).Font.Bold = True
            Else
                rg.Offset(0, nMileageOffset).Font.Bold = False
            End If
            rg.EntireRow.Hidden = False
        End If

        ' move down to the next row
        Set rg = rg.Offset(1, 0)
    Loop

    Set rg = Nothing
End Sub
```

Let me make a few comments before I analyze this listing. First, this listing uses a worksheet named "List Example" and *doesn't* validate this assumption, so be sure you have either changed the worksheet name in the code or named one of your worksheets "List Example". Then run the ListExample procedure to hide selected rows and the Reset procedure to display the worksheet as it originally appeared.

The heart of this example is the poorly named FilterYear procedure. Notice one of the variables is named nMileageOffset. The procedure uses the Offset property to observe the value in the Mileage column. Your Range object variable, rg, is located in column 1, so to use Offset to view the Mileage column, you need to look in the cell six columns to the right. It's a good idea, at a minimum, to store a value like this in a variable or a constant. That way if you need to change the value (perhaps you need to insert a column, for example), you only have to change it in one location. The FilterYear stores this mileage column offset in a variable named nMileageOffset.

The processing loop is a Do...Loop that terminates when it finds an empty cell. Each time through the loop, you set the rg variable to refer to the next cell down. The primary assumption that is made here is that you don't have any empty cells between the first and last row. If there is a chance that you may have empty cells, you need to use another method to process the list or put some appropriate checks in place.

The first piece of business inside the loop is to see if the value in the year column (the value in the range to which the rg variable refers) is less than the value passed in the nYear parameter. If it is, you can use the EntireRow property of your Range object to refer to a range that represents all of the cells in the row occupied by the rg variable. In the same statement, set the Hidden property to true to hide the row. If the value in the Year column is equal to or greater than nYear, check the value in the Mileage column and ensure that the row isn't hidden. The last thing to do inside the loop is advance the rg variable so that it refers to the next cell down the worksheet.

Notice in the Reset procedure that you can return a range that represents all of the rows in a worksheet or a selected row in the worksheet. This makes it very easy to unhide all of the rows at once. In order to remove any bold formatting that the FilterYear procedure applied, remove any bold formatting from any cell on the worksheet and then go back and apply it to the first row (the column headings). This is much easier and faster than looping through each cell individually and turning bold off if it is on. The output of Listing 8.6 is shown in Figure 8.9.

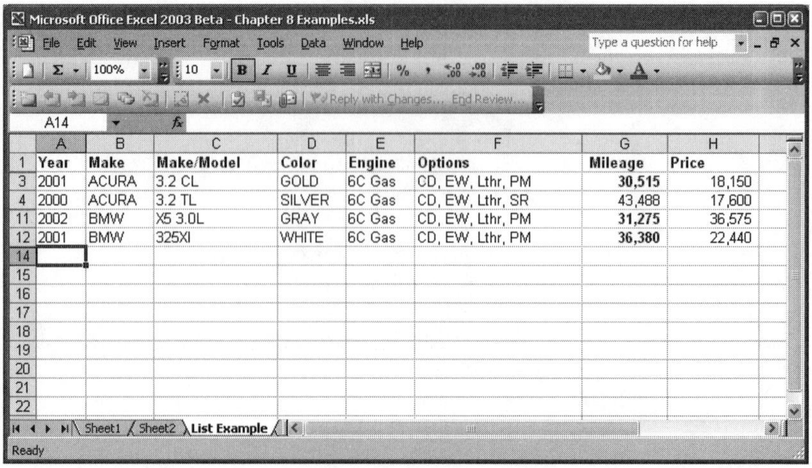

FIGURE 8.9

List processing can be performed very easily with just a little bit of code.

Last but Not Least—Finding the End

One property of the Range object that is extremely useful for navigational activities is the End property. If you are used to navigating around Excel using the Control key in conjunction with the arrow keys, you already know how End behaves—End is the programmatic equivalent of navigating using Control in conjunction with the arrow keys. If you don't know what I'm talking about, it'll be helpful to perform the following exercise to see for yourself.

1. On a blank worksheet in Excel, select the range A1:C10.

2. Press the numeral 1 key and then press Ctrl+Shift+Enter to populate every cell in the range with the value 1.

3. Also, place the value 1 in the cells A12:A15, B14, C12, and D13:D14, as shown in Figure 8.10.

4. Select cell A1.

5. Press Ctrl+Down Arrow to select cell A10.

6. Press Ctrl+Right Arrow to select cell C10.

7. Continue experimenting with Ctrl+(Up/Down/Right/Left) Arrow until you have a good feel for how this behaves.

The general algorithm of this functionality is as follows. If the current cell *is* empty, then select the first nonempty cell in the direction specified by the arrow key. If a nonempty cell can't be found, select the cell next to the boundary of the worksheet.

FIGURE 8.10

A simple list for testing the End property

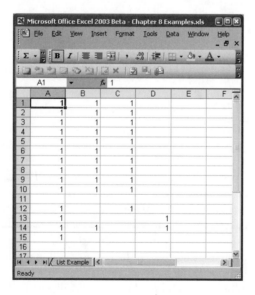

If the current cell *is not* empty, then see if the cell next to the current cell (in the direction specified by the arrow key) is empty. If the next cell is empty, then select the first nonempty cell. If a nonempty cell isn't found, select the cell next to the boundary of the worksheet. If the next cell is not empty, then select the last cell in the range of contiguous nonempty cells.

Listing 8.7 presents an example that uses the End property. I set this procedure up using the worksheet from the preceding exercise. You may need to update the procedure to refer to a different worksheet if you didn't use the first worksheet in the workbook.

LISTING 8.7: USING THE END PROPERTY TO NAVIGATE WITHIN A WORKSHEET

```
Sub ExperimentWithEnd()
    Dim ws As Worksheet
    Dim rg As Range

    Set ws = ThisWorkbook.Worksheets(1)
    Set rg = ws.Cells(1, 1)

    ws.Cells(1, 8).Value = _
        "rg.address = " & rg.Address

    ws.Cells(2, 8).Value = _
        "rg.End(xlDown).Address = " & rg.End(xlDown).Address

    ws.Cells(3, 8).Value = _
        "rg.End(xlDown).End(xlDown).Address = " & _
        rg.End(xlDown).End(xlDown).Address

    ws.Cells(4, 8).Value = _
        "rg.End(xlToRight).Address = " & rg.End(xlToRight).Address

    Set rg = Nothing
    Set ws = Nothing
End Sub
```

Listing 8.7 simply uses the End property to navigate to a few locations. It outputs the address of the range it navigates to as it goes. Notice that because the End property returns a Range object, you can use it multiple times in the same statement.

As you can see, using End is an efficient technique for finding the boundaries of a contiguous series of cells that contain values. It's also useful for finding the last row in a given column or the last column in a given row. When you use End to find the last used cell in a column or row, however, you need to be wary of empty cells.

In order to account for the possibility of empty cells, all you need to do to find the last cell is start at the boundary of the worksheet. So if you need to find the last row in a given column, use End, except start at the bottom of the worksheet. Similarly, to find the last column in a given row, start at the far right column of the worksheet.

Listing 8.8 presents two functions that return either a range that represents the last used cell in a column or the last used cell in a row, depending on which function you call.

LISTING 8.8: FINDING THE LAST USED CELL IN A COLUMN OR ROW

```
' returns a range object that represents the last
' non-empty cell in the same column
Function GetLastCellInColumn(rg As Range) As Range
    Dim lMaxRows As Long

    lMaxRows = ThisWorkbook.Worksheets(1).Rows.Count

    ' make sure the last cell in the column is empty
    If IsEmpty(rg.Parent.Cells(lMaxRows, rg.Column)) Then
        Set GetLastCellInColumn = _
            rg.Parent.Cells(lMaxRows, rg.Column).End(xlUp)
    Else
        Set GetLastCellInColumn = rg.Parent.Cells(lMaxRows, rg.Column)
    End If
End Function

' returns a range object that represents the last
' non-empty cell in the same row
Function GetLastCellInRow(rg As Range) As Range
    Dim lMaxColumns As Long

    lMaxColumns = ThisWorkbook.Worksheets(1).Columns.Count

    ' make sure the last cell in the row is empty
    If IsEmpty(rg.Parent.Cells(rg.Row, lMaxColumns)) Then
        Set GetLastCellInRow = _
            rg.Parent.Cells(rg.Row, lMaxColumns).End(xlToLeft)
    Else
        Set GetLastCellInRow = rg.Parent.Cells(rg.Row, lMaxColumns)
    End If
End Function
```

GetLastCellInColumn and GetLastCellInRow work almost identically, but are different in two ways. First, when you're looking for the last used cell in a column, you need to start at the bottom of the worksheet. For rows, you start at the far right edge of the worksheet instead. The second difference is the parameter you supply to the End property. For the last used cell in a column, you use xlUp; for the last used cell in a row you use xlToLeft. The most important statement in each of these functions is the one that uses the End property. I took the example shown here from the GetLastCellInRow function.

```
rg.Parent.Cells(rg.Row, lMaxColumns).End(xlToLeft)
```

The rg variable is a Range object supplied to the function as a parameter. Your objective with this statement is to move to the last possible cell in the row to which rg belongs and then use End to move to the first nonempty cell in the same row. You can see exactly how this objective is achieved by breaking the statement down from left to right:

1. First you receive a reference from rg.Parent to the worksheet that contains the range.

2. Next you use the Cells property of the worksheet object to specify the last possible cell in the row. Specify the specific cell by supplying a row number and a column number.

   1. You can determine the specific row number by using the Row property of the Range object.

   2. You can determine the last possible column by counting the number of columns on a worksheet. This is performed a few statements earlier and the result is assigned to the lMaxColumns variable.

3. Finally, use the End property to find the last nonempty cell in the row.

This is a good example of how you can get a lot done with one statement. As you progress and get more familiar with the Excel object model, putting these statements together will become second nature for you. 99 percent of the time, this statement alone would suffice. In order to account for the possibility that the last possible cell in the row or column isn't empty, you need to add an If…Then statement to check for this condition. If the last possible cell is nonempty and you use the End property on that cell, the function returns an incorrect result because it moves off of the cell to find the next nonempty cell.

Listing 8.9 adopts these functions so that they can be called from a worksheet. The main change you need to make is to return a numeric value that can be displayed on a worksheet rather than on a Range object.

LISTING 8.9: RETURNING THE LAST USED CELL IN A COLUMN OR ROW WITH WORKSHEET CALLABLE FUNCTIONS

```
' returns a number that represents the last
' nonempty cell in the same column
' callable from a worksheet
Function GetLastUsedRow(rg As Range) As Long
    Dim lMaxRows As Long

    lMaxRows = ThisWorkbook.Worksheets(1).Rows.Count

    If IsEmpty(rg.Parent.Cells(lMaxRows, rg.Column)) Then
        GetLastUsedRow = _
            rg.Parent.Cells(lMaxRows, rg.Column).End(xlUp).Row
    Else
        GetLastUsedRow = rg.Parent.Cells(lMaxRows, rg.Column).Row
    End If
End Function
```

```
' returns a number that represents the last
' nonempty cell in the same row
' callable from a worksheet
Function GetLastUsedColumn(rg As Range) As Long
    Dim lMaxColumns As Long

    lMaxColumns = ThisWorkbook.Worksheets(1).Columns.Count

    If IsEmpty(rg.Parent.Cells(rg.Row, lMaxColumns)) Then
        GetLastUsedColumn = _
            rg.Parent.Cells(rg.Row, lMaxColumns).End(xlToLeft).Column
    Else
        GetLastUsedColumn = rg.Parent.Cells(rg.Row, lMaxColumns).Column
    End If
End Function
```

These functions are handy because you can call them from a worksheet function. Figure 8.11 shows the results of calling these functions from the worksheet you created earlier to experiment with navigation using the Control key in conjunction with the arrow keys.

FIGURE 8.11

The GetLastUsed-Row and GetLastUsed-Column functions can be called from a worksheet.

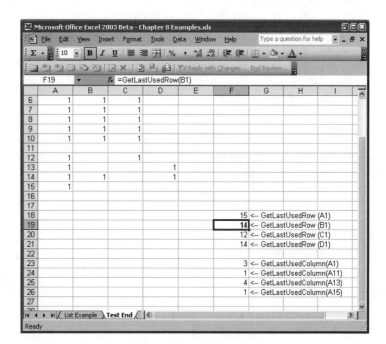

Input Easy; Output Easier

You now know everything that you *need* to know to learn how to collect worksheet-based input and display output. Worksheet-based input/output (I/O) draws on your knowledge of using the Application,

Workbook, Worksheet, and Range objects. Sure, the direct object you use is the Value property of the Range object, but you can't effectively and professionally do this without using all of the other objects I mentioned.

One of the reasons you need to draw on your knowledge of all of the objects we have covered so far is that I/O is a risky operation in terms of the potential for run-time errors and you need to program accordingly.

The other reason is that without giving some thought to I/O, it's easy to create rigid procedures that are error prone and hard to maintain. In order to avoid this problem, you should think about how your procedures handle I/O and what you can do to create reasonably flexible procedures that are easy to maintain.

In any event, you'll need to make certain assumptions regarding I/O, and you need to safeguard or enforce those assumptions to eliminate or significantly reduce the potential for run-time errors. This could be as simple as telling your users to modify the workbook structure at their own risk. On the other end of the spectrum, you could develop a complex workbook and worksheet protection scheme that only allows changes that are necessary to accomplish the objectives that the workbook was designed to accomplish. Ultimately, the choice comes down to a tradeoff between development time on the one hand, and the utility of increased flexibility and application robustness on the other. That said, let's see if I can highlight some of these tradeoffs as you explore some of the ways that you can perform I/O in Excel.

Output Strategies

You've already seen a few examples of simple, unstructured output. I'd define simple, unstructured output as output that uses the Value property of the Range object to a known worksheet without any regard for formatting and little regard for precise data placement.

For example, Listing 8.2 displayed a simple grid of data to a block of cells on a worksheet. Likewise, Listing 8.4 displayed the names in a given workbook as a simple list. Both of these examples had some output to display, and displayed it by dumping it in a range of contingent worksheet cells.

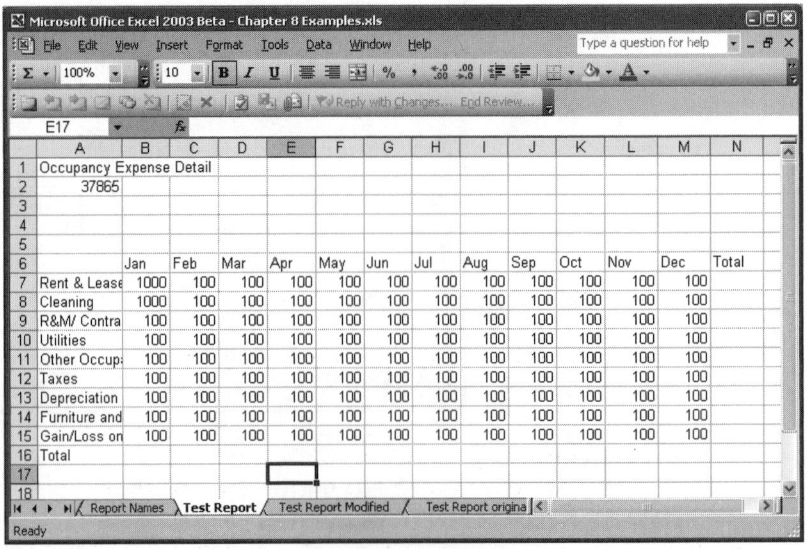

FIGURE 8.12

A raw, unformatted report in need of some help

In contrast to simple output, structured output is output to one or more worksheets that are rigidly structured, such as a report template. Structured output is more difficult in the sense that you need to be much more careful regarding the assumptions you make about where the output should go if one of your goals is a robust solution. Consider the raw, unformatted report shown in Figure 8.12. How might you go about formatting this report programmatically?

Earlier in this section, I cautioned against creating rigid, difficult to maintain procedures. Let's take a look at an example of a rigid procedure (see Listing 8.10).

LISTING 8.10: BE WARY OF PROCEDURES THAT CONTAIN A LOT OF LITERAL RANGE SPECIFICATIONS.

```
' this is an example of a rigid procedure
' rigid procedures are generally error prone
' and unnecessarily difficult to maintain/modify
Sub RigidFormattingProcedure()
    ' Activate Test Report worksheet
    ThisWorkbook.Worksheets("Test Report").Activate
    ' Make text in first column bold
    ActiveSheet.Range("A:A").Font.Bold = True
    ' Widen first column to display text
    ActiveSheet.Range("A:A").EntireColumn.AutoFit
    ' Format date on report
    ActiveSheet.Range("A2").NumberFormat = "mmm-yy"
    ' Make column headings bold
    ActiveSheet.Range("6:6").Font.Bold = True
    ' Add & format totals
    ActiveSheet.Range("N7:N15").Formula = "=SUM(RC[-12]:RC[-1])"
    ActiveSheet.Range("N7:N15").Font.Bold = True
    ActiveSheet.Range("B16:N16").Formula = "=SUM(R[-9]C:R[-1]C)"
    ActiveSheet.Range("B16:N16").Font.Bold = True
    ' Format data range
    ActiveSheet.Range("B7:N16").NumberFormat = "#,##0"
End Sub
```

If I could guarantee that the format of this report would never change, that none of the items on the report would ever appear in a different location, and that no other procedures in your entire project would reference the same ranges as this procedure, then I'd consider letting this procedure slide if it wasn't for the use of Activate in the first statement.

In practice however, it's rarely the case that anything remains static. Granted, often after the development process is complete, things may stay static for long periods of time. However, during the development and testing process, things change—perhaps repeatedly. It only takes one type of change to break nearly every line in this procedure—basically any change that results in the location of items shifting in the worksheet, such as when a new row or a new column is added. This may not seem like a big deal in this example because it's only one small procedure. Realistically though, your projects may consist of multiple modules, each containing a handful to dozens of procedures. Do you really want to revisit each procedure every time a change is made that violates your original assumptions?

FIGURE 8.13
Results of applying basic formatting to the report shown in Figure 8.12

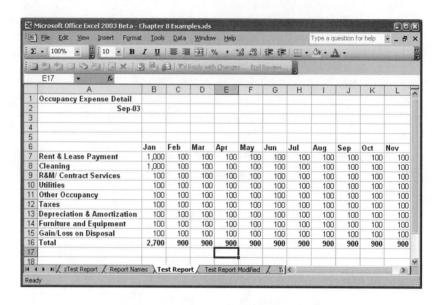

FIGURE 8.14
By naming sections of a report, you can help insulate your code from structural changes to the worksheet.

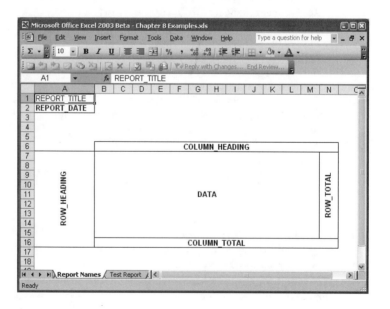

So, what could you do to minimize the impact of changes? First, you can place every literal or hard-coded value that you can't reasonably avoid in locations that are easy to modify if necessary—especially literal values used in more than one place. Second, you can seek to limit the use of hard-coded values in the first place.

TIP *I find that using syntax highlighting (in the VBE, select Tools ➤ Options and then choose the Editor Format tab) is a big help in quickly identifying/locating places in a project where literal values are being used. I prefer to set the background color to light gray and the foreground color to red for Normal Text. Then I set the background color to light gray for Comment Text, Keyword Text, and Identifier Text. Finally, I set the foreground color as I see fit. Hard-coded values are visually apparent now.*

Take a look back at Listing 8.10. One way you can protect yourself from this type of problem is to use named ranges. The benefit of using named ranges here is that if you insert or remove rows or columns, named ranges are much less likely to be affected. Figure 8.14 shows how you could name the various sections of this report.

Assuming you create the range names shown in Figure 8.14, Listing 8.11 provides you with an example of a much more robust procedure. This procedure uses the WorksheetExists procedure presented in the last chapter as well as the RangeNameExists procedure shown in Listing 8.5.

LISTING 8.11: A MORE FLEXIBLE PROCEDURE FOR WORKING WITH STRUCTURED RANGES

```vba
Sub RigidProcedureDeRigidized()
    Dim ws As Worksheet

    If Not WorksheetExists(ThisWorkbook, "Test Report") Then
        MsgBox "Can't find required worksheet 'Test Report'", vbOKOnly
        Exit Sub
    End If

    Set ws = ThisWorkbook.Worksheets("Test Report")

    If RangeNameExists(ws, "REPORT_TITLE") Then _
        ws.Range("REPORT_TITLE").Font.Bold = True

    If RangeNameExists(ws, "REPORT_DATE") Then
        With ws.Range("REPORT_DATE")
            .Font.Bold = True
            .NumberFormat = "mmm-yy"
            .EntireColumn.AutoFit
        End With
    End If

    If RangeNameExists(ws, "ROW_HEADING") Then _
        ws.Range("ROW_HEADING").Font.Bold = True
```

```
    If RangeNameExists(ws, "COLUMN_HEADING") Then _
        ws.Range("COLUMN_HEADING").Font.Bold = True

    If RangeNameExists(ws, "DATA") Then _
        ws.Range("DATA").NumberFormat = "#,##0"

    If RangeNameExists(ws, "COLUMN_TOTAL") Then
        With ws.Range("COLUMN_TOTAL")
            .Formula = "=SUM(R[-9]C:R[-1]C)"
            .Font.Bold = True
            .NumberFormat = "#,##0"
        End With
    End If

    If RangeNameExists(ws, "ROW_TOTAL") Then
        With ws.Range("ROW_TOTAL")
            .Formula = "=SUM(RC[-12]:RC[-1])"
            .Font.Bold = True
            .NumberFormat = "#,##0"
        End With
    End If

    Set ws = Nothing
End Sub
```

NOTE *See Listing 7.2 for the WorksheetExists procedure. See Listing 8.5 for the RangeNameExists procedure.*

This procedure fulfills the same responsibility as Listing 8.10. Yes, it is longer. Yes, it still contains literal values. However, the payoff is huge. Here is why. Rather than rigid range addresses, the literal values are now the names of named ranges. As you saw earlier, it's easy to validate named ranges. Further, named ranges insulate you from most of the effects of changing the worksheet's structure. If you add or remove rows or columns, the named ranges adjust accordingly. If you need to adjust the range boundaries of a named range, you can do it from the worksheet rather than modifying code. For example, let's say you need to add a new expense line and insert two more rows between the report title and the column headings. The new worksheet structure is shown in Figure 8.15. The new rows are highlighted. The original procedure is shown in Figure 8.16.

As you can see, a little extra work can really pay off. Because you used named ranges, you now have the ability to perform validation on the expected regions in your report and can make structural changes to the worksheet without having to modify your procedures. If need be, you can simply adjust the range that a named range refers to from Excel rather than modifying your code.

FIGURE 8.15
How will your two formatting procedures handle this new structure?

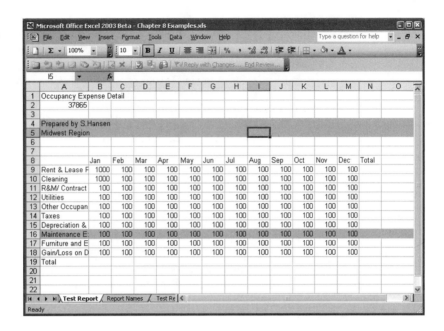

FIGURE 8.16
The original procedure fails miserably.

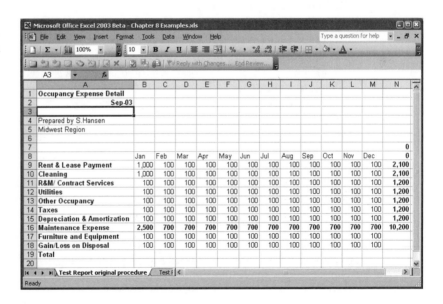

FIGURE 8.17

The revised procedure runs flawlessly.

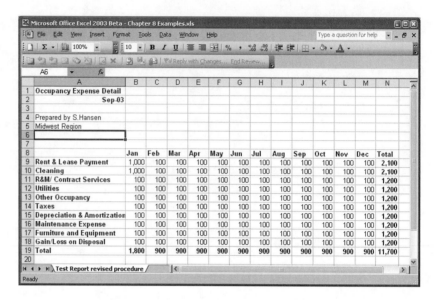

Accepting Worksheet Input

When you go to accept worksheet-based input, you'll encounter many of the issues that surround structured output. Chiefly, you need to develop a strategy for ensuring that the input is in the location you expect and that any supporting objects, such as specific worksheets or named ranges, are also present.

Another facet of accepting worksheet-based input makes accepting input slightly more difficult than displaying output. Usually your procedures expect input of a specific data type such as a date, a monetary amount, or text. If these procedures get an input that uses a different data type, a run-time error could occur. Therefore, you need to develop a way to either enforce the type of data that can be entered, account for the possibility of other data types in your procedures or, preferably, use a combination of these two strategies.

WARNING *You can't rely on Excel's Data Validation feature alone for validating input. You can easily circumvent the Data Validation feature by entering an invalid value in a cell that doesn't have any validation rules and copying/pasting into the cell containing validation. Because many people use copy/paste to enter values in Excel, this occurs more than you might think.*

One way in which you can enforce the value that can be entered in a worksheet is to write a procedure to validate the cell and hook that procedure up to the worksheet change event. For an extra level of protection, validate the cell's value before you use it in other procedures. For example, if you have a procedure that expects a currency value and you need to obtain this value from a worksheet cell, you may want to use a procedure to validate that the range has an appropriate value (see Listing 8.12).

LISTING 8.12: VALIDATING A RANGE FOR APPROPRIATE DATA

```
Function ReadCurrencyCell(rg As Range) As Currency
    Dim cValue As Currency

    cValue = 0

    On Error GoTo ErrHandler
    If IsEmpty(rg) Then GoTo ExitFunction
    If Not IsNumeric(rg) Then GoTo ExitFunction

    cValue = rg.Value

ExitFunction:
    ReadCurrencyCell = cValue
    Exit Function
ErrHandler:
    ReadCurrencyCell = 0
End Function
```

You are guaranteed to get a numeric value back when you use the ReadCurrencyCell function. This eliminates the problem caused when a range of interest either contains text data or doesn't contain any value at all. In both of these cases, the procedure returns a zero.

Summary

The Range object is the most important Excel object to know if you want to become proficient developing in Excel. As with most things, a solid understanding of the fundamentals is more important than knowledge of all of the exotic and little-used features or techniques. When it comes to the Range object, the fundamentals consist of referring to specific ranges, navigating around a worksheet, and handling input/output operations.

It's extremely easy to use the Range object to create rigid, though fragile, applications. You could refer to worksheets by name in your procedures and refer to ranges using standard A1-style addresses whenever you need to reference a certain range. Hopefully you have an appreciation of why it isn't a good idea to do this unless you are developing a quick, one-off utility for your own use. Referring to objects using literal values is error prone, makes modifications unnecessarily difficult, and can limit the potential for reuse.

In order to avoid creating fragile applications, you must consider how your procedures will interact with worksheets and ranges. In addition to the standard defensive tactics such as validating the existence of specific worksheets and named ranges, you can "feel" your way around a worksheet examining values, formatting, or identifying other characteristics to find a range of interest. In order to move around a worksheet, you can use the Cells property of the Worksheet object, the Range property of the Worksheet object, the End property of the Range object, and the Offset property of the Range object.

Displaying output to a worksheet is accomplished using the Value property of the Range object. Again, the primary difficulty is accounting for the possible actions an end user can take that have the possibility of causing run-time errors due to the assumptions you build into your procedures. If you collect input from a worksheet, the difficulty level increases because you need to account for the possibility that the data type may not be the type your procedure is expecting. Well-written procedures always contain a dose of defensive programming aimed at validating the assumptions made during the development process.

In the next chapter, you'll examine some of the more useful of the many properties and methods of the Range object.

Chapter 9

Practical Range Operations

NOW THAT YOU UNDERSTAND the fundamentals of using a Range object—referring to ranges, navigating a worksheet using ranges and basic input/output —you can start learning how to do all of the things you'd do with a range if you were doing it (i.e., using the Excel interface) manually. In this chapter, you'll learn how to use the Range object to cut, copy, paste, filter, find and sort data in Excel.

This chapter, when combined with the previous chapter, is really the bread and butter of Excel development. After reading this chapter, if you're comfortable with all of the topics presented, I'll consider this book a success. Everything else is bonus material. Now that's value! Seriously though, most of what you do in Excel involves manipulating data, and to do that you use the Range object.

Data Mobility with Cut, Copy, and Paste

Some of the most mind-numbing work I can think of is performing a long, manual, repetitive sequence of copy/paste or cut/paste. Have you ever experienced this? Maybe you receive a dump of data from some other system and need to systematically sort and group the data and then prepare a report for each grouping. Based on my observations, I'm not the only person who has suffered through this kind of activity. More than a few people have probably become attracted to the potential benefits of automation with VBA while enduring the mental pain associated with this activity.

If you know of a process or two that include large amounts of shuffling data around, automating these processes could be your first big win as an Excel developer. Usually it's fairly easy to automate these processes, and the time savings of automation versus doing it manually can be monumental.

To complete such a task, however, you need to learn how to use the Cut, Copy, and PasteSpecial methods of the Range object. Cut and Copy can be used identically. Use Cut when you want to move the range to a new location and remove any trace of it from its original location. Use Copy when you want to place a copy of the range in a new location while leaving the original range intact.

```
YourRangeObject.Cut [Destination]
YourRangeObject.Copy [Destination]
```

The optional Destination parameter represents the range that should receive the copied or cut range. If you don't supply the Destination parameter, the range is cut or copied to the Clipboard.

NOTE   An example of Copy is shown in the CopyItem procedure shown in Listing 9.1.

If you use Cut or Copy without specifying a destination, Excel will still be in cut/copy mode when your procedure finishes. You can tell when Excel is in cut/copy mode by the presence of a moving, dashed border around the range that has been copied (see Figure 9.1).

When I first started developing, it took me forever to figure out how to turn cut/copy mode off; when I did figure it out, I didn't even do it correctly. I used the SendKeys function to send the equivalent of the Escape keystroke to the active window. It did the job, but it wasn't very elegant. Anyway, the Application object has a property called CutCopyMode. You can turn cut/copy mode off by setting this property to false.

```
' Turn cut/copy mode off
Application.CutCopyMode = False
```

You can use PasteSpecial to copy the contents of the Clipboard to a range. PasteSpecial is quite flexible regarding how the contents of the Clipboard get pasted to the range. You can tell it to paste everything, comments only, formats only, formulas only, or values, among other things.

```
YourDestinationRange.PasteSpecial [Paste As XlPasteType], _
    [Operation As XlPasteSpecialOperation], _
    [SkipBlanks], [Transpose]
```

All of the parameters of PasteSpecial (listed momentarily) are optional. If you don't specify any of the parameters, the contents of the Clipboard will be pasted to the range as if you had used the Copy method.

Paste   You can use the Paste parameter to specify what gets pasted to the range. You can specify one of the xlPasteType constants: xlPasteAll (default), xlPasteAllExceptBorders, xlPasteColumnWidths, xlPasteComments, xlPasteFormats, xlPasteFormulas, xlPasteFormulasAndNumberFormats, xlPaste-Validation, xlPasteValues, and xlPasteValuesAndNumberFormats. I'll assume that you can figure out what each of these constants does.

FIGURE 9.1

The dashed border around this range indicates that Excel is in cut/copy mode.

Operation   The Operation parameter specifies whether to perform any special actions to the paste values in conjunction with any values that already occupy the range. You can use one of the xlPasteSpecialOperation constants: xlPasteSpecialOperationAdd, xlPasteSpecialOperationDivide, xlPasteSpecialOperationMultiply, xlPasteSpecialOperationNone (default), and xlPasteSpecialOperationSubstract.

SkipBlanks   This Boolean (true/false) parameter specifies whether or not to ignore any blank cells on the Clipboard when pasting. By default this parameter is false.

Transpose   Transpose is a slick, little-known (by Excel users in general anyway) feature. Like its regular Excel counterpart, this optional Boolean parameter transposes rows and columns. If you have a series of values oriented horizontally, and you paste it using the value true for the Transpose parameter, you'll end up with a series of values oriented vertically.

I suppose this would also be a good place to mention the Delete method. Delete has one optional parameter—Shift—that represents how remaining cells on the worksheet should be shifted to fill the void left by the deleted cells. You can use one of the defined xlDeleteShiftDirection constants: xlShiftToLeft or xlShiftUp.

Find What You Are Seeking

You can use many strategies to look for items of interest on a worksheet. The most obvious way is to loop through any cells that might contain the value you are seeking and observe the value of each cell. If your data is in a list, you could sort the data first, which would limit the number of cells you need to view. Another option is to use a filter. Or finally, you could always use the Find method. The Find method is your programmatic doorway to the same functionality found on the Find tab of the Find and Replace dialog box (CTRL+F in Excel), shown in Figure 9.2.

FIGURE 9.2
The Find method allows you to access all of the functionality found on the Find tab of the Find and Replace dialog box.

Here is the syntax of Find:

```
YourRangeToSearch.Find(What, [After], _
    [LookIn], [LookAt], [SearchOrder], _
    [SearchDirection As XlSearchDirection], _
    [MatchCase], [MatchByte], [SearchFormat]) _
    As Range
```

The Find method has a fair number of parameters. The parameters are described in the list below.

What   What is the only required parameter. This parameter is the data to look for—a string, integer, or any of the Excel data types.

After   This optional range parameter specifies the cell *after* which the range should be searched. In other words, the cell immediately below or to the right of the After cell (depending on the SearchOrder) is the first cell searched in the range. By default, After is the upper-left cell in the range.

LookIn   You can use the LookIn parameter to specify where to look for the item. You can use one of the defined constants xlValues, xlFormulas or xlComments.

LookAt   Use LookAt to specify whether Find should only consider the entire contents of a cell or whether it attempts to find a match using part of a cell. You can use the constants xlWhole or xlPart.

SearchOrder   The SearchOrder parameter determines how the range is searched: by rows (xlByRows) or by columns (xlByColumns).

SearchDirection   Do you want to search forward (xlNext) or backward (xlPrevious)? By default, the SearchDirection is forward.

MatchCase   This parameter is false by default; this means that normally the search is not case sensitive (A=a).

MatchByte   If you have selected or installed double-byte language support, this should be true to have double-byte characters match only double-byte characters. If this is false, double-byte characters match their single-byte equivalents.

SearchFormat   Use this value if you'd like to specify a certain type of search format. This parameter is not applicable to English language computers.

Find is a semi-smart method in that it remembers the settings for LookIn, LookAt, SearchOrder, and MatchByte between method calls. If you don't specify these parameters, the next time you call the method, it uses the saved values for these parameters.

To demonstrate Find, I have a rather lengthy example for you. When you're using Excel, you'll often need to find an item in one list and copy it to another. Rather than show you a simple Find example, I have an example that demonstrates this entire process. Though it is longer than other examples you've looked at so far, it's nice in that it draws on much of the knowledge you've acquired. Figure 9.3 shows a simple list that you'll use for this example and a later example that demonstrates the Replace method.

Your goal is to develop a process that reads the value in cell J1 and looks for the value in the Product column (column B) of the list located in the range A1:D17. Every time it finds the value in the list, it places a copy of the item in the list of found items (the "found list") that begins with cell H4. Listing 9.1 presents an example that illustrates the use of the Find method.

FIGURE 9.3

Simple list for experimenting with Find and Replace

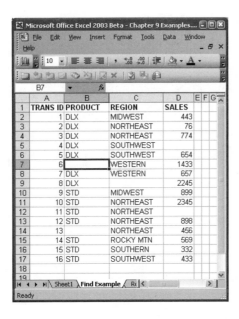

LISTING 9.1: USING FIND AND COPY

```
Option Explicit

' Name of worksheet
Private Const WORKSHEET_NAME = "Find Example"
' Name of range used to flag beginning of
' found list
Private Const FOUND_LIST = "FoundList"
' Name of range that contains the product
' to look for
Private Const LOOK_FOR = "LookFor"


Sub FindExample()
    Dim ws As Worksheet
    Dim rgSearchIn As Range
    Dim rgFound As Range
    Dim sFirstFound As String
    Dim bContinue As Boolean

    ResetFoundList
    Set ws = ThisWorkbook.Worksheets("Find Example")
    bContinue = True
```

```
      Set rgSearchIn = GetSearchRange(ws)

      ' find the first instance of DLX
      ' looking at all cells on the worksheet
      ' looking at the whole contents of the cell
      Set rgFound = rgSearchIn.Find(ws.Range(LOOK_FOR).Value, _
          , xlValues, xlWhole)

      ' if we found something, remember where we found it
      ' this is needed to terminate the Do...Loop later on
      If Not rgFound Is Nothing Then sFirstFound = rgFound.Address


      Do Until rgFound Is Nothing Or Not bContinue
          CopyItem rgFound

          ' find the next instance starting with the
          ' cell after the one we just found
          Set rgFound = rgSearchIn.FindNext(rgFound)

          ' FindNext doesn't automatically stop when it
          ' reaches the end of the worksheet - rather
          ' it wraps around to the beginning again.
          ' we need to prevent an endless loop by stopping
          ' the process once we find something we've already
          ' found
          If rgFound.Address = sFirstFound Then bContinue = False
      Loop

      Set rgSearchIn = Nothing
      Set rgFound = Nothing
      Set ws = Nothing
End Sub

' sets a range reference to the range containing
' the list - the product column
Private Function GetSearchRange(ws As Worksheet) As Range
      Dim lLastRow As Long

      lLastRow = ws.Cells(65536, 1).End(xlUp).Row
      Set GetSearchRange = ws.Range(ws.Cells(1, 2), _
          ws.Cells(lLastRow, 2))
End Function

' copies item to found list range
Private Sub CopyItem(rgItem As Range)
      Dim rgDestination As Range
      Dim rgEntireItem As Range
```

```vba
        ' need to use a new range object because
        ' we will be altering this reference.
        ' altering the reference would screw up
        ' the find next process in the FindExample
        ' procedure. also - move off of header row
        Set rgEntireItem = rgItem.Offset(0, -1)

        ' resize reference to consume all four
        ' columns associated with the found item
        Set rgEntireItem = rgEntireItem.Resize(1, 4)

        ' set initial reference to found list
        Set rgDestination = rgItem.Parent.Range(FOUND_LIST)

        ' find first empty row in found list
        If IsEmpty(rgDestination.Offset(1, 0)) Then
            Set rgDestination = rgDestination.Offset(1, 0)
        Else
            Set rgDestination = rgDestination.End(xlDown).Offset(1, 0)
        End If

        ' copy the item to the found list
        rgEntireItem.Copy rgDestination
        Set rgDestination = Nothing
        Set rgEntireItem = Nothing
End Sub


' clears contents from the found list range
Private Sub ResetFoundList()
    Dim ws As Worksheet
    Dim lLastRow As Long
    Dim rgTopLeft As Range
    Dim rgBottomRight As Range

    Set ws = ThisWorkbook.Worksheets(WORKSHEET_NAME)
    Set rgTopLeft = ws.Range(FOUND_LIST).Offset(1, 0)
    lLastRow = ws.Range(FOUND_LIST).End(xlDown).Row
    Set rgBottomRight = _
        ws.Cells(lLastRow, rgTopLeft.Offset(0, 3).Column)

    ws.Range(rgTopLeft, rgBottomRight).ClearContents

    Set rgTopLeft = Nothing
    Set rgBottomRight = Nothing
    Set ws = Nothing
End Sub
```

This whole process uses four procedures: CopyItem, FindExample, GetSearchRange, and Reset-FoundList. The FindExample procedure is the main procedure; ResetFoundList and Get-SearchRange are bit players in this example. Each of these procedures is only called once—though their roles are small they are important. ResetFoundList is called near the beginning of the FindEx-ample procedure to clear any contents from the found list. Like GetSearchRange, the primary task ResetFoundList needs to do is find the bottom of the list.

Notice that all of the procedures and the constants at the top of the listing are declared as private with the exception of the FindExample procedure. Hiding supporting procedures and constants in this manner is a good idea because it prevents the procedures from being called from other modules or from Excel's user interface—although any subroutine that requires a parameter can't be called from the Excel user interface anyway. For me, this practice is as much a mental aid as anything else. It gives me mental closure and helps me visualize the procedures within the module as having a specific pur-pose. I'm not always the neatest person in the world, but I like some semblance of order, and hiding procedures (by declaring them as private) that aren't meant to be called by external processes creates mental order for me.

The FindExample procedure is typical of many routines that use the Find method. The general approach is to set a reference to a range that represents the range in which you want to search. If you want to search an entire worksheet, you can use the Cells property of the Worksheet object. In this example, you're just looking in the Product column. Because Find returns a range object, you need to declare a Range object variable to hold the result.

The first thing to do is to use the Find method and see if you find anything. If Find doesn't find anything, the range variable holding the result is Nothing. Because Find doesn't automatically stop looking when it hits the beginning or end of the worksheet (depending on which direction you're going), if you find something the first time you call Find, you need to remember the address of what you found. That allows you to make sure that subsequent calls to FindNext don't result in an endless loop of finding the same things over and over again. All you need to do is compare the address of each found cell to the address of the first cell you found.

At this point, you create a loop that keeps calling FindNext. This loop is never entered if the orig-inal call to Find doesn't find anything. Inside the loop, you place any statements you want to execute (in this case, you simply call CopyItem), call FindNext, and compare the result's address to the address of the first found item. If the addresses match, a terminating condition is set to exit the loop. One more important comment—the call to FindNext must specify the range from which to start the search. In order to avoid finding the exact same thing over and over again, you need to start searching with the cell after the last cell that was found.

The CopyItem procedure performs a little dance with the item found by the Find and FindNext methods. Because it's important not to "disturb" or change the reference of the rgFound variable lest you create problems with FindNext, you create a range variable named rgEntireItem. You'll use this variable to create a reference to the entire record or item found rather than just the Product field or column held in the rgFound variable. To get a range that represents the entire record, you do two things. First, move over to the first column using Offset and specifying one column to the left. Next, resize the range. Instead of a range that is one row by one column (1×1), you need a range that is one row by four columns (1×4) because your list is four columns wide.

After all of this, you're nearly ready to copy the record to the found list. The only task left is to figure out exactly where you should copy the record. In this example, I created a named range called

FoundList that is the upper-left cell of the found list. This cell is the column header for the first column of the found list. All you need to do is go to that cell and then find the first empty cell below it and you'll have your destination.

Figure 9.4 shows the results of running the FindExample procedure. The range to search is the current region associated with cell A1 and the product to search for is indicated in cell J1. The found list is the current region associated with cell H4.

Don't Like It? Change It with Replace

Replace is a hard-working method as far as I'm concerned. This is one of those features that many general Excel users don't take advantage of. In case you're one of those, I better illustrate how useful this functionality is before I dive into how to use it programmatically. Figure 9.5 shows the Replace dialog box displayed by selecting Edit ➢ Replace from the Excel menu. You may need to click the Options button to view the Replace options shown in Figure 9.5.

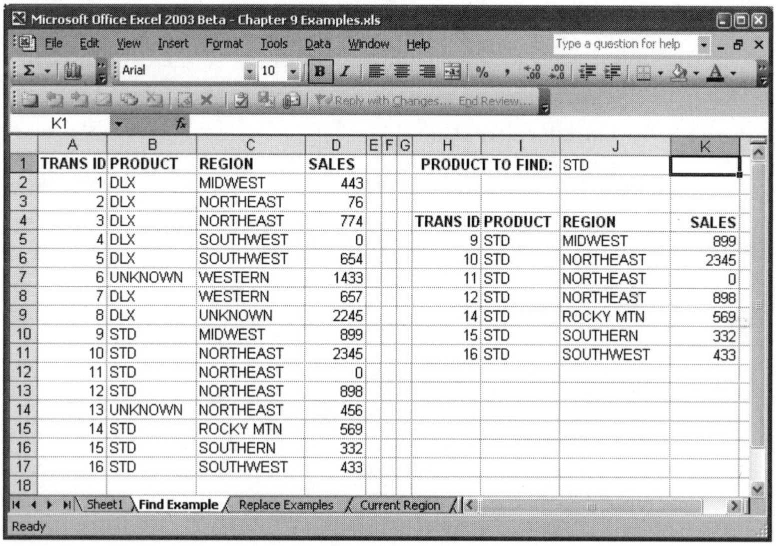

	A	B	C	D	E	F	G	H	I	J	K
1	TRANS ID	PRODUCT	REGION	SALES				PRODUCT TO FIND:		STD	
2	1	DLX	MIDWEST	443							
3	2	DLX	NORTHEAST	76							
4	3	DLX	NORTHEAST	774				TRANS ID	PRODUCT	REGION	SALES
5	4	DLX	SOUTHWEST	0				9	STD	MIDWEST	899
6	5	DLX	SOUTHWEST	654				10	STD	NORTHEAST	2345
7	6	UNKNOWN	WESTERN	1433				11	STD	NORTHEAST	0
8	7	DLX	WESTERN	657				12	STD	NORTHEAST	898
9	8	DLX	UNKNOWN	2245				14	STD	ROCKY MTN	569
10	9	STD	MIDWEST	899				15	STD	SOUTHERN	332
11	10	STD	NORTHEAST	2345				16	STD	SOUTHWEST	433
12	11	STD	NORTHEAST	0							
13	12	STD	NORTHEAST	898							
14	13	UNKNOWN	NORTHEAST	456							
15	14	STD	ROCKY MTN	569							
16	15	STD	SOUTHERN	332							
17	16	STD	SOUTHWEST	433							
18											

FIGURE 9.4 The results of FindExample, a procedure that performs functionality common to many applications—finding an item of interest in one list and copying it to another.

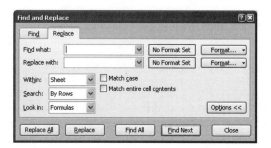

FIGURE 9.5 Once you file it in your mental toolbox, you'll find numerous ways to use Replace creatively.

One situation that I commonly run across is the need to replace null values (or empty cells) in a list with some default value such as zero. For example, in Figure 9.4 let's replace empty cells in column B and C with "UNKNOWN" and empty cells in column D with zero.

1. Select the range B2:C17

2. Press CTRL+H to view the Replace dialog box.

3. Leave the Find What text box empty.

4. Enter UNKNOWN in the Replace With text box.

5. Click Replace All.

6. Select D2:D17. You don't need to close the Replace dialog box first.

7. Enter 0 in the Replace With text box.

8. Click Replace All.

9. Click Close.

Figure 9.6 shows the results.

This functionality is invaluable when you're cleaning up data on a worksheet that consists of hundreds or thousands of rows. When you use the options available on the Replace dialog box, you'll find that you have quite a bit of flexibility. In fact, I've always appreciated the functionality of Replace. Replace is even capable of searching for and replacing particular formats. For example, you can find a cell that contains bold formatting and replace it with italic. This is especially helpful for highly formatted documents in which you can identify elements of interest according to the formatting applied.

As you can see here, Replace uses many of the same parameters that the Find method uses.

```
YourRangeToSearch.Replace What, Replacement, [LookAt], _
    [SearchOrder], [MatchCase], [MatchByte], [SearchFormat], _[ReplaceFormat] As
Boolean
```

To avoid duplication, I'll just note the parameters that I didn't cover when I discussed the Find method earlier.

Replacement   Replacement and What are the only required parameters for Replace. Replacement is the value substituted for the value supplied by the What parameter.

FIGURE 9.6

Replace can scrub your data in a matter of seconds.

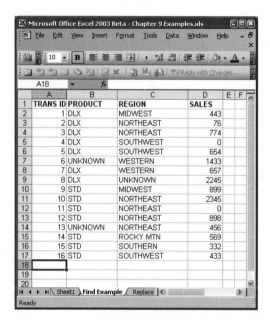

SearchFormat   SearchFormat is an optional Boolean value that instructs Replace to look for the format described by the Application.FindFormat object. See Listing 9.3 for an example of how you'd use SearchFormat and ReplaceFormat.

ReplaceFormat   ReplaceFormat is an optional Boolean value that instructs Replace to apply the format described by the Application.ReplaceFormat object to any cell in which Replace substitutes a value.

Now let's see how you can achieve the same results programmatically. Notice in the Replace exercise steps 1 and 6, that you selected just the range that represented your data range. When replacing empty cells, of course, if you didn't limit the range, Replace would fill up all of the empty cells on the worksheet with the value you supplied to the Replace With text box. When you are doing this programmatically, you need to be conscious of this issue. Listing 9.2 demonstrates how to go about setting the correct range.

LISTING 9.2: USING REPLACE PROGRAMMATICALLY TO SET THE CORRECT RANGE

```
Sub ReplaceExample()
    Dim ws As Worksheet
    Dim rg As Range
    Dim lLastRow As Long

    Set ws = ThisWorkbook.Worksheets("Replace Examples")
```

```
            ' determine last cell in data range
            ' assumes the would never be an empty cell
            ' in column 1 at the bottom of the list
            lLastRow = ws.Cells(65536, 1).End(xlUp).Row

            ' Replace empty cells in 2nd & 3rd columns
            Set rg = ws.Range(ws.Cells(2, 2), ws.Cells(lLastRow, 3))
            rg.Replace "", "UNKNOWN"

            ' Replace empty cells in 4th column
            Set rg = ws.Range(ws.Cells(2, 4), ws.Cells(lLastRow, 4))
            rg.Replace "", "0"

            Set rg = Nothing
            Set ws = Nothing
    End Sub
```

More times than not, when you're working with a list, at least one column always has a value for every row in the list. This is the column that you'll want to use to determine what the last row is. If you use a column that potentially has an empty value in the last cell, you won't be checking all of the rows in the list when you use Replace. In this example, the first column contains a value in every row, so it is the column you'd use to find the last row in the list. As you recall from the last chapter, the End property of the Range object is a convenient way to do this. All you do is start from the last row in the worksheet (I cheated here and hard coded the number of rows in a worksheet) and use the End property with the xlUp constant to find the first non-empty cell in the column. Because End returns a Range object, you use the Row property to give you your answer—a numeric value that represents the last row in your list.

Once you have the last row, it's simple to set the appropriate range references for use with the Replace method. First you set a range to the second and third columns. This is easily achieved by specifying the top-left and bottom-right cells that define the range.

```
    Set rg = ws.Range(ws.Cells(2, 2), ws.Cells(lLastRow, 3))
```

The top-left cell is given using the Cells property of your worksheet object and refers to the cell in row 2, column 2. The bottom-right cell is specified similarly except you use the value in the lLastRow variable for your row along with column 3. The range reference for the fourth column is set in the same manner.

The actual call to the Replace method is no big deal. All you need to do is tell Replace what to look for along with what value it should replace any instances it finds with.

OK, so that is easy enough. But what the heck is that Application.FindFormat thing all about? Application.FindFormat and Application.ReplaceFormat are objects that exist solely to allow you to describe what kind of formatting Replace should look for and then what kind of formatting should be applied to anything Replace finds. Listing 9.3 shows an example that looks on the active sheet for any cells that have bold, size 11 font and replaces the formatting with italic, size 8.

LISTING 9.3: USING REPLACE TO REPLACE FORMATTING

```vb
Sub ReplaceFormats()
    ' set formatting to look for
    With Application.FindFormat
        .Font.Bold = True
        .Font.Size = 11
    End With

    ' set formatting that should be applied instead
    With Application.ReplaceFormat
        .Font.Bold = False
        .Font.Italic = True
        .Font.Size = 8
    End With

    ActiveSheet.Cells.Replace What:="", Replacement:="", _
        SearchFormat:=True, ReplaceFormat:=True
End Sub
```

In the next chapter, you'll be looking at some of the formatting related objects in more detail. The main thing to point out here is that, when you only want to replace formats, you must use an empty string for both the What parameter and the Replacement parameter.

Would You Like Special Sauce with That?

Are you familiar with the Go To Special functionality in Excel? This is another chunk of functionality that many Excel users either don't know exists or don't take advantage of. Check it out in Excel; select Edit ➢ Go To and then click the Special button at the bottom left corner of the Go To dialog box. Figure 9.7 is the result.

FIGURE 9.7

Go To Special is another useful, yet underutilized, chunk of Excel functionality.

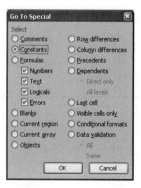

If you haven't used this yet, let me tell you—this handy little dialog box can be a real time-saver. Quick, what's the easiest way to select all of the text values in the range shown in Figure 9.8?

The answer? Press CTRL+G to display the Go To dialog box and then click the Special button. Choose the Constants option with only the Text checkbox checked and click OK. Figure 9.9 shows the results of this operation.

Most of the functionality served up by Go To Special can be accessed programmatically using the SpecialCells method.

```
YourSearchRange.SpecialCells(Type As XlCellType, [Value]) As Range
```

FIGURE 9.8

Ever needed to clear text values out of a range of otherwise numeric values?

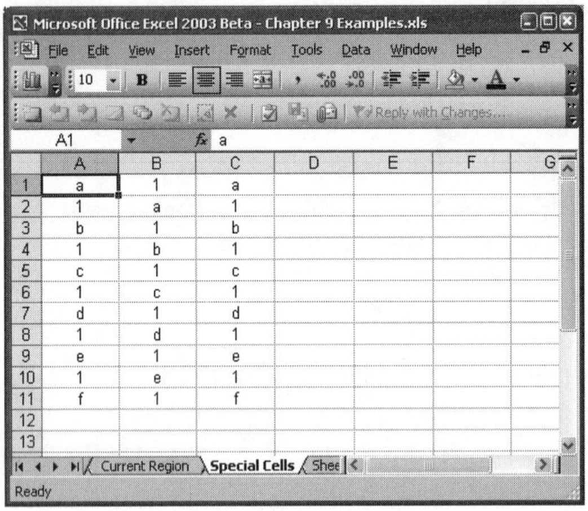

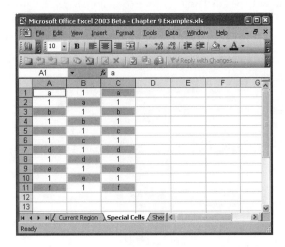

FIGURE 9.9

Among other things, you can employ Go To Special to help you clean up data in lists.

The Type parameter is required and should be one of the xlCellType constants shown in Table 9.1.

TABLE 9.1: xlCellType Constants for Use with the SpecialCells Method

CONSTANT	SELECTS
xlCellTypeAllFormatConditions	Cells of any format
xlCellTypeAllValidation	Cells using data validation
xlCellTypeBlanks	Empty cells
xlCellTypeComments	Any cell containing a comment
xlCellTypeConstants	Cells with constant (or literal) values
xlCellTypeFormulas	Cells with formulas
xlCellTypeLastCell	The last cell in the used range
xlCellTypeSameFormatConditions	Cells having the same format
xlCellTypeSameValidation	Cells having the same data validation criteria
xlCellTypeVisible	All visible cells

If you chose either xlCellTypeConstants or xlCellTypeFormulas for the Type parameter, you can further define which cells to select using the optional Value parameter. By default, all constants or formulas are selected. Use one or more of the following constants: xlErrors, xlLogical, xlNumbers, or xlTextValues. For example, to duplicate the functionality demonstrated in Figure 9.8, you'd use something similar to this:

```
ActiveSheet.Cells.SpecialCells(xlCellTypeConstants, xlTextValues)
```

Note that you can specify more than one kind of value by adding constants together.

```
ActiveSheet.Cells.SpecialCells(xlCellTypeConstants, _
    xlErrors + xlTextValues)
```

One more thing, SpecialCells requires special care. If SpecialCells doesn't find any special cells, it generates a run-time error, so be sure to use error handling in any procedure that uses SpecialCells. Listing 9.4 demonstrates one way to handle any run-time errors that SpecialCells may generate.

LISTING 9.4: USING ERROR HANDLING WHEN USING SPECIALCELLS

```
Sub SpecialCells()
    Dim ws As Worksheet
    Dim rgSpecial As Range
    Dim rgCell As Range

    On Error Resume Next
```

```
        Set ws = ThisWorkbook.Worksheets("Special Cells")
        Set rgSpecial = ws.Cells.SpecialCells(xlCellTypeFormulas, xlErrors)

        If Not rgSpecial Is Nothing Then
            rgSpecial.Interior.Color = vbRed
        Else
            MsgBox "Congratulations! " & ws.Name & _
                    " is an error-free worksheet."
        End If

        Set rgSpecial = Nothing
        Set rgCell = Nothing
        Set ws = Nothing
    End Sub
```

All this procedure does is look for any errors on a worksheet named Special Cells. If it finds any errors, it makes the background of the cells that contain an error red. Otherwise the procedure reports that it didn't find any errors.

The first thing this procedure needs to do is enable error handling. In this case, you instruct VBA to simply move to the following statement if a run-time error occurs. If SpecialCells generates an error, the Range variable rgSpecial never gets initialized. Using the Is Nothing statement, you can see if this is the case and take the appropriate action.

WARNING   *A run-time error (error number 1004: No Cells Were Found.) occurs if the SpecialCells method doesn't find any special cells. Consequently, you need to use error handling when you use this method.*

CurrentRegion: A Useful Shortcut

Depending on what you need to do, the CurrentRegion property may offer a shortcut that you can use instead of determining range boundaries manually. The current region represents the group of cells bounded on all sides by empty rows and columns.

Take a look at Figure 9.10. No matter which cell you select in the range B2:D4, the address of the CurrentRegion is B2:D4. Similarly, the two other shaded ranges represent the CurrentRegion associated with any cell within the shaded area.

When applied to a list, CurrentRegion is also handy when you are trying to determine the characteristics of the list. An example of this is shown in Listing 9.5.

LISTING 9.5: CALLING CURRENTREGION TO INSPECT A LIST'S USEFUL CHARACTERISTICS

```
Sub CurrentRegionExample()
    Dim rg As Range
    Dim ws As Worksheet

    Set ws = ThisWorkbook.Worksheets("Current Region")
```

```
    ' get current region associated with cell A1
    Set rg = ws.Cells(1, 1).CurrentRegion

    ' number of header rows
    ws.Range("I2").Value = rg.ListHeaderRows

    ' number of columns
    ws.Range("I3").Value = rg.Columns.Count

    ' resize to exclude header rows
    Set rg = rg.Resize( _
        rg.Rows.Count - rg.ListHeaderRows, _
        rg.Columns.Count).Offset(1, 0)

    ' number of rows ex header rows
    ws.Range("I4").Value = rg.Rows.Count

    ' number of cells ex header rows
    ws.Range("I5").Value = rg.Cells.Count

    ' number empty cells ex header rows
    ws.Range("I6").Value = Application.WorksheetFunction.CountBlank(rg)

    ' number of numeric cells ex header rows
    ws.Range("I7").Value = Application.WorksheetFunction.Count(rg)

    ' last row
    ws.Range("I8").Value = rg.Rows.Count + rg.Cells(1, 1).Row - 1

    Set rg = Nothing
    Set ws = Nothing
End Sub
```

This procedure demonstrates a number of range properties and a property of the Application object that I don't believe you've seen yet. The important statement, for the purposes of this example, is the one that sets the rg variable to refer to the current region associated with cell "A1." The List-HeaderRows property returns the number of rows that appear to be header rows. As you can see, you can use the value of this property to resize your Range object so that it represents data rows only.

The only other statements of interest are the ones that use the WorksheetFunction property of the Application object. This property provides programmatic access to the standard worksheet functions that you can use from a worksheet.

The output of the CurrentRegionExample is shown in Figure 9.11. The list is the current region associated with cell A1. The characteristics of the list are output beginning with cell H1.

FIGURE 9.10

A range of data for experimenting with CurrentRegion.

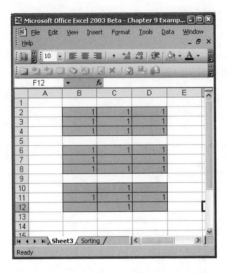

FIGURE 9.11

Output of the CurrentRegion-Example procedure

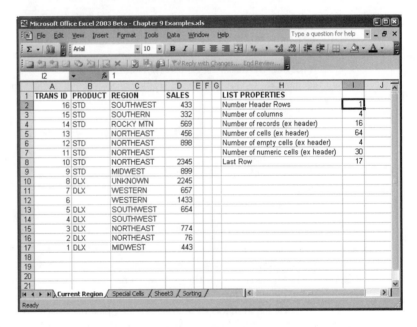

Sorting Lists Simplified

The Sort method looks rather intimidating at first glance. Fear not, however. It is a lot easier to use than it looks here because all the parameters are optional and you'll usually only use a handful of them.

```
YourRangeToSort.Sort [Key1], [Order1 As XlSortOrder], _
    [Key2], [Type], [Order2 As XlSortOrder], _
    [Key3], [Order3 As XlSortOrder], _
    [Header As XlYesNoGuess], [OrderCustom], [MatchCase], _
    [Orientation As XlSortOrientation], _
    [SortMethod As XlSortMethod], _
    [DataOption1 As XlSortDataOption], _
    [DataOption2 As XlSortDataOption], _
    [DataOption3 As XlSortDataOption]
```

Because you can sort on up to three columns, the first nine parameters consist of a set of three parameters repeated for each column that you want to include in the sort.

Below are descriptions of the parameters of the Sort method:

Key1, Key2, and Key3   You use Key1 to specify the first sort column. You can specify either a text value that identifies the column or a Range object. Likewise, Key2 specifies the second column and Key3 specifies the third column.

Order1, Order2, and Order3   Use the Order parameters to indicate how a field is sorted. You can use the defined constants xlDescending or xlAscending (default).

Type   This parameter is only applicable to sorting PivotTable reports. You can specify xlSort-Labels or xlSortValues.

Header   Use this parameter to indicate whether the range to sort has a header row or not. This parameter can't be used when sorting a PivotTable. You can use the defined constants xlGuess (Excel will try to determine whether or not a header row exists), xlYes or xlNo.

OrderCustom   The OrderCustom parameter is used to point the Sort method to a list of custom sort orders. It should be a 1-based offset to the list of custom sort orders.

MatchCase   Use this optional Boolean parameter to specify whether to do a case-sensitive sort (true) or not (false). This parameter can't be used against a PivotTable report.

Orientation   By default the Sort method assumes that your data is arranged vertically and sorts by row. If your data is arranged horizontally, you can use the Orientation parameter to specify this and it will sort by column. You can use either the xlSortRows defined constant or xlSortColumns.

SortMethod   This parameter is not applicable for English language computers and is used for some other languages.

DataOption1, DataOption2, and DataOption3   This parameter can be used to specify how text and numbers should be treated when you're sorting. If you specify xlSortTextAsNumbers, text is treated as numeric data for the sort. The default, xlSortNormal, sorts numeric and text data separately. DataOption1 is applicable to the Key1 parameter. DataOption2 is applicable to Key2 and DataOption3 is applicable to Key3.

FIGURE 9.12

Make sure you add Listing 9.6 to a Worksheet module rather than a standard module.

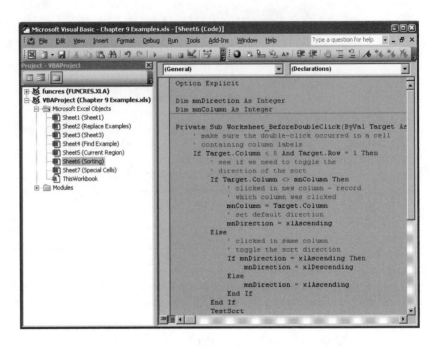

So shall we check this out? You know how many websites allow you to sort a particular column in a list simply by clicking the column label and each time you click the label it toggles the sort direction? Let's see how you can provide this functionality to an Excel list.

This is surprisingly easy functionality to implement. In order to demonstrate this, you'll add code to the module associated with the worksheet that contains the list. If you remember, each worksheet object has a module associated with it to which you can add code that is applicable to the worksheet. For this demo (see Figure 9.12), I've created a worksheet named Sorting and added the code shown in Listing 9.6 to the module associated with the worksheet.

LISTING 9.6: ADDING CLICKABLE SORTING TO WORKSHEET LISTS

```
Option Explicit

Dim mnDirection As Integer
Dim mnColumn As Integer

Private Sub Worksheet_BeforeDoubleClick(ByVal Target As Range, Cancel As Boolean)
    ' make sure the double-click occurred in a cell
    ' containing column labels
    If Target.Column < 5 And Target.Row = 1 Then
        ' see if we need to toggle the
        ' direction of the sort
        If Target.Column <> mnColumn Then
            ' clicked in new column - record
```

```
                ' which column was clicked
                mnColumn = Target.Column
                ' set default direction
                mnDirection = xlAscending
            Else
                ' clicked in same column
                ' toggle the sort direction
                If mnDirection = xlAscending Then
                    mnDirection = xlDescending
                Else
                    mnDirection = xlAscending
                End If
            End If
            TestSort
        End If
    End Sub

Private Sub TestSort()
    Dim rg As Range

    ' get current region associated with cell A1
    Set rg = Me.Cells(1, 1).CurrentRegion

    ' ok - sort the list
    rg.Sort Key1:=rg.Cells(1, mnColumn), _
            Order1:=mnDirection, _
            Header:=xlYes

    Set rg = Nothing
End Sub
```

I think this is a good example because it incorporates some of the things you learned earlier in the book but haven't used very much yet, such as event handling, an appropriate use of module-level variables, and the use of named parameter passing (as opposed to passing parameters by order). Oh, and I demonstrate the Sort method—the main purpose of this example.

The first thing to note is the two module-level integer variables: mnDirection and mnColumn. You'll use these two variables to store which column was last sorted and the direction in which it was sorted.

This functionality wouldn't be possible without the ability to capture the double-click event. The code within this event handler executes any time you double-click the worksheet. By inspecting the Column and Row properties of the Target parameter, you can figure out if the double-click occurred on the header row of your list or not. The Target parameter is a Range object that represents the cell that was double-clicked.

If the double-click occurred on one of the header row cells, the next task is to figure out whether it occurred in the same column as the last sort or not. If the double-click occurred in a different column, we need to update the mnColumn variable with the new column number and set the mnDirection variable to a default value (ascending). If the double-click occurred in the same column, you simply need to toggle the mnDirection variable. Note that you use the Excel-defined constants xlAscending and xlDescending to set the mnDirection variable. This helps make your code easier to read and understand.

The last thing to do is call the TestSort procedure that actually performs the sort. TestSort uses the CurrentRegion property of cell A1 to determine the boundaries of your list. For sorting, all you need to do is specify the key or column that should be sorted and the order of the sort, and then you should indicate whether or not there is a header row. Because you don't need to use many of the Sort method's parameters, it's better here to use the named parameter method of passing parameters rather than using a comma-separated ordered list as you have for most of the other examples in the book. You can see the intended result in Figures 9.13 and 9.14: a list that can be sorted just by clicking on the column headers.

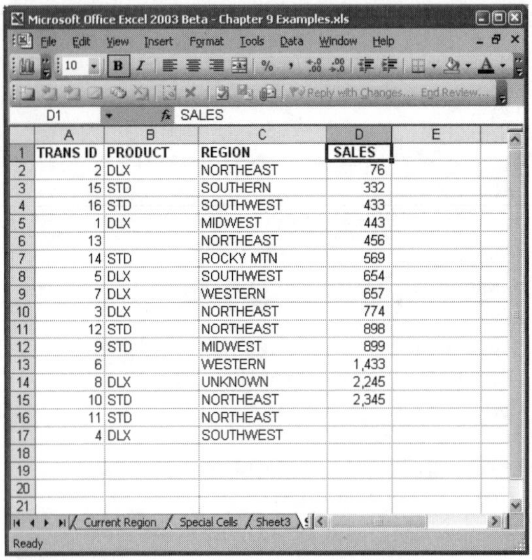

TRANS ID	PRODUCT	REGION	SALES
2	DLX	NORTHEAST	76
15	STD	SOUTHERN	332
16	STD	SOUTHWEST	433
1	DLX	MIDWEST	443
13		NORTHEAST	456
14	STD	ROCKY MTN	569
5	DLX	SOUTHWEST	654
7	DLX	WESTERN	657
3	DLX	NORTHEAST	774
12	STD	NORTHEAST	898
9	STD	MIDWEST	899
6		WESTERN	1,433
8	DLX	UNKNOWN	2,245
10	STD	NORTHEAST	2,345
11	STD	NORTHEAST	
4	DLX	SOUTHWEST	

FIGURE 9.13
Providing the custom sorting functionality in Excel is almost trivial it is so easy. I have double-clicked the Sales label in this picture.

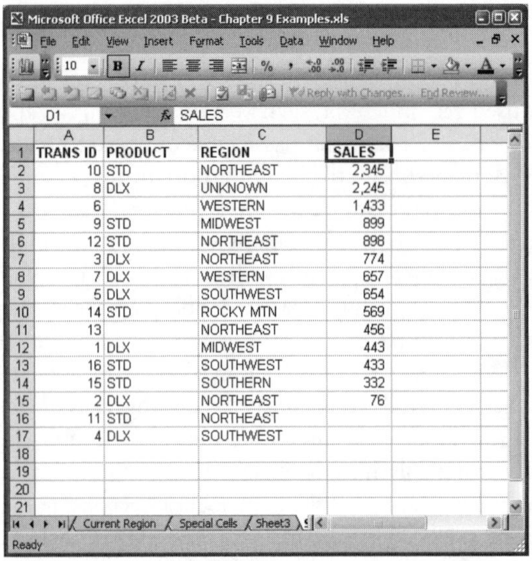

TRANS ID	PRODUCT	REGION	SALES
10	STD	NORTHEAST	2,345
8	DLX	UNKNOWN	2,245
6		WESTERN	1,433
9	STD	MIDWEST	899
12	STD	NORTHEAST	898
3	DLX	NORTHEAST	774
7	DLX	WESTERN	657
5	DLX	SOUTHWEST	654
14	STD	ROCKY MTN	569
13		NORTHEAST	456
1	DLX	MIDWEST	443
16	STD	SOUTHWEST	433
15	STD	SOUTHERN	332
2	DLX	NORTHEAST	76
11	STD	NORTHEAST	
4	DLX	SOUTHWEST	

FIGURE 9.14
If I Double-clicking Sales again, the sort order is reversed.

Summary

Data manipulation is one of the most common activities performed with Excel. Copy. Paste. Sort. Copy. Paste Special (values). Cut. Paste. Add Worksheet. Format range (bold). Sound familiar? This kind of process is a prime candidate for automation using VBA. Using the information presented in this and previous chapters, it's now within your reach to implement this kind of automation.

Cut, Copy, and PasteSpecial are germane to any process involving significant data manipulation. You use Cut when you want to move a range from one location to another whereas Copy is for copying (leaving the range in its original location and placing a copy in another location). PasteSpecial allows you to paste the contents of the clipboard to a given location. Using PasteSpecial, you can choose to paste only certain aspects of the clipboard such as values only, formulas, formats, or other aspects. When you're performing a lot of copying, keep in mind that you have another alternative—simply setting the Value property of one range equal to the Value property of another.

Between Find, Replace, SpecialCells, and Sort, you have a lot of power at your disposal for your various data manipulation needs. Don't let all of the parameters of these methods fool you into thinking they are difficult to use. Though they have many parameters, most of them are optional and you usually only use a few at a time.

In the next chapter, I'll wrap up coverage of the Excel object model by examining a handful of other common Excel objects including objects related to formatting, printing, and charts.

Chapter 10

Exploring Other Excel Objects

THE EXCEL OBJECT MODEL is very rich. To go into detail on all of the objects available would fill many more pages than I have targeted for this book. Besides, you already have Excel's detailed help files available to you. Therefore, I believe the way I can provide added value to you is to help you focus on some of the objects that you're likely to use in the course of your normal development activities and give you good advice regarding how you use these objects. So far, I've covered the most important objects: Application, Workbook, Worksheet, and Range. Now I need to show you some of the more common supporting objects.

In particular, you'll look at various objects you need to know about in order to make your worksheets visually appealing. To do this, you need to review how to use colors, fonts, interiors, borders, and charts. By applying nice formatting touches to your worksheets, your applications will look as good as they perform. This chapter gives you the knowledge you need to do this.

Make a Good First Impression

I find formatting to be an occasional source of frustration. You expend all this mental energy creating a superb application, and then your users complain about "trivial" formatting details. Well, it's better that they complain about minor formatting issues than fundamental issues that concern your application's functionality. So remember not to sweat the small stuff—formatting is a piece of cake to learn, implement, and modify.

Coloring Your World

Before I get to the actual formatting objects, I should tell you a little about the two ways to use colors programmatically in Excel - using RGB values or using a workbook's color palette. An RGB value is a way to express a color by defining its composition in terms of the amount of red, green, and blue it takes to define it. A function named RGB helps you create RGB color values.

```
RGB( red, green, blue)
```

Each of the three RGB parameters is an integer from 0 to 255 that indicates the extent that the parameter contributes to the final color. RGB returns a long integer you can use to specify a color to the various objects that have a Color property. Using RGB, you can theoretically produce 16,777,216 different colors (256 * 256 * 256). This number also happens to be the number of cells on a worksheet.

For the basic colors, you can use a defined constant rather than figuring out the appropriate values for red, green, and blue. The list of predefined colors (Table 10.1) is fairly sparse. However, I often have trouble matching my shoes to my belt. If you're like me, you'll find this list gives you plenty of opportunity to demonstrate your lack of color matching skills.

TABLE 10.1: PREDEFINED COLOR CONSTANTS

CONSTANT	COLOR
vbBlack	Black
vbBlue	Dark Blue
vbCyan	Light Blue
vbGreen	Green
vbMagenta	Magenta (kind of a pinkish color)
vbRed	Red
vbWhite	Opposite of black
vbYellow	Yellow

For fun, I developed a procedure that would theoretically color each cell a different color. I say theoretically because I didn't have the patience to wait for it to finish. Some night I may just let it run and see what happens. If you try this, be warned, it will produce a gigantic (in terms of memory required) workbook. Again, in theory anyway!

Listing 10.1 is for adventurous readers only—the kind that would climb a mountain to see if it could be climbed.

LISTING 10.1: FUN WITH COLORS

```
Sub ColorWorksheet()
    Dim lRow As Long
    Dim lColumn As Long
    Dim ws As Worksheet
    Dim lColor As Long

    Set ws = ThisWorkbook.Worksheets(1)
    lRow = 1
    lColumn = 1
    Application.ScreenUpdating = False
    Application.StatusBar = "On column 1"

    For lColor = 0 To 16777215
        ' record color
        ws.Cells(lRow, lColumn).Interior.Color = lColor
```

```
        ' move to next cell
        lRow = lRow + 1

        ' worksheet has 65,536 rows
        If lRow = 65537 Then
            lRow = 1
            lColumn = lColumn + 1
            Application.StatusBar = "On column " & lColumn
        End If
    Next

    Set ws = Nothing
    Application.StatusBar = False
    Application.ScreenUpdating = True
End Sub
```

You may have figured this out already, but if not, this is a good time to point this out. You can interrupt a running procedure by pressing the Escape (Esc) key. Doing so displays the following dialog box.

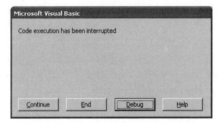

IGNORANCE IS BLISS. OR IS IT?

By default, anyone can interrupt program execution by pressing the Esc key. During the development process, this is a very good thing because it gives you the ability to interrupt endless loops or jump into Break mode on a whim. The question is, do you want your users to be able to do this? On the one hand, this gives them the opportunity to escape from long-running tasks or (gulp) your faulty program. On the other, this isn't a very graceful way to end an application—it's only slightly better than pressing Ctrl+Alt+Delete.

If you want more control over how your users interact with your program while it is running, you can instruct Excel to ignore any mouse or keyboard input other than actions required to operate forms or dialog boxes.

```
    Application.Interactive = False    ' Ignore keyboard and mouse input
```

The Interactive property prevents the user from interfering with the execution of your code. If you do use the Interactive property, be sure to set it back to true when you're done with it. If you do use this, you may also be interested in the DisplayAlerts property, which is also a property of the Application object. If you set DisplayAlerts to false, Excel won't display any prompts or messages during the execution of any code (such as it might if you closed a workbook without saving it). Instead, your code executes as if the prompt or message was displayed and the user chooses the default value or action (such as clicking Yes when asked about saving changes).

FIGURE 10.1

Each workbook has a color palette associated with it that can contain 56 different colors.

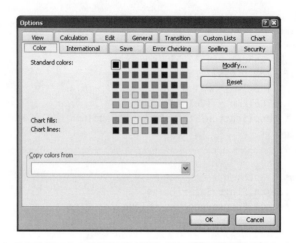

You can click Debug to enter Break mode (assuming the VBA project isn't locked for viewing), End to abruptly terminate the procedure, and Continue to, well, continue.

The second way to express a color programmatically is to use the color palette associated with a workbook. You can view this palette in Excel by viewing the Color tab of the Options dialog box (Tools ➢ Options...).

Color palettes are workbook specific and can contain 56 different colors. You can modify which colors your workbook palette contains. Because color palettes are workbook specific, it makes sense that to modify color palette colors programmatically, you access the color palette via the Workbook object using the Colors property.

NOTE   *Check out Listing 10.4 later in this chapter for an example of retrieving and displaying the colors that occupy a palette.*

Although you can modify aspects of the color palette through the Workbook object, objects that can display a color have a ColorIndex property. The value of the ColorIndex property corresponds to an index of the color palette. So if ColorIndex is 2, whatever color occupies the second spot in the palette is the color that is displayed by the given object.

When you use ColorIndex to specify colors, keep in mind that color palettes are workbook specific. This means that you aren't guaranteed that the color that occupies the second slot of the palette in one workbook equals the color in the second slot in another workbook.

WARNING   *Color palettes are workbook specific. Be careful if you make any assumptions regarding the color found at a specific index.*

Fiddling with Fonts

The Font object is probably a good place to start regarding formatting-oriented objects. One of the ways to learn the properties associated with the Font object that you visual learners might appreciate is to study the Font tab of the Format Cells dialog box (see Figure 10.2).

FIGURE 10.2
The Font object contains properties that represent all of the items found on the Font tab of the Format Cells dialog box.

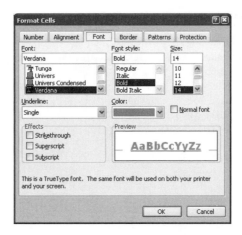

Most of the properties that correspond to items found on the Font tab of the Format Cells dialog box are named exactly the same. For example, the Font object has properties named Color, Size, and Underline. The most common properties of the Font object are shown in Table 10.2.

TABLE 10.2: COMMON PROPERTIES OF THE FONT OBJECT

PROPERTY NAME	DESCRIPTION
Bold	Set to true to make the font bold or false to turn bold off.
Color	Returns or sets the color of the font using an RGB value.
ColorIndex	Returns or sets the color of the font using a color from the workbook's color palette.
FontStyle	Returns or sets the font style.
Italic	Set to true to make the font italic or false to turn italic off.
Name	Returns or sets the name of the font.
Size	Returns or sets the size of the font in points.
Underline	Returns or sets the type of underline used by the font. Choose from xlUnderlineStyleNone, xlUnderlineStyleSingle, xlUnderlineStyleDouble, xlUnderlineStyleSingleAccounting, or xlUnderlineStyleDoubleAccounting.

No real surprises here, no tricks to learn and no gotchas. Take a look at Listing 10.2 for a simple example that uses the Font object.

LISTING 10.2: THE FONT OBJECT—A SIMPLE, STRAIGHTFORWARD OBJECT

```
Sub DemonstrateFontObject()
    Dim nColumn As Integer
    Dim nRow As Integer
    Dim avFonts As Variant
```

```
    Dim avColors As Variant

    For nColumn = 1 To 5
        With ThisWorkbook.Worksheets(1).Columns(nColumn).Font
            .Size = nColumn + 10

            If nColumn Mod 2 = 0 Then
                .Bold = True
                .Italic = False
            Else
                .Bold = False
                .Italic = True
            End If
        End With
    Next

    avFonts = Array("Tahoma", "Arial", "MS Sans Serif", _
        "Verdana", "Georgia")
    avColors = Array(vbRed, vbBlue, vbBlack, vbGreen, vbYellow)

    For nRow = 1 To 5
        With ThisWorkbook.Worksheets(1).Rows(nRow).Font
            .Color = avColors(nRow - 1)
            .Name = avFonts(nRow - 1)

            If nRow Mod 2 = 0 Then
                .Underline = True
            Else
                .Underline = False
            End If
        End With
    Next
End Sub
```

The output of Listing 10.2 is shown in Figure 10.3. One thing that this example demonstrates is the use of the With…End With statement. When you perform formatting operations, you'll commonly need to execute multiple formatting statements on a given range. Using With…End With saves time in the development process by reducing the amount of keystrokes you need to enter, and it also performs better at run-time.

The DemonstrateFontObject procedure demonstrates a few things that you haven't looked at for a while. The VBA Mod operator divides one number by another and returns the remainder. In this procedure Mod is used to check whether a number is even or odd.

Another technique you haven't used for a while is the use of a variant array. DemonstrateFont-Object uses two variant arrays—one to store five colors and another to store five font names. Notice that you can use the Array function to create the array. By placing these items in an array you can easily assign font names and colors as you loop through the rows in Listing 10.2.

FIGURE 10.3

This is the output of the Demonstrate-FontObject procedure.

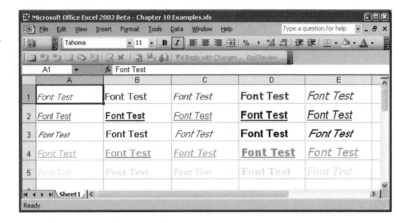

FIGURE 10.4

The Patterns tab of the Format Cells dialog box is the public face of the functionality afforded by the Interior object.

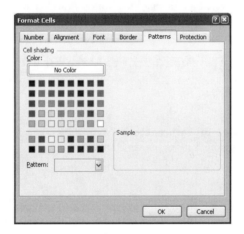

TIP *The Macro Recorder is an excellent tool for learning about many of the objects covered in this chapter. I frequently use the Macro Recorder when I need to perform extensive formatting—especially on objects that I haven't had to use for a while. Though the code produced by the Macro Recorder is usually inefficient and rigid, it is easy to tweak the resulting code to your needs. If nothing else, it is an easy way to discover the objects, properties, or methods that you need to use to achieve the task at hand.*

Interior Decorating

The Interior object is your object of interest if you need to modify the background or interior of a range or other object. The Interior object is your programmatic equivalent of the Patterns tab of the Format Cells dialog box (see Figure 10.4).

The Interior object is used for two types of activities: changing the color of a range or changing the background pattern of a range. Table 10.3 lists the handful of useful properties you may need to use. Note, this list is not inclusive of all of the properties of the Interior object, just the ones that you are most likely to use.

TABLE 10.3: USEFUL INTERIOR PROPERTIES

PROPERTY NAME	DESCRIPTION
Color	Returns or sets the primary color of the interior using an RGB value.
ColorIndex	Returns or sets the color of the interior using a color from the workbook's color palette.
Pattern	Returns or sets the interior's pattern.
PatternColor	Returns or sets the color of the interior's pattern using an RGB value.
PatternColorIndex	Returns or sets the color of the interior's pattern using a color from the workbook's color palette.

As you can see, there isn't much here. Most of the functionality here lies in the various patterns that can be created. It would probably be helpful to know what those patterns are. Listing 10.3 creates an example of each pattern available. As an added bonus, it also creates an example of each defined VB color constant (as listed in Table 10.1).

LISTING 10.3: USING THE INTERIOR OBJECT TO ALTER THE BACKGROUND OF A RANGE

```
Sub InteriorExample()
    Dim rg As Range

    ' create examples of each pattern
    Set rg = ThisWorkbook.Worksheets("Interior"). _
        Range("ListStart").Offset(1, 0)

    Do Until IsEmpty(rg)
        rg.Offset(0, 2).Interior.Pattern = rg.Offset(0, 1).Value
        rg.Offset(0, 3).Interior.Pattern = rg.Offset(0, 1).Value
        rg.Offset(0, 3).Interior.PatternColor = vbRed
        Set rg = rg.Offset(1, 0)
    Loop

    ' create examples of each VB defined color constant
    Set rg = ThisWorkbook.Worksheets("Interior"). _
        Range("ColorListStart").Offset(1, 0)

    Do Until IsEmpty(rg)
        rg.Offset(0, 2).Interior.Color = rg.Offset(0, 1).Value
        Set rg = rg.Offset(1, 0)
    Loop

    Set rg = Nothing
End Sub
```

This listing loops through two lists that I've created on a worksheet named "Interior". The first list, whose top left cell is named "ListStart", is a list of all of the xlPattern constants and their associated values. The second list, whose top left cell is named "ColorListStart", is a list of the VB-defined color constants and their associated values. This procedure loops through each of the lists. For each row, it applies the constant value in the second column to either the Pattern property or the Color property of the Interior object. The output of this procedure is shown in Figures 10.5 and 10.6.

FIGURE 10.5

An example of the various background patterns available in Excel

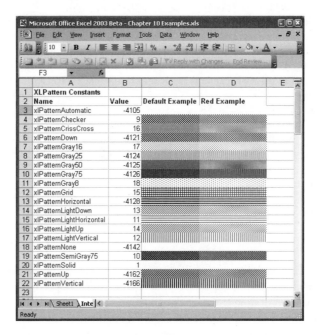

FIGURE 10.6

The basic colors are predefined.

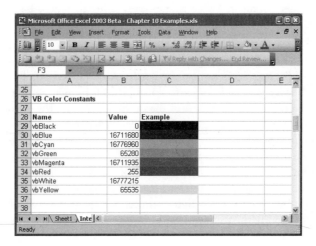

This section wouldn't be complete without looking at a way to display the colors occupying a workbook's color palette. Listing 10.4 loops through all of the colors on a palette and outputs each one's color index, color, and color value.

LISTING 10.4: STROLLING THROUGH THE COLOR PALETTE

```
Sub ViewWorkbookColors()
    Dim rg As Range
    Dim nIndex As Integer

    Set rg = ThisWorkbook.Worksheets("Interior"). _
        Range("ColorIndexListStart").Offset(1, 0)

    For nIndex = 1 To 56
        rg.Value = nIndex
        rg.Offset(0, 1).Interior.ColorIndex = nIndex
        rg.Offset(0, 2).Value = rg.Offset(0, 1).Interior.Color
        Set rg = rg.Offset(1, 0)
    Next

    Set rg = Nothing
End Sub
```

As you can see, I have coded this procedure to work using a worksheet named "Interior" and a range named "ColorIndexListStart" that represents the upper-left cell of the list. Hopefully you are not sick of me repeating this, but I'm violating best practices in many of these examples in order to save space and make the examples more self-contained. A robust procedure would never use a worksheet name or named range in this manner without first validating that they exist.

One thing to note here is that the loop through the colors is hard coded from 1 to 56. This is another instance of an array that is one-based rather than zero-based.

No Visa Required For These Borders

The Range object has a property and a method that you can use to manipulate range borders—specifically, the Borders property and the BordersAround method. The Borders property returns a collection of Border objects. In order to do any serious border manipulation you'll work with a Border object. In keeping with the theme of the previous sections, the Border object is your programmatic equivalent of the Border tab of the Format Cells dialog box in Excel (see Figure 10.7).

To modify a border, you first must obtain a Range object that refers to the cells containing the border. Then you use the Borders property, which refers to a Borders collection object. In order to specify a particular border, you can use one of the XLBordersIndex constants listed in Table 10.4.

Once you have a border to work with, you can perform a handful of actions. You can set its color using either the Color or ColorIndex properties, change the style of the border using the LineStyle property, or modify the thickness of the border using the Weight property.

FIGURE 10.7
The Border tab of
the Format Cells
dialog box.

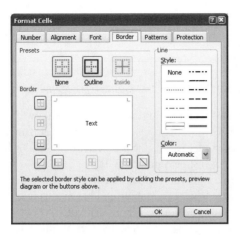

TABLE 10.4: XLBORDERSINDEX CONSTANTS THAT SPECIFY BORDERS

CONSTANT	USED TO
xlDiagonalDown	A diagonal line through the range starting at the upper-left corner and ending in the bottom-right corner.
xlDiagonalUp	A diagonal line through the range starting at the bottom-left corner and ending in the top-right corner.
xlEdgeBottom	The bottom edge of a range.
xlEdgeLeft	The left edge of a range.
xlEdgeRight	The right edge of a range.
xlEdgeTop	The top edge of a range.

To change the LineStyle property, you use one of the XLLineStyle constants. Listing 10.5 shows an example that demonstrates all of the various line styles.

LISTING 10.5: THE VARIOUS PROPERTIES ASSOCIATED WITH THE BORDER OBJECT

```
Sub BorderLineStyles()
    Dim rg As Range

    Set rg = ThisWorkbook.Worksheets("Borders"). _
        Range("LineStyleListStart").Offset(1, 0)

    Do Until IsEmpty(rg)
        rg.Offset(0, 2).Borders(xlEdgeBottom).LineStyle = _
            rg.Offset(0, 1).Value
```

```
        Set rg = rg.Offset(1, 0)
    Loop

    Set rg = Nothing
End Sub
```

You've seen a number of examples in this chapter that follow this pattern, so there is not a whole lot to talk about here. This procedure operates on a worksheet named Borders. In particular it is looking for a range named LineStyleListStart, which I have defined as cell A12 in Figure 10.8 below. The output of BorderLineStyles is shown in Figure 10.8.

It just dawned on me that by looping though a range like this to demonstrate all of the various choices available for the properties you've been looking at, I haven't made it very clear how you use the defined constants. I wouldn't want to lead you to believe that you have to get the value of the constant before using it. So, to make it clear, Listing 10.6 demonstrates an alternate way to write Listing 10.5.

LISTING 10.6: AN ALTERNATIVE APPROACH TO LISTING 10.5

```
Sub BorderLineSytlesII()
    Dim rg As Range

    Set rg = ThisWorkbook.Worksheets("Borders"). _
        Range("LineStyleListStart")

    rg.Offset(1, 2).Borders(xlEdgeBottom).LineStyle = xlContinuous
    rg.Offset(2, 2).Borders(xlEdgeBottom).LineStyle = xlDash
    rg.Offset(3, 2).Borders(xlEdgeBottom).LineStyle = xlDashDot
    rg.Offset(4, 2).Borders(xlEdgeBottom).LineStyle = xlDashDotDot
    rg.Offset(5, 2).Borders(xlEdgeBottom).LineStyle = xlDot
    rg.Offset(6, 2).Borders(xlEdgeBottom).LineStyle = xlDouble
    rg.Offset(7, 2).Borders(xlEdgeBottom).LineStyle = xlLineStyleNone
    rg.Offset(8, 2).Borders(xlEdgeBottom).LineStyle = xlSlantDashDot

    Set rg = Nothing
End Sub
```

Hopefully if I lost you by using the values of the constants rather than specifying the names of each constant in the examples in this chapter, it is all clear now.

As I mentioned at the beginning of this section, the Range object also has a method associated with it called BordersAround; you can use it to create a border around a range.

```
SomeRangeObject.BordersAround [LineStyle], [Weight], _
    [ColorIndex], [Color]
```

FIGURE 10.8

A visual representation of the XLLineStyle constants

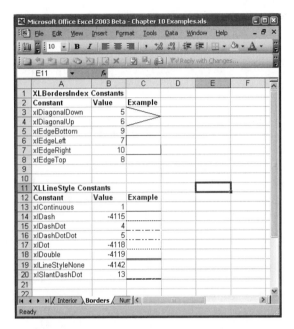

The parameters of the BordersAround method are described in the following list.

LineStyle The line style for the border. You can either use the LineStyle parameter or the Weight parameter, not both. Choose from one of the XLLineStyle constants shown in Figure 10.8.

Weight The weight, or thickness of the border. You can either use the LineStyle parameter or the Weight parameter, not both. Choose from one of the XLBorderWeight constants: xlHairline, xlMedium, xlThick, or xlThin (default).

ColorIndex The color of the border using an index that indicates which of the color palette's colors to use. If you supply the ColorIndex, don't supply the Color parameter.

Color The color of the border using a RGB value. If you supply the Color, don't supply the ColorIndex parameter.

Formatting Those Figures

Excel is all about numbers, so it comes as no surprise that you can format a number in Excel in about a million different ways. Well, maybe not a million, but you can get pretty creative. Believe it or not, though, you only need to use one property of the Range object to have complete control of the various ways you can format a number. That property is the NumberFormat property. Can you guess which tab of the Format Cells dialog box provides functionality similar to the NumberFormat property? The answer is shown in Figure 10.9.

FIGURE 10.9
Use the Number-
Format property to
format a range much
as you would using
the Number tab
of the Format
Cells dialog box.

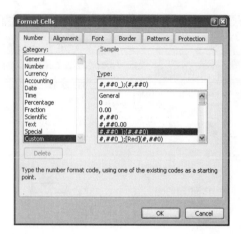

If you understand how to create a custom format code in Excel, you won't have a problem transferring your knowledge here. You can simply assign the format code to the NumberFormat property to achieve the same result programmatically. A basic understanding of number format codes is definitely in order before you use the NumberFormat property. Number format codes are composed of a combination of special characters. Table 10.5 lists the most commonly used characters.

TABLE 10.5: SPECIAL CHARACTERS FOR CREATING NUMBER FORMAT CODES

CHARACTER	USE
#	A placeholder for significant digits only—doesn't display insignificant zeroes.
0	A placeholder for all digits. If a number doesn't have enough significant digits to fill the placeholder, a zero is displayed.
?	A placeholder that adds space for, but doesn't display, insignificant digits. You use this to line up decimal points when you have a column of numbers that deal with differing numbers of significant digits.
. (decimal point)	Placeholder used to indicate how many digits should be displayed before and after the decimal point.
, (comma)	Placeholder used to indicate whether the thousands separator should be displayed or not. Also used to scale numbers (without changing the fundamental value of the underlying number).
_ (underscore)	Used to create space in a number format. For example, if you format negative numbers in parentheses you need to add the space equal to the width of the closing parenthesis to positive numbers in order to have the numbers line up.

Table 10.5 is not an exhaustive list; rather it contains enough to get you on your way. I'd encourage you to look in Excel's help files for more information regarding number format codes because they afford a ton of flexibility.

FIGURE 10.10

Number format code
examples

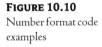

	A	B	C	D	E
1	**Number Format Code Examples**				
2	**The actual number in all cells is 1234.4321.**				
3					
4	**Format Code**	**Positive Number**	**Negative Number**	**Zero**	
5	0	1234	-1234	0	
6	#,##0	1,234	-1,234	0	
7	#,##0_);(#,##0)	1,234	(1,234)	0	
8	#,##0_);[Red](#,##0)	1,234	(1,234)	0	
9	#,##0_);[Red](#,##0); " - "	1,234	(1,234)	-	
10	???.???	1234.432	-1234.432	.	
11	#,##0.00_);(#,##0.00)	1,234.43	(1,234.43)	0.00	
12	#,	1	-1		
13					
14					

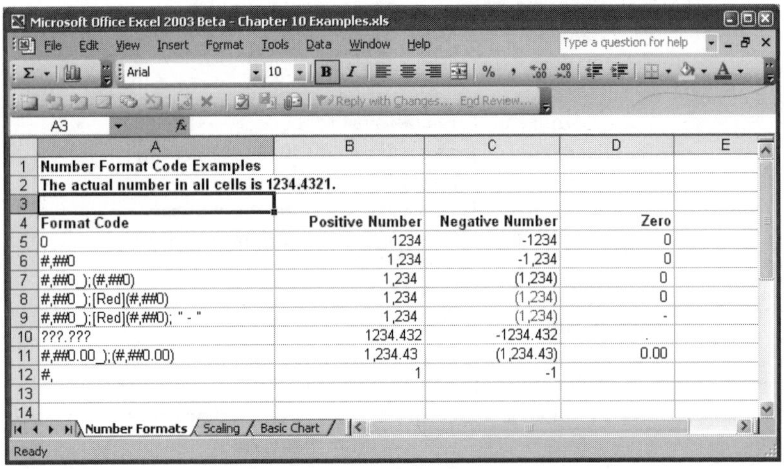

NOTE   *Check out the Excel help topic "Create or delete a custom number format" for more information regarding custom number format codes.*

On more than one occasion, I've seen people go through an obscene amount of effort to display data a certain way that could have been easily achieved using a custom number format.

A format code can have up to four sections each separated by a semicolon (;): the first section specifies how positive numbers are formatted; the second specifies how negative numbers are formatted; the third specifies how zero is formatted; and the last details how nonnumeric values should be formatted. Figure 10.10 shows some examples of various format codes.

In order to experiment with format codes, why not put together a little procedure that attempts to apply a number format code to a range of numbers as you enter various format codes? Check out Listing 10.7. If you're going to try it out, you need to enter the code into the module associated with a Worksheet (so that you can catch the Worksheet Change event). Also, the worksheet should have two named ranges. "FormatCode" is the cell containing the number format code that you want to apply to the range named 'TestFormatCode'. Figure 10.11 depicts the worksheet I used for this example.

LISTING 10.7: EXPERIMENTING WITH FORMAT CODES

```
Private Sub Worksheet_Change(ByVal Target As Range)
    If Target.Address = Me.Range("FormatCode").Address Then
        ApplyFormatCode
    End If
End Sub


Private Sub ApplyFormatCode()
    ' if we attempt to apply an invalid
```

```
                    ' number format code an error will
                    ' occur - we need to catch it
                    On Error GoTo ErrHandler

                    ' clear any prior invalid code message
                    Me.Range("FormatCode").Offset(0, 1).Value = ""
                    ' attempt to apply the format code
                    Me.Range("TestFormatCode").NumberFormat = _
                        Me.Range("FormatCode").Value
                    Exit Sub

                ErrHandler:
                    ' oops - invalid format code
                    ' set the format to General
                    Me.Range("TestFormatCode").NumberFormat = "General"
                    ' let the user know what happened
                    Me.Range("FormatCode").Offset(0, 1).Value = "Invalid Format Code!"
                End Sub
```

TIP   *Rather than struggle through creating a complex format code from scratch, see if you can start with one of the pre-defined codes defined on the Number tab of the Format Cells dialog box. Once you select one of the predefined number formats, you can switch to the Custom category and the format code of the number format you selected will be displayed in the Type text box. You can copy the format code displayed into your code or use it as the basis for your more complex format code.*

FIGURE 10.11

Testing number format codes using the ApplyFormatCode procedure

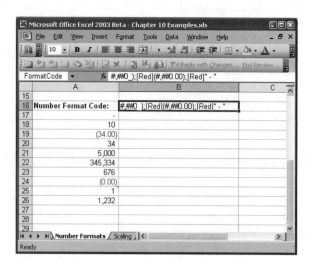

Save Tons of Time When Scaling Worksheets

How many worksheets have you seen or created that multiplied each value by .001 or divided by 1000 to scale a worksheet by 1000? There is a much, much better way to do this. Scaling cell values by modifying the actual value of the cell in this manner is not a good idea. Although it solves the presentation aspect by showing numbers in thousands, it creates other problems. One of the biggest is that any dependent ranges need to know how the worksheet was scaled and act accordingly. In a large, complex model this can get messy really fast. Another problem is that in some instances, you may want to see the real, unscaled value. For example, if you're viewing an income statement for a large division in a company, scaling the numbers makes sense. On the other hand, the manager of a single cost center or department may be managing to the dollar (or hundreds of dollars) and is interested in seeing the unscaled numbers. The process of using formulas to scale values doesn't lend itself to switching back and forth very easily.

The answer, of course, is to leave the underlying values alone and scale numbers for presentation purposes using number formats. That's right, you can scale numbers using number formats. Take a look back at Figure 10.10 row 12. The underlying value is 1,234, but the value displayed is 1.

You can easily scale worksheets on the fly if you know ahead of time the range that contains the values to be scaled. For example, consider the worksheet shown in Figure 10.12.

It is a piece of cake to provide scaling capability to this report. Notice that the selected range is named ScaleRange. All you need to do is create a procedure that sets a reference to the ScaleRange and sets its number format appropriately.

FIGURE 10.12
A simple income statement report

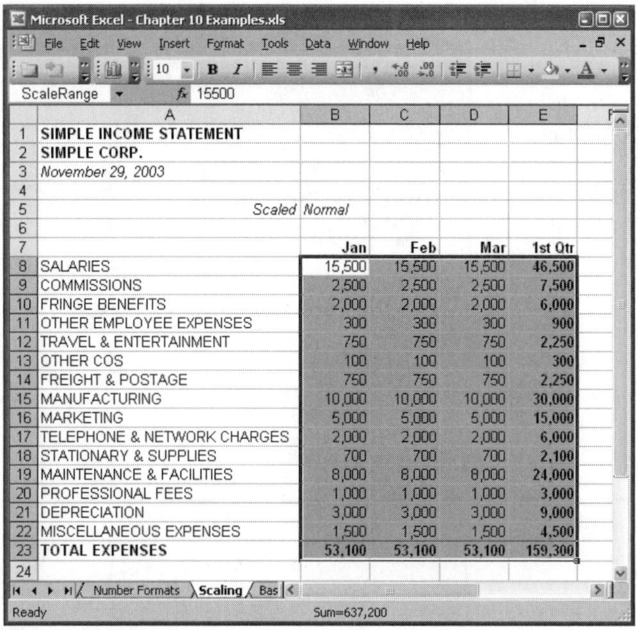

	A	B	C	D	E
1	**SIMPLE INCOME STATEMENT**				
2	**SIMPLE CORP.**				
3	*November 29, 2003*				
4					
5	*Scaled*	*Normal*			
6					
7		**Jan**	**Feb**	**Mar**	**1st Qtr**
8	SALARIES	15,500	15,500	15,500	**46,500**
9	COMMISSIONS	2,500	2,500	2,500	**7,500**
10	FRINGE BENEFITS	2,000	2,000	2,000	**6,000**
11	OTHER EMPLOYEE EXPENSES	300	300	300	**900**
12	TRAVEL & ENTERTAINMENT	750	750	750	**2,250**
13	OTHER COS	100	100	100	**300**
14	FREIGHT & POSTAGE	750	750	750	**2,250**
15	MANUFACTURING	10,000	10,000	10,000	**30,000**
16	MARKETING	5,000	5,000	5,000	**15,000**
17	TELEPHONE & NETWORK CHARGES	2,000	2,000	2,000	**6,000**
18	STATIONARY & SUPPLIES	700	700	700	**2,100**
19	MAINTENANCE & FACILITIES	8,000	8,000	8,000	**24,000**
20	PROFESSIONAL FEES	1,000	1,000	1,000	**3,000**
21	DEPRECIATION	3,000	3,000	3,000	**9,000**
22	MISCELLANEOUS EXPENSES	1,500	1,500	1,500	**4,500**
23	**TOTAL EXPENSES**	**53,100**	**53,100**	**53,100**	**159,300**
24					

LISTING 10.8: PROVIDING DYNAMIC SCALING TO YOUR WORKSHEETS

```
Private Sub Worksheet_Change(ByVal Target As Range)
    If Target.Address = Me.Range("ScaleFactor").Address Then
        ScaleData
    End If
End Sub

Private Sub ScaleData()
    If Me.Range("ScaleFactor").Value = "Normal" Then
        Me.Range("ScaleRange").NumberFormat = "#,##0"
    Else
        Me.Range("ScaleRange").NumberFormat = "#,"
    End If
End Sub
```

How easy is that? Just place this code in the worksheet's code module and set up two named ranges. ScaleRange is the range containing the data to be scaled while ScaleFactor is the range that specifies how to scale it. For this example, I just applied a data validation list on the ScaleFactor cell to provide a drop-down list with the scaling options. As Figure 10.13 demonstrates, this is just a simple example of how to do it. Apply your imagination and I bet you can come up with some excellent ideas that are easy to implement.

FIGURE 10.13

From the user's perspective, toggling back and forth is as simple as choosing from a drop-down list.

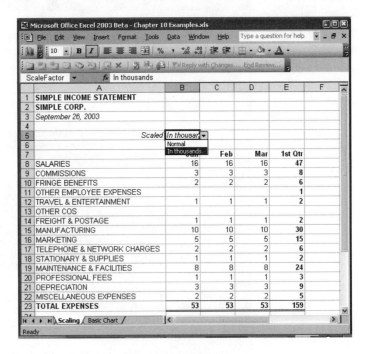

Chart Manipulation

Usually any programmatic manipulation with a chart is relatively minor. Your needs may be totally different than anything I've ever done, but when I have had applications that use charts in the past, usually the charts are precreated and then displayed or hidden as needed. You can manage which data is displayed in a chart by having a static chart source range and then programmatically managing which data appears in the chart source range. In this way, you can avoid all of the details of having to create a chart on the fly.

Why do you want to avoid creating charts on the fly? Although it is easy to create a simple chart on the fly, it is difficult to create a *nice* chart on the fly. If you've ever had to create a series of presentation quality charts, think about how many revisions you went through before you finally had a chart that looked good. The fact is, because charts are such a visual medium, you can't really go about developing the code to create a chart without first developing the chart manually to make sure you're happy with the end product. Because you have to do this anyway and because it's such a trivial task to modify many aspects of the chart once it is created, I think you'll find that usually your chart-related programming tasks will be involved with manipulating an existing chart.

A lot of chart-related objects exist. One of the first orders of business is to link these various chart objects to the actual chart elements that they represent. That is 90 percent of the battle. To do this, begin by studying a picture of a chart like the one in Figure 10.14.

As long as you know the "official" names of all of the elements that make up a chart, finding the VBA counterpart to the chart element is pretty easy. In most instances, the VBA object is named the same thing with the spaces removed (i.e., Plot Area becomes PlotArea). You can see for yourself by taking a look at the chart object model shown in Figure 10.15.

FIGURE 10.14

Elements of a chart

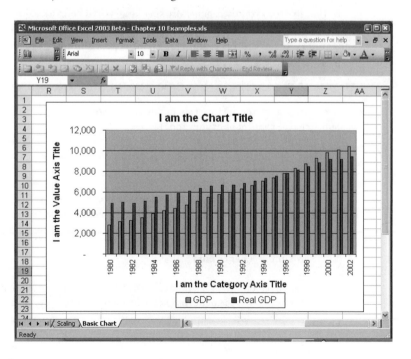

FIGURE 10.15
The chart object model

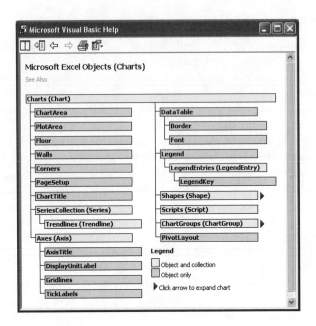

Creating a Chart from Scratch

Now that I've told you that, generally speaking, you'll be working with existing charts, it would probably be a good training exercise to create a chart from scratch. In fact, Listing 10.9 creates the chart shown in Figure 10.14 programmatically, except with more appropriate titles (chart and axis titles).

LISTING 10.9: CREATING A NEW CHART USING THE CHARTWIZARD METHOD

```
' creates a chart using the ChartWizard Method
Sub CreateExampleChartVersionI()
    Dim ws As Worksheet
    Dim rgChartData As Range
    Dim chrt As Chart

    Set ws = ThisWorkbook.Worksheets("Basic Chart")
    Set rgChartData = ws.Range("B1").CurrentRegion

    ' create a new empty chart
    Set chrt = Charts.Add

    ' embed chart in worksheet - this creates a new object
    Set chrt = chrt.Location(xlLocationAsObject, ws.Name)
```

```
    With chrt
        ' use chart wizard to populate/format empty chart
        .ChartWizard _
            Source:=rgChartData, _
            Gallery:=xlColumn, _
            Format:=1, _
            PlotBy:=xlColumns, _
            CategoryLabels:=1, _
            SeriesLabels:=1, _
            HasLegend:=True, _
            Title:="Gross Domestic Product Version I", _
            CategoryTitle:="Year", _
            ValueTitle:="GDP in billions of $"
    End With

    Set chrt = Nothing
    Set rgChartData = Nothing
    Set ws = Nothing
End Sub
```

You probably already know this, but a chart can assume two forms: it can be created as a chart sheet or it can be embedded within a worksheet. One thing that is kind of odd regarding the process of creating a chart is that you don't have any control over what kind of chart is created when you use Charts.Add. This statement creates an empty chart sheet. This is fine and dandy if you want a chart sheet, but what if you want to embed it into a worksheet? That is what the Location method is for.

```
YourChartObject.Location([Where], [Name])
```

The Where parameter can be either xlLocationNewSheet (creates a chart sheet), xlLocationAsObject (embeds in a worksheet), or xlLocationAutomatic. The Name parameter is the name of the new chart sheet if you use xlLocationNewSheet. If you use xlLocationAsObject, the Name parameter should be the name of the worksheet in which you want to embed the chart. Another somewhat peculiar aspect of creating a chart is that Location creates a new Chart object from a programmatic perspective. If you are using a Chart object variable to refer to a chart, you need to reset it when you use Location. That's the reason for the following statement in the CreateExampleChartVersionI procedure.

```
' embed chart in worksheet - this creates a new object
Set chrt = chrt.Location(xlLocationAsObject, ws.Name)
```

Now that you have the chart where you want it, it is time to employ the ChartWizard method to give the chart some personality. As you can see in this example, the ChartWizard method has a lot of parameters and you'll probably use most of them. Note, however, that all of the parameters are optional.

```
YourChartObject.ChartWizard [Source], [Gallery], [Format], _
    [PlotBy], [CategoryLabels], [SeriesLabels], [HasLegend], _
    [Title], [CategoryTitle], [ValueTitle], [ExtraTitle]
```

The parameters of the ChartWizard method are detailed in the following list.

Source   This is an optional parameter that represents the range that contains the source data for the chart.

Gallery   Gallery is the type of chart to create. Choose from xlArea, xlBar, xlColumn, xlLine, xlPie, xlRadar, xlXYScatter, xlCombination, xl3DArea, xl3DBar, xl3DColumn, xl3DLine, xl3DPie, xl3DSurface, xlDoughnut, or xlDefaultAutoFormat.

Format   The option number for the type of chart you specified using Gallery. This can be a number from 1 through 10 depending on the type of chart.

PlotBy   Use xlRows or xlColumns to specify how the data is oriented.

CategoryLabels   Use this parameter to indicate the number of rows or columns in the source data range that consist of category labels.

SeriesLabels   Use this parameter to indicate the number of rows of columns in the source data range that contain series labels.

HasLegend   HasLegend should be true to include a legend, false to exclude it.

Title   The title of the chart can be specified with this parameter.

CategoryTitle   The category axis title.

ValueTitle   The value axis title.

ExtraTitle   The series title for 3-D charts or the second value axis title for 2-D charts.

Figure 10.16 shows an example of a chart created using the ChartWizard method. This chart was generated using the CreateExampleChartVersion1 procedure from Listing 10.9.

FIGURE 10.16
This is the chart created by Listing 10.9.

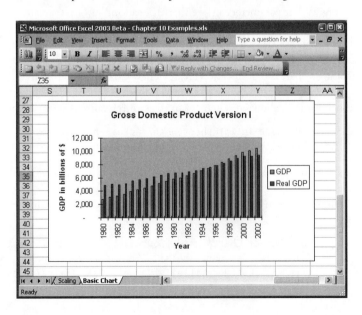

You don't necessarily need to use the ChartWizard method to create your chart. Well, technically the ChartWizard doesn't create the chart, but it certainly does all of the heavy lifting. Another way to achieve the same result is to do it yourself using other properties and methods of the Chart object. Take a look at Listing 10.10.

LISTING 10.10: CREATING A CHART USING THE CHART OBJECT

```vba
' creates a chart using basic Chart properties and methods
Sub CreateExampleChartVersionII()
    Dim ws As Worksheet
    Dim rgChartData As Range
    Dim chrt As Chart

    Set ws = ThisWorkbook.Worksheets("Basic Chart")
    Set rgChartData = ws.Range("B1").CurrentRegion

    ' create a new empty chart
    Set chrt = Charts.Add

    ' embed chart in worksheet-this creates a new object
    Set chrt = chrt.Location(xlLocationAsObject, ws.Name)

    With chrt

        .SetSourceData rgChartData, xlColumns
        .HasTitle = True
        .ChartTitle.Caption = "Gross Domestic Product Version II"
        .ChartType = xlColumnClustered

        With .Axes(xlCategory)
            .HasTitle = True
            .AxisTitle.Caption = "Year"
        End With

        With .Axes(xlValue)
            .HasTitle = True
            .AxisTitle.Caption = "GDP in billions of $"
        End With

    End With

    Set chrt = Nothing
    Set rgChartData = Nothing
    Set ws = Nothing
End Sub
```

As you can see in Figure 10.17, this listing produces the same result as Listing 10.9. Personally, I prefer this listing over the ChartWizard method. You have more flexibility doing it manually as we do here, and I think it's easier to read and understand.

FIGURE 10.17
An exact match. This is the chart produced by Listing 10.10.

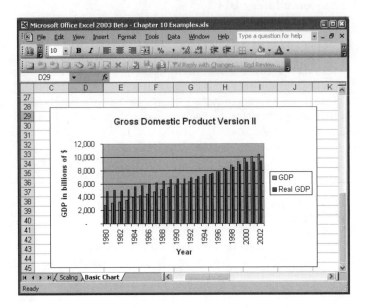

Chart Hunting

As you know, a chart can take up residence in two locations: as a chart sheet in the workbook, or as an embedded chart on a worksheet. Setting a reference to an existing chart varies according to what kind of location the chart lives in. For chart sheets, you can refer to them almost like a worksheet as the following code snippet demonstrates.

```
Dim chrt1 As Chart
Dim chrt2 As Chart

' set a reference to the chart sheet named Chart4
Set chrt1 = ThisWorkbook.Charts("Chart4")

' set a reference to the 2nd chart sheet in the wb
Set chrt2 = ThisWorkbook.Charts(2)
```

If your chart is embedded in a worksheet, however, you need to go through the ChartObjects collection, which is a property of the Worksheet object that contains the embedded chart. An example of this method is shown in the following snippet.

```
Dim chrt1 As Chart
Dim chrt2 As Chart
```

```
Dim ws As Worksheet

Set ws = ThisWorkbook.Worksheets(1)

' set a reference to the embedded chart named Chart4
Set chrt1 = ws.ChartObjects("Chart4").Chart

' set a reference to the 2nd embedded chart
Set chrt2 = ws.ChartObjects(2).Chart
```

Notice that to get to the actual chart object you need to locate a specific ChartObject first. You can think of a ChartObject as a special object that exists merely to contain a chart on a worksheet. Much like a flea needs a dog, a Chart needs a ChartObject to reside on a worksheet.

You can apply all of the techniques you learned about looking for specific worksheets in a workbook to looking for chart sheets. Looking for embedded charts is another story due to two minor complications. First, it isn't practical to know the index order of the chart objects on a worksheet. If you only have one chart on a worksheet, you're fine (but who's to say that another chart doesn't get added unbeknownst to you?). Second, unless you named the chart when you created it, you can't refer to it by name.

What to do? Simple, create a procedure that returns a chart based on some identifying characteristic. For example, you could retrieve charts according to the chart title, one of the axis titles, the source data range, or any of the other identifying characteristics. Listing 10.11 presents an example of a procedure that searches for and returns a chart based on a chart title.

LISTING 10.11: SEACHING FOR CHARTS USING THE CHART TITLE

```
' searches charts on a worksheet by chart title
Function GetChartByCaption(ws As Worksheet, sCaption As String) _
    As Chart

    Dim chtObj As ChartObject
    Dim cht As Chart
    Dim sTitle As String

    Set cht = Nothing

    ' loop through all chart objects on the ws
    For Each chtObj In ws.ChartObjects

        ' make sure current chart object chart has a title
        If chtObj.Chart.HasTitle Then

            sTitle = chtObj.Chart.ChartTitle.Caption

            ' is this title a match?
            If StrComp(sTitle, sCaption, vbTextCompare) = 0 Then
```

```
                        ' bingo
                        Set cht = chtObj.Chart
                        Exit For
                    End If

                End If

            Next

            Set GetChartByCaption = cht
            Set cht = Nothing
            Set chtObj = Nothing

    End Function

    Sub TestGetChartByCaption()
        Dim cht As Chart
        Dim ws As Worksheet

        Set ws = ThisWorkbook.Worksheets("Basic Chart")
        Set cht = GetChartByCaption(ws, "I am the Chart Title")

        If Not cht Is Nothing Then
            MsgBox "Found chart"
        Else
            MsgBox "Sorry - chart not found"
        End If

        Set ws = Nothing
        Set cht = Nothing
    End Sub
```

This function works by looping through all of the ChartObjects and their associated charts on the specified worksheet. For each chart, it checks to make sure the chart has a title, and if it does, the function checks the title for a match. The TestGetChartByCaption procedure provides an example of how you could use the GetChartByCaption function. Basically, all you need to do is make sure that a chart was found by comparing the result to Nothing.

Once you've found a chart to manipulate, the actual manipulation is quite easy now that you're familiar with what I've covered earlier in the chapter regarding the use of colors, the Font object, the Interior object, and the Border object. Listing 10.12 provides a basic example of some chart formatting.

After looking over this listing, I am quite confident that you'll recognize the chart objects and the chart elements to which they apply as shown in Figure 10.14. Also, notice how many of the chart objects, being visual in nature, use the various objects that I covered earlier in the chapter.

LISTING 10.12: FORMATTING A BASIC CHART

```vba
Sub FormattingCharts()
    Dim cht As Chart
    Dim ws As Worksheet
    Dim ax As Axis

    Set ws = ThisWorkbook.Worksheets("Basic Chart")
    Set cht = GetChartByCaption(ws, "GDP")

    If Not cht Is Nothing Then

        ' format category axis
        Set ax = cht.Axes(xlCategory)
        With ax
            .AxisTitle.Font.Size = 12
            .AxisTitle.Font.Color = vbRed
        End With

        ' format value axis
        Set ax = cht.Axes(xlValue)
        With ax
            .HasMinorGridlines = True
            .MinorGridlines.Border.LineStyle = xlDashDot
        End With

        ' format plot area
        With cht.PlotArea
            .Border.LineStyle = xlDash
            .Border.Color = vbRed
            .Interior.Color = vbWhite
            .Width = cht.PlotArea.Width + 10
            .Height = cht.PlotArea.Height + 10
        End With

        ' format misc other
        cht.ChartArea.Interior.Color = vbWhite
        cht.Legend.Position = xlLegendPositionBottom
    End If

    Set ax = Nothing
    Set cht = Nothing
    Set ws = Nothing
End Sub
```

Although all of this should appear relatively straightforward, I hope that you don't have to do much chart manipulation via code for the reasons given earlier. Creating presentation-quality charts requires an iterative design approach that can only be done manually (at least the first time). The approach is to design a nice chart manually that you then use as a template when you need to, reserving any code manipulation for relatively minor changes such as changing titles, colors, or perhaps changing the source data range.

Summary

It's easy to get so involved polishing your application from a programmatic standpoint that you neglect the part most noticeable to users—the look. Though it may seem trivial, the formatting of your various worksheets can go a long way toward influencing how your hard work is perceived by your end users. Therefore, it pays to make sure you give this area some attention and don't downplay these issues.

One way that you can spice up a worksheet is by applying color to its various components. You can color fonts, cell interiors, gridlines, drawing objects, and all of the visual chart-related objects and borders, among other things. Any object that has a Color property also contains a ColorIndex property. The difference is that you can specify Color using an RGB value, whereas you specify ColorIndex using an index that refers to a color occupying the workbook's color palette.

Other ways that you can dress up a worksheet include using a pleasing mix of fonts (Font.Name), font sizes (Font.Size), interior patterns (Interior.Pattern), and borders. To apply these effects, use the appropriate object and property applied to a given Range object. Oh, and don't forget about those number formats. You can set them using the NumberFormat property of the Range object.

Regarding charts, although you can create them on the fly, it is best to create charts during the development process and then use them as templates, so to speak. This is because creating visually pleasing charts requires an iterative design process that requires your visual senses—a task that can't be replaced by a computer.

The conclusion of this chapter marks the end of the Excel object model section of this book. The next section covers some more advanced topics including interacting with external programs, developing class modules, adding user personalization, and some Excel development best practices. I'll kick this section off with a chapter that teaches you how to create and use your own classes.

Part 3

Advanced Excel Programming Techniques

Chapter 11

Developing Class Modules

"Uh-oh. Class modules? That sounds difficult. I don't need no stinkin' class modules—I'm creating wonderful applications without them. What do I need class modules for?"

Do you hear that voice? Don't listen to it. Although it's true that developing and then using class modules requires you to think about programming in a different manner, that doesn't mean it is more difficult. Although you can create wonderful applications without using class modules, class modules bring enough benefits to the table to warrant their use.

The objective of this chapter is threefold. First, I want you to understand exactly what class modules are. Second, I want you to recognize the benefits of using class modules. Finally, you'll learn the mechanics of creating your own objects using class modules.

Class Modules Are for Creating Objects

I dreamed I was on Jeopardy the other night playing against Bill Gates and Scott McNealy (CEO of Sun Microsystems and a bitter, relentless Microsoft basher). I managed to take control of the game after Scott insulted Bill's mother and a Jerry Springer–style brawl ensued.

I said, "I'll take programming paradigms for $1,000,000, Alex."

"These modules are used for creating your own objects in VBA," replied Alex.

Da, da, da, da, da, da, daaa (hum the Jeapoardy theme here).

For a million bucks I replied, "What are class modules?"

I was feeling pretty good about myself until Bill looked at me and chuckled, "My accountants consider a million bucks a rounding error."

Wouldn't it be nice if it were just that simple? Well, it is that simple, I suppose, if you know what objects are and you just want to know what class modules are for. One thing that my five-year-old boy has taught me is that answers merely beget more questions. What are objects? That's the real question. It is quickly followed by these: How are objects any different from the collection of procedures I've tied together in regular procedures throughout this book? Is this what they mean by object-oriented programming?

Throughout the book, you've been using objects that are intrinsic to Microsoft Excel. You've used the Application, Workbook, Worksheet, Range, and other objects with nary a thought to the mindset regarding the underlying paradigm. For the most part, didn't it just feel natural to program in this manner and use these objects? Can you imagine any other way to think about how you'd program

Microsoft Excel? If a Worksheet object didn't exist, how would you manipulate a worksheet? Thank goodness you, as an Excel developer, don't have to learn C, Assembly language, or some other lower-level language that doesn't have as much correlation between how you think about a given object and how you implement those thoughts programmatically.

The point is that, without realizing it, you're already thinking in terms of objects. So far, you've been consumers of objects that other programmers have thoughtfully created for you to shield you from the underlying complexity of dealing with the inner workings of Excel. Wouldn't it be nice to create your own objects that allow this same level of convenience regarding the specifics of your application? You can do it using class modules.

A Linguistic Foundation

Before I get too far, I should probably synchronize our vocabulary a bit. Until now, I've been a little general regarding some of the terms used to describe object-oriented programming concepts. In order to discuss object-oriented programming concepts in any detail, I need to be a little more precise with my vocabulary. The following list represents the most common object-oriented terms that I'll use in this chapter and throughout the rest of the book.

Class   A class is the programmatic definition of an object. A class doesn't become an object until a client application or process instantiates the class. The common metaphor is to think of a class as a cookie cutter and an object as a cookie.

Class module   A class module is your canvas, so to speak. It's a special code module in the development environment that is used solely to define classes.

Instantiate   To instantiate an object is to give it life. Using the cookie cutter metaphor, a cookie is instantiated when you use the cookie cutter to create the cookie by separating it from the mass of cookie dough. There are a few ways that you can instantiate an object. Generally objects are instantiated using the New keyword. I'll show you the specifics of instantiation later in this chapter.

Interface   An interface is the public face of a class. It represents the parts of the class that can be accessed by external processes.

Member   A member refers to either a method or a property. The members of a class are the combination of all of the properties and methods of the class.

Method   A method is an action that can be performed on or with an object.

Object   To be precise, an object represents a specific instantiation of a class. However, many times the term *object* is used in conversation (and in writing) to refer to what is technically a class.

Object-Oriented Programming   This is a programming paradigm in which a program is developed by creating numerous objects that work together to provide the desired functionality. An object comprises the data structures and algorithms necessary for the object to exhibit properties and methods that model the natural characteristics and actions of the object. VBA lacks a few capabilities that prevent it from being classified as a true object-oriented programming language.

Nonetheless, it has enough object-oriented features to allow you to think in terms of objects and realize much of the value of object-oriented programming.

Property   A property is a characteristic of an object such as color, height, or name.

What's the Big Deal? Why Use Objects?

It took me a long time to appreciate the power that classes can provide. I believe part of the reason that it takes beginning programmers a long time to fully comprehend the benefits of creating your own classes is that until you are knee-deep in a runaway development effort, it's hard to relate to the problems that using classes can solve. The simple fact is that when you're learning, you tend to work with smaller, easier-to-understand programming tasks. If you shoot yourself in the foot developing one of these applications, no big deal—you can recode it in a few hours. In larger development efforts, you don't have this luxury. A poorly implemented program may take days or weeks to correct.

In my experience, it's a lot easier to appreciate problems and their solutions when you have first-hand experience with the problem. Thus, until I experienced the problems that other programmers had tried to warn me about, I didn't care much about using classes. Hopefully you won't follow my footsteps; instead, I hope you'll start experimenting with classes now.

Classes Unite

One of the benefits of developing classes is that they serve as a formal way to unite data and behavior associated with a given object. Although you can informally try and imitate the same kind of thing using a standard module and a collection of module-level variables, subroutines, and functions, the resulting module would only be an object to you. Nothing would identify the "fake" object to VBA or other programmers as an object. It would appear as just what it is: a collection of procedures and variables with no explicit relationship.

By developing a class, you're formally declaring the collection of variables and procedures as a group of programmatic elements that are inherently related to each other and work symbiotically with one another to provide a programmatic representation of a tangible or intangible object. Wow. That was a mouthful. Sorry about that one.

By uniting a group of programmatic elements inside a class, you allow other procedures that need to use the class to create a single, addressable object. This allows procedures to work with multiple copies of the class where each copy is seen as a separate entity. This makes programming easier because you don't have to remember which module contains the procedure you're looking for. With an object, all of the appropriate properties and methods are available to you directly through the object variable.

For example, consider how hard it would be to develop Excel applications if Excel didn't have an object model. Instead of an object model, it would have a handful of modules, and each one would contain hundreds of procedures. Or maybe one module would have thousands of procedures. If you thought the Range object has a lot of properties and methods, just think about how difficult it would be to look through an Auto List Members list of hundreds of procedures to find what you're looking for. Instead of Workbook.Name and Worksheet.Name to retrieve the name associated with each object, you'd need to have special procedures such as GetWorkbookName, GetWorksheetName, GetChartName, GetRangeName, GetAddInName, GetApplicationName, GetFontName, GetPivot-TableName, and GetQueryRangeName. Well, you get the picture.

Classes Hide the Details

Another benefit of developing class modules is that they hide the details of their implementation. You don't care about hiding details because you're a Draconian, paranoid programmer (well, maybe some of you are). You care about hiding details to protect you from yourselves and your programming colleagues. When you instantiate an object from a class in a procedure (the consumer procedure or just consumer), the consumer can only see or use those object members that the class developer deems appropriate. This is a good thing because it allows you to create a layer of abstraction between the interface (the procedures that can be seen by consumers) and the implementation of the interface.

Hiding the details prevents developers from calling procedures in your class that were never meant to be used outside the class. This is great because as long as you keep the interface the same, you're free to change the implementation details without fear of breaking any dependent code in consumer procedures.

Hiding details is also helpful from a mental standpoint. Rather than re-creating a difficult process and struggling through the specifics of the necessary code, you can develop a class that hides the implementation complexities and exposes only a simpler, nicer interface for use in all future procedures that need to use the object's functionality.

Classes Enable Collaboration

In larger development efforts that require multiple developers, using classes makes collaboration easier. Developers can define the necessary interface that classes require and then split the development chores between each other along class lines, with each developer coding under the assumption of the agreed-upon interfaces. So long as they create classes that stick to the originally defined interface, it's easy to snap the classes in place as they are completed. Further, because a class is a discrete component, it's relatively easy to create test routines to test the classes individually.

Collaboration without using classes is much harder because you need to coordinate the process of merging code into standard modules or else you'll have a mish-mash of related procedures living in separate modules. Also, it's tempting for other programmers to use routines that weren't meant to be used by the original developer. If the original developer modifies the routine (not knowing that other developers are building dependencies on the routine), dependent procedures may break.

Creating a Simple Object

Ok, let's test the water by creating a simple object and then using it within a standard module. By the powers vested in me, I hereby pronounce you a banker. Umm, make that a bank programmer. I know you would prefer the banker's hours, but without the well-oiled systems that you develop, those bankers wouldn't be able to get on the links so early (banker's hours are traditionally 9:00 A.M. to 3:00 P.M.— of course, these days bankers work just as hard as anyone else).

Your goal is to create a simple Loan object. So what are some ways to describe a loan? Principal amount, interest rate, term, payment, and loan number (aka account number) are a few things that come to mind. You'll make all of these items properties.

To begin, insert a new class module in the VBE. The first order of business is to name the class. I prefer to use a name that's as close as possible to how you'd normally refer to the object. For the simple Loan object, set the name to SimpleLoan (not Loan because you'll create a more complex Loan object later in the chapter) as shown in Figure 11.1. Leave the Instancing property set to 1 - Private. This property is used to allow the ability to share a class between VBA projects using project references.

One advantage of using objects is that they have two event procedures you can attach code to: an Initialize event and a Terminate event (see Figure 11.2). For your Loan object, you'll take advantage of the Initialize event to set default values for all of the Loan's properties. To add the Initialize event procedure, select the Class object from the Object drop-down list. The VBE will automatically enter the Initialize event procedure for you. If you want to add the Terminate event procedure, you need to select Terminate from the Procedure drop-down list.

FIGURE 11.1

The beginnings of one fine Loan object

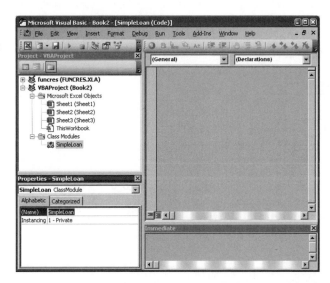

FIGURE 11.2

Class modules allow you to attach event procedures to the Initialize and Terminate events.

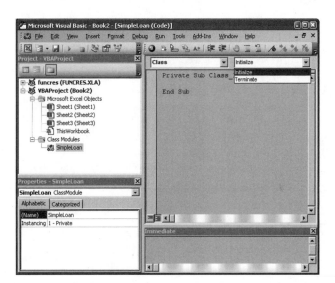

The easiest way to add properties to a class is to just declare some public variables. You can use this method for all of your properties except the Payment property. Because a loan payment is a function of the principal amount, term, and interest rate, it won't suffice to use a public variable declaration to create this property. Instead you'll need to use another method of creating a property—you need to use a Property Get procedure. This is a special kind of procedure used to create properties in class modules. You'll take a detailed look at this method later in the chapter. Listing 11.1 presents the SimpleLoan class in its entirety.

LISTING 11.1: THE SIMPLELOAN CLASS

```
Option Explicit

' Loan Properties
Public PrincipalAmount As Variant
Public InterestRate As Variant
Public LoanNumber As Variant
Public Term As Variant

Private Sub Class_Initialize()
    ' set default principal amount to 0
    PrincipalAmount = 0
    ' set default interest rate to 8% annually
    InterestRate = 0.08
    ' set loan number to 0
    LoanNumber = 0
    ' set default term to 36 months
    Term = 36
End Sub

Public Property Get Payment() As Variant
    Payment = Application.WorksheetFunction.Pmt _
        (InterestRate / 12, Term, -PrincipalAmount)
End Property
```

Are you surprised at all? I mean, that isn't much code. Granted, this is a simple class, but the way you hear some people talk, they'd have you believe that it takes a Ph.D. I know what you are thinking. I mean, I think I know what you are thinking. You still don't see how this can help you or how it's better than just throwing a simple CalculatePayment function in a procedure. Well, now that you have something to experiment with, let's see if you can't demonstrate some of the advantages.

Using Your Object

Using your own objects is a little different than using intrinsic Excel objects. With all of the Excel objects you've used, the object already existed before you used it. All you had to do was set a reference to the object using the Set keyword. When you did add a new Excel object such as a worksheet, you used the Add method of one of the various Collection objects (such as Worksheets). Collection objects provide methods for creating and adding a new object to the collection.

When you use your own object or, as you'll see later, an object from a class library other than Microsoft Excel, you need to use the New keyword to create or instantiate an object. You can instantiate an object in one of two ways.

First, you can use the New keyword in the declaration of the variable that you'll use to refer to the object. The second way is to declare the variable as you would any other variable and then, before using the variable, explicitly create the object and point the variable to it. Listing 11.2 shows an example of both methods. As you enter this listing, you'll witness another minor benefit of developing and using classes. Look at what you find in the Auto List Members dropdown list. Do you see it in Figure 11.3? That new object named SimpleLoan that looks like it is a native object in Excel?

LISTING 11.2: TWO WAYS TO USE AN OBJECT

```
Sub TestSimpleLoan()
    ' declare a loan variable and explicitly
    ' create the object that the variable
    ' will refer to.
    Dim objLoan1 As New SimpleLoan

    ' declare a loan variable
    Dim objLoan2 As SimpleLoan

    ' create the object that objLoan2
    ' will refer to.
    Set objLoan2 = New SimpleLoan

    ' demonstrate that the two
    ' loans are separate objects
    objLoan1.LoanNumber = 1
    objLoan2.LoanNumber = 2
    Debug.Print "objLoan1.LoanNumber is: " & objLoan1.LoanNumber
    Debug.Print "objLoan2.LoanNumber is: " & objLoan2.LoanNumber

    ' terminate the objects and
    ' free the memory associated with
    ' the object variables
    Set objLoan1 = Nothing
    Set objLoan2 = Nothing
End Sub
```

FIGURE 11.3
By developing and
using classes, you
automatically get
the benefit of having
your classes appear
in the Auto List
Members list.

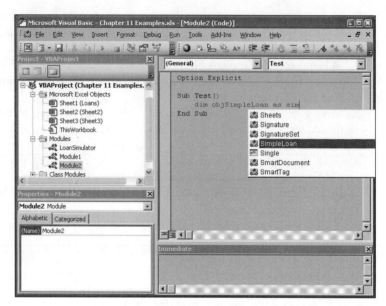

This listing produces the following output:

```
objLoan1.LoanNumber is: 1
objLoan2.LoanNumber is: 2
```

You may be tempted to use the method used for instantiating objLoan1. After all, it takes only one line of code to do this versus two lines of code for the method used with objLoan2. In many cases, absolutely nothing is wrong with this. However, it would be a good exercise for you to step through this code in Break mode and observe the behavior of each method. What you'll find is that when you use the first method, the object is not instantiated when you declare the variable with the New keyword. Instead, it's instantiated the first time the variable is used. However, the second method instantiates the object in the statement that sets the variable to refer to a newly created object.

The point to remember here is that when you use the one-line method of instantiation, it can be difficult to know when the object is instantiated because it happens implicitly the first time the object is used. The two-line method is much clearer because it makes instantiation an explicit occurrence.

I prefer to use the one-line method only in small simple procedures where the object is instantiated and terminated all in the same procedure and is not passed to other procedures as a variable. Otherwise, for debugging and mental simplification purposes, I prefer the two-line method.

A Better, Smarter Object

You get what you pay for, and creating object properties by simply declaring public variables inside a class module is a good example. It's quick and easy but doesn't give you much in return. On the other hand, you can create object properties using Property Get/Let/Set procedures. These types of procedures take a *little* more effort to set up, but they provide you with a lot more flexibility.

Property Get/Let/Set procedures give you two powerful capabilities. First, when you create an object property using Property Get/Let/Set, you can decide whether the property is read/write, read-only, or write-only by implementing one or two procedures (see Table 11.1). A Property Get procedure provides read access to a property. A Property Let/Set procedure provides write access to a property. You use Property Let when the property's data type is one of the basic data types (Integer, String, Variant, etc.) and Property Set when the underlying data type is an object (Worksheet, Range, etc.).

TABLE 11.1: IMPLEMENTING READ/WRITE COMBINATIONS WITH PROPERTIES

READ/WRITE CAPABILITY	IMPLEMENTATION
Read/Write	Property Get/Property Let
Read-only	Property Get
Write-only	Property Let

Second, when you use Property procedures, your class is aware of changes made to a property value. If you use public variables, you have no way of knowing when a consumer procedure changes a given property's value. When you use Property Let to define write-access to a property, the only way to change the property's value is to go through the Property Let procedure. This allows you to do things like perform data validation.

To demonstrate how to use Property procedures, let's create a Loan object that has the same properties as SimpleLoan but uses Property procedures rather than public variables. Go ahead and insert a new class module into your VBA project and name it Loan.

I prefer to add stubs for all of the Property procedures before adding any of the implementation details. By stub, I'm referring to the opening and closing statement of each property. Let's go ahead and add all of the stubs.

1. Select Insert ➢ Procedure from the VBE menu.

2. Enter **PrincipalAmount** in the Name text box.

3. Select Property as the Type.

4. Select Public as the Scope and click OK.

5. Repeat steps 1–4 for interest rate (InterestRate), term (Term), payment (Payment), and loan number (LoanNumber). Figure 11.4 shows a picture of the VBE after I've added the stubs for the PrincipalAmount property.

So now you have stubs for all of the properties. You need to get a little more specific regarding your specification before you go any further. Although you may consider what the loan payment will be when you're deciding on how much to borrow and for how long, ultimately the loan payment is a function of the amount you borrow, the term or length of the loan (or number of payments), and the interest rate. Therefore, it makes sense to make this a calculated amount and not an amount that you can change—it's a read-only property. As you recall, properties can be read/write, read-only, or write only. In order to make the Payment property read-only, go ahead and delete the Property Let stub for the Payment property. As an alternative, consider commenting out the Property Let stub in case you decide to add it back later. This is a good idea because it makes it clear that you're intending to implement a read-only property.

```
' this stub should be deleted or commented out
Public Property Let Payment(ByVal vNewValue As Variant)

End Property
```

After the stubs are all ready, it's time to add some private module-level variables to hold the value associated with each property. The idea behind using private class variables is that it provides a level of abstraction and ensures that all class implementation details are hidden. Enter the following code underneath the Option Explicit statement at the top of the class module (you are using Option Explicit, right?).

FIGURE 11.4

The Loan object is taking shape. Here you see the Loan object with stubs for the Initialize event and the Principal-Amount property.

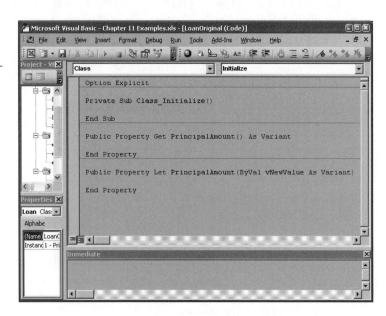

```
' private class variables to hold property values
Dim mvPrincipalAmount As Variant
Dim mvInterestRate As Variant
Dim mvLoanNumber As Variant
Dim mvTerm As Variant
```

Now you're ready to fill in the implementation details. First, let's knock out the initialization event procedure. Locate the Class_Initialize procedure and modify it so that it matches the following procedure.

```
Private Sub Class_Initialize()
    ' set default principal amount to 0
    mvPrincipalAmount = 0
    ' set default interest rate to 8% annually
    mvInterestRate = 0.08
    ' set loan number to 0
    mvLoanNumber = 0
    ' set term to 0
    mvLoanNumber = 0
End Sub
```

You may be surprised, but many times it only takes a line or two to implement each of those Property Let and Property Get procedures. Listing 11.3 shows the implementation of all of the Property procedures.

LISTING 11.3: LOAN OBJECT IMPLEMENTATION DETAILS

```
Public Property Get PrincipalAmount() As Variant
    PrincipalAmount = mvPrincipalAmount
End Property

Public Property Let PrincipalAmount(ByVal vNewValue As Variant)
    mvPrincipalAmount = vNewValue
End Property

Public Property Get InterestRate() As Variant
    InterestRate = mvInterestRate
End Property

Public Property Let InterestRate(ByVal vNewValue As Variant)
    mvInterestRate = vNewValue
End Property

Public Property Get LoanNumber() As Variant
    LoanNumber = mvLoanNumber
End Property

Public Property Let LoanNumber(ByVal vNewValue As Variant)
    mvLoanNumber = vNewValue
```

```
    End Property

    Public Property Get Term() As Variant
        Term = mvTerm
    End Property

    Public Property Let Term(ByVal vNewValue As Variant)
        mvTerm = vNewValue
    End Property

    Public Property Get Payment() As Variant
        Payment = Application.WorksheetFunction.Pmt _
            (mvInterestRate / 12, mvTerm, -mvPrincipalAmount)
    End Property
```

As you can see, using Property procedures is a little more work, but not much, considering you can now implement read/write, read-only, or write-only procedures. Plus, you can perform data validation on any incoming values before you officially accept the value by assigning it to the private module-level variable created to store the value.

An Object Showdown

Is it possible to demonstrate any compelling benefits with such a simple object? Perhaps a few test scenarios will illustrate some clear benefits. With such a simple object, it is trivial to code a "normal" set of procedures that deliver the main functionality that the Loan class delivers. To summarize, the only thing the Loan class does is remember who it is (LoanNumber), how much it is for (PrincipalAmount), what interest rate it carries (InterestRate), how long it is for (Term), and finally, what the loan payment is (Payment).

For the first scenario, you'll just loop through a list of loans and calculate payment amounts. Figure 11.5 shows the worksheet I created for this example. Notice that it contains a named range "LoanListStart" that refers to cell A1.

FIGURE 11.5

A list of loans for testing the Loan object

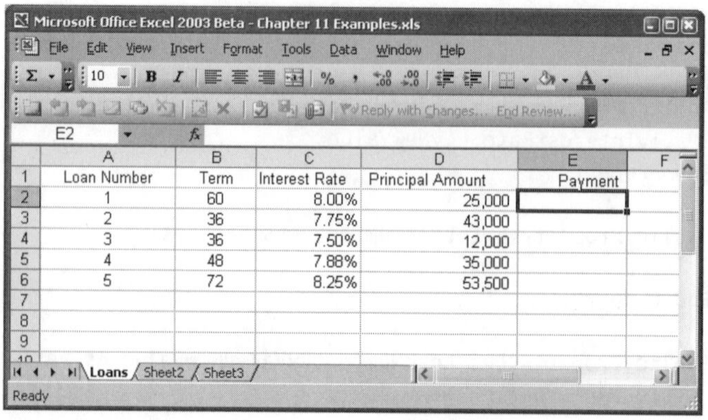

Listing 11.4 presents a procedure that loops through loan data on a worksheet and calculates the payment amount associated with each loan.

LISTING 11.4: CALCULATING THE LOAN PAYMENTS USING THE LOAN OBJECT

```
Sub Test1LoanObject()
    Dim rg As Range
    Dim objLoan As Loan

    Set rg = ThisWorkbook.Worksheets("Loans"). _
        Range("LoanListStart").Offset(1, 0)
    Set objLoan = New Loan

    Do Until IsEmpty(rg)
        With objLoan
            .Term = rg.Offset(0, 1).Value
            .InterestRate = rg.Offset(0, 2).Value
            .PrincipalAmount = rg.Offset(0, 3).Value
            rg.Offset(0, 4).Value = .Payment
        End With
        Set rg = rg.Offset(1, 0)
    Loop

    Set objLoan = Nothing
    Set rg = Nothing
End Sub
```

This listing loops through the list of loans until it comes across an empty cell. For each loan, it reads in the various loan values and assigns them to the appropriate loan property. The loan payment is calculated and written to the worksheet before moving on to the next loan.

Listing 11.5 presents a procedure that duplicates the functionality found in Listing 11.4 except that it doesn't use the Loan object. For the purposes of this example, the only functionality that you really need to replace is the Payment function.

LISTING 11.5: CALCULATING LOAN PAYMENTS WITHOUT USING THE LOAN OBJECT

```
Public Function Payment(vInterestRate As Variant, vTerm As Variant, _
    vPrincipalAmount) As Variant

    Payment = Application.WorksheetFunction.Pmt _
        (vInterestRate / 12, vTerm, vPrincipalAmount)
End Function

Sub Test1NoObject()
```

```
        Dim rg As Range
        Dim vTerm As Variant
        Dim vInterestRate As Variant
        Dim vPrincipalAmount As Variant

        Set rg = ThisWorkbook.Worksheets("Loans"). _
            Range("LoanListStart").Offset(1, 0)

        Do Until IsEmpty(rg)
            vTerm = rg.Offset(0, 1).Value
            vInterestRate = rg.Offset(0, 2).Value
            vPrincipalAmount = rg.Offset(0, 3).Value
            rg.Offset(0, 4).Value = _
                Payment(vInterestRate, vTerm, vPrincipalAmount)
            Set rg = rg.Offset(1, 0)
        Loop

        Set rg = Nothing
    End Sub
```

This listing works much the same as the previous listing, except it doesn't use the Loan object. Therefore a subtle, yet mentally significant difference exists between these two. When the Loan object is used, the variables that are attributable to a loan (such as variables representing the term and interest rate) are directly attached to the Loan object. Without a Loan object, you need to use variables that, though appropriately named, have no inherent relationship to one another. Likewise, the Payment function exists as just another function in a collection of procedures within a standard module. Further, you need to be aware of the parameters required by the Payment function. Take a minute to ponder these mental differences between the two listings.

Collecting Your Objects

One big advantage of using classes is that they lend themselves very nicely to using the Collection object. You've seen collection objects earlier in the book, such as Workbooks and Worksheets. The Collection object is an easy-to-use, generic object that you can use to contain a group of objects.

The advantage of using a collection of objects will be more apparent later on when you look at reading/writing to external data sources. For now, imagine a scenario in which you need to hold more than one Loan object in memory. By using the Collection object and classes, this is easily achieved.

Listing 11.6 demonstrates how to use the Collection object. The first procedure, TestCollection-Object, calls the CollectLoanObjects procedure to retrieve a Collection object that contains all of the loans in the list starting just below the range named LoanListStart. Then TestCollectionObject iterates through all of the loans in the Collection object and outputs the loan number and payment amount to the Immediate window.

LISTING 11.6: USING THE COLLECTION OBJECT TO SERVE AS A CONTAINER FOR MULTIPLE OBJECTS

```vba
Sub TestCollectionObject()
    Dim rg As Range
    Dim objLoans As Collection
    Dim objLoan As Loan

    Set rg = ThisWorkbook.Worksheets("Loans"). _
        Range("LoanListStart").Offset(1, 0)

    ' get the collection of loan objects
    Set objLoans = CollectLoanObjects(rg)

    Debug.Print "There are " & objLoans.Count & _
        " loans."

    ' iterate through each loan
    For Each objLoan In objLoans
        Debug.Print "Loan Number " & objLoan.LoanNumber & _
            " has a payment of " & Format(objLoan.Payment, "Currency")
    Next

    Set objLoans = Nothing
    Set objLoan = Nothing
    Set rg = Nothing
End Sub

Function CollectLoanObjects(rg As Range) As Collection
    Dim objLoan As Loan
    Dim objLoans As Collection

    Set objLoans = New Collection

    ' loop until we find an empty row
    Do Until IsEmpty(rg)
        Set objLoan = New Loan
        With objLoan
            .LoanNumber = rg.Value
            .Term = rg.Offset(0, 1).Value
            .InterestRate = rg.Offset(0, 2).Value
            .PrincipalAmount = rg.Offset(0, 3).Value
        End With

        ' add the current loan to the collection
        objLoans.Add objLoan, CStr(objLoan.LoanNumber)

        ' move to next row
```

```
        Set rg = rg.Offset(1, 0)
    Loop

    Set objLoan = Nothing
    Set CollectLoanObjects = objLoans
    Set objLoans = Nothing
End Function
```

The output of the TestCollectionObject procedure is as follows.

```
There are 5 loans.
Loan Number 1 has a payment of $506.91
Loan Number 2 has a payment of $1,342.51
Loan Number 3 has a payment of $373.27
Loan Number 4 has a payment of $852.40
Loan Number 5 has a payment of $944.57
```

The procedure of interest in this listing is CollectLoanObjects. Notice that the Collection object needs to be instantiated using the New keyword. The other statement to pay attention to is the one you use to add the current loan in the objLoan variable to the objLoans collection. This statement uses the Add method of the Collection object.

```
objCollection.Add item,[key],[before],[after]
```

The parameters of the Add method are explained in the following list.

Item   Item is required and represents the object to add to the collection.

Key   Key (optional) is a unique string that can be used to refer to the item using the key value rather than the index number of the item.

Before   Use Before to insert the new object at the position before the item given by this parameter. You can specify either an index number or a key value. You can't specify After if you specify Before.

After   Use After to insert the new object at the position after the item given by this parameter. You can specify either an index number or a key value. You can't specify Before if you specify After.

Now, you can still perform this same kind of thing without using classes. However, I think you'll agree that things start getting tricky and the result is two procedures that are much harder to read than the two presented in Listing 11.6. Listing 11.7 produces exactly the same output as Listing 11.6.

LISTING 11.7: COLLECTING LOANS THE HARD WAY

```
Sub TestCollectLoansTheHardWay()
    Dim rg As Range
    Dim vLoans() As Variant
    Dim nLoan As Integer
    Dim dPayment As Double
```

```
    Set rg = ThisWorkbook.Worksheets("Loans"). _
        Range("LoanListStart").Offset(1, 0)

    vLoans = CollectLoansTheHardWay(rg)

    Debug.Print "There are " & UBound(vLoans) + 1 & " loans."

    For nLoan = 0 To UBound(vLoans)
        dPayment = Payment(vLoans(nLoan, 2), _
            vLoans(nLoan, 1), vLoans(nLoan, 3))
        Debug.Print "Loan Number " & vLoans(nLoan, 0) & _
            " has a payment of " & Format(dPayment, "Currency")
    Next nLoan

    Set rg = Nothing
End Sub

Function CollectLoansTheHardWay(rg As Range) As Variant()
    Dim vTerm As Variant
    Dim vInterestRate As Variant
    Dim vPrincipalAmount As Variant
    Dim vLoans() As Variant
    Dim nRows As Integer
    Dim nItem As Integer

    ' figure out how many rows there are
    nRows = rg.End(xlDown).Row - rg.Row

    ' resize the array to reflect the number
    ' of rows.
    ReDim vLoans(nRows, 3)

    ' initialize array loan index
    nItem = 0

    ' ok - read in the values
    Do Until IsEmpty(rg)
        ' loan number
        vLoans(nItem, 0) = rg.Value
        ' term
        vLoans(nItem, 1) = rg.Offset(0, 1).Value
        ' interest rate
        vLoans(nItem, 2) = rg.Offset(0, 2).Value
        ' principal amount
        vLoans(nItem, 3) = rg.Offset(0, 3).Value
        Set rg = rg.Offset(1, 0)
```

```
            nItem = nItem + 1
        Loop

        CollectLoansTheHardWay = vLoans
    End Function
```

Flip back and forth between this listing and the previous listing. If I took out all of the comments, to what extent could you tell exactly what was going on in each of these listings? Trust me, as your projects get more complex, the mental simplification that using classes affords is a huge deal.

There is another significant difference between this listing and the previous listing. Listing 11.7 is bound to the display of the data in two procedures versus only one procedure in the previous listing. So if the layout of the data changes (the term and interest rate swap columns, for example), you need to fix two procedures. This issue would become a big deal in a more complicated (in other words, real-life) application. You'd basically need to review and repair any procedure that used the array of loan data. With a collection of Loan objects, the only thing you'd need to do is adjust the procedure that reads the data from the worksheet.

Of course, you could mitigate the impact of this problem using constants that map a constant name to a column number (for example, CONST INTEREST_RATE = 3). This would help, but you still wouldn't have nearly as much flexibility as you do when you're using an object.

Implementing More Accurate Properties

Using the Loan object is easy enough, but it could be easier and more precise. In order to keep it simple, you use the Insert ➤ Procedure functionality in the VBE when you create your Loan object. Although this is a convenient way to insert subroutines, functions, and properties, you may not find that the resulting property stubs meet your needs as well as you'd like.

When I review the Loan object, I am not happy about a few things. Specifically, I don't like the fact that all of the properties and parameters to the Property Let statements use the Variant data type. Consider the interest rate parameter. Interest rates are numeric values. When you use the Variant data type, what prevents a programmer from passing in a string value? If you pass a string value and then try to retrieve the value of the Payment property, a type mismatch error occurs.

Another thing that I'm not exactly thrilled about is the parameter name vNewValue used for the Property Let statements. Notice that all of Excel's inherent objects generally use parameter names that add meaning to the parameter. Your Loan object should also provide more meaningful parameter names.

You also haven't done any data validation on the incoming values. For example, maybe your bank has minimum and maximum interest rates, minimum and maximum loan limits, or has set loan terms such as 24, 36, 48, 60, and 72 months. When invalid values are found, the class should raise an error informing the consumer procedure that an invalid value was entered.

Listing 11.8 implements all of these changes in the Loan object. Along the way, you'll stumble across two new capabilities of VBA: enumerations and raising errors.

```vba
Option Explicit

' private class variables to hold property values
Dim mcPrincipalAmount As Currency
Dim mdInterestRate As Double
Dim mlLoanNumber As Long
Dim mnTerm As Integer

' create an enumeration of loan terms
' set each value equal to the term in months
Enum lnLoanTerm
    ln2Years = 24
    ln3Years = 36
    ln4Years = 48
    ln5Years = 60
    ln6Years = 70
End Enum

' Lending limits
Private Const MIN_LOAN_AMT = 5000
Private Const MAX_LOAN_AMT = 75000

' Interest rate limits
Private Const MIN_INTEREST_RATE = 0.04
Private Const MAX_INTEREST_RATE = 0.21


Private Sub Class_Initialize()
    ' set default principal amount to 0
    mcPrincipalAmount = 0
    ' set default interest rate to 8% annually
    mdInterestRate = 0.08
    ' set loan number to 0
    mlLoanNumber = 0
    ' set default term to 36 months
    mnTerm = ln3Years
End Sub

Public Property Get PrincipalAmount() As Currency
    PrincipalAmount = mcPrincipalAmount
End Property

Public Property Let PrincipalAmount(ByVal PrincipalAmt As Currency)
    If PrincipalAmt < MIN_LOAN_AMT Or PrincipalAmt > MAX_LOAN_AMT Then
        ' don't change value
```

```vba
            ' raise error
            Err.Raise vbObjectError + 1, "Loan Class", _
                "Invalid loan amount. Loans must be between " & _
                MIN_LOAN_AMT & " and " & MAX_LOAN_AMT & _
                " inclusive."
        Else
            mcPrincipalAmount = PrincipalAmt
        End If
End Property

Public Property Get InterestRate() As Double
    InterestRate = mdInterestRate
End Property

Public Property Let InterestRate(ByVal Rate As Double)
    If Rate < MIN_INTEREST_RATE Or Rate > MAX_INTEREST_RATE Then
        ' don't change value
        ' raise error
        Err.Raise vbObjectError + 2, "Loan Class", _
            "Invalid interest rate. Rate must be between " & _
            MIN_INTEREST_RATE & " and " & MAX_INTEREST_RATE & _
            " inclusive."
    Else
        mdInterestRate = Rate
    End If
End Property

Public Property Get LoanNumber() As Long
    LoanNumber = mlLoanNumber
End Property

Public Property Let LoanNumber(ByVal LoanNbr As Long)
    mlLoanNumber = LoanNbr
End Property

Public Property Get Payment() As Currency
    Payment = Application.WorksheetFunction.Pmt _
        (mdInterestRate / 12, mnTerm, -mcPrincipalAmount)
End Property

Public Property Get Term() As lnLoanTerm
    Term = mnTerm
End Property

Public Property Let Term(ByVal Term As lnLoanTerm)
    Select Case Term
```

```
        Case ln2Years
            mnTerm = Term
        Case ln3Years
            mnTerm = Term
        Case ln4Years
            mnTerm = Term
        Case ln5Years
            mnTerm = Term
        Case ln6Years
            mnTerm = Term
        Case Else
            ' don't change current value
            ' raise error
            Err.Raise vbObjectError + 3, "Loan Class", _
                "Invalid loan term. Use one of the " & _
                "lnLoanTerm values."
    End Select
End Property
```

Whew! I have a lot to cover on this one. Starting at the top, the first thing I'd like to point out is that I renamed the module-level variables to match the new data types. For example mvInterestRate, originally a Variant, became mdInterestRate (a double). This is the biggest drawback to using naming conventions that indicate a variable's data type. If you change the data type, you either have to change the variable name and then fix it everywhere it appears in your code (Edit ➢ Replace can do this trick nicely) or don't change the variable name and live with a variable name that is conveying misinformation. Either way, it's a pain. The moral of the story is choose your data types wisely to begin with if you use a naming convention that reflects the underlying value's data type.

The next interesting aspect of this listing is the lnLoanTerm enumeration. Enumerations provide you with a convenient way to indicate the valid values that a property can assume when you have a property that can assume only a handful of possible values.

End users of your class (you or other developers) will benefit from your use of enumerations because the Auto List Members feature understands enumerations and lists the enumerated choices for them when appropriate, as demonstrated in Figure 11.6.

Although I specified values for each enumeration in this listing, this isn't required. For example, if you wanted a simple list of region choices and didn't care what the value of each choice was, you could create an enumeration such as the following.

```
Enum rgRegions
    rgEast
    rgMidwest
    rgNorth
    rgNorthwest
    rgSouth
    rgWest
End Enum
```

FIGURE 11.6

Using enumerations has the added benefit of enabling the Auto List Members feature to provide extra help.

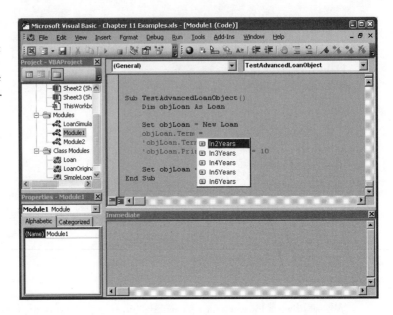

When creating enumerations, keep in mind that the enumeration names must be unique compared to any other enumeration names that are in scope. In order to help guarantee unique names, it is helpful to prefix the enumeration with a few letters such as I did for the loan term enumeration (lnLoanTerm).

After I created the lnLoanTerm enumeration in Listing 11.8, I defined a few private constants that represent the minimum and maximum values for loan amount and interest rate. You'll use these in the appropriate Property Let statements to perform some data validation before you accept the incoming value.

As you peruse the various Property procedures, notice that I've modified the Property Get procedures to return a more specific data type that is appropriate for the given property. Likewise, the Property Let procedures now have parameters that use more specific data types.

The PrincipalAmount, InterestRate, and Term Property Let procedures are interesting in that they use the Err object to generate an error. What!? You're writing code to intentionally raise an error? That's right. Keep in mind that when you develop your own classes, you're developing for a different audience—yourself and other programmers. If a procedure passes an invalid value to a property, you need to notify the offending procedure of the error so that it doesn't go on assuming that everything is fine. By raising an error, you give the other procedure a chance to correct the problem in an error-handling routine. Alternatively, the programmer using the object gets the error during the development and testing process and modifies her code to handle invalid values correctly. The syntax of Err.Raise is as follows.

```
Err.Raise number, [source], [description], [helpfile], [helpcontext]
```

The parameters of the Raise method are described in the following list.

Number This is a long integer that identifies the error. This should be a value between 513 and 65,535. When using Err.Raise from within a class module, you should use the vbObjectError constant in conjunction with the desired error number.

Source   This is an optional string value that you can use to identify the source of the error.

Description   This is an optional string that describes the error.

Helpfile   This is an optional string that is the fully qualified path to the help file that describes the error.

Helpcontext   This is an optional context ID that identifies a topic within the help file that contains information on the error.

My final comment regarding Listing 11.8 relates to the Property Get/Let procedures for the Term property. In order to take advantage of the lnLoanTerm enumeration I set up, you need to specify that the Property Let procedure requires a lnLoanTerm value as a parameter. One benefit of this is that users of your class can take advantage of the Auto List Members feature when they're specifying a new Term value. Of course, once the code is entered, enumerations add to the readability of your code.

When you use enumerations in Property Let procedures, it's possible that an invalid value will be passed to the parameter. Consequently, you need to use a Select Case structure to check the value against the possible enumeration values. Use a final Case Else statement to catch any value that doesn't have an enumeration value defined for it and raise an error or take appropriate action.

This Loan object is a great improvement over your original Loan object. For one thing, when you use the Term property, the Auto List Members feature displays a list of valid choices for you.

Additionally, you have implemented data validation that validates the interest rate, principal amount, and the term. If you pass an invalid value, the Loan object raises an error notifying you of the situation as the following screenshots demonstrate.

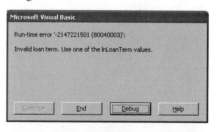

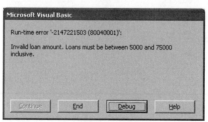

Finally, you've defined the various properties with a data type appropriate for the kind of data that each property will hold.

Summary

VBA provides class modules to enable you to enjoy many, but not all, of the benefits of object-oriented programming. So far throughout this book, you've been working with and enjoying the benefits of objects that other programmers have created. You've used the Application object, Workbook object, Worksheet object, and Range object, among others. I think you'd agree that using these objects seemed, for the most part, a natural experience. Well-designed objects feel natural to use because they have properties and methods that work and are named just as you'd normally think about them.

Although it is natural to use objects, many beginning programmers have a difficult time approaching objects from the other perspective—that is, as a developer of classes that will be used by yourself or other programmers. The terms *class* and *object* are often used in the same context. To be precise, however, a class is like an object template, whereas an object is a class that has been instantiated (created) using the object template (class). Objects are instantiated in VBA using the New keyword.

Part of the problem that beginning programmers may have with objects is that they haven't experienced some of the pain that object-oriented programming techniques can relieve. Therefore, it's harder to comprehend how the extra effort involved in developing classes is beneficial. That said, the extra effort is minimal. Classes are really not any more difficult to develop. They're just different. Remember, different doesn't equal difficult.

If you are still a little fuzzy on classes after this chapter, don't worry—practice makes perfect. In the next chapter, you'll get some more practice with classes by developing a class that you can use to, among other things, implement user personalization in your Excel application.

Chapter 12

Adding User Personalization to Your Application

IN MOST APPLICATIONS YOU usually need to remember user settings or other configurable values between uses of the application. Old-school Windows applications used initialization files (*.INI files); modern Windows applications use the system registry and web-based applications to store this kind of information either in a database on the server or as cookies on the user's computer.

For Excel-based applications, these methods aren't usually needed. In this chapter, you'll get some valuable practice creating classes that can be used to remember user preferences and other configurable values.

The Need for Persistence

Because your code lives in a workbook, why not store user settings there? In fact, why stop with user settings? Why not put any configurable setting on a worksheet where it can be easily modified as needed? You'll encounter certain situations in which this is not a good idea or not practical, but for many Excel applications this is a useful way to store this information in a manner that is easy and portable (the settings "travel" with the workbook). By portable, I mean that the workbook doesn't have any dependencies on other files or registry entries or anything else external to the workbook file.

You may want to think about storing many nuggets of information. Basically, any constant or semi-constant value in your code can be pulled out of the VBE and onto a worksheet. When you put this information on a worksheet, you're able to change the behavior of your application without getting knee-deep in the code. Some people refer to this type of programming as table-driven programming. One of the benefits of this method of programming is that you don't have to be a programmer to change the configuration of the program and thus its behavior.

In order to facilitate this type of programming, I've created a few easy-to-use classes. The Setting class is the primary class that allows you to manipulate Setting objects. The Settings class is a pseudo-collection class that manages a collection of Setting objects.

Class Semi-Specification

Prior to coding any class, consider what kind of public face or interface the class should have. This decision is very important. Once you've decided on an interface, making any changes may break any procedures that use the class. The only "safe" changes to a class interface are additions to the class—new methods or properties. The bottom line is that a switching cost (in terms of time and effort) is associated with changing a class interface. The more procedures that use a class, the higher the switching cost of changing the interface.

As a collection-type class, the Settings class should implement many of the common features of a collection object. Table 12.1 shows the members needed for the Settings class. One member that may stand out to you is the ItemByValue method. I've encountered instances in which I need to perform a reverse lookup, meaning I must retrieve a Setting according to its value instead of its name.

TABLE 12.1: MEMBERS OF THE SETTINGS CLASS

MEMBER NAME	TYPE	PURPOSE
Add	Method	To add a new Setting to the collection
Count	Property	To count the number of settings
Delete	Method	To delete all of the settings
Item	Method	To return a Setting object by index number or name
ItemByValue	Method	To return a Setting object by setting value

You may wonder about my choice of member type for the Item member. If you browse through the various Item members for all of the Excel classes that implement this member (Figure 12.1), you'll find that about half implement Item as a property and half implement it as a method.

FIGURE 12.1
Based on Excel's existing classes, you could just as well flip a coin when choosing between making Item a property or method.

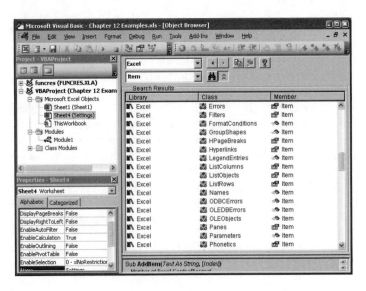

What characteristics do you think would be useful for the Setting object? Some of the obvious ones include a Name property, a Value property, and a Delete method. A Description property would also be useful.

In order to implement different kinds of settings, I've also included a SettingType property. Using this property allows you to implement read-only or read-write settings. Table 12.2 shows members needed by the Setting class.

TABLE 12.2: MEMBERS OF THE SETTING CLASS

MEMBER NAME	TYPE	PURPOSE
ChangeEditMode	Method	To turn on/off the ability to edit the setting.
Delete	Method	To delete the setting.
Description	Property	The description of the setting.
GetSetting	Method	This method initializes the object.
Index	Property	The index of the setting.
Name	Property	The name of the setting.
SettingType	Property	The type of setting (private, read-only, read-write, or read-protected write).
Value	Property	The value of the setting.

I didn't completely specify the class interfaces here. In particular, I left out the data types of the properties; nor did I specify any of the necessary parameters or their data types or the data type returned by each of the methods. I'll discuss these details as I dig into each object. Additionally, I left out an important property of the Setting class as a special surprise for later in the chapter.

Planning the Plumbing

Because the settings will be stored in a worksheet, the Settings and Setting classes need to know a few things about the worksheet if they're to work with it. For one thing, the classes need to know how to obtain a reference to the worksheet. As I mentioned earlier in the book, you can set a reference to a worksheet in a few ways. One way to refer to it is using its code name. You set the code name by changing the Name property of the worksheet in the Properties window of the VBE. Another way to set a reference is to use the Worksheets collection object and refer to a Worksheet object by index number. A final way to set a reference is to use the Worksheets object and refer to the worksheet using the name displayed on the worksheet tab.

The Settings and Setting objects use the final method of referring to a worksheet. That is, you'll assume that the worksheet has a certain name; specifically, you'll assume that the worksheet is named Settings. Of course, your class will validate that this worksheet exists before it ever uses it.

This worksheet is just a simple list of settings (as shown in Figure 12.2). The list needs to contain the following columns: Name, Value, Type, Description, and Setting Change Event.

FIGURE 12.2

The Settings worksheet is just a simple list that stores the data associated with each setting.

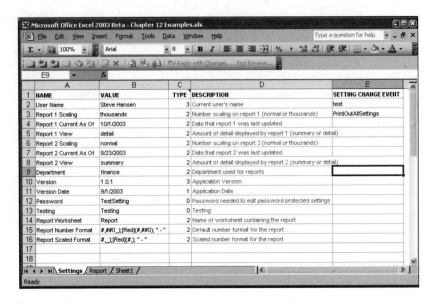

Security Considerations

Because you don't particularly want your users modifying the Settings worksheet on a whim, normally this worksheet is very hidden (xlVeryHidden—so hidden it doesn't show up when you select Format ➤ Sheet ➤ Unhide). Although I haven't done so here, you could extend the final product to use a protection scheme on this worksheet as well so that it can't be changed without using a password.

While I'm on the subject, this method of storing data is *not* inherently secure. Ninety-nine percent of general Excel users won't have a clue as to how this functionality is implemented or that the Settings worksheet even exists. To further prevent the Settings worksheet from being "discovered" by curious users, you should lock the VBA project so that you can't stumble across it in the code or as one of the Microsoft Excel objects in the Project window.

Even when you take these measures, it's still possible for people knowledgeable about VBA to discover the Settings worksheet. Once they know that a worksheet exists, anyone can at least read its contents by setting up formulas that link to that worksheet from another worksheet. Therefore, don't put anything on the Settings worksheet that you can't take any chances about other people discovering. That said, it's still highly unlikely that most people will even know it exists, so for the purposes for which you're planning on using it, I don't think this is a problem. It's certainly less visible than INI files that can be opened and inspected using Notepad.

The Setting Class

I haven't pulled any punches with the Setting class. This is an example of "real" code that you can put to work in real applications. You're going to use all sorts of techniques that I've covered so far including classes (obviously), enumerations, and error handling. Anyway, because this is production code, or code you can use for "real" applications, it's meant to be robust yet readable. Consequently, this class is longer than other code listings you've seen so far.

I debated the merits of presenting this class piece by piece versus showing it all at once and decided on the latter. From my own experience reading other programming books, I know that I always seem to forget something when I'm trying to put together long passages of code that are presented piecemeal.

As you browse over the code in Listing 12.1, notice that most of the Property Let procedures are implemented nearly identically. Likewise, most of the Property Get procedures are very similar.

LISTING 12.1: THE COMPLETE SETTING CLASS

```
Option Explicit

' private class variables
Private mwsSettings As Worksheet
Private mrgSetting As Range
Private mbAllowEditing As Boolean

' private class constants
Private Const SETTINGS_WORKSHEET = "Settings"
Private Const VALUE_OFFSET = 1
Private Const TYPE_OFFSET = 2
Private Const DESCRIPTION_OFFSET = 3
Private Const CHANGE_EVENT_OFFSET = 4

' Enumeration for the kinds of Setting types
Enum setSettingType
    setPrivate = 0              ' don't display in user inteface
    setReadOnly = 1            ' read-only setting
    setReadWrite = 2          ' read-write setting
    setReadProtectedWrite = 3  ' read-write with password
End Enum

' Setting Description
Property Get Description() As String
    If mrgSetting Is Nothing Then
        Description = ""
    Else
        Description = mrgSetting.Offset(0, DESCRIPTION_OFFSET).Value
    End If
End Property

Property Let Description(PropertyDescription As String)
    If mrgSetting Is Nothing Then
        UninitializedError
    Else
```

```vba
        ' mbAllowEditing is managed by the
        ' EditMode method.
        If mbAllowEditing Then
            mrgSetting.Offset(0, DESCRIPTION_OFFSET).Value = _
                PropertyDescription
        Else
            ReadOnlyError
        End If
    End If
End Property


' setting EventHandler - represents a procedure that
' gets called automatically when the setting's value
' changes
Property Get EventHandler() As String
    If mrgSetting Is Nothing Then
        EventHandler = ""
    Else
        EventHandler = mrgSetting.Offset(0, CHANGE_EVENT_OFFSET).Value
    End If
End Property

Property Let EventHandler(EventHandlerProcedure As String)
    If mrgSetting Is Nothing Then
        UninitializedError
    Else
        ' mbAllowEditing is managed by the
        ' EditMode method.
        If mbAllowEditing Then
            mrgSetting.Offset(0, CHANGE_EVENT_OFFSET).Value = _
                EventHandlerProcedure
        Else
            ReadOnlyError
        End If
    End If
End Property


' The settings are ordered by row
' on the Settings worksheet. Because this worksheet
' includes one row for column headings, you can
' get the index of the setting by looking at
' the row of the setting and subtracting one.
Property Get Index() As Long
    If mrgSetting Is Nothing Then
        Index = -1
    Else
        Index = mrgSetting.Row - 1
    End If
```

```
End Property

Property Get Name() As String
    If mrgSetting Is Nothing Then
        Name = ""
    Else
        Name = mrgSetting.Value
    End If
End Property

Property Let Name(PropertyName As String)
    ' Name is implemented as a read-only property
    ' so you can create dependencies on Setting
    ' names in your code.
End Property

Property Get SettingType() As setSettingType
    If mrgSetting Is Nothing Then
        SettingType = -1
    Else
        SettingType = mrgSetting.Offset(0, TYPE_OFFSET)
    End If
End Property

Property Let SettingType(SettingType As setSettingType)
    If mrgSetting Is Nothing Then
        UninitializedError
    Else
        If mbAllowEditing Then
            mrgSetting.Offset(0, TYPE_OFFSET).Value = SettingType
        Else
            ReadOnlyError
        End If
    End If
End Property

Property Get Value() As Variant
    If mrgSetting Is Nothing Then
        Value = ""
    Else
        Value = mrgSetting.Offset(0, VALUE_OFFSET)
    End If
End Property

Property Let Value(PropertyValue As Variant)
    If mrgSetting Is Nothing Then
        UninitializedError
    Else
```

```
        If mbAllowEditing Then
            ' ok, change the value
            mrgSetting.Offset(0, VALUE_OFFSET).Value = PropertyValue
            ' call any procedures specified by the setting
            ' in the event of a change
            ExecuteEventHandler
        Else
            ReadOnlyError
        End If
    End If
End Property

Public Function Delete() As Boolean
    Delete = False
    If mrgSetting Is Nothing Then
        UninitializedError
    Else
        If mbAllowEditing Then
            mrgSetting.EntireRow.Delete xlUp
            Set mrgSetting = Nothing
            Delete = True
        Else
            ReadOnlyError
        End If
    End If
End Function

Public Function ChangeEditMode(AllowEditing As Boolean, _
    Optional Password As Variant) As Boolean

    If AllowEditing Then
        Select Case Me.SettingType
            Case setSettingType.setPrivate
                ' Private settings are settings used
                ' for programatic purposes or otherwise
                ' that should not be displayed on any
                ' user interface but can be freely
                ' modified programmatically
                mbAllowEditing = True

            Case setSettingType.setReadOnly
                ' Settings that are not intended to
                ' be changed by users but are useful
                ' to know. Never allow EditMode on these.
                mbAllowEditing = False

            Case setSettingType.setReadWrite
                ' Settings that can be freely modified
```

```
                          ' by the user
                          mbAllowEditing = True

                  Case setSettingType.setReadProtectedWrite
                      ' Settings that can be read but only
                      ' changed by users that know the password
                      If IsMissing(Password) Then
                          mbAllowEditing = False
                      Else
                          If ValidPassword(CStr(Password)) Then
                              mbAllowEditing = True
                          Else
                              mbAllowEditing = False
                          End If
                      End If
                  Case Else
                      ' unknown setting type
                      mbAllowEditing = False
              End Select

      Else
          mbAllowEditing = False
      End If
      ChangeEditMode = mbAllowEditing
End Function

Public Function GetSetting(SettingName As String) As Boolean
    Dim lRow As Integer
    Dim bFoundSetting As Boolean

    Set mrgSetting = Nothing
    bFoundSetting = False
    mbAllowEditing = False

    lRow = 2
    Do Until IsEmpty(mwsSettings.Cells(lRow, 1))
        If UCase(mwsSettings.Cells(lRow, 1).Value) = _
            UCase(SettingName) Then

            Set mrgSetting = mwsSettings.Cells(lRow, 1)
            bFoundSetting = True
            Exit Do

        End If
        lRow = lRow + 1
    Loop

    GetSetting = bFoundSetting
```

```vb
End Function

Private Sub UninitializedError()
    Err.Raise vbObjectError + 101, "Setting Class", _
        "The setting has not been properly initialized. " & _
        "Use the GetSetting method to initialize the setting."
End Sub

Private Sub ReadOnlyError()
    Err.Raise vbObjectError + 102, "Setting Class", _
        "The setting you are trying to change is " & _
        "either read-only, requires a password, or " & _
        "you have not put the object in edit mode " & _
        "using the EditMode method."
End Sub

Private Sub Class_Initialize()
    ' do not allow editing by default
    mbAllowEditing = False

    ' need to point the mws worksheet variable to the
    ' Settings worksheet
    If WorksheetExists(ThisWorkbook, SETTINGS_WORKSHEET) Then
        Set mwsSettings = ThisWorkbook.Worksheets(SETTINGS_WORKSHEET)
    Else
        Set mwsSettings = Nothing
        Err.Raise vbObjectError + 100, "Setting Class", _
        "The worksheet named " & SETTINGS_WORKSHEET & _
        " could not be located."
    End If
End Sub

' Determines if a given worksheet name exists in a workbook
Private Function WorksheetExists(wb As Workbook, sName As String) _
    As Boolean
    Dim s As String

    On Error GoTo WorksheetExistsErr

    s = wb.Worksheets(sName).Name

    WorksheetExists = True
    Exit Function

WorksheetExistsErr:
    WorksheetExists = False
End Function
```

```
' Validate password by comparing it against the value
' given by the Password setting on the Settings worksheet.
' Obviously, this assumes that the worksheet is managed such
' that it cannot be easily retrieved/discovered.
' WARNING: this provides only very basic security and should
' not be used to protect sensitive data.
Private Function ValidPassword(sPassword As String) As Boolean
    Dim oSetting As Setting
    Dim bValid As Boolean

    bValid = False
    Set oSetting = New Setting

    If oSetting.GetSetting("Password") Then
        If oSetting.Value = sPassword Then
            bValid = True
        Else
            bValid = False
        End If
    Else
        bValid = False
    End If

    Set oSetting = Nothing
    ValidPassword = bValid
End Function

Private Sub ExecuteEventHandler()
    On Error Resume Next
    ' make sure there is an Event Handler
    ' for the setting
    If Len(Me.EventHandler) <> 0 Then
        ' call the procedure specified
        ' by the EventHandler property
        Application.Run Me.EventHandler
    End If
End Sub
```

The key to the implementation of this class is the class variable mrgSetting, a range object that represents the cell associated with the current setting's name. When you use the x_OFFSET constants defined near the top of the class, it is possible to use the Offset method on the mrgSetting object to retrieve all of the other information associated with the Setting object.

Because the mrgSetting variable is absolutely essential to the operation of this class, it is imperative that you make sure that this range is actually pointing to something in nearly every procedure. You may wonder then, why the Class_Initialize procedure doesn't set this variable. The reason is that you have no way to specify which range the Class_Initialize procedure should point mrgSetting to. It would be nice to have a way to specify an input parameter to this procedure. Unfortunately, this is a limitation of VBA in regards to developing classes. In other languages, such as C++, for example, you can create initialization procedures that have input parameters.

In order to get around this limitation you need to use a method named GetSetting. This method's sole purpose is to set the mrgSetting variable so it refers to the setting with the specified name. You'll see that the Settings object knows how to call this method in the Item property so that end users (developers who use the class) won't need to perform the awkward process of creating the object and then using GetSetting to properly "initialize" it.

If a procedure notices that the mrgSetting variable is not set up correctly, it either raises an error (using the UninitializedError procedure) in the case of a Property Let procedure, or it reports either an empty string or the value –1 in the case of a Property Get procedure.

Another piece of functionality that needs special attention is the process of implementing the SettingType property. The SettingType property allows you to designate a setting as private, read-only, read-write, or read-protected write. Consequently, it won't suffice to create any old Property Let procedures. You need to be conscious of the fact that it may or may not be possible to modify the value depending on the value of the SettingType property and whether or not an appropriate password was supplied. In order to keep track of whether or not the Setting can be edited, the class uses a Boolean variable named mbAllowEditing. This variable is false by default and can only be changed using the ChangeEditMode method.

ChangeEditMode is the method in charge of determining whether or not a setting can be modified. The AllowEditing parameter is a required Boolean parameter. The Password parameter is optional and is only required or applicable if the setting's type is read-protected write. Notice the use of the IsMissing function in the setSettingType.setReadProtectedWrite case. IsMissing is a VBA function you can use to test whether or not optional parameters were passed into the procedure.

NOTE *Parameters specified with the Optional keyword can't have any required parameters after them in the parameter list.*

WARNING *IsMissing only works with Variant data types. If you use it against other data types, it always returns false.*

If the password is present and the setting type is read-protected write, then ChangeEditMode relies on the ValidPassword method to validate the password. ValidPassword is a private method and can't be seen or called from procedures external to the Setting class. ValidPassword assumes a setting on the Settings worksheet called Password. If this setting isn't present, it won't validate the password.

This password validation scheme highlights an important benefit of using classes. As I mentioned in the last chapter, because consumers of classes depend on the interface of a class and not its implementation, you can change implementation details without breaking any code that uses the class. If you require a more secure scheme to password-protect settings, you can change the implementation details of the ValidPassword function.

Fake Is Fine

The Setting class contains a powerful capability—so powerful that it needs its own section. This is the surprise I mentioned earlier in the chapter and it is huge. While perusing Listing 12.1, did you pick up on the EventHandler property and the private ExecuteEventHandler procedure? Are you hoping it is what you thought it was? That is, a way to dynamically execute a setting-specific procedure whenever the setting's value changes? Although you can't create "real" events for your classes with VBA, you can fake it—and for most purposes, faking it does just fine.

The Setting class knows when setting values change because it controls how they get set with the Property Let procedure. As mentioned in the last chapter, this is a key benefit of using Property procedures versus implementing class properties using public variables. This means that any property implemented using Property Let/Set provides you with the opportunity to create functionality similar to events. The question is how will you decide which procedure to call when an event occurs?

You could hard code the appropriate event procedures within the class, but this would be problematic. When developing your own classes, one of your goals is that after you create them, you leave them alone. Therefore, you don't want to put anything in the class that might change. So you certainly don't want to hard code event procedures in the class that are likely to be application specific. That's where the Run method of the Application object comes into play.

The Run method provides you with the ability to call any public procedure in the current project. Because you can pass variables to the Run method, you don't need to know the procedure names at development time. Instead, you can place these procedures in a handy place (like the Settings worksheet) and look them up dynamically from your procedures. For the Setting class, it makes sense to include the setting's change event procedure as a property of the Setting itself. Then, in order to call the appropriate event procedure, all you need to do is call the procedure given by the setting's EventHandler property using Application.Run whenever the setting's value changes.

Collect Those Setting Objects with Settings

The Settings class is a pseudo-collection class that manages all of the Setting objects. I'll discuss why I call this a pseudo-collection class later in the chapter. For the most part, however, this class operates much like any other collection class. It has all of the common members found in a collection class: Add, Count, Delete, and Item. The complete class is shown in Listing 12.2.

LISTING 12.2: THE SETTINGS CLASS—A PSEUDO-COLLECTION OF SETTING OBJECTS

```
Option Explicit

' class constants
Private Const SETTINGS_WORKSHEET = "Settings"
Private Const NAME_COLUMN = 1
Private Const VALUE_COLUMN = 2

' class variables
Private mwsSettings As Worksheet

' count of settings
Property Get Count()
    Count = mwsSettings.Cells(65536, 1).End(xlUp).Row - 1
End Property
```

```vb
' adds a new setting. returns setting object
' associated with the new setting.
Public Function Add(Name As String) As Setting
    Dim lRow As Long
    Dim oSetting As Setting

    ' make sure a setting with this name
    ' doesn't already exist
    'Set oSetting = Me.Item(Name)

    If Not SettingExists(Name) Then
        ' find the last used row and move down one row
        lRow = mwsSettings.Cells(65536, 1).End(xlUp).Row + 1
        ' add the name of the new setting
        mwsSettings.Cells(lRow, 1) = Name
        ' set a reference to it
        Set oSetting = Me.Item(Name)
    Else
        ' the item already exists
        Err.Raise vbObjectError + 201, "Settings Class", _
        "A setting named " & Name & " already exists."
        Set oSetting = Nothing
    End If
    Set Add = oSetting
End Function


' deletes ALL settings
Public Function Delete() As Boolean
    mwsSettings.Range(mwsSettings.Cells(2, 1), _
        mwsSettings.Cells(65536, 4)).ClearContents
    Delete = True
End Function


' retrieves a setting by index or name
' retrieves by index if Index is numeric
' retrieves by name if Index is not numeric
Public Function Item(Index As Variant) As Setting
    Dim lRow As Long
    Dim lFoundRow As Long
    Dim oSetting As Setting
    Dim sName As String

    Set oSetting = New Setting

    ' if Index is numeric then assume
    ' that we are looking by index
    ' if Index is not numeric then assume
    ' that we are looking by name
```

```
    If IsNumeric(Index) Then
        ' get the name of the setting associated with
        ' the index. Row of setting = Index + 1 (header row)
        sName = mwsSettings.Cells(Index + 1, 1).Value
        ' make sure we got a name rather than an empty
        ' cell
        If Len(sName) <> 0 Then
            ' set a reference to the setting
            If oSetting.GetSetting(sName) Then
                Set Item = oSetting
            Else
                Err.Raise 9, "Settings Class", _
                    "Subscript out of range."
            End If
        Else
            Err.Raise 9, "Settings Class", _
                "Subscript out of range."
        End If
    Else
        If oSetting.GetSetting(CStr(Index)) Then
            Set Item = oSetting
        Else
            Err.Raise 9, "Settings Class", _
                "Subscript out of range."
        End If
    End If
End Function

' performs a reverse-lookup. looks up a setting by value
' rather than by name.
Public Function ItemByValue(Value As Variant) As Setting
    Dim lRow As Long
    Dim oSetting As Setting
    Dim bFound As Boolean

    Set oSetting = New Setting
    bFound = False

    For lRow = 2 To mwsSettings.Cells(65536, 1).End(xlUp).Row
        If Value = mwsSettings.Cells(lRow, VALUE_COLUMN).Value Then
            If oSetting.GetSetting( _
                mwsSettings.Cells(lRow, NAME_COLUMN).Value) Then
                Set ItemByValue = oSetting
            Else
                Err.Raise 9, "Settings Class", _
                    "Subscript out of range."
            End If
            bFound = True
```

```vb
                Exit For
            End If
        Next

        If Not bFound Then
            Set ItemByValue = Nothing
            Err.Raise 9, "Settings Class", _
                "Subscript out of range."
        End If
End Function

Private Sub Class_Initialize()
    ' need to point the mws worksheet variable to the
    ' Settings worksheet
    If WorksheetExists(ThisWorkbook, SETTINGS_WORKSHEET) Then
        Set mwsSettings = ThisWorkbook.Worksheets(SETTINGS_WORKSHEET)
    Else
        Set mwsSettings = Nothing
        Err.Raise vbObjectError + 200, "Settings Class", _
            "The worksheet named " & SETTINGS_WORKSHEET & _
            " could not be located."
    End If
End Sub

' Determines if a given worksheet name exists in a workbook
Private Function WorksheetExists(wb As Workbook, _
    sName As String) As Boolean

    Dim s As String

    On Error GoTo bWorksheetExistsErr

    s = wb.Worksheets(sName).Name

    WorksheetExists = True
    Exit Function

bWorksheetExistsErr:
    WorksheetExists = False
End Function

Private Function SettingExists(SettingName As String) As Boolean
    Dim oSetting As Setting

    On Error GoTo ErrHandler
    Set oSetting = Me.Item(SettingName)
```

```
        SettingExists = True
        Set oSetting = Nothing
        Exit Function
    ErrHandler:
        SettingExists = False
    End Function
```

This class has a couple of noteworthy sections starting with the Add method. One of the rules enforced by the Add method is that setting names must be unique. In order to check if the name provided to Add is unique, the Add method calls the private function SettingExists. SettingExists tries to set a reference to it using the Item method of the Settings class. The keyword Me is simply a convenient way to refer to the class from within the class itself. Anyway, if an error is generated, then SettingExists reports that the setting doesn't exist. This algorithm is identical to the one used by WorksheetExists.

When the setting is added, basically all that happens is that you find the first empty row, enter the setting name in the first column or the first empty row, and then set a reference to the newly added setting.

The Item method is the other noteworthy passage. Just like real collection classes, the goal here is to allow the ability to use either an index number or a setting name as a parameter. For example, if a setting named "Fiscal Year" is the second setting, you want to be able to refer to it using either of the following statements.

```
' refer to a setting by index number
Set setFiscalYear = MySettings.Item(2)
' refer to a setting by name
Set setFiscalYear = MySettings.Item("Fiscal Year")
```

In order to achieve this goal, the input parameter (named Index as is customary with collection classes) must be declared as a Variant data type. The Item method assumes that if the parameter is a number, then it must represent the setting index. Otherwise it treats the parameter as a setting name. The implication of this is that it is wise to avoid using numeric setting names. If a setting name is a number, the only way to set a reference to that setting is by using the index number. For example, if you have a setting named 423 and try to set a reference by name (e.g., MySettings.Item("423")), the Item method would try and retrieve the setting associated with the 424th row, which may or may not contain a setting. If it does contain a setting, chances are that it will be the wrong one. If the specified setting isn't found, Item raises a "Subscript out of range" error, much as other collection classes would.

The ItemByValue method is a way to retrieve a setting by looking at setting values rather than setting names. This method loops through the setting values until it finds a value that matches, and then it returns a reference to the associated setting. If the value is not found, a "Subscript out of range" error is raised.

The Delete method is simple—just clear the contents of the cells representing A2:D65536. The Count property is also trivial. The Count of the settings is just the row number of the last used row minus one for the heading row (row 1).

Pseudo? Says Who?

Although the Settings object exhibits the typical methods and properties of a collection object, you can't iterate over all of the Setting objects in the Settings object collection using the For Each...Next method as is shown in Listing 12.3. That is why I refer to this class as a pseudo-collection class.

LISTING 12.3: FUTILE ATTEMPT TO ITERATE OVER SETTINGS

```
' This does not work. The Settings object does
' not natively know how to iterate over all of
' the objects it contains.
Sub BadPrintOutAllSettings()
    Dim oSettings As Settings
    Dim oSetting As Setting
    Dim nIndex As Integer
    Dim ws As Worksheet

    Set oSettings = New Settings

    ' this does not work
    For Each oSetting In oSettings
        Set oSetting = oSettings.Item(nIndex)
        Debug.Print oSetting.Name & " = " & oSetting.Value
    Next

    Set oSetting = Nothing
    Set oSettings = Nothing
End Sub
```

Real collection objects support this method of iterating over the objects in the collection. If you try this using the Settings object you get the following error.

To iterate over all of the Setting objects in the Settings collection, you need to use a For...Next loop from 1 to a count of the number of Setting objects. Then you need to use the Item property with the index value to retrieve each Setting object. Because most collection objects are one-based rather than zero-based, I implemented the Settings object as a one-based collection. Listing 12.4 demonstrates an example of this method of iterating over the Setting objects.

LISTING 12.4: SUCCESSFUL (MANUAL) ITERATION OVER SETTINGS

```
Sub PrintOutAllSettings()
    Dim oSettings As Settings
    Dim oSetting As Setting
    Dim nIndex As Integer

    Set oSettings = New Settings

    For nIndex = 1 To oSettings.Count
        Set oSetting = oSettings.Item(nIndex)
        Debug.Print oSetting.Name & " = " & oSetting.Value
    Next

    Set oSetting = Nothing
    Set oSettings = Nothing
End Sub
```

This procedure produced the following output based on the Settings worksheet shown in Figure 12.2.

```
User Name = Steve Hansen
Report 1 Scaling = thousands
Report 1 Current As Of = 10/1/2003
Report 1 View = detail
Report 2 Scaling = normal
Report 2 Current As Of = 9/23/2003
Report 2 View = summary
Department = finance
Version = 1.0.1
Version Date = 9/1/2003
Password = TestSetting
Testing = Testing
Report Worksheet = Report
Report Number Format = #,##0_);[Red](#,##0); " - "
Report Scaled Format = #,_);[Red](#,); " - "
```

Put Those Settings to Work

I have really talked these classes up because I've used them (or their predecessors) in nearly every project over the past few years. Now it's time to look at an example of how to use them. Listing 12.5 shows how to add, manipulate, and then delete a setting.

LISTING 12.5: QUALITY CLASSES 'FEEL' LIKE NATIVE EXCEL FUNCTIONALITY

```vba
Sub DemonstrateSettings()
    Dim oSettings As Settings
    Dim oSetting As Setting

    Set oSettings = New Settings

    ' Add a setting
    Set oSetting = oSettings.Add("Test New Setting")
    With oSetting
        .ChangeEditMode True
        .Description = "This is a test setting."
        .Value = "Testing"
        .EventHandler = "SayHello"
    End With

    ' Check out EventHandler
    oSetting.Value = "Show me the event handler!"

    ' Delete the setting
    oSetting.Delete

    Set oSetting = Nothing
    Set oSettings = Nothing
End Sub

Sub SayHello()
    MsgBox "Hello"
End Sub
```

It would be a good idea to step through this listing to get a good feel for the flow of everything, particularly the execution path when you're using the EventHandler property. As you can see, it is very easy to use these classes.

Let's review. To use the Settings and Setting classes in a project you need to do the following.

1. Ensure that one of the worksheets in the workbook is named "Settings". You can either copy an existing Settings worksheet (from a different workbook) into the workbook or name one of the existing sheets "Settings". If you rename one of the existing sheets, be sure to populate the first row in the worksheet with the appropriate column names: Name, Value, Type, Description, and Setting Change Event.

2. Import the Setting and Settings classes into the VBA project. You can achieve this by opening an existing project that uses the classes and dragging and dropping the class modules from one project to the next. Alternatively, you can use File ➤ Import File... from the VBE menu and

locate the code files. This method assumes that you have exported the files at some point using File ➤ Export File.

3. Before distributing the file, you'll probably want to hide the Settings worksheet.

If you find yourself using the Setting and Settings classes in every project, you may want to set up a workbook with all of the required components and then save the workbook as a template. Then, when you begin working on a new development project, you can start by creating a new workbook based on your development template.

I'll be using both of these classes for many other examples in the remainder of this book. You'll really get a kick out of this in Chapter 20 when I present a user interface you can use with these classes. Figure 12.3 provides a hint of what's to come in that chapter.

FIGURE 12.3

Once you get a user interface hooked up to the Settings class, things will really fall into place.

Summary

An application that allows its end users to customize it to their preferences exudes an air of professionalism. If you're working with a tightly locked-down workbook, this functionality assumes even greater importance because it may be the only way that users can customize the look of the application.

Not only can this kind of functionality enhance the professionalism of your applications, it also has the ability to save you time by reducing the amount of change requests you receive. For every person that wants data formatted or calculated a certain way, there is always someone else who wants it formatted the exact opposite or calculated in a different manner.

The fact that you can provide personalization in your applications is a prime example of the benefit of using classes. You can create classes that wrap up all of the necessary functionality and then drop these classes in any project that requires them. As you'll soon see, these classes are much more beneficial than I originally intended them to be. When you use the Setting and Settings classes, you can conceivably pull any variable you use in your program out of the VBE environment (your code) and onto a worksheet managed by these classes. This approach, often referred to as table-driven programming, allows people other than programmers to configure and modify the behavior of the application without having to understand the VBA code. In Chapter 20, you'll develop a User Form that works with these classes to manage the Settings visually.

In Chapter 13, you'll review some Excel development best practices. Some of this material will serve as a review of some of the best tips I've already given you. In addition, I'll discuss other development techniques that I've found valuable while developing Excel applications.

Chapter 13

Excel Development Best Practices

As you advance your Excel development skills, you'll experience *dramatic* increases in productivity. These increases come from knowing more about various Excel objects and their properties and methods, being able to apply the *correct* object to the task at hand, and realizing more efficient development methodologies.

The goal of this chapter is to present tips, techniques, and other knowledge that I've found useful. Hopefully this will save you a lot of time and save you from just stumbling across these techniques through trial and error.

Deactivate Activate; Don't Select Select

The use of the Activate and Select methods are the two most common blunders I see. Activate is used to activate a workbook, worksheet, or range. Select is used to select a range. Once a range is selected, it can be manipulated using the Selection property of the Application object. Manipulating Excel objects using Activate, Select, and Selection is slow, error-prone, and usually results in code that is difficult, at best, to maintain.

The biggest offender of this guidance is Excel's macro recorder. This feature generates a lot of inefficient, error-prone, and unmaintainable code. To be fair, the macro recorder also creates a lot of value, because for many people, it's the only way to automate otherwise tedious, manual tasks.

Because many people learn by studying the output of the macro recorder, using Select and Selection are the most common bad habits exhibited by most beginning Excel developers.

If you've read this book sequentially up to this point, you know that you don't need to activate or select worksheets and ranges to manipulate them programmatically. Instead, you can create a variable of the appropriate object type (workbook, worksheet, or range), point the variable to the desired object, and then manipulate the object through the variable.

Listing 13.1 provides an example of some code recorded by the Macro recorder and an equivalent procedure that avoids using Select. These two procedures just go to various worksheets in a workbook, select a column, and make the font of the column bold. To demonstrate a quantifiable difference, I've also included a couple of procedures to time each procedure, both with and without screen updating.

LISTING 13.1: AVOIDING SELECT AND SELECTION

```vb
Option Explicit

Sub RecorderCode()
'
' RecorderCode Macro
' Macro recorded 10/12/2003 by Steven M. Hansen
'

'
    Sheets("Sheet1").Select
    Columns("A:A").Select
    Selection.Font.Bold = True
    Sheets("Sheet2").Select
    Columns("B:B").Select
    Selection.Font.Bold = True
    Sheets("Sheet3").Select
    Columns("C:D").Select
    Selection.Font.Bold = True
    Range("A1").Select
    Sheets("Sheet4").Select
    Columns("D:D").Select
    Selection.Font.Bold = True
    Range("A1").Select
End Sub

' A more efficient version of RecorderCode
Sub RecorderCodeII()
    With ThisWorkbook
        .Worksheets("Sheet1").Range("A:A").Font.Bold = True
        .Worksheets("Sheet2").Range("B:B").Font.Bold = True
        .Worksheets("Sheet3").Range("C:D").Font.Bold = True
        .Worksheets("Sheet4").Range("D:D").Font.Bold = True
    End With
End Sub

Sub TestProcedures()
    Dim dResult As Double

    dResult = TestProcedure(1, True)
    Debug.Print "RecorderCode w/screen updating: " & _
        Format(dResult, "0.00") & " seconds."

    dResult = TestProcedure(2, True)
    Debug.Print "RecorderCodeII w/screen updating: " & _
        Format(dResult, "0.00") & " seconds."
```

```
        dResult = TestProcedure(1, False)
        Debug.Print "RecorderCode w/o screen updating: " & _
            Format(dResult, "0.00") & " seconds."

        dResult = TestProcedure(2, False)
        Debug.Print "RecorderCodeII w/o screen updating: " & _
            Format(dResult, "0.00") & " seconds."
End Sub

Function TestProcedure(nVersion As Integer, _
    bScreenUpdating As Boolean) As Double

        Dim nRepetition As Integer
        Dim ws As Worksheet
        Dim dStart As Double

        ' Set screen updating
        Application.ScreenUpdating = bScreenUpdating

        ' Record the start time
        dStart = Timer

        ' Loop through procedure 100 times
        For nRepetition = 1 To 100
            If nVersion = 1 Then
                RecorderCode
            Else
                RecorderCodeII
            End If
        Next

        ' Return elapsed time since procedure started
        TestProcedure = Timer - dStart

        ' Make sure ScreenUpdating is on
        Application.ScreenUpdating = True

        Set ws = Nothing

End Function
```

Running this TestProcedures routine produces the following output on my computer.

```
RecorderCode w/screen updating: 2.96 seconds.
RecorderCodeII w/screen updating: 0.10 seconds.
RecorderCode w/o screen updating: 0.45 seconds.
RecorderCodeII w/o screen updating: 0.04 seconds.
```

As you can see, the procedure that doesn't use Select is significantly faster, regardless of the screen updating setting. From a maintenance perspective, which of the two procedures would you rather have in your project?

Manage the Display

Good Excel applications exhibit a fit and finish that can be achieved only by paying attention to how information does (or doesn't) get displayed. Not only does this result in better-looking applications, it also results in better performance.

The first thing to do is manage screen updating. When you don't manage screen updating, often the screen flashes like a vintage disco strobe light—except when this happens, it's *not* cool. To give your application a better fit and finish, make sure you turn off screen updating as your code executes.

You can see the performance benefits of managing screen updating by examining the output of Listing 13.1. Just by turning off screen updating, you can increase the performance of an application significantly.

Another thing to pay attention to is the use of message boxes and forms. Use them judiciously. In a long process, try and arrange the process so that any message boxes or forms are displayed at the beginning or the end of a process if at all. That way, end users don't feel like they have to "baby-sit." Additionally, although forms offer a great deal of functionality, they also cause the size of the file to bloat.

One more practice that I've really come to appreciate is sizing the worksheet, which is the practice of hiding unused columns and rows. Sizing the worksheet offers a few benefits. First, it focuses the user on the data range and visually enforces to the user that they don't need to be concerned with anything else on the worksheet. It provides great mental closure. Second, users who navigate using the keyboard will appreciate the fact that they can easily get to the boundaries of the data range without zipping down to the 65,536th row or column IV. Finally, when filling a series using the mouse, you don't experience that frustrating problem of oscillating back and forth trying to fill down to the exact row. Figure 13.1 shows an example of a sized worksheet.

Shortcut keys make sizing a worksheet a five-second (or less) task. Table 13.1 lists the shortcut keys that are useful when sizing worksheets.

TABLE 13.1: Useful Shortcut Keys for Sizing Worksheets

SHORTCUT	PURPOSE
CTRL+↓	Move to bottom of current region.
CTRL+→	Move to right edge of current region.
CTRL+SHIFT+↓	Select cells to bottom of current region.
CTRL+SHIFT+→	Select cells to right edge of current region.
CTRL+(	Hide the selected rows.
CTRL+SHIFT+(	Unhide the selected rows.
CTRL+)	Hide the selected columns.
CTRL+SHIFT+)	Unhide the selected columns.

FIGURE 13.1

A sized worksheet offers nice navigational benefits and provides users with mental closure.

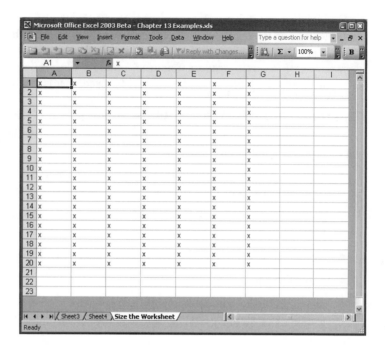

Design for Portability

When it comes to Excel applications, portability should be an important design consideration. That is, aim to develop Excel applications that don't make any assumptions regarding the location from which they are running. An application should not care which computer it runs on, where the workbook is stored on the filesystem, or make any assumptions about the location of other files other than relative paths (which should be user configurable). There are many reasons why it behooves you to follow this advice.

In the corporate world, Excel workbooks are nearly equivalent to Adobe Acrobat files (`*.pdf`) in terms of portability. They are e-mailed, shared on file servers, and posted to the corporate intranet. Excel and the other Microsoft Office applications are often mediums of collaboration. In fact, Microsoft is touting collaboration as a key benefit of the Office 2003 system. In this environment, portability is paramount. Ideally, an Excel application contains everything it needs to work within the workbook. If so, you can distribute your Excel application much the same as you would any other workbook.

In addition to the vast amount of collaboration and sharing that occurs with Excel workbooks, many people have more than one computer. They may have a laptop and a desktop computer, or a work computer and a home computer. In either of these scenarios, chances are that they often transfer files between the two computers. You can make it much easier on your users by designing an application that doesn't require any special setup procedures or installation process.

Finally, chances are that the version of Microsoft Windows you use is geared toward supporting multiple users on the same computer. In order to support this capability, each user's files should be kept separate from other users' files. In order to play by the rules, your application shouldn't force users to store user-specific information in a "common" file location. For example, it shouldn't force everyone to store their files in a folder named `C:\Excel Application\Reports`.

Tips for Creating Portable Applications

So what can you do to create portable applications? Here are a few things to keep in mind when coding for workbook portability.

◆ Use configurable *relative* paths to any application-specific folders. It is easy to allow the user to choose the names of these folders.

◆ If you do use application-specific folders, check for the presence of these folders in the Workbook Open event. If they don't exist, offer to create them.

◆ Always validate file locations and check to make sure files exist before using them.

◆ Avoid using registry keys or INI files.

◆ If you can't create a portable application, provide a way for users to export key sections of the workbook (such as reports) to code- and link-free workbooks.

Test the Water before Jumping In

I've analyzed several procedures related to validating object names before setting a reference to an object by name. Remember, always check worksheet names, range names, filenames, Setting names (if you're using the Settings class from the last chapter), and any other object name before you explicitly set an object reference using the name.

One of the differences between developing in VBA with Excel as a host and developing a stand-alone application with a traditional programming language is that when you develop in Excel, you don't have 100-percent control over how a user interacts with your application; therefore you need to be wary of things that the end user could do that would affect whether your program operates properly. When you develop a stand-alone application using Visual Basic or some other programming language, you have total control over everything. The drawback of having all of the control is that you have to write a lot more code.

Because validating objects is such a common task, I place all of my validation procedures together in a module that I include in every project I work on. This module contains most of the generic procedures presented in this book such as WorksheetExists, RangeNameExists, and WorkbookExists.

Remember Your Math

Think back to your school days. Remember algebra? Trying hard to forget? One of the concepts taught in my algebra classes was a concept called *factoring*. Factoring is the process of taking a long equation and rearranging it so that it can't be rearranged in a more concise way. For example, the polynomial $2xy + 2xy$ can be factored to $4xy$.

You should approach your VBA modules with the same mindset. How can my procedures be rearranged so that there is no duplication of code? The best way to achieve this is to create small, focused procedures that each perform only one dedicated task.

There are many benefits to factoring your code. In my opinion, the three most important benefits of creating factored code are increased reuse opportunity, reduced complexity, and improved tuning ability.

There are two different levels of reuse: the first level is reuse within the same module or project and the second level is reuse within other projects. An exciting thing happens with factored code—you experience a wonderful snowball effect. You'll find that as soon as you get a critical mass of small, focused procedures, lights will go on that wouldn't have been activated if your code consisted of long, complicated routines. You'll see new ways to combine these small procedures to provide new levels of functionality, without incurring a significant development burden.

The second level of reuse is significant because you can dramatically reduce the development time of future projects by collecting all of those useful, common routines and using them together as a springboard to jumpstart your next project. This book has presented a decent number of common Excel routines that can seed your collection. For example, the WorksheetExists function that I've mentioned numerous times in this book is something that I need to use in nearly every project.

Another benefit of factored routines is that they reduce complexity and are therefore much easier to maintain. The benefit of this is that it's easier for you or someone else to figure out how a procedure works six months or a year later when updates or modifications need to be made. I've seen my share of programs using huge everything-but-the-kitchen-sink procedures that were basically scrapped rather than updated because it was easier to rewrite than it was to figure out what was going on. This is an avoidable shame.

Finally, by factoring your code, you have an increased ability to improve performance. For example, you may have an application that calls a routine to find a particular item in a range. In an unfactored application, different procedures may implement their own search algorithm to find an item in a range. It may not be an easy matter to modify each procedure to use a more efficient search algorithm. A factored application has one search method that's used by any procedure that needs to search a range. By modifying the search algorithm in the search method, all of the procedures using the method will benefit from the increased performance.

Think Like an Environmentalist

One of the quickest ways an application can annoy or alienate a user is by operating like a toxic manufacturing factory located in Yellowstone National Park. Like a contemptible website that spawns countless pop-up windows, these programs go about rearranging options, menus, shortcut keys, and other aspects of Excel with reckless abandon.

Programs should respect the environment that they operate in and respect the settings and preferences of the user. A conscientious program should

- Leave things as it finds them including menus and Excel option settings.

- Not reassign existing shortcut keys or mouse actions unless it gives the user the opportunity to turn this functionality on/off.

- Provide the user with reasonable preference/configuration options.

- Keep the user informed as to what is going on in an unobtrusive way such as by using the status bar.

NOTE *User interface coverage begins in Chapter 18.*

The goal is that when a user closes the application's workbook (or turns off the add-in), the Excel user interface should look exactly like it did before the application started—down to the last setting.

Use Literal Values with Care

Literal ("hard-coded") values can be maintenance nightmares and should be used cautiously. You can use literal values in many different ways. Some of the more common uses for these values within an Excel application include

♦ Range addresses

♦ Row numbers

♦ Column numbers

♦ Worksheet names

♦ Workbook names

♦ Database connection information

In the last chapter, I presented the Setting and Settings classes. You can use these classes to move these kinds of things out of your VBA code and onto a worksheet where you can manage them better. Although this has the benefit of centralizing the handling of literal values, it doesn't eliminate literal values from your code, because setting names are literal values. However, you can validate that a setting name exists before you use it to eliminate the risk normally associated with using a literal value.

Use Syntax Highlighting

In Chapter 2, I mentioned that syntax highlighting is something that offers a lot of benefit, but that I rarely see people take advantage of it. Well, I should clarify. Nearly everyone uses syntax highlighting; it's just that hardly anyone deviates from the default settings. The chief benefit of using syntax highlighting is that you can instantly identify literal values in your code. Now, literal values aren't always a bad thing. However, they can be problematic when it comes to maintaining an application.

Unfortunately, the black and white pictures in this book aren't going to help prove how useful syntax highlighting is. It's really something you need to try for yourself. Table 13.2 shows the syntax highlighting settings that I like to use. Try these out to start with.

TABLE 13.2: EXAMPLE CODE COLOR SETTINGS

CODE ELEMENT	FOREGROUND COLOR	BACKGROUND COLOR
Normal Text	Red	Light Gray
Comment Text	Light Green	Light Gray
Keyword Text	Bright Blue	Light Gray
Identifier Text	Black	Light Gray

Using this syntax-highlighting scheme, when you view code in the VBE, literal values will stand out like a sore thumb because they'll appear as red text. Anywhere you see red text, you should pause and consider the way the literal value is being used and evaluate the likelihood that it will be a source of maintenance problems down the road.

Manage Literal Values Centrally

One of the risks associated with literal values is that if you need to modify a specific literal value, you need to be sure to look in every possible procedure that may be using the literal value to make sure each instance gets updated. This has two drawbacks: first, you may not get everything updated correctly because it can be easy to overlook something; and second, it's not very efficient to look through all of the procedures in a project. You can use Edit ➤ Replace to help ease this issue, but even this method isn't foolproof.

It's far more efficient to manage literal values centrally. You can do this in a lot of different ways including using private or public constants, storing data on a worksheet, using workbook names, or using the Windows registry. Occasionally, you'll need to employ more than one of these methods. I'll cover each of these methods in more detail in the following sections.

PRIVATE CONSTANTS

At a minimum, it's a good idea to assign literal values to constants at the top of a module. Additionally, you should use the Private keyword in the declaration so that the constant can't be seen by other procedures outside the module. The main benefit of using constants in your code rather than one of the other methods listed is that constants give you the best performance.

You should consider using private constants when the constant value and name is unique to the given module and you don't want the value to be used by procedures in any other modules.

PUBLIC CONSTANTS

If you need to refer to a literal value, you can assign a literal value to a public global constant rather than a private module-level constant. If you use global constants rather than private constants, then conceivably you might need to go to only one location in your project to update constant values. Like module-level constants, global constants offer the best performance when compared to the methods presented in the following sections.

You should consider using public constants over private constants for two reasons. One scenario is where you need to define a constant that procedures will use in more than one module. For example, perhaps you define a constant that defines the application's name:

```
Public Const APP_NAME = "Budget Plus"
```

Another reason to use public constants instead of private constants is that you can consolidate all of the constants in your application in one physical location. For example, you could create a module named CONSTANTS that serves as a container for all of the defined constants in your application. The benefit of this is that you don't have to search for constants in each module to make any updates. If you're in doubt about whether to define a private versus a public constant, I'd suggest that you make the constant public.

WORKSHEET-BASED VALUES

The Setting and Settings classes presented in the last chapter are a prime example of the worksheet-based approach. The advantage of this approach is that it removes literal values from the code. This allows someone to maintain or alter the literal values without using the VBE. You'll find this handy on occasions when the person who needs to modify the values isn't a developer and isn't comfortable working in the VBE. Alternatively, maybe you want to allow someone the ability to change these values but you don't want to give them the ability to view the code (i.e., you locked the VBA project for viewing). In these situations, you can place literal values on a worksheet and have procedures refer to the appropriate location on a worksheet to read the literal value.

NOTE Check out the Setting and Settings classes. They are presented in detail in Chapter 12.

If you don't need the comprehensive functionality provided by the Setting and Settings classes, you could do something as simple as defining a range name that refers to the range where the value is located. For example, let's say you created a range name "FISCAL_YEAR" that refers to a cell that stores the current fiscal year. You could easily retrieve the value in your code using the following statement.

```
ThisWorkbook.Names("Fiscal_Year").RefersToRange
```

In order to be a little more robust, you could validate that the name exists before using it in this manner. You may wonder if this really helps manage literal values. After all, isn't the name of the named range (Fiscal_Year) a literal value? Yes, the name of the named range is a literal value, but it's a good literal value if used correctly. The reason that this is a good literal value is that it's a literal value that can be validated before using it in your code. Additionally, it enables us to move the real value (i.e., fiscal year = 2003) into a more easily accessible place where it is easier to manage.

NOTE The use of named ranges is covered extensively in Chapter 8.

WORKBOOK NAME DEFINITIONS FOR SETTING STORAGE

Another way to store settings is by using workbook or worksheet name definitions. I feel this is a little bit sneaky, but once in a while, it's fun to be sneaky. Most Excel users aren't aware that you can set up constants in a workbook using the name functionality. For example, you could create a name called SalesTaxRate and have it refer to the value .06 rather than a cell or range in the workbook, as shown in Figure 13.2. Figure 13.3 shows an example of how you use the name from a worksheet.

FIGURE 13.2

You can set up names that refer to a value rather than a cell or range on a worksheet.

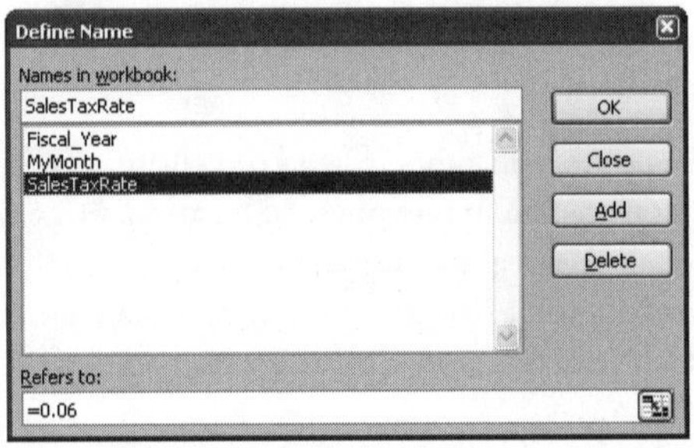

FIGURE 13.3

When you use the name in the workbook, you get the value you assigned to it.

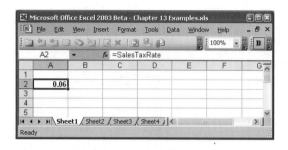

If you do use this method of storing values, you need to use the Evaluate method of the Application object to retrieve the value associated with the name. Listing 13.2 demonstrates this.

LISTING 13.2: RETRIEVING VALUES STORED AS A WORKBOOK NAME USING THE EVALUATE METHOD

```
Sub TestWorkbookNameValue()
    Dim vValue As Variant

    vValue = Application.Names("SalesTaxRate").RefersTo
    Debug.Print "Value retrieved using RefersTo: " & vValue

    vValue = Application.Names("SalesTaxRate").Value
    Debug.Print "Value retrieved using Value: " & vValue

    ' this next line doesn't work because the name
    ' doesn't refer to a range. Intentionally commented out.
    ' vValue = Application.Names("SalesTaxRate").RefersToRange

    vValue = Application.Evaluate("SalesTaxRate")
    Debug.Print "Value retrieved using Evaluate: " & vValue
End Sub
```

This listing produces the following output.

```
Value retrieved using RefersTo: =0.06
Value retrieved using Value: =0.06
Value retrieved using Evaluate: 0.06
```

Notice that if you do not use Evaluate, the value retrieved from the Name will include an equals sign (=). If the value is text data, you'll also get the value enclosed in quotes.

One of the primary benefits of this method is that you can be consistent in how you use literal values within the workbook and your VBA code. For example, the SalesTaxRate name in Listing 13.2 could also be used in any worksheet formulas that need to reference the sales tax rate.

FIGURE 13.4
Excel uses the registry
to store configuration
information.

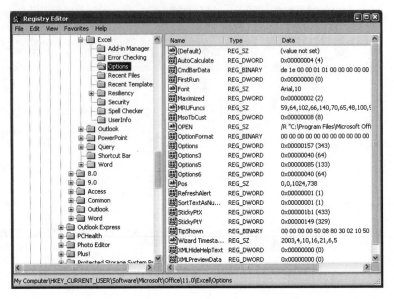

USING THE WINDOWS REGISTRY FOR STORING VALUES

Another option for storing literal values is the Windows registry. In fact, if you browsed the registry using the Registry Editor, you'd see that this is a common way for Windows programs to store configuration information. In Figure 13.4, you can see some of the registry settings used by Excel.

NOTE   *To view the registry, choose Start ➢ Run, type **regedit**, and click OK.*

WARNING   *Use extreme caution using the Registry Editor. Never modify registry information unless you are 100 percent sure of the consequences.*

Individual settings in the registry are referred to as keys. VBA provides a few functions for writing to and reading from the registry. The function SaveSetting creates a new registry key or updates an existing registry key. The function GetSetting retrieves the value associated with a registry key. I'll let you take a stab at what DeleteSetting does. Finally, a function called GetAllSettings retrieves a list of keys and the values associated with a certain application and section. These functions are pretty easy to use as is demonstrated by Listing 13.3.

LISTING 13.3: WORKING WITH THE REGISTRY USING THE VBA REGISTRY FUNCTIONS

```
Sub ExperimentWithRegistry()
    Dim vaKeys As Variant

    ' create new registry entries
```

```vb
        SaveSetting "XLTest", "General", "App_Name", "XLTest"
        SaveSetting "XLTest", "General", "App_Version", "1.0.0"
        SaveSetting "XLTest", "General", "App_Date", "10/11/2003"

        PrintRegistrySettings

        ' update a setting
        SaveSetting "XLTest", "General", "App_Version", "1.0.1"

        PrintRegistrySettings

        ' get all settings in an array
        vaKeys = GetAllSettings("XLTest", "General")
        PrintAllSettings vaKeys

        ' delete settings
        DeleteSetting "XLTest", "General", "App_Name"
        DeleteSetting "XLTest", "General", "App_Version"
        DeleteSetting "XLTest", "General", "App_Date"

        PrintRegistrySettings
End Sub

Sub PrintRegistrySettings()
    On Error Resume Next
    Debug.Print "Application Name: " & _
        GetSetting("XLTest", "General", "App_Name")
    Debug.Print "Application Version: " & _
        GetSetting("XLTest", "General", "App_Version")
    Debug.Print "Application Date: " & _
        GetSetting("XLTest", "General", "App_Date")
    Debug.Print "------------------------"
End Sub

Sub PrintAllSettings(vaSettings As Variant)
    Dim nItem As Integer

    If IsArray(vaSettings) Then
        For nItem = 0 To UBound(vaSettings)
            Debug.Print vaSettings(nItem, 0) & ": " & _
                vaSettings(nItem, 1)
        Next
    End If
    Debug.Print "------------------------"
End Sub
```

This listing produces the following output:

```
Application Name: XLTest
Application Version: 1.0.0
Application Date: 10/11/2003
------------------------
Application Name: XLTest
Application Version: 1.0.1
Application Date: 10/11/2003
------------------------
App_Name: XLTest
App_Version: 1.0.1
App_Date: 10/11/2003
------------------------
Application Name:
Application Version:
Application Date:
------------------------
```

Notice that if you use the GetAllSettings function, a two-dimensional variant array is returned. The first dimension represents each setting returned whereas the second dimension is one of two items: the key name or the key value.

NOTE *Registry entries created with SaveSetting are written to* HKEY_CURRENT_USER\Software\VB *and* VBA Program Settings\.

LOOKING UP VALUES FROM A DATABASE

It's possible to store these kinds of values in a database. The benefit of this approach is that it's possible to change the settings for all of the users without having to distribute new copies of the workbook or application. It also offers the most flexibility regarding securing the values. The main drawbacks of this method are that it requires a database connection and it's slower than the other methods. If you don't want to assume a constant database connection, you could use one of the other approaches for short-term needs and occasionally connect to the database for updates.

Consider using a database to store literal values that have short half-lives. That is, literal values that are likely to change over the life of the application. The more difficult it is to distribute new versions of the application, the more attractive this option becomes. For example, if the application is distributed to hundreds or thousands of users across the organization, it may be cost-effective to have an application that knows how to update itself rather than redistribute new versions of the application or otherwise force users to always "check the intranet for the latest version."

NOTE *Database coverage begins in Chapter 16.*

USING XML FOR PERSISTENT SETTINGS

One of the many things that you can use XML (Extensible Markup Language) for is to create a modern-day initialization file. In fact, some of the most exciting new features in Excel 2003 rely heavily on XML for this purpose.

Though the Windows registry was meant to replace INI (initialization) files, they are still in widespread use. One of the strengths of INI files versus the registry is that, because INI files are simple text, they can be easily inspected and modified using a text editor such as Notepad. INI files can also be copied with ease to other computers.

XML files offer the same conveniences as INI files do while delivering increased flexibility. Whereas data stored in INI files has to conform to the section, key, and value model (much like the registry), XML files can assume a form of your own choosing.

NOTE *In Chapters 17 and 21, I'll show the various ways in which you can use XML with Excel.*

Smart Workbook Design

Although this book focuses on the VBA aspect of developing Excel applications, this chapter wouldn't be complete without mentioning some practical advice regarding the general layout of an Excel application. In Chapter 22, I describe various application-distribution strategies and techniques such as templates, add-ins, and standard Excel workbooks. For the purposes of this section, I'm assuming that you're developing a standard Excel workbook. By standard Excel workbook, I mean an application whose "life-form" is a standard Excel workbook or file.

There are many schools of thought on the "proper" way to lay out or design a spreadsheet. Over the course of my career, I've experimented with many different strategies to design a spreadsheet. So if you want to know the *best* approach to designing a robust, efficient, and easy-to-maintain spreadsheet, I can say with 100 percent confidence that it depends. Among other things, it depends on the ultimate purpose of the spreadsheet, the potential value of the spreadsheet versus the extra time and effort (costs) required to implement the various characteristics, and the amount of data being analyzed. For example, sometimes you'll value clarity above everything else, other times ease-of-use will be your most important design objective. The best approach for designing and building the spreadsheet depends on your prioritization of the various design objectives.

That said, I believe most of the following design tips should apply to nearly every spreadsheet.

Spreadsheets should flow top to bottom, left to right. This seems natural, right? Almost too obvious to include here? However, an important point is implicit in this statement that I need to point out. Formulas in cells should refer only to cells that are upstream from them. So a formula in cell B10 should refer only to a cell in the range A:B9 on the current worksheet or any cell in one of the previous worksheets (a worksheet to the left of the current worksheet, assuming that the worksheets are in order of the flow of the worksheet).

Separate input, calculations, and output. This is good advice for a few reasons. First, it helps facilitate discussion when you're constructing the spreadsheet. It's natural to think in terms of these concepts. What do I have/need? That is your input. Where do I need to go? That is your desired output or reports. How do I get there? These are your calculations. Second, it is easy to understand, document, and explain the final product. And finally, it facilitates many of the techniques mentioned within this section.

Keep time periods consistent between worksheets. If the columns in your workbook represent a time series and this time series is repeated between worksheets, make sure that like time periods occupy the same column on every worksheet. If January 2004 is column D on Sheet1, it should be column D on Sheet2. The benefits of this practice are that it makes it much easier to construct formulas during the build process, it facilitates formula auditing, and makes it easier to refer to individual time periods programmatically.

Avoid blank columns.   One common practice is to insert blank columns in between sections of data to create visual separation between the sections. This is especially true if each column represents a period of time in a time series. For example, if you have two years of data by month, do not insert an empty column between each year of data. You can create the desired separation using column widths and cell indenting. I prefer to keep all of the months as one unit and then show summaries (such as by quarter or by year) in the columns to the right of the data range. The benefit is that it is easier to create and audit formulas and easier to work with the data programmatically because you don't have to worry about blank columns or columns that represent summarized data. This strategy is easiest to implement when you break a workbook into input, calculation, and output sections. Assuming the monthly time series scenario, usually the only time that you need to display summaries (by quarter or by year) is on the output or reports.

Don't scale numbers using formulas.   In Chapter 10, I demonstrated that you can easily display scaled values using a number format rather than physically adjusting the true value of the number (such as multiplying by 0.001 or dividing by 1000).

Monster formulas are not cool.   Earlier in my career, I thought that the ability to create huge, complex formulas was a way to prove how "advanced" my Excel skills were. Big mistake. It is much better for everyone, including yourself, to use a series of separate, intermediate calculations. If you follow the input, calculation, and output theme just discussed, using a few extra columns or rows to perform intermediate calculations shouldn't be an issue. Calculation worksheets are just that— places in a workbook for calculation purposes only. In order to get the most bang for the buck, you should lay out calculation sections in a manner that facilitates understanding and auditing. Unless you have more than 65,536 rows or 256 columns, why consolidate intermediate calculations into one mega formula? It is true that you'll get a marginal benefit in calculation time; however, this benefit comes at a huge cost, in my opinion.

As I alluded to earlier, one size doesn't fit all. If I had to try and make one size fit all, I'd use the one high-level design that seems to work for me more times than not. This design includes a menu worksheet, an input worksheet(s), a calculation worksheet(s), a report worksheet(s), and the Settings worksheet used by the Setting and Settings classes presented in Chapter 12.

By default, the menu worksheet is what is displayed when the workbook is opened. Giving a nod to the value of the first impression, the menu worksheet should be visually pleasing and have a little "WOW!" aspect to it. The menu worksheet can serve numerous purposes. If the application doesn't use its own Excel menu or toolbar, the menu worksheet serves as a switchboard to help users navigate to various sections of the workbook. Even if the workbook does have a more sophisticated user interface, the menu can provide an additional way to navigate to other locations in the workbook. It could also be used to navigate to external documents.

Another possible function of the menu worksheet is to collect high-level user information. For example, in a budgeting application, the menu worksheet might be the location where the user enters his name and the name of the entity or department that he is creating a budget for.

In addition, I feel that the menu should, if possible, convey the overall message that the workbook aims to convey. For example, in a budgeting workbook, you may include a small graph on the menu worksheet that shows next year's budget against this year's, along with a few key performance indicators (KPIs).

Finally, you can use the menu worksheet to display general application information such as the current version, version date, or other useful nuggets of information. In one application I built, the menu worksheet included dynamic comments retrieved from a database that notified users of important information related to the model. Figure 13.5 shows an example of a menu worksheet.

After the menu worksheet, I'll have one or more input worksheets. Input can come from multiple places including databases, text files, other Excel workbooks, user input, or an XML file. I like to keep each set of data on a separate worksheet. This makes things easier to work with programmatically.

Input worksheets should be the raw input data and nothing else. Perform any supporting calculations on separate worksheets. The calculation worksheets should be laid out in a manner that facilitates understanding. Don't worry about eye candy when it comes to calculation worksheets. Calculation worksheets can be kept hidden and displayed only when necessary.

The next set of worksheets represents the output or reports. These worksheets are organized in a manner that conveys the information that the spreadsheet was designed to convey. Output worksheets should be well formatted and print ready.

The last worksheet in the workbook is the Settings worksheet. This worksheet stores any configurable settings used in the workbook. I usually use the Settings worksheet in conjunction with the Setting and Settings classes presented in Chapter 12.

FIGURE 13.5

I like to think of the menu worksheet as a portal to the rest of the workbook.

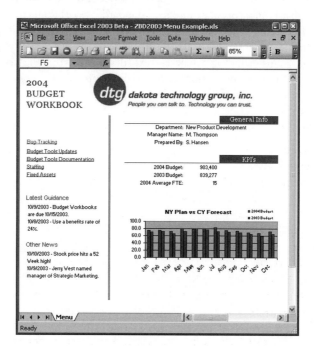

Summary

It can be very easy to write some VBA code to achieve a desired outcome. Writing robust yet readable and maintainable applications requires a little extra thought and planning. You can get off to a good start, however, by incorporating some of the ideas suggested in this chapter.

The most common problem that I see in poorly developed Excel applications is the use of Select and Selection to manipulate objects in Excel. This can be the result of using the Excel's macro recorder or the product of a beginning developer who has learned by studying the output of the macro recorder. It isn't necessary to select objects before you manipulate them programmatically. A better approach is to create a variable of the appropriate object type (workbook, worksheet, or range), set the variable to refer to the desired object, and then manipulate the object using the variable.

Another problem exhibited by some Excel applications is the failure to manage the display of information. This can lead to poor performance and it looks awful from the user's perspective. Thankfully, it's a simple problem to solve using the ScreenUpdating property of the Application object.

Regarding the organization of your code, using more procedures is better. Write lots of small, focused procedures rather than a single monolithic procedure that does everything. Modular procedures offer more opportunity for reuse, are more readable, and facilitate code optimization for greater performance.

As you develop your program design skills, you'll find that you can apply the same design skills to the design and construction of spreadsheets in general. The design of a spreadsheet plays a huge part in determining the difficulty of applying automation to it using VBA.

Hopefully the techniques in this chapter will be as valuable to you as they are to me. Nonetheless, I think it pays to experiment. I try new approaches all of the time. With each new approach, I find something I like that I can incorporate into my "standard" way of doing things. That's how we all evolve and learn. Look at finding your own best practices as a journey rather than a destination. Enjoy the trip!

With the next chapter, I'll begin my coverage of the techniques related to working with external data and programs including databases, text files, and XML. The first topic in this part, however, is integrating with other applications such as Microsoft Word.

Part 4

Working with External Data

Chapter 14

Integrating with Other Applications

ALTHOUGH EXCEL IS A versatile application, try as some people might, they can't make it do everything. Thankfully, it's possible to embed or link documents created using other applications into an Excel document. Documents created using multiple applications are referred to as compound documents.

It's also possible to control other applications programmatically. This is helpful when you need to automate a process that involves multiple applications. The act of programmatically controlling one application from within a different application is referred to as automation.

This chapter provides an overview of the technologies associated with creating compound documents and automation as well as examples of each technique.

A Primer to Office Automation

Microsoft has referred to the technology and techniques I cover in this section using numerous terms over the years. If you look in other books or articles, you may see this technology referred to using one of the following names, depending on the date the information was published.

Object Linking and Embedding (OLE)   Although object linking and embedding has always referred to the concept of a compound document, depending on the time period it was used, the acronym OLE may have referred to a much broader range of technologies.

ActiveX   Just as people were getting used to the term OLE, Microsoft began to refer to the same technology using the term ActiveX. This move was intended to reflect the wider scope of functionality that the underlying technologies enabled, and to try and capitalize on the possibilities that ActiveX provided in terms of providing dynamic content to web pages. ActiveX was more of a marketing term.

Component Object Model (COM)   COM is a specification for a software component architecture. COM is the foundation of all of the other technologies described in this chapter.

COM+   An updated version of COM that came into existence with Windows 2000.

Automation   Automation is the term that refers to the concept of controlling one application from within another application.

NOTE *Microsoft has a newer software architecture called .NET. .NET is a totally new architecture that is not directly compatible with COM technologies (though you can have the two technologies co-exist by using a translation layer called an interop assembly). As Microsoft Office is COM-based software, the topics in this chapter stick to the COM side of the fence.*

Note that these names refer to a set of technologies that encompass more, perhaps much more, than the small subset of functionality this book will cover.

I feel compelled to tell you that I am attempting to simplify this information to a reasonable extent. If you are the type who enjoys digging into the underlying details, you will have a field day studying this technology. It gets complicated really quickly. Entire books have been written on the intricacies of COM.

Why are there so many names associated with this technology? To help you understand, let me review a little about the history of the technology. In the late 1980s, if you wanted to use data from one application inside another, you were pretty much up the proverbial creek. The only mechanism that general users had was the clipboard. You could cut or copy some text from one application and paste it into another. For some uses this worked just fine, but users demanded more. Among other things, if data changed in one document, you had to manually update the dependent document. Thus, it was a tedious task to keep related documents up-to-date.

In order to solve the problem of keeping the same "nugget" of information up-to-date in dependent documents when information was changed in the source document, Microsoft created dynamic data exchange (DDE) and the initial version of object linking and embedding (OLE). Although DDE could help solve the problem, it wasn't the easiest technology to work with.

The initial version of OLE was significant in that this is where Microsoft created the concept of compound documents. A compound document is a document created using multiple applications. This meant that you could have a Word document that contained an embedded Excel chart or worksheet such as the document pictured in Figure 14.1. This was a wonderful idea. Unfortunately, it was a little ahead of its time. Most of the PCs in use in this era had a difficult time, at best, handling compound documents. I can remember some of my greatest demonstrations of patience occurring when I was trying to create impressive compound documents.

From the momentum generated by the initial version of OLE came an enhanced version of OLE. This time, Microsoft dropped the "Object Linking and Embedding (OLE)" references and simply called the technology OLE, recognizing that the technology was really about much more than simply creating compound documents. OLE represented a fundamental shift in thinking. Microsoft developers who worked on the original version of OLE came to view the parts of a compound document as software *components*. Out of this shift in vision, they set about specifying a way for software components to "talk" to each other and discover the services that each offers. Microsoft developed a specification known as the Component Object Model (COM). The second version of OLE was build upon COM underpinnings.

In the mid 90s Microsoft came up with the term ActiveX and thoroughly confused everyone (once again). ActiveX controls, ActiveX documents, ActiveX scripting. Everything was ActiveX. I think the Xbox was also in development about this time. Do you suppose the secret code name to that project was the ActiveXbox?

What is the difference between ActiveX controls and OLE controls? Nothing. Why the change? Marketing. Oh, and in ActiveX, OLE once again refers only to object linking and embedding—not to the broad range of things it used to. At the time, Homer Simpson was quoted as saying "DOOUGH!"

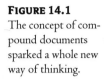

FIGURE 14.1
The concept of compound documents sparked a whole new way of thinking.

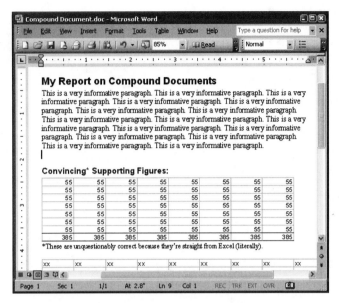

For the purposes of this chapter, the main thing to take out of this section is that no matter what technical or marketing name you want to use, the concept we are talking about deals primarily with one of two things: First, the creation and manipulation of compound documents, and second, the automation of one application from within another application.

Expounding On Compound Documents

As I mentioned in the previous section, compound documents are created using multiple applications yet they appear as a single cohesive document in the compound document's host application. You use a document's host application to view the document in its entirety.

A compound document can store its components in two different ways. The first way is via linking. When you create a compound document in which a component of the document is linked to another document, the compound document stores the link details in the document file. The linked component's details are stored in a separate file.

The other way a compound document can store a component is by embedding the component's file inside the compound document's file. Hence you have object linking and embedding (OLE)—a boring but descriptive name when it comes to talking about compound documents.

A compound document can consist of multiple components. If you are feeling adventurous or maybe you're just bored, you can do all sorts of weird things. For example, Figure 14.2 is an Excel worksheet inside an embedded Word document inside another Excel worksheet. The son-in-law of my friend's cousin's girlfriend showed me that trick.

FIGURE 14.2
Embed Excel in
Word in Excel? You
can create all sorts
of combinations by
embedding different
combinations inside
one another.

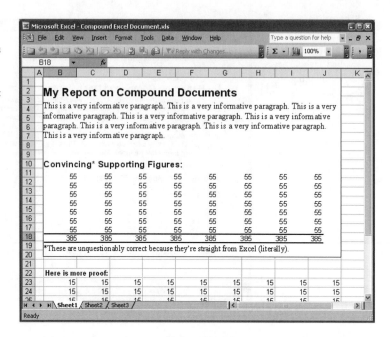

Depending on whether a component is embedded or linked, you can perform various actions on the component. Embedded components can be edited in-place, as in Figure 14.3, or opened up in a full instance of their native application for editing.

FIGURE 14.3
Embedded objects
can be edited in place.

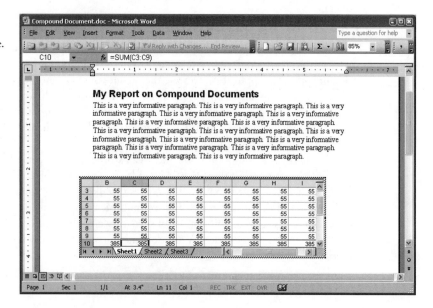

In-place editing is really an impressive development feat as far as I am concerned. Look what happens in Figure 14.4 when you edit an Excel worksheet embedded inside a Word document. Word morphs into an Excel environment. The menu in Figure 14.3 is an Excel menu, but I never did anything to leave the Word environment. You can see the Word icon in the upper-left corner of Figure 14.4.

FIGURE 14.4

In-place editing of embedded components in a compound document is a truly impressive capability.

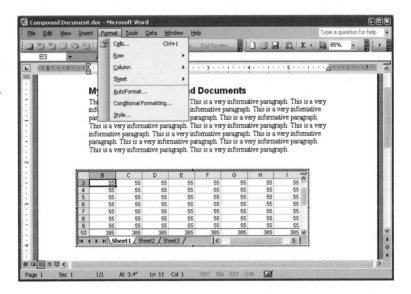

Linked components can also be edited. However, they can't be edited in place as embedded components can. The main advantage of linked components is that you can create a "living" document that is aware of its linked components. As a linked component gets modified, the compound document can display the updated values without your intervention.

Crafting Compound Documents Programmatically

From a developer standpoint, wouldn't it be nice to tap into the functionality related to object linking and embedding? True to form, it is surprisingly easy to programmatically embed or link a document inside another document. The Excel object model contains two objects related to object linking and embedding: OLEObject and OLEObjects. OLEObjects is a collection object that contains OLE-Object objects. Just like the other collection objects you've seen so far, OLEObjects contains an Add method that you can use to add a new OLEObject to a worksheet. Although the Add method has a lot of parameters, they are all optional, sort of, and you usually only need to specify a few of them. I say "sort of" because you do need to specify either ClassType or FileName. Here is the syntax of the Add method:

```
SomeWorksheetObject.OLEObjects.Add [ClassType], [FileName], [Link],
[DisplayAsIcon], [IconFileName], [IconIndex], [IconLabel], [Left], [Top], [Width],
[Height]
```

The parameters of the Add method are detailed in the following list.

ClassType The programmatic identifier of the object to be created. If ClassType is specified, FileName and Link are ignored. You must specify either the ClassType parameter or the File-Name parameter. Use the ClassType parameter when you want to add an OLE object to the worksheet that is not based on an existing document. For example, if you specified "Word.Document" as the ClassType, an empty Word document would be embedded in the worksheet.

FileName The name of the file that the OLE object is based on or linked to. You must specify either the ClassType parameter or the FileName parameter. Use FileName when you want to embed or link to an existing document.

Link Link is only used if the FileName parameter is specified. If you want to embed the document into the worksheet, Link should be false. If you want an OLE object that is linked to the source document, Link should be true. The default value is false.

DisplayAsIcon This should be true to display the new OLE object either as an icon, and false to display the object normally. If this argument is true, IconFileName and IconIndex can be used to specify an icon. The default value is false.

IconFileName The filename of the file that contains the icon to be displayed. This argument is used only if DisplayAsIcon is true.

IconIndex The index number of the icon in the icon file. IconIndex is used only if Display-AsIcon is true and IconFileName refers to a valid file that contains icons.

IconLabel IconLabel should be a string that contains the text to display beneath the icon. Icon-Label is used only if DisplayAsIcon is true. By default, no label is displayed.

Left The distance in points of the left edge of the object from the left edge of the worksheet. By default the left value of the ActiveCell is used (ActiveCell.Left).

Top The distance in points of the top edge of the object from the top edge of the worksheet. By default the top value of the ActiveCell is used (ActiveCell.Top).

Width The initial width of the object in points.

Height The initial height of the object in points.

TIP Don't have a clue how to estimate distances in points? Don't fret, I don't either. Assuming you are an American or are otherwise familiar with our unique way of measuring distances, you'll feel more at home using Application. InchesToPoints to specify distances. For example, if you want an OLE object to appear 1/2 inch from the top of the worksheet, you can use a statement similar to `MyOLEObject.Top = Application.InchesToPoints(0.50)`.

Listing 14.1 demonstrates how to programmatically embed a Word document inside an Excel worksheet using the Add method of OLEObjects.

```vba
Sub CreateCompoundDocument()
    Dim rg As Range
    Dim obj As OLEObject

    ' Set up a range that will indicate the
    ' top left corner of the OLEObject
    Set rg = ThisWorkbook.Worksheets(1).Cells(2, 2)

    ' Insert OLEObject
    Set obj = InsertObject(rg, "C:\testdoc.doc", False)

    ' Demonstrate that the object was inserted (or not)
    If Not obj Is Nothing Then
        Debug.Print "Object inserted."
    Else
        Debug.Print "Sorry - the object could not be inserted."
    End

    ' Clean up
    Set obj = Nothing
    Set rg = Nothing
End Sub

Function InsertObject(rgTopLeft As Range, sFile As String, _
    bLink As Boolean) As OLEObject

    Dim obj As OLEObject

    On Error GoTo ErrHandler

    ' Insert the object
    Set obj = rgTopLeft.Parent.OLEObjects.Add( _
        Filename:=sFile, _
        Link:=bLink)

    ' Don't specify these in the Add method
    ' above - it causes an error.
    obj.Top = rgTopLeft.Top
    obj.Left = rgTopLeft.Left

    ' Return a reference to the inserted OLEObject
    Set InsertObject = obj
    Exit Function

ErrHandler:
```

```
        ' Tarter sauce! An error occurred.
        Debug.Print Err.Description
        Set InsertObject = Nothing
    End Function
```

FIGURE 14.5

Creating a compound document is a piece of cake using the OLE-Objects object.

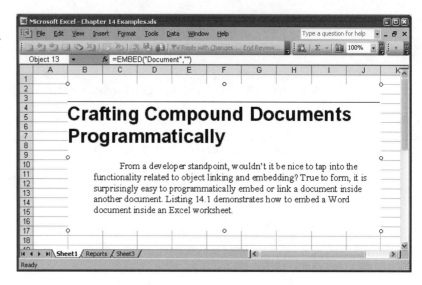

The objective of this listing is to embed the document "C:\testdoc.doc" (you'll need to update this if you try this listing), a Word document, into the first worksheet of a workbook with the top-left corner of the embedded Word document located at cell B2. So that you can do this, I've created a function called InsertObject that actually embeds or links a document inside the worksheet on which the range object is located. The CreateCompoundDocument procedure sets the appropriate parameters necessary to give the InsertObject function a test drive. Figure 14.5 shows the result of my test drive.

One of the interesting points regarding Listing 14.1 is that you don't have to specify the application or class that created the document you're inserting. For example, if you specify a PowerPoint file to the InsertObject function, it'll work without a hitch and embed a PowerPoint document into the spreadsheet (see Figure 14.6). Well, actually, the Add method of the OLEObjects object works without a hitch because this is the method called by InsertObject.

OLE Is Great; Automation Is Better

Linking and embedding objects is great and all, but what if you need to perform an action on a linked or embedded document? Or, what if your code needs to use functionality provided by another application? For these types of tasks, you need to move beyond linking and embedding into an area generally referred to as automation. Automation refers to the process of accessing the object model associated with another application or software component.

FIGURE 14.6

Why stop with Word documents? You can embed documents created with other applications including PowerPoint.

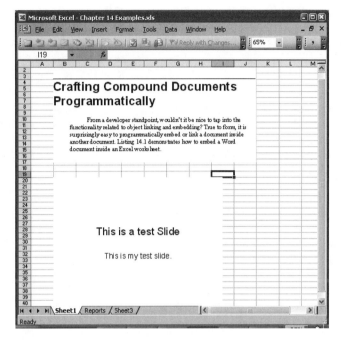

Once you learn the mechanics of accessing another application's class library, you are home free. From there, you use the class library as if you were using it natively. This, of course, assumes that you're familiar with the other application's class library. Just as it's hard to do anything in Excel without some knowledge of Excel's object model, it's difficult to do anything useful in Word without some knowledge of Word's object model.

So how do you access another application's class library? Well, it depends on how you'd like to bind to that library.

Binding to a Class Library

One important concept to understand is the concept of binding. Binding occurs when the controlling application (or client) learns about the objects, properties, and methods that are present within the controlled application's (or server) object model.

There are two types of binding: early binding and late binding. Early binding occurs during the development process and (usually) requires the developer to set a reference to the type library associated with the server. Late binding occurs at run-time.

Most of the time you should use early binding. Early binding offers two main benefits: first, it offers much faster performance; second, it allows you to take advantage of all the helpful VBE features such as Auto Syntax Check, Auto List Members, and quick access to the server's context-sensitive help files. However, early binding does have a downside—if you deploy the application on a PC that doesn't have the server application installed, the application won't run and an error will be displayed as soon as you open the application file. This is because VBA checks the validity of any early-bound objects when the file is opened.

You can enable early binding by setting a reference to the server's type library. To set a reference, select Tools ➤ References from the VBE menu. This displays a References dialog box similar to the one shown in Figure 14.7.

To enable early binding, scroll down the list of available references and place a check mark next to the appropriate type library. You should only select type-libraries that you are actually going to use. In Figure 14.8, I have set a reference to Microsoft Word.

Not every server supports early binding. For the servers that don't, you must use late binding. Late binding is slower than early binding because a special validation process occurs under the covers for each line of your code that uses the server.

So, back to the original question. How do you access an external application's class library? Listing 14.2 shows how to access Word's class library in two ways.

FIGURE 14.7

Enable early binding using the References dialog box.

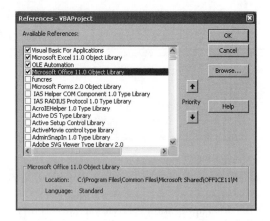

FIGURE 14.8

All of the selected available references are early bound.

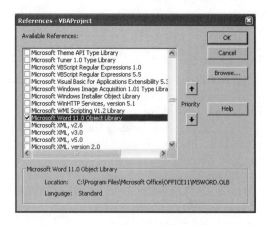

LISTING 14.2: EARLY VS. LATE BINDING

```
Sub WordEarlyBound()
    Dim wd As Word.Application
    Dim doc As Word.Document

    ' Create new instance of Word
    Set wd = New Word.Application

    ' Add a new document
    Set doc = wd.Documents.Add

    ' Save & close the document
    doc.SaveAs "C:\testdoc1.doc"
    doc.Close

    ' Clean up
    Set doc = Nothing
    Set wd = Nothing
End Sub

Sub WordLateBound()
    Dim objWord As Object
    Dim objDoc As Object

    ' Create a new instance of Word
    Set objWord = CreateObject("Word.Application")

    ' Add a new document
    Set objDoc = objWord.Documents.Add

    ' Save & close the document
    objDoc.SaveAs "C:\testdoc2.doc"
    objDoc.Close

    ' Clean up
    Set objDoc = Nothing
    Set objWord = Nothing
End Sub
```

The WordEarlyBound procedure assumes that you have already set a reference to the Microsoft Word Object Library by selecting it in the References dialog box as shown in Figure 14.8. You can always tell when early binding is being used by looking at the variable declarations. By setting a reference to the Microsoft Word Object Library, you allow VBA to have knowledge of the Word object model. As a result, you can declare variables using the specific object associated with each variable rather than declaring each variable using the generic Object object.

The WordLateBound procedure doesn't require you to set a reference. On the flip side, the variables must be declared as Object objects. Further, because VBA has no knowledge of the properties and methods associated with the variables, the VBE can't provide any help in the form of Auto List Members or Auto Syntax Checking. Writing code when you are using late bound objects is old-school. You either memorize object libraries or else spend a lot of time in the help files looking up properties, methods, and method parameters.

An Automation Example: Presentation Automation

It's time to break out the role playing hats and take a look at an example in which automation may be a good solution. For this example, you're a financial analyst at a large retailer—Bullseye Corporation. One of your many tasks is to prepare a presentation each month for your boss who then presents the data to upper management. This report details sales information such as same-store sales comparisons, revenue per store, and other key indicators.

Most of the presentation involves financial data that you prepare in Excel. Because your company has invested in Microsoft Analysis Services to facilitate rapid analysis in Excel, it only takes you a matter of minutes to gather the data required for the report.

THE PROBLEM

The problem is that the presentation needs to use PowerPoint. Consequently, you spend most of your time shuffling data from Excel to PowerPoint manually. You have already experimented with object linking and embedding as a way to eliminate or reduce the amount of tedious copying and pasting required of the task.

For example, you tried to create a single Excel workbook and a single PowerPoint presentation. The presentation contains linked Excel data. Each month, all you need to do is refresh the data in Excel and the PowerPoint presentation updates automatically. Then all you need to do is change the bullet points in the presentation as necessary. In theory, this should work just fine. However, you encounter two problems with this approach that prevent it from being as useful as you first thought it would be.

First of all, like most financial analysts, you are a pack rat by necessity. You need to keep a copy of every report that you produce along with all of the supporting detail you need to produce the report. That way, if anyone ever questions you about the report, you can go back and retrace your steps. The single workbook/single presentation approach doesn't work well for you because in the process of updating for the current month, you destroy the prior month. The elaborate folder system you have created for storing files also means that linking files can be problematic. Any time you copy files to a new location, you run the risk of error either by breaking links, or worse, by using links that mistakenly point to the wrong file. For example, October's presentation may have a link to September's Excel workbook.

The second problem is also related to linking. The presentation file needs to be portable so that your boss and others can use it without having to distribute the Excel file as well. This means you really need to embed the Excel file rather than link to it. If you embed, of course, you don't get the intended benefit of eliminating all of the copying and pasting because you'll need to re-create the presentation each month.

THE SOLUTION

The solution to this problem is to employ automation in Excel that will automatically create the presentation based on data in your Excel workbook. Using VBA you can write code that will

◆ Create an instance of PowerPoint.

◆ Create an empty presentation using the designated template.

◆ Create a title slide.

◆ Create a slide for each report you have created in Excel.

◆ Save the presentation to a location of your choosing.

Ideally, the only thing you'll need to do is add any content to the presentation that doesn't come from Excel.

THE SAMPLE WORKBOOK

For the purposes of this example, I created three sample reports—all on a single worksheet named "Reports". The range of the first report is named "Sales_Summary". This report is shown in Figure 14.9, along with another report that is a chart based on the Sales Summary data.

The third report is a listing of the top five stores based on sales. The range name for this report is "Top_Five". This report is shown in Figure 14.10.

FIGURE 14.9

The Sales Summary report and graph

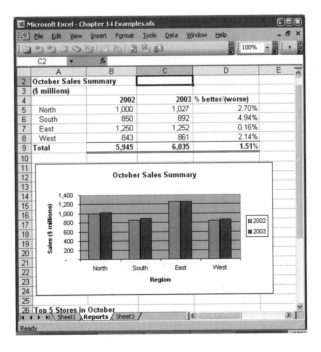

FIGURE 14.10

The Top 5 Stores report

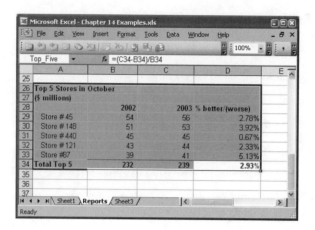

The code to implement the solution is shown in Listing 14.3. This listing uses early binding to establish a reference to PowerPoint, so if you try this yourself, be sure to set a reference to PowerPoint by selecting Tools ➤ References from the VBE and placing a check mark next to the Microsoft PowerPoint 11.0 Object Library in the list of available references. If you're using a version of Microsoft Office other than Office 2003, you'll have a different version of PowerPoint such as Microsoft PowerPoint 10.0 Object Library.

LISTING 14.3: AUTOMATING POWERPOINT PRESENTATION CREATION FROM EXCEL

```
Option Explicit

Sub CreatePresentation()
    Dim ppt As PowerPoint.Application
    Dim pres As PowerPoint.Presentation
    Dim sSaveAs As String
    Dim ws As Worksheet
    Dim chrt As Chart
    Dim nSlide As Integer

    On Error GoTo ErrHandler

    Set ws = ThisWorkbook.Worksheets("Reports")

    ' Create a new instance of PowerPoint
    Set ppt = New PowerPoint.Application

    ' Create a new presentation
    Set pres = ppt.Presentations.Add
    pres.ApplyTemplate _
        "c:\program files\microsoft office\templates" & _
```

```
            "\presentation designs\maple.pot"

    With pres.Slides.Add(1, ppLayoutTitle)
        .Shapes(1).TextFrame.TextRange.Text = "October Sales Analysis"
        .Shapes(2).TextFrame.TextRange.Text = "11/5/2003"
    End With

    ' Copy data
    CopyDataRange pres, ws.Range("Sales_Summary"), 2, 2
    CopyChart pres, ws.ChartObjects(1).Chart, 3, 1
    CopyDataRange pres, ws.Range("Top_Five"), 4, 2

    ' Save & close the presentation file
    sSaveAs = GetSaveAsName("Save As")
    If sSaveAs <> "False" Then
        pres.SaveAs sSaveAs
    End If
    pres.Close

ExitPoint:
    Application.CutCopyMode = False
    Set chrt = Nothing
    Set ws = Nothing
    Set pres = Nothing
    Set ppt = Nothing
    Exit Sub
ErrHandler:
    MsgBox "Sorry the following error has occurred: " & _
    vbCrLf & vbCrLf & Err.Description, vbOKOnly
    Resume ExitPoint
End Sub

Private Sub CopyDataRange(pres As PowerPoint.Presentation, _
    rg As Range, nSlide As Integer, _
    dScaleFactor As Double)

    ' copy range to clipboard
    rg.Copy

    ' add new blank slide
    pres.Slides.Add nSlide, ppLayoutBlank

    ' paste the range to the slide
    pres.Slides(nSlide).Shapes.PasteSpecial ppPasteOLEObject

    ' scale the pasted object in PowerPoint
    pres.Slides(nSlide).Shapes(1).ScaleHeight dScaleFactor, msoTrue
    pres.Slides(nSlide).Shapes(1).ScaleWidth dScaleFactor, msoTrue
```

```
    ' Center Horizontally & Vertically
    ' Might be a good idea to move this outside this procedure
    ' so you have more control over whether this happens or not
    CenterVertically pres.Slides(nSlide), _
        pres.Slides(nSlide).Shapes(1)
    CenterHorizontally pres.Slides(nSlide), _
        pres.Slides(nSlide).Shapes(1)

End Sub

Private Sub CopyChart(pres As PowerPoint.Presentation, _
    chrt As Chart, nSlide As Integer, _
    dScaleFactor As Double)

    ' copy chart to clipboard as a picture
    chrt.CopyPicture xlScreen

    ' add slide
    pres.Slides.Add nSlide, ppLayoutBlank

    ' copy chart to PowerPoint
    pres.Slides(nSlide).Shapes.PasteSpecial ppPasteDefault

    ' scale picture
    pres.Slides(nSlide).Shapes(1).ScaleHeight dScaleFactor, msoTrue
    pres.Slides(nSlide).Shapes(1).ScaleWidth dScaleFactor, msoTrue

    ' Center Horizontally & Vertically
    ' Might be a good idea to move this outside this procedure
    ' so you have more control over whether this happens or not
    CenterVertically pres.Slides(nSlide), _
        pres.Slides(nSlide).Shapes(1)
    CenterHorizontally pres.Slides(nSlide), _
        pres.Slides(nSlide).Shapes(1)

End Sub

Private Function GetSaveAsName(sTitle As String) As String

    Dim sFilter As String

    sFilter = "Presentation (*.ppt), *.ppt"

    GetSaveAsName = _
        Application.GetSaveAsFilename(filefilter:=sFilter, _
        Title:=sTitle)
End Function
```

```
Private Sub CenterVertically(sl As PowerPoint.Slide, _
    sh As PowerPoint.Shape)

    Dim lHeight As Long

    lHeight = sl.Parent.PageSetup.SlideHeight
    sh.Top = (lHeight - sh.Height) / 2
End Sub

Private Sub CenterHorizontally(sl As PowerPoint.Slide, _
    sh As PowerPoint.Shape)

    Dim lWidth As Long

    lWidth = sl.Parent.PageSetup.SlideWidth
    sh.Left = (lWidth - sh.Width) / 2
End Sub
```

CreatePresentation is the main procedure of this listing. Right off the bat, you can tell that this procedure is using early binding just by looking at the variable declarations. CreatePresentation uses two variables that represent a PowerPoint object. The first, ppt, represents the PowerPoint.Application object. Like the Application object from the Excel object model, PowerPoint.Application is at the top of the PowerPoint object model. The second variable that represents a PowerPoint object is named pres and represents a PowerPoint Presentation object. The Presentation object is roughly analogous to the Workbook object in Excel.

After the variables are declared, the next task is to enable some sort of error handling. You'll encounter an increased probability of errors in code that deals with automation. For this example, I just trap the error, display the error message, and then run the clean-up code denoted by the ExitPoint label.

After I set a reference to the Reports worksheet, it's time to create a new instance of PowerPoint and point your ppt variable to it. Once I have PowerPoint up and running, I create a new presentation using the fall inspiring maple template (which is appropriate for October) and add the title slide.

At this point, I can copy in the data from Excel. Because I need to do a number of things when I'm copying from Excel to PowerPoint, it's a good idea to create a procedure that wraps this task up. To do so, I enter the CopyDataRange procedure. Copying from Excel to PowerPoint is a two statement process.

```
' copy range to clipboard
rg.Copy
...
' paste the range to the slide
pres.Slides(nSlide).Shapes.PasteSpecial ppPasteOLEObject
```

The first step is to copy the range in Excel to the clipboard. The transfer is completed in PowerPoint by using the PasteSpecial method of the Shapes object and specifying the OLE object option. The remainder of this procedure deals with sizing and positioning (via the CenterVertically and Center-Horizontally procedures). In order to make this procedure more generic (and therefore increase the potential for reuse) it would be a good exercise to either remove the positioning statements or add a parameter that allows you to copy the range onto the slide without repositioning.

The CopyChart procedure is very similar to CopyDataRange. The first difference is that this procedure requires a Chart object as a parameter rather than a Range object. The other difference is in the copy/paste operation.

```
' copy chart to clipboard as a picture
chrt.CopyPicture xlScreen
...
' copy chart to PowerPoint
pres.Slides(nSlide).Shapes.PasteSpecial ppPasteDefault
```

I have used the CopyPicture method of the Chart object, which copies a picture of the chart to the clipboard. Rather than the OLE object option, I pasted the chart using the default option.

THE RESULT

Listing 14.3 produces a new PowerPoint presentation with a title slide and three additional slides corresponding to the reports in Excel. Figure 14.11 shows what the slides look like in PowerPoint.

Although the chart was embedded in the presentation in a picture format, the Sales Summary and Top 5 Stores reports are embedded in the presentation as Excel documents. This means that you can take advantage of in-place editing directly in PowerPoint as I am doing in Figure 14.12.

FIGURE 14.11
This is the presentation created by Listing 14.3.

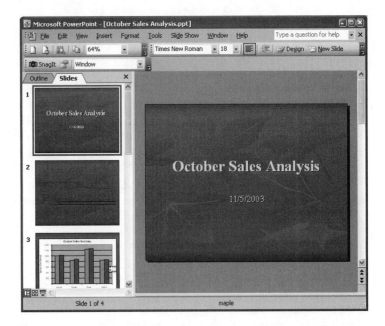

FIGURE 14.12

You can edit the reports directly in PowerPoint if desired.

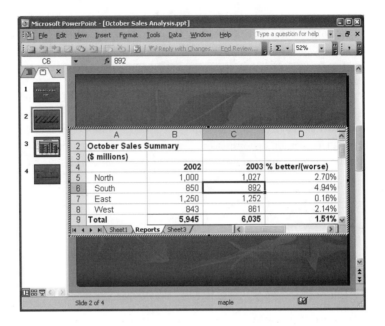

Although this is rather rudimentary as far as PowerPoint presentations go, it is not that much of a stretch to see how you might apply automation to your reporting and presentation cycles.

Summary

Object linking and embedding is a great way to use the strengths of various Microsoft Office applications where it makes sense, yet still retain the ability to bring everything together into a unified document. A document that contains components created using different applications is referred to as a compound document.

Object linking and embedding is enabled thanks to a powerful architecture referred to as the Component Object Model (COM). Over the years, Microsoft has kept everyone confused by naming, renaming, and shifting definitions of various COM-related technologies—especially the functionality related to object linking and embedding (OLE).

Although OLE is helpful in many situations, you'll undoubtedly run into situations where OLE doesn't quite cut it. In these instances, you may need to employ a concept commonly know of as automation. Automation involves controlling one application using code that "lives" within a different application. For example, you could conceivably create a Microsoft Word application implemented entirely in VBA that runs from Excel. Not that you would actually want to do this. When developing solutions involving multiple Microsoft Office applications, generally one of the applications (Access, Excel, Word, etc.) will emerge as the dominant application for the solution and usually the dominant application contains the code that implements the solution.

One key concept of automation is the concept of binding. Binding refers to the process of "introducing" an external class library (such as Word) to the environment in which your code runs. There are two classifications of binding. Early-bound objects are objects that are bound during development by setting a reference to the object's class library in the VBE. Late-bound objects are objects that are bound at run-time by explicitly creating an instance of the object using CreateObject. For performance reasons, early binding is the most commonly used way to bind external class libraries to VBA projects.

OLE and automation are great for getting at data embedded in other Microsoft Office applications (or other applications that support OLE and automation), however, the world is much, much bigger than the data embedded in these applications. To explore other data in the universe you need to find a common denominator. The common denominator has historically been the simple text file. In the next chapter, I cover issues related to working with and creating text files.

Chapter 15

Incorporating Text Files in Your Solution

THE LOWLY TEXT FILE is a tried and true method of transferring data between disparate applications. When all else fails, chances are you'll be able to shuffle data by exporting it from one application into a text file and then importing the text file into the destination application. In heterogeneous environments, working with text files may be an everyday occurrence. Though XML is being pushed as a better way to transfer data, it is impractical to add XML capabilities to every existing system. Consequently, the ability to work with text files will not become irrelevant any time soon.

Excel provides many features aimed at facilitating the ability to use text files. In addition, the VBA language has features above and beyond those offered by Excel that you can take advantage of to easily read and write text files. In addition to teaching you about the mechanics of using text files in Excel and VBA, this chapter also covers some of the various text functions that you will find useful when working with text files.

Versatile Simplicity

The simple, yet versatile, text file. You have probably opened countless text files. They come in all shapes and sizes and are used for everything—instructions, notes (such as readme.txt files), application configuration, and last but not least, storing data.

Although flexibility is one of the strengths of a text file as a means of storing data, text files are generally structured like a list in Excel or a database table where each row in the list represents one item or record. The question is, how do you specify where one field ends in a given record and where the next begins? Without knowing the answer to this question, applications such as Excel have no way of parsing the file or breaking each record down into individual fields.

Parsing the data is the process of extracting the field information from each record. Prior to being parsed, each record looks like a single chunk of data. You have probably seen this occasionally when you are trying to copy data into Excel and the whole chunk ends up stuffed into a single cell or column of cells. After parsing the data, each record consists of a number of distinct fields or columns.

You can use one of two methods to separate fields in a text file. One method is to place a delimiter between each field. A delimiter is a token character that denotes the end of a field; for example, each field may be separated by a comma or a tab. An example of a delimited file is shown in Figure 15.1.

FIGURE 15.1

A comma-delimited text file

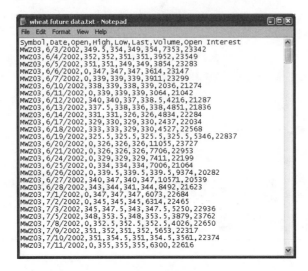

FIGURE 15.2

A fixed-width text file

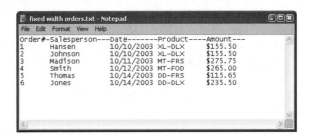

Delimited files are the most efficient way of storing data from a storage space standpoint because you do not need to pad fields with extra spaces as you need to do with the fixed-width method described next. When viewed in a text editor such as Notepad, however, delimited files do not look very attractive.

The second method is to assume that each field has a set amount of characters. This kind of file is referred to as a fixed-width file. The number of spaces allocated to each field is specified by the application that creates the file. For example, a field that contains last names may have 35 characters allocated to it. Any unused space in a field is filled with blank spaces, as if you pressed the spacebar until all 35 characters were used. So the last name "Davis" would have five characters for the actual name and 30 space characters. An example of a fixed-width text file is shown in Figure 15.2.

Fixed-width files have the advantage of being easier to read when viewed in a text editor such as Notepad. On the other hand, they take up more storage space and are not quite as easy to work with.

The mechanics of importing a text file differ slightly depending on the method you use to separate fields in a text file. You can incorporate data from a text file into Excel in three ways. In the next section,

I'll cover the most common way—opening the text file using File ➢ Open. You can also import text data or copy/paste text data onto a worksheet. These two methods will be covered later in this chapter.

Opening Text Files in Excel

Even if you are already familiar with the mechanics of opening a text file in Excel, it is a good idea to refresh your knowledge here because the process of opening these files programmatically depends on your familiarity with the manual process.

I will demonstrate the mechanics of opening up a delimited file using the file shown in Figure 15.1. For any text file, you begin the process by selecting File ➢ Open in Excel and then you change the Files of Text drop-down box to Text Files (*prn., *.txt, *.csv) as shown in the following graphic.

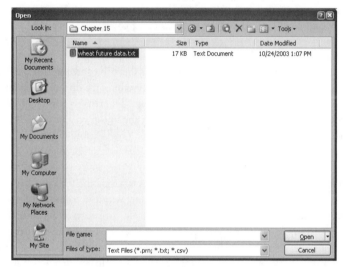

Once you pick a file and click Open, the first step of the Text Import Wizard is displayed. This step looks the same whether the file is delimited or fixed-width.

FIGURE 15.3

Opening a delimited file—step 1

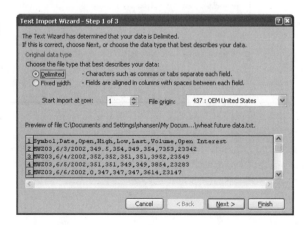

Usually you can tell by looking at the preview in the bottom half of Figure 15.3 whether the file's type is delimited or fixed-width. This can be tricky with tab-delimited files, however, as they can look a bit like a fixed-width file. If in doubt, you can always select delimited and move on to the next step. If you select the tab delimiter and the file does not get parsed (the field separation lines do not appear), then go back to step 1 and choose fixed-width. Most of the time you don't need to do anything, however, because Excel determines which type of file you are opening and makes the correct choice to begin with. The file in Figure 15.1 is a comma-delimited text file.

NOTE *CSV stands for comma-separated values. Files with a .csv extension are comma-delimited text files. Excel automatically opens files with a .csv extension without requiring the use of the Text Import Wizard.*

TIP *You can bypass the Text Import Wizard when opening text files by holding down the Shift key when you open the file. This is helpful for tab-delimited files that will be parsed by default.*

Notice that you can specify which row to begin importing. This allows you to skip any header rows if you do not want them in the resulting worksheet. Regarding the file origin, most of the time you never need to change this. If the text file was generated on a different platform (operating system), however, you may need to make an adjustment here. The reason for this is that different operating systems have different conventions for representing the line-feed character. This is significant because the line-feed character signifies the end of a record. You'll know when you haven't set this correctly because Excel interprets the entire contents of the file as a single record.

The main task in step 2 (shown in Figure 15.4) is to specify the character that is used to delimit the file. When you check a delimiter, Excel attempts to parse the file, and then shows the results in the data preview. Excel places vertical lines in the preview window to indicate how the data will be lined up in columns. You can also tell Excel how to handle consecutive delimiters and indicate how text is qualified. For example, if your file is space delimited and one of the fields contained text data, you would not want Excel to interpret the spaces in the text field as delimiters. To prevent this, the system that created your text file usually wraps text data in a qualifier such as single or double quotes.

FIGURE 15.4

Opening a delimited file—step 2

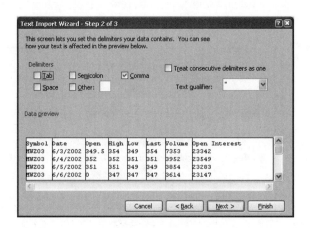

FIGURE 15.5

Opening a delimited file—step 3

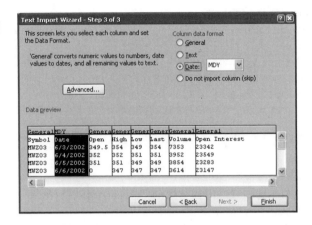

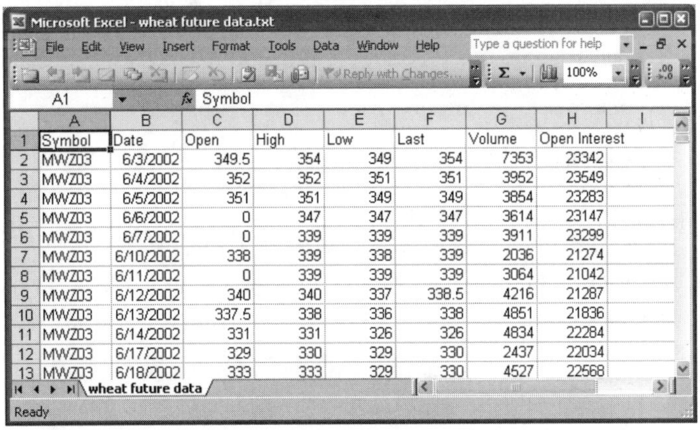

FIGURE 15.6

An imported text file in Excel

The final step is to identify the data format of each field as shown in Figure 15.5. This step is particularly important when you have fields containing numeric data that should be treated as text. For example, maybe your company uses a numeric code to identify products and one particular product line uses three leading zeros as part of its product code (e.g., 0005700). If you leave the column's data format set at general, when you import the data into Excel, the leading zeroes will be stripped off (e.g., 5700). In order to prevent this, select the column and change the column data format to Text.

In Figure 15.5, I have changed the column data format to Date for the field containing dates. Figure 15.6 shows the text data that results after I click Finish.

The main difference when opening a fixed-width file is that you have to specify where one field ends and the next begins. To demonstrate, I will use the file shown in Figure 15.2. To open a fixed-width text file, you begin the same way as with a delimited text file—by selecting File ➢ Open in Excel and then changing the Files of Text drop-down box to Text Files (*.prn., *.txt, *.csv). In step 1 of the Import Text Wizard (Figure 15.3) select fixed-width rather than delimited. It is not until step 2 (Figure 15.7) that things look a bit different. Because Excel has no way of knowing where one column ends and the next begins, it is up to you to place markers between the columns. Excel refers to these markers as break lines. Click once at the desired location to place a break line. Double-click a break line to remove it. Finally, you can move a break line by dragging and dropping it.

After you have set all your break lines, you will find yourself back in familiar territory. The remainder of the process is the same as it was with a delimited file.

Importing Text Data onto a Worksheet

Similar to how you opened a text file in the previous section, you can also import text into an existing worksheet. This process involves many of the steps that you go through to open a text file directly. However, importing data onto an existing worksheet provides you with an added capability that you don't have when you open a text file directly. When you import text data onto an existing worksheet, the range that contains the imported text data is considered a data range. Among other things, you can instruct a data range to refresh itself automatically at specific intervals or whenever you open the workbook; and you can do this without repeating all of the normal steps associated with opening or importing text files.

To demonstrate this process, I'll import the data shown in Figure 15.1 into a worksheet.

1. Select Data ➢ Import External Data ➢ Import Data….

2. Change the Files of Type drop-down list to Text Files, locate the text file to import, and click Open.

3. Perform the three steps of the Import Text Wizard (see Figures 15.3, 15.4, and 15.5).

4. Select a location for the data to be imported as shown in the following screen shot and click OK.

Figure 15.8 shows an example of text data that has been imported into a workbook. One of the first things you will notice after importing the data (assuming you are using all of the default option settings) is that a new toolbar appears—the External Data toolbar. The appearance of this toolbar is a sign that the data you just imported is associated with a data range.

FIGURE 15.7

Opening a fixed-width file—step 2

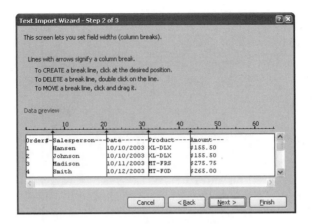

FIGURE 15.8

When you import a text file, the data is associated with a data range.

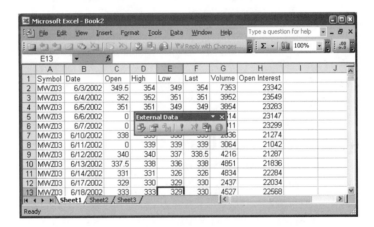

A data range has a number of capabilities associated with it. To get an idea of these capabilities, look at Figure 15.9. One thing to point out is the name of the data range. As part of the process of importing data, Excel creates a named range that is equivalent to the name of the file imported. Well, almost equivalent. The named range has underscores where the spaces are. For example, the data range in Figure 15.9 is "wheat futures data" while the named range that refers to the data is named "wheat_futures_data".

Another useful capability of a data range is that you can set it up to automatically refresh the data. This is useful in many different scenarios. For example, many servers and applications produce log files that change frequently. If you were importing this data into Excel, you could set the data range to refresh itself automatically every few minutes.

FIGURE 15.9
Data ranges offer a
number of useful
capabilities.

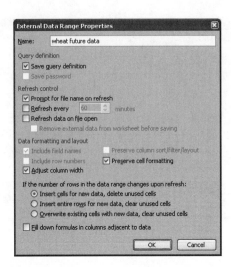

TIP   If you are working with a large text file, you can reduce the size of your Excel file by selecting the Refresh Data on File Open and Remove External Data from Worksheet Before Saving options from within the External Data Range Properties dialog box. When you do this, the data from the text file is not saved with the Excel file; rather, it is automatically imported every time you open the file.

Automatic Text Files

Now that you have reviewed how to open text files manually, opening text files programmatically isn't much of a stretch. To open text files programmatically, use the OpenText method of the Workbooks object. The syntax of OpenText is as follows.

```
Application.Workbooks.OpenText Filename, [Origin], _
    [StartRow], [DataType], [TextQualifier], _
    [ConsecutiveDelimiter], [Tab], [Semicolon], [Comma], _
    [Space], [Other], [OtherChar], [FieldInfo], _
    [TextVisualLayout], [DecimalsSeparator], _
    [ThousandsSeparator], [TrailingMinusNumbers], [Local]
```

As you can see, OpenText has quite a few parameters—more than any other method you have seen so far. The parameters are explained in the following list. In order to conserve some space, I have combined related parameters.

Filename   This is the only required parameter. Obviously this is used to tell OpenText which file to open.

Origin   Origin is an optional parameter that specifies either the file origin (or platform) or the code page used to encode the text file (such as OEM United States, Korean, or Nordic). If you need to specify the platform used, you can use one of the xlPlatform constants: xlMacintosh, xlWindows, or xlMSDOS. To specify a particular code page, you need to pass in the integer value associated with the desired code page. The best way to figure out the value is to find the code page you need in the file origin drop-down list of step 1 (Figure 15.3) of the Text Import Wizard; for example, the integer value associated with the OEM United States code page is 437.

StartRow   StartRow is an optional parameter that specifies the row in the text file to begin importing. The default value is 1.

DataType   DataType is an optional parameter that specifies how columns are organized in the text file. You can use one of the xlTextParsingType constants: xlDelimited or xlFixedWidth. By default, Excel attempts to determine the type when it opens the file.

TextQualifier   This is an optional parameter that specifies how text is qualified in the file. You can use one of the xlTextQualifier constants: xlTextQualifierDoubleQuote, xlTextQualifier-None, or xlTextQualifierSingleQuote. The default value is xlTextQualifierDoubleQuote.

ConsecutiveDelimiter   This is an optional parameter that instructs Excel how to handle consecutive delimiters. Use true to instruct Excel to treat consecutive delimiters as a single delimiter. The default value is false.

Tab, Semicolon, Comma, and Space   These optional parameters are only relevant if the DataType parameter is xlDelimited. Set the desired parameter to true to have Excel consider the character a valid delimiter in the text file. The default value for all of these parameters is false.

Other and OtherChar   If the text file is delimited by a character other than a tab, semicolon, comma, or space (for example, I am partial to the pipe character " | ") you can use these two optional parameters to specify that a different character is used (Other = true) and what the character (OtherChar = " | ") is. Note that OtherChar is required if Other is true. By default Other is false.

FieldInfo   FieldInfo is technically an optional parameter; however, if the file you are opening is a fixed-width text file, you might as well consider this a required parameter because you will use it to instruct Excel on where each column starts. FieldInfo is also used to indicate each column's data type. As you may have presumed, FieldInfo is a little more complicated than your typical parameter. FieldInfo should be an array of two element arrays. The interpretation of the array depends on the value of the DataType parameter.

If DataType = xlDelimited than the first element represents the column number and the second element represents the column's data type. To specify a data type, use one of the xlColumn-DataType constants: xlGeneralFormat, xlTextFormat, xlSkipColumn, xlMDYFormat, xlDMY-Format, xlYMDFormat, xlMYDFormat, xlDYMFormat, xlYDMFormat, or xlEMDFormat (applicable only if you have installed and selected Taiwanese language support).

If DataType = xlFixedWidth than the first element specifies the starting character of the column and the second element specifies the column's data type.

TextVisualLayout   An optional parameter that specifies the visual layout of the text.

DecimalsSeparator, ThousandsSeparator, and TrailingMinusNumbers These optional parameters specify the character used as a decimal separator or thousands separator and whether negative numbers have a trailing minus sign.

Local This is a mysterious optional parameter for which there isn't any documentation.

The parameters of OpenText are quite a mouthful. Generally I only use a handful of them; therefore, I find it is easier to wrap this method up in my own function. I have one function for opening delimited files and another for opening fixed-width files. Listing 15.1 presents the function for opening delimited files along with a procedure for testing it.

LISTING 15.1: OPENING DELIMITED FILES SIMPLIFIED

```
Sub TestOpenDelimitedFile()
    Dim wb As Workbook
    Dim vFields As Variant

    ' The third column of the orders file
    ' is a date column (MM/DD/YYYY).
    ' The rest are general (default)
    vFields = Array(Array(3, xlMDYFormat))

    Set wb = OpenDelimitedFile("C:\tab delimited orders.txt", 2, _
        xlTextQualifierNone, False, vbTab, vFields)

    Set wb = Nothing
End Sub


Function OpenDelimitedFile(sFile As String, _
                          lStartRow As Long, _
                          TxtQualifier As XlTextQualifier, _
                          bConsecutiveDelimiter As Boolean, _
                          sDelimiter As String, _
                          Optional vFieldInfo As Variant) As Workbook

    On Error GoTo ErrHandler

    If IsMissing(vFieldInfo) Then

        Application.Workbooks.OpenText _
            Filename:=sFile, _
            StartRow:=lStartRow, _
            DataType:=xlDelimited, _
            TextQualifier:=TxtQualifier, _
            ConsecutiveDelimiter:=bConsecutiveDelimiter, _
            Other:=True, _
            OtherChar:=sDelimiter
```

```
    Else

        Application.Workbooks.OpenText _
            Filename:=sFile, _
            StartRow:=lStartRow, _
            DataType:=xlDelimited, _
            TextQualifier:=TxtQualifier, _
            ConsecutiveDelimiter:=bConsecutiveDelimiter, _
            Other:=True, _
            OtherChar:=sDelimiter, _
            FieldInfo:=vFieldInfo

    End If

    Set OpenDelimitedFile = ActiveWorkbook
ExitPoint:
    Exit Function
ErrHandler:
    Set OpenDelimitedFile = Nothing
    Resume ExitPoint
End Function
```

NOTE *Listings 15.1 and 15.2 refer to sample data files located in the root directory of your C:\ drive. You should update the file location of these files accordingly if you try these listings.*

The OpenDelimitedFile in Listing 15.1 reduces the number of parameters from 18 to 6, and one of the parameters is optional— the vFieldInfo parameter. This is helpful because out of all the parameters, vField-Info is the most tedious to prepare. Because I don't use the field info parameter very much, it made sense to make this parameter optional in order to make this function easier to use. After turning error handling on, the next thing to do is check to see whether vFieldInfo was specified using the VBA IsMissing function. The call to OpenText is the same in both cases other than the inclusion of the FieldInfo parameter. Assuming all goes well, OpenDelimitedFile sets a reference to the ActiveWorkbook. Opening a file always results in the ActiveWorkbook being set to the opened file. If an error occurs, however, the error-handling code merely sets the return value to Nothing and then exits the function at the exit point.

One other comment regarding this listing is the use of the Other and OtherChar parameters in the OpenText method call. Rather than fiddling with setting the Tab, Semicolon, Comma, or Space parameters of the OpenText method, it is easier to just use the Other and OtherChar parameters. The only trick is specifying a tab delimiter when calling OpenDelimitedFile. In order for this to work you can use the VB-defined constant vbTab.

The test data I used is a tab-delimited file containing a header row and a date field in the third column. An example of this file is shown in Figure 15.10. Because I would like the date field treated as a date, the TestOpenDelimitedFile procedure prepares the vFieldInfo parameter by using the Array function. Remember that the field info parameter requires an array of two-element arrays. That is why you see two calls to the Array function.

FIGURE 15.10

A tab-delimited text file

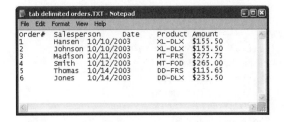

FIGURE 15.11

The result of using OpenDelimitedFile on the sample data

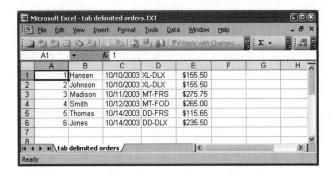

As you can see in Figure 15.11, the test is successful and the OpenDelimitedFile procedure successfully opens the orders file shown in Figure 15.10. Because I specified that it should start with the second row, the header row has been skipped.

For fixed-width files, the FieldInfo parameter of OpenText assumes paramount importance. If you don't provide the FieldInfo parameter, Excel opens the file with everything squeezed into the first column. Consequently, the OpenFixedWidthFile procedure shown in Listing 15.2 requires a parameter, vFieldInfo, which it merely passes to OpenText as the FieldInfo parameter. Notice that the OpenFixedWidthFile procedure only has three parameters versus six for OpenDelimitedFile. This is because you do not need to worry about specifying any delimiter-related information.

LISTING 15.2: OPENING FIXED-WIDTH FILES SIMPLIFIED

```
Sub TestOpenFixedWidthFile()
    Dim wb As Workbook
    Dim vFields As Variant

    ' The third column of the orders file
    ' is a date column (MM/DD/YYYY).
    ' The rest are general (default)
```

```
    vFields = Array( _
        Array(0, xlGeneralFormat), _
        Array(7, xlGeneralFormat), _
        Array(21, xlMDYFormat), _
        Array(32, xlGeneralFormat), _
        Array(43, xlGeneralFormat))

    Set wb = OpenFixedWidthFile( _
        "C:\fixed width orders.txt", 1, vFields)

    Set wb = Nothing
End Sub

Function OpenFixedWidthFile(sFile As String, _
                            lStartRow As Long, _
                            vFieldInfo As Variant) As Workbook

    On Error GoTo ErrHandler

    Application.Workbooks.OpenText _
        Filename:=sFile, _
        StartRow:=lStartRow, _
        DataType:=xlFixedWidth, _
        FieldInfo:=vFieldInfo

    Set OpenFixedWidthFile = ActiveWorkbook
ExitPoint:
    Exit Function
ErrHandler:
    Set OpenFixedWidthFile = Nothing
    Resume ExitPoint
End Function
```

The OpenFixedWidthFile procedure is smaller than OpenDelimitedFile because OpenFixedWidth-File doesn't have an optional parameter. Although OpenFixedWidthFile is smaller and has fewer parameters than OpenDelimitedFile, it is definitely more tedious to call it. This is because you need to set up the vFieldInfo parameter. In order to set it up, you need to know where each column of data is located in the source file. For example, in my sample data file (Figure 15.2), the first column of data begins at zero and the second column of data begins with the seventh character. Obviously, this isn't the kind of thing you can determine dynamically—you need to know what the specifications are or have a sample of the text file at development time. Figure 15.12 shows the result of the OpenFixedWidthFile on my sample data file.

The Old Standby—Copy/Paste

So far, you have seen that you can open text files directly or you can import them as a data range. Of course, you can always copy data from a text file and paste it into Excel. Then, if the data is not parsed, you can select Data ➤ Text to Columns... to launch a wizard that will allow you to instruct Excel how to parse the data. The wizard that performs this? The Convert Text to Columns Wizard (a.k.a. the Text Import Wizard).

I will not bore you by describing the details because they are nearly identical to what you would do when you open a text file. The only difference here is that you need to select the range that you need to convert to columns and then use Data ➤ Text to Columns... to launch the wizard (rather than File ➤ Open and choosing a text file). Figures 15.13 and 15.14 show a before and after shot of text data that was pasted into Excel and then converted to columns using Text to Columns.

FIGURE 15.12

The result of using OpenFixedWidth-File on the sample data

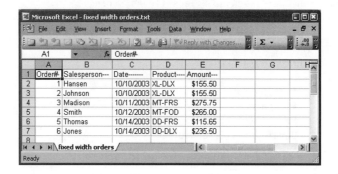

FIGURE 15.13

Text data that needs parsing

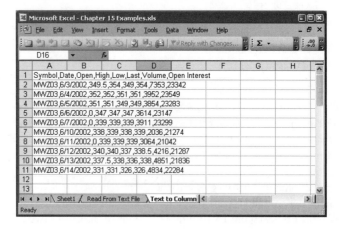

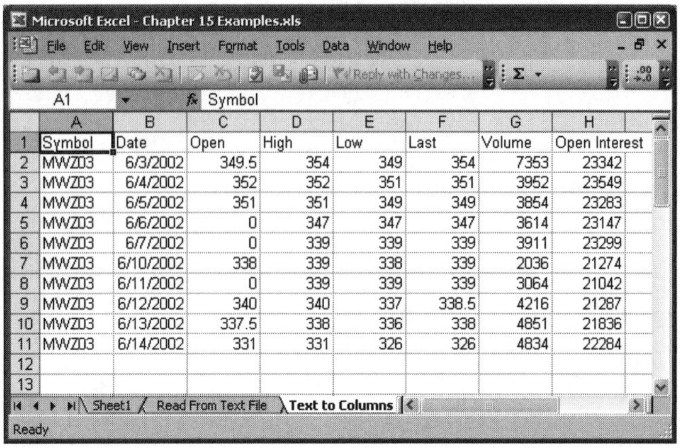

FIGURE 15.14

Text data parsed using Text to Columns

The Range object has a TextToColumns method that allows you to do this programmatically. The syntax of TextToColumns is as follows.

```
rg.TextToColumns [Destination], [DataType], [TextQualifier], _
    [ConsecutiveDelimiter], [Tab], [Semicolon], _
    [Comma], [Space], [Other], [OtherChar], [FieldInfo], _
    [DecimalSeparator], [ThousandsSeparator], _
    [TrailingMinusNumbers]
```

So what do you think, shall we review all of these parameters (again)? We should probably move onward. Just in case you need a review, please refer back to the parameters of the OpenText method in the previous section entitled "Automatic Text Files."

The TextToColumns method does have one parameter that is specific to this function, the Destination parameter. Destination is an optional parameter that specifies the cell representing the upper-left cell of the parsed data. If the range passed to Destination is larger than a single cell, the upper-left cell of the range is used. By default, the destination is the upper-left cell of the Range object that the TextToColumns method operates on. Perhaps an example will make this more clear. Listing 15.3 demonstrates the use of the Destination parameter by converting a range of text to columns not once, but twice. The first time, it converts the text but places the results in a new range. The second time it converts the text but replaces the original text with the converted text.

LISTING 15.3: TEXTTOCOLUMNS EXAMPLE

```
Sub TestTextToColumns()
    Dim rg As Range

    Set rg = ThisWorkbook.Worksheets("Text to Columns"). _
        Range("a20").CurrentRegion

    ' Converts text to columns but
    ' leaves the original text untouched
```

```
    CSVTextToColumns rg, rg.Offset(15, 0)

    ' Converts text to columns.
    ' Replaces original text with converted text.
    CSVTextToColumns rg

    Set rg = Nothing
End Sub

' Converts text to columns assuming the text
' to be converted is comma delimited.
Sub CSVTextToColumns(rg As Range, Optional rgDestination As Range)
    If IsMissing(rgDestination) Or rgDestination Is Nothing Then
        rg.TextToColumns , xlDelimited, , , , , True
    Else
        rg.TextToColumns rgDestination, xlDelimited, , , , , True
    End If
End Sub
```

One interesting thing in this listing is the optional rgDestination parameter used by the CSVText-ToColumns procedure. You may wonder why you need to check rgDestination against Nothing in addition to seeing if it is missing in the If…Then statement. Shouldn't the use of IsMissing be sufficient? IsMissing is only accurate when you use it on Variant variables. On variables using other data types, IsMissing always returns false. By making rgDestination optional, the only thing I have done is made it easier to call the procedure if you do not want to specify a destination. Another option is to make the rgDestination a Variant (which has the capability to represent range objects) rather than a Range. Figure 15.15 shows the results of the TextTextToColumns procedure.

FIGURE 15.15
The results
of TestTextTo-
Columns

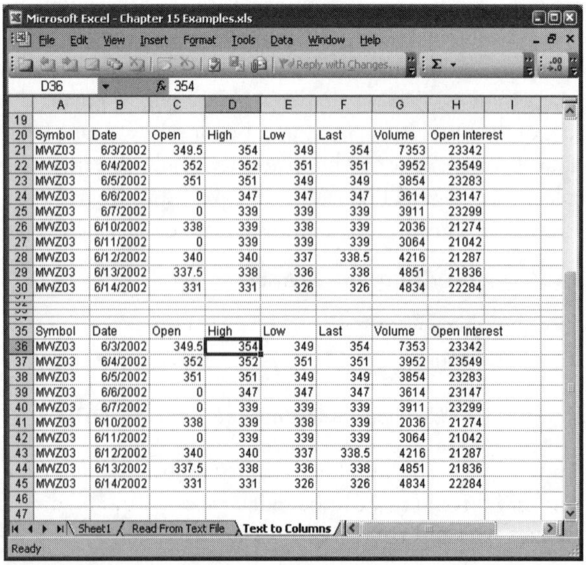

Opening Files Under the Covers

So far this chapter has been primarily geared towards working with structured text files. Structured text files are usually used to move data between incongruent applications that do not have a built-in facility for sharing data with each other. As a developer, structured text files are likely to be the most frequent type of text file you work with. You saw earlier in this chapter that Excel has a native ability to open structured text files. The examples so far used Excel to open the text files. This is fine if you want or do not mind the end user viewing the contents of the text file. For those times when you want to examine or modify a text file without displaying it to the user ,you can open the text file under the covers using VBA.

Additionally, you may need to work with unstructured text files include text files that have a formalized structure—just not a structure that Excel knows how to work with. In order to work with unstructured text files, you need to open them and inspect or modify them using VBA.

In order to perform these feats, you need to learn how to use the text file functionality offered by VBA. VBA provides read/write support for text files. In particular, you need to be familiar with the following VBA language elements:

Open   Enables input/output to a file.

Close   Closes a file opened using Open.

FreeFile   Returns an Integer representing the next file number available for use by Open.

Input and Input #   Returns a String containing text read from a file.

LineInput   Returns a String representing an entire line of text read from a file.

Print   Writes display-formatted data to a file.

Write #   Writes data to a file.

Open for Business

The first thing you need to do to work with any file is open it. Opening text files in VBA is a little different than opening a workbook in Excel or opening a text file in Excel. For starters, the fundamental concept of *open* is different. Previously in this chapter when a file was opened, it was opened and displayed visibly on the screen. In this section, when a file is opened, it is opened in memory only. Unless you take programmatic action on your own, the file will not be displayed on the screen, and the user (or the developer for that matter) gets no visual indication that the file is open.

The mechanics of opening a file are also different. This is primarily due to the convention used for referring to open files. Once opened, files are referred to by a number which you assign in the process of opening them.

To open a file, use the VBA Open statement. This is not the same thing as the Open method of the Workbooks object. The syntax of the Open statement is as follows.

```
Open Pathname For Mode [Access] [Lock] As [#]Filenumber [RecLength]
```

The following list describes the various parameters of Open.

Pathname   This is a required parameter that specifies the name of the file to open. It may include a directory and drive. If you do not include a directory and drive, it uses the value given by the VBA function CurDir (CurDir returns the current path).

Mode   Mode is a keyword specifying the mode that the file should be opened in. You can use Append, Binary, Input, Output, or Random. If Mode is unspecified, the file is opened in Random mode. For text files, you should use one of the sequential modes: Input, Output, or Append. Input mode restricts file operations to read only. Output mode creates a new file, overwriting any file in the directory that has the same filename. Append allows you to add text to the end of an existing file. Binary mode is for, well, binary files or any situation in which you need to read/write individual bytes. Random mode is usually used for files that contain fixed-length data structures.

Access   Access is an optional parameter that specifies the kind of operations that you can perform on the file. You should specify one of these: Read, Write, or Read Write.

Lock   Lock is an optional parameter that specifies the restrictions placed on the file if it is accessed by other processes. Lock can be Shared, Lock Read, Lock Write, or Lock Read Write.

Filenumber   Filenumber is required and should be a value between 1 and 511 inclusively. It is best to use the FreeFile function to obtain the next available file number.

RecLength   RecLength is an optional parameter that represents the record length when used with Random files, and the length of the buffer when used with sequential files.

I find VBA's Open statement to be rather awkward to use. Perhaps this is because I do not use it very often, or maybe it is just because the syntax of it is downright discomfited (much like the word discomfited itself). Most of the time, you can get the job done by modifying one of the simple forms shown in Listing 15.4.

LISTING 15.4: EXAMPLES OF THE VBA OPEN STATEMENT

```
Sub SimpleOpenExamples()
    Dim lInputFile As Long
    Dim lOutputFile As Long
    Dim lAppendFile As Long

    ' Get a valid file number
    lInputFile = FreeFile
    ' Open MyInputFile.txt for input
    Open "C:\MyInputFile.txt" For Input As #lInputFile

    ' Get another valid file number
    lOutputFile = FreeFile
    ' Create a new file for output
    Open "C:\MyNewOutputFile.txt" For Output As #lOutputFile

    ' Get another valid file number
    lAppendFile = FreeFile
    ' Open MyAppendFile.txt to append data to it
    ' or create new file if MyAppendFile doesn't exist
    Open "C:\MyAppendFile.txt" For Append As #lAppendFile
```

```
    ' Close the files
    Close lInputFile, lOutputFile, lAppendFile
End Sub
```

The SimpleOpenExamples procedure opens three files. The first example opens a file named MyInputFile.txt for input. This statement generates a run-time error if the file is not found, so it would be best to use an error-handling mechanism. The second example opens a new file for output, overwriting any existing file with the same name in the same directory without any warning. The third example opens a file in Append mode. If an existing file is present, the existing file is used; otherwise a new file is created.

WARNING *Opening files is an error-prone process. You would be wise to use an error-handling mechanism in any procedure that uses Open.*

Most businesses are not open 24/7/365 and your text files should not be either. Closing files that you have opened is easily achieved by using VBA's Close statement followed by the file number you want to close. The official syntax of Close is

```
Close [FilenumberList]
```

where FilenumberList is a comma-separated list of file numbers to close. If you do not specify any file numbers, Close will close all active files that were opened using Open. Obviously, after you call Close with a file number, the file number no longer ceases to be associated with the file that was closed.

File I/O

Opening and closing files does not do any good unless you can read or write from those files. Depending on what you are doing, you will use Input, Input #, Line Input #, Print #, or Write # to read from or write to a file. The use of these statements is detailed in the following list.

Input   The Input statement is used to read data from a text file *n* characters at a time where *n* is the number of characters to read. Input returns any character it comes across such as commas, tabs, quotation marks, linefeeds, and spaces in addition to normal text. You can use the VBA functions EOF and LOF to determine if you have reached the end of file and to determine the length (size) of the file.

Input #   The Input # statement is more sophisticated than Input. Input # knows how to read data into a series of variables. It also removes quotes and converts date strings to VBA dates. Use Input # on files created using the Write # statement.

Line Input #   The Line Input # statement is meant for reading entire lines of data at once from a text file. Line Input # is usually used against text files written using the Print # statement.

Print #   Print # is used to write display-formatted data to a text file. Print # is usually used to create files for use with the Input statement.

Write #   Write # is meant for creating data-oriented text files. Files created using Write # can be easily read using the Input # statement.

Listing 15.5 presents an example that uses Write # to create a comma-delimited file based on the worksheet shown in Figure 15.16. After creating a new file, a second procedure opens the file and writes the data from the file onto a new worksheet using Input #.

FIGURE 15.16

Sample data for experimenting with Write # and Input #

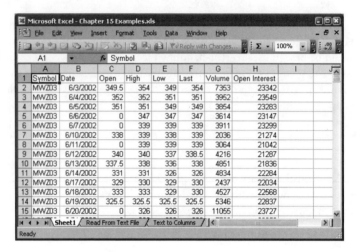

LISTING 15.5: AN EXAMPLE USING WRITE # AND INPUT #

```
Sub TestWriteInput()
    WriteExample
    InputExample
End Sub


' Creates a comma-delimited file based
' on a range in Excel that is 8
' columns wide
Sub WriteExample()
    Dim lOutputFile As Long
    Dim rg As Range

    ' Set rg to refer to upper-left cell of range
    Set rg = ThisWorkbook.Worksheets(1).Range("a1")

    ' Get a valid file number
    lOutputFile = FreeFile

    ' Create a new file for output
    Open "C:\Write Example.txt" For Output As #lOutputFile

    ' Loop until there isn't any data in the first column
```

```vb
    Do Until IsEmpty(rg)

        ' Write the data to the file
        Write #lOutputFile, rg.Value, _
            rg.Offset(0, 1).Value, _
            rg.Offset(0, 2).Value, _
            rg.Offset(0, 3).Value, _
            rg.Offset(0, 4).Value, _
            rg.Offset(0, 5).Value, _
            rg.Offset(0, 6).Value, _
            rg.Offset(0, 7).Value

        ' Move down to next row
        Set rg = rg.Offset(1, 0)
    Loop

    Set rg = Nothing
    Close lOutputFile
End Sub

Sub InputExample()
    Dim lInputFile As Long
    Dim rg As Range
    ' Variant variables for reading
    ' from text file
    Dim v1, v2, v3, v4
    Dim v5, v6, v7, v8

    ' Set rg to refer to upper-left cell of range
    Set rg = ThisWorkbook.Worksheets(2).Range("a1")

    ' Clear any existing data
    rg.CurrentRegion.ClearContents

    ' Get a valid file number
    lInputFile = FreeFile

    ' Create a new file for input
    Open "C:\Write Example.txt" For Input As lInputFile

    ' Loop until you hit the end of file
    Do Until EOF(lInputFile)

        ' Read the data to the file
        ' Have to read into a variable - can't assign
        ' directly to a range
        Input #lInputFile, v1, v2, v3, v4, v5, v6, v7, v8
```

```
                    ' Transfer values to that worksheet
                    rg.Value = v1
                    rg.Offset(0, 1).Value = v2
                    rg.Offset(0, 2).Value = v3
                    rg.Offset(0, 3).Value = v4
                    rg.Offset(0, 4).Value = v5
                    rg.Offset(0, 5).Value = v6
                    rg.Offset(0, 6).Value = v7
                    rg.Offset(0, 7).Value = v8

                    ' Move down to next row
                    Set rg = rg.Offset(1, 0)
            Loop

            Set rg = Nothing
            Close lInputFile
    End Sub
```

CREATING OLAP QUERY FILES WITH PRINT

Just today, I needed to write a small utility that would automatically create a Microsoft Office Excel OLAP Query File (*.oqy). A query file is a file that Excel uses to store information related to the details associated with a connection to a Microsoft Analysis Services OLAP database. Anyway, this utility is handy because it eliminates the need to physically create the file for users or instruct them how to create it themselves.

NOTE   *See Chapter 16 for more information on working with OLAP databases.*

In order to create the query file, the utility needed to open a new file in Output mode, write (using Print #) information to the file, and then close the file. Listing 15.6 presents the procedure.

LISTING 15.6: CREATING AN OLAP QUERY FILE

```
    Option Explicit

    Sub CreateOQY()
        Dim lFileNumber As Long
        Dim sText As String
        Dim oSettings As New Settings
        Dim sFileName As String

        On Error GoTo ErrHandler

        ' Obtain a file number to use
        lFileNumber = FreeFile
```

```
    ' Determine the file name and folder location.
    sFileName = QueriesPath & oSettings.Item("OQYName").Value & ".oqy"

    ' Open the file. Note - this overwrites any existing file
    ' with the same name in the same folder
    Open sFileName For Output As #lFileNumber

    ' Output the OQY details
    Print #lFileNumber, "QueryType=OLEDB"
    Print #lFileNumber, "Version=1"
    Print #lFileNumber, "CommandType=Cube"
    Print #lFileNumber, "Connection=Provider=MSOLAP.2;" & _
    "Data Source="; oSettings.Item("Database").Value & ";" & _
    "Initial Catalog=" & oSettings.Item("Database").Value & _
    ";Client Cache Size=25;Auto Synch Period=10000"
    Print #lFileNumber, "CommandText=" & oSettings.Item("Cube").Value

    ' Close the file
    Close lFileNumber

    Set oSettings = Nothing
    MsgBox "Your OLAP connection has been created.", vbOKOnly
    Exit Sub
ErrHandler:
    MsgBox "An error occured while creating your OLAP connection. " _
        & Err.Description, vbOKOnly
End Sub

' The file should be stored in the Queries folder associated with
' the current user. For example, assuming user name = shansen,
' the OQY file should be store in:
' C:\Documents and Settings\shansen\ _
'    Application Data\Microsoft\Queries
Function QueriesPath() As String
    Dim sLibraryPath As String

    ' Get the AddIns path associated with the current user
    sLibraryPath = Application.UserLibraryPath

    ' The Queries path is a peer of AddIns
    QueriesPath = Replace(sLibraryPath, _
        "\Microsoft\AddIns\", "\Microsoft\Queries\")
End Function
```

FIGURE 15.17

The settings used by CreateOQY

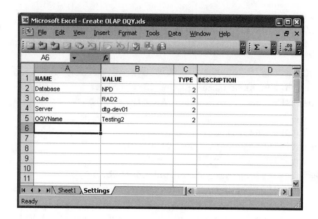

NOTE *Listing 15.6 requires the Setting and Settings classes along with the Settings worksheet that were presented in Chapter 12.*

Figure 15.17 shows a picture of the Settings worksheet used for this utility.
CreateOQY creates a file with the following output when used with the settings shown in Figure 15.17.

```
QueryType=OLEDB
Version=1
CommandType=Cube
Connection=Provider=MSOLAP.2;Data Source=dtg-dev01; _
    Initial Catalog=NPD;Client Cache Size=25;Auto Synch Period=10000
CommandText=RAD2
```

NOTE *The Connection line has been split onto two lines for the purposes of displaying it in this book. The actual output does not split this line.*

String Functions Offering Utility

With all of this talk about text files, it seems like this would be a good place to mention some useful string functions. Rare is the procedure that reads/writes from a text file that does not use one of the functions listed in Table 15.1.

TABLE 15.1: USEFUL STRING FUNCTIONS

FUNCTION	USE
Left	Returns x characters from the left of a string
Len	Returns the length of a string
LTrim	Trims any spaces from the left of a string

TABLE 15.1: USEFUL STRING FUNCTIONS *(continued)*

FUNCTION	USE
Mid	Returns *x* characters from the middle of a string starting with character *y*
Right	Returns *x* characters from the right of a string
RTrim	Trims any spaces from the right of a string
Split	Splits a delimited string into an array of individual values
StrConv	Converts a string to the specified format
Trim	Trims any spaces from the left and right of a string

This is not a complete list of string functions; rather, it is a list of the functions I use the most when working with text files. Listing 15.7 provides an example of these functions.

NOTE   For further reference, check out VBA Developer's Handbook, Second Edition *by Ken Getz and Mike Gilbert (Sybex, 2001). They have a whole chapter dedicated to working with strings.*

LISTING 15.7: AN EXAMPLE OF USEFUL STRING FUNCTIONS

```vba
Sub UsefulStringFunctions()
    Dim sTestWord As String

    sTestWord = "filename"

    ' Len demonstration
    Debug.Print sTestWord & " is " & Len(sTestWord) & _
        " characters long."

    ' Mid & concatenation demonstration
    Debug.Print Mid(sTestWord, 3, 1) & Right(sTestWord, 3)

    ' Left demonstration
    Debug.Print Left(sTestWord, 4)

    ' Right demonstration
    Debug.Print Right(sTestWord, 4)

    ' Trim demonstration
    sTestWord = "    padded    "

    Debug.Print ">" & sTestWord & "<"
    Debug.Print ">" & LTrim(sTestWord) & "<"
    Debug.Print ">" & RTrim(sTestWord) & "<"
    Debug.Print ">" & Trim(sTestWord) & "<"
```

```
    ' StrConv demonstration
    sTestWord = "The moon over Minneapolis is big and bright."
    Debug.Print StrConv(sTestWord, vbLowerCase)
    Debug.Print StrConv(sTestWord, vbUpperCase)
    Debug.Print StrConv(sTestWord, vbProperCase)

    ' Split demonstration
    sTestWord = "One, Two, Three, 4, Five, Six"
    DemoSplit sTestWord
End Sub

Sub DemoSplit(sCSV As String)
    Dim vaValues As Variant
    Dim nIndex As Integer

    ' Split the values
    vaValues = Split(sCSV, ",")

    ' Loop through the values
    For nIndex = 0 To UBound(vaValues)
        Debug.Print "Item (" & nIndex & ") is " & vaValues(nIndex)
    Next
End Sub
```

SubUsefulStringFunctions produces the following output:

```
filename is 8 characters long.
lame
file
name
>     padded    <
>padded    <
>     padded<
>padded<
the moon over minneapolis is big and bright.
THE MOON OVER MINNEAPOLIS IS BIG AND BRIGHT.
The Moon Over Minneapolis Is Big And Bright.
Item (0) is One
Item (1) is  Two
Item (2) is  Three
Item (3) is  4
Item (4) is  Five
Item (5) is  Six
```

Between Table 15.1 and Listing 15.7 the purpose and use of the functions are pretty self-evident. However, Split is such a powerful function that it deserves a little more detail. Split is extremely handy when you are working with delimited files that you open using the VBA Open statement (rather than the OpenText method of the Workbooks object). The syntax of Split is as follows.

```
Split(Expression, [Delimiter], [Limit], [Compare])
```

The parameters of Split are explained in the following list.

Expression Expression is a required parameter. It is the string that you would like to split apart. Expression should be a string consisting of subparts and delimiters such as one line from a delimited text file.

Delimiter Delimiter is an optional parameter. Set the Delimiter parameter equal to the character used to delimit the string given by Expression. By default, Split assumes that Expression is space delimited.

Limit Limit is an optional parameter that can be used to specify how many subparts to return.

Compare Compare is an optional parameter that can be used to specify the type of comparison to use when comparing substrings. Use one of the following: vbUseCompareOption, vbUseBinaryCompare, vbUseTextCompare, or vbUseDatabaseCompare.

Summary

Working with text files can be more tedious than working with other data transfer mechanisms such as using a database or XML. Nonetheless, working with text files offers some advantages. For one, text files are universally supported. If you need to get data from one application to another, if nothing else, you can export data to text and then import it in the other application. Another advantage of using text files is that Excel can open delimited and fixed-width files without writing any special VBA code. Yet another advantage of using text files is that operations on text files are fast.

You can use text files in your application in two ways. One way is to open the text file in Excel, much like you would an Excel workbook. You can open the file manually or you can open it programmatically using the OpenText method of the Workbooks object. The second way to use a text file can only be achieved programmatically—you open the text file using VBA's Open statement. This method opens the file without actually displaying it. Your code can work with the text file and then close it when finished without the user knowing that it is even being used.

VBA provides lots of native abilities for working with strings (all text file data is essentially a string right?). When you use functions like Left, Right, Mid, Split, and the various Trim functions, you will have no problem slicing and dicing text files.

In the next chapter, things get a little more interesting as you learn how to retrieve data from databases. Combining Excel with the data retrieval capabilities of a database opens up a new world of possibilities in terms of the sophistication, scale, and functionality you can offer with your custom solution. As you'll see, VBA is the glue that makes it all work.

Chapter 16

Dealing with Databases

YOUR SKILLS AS A developer reach a new level when you learn how to develop solutions that harness the power of a database to handle an application's data storage and management chores. By designing solutions that utilize Excel's analytical and presentation capabilities and the data management capabilities of a database, you can create applications that perform faster, support more users, handle vast amounts of data, and enable sophisticated application functionality.

I aim to do three things with this chapter. First, I'll provide an overview of databases in general so that I can establish some common ground. Second, I'll show you the multiple ways that you can interact with a database from Excel without writing a line of code. Finally, I'll provide the details you need to programmatically interact with a database. As a special treat, I'll end the chapter by demonstrating how to work with Microsoft Analysis Services. Analysis Services is an online analytical processing (OLAP) product that enables rapid data analysis.

Database Basics

The simplest definition of a database is that it is one or more sets of persistent, related data. By that definition, text files and even a list in Excel could qualify as a database. However, generally when the term database is used, it also refers to the software used to create and manage the database. This type of software is referred to as database management systems (DBMS). Most databases created using a DBMS are *relational* databases. A relational database is a database that allows the database developer to create relationships between tables. For example, if you have a salesperson table and an orders table, you can define a relationship between the tables that would associate a salesperson with the orders she generated. Further, the database developer can specify certain rules that should be enforced by the relationship. For example, what would happen if you tried to add a record to the orders table that wasn't associated with a salesperson? You can create relationships that would either allow or disallow the record from being added. Benefits of a relational database include the following:

Relational integrity   You can ensure that the data in a relational database conforms to certain business rules (i.e., all orders must be associated with a salesperson).

Data integrity   A relational database allows you to define rules and data types specific to a particular field in a table. For example, you could specify that a particular field can only contain integers and that it can't contain a null value. Further, you can define constraints such that the field must be within a certain range of values.

Scalability   Most database products are designed to handle a great deal more data than Excel can handle. For example, Excel has 65,536 rows. Have you ever used all of them? If so, what happened? The size of the spreadsheet increased dramatically and your computer's performance probably slowed to a crawl. Even basic database products such as Microsoft Access can handle hundreds of thousands of rows. Unlike with Excel, a database does not necessarily load the entire contents of the database into memory.

Performance   Databases offer increased data retrieval speed, faster and more comprehensive sorting capabilities, and increased data manipulation performance.

Stability   Many database products have extensive logging, backup, and transactional features that help ensure the integrity of a database in the event of software or hardware failure.

Collaboration   Though Excel offers some multiuser capabilities, data in a database can be accessed by many people at once. By storing data in a central location (rather than distributing it among many spreadsheets), your organization gains the benefit of making the data available to many different kinds of applications in addition to Excel.

Once you've decided to use a database, you'll find many database products on the market from which to choose. There are not any hard and fast guidelines for choosing a database product. Many factors may weigh into the final decision including these:

◆ Expected database usage

◆ Number of concurrent users

◆ Amount of data to be stored

◆ Skill set of the technical staff

◆ The cost of the software

For learning purposes and departmental databases, Microsoft Access is a common choice. Access is an easy-to-use and widely available (it was probably installed along with Excel) database. Access and Excel are tightly integrated, which means that you have more options for moving data between the two applications. For example, you can copy/paste entire worksheets into Access and Access will create a table out of them.

Microsoft SQL Server is more of an industrial strength database. You can use SQL Server for everything from a personal database using SQL Server Personal Edition, to enterprise databases using SQL Server Standard or Enterprise Edition. SQL Server is not as easy to use as Access, but it offers much more in terms of database development flexibility, database management features, security, and scalability.

Of course, you have tons of other choices from other vendors including IBM, Oracle, and Sybase. You'll even come across open source products such as MySQL. In theory, you'll be able to write applications that will work with any of these databases. That said, you may encounter slight functional differences between products, so the actual mechanics involved may vary somewhat from product to product.

NOTE *The examples in this chapter use Microsoft Access. The final section of the chapter demonstrates how to retrieve data from Microsoft Analysis Services, a special kind of database product that ships with Microsoft SQL Server.*

Data in a database is manipulated using Structured Query Language (SQL). Although your efficiency will improve as you learn to craft SQL statements by hand, most database products ship with some sort of visual query tool that allows you to build SQL statements (aka queries) visually.

Though you can get by using visual query tools to build queries, I feel it is also important to learn how to write them by hand. One of the reasons it is important to learn the syntax of SQL so that you can write queries manually is that, as a developer, you'll typically need to write SQL statements that you pass to the database via an intermediate mechanism. If you can't write queries by hand, you have to build them in your visual query tool and then copy/paste them into the VBE. In the process of copying and pasting, chances are you'll need to do a little rearranging of the query once it is in the VBE. This whole process is rather inefficient.

NOTE *The intermediate mechanism that will be presented in this chapter is known as ActiveX Data Objects (ADO). ADO is a set of objects that you can use programmatically to work with a database. Basically, it is an abstraction layer between your code and the database. One of the benefits of an abstraction layer is that it shields you from the necessity of becoming intimately familiar with the particular details of working with different database products. Instead you learn how to use ADO and let your ADO provider worry about handling the details. I'll go over this in more detail later in the chapter.*

Another reason it is beneficial to learn how to write queries manually is that visual query tools don't always write the best SQL for the task at hand. In fact, sometimes you won't even be able to design a given query using a visual query tool. Armed with a better understanding of writing your own SQL, you can easily get around these query tool shortcomings. Without this understanding, you're at the mercy of your tool of choice.

Developing Your Skills

In order to develop the skills necessary to incorporate database functionality into your solutions, you must invest time learning many new things. Some of the areas that you may need to learn or brush up on include the following:

- The general use of one or more database products such as Microsoft Access or Microsoft SQL Server

- Database design and development techniques. Unless you are using a database that someone else put together, you'll need to create and populate the tables in a database.

- Structured Query Language (SQL)

- ActiveX Data Objects (ADO)

Entire books have been written on each of the items mentioned, so you can correctly surmise that it is impossible for me to tell you all that you need to know about each topic in one chapter. Hopefully you'll find enough material in this chapter to help you solve a current problem or get you started in the right direction.

NOTE *Check out the informative, developer-oriented book, the Access 2002 Developer's Handbook Set, by Paul Litwin, Ken Getz, and Mike Gunderloy (Sybex, 2001), for in-depth coverage of Microsoft Access. Alternatively, Mastering SQL Server 2000, by Mike Gunderloy and Joseph L. Jorden (Sybex, 2000) provides a wide range of information related to Microsoft SQL Server.*

If you are totally new to working with databases and this all seems overwhelming, it is important that you just start learning and trust that it will become clear. It gets easier. Synergies exist between all of the items I just mentioned. As you learn more about one of them, you'll find that it gets easier and easier to learn about the others.

Native Excel Database Integration

Once you put your data in a database, you need an efficient way to get it out. Without writing a single line of code, you can easily incorporate data from a database into an Excel workbook using Microsoft Query (MS Query).

MS Query is included with every edition of Microsoft Office. As you can see in Figure 16.1, MS Query is a visual query tool that looks similar to the query design view in Access. Using MS Query, you can define a query that runs and returns data to Excel. A query is basically a question that is phrased in terms that a database can understand. The data that a query returns is referred to as a result set or a recordset.

FIGURE 16.1

Microsoft Query in action

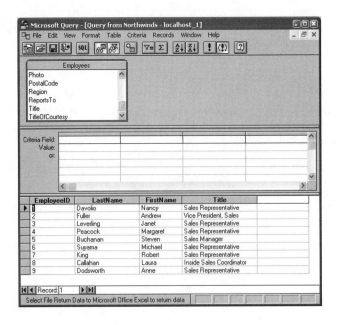

MS Query is a useful, but for some reason, underused application. This may reflect the general user's lack of understanding about databases. Alternatively, MS Query may turn some people off because of some of its usage quirks. However, if you give MS Query a chance and invest some time learning how to use it, you'll find that it allows you to do many useful things.

Data retrieved using MS Query is associated with an external data range. As you learned in the last chapter, an external data range is a range of data in Excel that is somehow associated with an external data source. You can set up an external data range so that it refreshes itself at specific times to ensure that it always contains the most up-to-date data. In addition, MS Query allows you to harness the power of parameter queries.

A parameter query is a query that is set up to prompt for or accept some criteria when the query executes. This allows you to use the same query to return data associated with a specific data item. For example, rather than creating 12 queries where each returns a specific month's data, you could create a single query that prompts you to enter the month desired. When you create a parameter query in Microsoft Query, you can instruct Excel to retrieve the parameter from a particular cell. Further, you can set up the external data range associated with the data to refresh the data whenever the cell containing the parameter changes. This is powerful stuff. I'll demonstrate an example of this later in the chapter.

NOTE *Microsoft Query is not installed by default. You may require your Microsoft Office setup CD to install MS Query the first time you try and use it.*

Excel, Meet My Database. Database, This Is Excel

To use MS Query, select Data ➤ Import External Data ➤ New Database Query from the Excel menu. If this is the first time you're querying a particular data source, you need to set up a new data source by choosing New Data Source as shown in Figure 16.2. This displays the Create New Data Source form shown in Figure 16.3.

In step one in Figure 16.3, you provide a name for the database. The name you put here is the name that shows up in the list of databases that you can see in Figure 16.2. I like to use the name of the database followed by the server or computer on which the database resides. This practice is handy in the development process because you may have two copies of a given database; one for testing and another "production" or live version.

FIGURE 16.2

Selecting a database

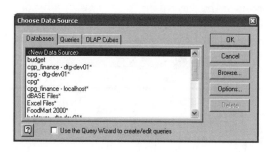

FIGURE 16.3

Creating a new data source

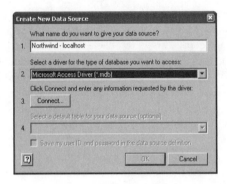

FIGURE 16.4

Connecting to an Access database

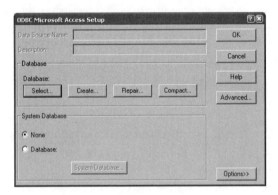

In step two, you select a driver for the database. The choice of a driver is critical because the driver handles all of the communication between MS Query and the database. Database vendors usually provide drivers that are specific to their product. For connecting to an Access database select the Microsoft Access Driver (*.mdb).

In step three, you specify where the database resides and any other connection-related details. This step is database specific. If you selected the Access driver, the dialog box shown in Figure 16.4 appears.

For an Access database, most of the time all you need to do is click Select and locate the desired database on your filesystem. In the following screen shot, I've located the Northwind sample database.

FIGURE 16.5

Choosing a data source

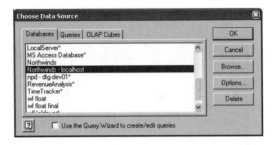

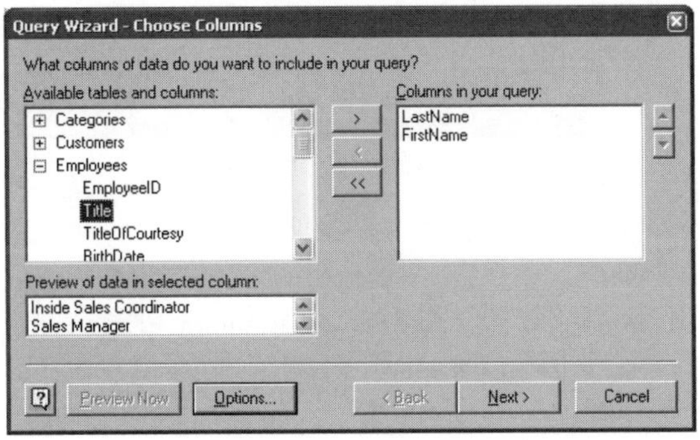

FIGURE 16.6

The Query Wizard leads you through the process of creating elementary queries.

NOTE   The Northwind sample database ships with Microsoft Access. It will be used for all Access examples.

In step four, you indicate a default table. This is an optional step. If you are sure that you'll always use the same table, go ahead and select it here; otherwise leave it blank. When you're finished creating the new data source, it will appear in the list of databases as shown in Figure 16.5. At this point you're ready to select the desired database and define your query.

You Are an Advanced Player

See that check box at the bottom of Figure 16.5? The one that says "Use the Query Wizard to create/edit queries?" If you just need to return data associated with a single table or view in the database, you could use the Query Wizard. The Query Wizard (Figure 16.6) is a tool meant to make it easier to create simple queries.

Although Query Wizard does make it easier, it also limits you to the most elementary types of queries. I'd encourage you to avoid the Query Wizard and learn how to use MS Query's normal design view (Figure 16.1).

There are five basic steps to creating a query using MS Query. To illustrate the process, I'll create a query that summarizes sales in the US by an employee in the Northwind database.

FIGURE 16.7

After adding tables, you are ready to add fields to the result set.

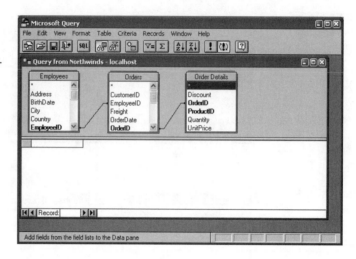

STEP ONE: ADD TABLES

Immediately after you select a database and assuming you're not using the Query Wizard, MS Query prompts you to add tables to the query. To add tables, double-click the table(s) you'd like to use. After you've added all the tables you need, click the Close button. An example of the Add Tables dialog box is shown here.

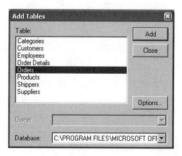

MS Query automatically recognizes any defined relationships between the tables and displays them in the MS Query window. In Figure 16.7, I've added three tables to the query. If you need to remove a table from the query, click once on the table and press Delete.

To summarize sales by an employee in the Northwinds database, I need the Employees, Orders, and Order Details tables.

STEP TWO: SELECT FIELDS TO INCLUDE IN THE RESULT SET

The next step is to select the fields that you want to include in the result set. You can select fields several ways:

♦ Double-click the field name in the Table pane. This makes the selected field the last column of the result set.

♦ Drag the field name(s) from the Table pane to the Data pane. This allows you to place the field(s) before the first column, between existing columns, or after the last column. To select multiple contiguous fields, press and hold Shift and then select the first and last fields that you want to include. To select multiple noncontiguous fields, press and hold Control while selecting the fields you want to include.

♦ Click in the first empty column of the Data pane and choose from the list of fields in the drop-down control. An example of this method is shown in Figure 16.8.

♦ To remove a column from the Data pane, click the column label to select the entire column and then press Delete.

For my query, I need Employees.LastName, Employees.FirstName, and Orders.ShipCountry. Thankfully, you can also create calculated fields. For example, to summarize sales by employee, I need to determine the amount of each order detail item. The amount of each order detail item is determined by multiplying the quantity field by the unit price field and then applying the discount for the item (multiply by 1 minus the discount field). To create a calculated field, click in an empty column and enter the desired formula (see Figure 16.9).

After you enter the formula, you can double-click the formula you just entered. Doing so displays a dialog box (Figure 16.10) that allows you to change the column heading that is displayed in the result set. In fact, you can double-click any column heading in the Results pane to change the column heading that will be displayed or to indicate whether the results should be summarized in some way (sum, average, count, etc.). I added the column heading OrderTotal to the calculated field.

FIGURE 16.8

Selecting fields to include in the result set

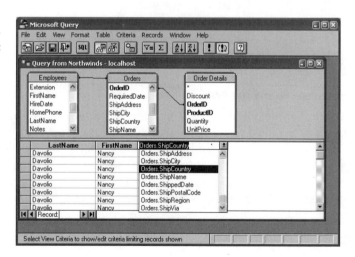

FIGURE 16.9
Specifying a
calculated field.

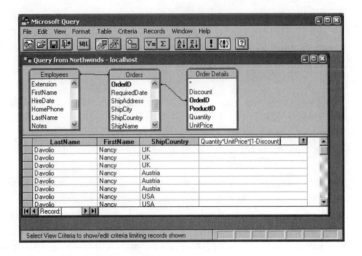

FIGURE 16.10
The Edit Column
dialog box allows
you to edit column
attributes.

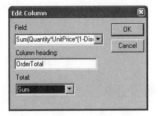

STEP THREE: FILTER THE RESULTS

If you need to filter the results that are returned, you need to display the Criteria pane (View ➤ Criteria). You can add fields to the Criteria pane in a way similar to how you added fields to the Data pane. You only need to add fields that will be used in the filter. Table 16.1 contains examples of the operators you can use in the Criteria pane to filter the results returned by the query.

TABLE 16.1: USING OPERATORS IN THE CRITERIA PANE

TO SPECIFY THIS	ENTER THIS	EXAMPLE	INTERPRETATION
Equals	=	=West	Return only the records with the value West in the Criteria field.
Is not equal to	<>	<>North	Return only the records that do not have North in the Criteria field.

TABLE 16.1: USING OPERATORS IN THE CRITERIA PANE *(continued)*

TO SPECIFY THIS	ENTER THIS	EXAMPLE	INTERPRETATION
Is greater than	>	>100	Return only the records whose Criteria field value is greater than 100.
Is greater than or equal to	>=	>=0	Return only the records whose Criteria field value is greater than or equal to 0.
Is less than	<	<0	Return only the records whose Criteria field value is less than 0.
Is less than or equal to	<=	<=10	Return only the records whose Criteria field value is less than or equal to 10.
Is one of	In()	In('East', 'West')	Return only the records whose Criteria field value is East or West.
Is between	Between	Between 5 and 10	Return only the records whose Criteria field value is between 5 and 10.
Begins with	Like	Like A*	Return only the records whose Criteria field value begins with A (or a).
Ends with	Like	Like *A	Return only the records whose Criteria field value ends with A (or a).
Contains	Like	Like *oo*	Return only the records whose Criteria field value contains the string oo (or OO).
Is null	Is Null	Is Null	Return only the records whose Criteria field value is empty.
Is not null	Is Not Null	Is Not Null	Return only the records whose Criteria field value is not empty.

Note that you can apply criteria to fields which are not included as part of the result set. Also, you can create complex criteria by using multiple fields as part of the criteria expression. Criteria listed in different columns but on the same row are considered an And condition. Criteria listed in the same column but on different rows indicate an Or condition.

NOTE *The Not operator can be applied in front of any expression to return the opposite values. For example you could specify Not Between 5 and 10 to return only those records whose Criteria field value is not between 5 and 10.*

In Figure 16.11, I've placed a filter on the ShipCountry field to limit the results to just those order records that were shipped to the USA. Note that the quotes around USA were automatically added by MS Query after I entered =USA.

FIGURE 16.11

Filtering the results returned using the Criteria pane of MS Query

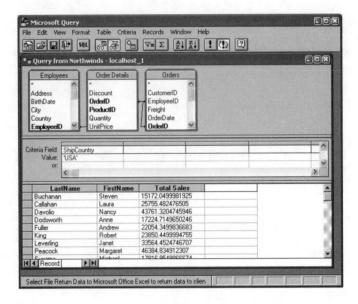

STEP FOUR: SET THE SORT ORDER

You can return a result set that is sorted using one or more fields. Sorting is optional of course. You could just return the results to Excel in the default order that they came from the database. The default order depends on the underlying table structure of the table(s) used in the query.

To sort the result set on a single field, click in any record in the field you want sorted, and then click either the Ascending or Descending toolbar buttons depending on how you want it sorted.

To sort the result set on multiple fields, start by sorting on the most important field. Then, while holding down the Ctrl key, sort additional fields in order of importance. When you hold down the Ctrl key, MS Query preserves any existing sort orders.

You can also define a sort order by choosing Records ➤ Sort from the MS Query menu. This displays the following Sort dialog box. For my query, I specified a sort on the LastName column as shown in the following screenshot.

Starting with the primary sort column, select the column to include in the sort, select Ascending or Descending, and then click Add.

STEP FIVE: RETURN THE RESULT SET TO EXCEL

Once you're satisfied that the query is retrieving the data you want the way you want it, select File ➤ Return Data to Microsoft Office Excel and then indicate where to place the data as shown in the following screenshot.

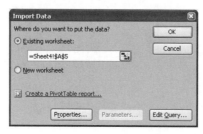

Note that you can also save the query (by choosing File ➤ Save in MS Query) so that it can be used from other workbooks without going through all of the steps to set it up again. Any queries you save will show up on the Queries tab when you select Data ➤ Import External Data ➤ New Database Query in Excel.

Turbo Charge Your Data Range

While using MS Query to retrieve data is a powerful capability, you can add more horsepower to your solution by using parameter queries. A parameter query is a query that allows you to specify one or more of the criteria values each time the query is executed.

You want to see sales figures for the Midwest division? Fine, run the query and specify "Midwest" for the division criteria. What's that? You want to see sales for the Northwest instead? No problem, refresh the query and specify "Northwest" for the division criteria. Parameter queries allow you to develop this kind of "push-button" reporting in which your end users can easily get the data they are interested in with a few clicks of the mouse.

For the most part, parameter queries are created just like any other query using MS Query. The key difference is how you specify the criteria on the field that you would like to use as a parameter field. In Figure 16.11, I used the ShipCountry field to filter the result set so that only records shipped from the USA were included. This query can be easily converted to a parameter query by making the modification shown in Figure 16.12.

Rather than hard-code USA as a value, I've entered a prompt in brackets. When you execute this query, MS Query will prompt you for the value to use using the text you supplied in between the brackets.

FIGURE 16.12
A basic parameter
query

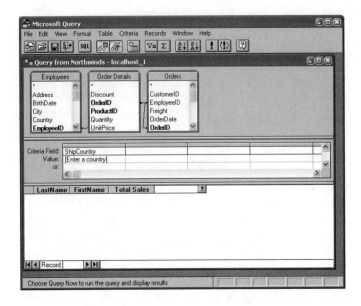

FIGURE 16.13
The Parameters
dialog box

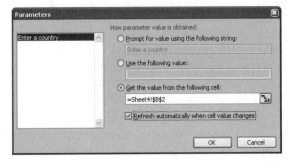

Once you return the data to Excel, things get even more interesting. If you right-click anywhere in the external data range and choose Parameters, a dialog box similar to the one shown in Figure 16.13 will display.

In Figure 16.13, I've instructed the data range to retrieve the value to pass on as the parameter from cell B2. Also, if the cell's value changes, I've set it up to rerun the query with the new value. To really make this easy from a user's perspective, you could use the Data Validation feature on the cell used for the parameter value. In Figure 16.14, I've filled in the necessary Data Validation values. The end result (Figure 16.15) is an interactive worksheet that allows users to easily retrieve just the data they're interested in seeing. All without a single line of code!

FIGURE 16.14
Use Data Validation
on the parameter cell.

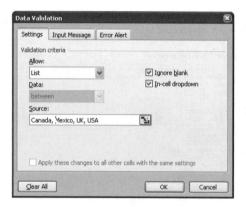

FIGURE 16.15
MS Query +
Parameter Query +
Data Validation =
Power

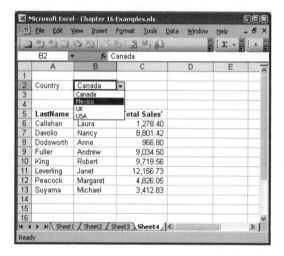

Work Magic with ADO

I feel it is important to learn how to use MS Query. I've seen numerous VBA applications that were created to retrieve data from a database into Excel that could have been done using MS Query alone. There's no sense in writing custom code to work with a database if you can achieve the same results with MS Query.

For those times when MS Query won't cut it, you can turn to ADO. ADO is a set of objects that you can use to interact programmatically with a database. The ADO object model is shown in Figure 16.16.

FIGURE 16.16
The ADO Object Model

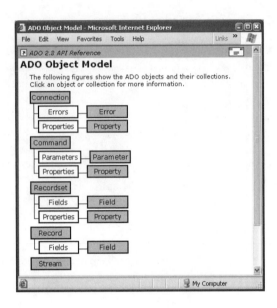

Now, I must tell you that ADO is a much bigger topic than can possibly be covered in one chapter. In fact, entire books have been written on the use of ADO. The content presented here should be enough to get you off to a good start. In particular, you'll find examples that show you how to open a connection to a data source, retrieve data from a data source, and copy it to the worksheet, as well as run action queries against the data source that insert new records or modify existing records.

The first thing you need to do to use ADO is set a reference to the ADO object library. Select Tools ➤ References from within the VBE. As you can see in Figure 16.17, there will likely be a few versions of ADO present on you computer. You should choose a version that you know will be installed on your user's computer. If you have a compelling reason to use a newer version of ADO that isn't installed on your users' computers, your users will need to install the required version of ADO before using your application. ADO version 2.1 was distributed with Office 2000 whereas version 2.5 was distributed with Office XP and Office 2003.

FIGURE 16.17
You will probably have many versions of ADO available on your PC.

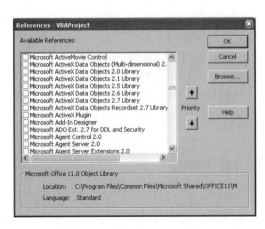

ADO has a very flexible object model. For many tasks, you could go about completing them multiple ways. For this reason, it can be difficult to understand how to use ADO at first. I guarantee that you'll see various ways for completing tasks with ADO if you look at online help, other developer books, and so on. My advice to you is to keep in mind that ADO is meant to be flexible—don't get too hung up or surprised when you see people use different methods for performing various actions with ADO.

In general, you need to know three main objects to begin using ADO: Command, Connection, and Recordset. Many times the Connection object is the first object you need to worry about. A Connection object contains properties and methods that allow you to manage the details associated with a unique connection to a data source. I say data source rather than database because ADO allows you to connect to other stores of data besides databases.

The Command object contains properties and methods that allow you to create or modify a statement that will be sent to the data source defined by the Command's associated Connection object. Command objects are useful for executing update and insert SQL statements and stored procedures, and for setting parameters for a parameter query.

A Recordset has the properties and methods you need to work with the result set retrieved from the data source. Recordset objects consist of records (rows) and fields (columns).

Make the Connection

As the top-level object of the ADO object library, you always need a Connection on which to operate in order to do anything else. You can obtain a Connection in two ways: you can explicitly create a Connection object, or you can implicitly create one when you're using one of the lower-level objects such as a Recordset by providing the object with the detail necessary to create a Connection. Table 16.2 provides a list of some key properties and methods of the Connection object.

Easily the most important part of creating a Connection object is specifying the ConnectionString, a property that contains essential details that let ADO know where the data source is located.

TABLE 16.2: Key Connection Object Properties and Methods

PROPERTY/METHOD	DESCRIPTION
ConnectionString Property	Provides the details used to establish a connection to the data source.
Provider Property	Sets or returns the name of the provider used for the connection. A provider is a software component that operates between ADO and the data source.
State Property	Indicates whether the connection is open (adStateOpen) or closed (adStateClosed).
Close Method	Closes the connection and any dependent objects.
Execute Method	Executes a SQL statement or stored procedure on the connection.
Open Method	Opens a connection to the data source.

Listing 16.1 presents a simple example that creates a Connection to the Northwind database. This listing just creates a new Connection, and opens and then closes the connection.

LISTING 16.1: A SIMPLE CONNECTION EXAMPLE

```
Sub MakeConnectionExample()
    Dim conn As ADODB.Connection

    On Error GoTo ErrHandler

    Set conn = New ADODB.Connection

    conn.Provider = "Microsoft.Jet.OLEDB.4.0;"
    conn.ConnectionString = "Data Source=C:\Program Files\" & _
        "Microsoft Office\OFFICE11\SAMPLES\northwind.mdb"
    conn.Open

    If conn.State = adStateOpen Then
        MsgBox "Connected!", vbOKOnly
        conn.Close
    Else
        MsgBox "Not connected!", vbOKCancel
    End If

    Set conn = Nothing
    Exit Sub

ErrHandler:
    MsgBox "Could not connect to database. " & Err.Description, _
        vbOKOnly
End Sub
```

I could have made this even easier, but I wanted to demonstrate two things that will be useful later on. First, I used the Provider property of the Connection object to specify the provider to use. A provider is generally a product-specific driver used by ADO to communicate with the database specified by the data source property embedded in the connection string. It's possible to embed the provider in the connection string. For example, I could have eliminated the statement that set the Provider property and assign the following value to the ConnectionString property.

```
conn.ConnectionString = "Provider=Microsoft.Jet.OLEDB.4.0;" & _
    "Data Source=C:\Program Files\" & _
    "Microsoft Office\OFFICE11\SAMPLES\northwind.mdb"
```

The second thing that I'd like to point out is the If…Then statement that compares the Connection State to the defined constant adStateOpen. For the purposes of the example, I could have simply displayed the "Connected!" message at this point. After the conn.Open statement, there are only two possible outcomes: either the connection is open or an error occurs. Because I've enabled error handling, if the line following the Open statement is executed, it's safe to assume that the connection is open. Nonetheless, I used the State property of the Connection object as a way to demonstrate that it exists and how you use it.

The State property is important because it's possible for a Connection to close without your knowledge. For example, perhaps a connection to a data source automatically closes or times out after a specified period of inactivity. Consequently, it's important that you check the State of a Connection before you use it and refresh (or reopen) the connection as needed.

Ready, Set, Query!

When retrieving data using ADO, the majority of your code will be operating on a Recordset object. Using the Recordset object, you'll specify the SQL statement you want to send to the data source, execute the query using the Open method, and then examine the results using various navigational properties and methods. The Recordset object is probably the largest of the ADO objects in terms of number of properties and methods. Table 16.3 lists some of the most commonly used properties and methods of the Recordset object.

TABLE 16.3: KEY RECORDSET OBJECT PROPERTIES AND METHODS

PROPERTY/METHOD	DESCRIPTION
ActiveConnection Property	Returns/sets the Connection with which the object is associated.
BOF/EOF Properties	Positional indicators. BOF indicates that the current record position is before the first record. EOF indicates that the current record position is after the last record.
CursorType Property	Indicates the type of cursor used. A cursor is a database object used to aid in record navigation and update records in a recordset. Can be one of the following: adOpenForwardOnly, adOpenKeyset, adOpenDynamic, or adOpenStatic. Not all providers support all types of cursors.
Fields Property	Returns a Fields object that is a collection of Field objects associated with a Recordset object.
RecordCount Property	Returns the number of records in the recordset.
Source Property	Sets/returns the data source (a Command object, SQL statement, stored procedure, or table name) for the recordset.
State Property	Indicates whether the connection is open (adStateOpen) or closed (adStateClosed).
AddNew Method	Creates a new record in an updateable recordset.
Close Method	Closes the recordset.
Delete Method	Deletes the current record or a group of records.

TABLE 16.3: KEY RECORDSET OBJECT PROPERTIES AND METHODS *(continued)*

PROPERTY/METHOD	DESCRIPTION
Move Method	Moves the position of the current record.
MoveFirst, MoveLast, MoveNext, or MovePrevious	Moves the current record to the first, last, next, or previous record.
Open Method	Opens a cursor on the recordset.
Requery Method	Updates the data by reexecuting the query on which the object is based.
Update Method	Saves any changes you make to the current record.

Listing 16.2 demonstrates the Recordset object by retrieving a list of employees from the Northwind database and copying the data onto a worksheet.

LISTING 16.2: USING A RECORDSET TO EXECUTE AND DISPLAY A QUERY

```
Sub RecordsetExample()
    Dim rst As ADODB.Recordset
    Dim sConn As String
    Dim sSQL As String
    Dim rg As Range

    On Error GoTo ErrHandler

    Set rg = ThisWorkbook.Worksheets(1).Range("a1")

    ' Create a new recordset object
    Set rst = New ADODB.Recordset

    ' Connection details - this is the kind of thing
    ' that you can use the Settings class for
    sConn = "Provider=Microsoft.Jet.OLEDB.4.0;" & _
        "Data Source=C:\Program Files\" & _
        "Microsoft Office\OFFICE11\SAMPLES\northwind.mdb"

    ' SQL statement to retrieve list of employees
    sSQL = "SELECT LastName, FirstName, Title FROM employees"

    ' Open the recordset
    rst.Open sSQL, sConn

    ' Copy recordset to the range
    rg.CopyFromRecordset rst
```

```
' Adjust column sizes
rg.CurrentRegion.Columns.AutoFit

' Close the recordset
rst.Close

' Clean up.
Set rst = Nothing
Set rg = Nothing
Exit Sub

ErrHandler:
    MsgBox "Sorry, an error occured. " & Err.Description, vbOKOnly
End Sub
```

This procedure is a good example of the flexibility of the ADO object model. Rather than explicitly creating a Connection object, it's implicitly created when the recordset is opened. The Open method of the Recordset object allows you to pass a connection string as the second parameter. Using the connection string, ADO creates a Connection object behind the scenes and then opens the recordset against it.

Once the recordset is opened, you can use the CopyFromRecordset method of the Range object to automatically copy the data to the range. The output of the RecordsetExample procedure is shown in Figure 16.18.

The CopyFromRecordset method is handy when you want to copy data to a worksheet exactly as it appears in the recordset. Many times, however, you'll need to do things like rearrange the order of the fields or examine individual records before copying them to a worksheet. Listing 16.3 demonstrates how you can loop through a recordset and manually transfer data to a worksheet.

FIGURE 16.18

Output of the RecordsetExample procedure

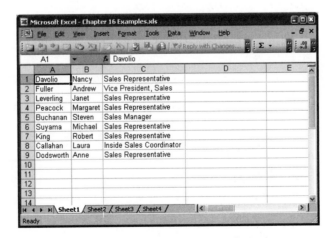

LISTING 16.3: LOOPING THROUGH A RECORDSET

```
Sub LoopThroughRecordset(rst As ADODB.Recordset, rg As Range)
    Dim nColumnOffset As Integer
    Dim fld As ADODB.Field

    ' Use With...End With on rst to
    ' save typing & increase performance
    ' Downside - harder to read.
    With rst

        ' Loop until we hit the end of the
        ' recordset
        Do Until .EOF

            ' Loop through each field and retrieve it's value
            nColumnOffset = 0
            For Each fld In .Fields
                rg.Offset(0, nColumnOffset).Value = fld.Value
                nColumnOffset = nColumnOffset + 1
            Next

            ' Move down one row on the worksheet
            Set rg = rg.Offset(1, 0)

            ' Move to the next record
            .MoveNext
        Loop

    End With

    ' Clean up.
    Set fld = Nothing

End Sub
```

You can test the LoopThroughRecordset procedure by replacing the statement

```
' Copy recordset to the range
rg.CopyFromRecordset rst
```

in the RecordsetExample procedure shown in Listing 16.2 with the following statement:

```
' Copy recordset to the range
LoopThroughRecordset rst, rg
```

After you do this, if you run the RecordsetExample procedure, it produces exactly the same output as it did using the CopyFromRecordset method (Figure 16.18). Of course, you now have unlimited control over the exact output because you can examine the records row by row, field by field.

As Listing 16.3 demonstrates, there are two key parts to setting up a loop to walk through the data in a recordset. The first part is setting up the Do…Loop statement to loop until the EOF property of the Recordset object is true. If you run a query that doesn't return any records, EOF will be true right from the get go, otherwise the recordset will be returned and the first record in the result set will be the current record. The second part is to make sure you advance the current record with each pass through the Do…Loop. You advance the current record by using the MoveNext method of the Recordset object. Without this statement the loop will repeat endlessly, so I like to add this statement immediately after creating the Do…Loop.

As an alternative to looping through the fields, you can also access individual fields. The Fields object is a collection of Field objects. As you have seen throughout the book, you can access a particular object in a collection using either its name or index. Consequently, if you were just interested in the LastName field, you could retrieve its value using one of the following statements.

```
' Retrieve last name by name
sLastName = rst.Fields("LastName").Value

' Retrieve last name by field index
sLastName = rst.Fields(0).Value
```

You can determine the index of a particular field by looking at the SQL statement used to retrieve the data. The first field mentioned after the SELECT statement will have an index of 0, the second field will have an index of 1, and so on.

It's Not Just about Retrieving

Reading data from a database is just half the story. You may also need to modify existing data or add new data to a database. Many times I see beginners open a table using the Recordset object, locate the record they want to change, and then make the desired change. Alternately, they will open up a table using the Recordset object and then add a new record on to the end of it. Although these methods work, they are extemely inefficient. It is much better to construct a SQL statement to do the job and then send the SQL statement to the data source and let the data source worry about making the changes. After all, managing data is what the data source is designed to do.

Queries that involve updating, inserting, and deleting records are commonly referred to as action queries. In order to execute action queries with ADO, you use the Command object. The Command object has a CommandText property. To execute a Command object you set the CommandText property equal to the SQL statement you wish to execute and then provide either a connection string or a Connection object to the Command's ActiveConnection property. Once you have set the CommandText and ActiveConnection properties you're ready to call Command's Excecute method. Table 16.4 lists the most commonly used Command properties and methods.

Listing 16.4 provides an example of using the Command object. The ActionQuery function executes the supplied action query (a SQL statement) against the supplied Connection object and returns the number of records that were affected by the query. TestActionQuery demonstrates how to use ActionQuery by adding a new record to the Catagories table in the Northwind database and then editing an existing record.

TABLE 16.4: KEY COMMAND OBJECT PROPERTIES AND METHODS

PROPERTY/METHOD	DESCRIPTION
ActiveConnection property	Returns/sets the connection with which the object is associated.
CommandText property	Returns/sets the text of the command to be issued to the data source.
CommandType property	Indicates the type of command. Generally the command type will be either adCmdText for SQL statements or adCmdStoredProc for stored procedures.
Parameters property	Returns a collection of Parameter objects associated with the Command object.
CreateParameter method	Creates a new Parameter object with the specified properties.
Execute method	Executes the command against the data source.

LISTING 16.4: EXECUTING ACTION QUERIES

```
Sub TestActionQuery()
    Dim conn As ADODB.Connection
    Dim lRecordsAffected As Long
    Dim sSQL As String

    On Error GoTo ErrHandler

    Set conn = New ADODB.Connection

    conn.ConnectionString = "Provider=Microsoft.Jet.OLEDB.4.0;" & _
        "Data Source=C:\Program Files\" & _
        "Microsoft Office\OFFICE11\SAMPLES\northwind.mdb"
    conn.Open

    If conn.State = adStateOpen Then
        ' Add a new category
        sSQL = "INSERT INTO Categories" & _
            "([CategoryName], [Description]) " & _
            "VALUES ('Jerky', 'Beef jerky, turkey jerky, " & _
            "and other tasty jerkies');"
        lRecordsAffected = ActionQuery(conn, sSQL)
        MsgBox "Added " & lRecordsAffected & " record(s).", vbOKOnly

        ' Edit an existing category
        sSQL = "UPDATE Categories SET [Description] = " & _
```

```
                "'Prepared meats except for jerky' " & _
                "WHERE [CategoryName]='Meat/Poultry';"
            lRecordsAffected = ActionQuery(conn, sSQL)
            MsgBox "Updated " & lRecordsAffected & " record(s).", vbOKOnly

            conn.Close
        End If

        Set conn = Nothing
        Exit Sub

ErrHandler:
        MsgBox "Could not connect to database. " & Err.Description, _
            vbOKOnly
End Sub

'/ returns number of records affected
Public Function ActionQuery(conn As ADODB.Connection, _
        sSQL As String) As Long

        Dim lRecordsAffected As Long
        Dim cmd As ADODB.Command

        On Error GoTo ErrHandler

        lRecordsAffected = 0

        Set cmd = New ADODB.Command

        With cmd
            .ActiveConnection = conn
            .CommandText = sSQL
            .CommandType = adCmdText
            .Execute lRecordsAffected
        End With

        ' Clean up.
        Set cmd = Nothing

ExitPoint:
        ActionQuery = lRecordsAffected
        Exit Function
ErrHandler:
        Debug.Print "ActionQuery error: " & Err.Description
        Resume ExitPoint
End Function
```

I Like Treats

At this point, I would like to share a treat with you by introducing you to a special product—Microsoft Analysis Services. Analysis Services is a special kind of database product that ships in the box with Microsoft SQL Server. Analysis Services is an OLAP product. OLAP stands for Online Analytical Processing. OLAP applications enable rapid analysis of numerical data along multiple dimensions. For example, an OLAP database may be designed to summarize financial data that can be viewed by product, business line, customer, and time period.

Analysis Services is rapidly gaining market share over traditional expensive, arcane OLAP products such as Hyperion Essbase due to its ease of use, performance, and price. Analysis Services ships with every version of SQL Server (Developer, Enterprise, Personal, and Standard). If you're building an analytical application that uses a large amount of data, I'd encourage you to give Analysis Services a look. If you don't have SQL Server, you can get a free trial version from Microsoft's website (`http://www.microsoft.com/sql/`).

Analysis Services is a very complimentary product to Excel. Many, if not most, Excel applications are analytical and numerical in nature. With Analysis Services, you can analyze an obscene amount of data using Analysis Services to serve the data and Excel to view the data. Excel can natively connect to Analysis Services via a PivotTable. Figure 16.19 shows an example of Analysis Services data as viewed through a PivotTable.

Microsoft also has an Excel add-in called CubeCellValue that you can download (`http://www.microsoft.com/downloads/details.aspx?displaylang=en&familyid=3c4bbc1c-24da-4e44-8f9b-995341ff2c67`); this allows you to retrieve Analysis Services data using cell formulas. In Figure 16.20, I've created a simple report that retrieves all of its values from Analysis Services using the CubeCellValue function from within Excel.

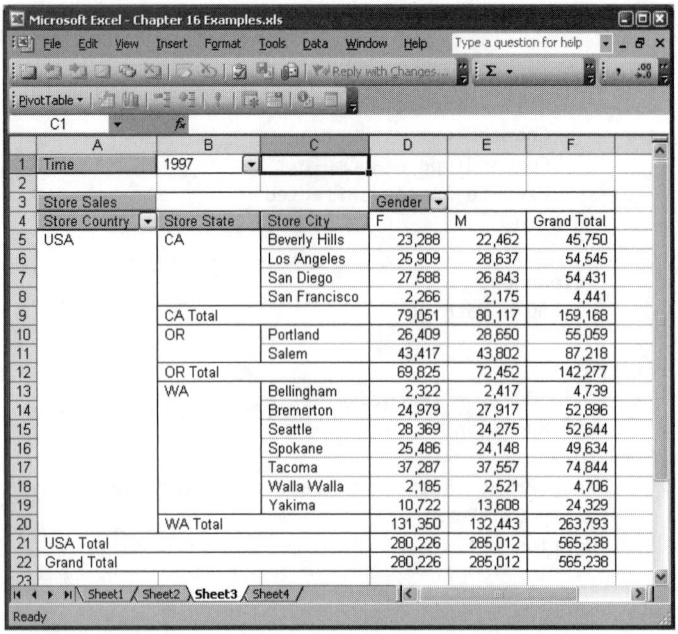

Time	1997				
Store Sales			Gender		
Store Country	Store State	Store City	F	M	Grand Total
USA	CA	Beverly Hills	23,288	22,462	45,750
		Los Angeles	25,909	28,637	54,545
		San Diego	27,588	26,843	54,431
		San Francisco	2,266	2,175	4,441
	CA Total		79,051	80,117	159,168
	OR	Portland	26,409	28,650	55,059
		Salem	43,417	43,802	87,218
	OR Total		69,825	72,452	142,277
	WA	Bellingham	2,322	2,417	4,739
		Bremerton	24,979	27,917	52,896
		Seattle	28,369	24,275	52,644
		Spokane	25,486	24,148	49,634
		Tacoma	37,287	37,557	74,844
		Walla Walla	2,185	2,521	4,706
		Yakima	10,722	13,608	24,329
	WA Total		131,350	132,443	263,793
USA Total			280,226	285,012	565,238
Grand Total			280,226	285,012	565,238

FIGURE 16.19
Analysis Services data viewed through a PivotTable

FIGURE 16.20
The CubeCellValue
add-in allows you
to use formulas to
retrieve data.

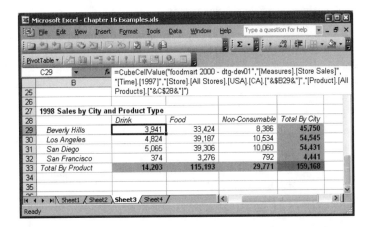

Although PivotTables and the CubeCellValue are useful ways to access Analysis Services, they don't serve all purposes. For other purposes, you can use your VBA skills in conjunction with ADO to retrieve Analysis Services data just the way you (or your users) want it. From a developer perspective, data in Analysis Services is much easier to work with when compared to the same data from a traditional database. SQL statements can get pretty complex when working with data that your users want to view along different dimensions and at different levels of detail.

There is a catch to writing your own queries for Analysis Services. You have to learn a different query language. To query an Analysis Services database you use a language known as MDX (multidimensional expression). It's not very difficult to learn enough basic MDX to start becoming productive.

NOTE   *If you are totally new to Analysis Services and want to learn more, I recommend* Microsoft SQL Server 2000 Analysis Services Step by Step *by Reed Jacobson (Microsoft Press, 2000).*

NOTE   *A good MDX book is* MDX Solutions: With Microsoft SQL Server Analysis Services *by George Spofford (John Wiley & Sons, 2001).*

Analysis Services ships with a sample database named FoodMart. Listing 16.5 presents an example that connects to FoodMart, queries FoodMart, and displays the results on an Excel worksheet. As an example of the versatility of ADO, Listing 16.5 uses standard ADO objects and methods to query the Analysis Server.

LISTING 16.5: A BASIC EXAMPLE USING DATA FROM ANALYSIS SERVICES

```
Option Explicit

Private Const msCONNECTION = _
    "Data Source=localhost;Initial Catalog=FoodMart 2000;Provider=msolap;"

Sub BasicQueryExampleI()
```

```
    Dim rst As ADODB.Recordset
    Dim sMDX As String
    Dim ws As Worksheet

    On Error GoTo ErrHandler

    Set ws = ThisWorkbook.Worksheets(2)

    ' An Analysis Services query
    sMDX = "SELECT { [Measures].[Units Shipped], " & _
        "[Measures].[Units Ordered] } on columns, " & _
        "NON EMPTY [Store].[Store City].members on rows " & _
        "from Warehouse"

    ' You can use ADODB.Recordset or ADOMD.Cellset
    Set rst = New ADODB.Recordset

    ' Open the recordset - implicit Connection object creation
    rst.Open sMDX, msCONNECTION

    ' Use of the Recordset object is handy because
    ' it allows use of the CopyFromRecordset method
    ws.Cells(1, 1).CopyFromRecordset rst

    rst.Close

ExitPoint:
    Set rst = Nothing
    Set ws = Nothing
    Exit Sub
ErrHandler:
    MsgBox "An error occured - " & Err.Description, vbOKOnly
    Resume ExitPoint
End Sub
```

Did you get a sense of déjà vu reading over this listing? In a true testament to the versatility of ADO, this listing is extremely similar to Listing 16.2. The output of BasicQueryExampleI is shown in Figure 16.21.

The reason ADO works with so many diverse data sources is because there is an abstraction layer between the data source and ADO. The provider specified in the connection string handles all of the details associated with performing various tasks using ADO. This makes your job easier because you don't have to learn a new object model for each type of data source. However, because OLAP data is so different from traditional data sources, ADO alone won't handle all of the tasks you may need to perform when working with data from Analysis Services.

FIGURE 16.21

The output of List-
ing 16.5

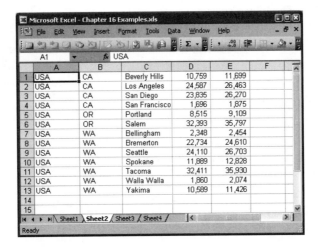

Consequently, there is a special version of ADO that can be used specifically to work with Analysis Services data. This version is called ADOMD. On one hand, ADOMD is a little more difficult to work with; on the other, it provides a richer object model that gives you more flexibility and control when you're working with data served from an analysis server. Key ADOMD objects are listed in Table 16.5. The most noticeable difference between ADO and ADOMD is that ADOMD uses a Cellset object to represent the data retrieved from a data source rather than a Recordset object as you saw with ADO.

TABLE 16.5: KEY ADOMD OBJECTS

OBJECT*	PARENT	DESCRIPTION
Catalog	None	Contains multidimensional schema information specific to a multidimensional data provider
CubeDef(s)	Catalog	Represents a cube from a multidimensional schema
Dimension(s)	CubeDef	Represents one of the dimensions of a cube
Hierarchy (Hierarchies)	Dimension	Represents one way in which the members of a dimension can be aggregated
Level(s)	Hierarchy	Contains a set of members, each of which has the same rank within a hierarchy
Cellset	None	Embodies the results of a multidimensional query
Cell	Cellset	Represents the data at the intersection of axis coordinates in a cellset
Axis (Axes)	Cellset	Represents a positional or filter axis of a cellset

TABLE 16.5: KEY ADOMD OBJECTS *(continued)*

OBJECT*	PARENT	DESCRIPTION
Position(s)	Axis or Cell	Represents a set of one or more members of different dimensions that defines a point along an axis
Member(s)	Level or Position	Represents a member of a level in a cube

Listing 16.6 presents an example that uses ADOMD. In order to use this example, you need to set a reference (Tools ➢ References in the VBE) to Microsoft ActiveX Data Objects (Multi-dimensional) 2.7 Library.

LISTING 16.6: A BASIC EXAMPLE USING ADOMD

```
Option Explicit

Private Const msCONNECTION = _
    "Data Source=localhost;Initial Catalog=FoodMart 2000;Provider=msolap;"

Sub BasicQueryExampleII()
    Dim cst As ADOMD.Cellset
    Dim cat As ADOMD.Catalog
    Dim sMDX As String
    Dim ws As Worksheet

    On Error GoTo ErrHandler

    Set ws = ThisWorkbook.Worksheets(2)

    ' An analysis services query
    sMDX = "SELECT { [Measures].[Units Shipped], " & _
        "[Measures].[Units Ordered] } on columns, " & _
        "NON EMPTY [Store].[Store City].members on rows " & _
        "from Warehouse"

    ' Unfortunately you need to explicitly create
    ' this object for the Cellset object (a Cellset
    ' object can't implicitly create a connection
    ' like a Recordset object can)
    Set cat = New ADOMD.Catalog
    cat.ActiveConnection = msCONNECTION

    ' Create new cellset and query away
    Set cst = New ADOMD.Cellset
    cst.Open sMDX, cat.ActiveConnection
```

```
    ' Call procedure to display the data
    DisplayCellset cst, ws.Cells(1, 1)

    cst.Close

ExitPoint:
    Set cat = Nothing
    Set cst = Nothing
    Set ws = Nothing
    Exit Sub
ErrHandler:
    MsgBox "An error occured - " & Err.Description, vbOKOnly
    Resume ExitPoint
End Sub

Sub DisplayCellset(cst As ADOMD.Cellset, rgTopLeft As Range)
    Dim nRow As Integer
    Dim nRowDimensionCount As Integer
    Dim nColumnMember As Integer
    Dim nRowDimension As Integer
    Dim nRowMember As Integer

    On Error GoTo ErrHandler

    nRowDimensionCount = cst.Axes(1).DimensionCount

    ' Loop through the rows contained in the cellset
    For nRow = 0 To cst.Axes(1).Positions.Count - 1

        ' Display labels for each row item
        For nRowDimension = 0 To nRowDimensionCount - 1
            rgTopLeft.Offset(nRow, nRowDimension).Value = _
                cst.Axes(1).Positions(nRow) _
                    .Members(nRowDimension).Caption
        Next

        ' Display values at each dimension intersection
        For nColumnMember = 0 To cst.Axes(0).Positions.Count - 1
            rgTopLeft.Offset _
                (nRow, nRowDimensionCount + nColumnMember).Value = _
                    cst.Item(nColumnMember, nRow).FormattedValue
        Next
    Next
ExitPoint:
    Exit Sub
ErrHandler:
    Debug.Print "DisplayCellset Error: " & Err.Description
    Resume ExitPoint
End Sub
```

FIGURE 16.22

The output of Basic-QueryExampleII

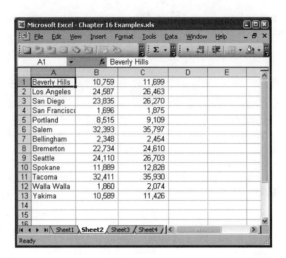

Looking at this listing, you can really appreciate the convenience of the CopyFromRecordset method used in the prior listing. Rather than one simple statement to transfer the result set to the worksheet, this listing requires an entire procedure. The output of BasicQueryExampleII is shown in Figure 16.22.

One of the nuances that you need to be aware of when using the Cellset object is that you can't use the ActiveConnection property the same way as you could with a Recordset. In ADO, you can implicitly create a Connection object by passing a connection string to a Recordset's ActiveConnection property. With ADOMD, you must set the Cellset's ActiveConnection using an explicitly created Catalog object. That is why a Catalog object is explicitly created in the BasicQueryExampleII procedure. A Catalog is roughly analogous to a Connection object in ADO.

The DisplayCellset procedure is a bit more difficult to understand then its ADO counterpart, the LoopThroughRecordset procedure presented in Listing 16.3. The extra difficulty comes from the need to handle data that is multidimensional. An ADO recordset is a two-dimensional entity. The two dimensions are fields (columns) and records (rows). A Cellset, on the other hand, can represent many dimensions. Consequently, the Cellset object uses more generic terminology to refer to items. To retrieve data out of a cellset, you need to examine the cellset's axes. An axis can be composed of one or more dimensions from the multidimensional data source. Depending on what you need to examine in a cellset, you use the Positions and Members objects or you can use the Item method of the Cellset object to retrieve a particular Cell object.

Summary

Although Excel has some data management capabilities, they are no where near the capabilities of even the most elementary database product. The more data you are working with, the more evident Excel's weaknesses become. This isn't a strike against Excel. Excel simply wasn't designed to be a database. By learning how to use Excel in conjunction with a database, you'll be able to create a whole new class of solutions that would be difficult if not impossible to do using just Excel.

The easiest way to incorporate data from a database in Excel is to use Microsoft Query (MS Query). MS Query is a visual query-building tool that ships with Microsoft Office. MS Query provides the capability to design and execute queries. The query results are delivered right to a worksheet in the form of an external data range.

Although MS Query is a powerful feature, you can make it even more useful by developing parameter queries with it. A parameter query is a query that allows you to specify one or more of the criteria values each time the query is executed. You can map parameter query inputs to certain cells in Excel. Further, you can set the data range up so that when a parameter's source cell changes, the external data range refreshes itself.

For programmatic access to databases, look to ActiveX Data Objects (ADO). ADO is an object library used for working with data sources. Although ADO is an extensive object model, you only need to know three main objects: the Connection object represents the details associated with a data source; the Recordset object represents a chunk of data retrieved from a given data source; and the Command object represents a command that you execute against a given data source. Command objects are used to execute action queries, stored procedures, or parameter queries.

Because most Excel applications are fundamentally numeric in nature, I encourage you to look into Microsoft Analysis Services if you are working on a problem that involves a large amount of data. Analysis Services is a special kind of database product called an OLAP database. OLAP databases are exceptional tools to use when you need to slice and dice large amounts of data (millions of records). Analysis Services and Excel are two complimentary products. You can use PivotTables to connect to an analysis server without writing any code. For programmatic access to an analysis server consider using either ADO or ADOMD, a flavor of ADO intended for Analysis Services.

Excel's XML capabilities received a huge boost with the release of Excel 2003. As more and more data is either stored or transmitted in XML, it is likely that if you aren't already working with XML, you will be soon. In the next chapter, I'll round out my coverage of working with external data by covering Excel's XML capabilities.

Chapter 17

XL(M) = XML

Extensible Markup Language (XML) is a technology that has created quite a bit of buzz over the past five years or so. Well, buzz is probably a bit of an understatement. Basically, XML has been hyped over this time period.

XML is a plain-text, Unicode-based metalanguage that you can use, among other things, to store and transmit tabular and semistructured data. Because XML is not associated with a programming language, operating system, or software vendor, it is particularly useful for transmitting data between widely disparate systems. Microsoft has embraced XML as a way to allow its various applications to collaborate on a document's data in ways that are not possible using Object Linking and Embedding (OLE) as I mentioned in Chapter 14. Of course, Excel (aka XL) has functionality that allows Excel to work with and create XML data. In this chapter, I will provide an elementary overview of XML followed by a look at the new XML functionality in Excel 2003. The chapter concludes with coverage of the new XML-related objects in Excel's object model.

Y XML?

As the father of a five-year-old, I've seen my share of SpongeBob episodes. In one episode, Squidward, an artsy, highbrow wannabe, is trying to create a marching band with a bunch of horrible musicians. Realizing that the situation is hopeless, he comes up with an idea. He asks how people try to sound intelligent. Plankton, a pseudo-intellectual bent on world-domination, speaks loudly. "They speak loudly," he says. The band then attempts to play as loudly as possible in order to make people think they're good.

I have a theory that another way people try to look intelligent is to use lots of acronyms. This approach is used at corporate business meetings on a daily basis. It is also why mathematicians seem so smart. They don't even bother with acronyms—they extend the concept by using letters to represent numbers and other objects of interest. The practice of looking intelligent by the overuse of acronyms is the theme of this chapter. XML is so simple it's difficult. When you see it, you're left wondering where the rest of it is. Listing 17.1 shows an example of an XML file.

LISTING 17.1: NEW-SCHOOL REINDEER DATA

```xml
<?xml version="1.0" encoding="UTF-8" ?>
<DataRoot>
   <Reindeer>
      <Name>Dasher</Name>
      <Disposition>Contemptuous</Disposition>
      <NoseColor>Black</NoseColor>
   </Reindeer>
   <Reindeer>
      <Name>Donner</Name>
      <Disposition>Optimistic</Disposition>
      <NoseColor>Black</NoseColor>
   </Reindeer>
   <Reindeer>
      <Name>Rudolph</Name>
      <Disposition>Cheerful</Disposition>
      <NoseColor>Bright Red</NoseColor>
   </Reindeer>
</DataRoot>
```

Without knowing anything about XML, it is easy to tell that this is a collection of reindeer, and for each reindeer, three characteristics are provided—the name of the reindeer, the disposition of the reindeer, and the color of its nose. If this data were in a standard text file, it might look something like Listing 17.2.

LISTING 17.2: OLD-SCHOOL REINDEER DATA

```
"Dasher", "Contemptuous", "Black"
"Donner", "Optimistic", "Black"
"Rudolph", "Cheerful", "Bright Red"
```

Although Listing 17.2 is more compact than its XML counterpart, if you weren't familiar with the underlying data, which way would you prefer to receive it? How would you know what the data was in Listing 17.2? Many times, I've received text files to work with that didn't contain field names as the first row. I could ask the person who gave it to me to include field names, but this isn't always practical.

XML has another big benefit over a standard text file—it can display relationships between individual elements in a file. As an example, consider Listing 17.3.

LISTING 17.3: EXTENDED REINDEER DATA

```xml
<?xml version="1.0" encoding="UTF-8" ?>
<DataRoot>
```

```
<Reindeer>
    <Name>Dasher</Name>
    <Disposition>Contemptuous</Disposition>
    <Nose>Black</Nose>
    <Children>
        <Son>Mickey</Son>
        <Son>Mikey</Son>
        <Daughter>Mindy</Daughter>
    </Children>
</Reindeer>
<Reindeer>
    <Name>Donner</Name>
    <Disposition>Optimistic</Disposition>
    <Nose>Black</Nose>
    <Children>
        <Daughter>Dorothy</Daughter>
    </Children>
</Reindeer>
<Reindeer>
    <Name>Rudolph</Name>
    <Disposition>Cheerful</Disposition>
    <Nose>Bright Red</Nose>
</Reindeer>
</DataRoot>
```

Listing 17.3 includes each reindeer's children and whether each child is a son or a daughter. Because each reindeer has a different number of children (or none at all), you can't create this kind of relationship in a standard delimited text file.

As you can see, XML is a powerful, yet simple, way to structure data. Because technologists have a hard time with simplicity, it's important to create confusion by inventing a number of related technologies, each with an acronym of its own. There is definitely no shortfall of acronyms related to XML. The next list covers some of the common acronyms you may come across.

DTD   DTD stands for Document Type Declaration. A DTD is a document that specifies all of the characteristics of the data elements within an XML file associated with the DTD. DTD has been pretty much relegated to little more than a historical role for two reasons: first, DTD is a rather cryptic way to specify an XML schema; second, DTD itself is not an XML document. This is a PITA (Pain In The Asp—where an asp is, of course, a feisty, venomous snake) because you can't use standard XML parsers to work with DTD files.

XDR   XDR refers to Microsoft's XML Data-Reduced schema.

XMLSS   XMLSS stands for XML Spreadsheet Schema. XMLSS was introduced by Microsoft with Excel 2002 as a way to save workbooks as XML documents.

XPath   XML path language, aka XPath, is a technology for querying XML data.

XSD XSD refers to the XML Schema Definition language. DTD, XDR, and XSD are all used to specify the allowable structure and content of an XML document. XSD is currently the preferred method for defining a schema. One advantage of XSD is that XSD files are themselves XML documents.

XSL Extensible Stylesheet Language (XSL) is a technology that provides methods for transforming XML data. XSL is used primarily to define the formatting and presentation of XML documents.

XSLT XSLT stands for XSL Transformations. XSLT is a subset of XSL. XSLT style sheets consist of a series of template rules and commands used to select and manipulate the structure of XML data.

Out of all of these acronyms, I'll only talk about XSD and XPath in this chapter. Now it is time to see how to marry XML with Excel.

XML in XL

As XML has become more prevalent, Microsoft has enhanced Excel's (and all other Office applications', for that matter) capability to work with XML. In Excel 2002, the primary XML support was the ability to use an XML file format that adhered to Microsoft's XMLSS. You could also import and open (but not save) XML files.

Excel 2003 extends XML support by offering you the ability to work with your own schemas. This is a significant extension. Because this is all new functionality, it's a good idea to go over some of these interesting features prior to covering them from a VBA standpoint. In particular, I'd like to examine three types of tasks you can perform.

Viewing and editing XML data Basic XML functionality that allows you to open an XML file, edit the data in Excel, and then save the data as XML. This functionality is covered in the "Easy XL XML" section.

Importing and mapping XML data This functionality extends the ability to work with XML data by allowing you to import XML data into the location of your choice. Further, you can map specific XML elements to cells on a worksheet. This functionality is covered in the section "XL XML Maps."

Exporting worksheet data back out to an XML file For this functionality, refer to the mysteriously named section "$4X^3M^2L^3$." Sounds pretty intelligent, eh?

After you learn how to perform these three tasks, I'll show you how to do the same thing programmatically.

Easy XL XML

The most basic XML functionality is the ability to open XML files. Depending on the structure of your XML file, you may or may not be able to modify the data and then save it as XML. The key determining factor is whether the XML contains a mixture of repeating and nonrepeating elements. If the XML file consists solely of repeating elements, you'll be able to modify the data and then resave it as XML. Listing 17.1 is a good example of an XML file that consists solely of repeating elements. This listing contains reindeer data and each reindeer element contains the same subelements.

If the XML file consists of a mixture of repeating and nonrepeating elements, you won't be able to make changes and then resave it as XML, but you will be able to open it. Listing 17.3 contains XML that consists of a mixture of repeating and nonrepeating elements. This listing contains reindeer data like Listing 17.1, but each reindeer item may or may not contain a Children element. Further, a Children element may contain any number of Son or Daughter elements.

To begin with, I'll demonstrate the steps required to open an XML file consisting solely of repeating elements.

1. Choose File ➤ Open from the Excel menu.

2. Locate and select the XML file you want and click Open.

3. In the Open XML dialog box, use the As an XML List option and click OK as shown in the following screen shot.

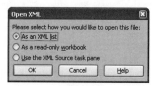

4. If your XML file doesn't refer to a schema or there is a problem with the schema, Excel may display the message shown in Figure 17.1; this alerts you of the problem and lets you know that it will create a schema for you.

As you can see in Figure 17.2, Excel opens the file and associates it with a list that you can sort, filter, and modify like any other list. Further, if you add a new item to the list or edit an existing item, you can save the data back to an XML file.

For example, in Figure 17.3, I've edited the first item and added a new item. To save the data back out to XML, choose Data ➤ XML ➤ Export, and then provide a filename and storage location for the file. When you do this, Excel exports the data back into an XML file that conforms to the schema of the original XML file.

When you open an XML file that consists of a mixture of repeating and nonrepeating elements, Excel flattens the structure so that it can be shown using the list functionality. You can use the same process to open the file. Unfortunately, you can't save back to the original XML structure when opening this type of XML file in this manner. Fret not, however; you can edit these types of XML files by using the process described in the next section. Figure 17.4 shows an example of a flattened file. The file shown is the XML from Listing 17.3. Notice that the first three rows are associated with Dasher.

FIGURE 17.1

Excel can create a schema based on your XML file.

FIGURE 17.2
Excel presents XML
data in a list format.

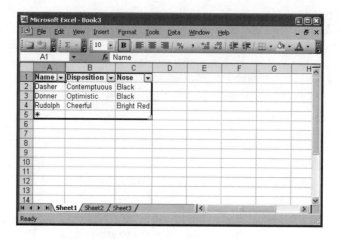

FIGURE 17.3
You can edit the data
in the list like any
other list in Excel.

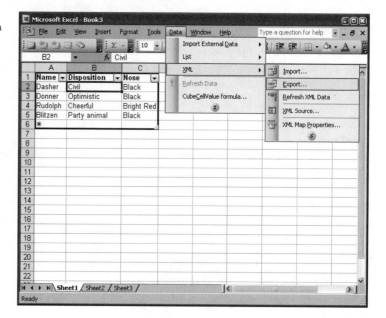

XL XML Maps

Although the functionality explained in the previous section is exciting, it is also quite limiting regarding the type of XML structures that you can use. In order to be truly useful, you need to be able to do more than just open mixed XML files; you need to be able to edit them and save them back to XML using the same file schema. Thankfully, you can use mixed XML files.

FIGURE 17.4

A flattened XML file in Excel

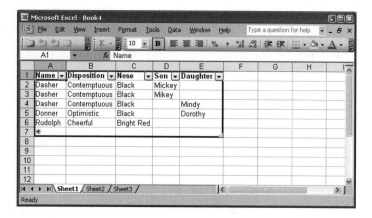

FIGURE 17.5

Excel's XML Source task pane

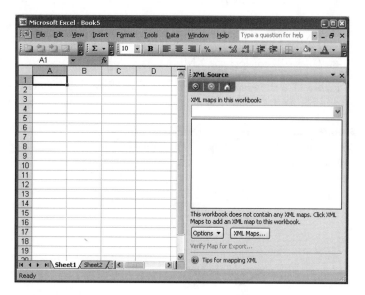

Although reindeer XML files may be interesting around the holiday season, in order to add a little realism to the remaining examples, the next two sections will use XML data that represents price observations of a wheat futures contract. If you're not familiar with futures contracts, don't fret. Price observation data is common to anything that is exchanged for money, so you can surely substitute an object that interests you—a stock or stock index, gold, or the going rate for a 2001 Porsche 996 Turbo.

In order to tap in to the real power of Excel's XML functionality, you define XML Maps using Excel's XML Source task pane (Figure 17.5). To display the XML Source task pane, select Data ➢ XML ➢ XML Source.

You can define an XML map using either an XML schema (an XSD file) or by having Excel derive a schema from a regular XML file. The process of defining an XML Map is as follows.

1. Click XML Maps on the XML Source task pane to display the XML Maps dialog box shown in the following screen shot.

2. Click Add on the XML Maps dialog box.

3. Select the XSD or XML file that you want to map into the current workbook from the Select XML Source dialog box and click Open.

4. Click OK to close the XML Maps dialog box.

Figure 17.6 shows an example of the XML Source task pane after a schema has been added to a workbook. At this point, you're ready to map the elements on to your worksheet.

FIGURE 17.6

A locked and loaded XML Source task pane

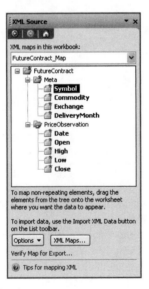

As noted in the XML Source task pane, the process of actually mapping XML elements to specific locations on the worksheet is as easy as dragging each desired XML element from the XML Source task pane to a location on the worksheet. One nice extra touch is the smart tag that appears when you drop an element on a cell. The smart tag allows you to display the element's name above or to the left of the cell (or not at all). An example of this is shown in Figure 17.7 where I have mapped the general futures contract items to the worksheet.

NOTE *The process of mapping XML elements to a worksheet doesn't retrieve data. At this point, you're merely telling Excel where it should put the elements when it does retrieve them from an XML data source whose structure conforms to the XML Map.*

FIGURE 17.7

The smart tags help you build an XML-based worksheet fairly quickly.

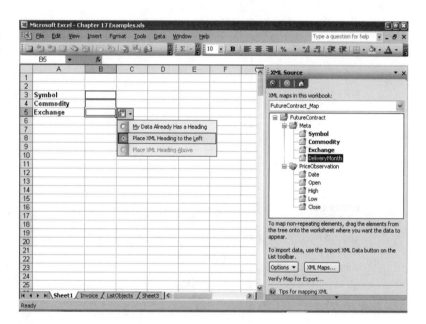

Mapping repeated XML elements is a little bit different. When you drag a repeating XML element onto the worksheet, Excel creates a list for the element. You do not need to map all of the repeated XML elements in one contiguous list. Also, you do not have to map every element. Just pick the ones you need for the task at hand. In Figure 17.8, I've finished mapping the elements in my map.

NOTE *Although I've demonstrated how to map XML data to a blank worksheet, mapping also allows you to map XML data to existing templates or worksheets you may have.*

All right, then. Here's where the fun begins. In the few minutes it took to create an XML Map and map the elements to areas on a worksheet, I gained the ability to retrieve data from any conforming XML file (conforming to the XML Map, that is) directly into my worksheet with each element placed in the exact location I chose.

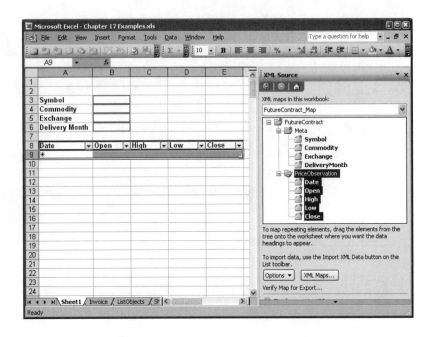

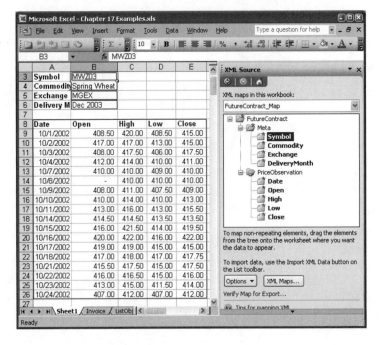

To import XML data, you need to follow these steps:

1. Select Data ➢ XML ➢ Import from the Excel menu.

2. Select the XML file that contains the data you want and click Import.

Figure 17.9 shows the payoff—XML data in the worksheet. Once you've imported the data, you can refresh it by clicking Data ➢ XML ➢ Refresh XML Data.

Pretty neat stuff, eh? As impressive as this functionality is, it gets better.

4X³M²L³

If you like puzzles, you can try and figure out how I arrived at this section's title. Otherwise you can keep reading. Do you remember the movie *Jerry Maguire*? Excel's XML functionality reminds me of a scene from that movie. There is a scene where Jerry (Tom Cruise) is elaborately pleading his case to his wife, Dorothy Boyd (René Zellweger), as to why she should take him back. Finally, she stops him and tells him to shut up. After a moment of stunned silence, she relays to him that he had her at "hello."

Although I'm not quite as much of a pushover as Dorothy Boyd, the XML functionality I've covered thus far is enough to win me over. Additionally, the fact that you can edit imported XML data and then turn around and save it back to XML is a much-appreciated bonus.

To see a demonstration of this functionality, consider the futures data shown in Figure 17.9. Let's say that after you received the XML file that contains pricing data, you needed to add another week's worth of data to the XML file. To do this, all you need to do is add the data to the bottom of the list and then select Data ➢ XML ➢ Export from Excel's menu. After selecting a storage location and providing a filename, Excel saves the data as an XML file that conforms to the structure of the original XML file or schema. In Figure 17.10, I've added another week's worth of data and am ready to export the data back to an XML file.

FIGURE 17.10

Updated data can be sent back to XML using the XML ➢ Export feature.

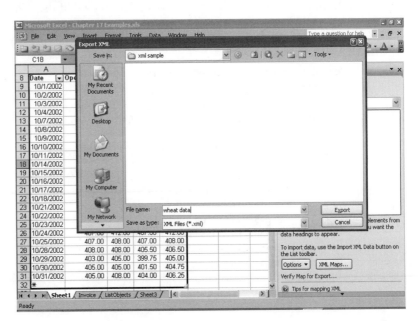

Now that you're familiar with Excel's new XML functionality, it's time to explore Excel's XML functionality from a VBA standpoint.

TIP *Still wondering what this section's title stands for? Reverse factor it and think roundtrip XML in XL.*

XML VBA Style

New functionality in Excel means new objects in the Excel object model. Most of the new functionality in Excel 2003 is XML-oriented, and therefore, most of the new objects in the object model are XML objects. Table 17.1 lists the key XML-oriented objects in the Excel object model.

TABLE 17.1: KEY XML OBJECTS

OBJECT	DESCRIPTION
XmlDataBinding	Represents the connection to the source data for an XmlMap object
XmlMap(s)	Represents an XML map that has been added to a workbook
XmlNamespace(s)	Represents a namespace that has been added to a workbook
XmlSchema(s)	Represents an XML schema contained by an XmlMap object
XPath	Represents an XPath expression that has been mapped to a Range or ListColumn object

In order to understand how to use VBA to manipulate XML data, you need to understand XPath. XPath is kind of like a query language on XML documents. For example, consider the Invoice XML in Listing 17.4. This XML file will be used for several of the following examples and listings.

LISTING 17.4: AN INVOICE XML

```
<?xml version="1.0" encoding="UTF-8" ?>
<Invoice>
   <InvoiceNumber>5050</InvoiceNumber>
   <InvoiceDate>10/31/03</InvoiceDate>
   <Customer>
      <CustomerName>Joe Smith</CustomerName>
      <Address>
         <Street>111 Maple Ln</Street>
         <City>Apple Valley</City>
         <State>MN</State>
         <Zip>55021</Zip>
         <Phone>(612)555-5555</Phone>
      </Address>
   </Customer>
   <Items>
      <Item>
```

```
            <Qty>2</Qty>
            <Description>XL Red Shirt</Description>
            <Price>10.00</Price>
            <ItemTotal>20.00</ItemTotal>
        </Item>
        <Item>
            <Qty>1</Qty>
            <Description>Lg Blue Sweatshirt</Description>
            <Price>24.00</Price>
            <ItemTotal>24.00</ItemTotal>
        </Item>
        <Item>
            <Qty>1</Qty>
            <Description>Boots</Description>
            <Price>99.00</Price>
            <ItemTotal>99.00</ItemTotal>
        </Item>
    </Items>
</Invoice>
```

Using XPath, you can address specific elements of an XML file much like you would specify where a certain file is located on your filesystem. Using XPath, you can retrieve the value of the customer name using the syntax /Invoice/Customer/CustomerName.

When you map elements of an XML file to cells on the worksheet, you are really associating XPath queries with worksheet ranges. Then, when you import an XML file, Excel applies the XPath queries that you mapped to the XML file and displays the matches.

Before you can map elements of an XML file to cells on a worksheet, you need to associate an XmlMap object with the workbook. This can be accomplished using the Add method of the Xml-Maps object as demonstrated in Listing 17.5. The Add method takes two parameters: *Schema* and *RootElementName*. Schema should be a string that represents either the path to the schema file or the schema itself. The path can be specified in the Universal Naming Convention (UNC) or Uniform Resource Locator (URL) format. Excel can build a schema for you given an XML file or you can use an XSD file.

The RootElementName parameter is optional and can be ignored if the schema contains only one root element. If the schema allows for the possibility of one of several root elements in an instance document (an XML document that conforms to the schema), the element referred to by RootElementName will be used as the root element.

LISTING 17.5: ADDING A SCHEMA TO A WORKBOOK

```vba
Sub ImportXMLSchema()
    Dim xmMap As XmlMap

    ' Turn off display alerts - otherwise if you
    ' use an XML file rather than an XSD file,
```

```
' Excel asks you about creating a schema
Application.DisplayAlerts = False

' Add a map based on an xml file
' Alternatively, an XSD file would work
Set xmMap = ActiveWorkbook.XmlMaps.Add("C:\invoice.xml", "Invoice")

' Turn DisplayAlerts back on
Application.DisplayAlerts = True

' Set any desired Map properties
xmMap.AdjustColumnWidth = False
xmMap.PreserveNumberFormatting = True

Set xmMap = Nothing
End Sub
```

Listing 17.5 turns off Application.DisplayAlerts to prevent Excel from showing the dialog box that asks you if you would like Excel to create a schema based on the supplied XML file (Figure 17.1). Depending on your needs, you may want to take the opportunity to set a number of the Xml-Map's properties after you create the map. If the map will be associated with a template-oriented worksheet, for example, you'll probably want to set AdjustColumnWidth to false and PreserveNumberFormatting to true to preserve the settings associated with the worksheet. Table 17.2 lists some of the properties available to you.

Once you associate an XmlMap object with the workbook, you can map XML elements to specific locations in the workbook. The process of mapping elements to ranges depends on whether you are mapping a repeated or nonrepeated element. Common to each process, however, is the necessity to set an XPath value.

TABLE 17.2: XMLMAP OBJECT PROPERTIES

PROPERTY	DESCRIPTION
AdjustColumnWidth	A read/write Boolean property that indicates whether column widths are automatically adjusted every time you import or refresh the XML map. The default setting is true.
AppendOnImport	A read/write Boolean property that indicates whether data overwrites existing data or is appended to it.
PreserveColumnFilter	A read/write Boolean property that indicates whether Excel should preserve filter settings when importing or refreshing the XML map.
PreserveNumberFormatting	A read/write Boolean property that indicates whether Excel should preserve number formatting when importing or refreshing the XML map. The default setting is false.
SaveDataSourceDefinition	A read/write Boolean property that indicates whether the XML schema map is saved with the workbook. The default setting is true.

Listing 17.6 demonstrates how to map elements to workbook locations using the invoice XML file shown in Listing 17.4. The worksheet that I'm binding the invoice XML to is shown in Figure 17.11.

FIGURE 17.11

An invoice template to bind XML data to

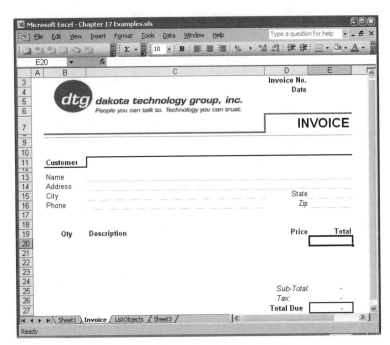

LISTING 17.6: ASSOCIATING XML ELEMENTS WITH RANGES

```
Sub MapRanges()
    Dim xmMap As XmlMap
    Dim ws As Worksheet
    Dim sPath As String
    Dim loList As ListObject

    Set ws = ThisWorkbook.Worksheets("Invoice")
    Set xmMap = ThisWorkbook.XmlMaps("Invoice_Map")

    Application.DisplayAlerts = False

    sPath = "/Invoice/Customer/CustomerName"
    MapRange ws.Range("CustomerName"), xmMap, sPath

    sPath = "/Invoice/Customer/Address/Street"
    MapRange ws.Range("Address"), xmMap, sPath
```

```
        sPath = "/Invoice/Customer/Address/City"
        MapRange ws.Range("City"), xmMap, sPath

        sPath = "/Invoice/Customer/Address/State"
        MapRange ws.Range("State"), xmMap, sPath

        sPath = "/Invoice/Customer/Address/Zip"
        MapRange ws.Range("Zip"), xmMap, sPath

        sPath = "/Invoice/Customer/Address/Phone"
        MapRange ws.Range("Phone"), xmMap, sPath

        sPath = "/Invoice/InvoiceNumber"
        MapRange ws.Range("Number"), xmMap, sPath

        sPath = "/Invoice/InvoiceDate"
        MapRange ws.Range("Date"), xmMap, sPath

        Set loList = ws.ListObjects.Add(xlSrcRange, _
            ws.Range("Qty").Resize(2, 4), , xlYes)

        sPath = "/Invoice/Items/Item/Qty"
        MapRepeatingRange loList.ListColumns(1), xmMap, sPath

        sPath = "/Invoice/Items/Item/Description"
        MapRepeatingRange loList.ListColumns(2), xmMap, sPath

        sPath = "/Invoice/Items/Item/Price"
        MapRepeatingRange loList.ListColumns(3), xmMap, sPath

        sPath = "/Invoice/Items/Item/ItemTotal"
        MapRepeatingRange loList.ListColumns(4), xmMap, sPath

        Application.DisplayAlerts = True

        Set xmMap = Nothing
        Set ws = Nothing
        Set loList = Nothing
    End Sub

    Function MapRange(rg As Range, xmMap As XmlMap, sPath As String) _
        As Boolean

        On Error GoTo ErrHandler

        ' If the range isn't already mapped
        ' it's ok to use SetValue...
        If rg.XPath.Value = "" Then
```

```
            rg.XPath.SetValue xmMap, sPath
        Else
            ' otherwise you need to clear
            ' the existing mapped item
            rg.XPath.Clear
            ' before using SetValue
            rg.XPath.SetValue xmMap, sPath
        End If
        MapRange = True
        Exit Function
ErrHandler:
        MapRange = True
End Function


Function MapRepeatingRange(lcColumn As ListColumn, xmMap As XmlMap, _
    sPath As String) As Boolean

    On Error GoTo ErrHandler

    ' Map a ListObject column to an XLM element
    lcColumn.XPath.SetValue xmMap, sPath


    Exit Function
    MapRepeatingRange = True
ErrHandler:
    Debug.Print Err.Description
    MapRepeatingRange = False
End Function
```

Though this is a longer listing then average, it is fairly simple to understand. The length comes from the MapRanges procedure. The length of MapRanges comes from the need to map so many XML elements to different locations on the worksheet. Consequently, the code contained in MapRanges is highly repetitive. MapRanges doesn't actually do the mapping; rather, it delegates this responsibility to MapRange or MapRepeatingRange depending on the type of XML element being mapped. The reason that Application.DisplayAlerts is turned off is that, depending on the formatting in your worksheet and the data type specified in the XML schema for a given element, Excel may display an alert telling you that there is a discrepancy between the formats. Depending on your needs, you can either ignore this alert or you may want to adjust formatting on the worksheet.

As I mentioned earlier in this section, understanding XPath is really the key to being able to perform the mapping process programmatically. To map an element to a range, you use the SetValue method of the XPath object associated with a range or a ListColumn. The MapRange function is used to map a single, nonrepeating XML element to a range. Before you attempt to use SetValue on a range, you should first check to see whether the range has already had its XPath set. If you attempt to use SetValue on a range that already has an XPath value, an error will occur. To clear an XPath value, use the Clear method of the XPath object.

The syntax of SetValue is as follows:

```
rg.SetValue Map, XPath, [SelectionNamespace], [Repeating]
```

The parameters of SetValue are detailed in the following list.

Map   Map is a required parameter that should be an XmlMap object. Map represents the schema documenting the XML file. The XPath parameter will be evaluated against the schema indicated by this parameter.

XPath   XPath is a required parameter that specifies the XPath query that can be used to retrieve the element of interest that you would like to map to the range or list object.

SelectionNamespace   SelectionNamespace is an optional variant parameter that specifies any namespace prefixes used in the XPath query. Namespaces allow you to uniquely identify elements that use the same name but come from different sources. If your XPath query doesn't use any namespace prefixes or uses Excel prefixes, you can omit this parameter.

Repeating   Repeating is an optional Boolean parameter that specifies whether the element is to be bound to a column in an XML list (Repeating = true) or mapped to a single cell (Repeating = false). The default value is false.

Although in theory you could use the same function to map both repeating and nonrepeating elements, I separated these responsibilities in Listing 17.6 so that you could have more control over the list object that is created when you map a repeating element. In the MapRepeatingRange function, you can see that I mapped elements to individual columns in the list. Depending on the worksheet you are mapping, you may find this approach helpful. Figure 17.12 shows the Invoice worksheet after running the ImportXMLSchema (Listing 17.5) and MapRanges (Listing 17.6) procedures.

NOTE   Because using the list object is so critical to mapping repeating XML elements, I have included a section covering the ListObject object at the end of this chapter.

LISTING 17.7: IMPORTING AN XML DATA FILE

```
Sub ImportXMLData()
    Dim xlImportResult As XlXmlImportResult

    xlImportResult = ThisWorkbook.XmlMaps("Invoice_Map") _
        .Import("C:\invoice.xml", True)

    Select Case xlImportResult
        Case xlXmlImportElementsTruncated
            Debug.Print _
                "XML data items imported with truncation."
        Case xlXmlImportSuccess
            Debug.Print _
                "XML data items imported successfully."
        Case xlXmlImportValidationFailed
            Debug.Print _
```

```
            "XML data items not imported. Validation failed."
    Case Else
        Debug.Print _
            "Data import process reported an unknown result code."
    End Select

    Set xlImportResult = Nothing
End Sub
```

After adding a schema and mapping XML elements to cells on a worksheet, the next logical thing to do is to import some XML data. Importing data is the easy part, as demonstrated by Listing 17.7.

To import XML data, the XmlMap object provides the Import method. The syntax of Import is as follows:

```
XlXmlImportResult = XmlMapObject.Import(URL, [Overwrite])
```

The two parameters of Import are described in the following list.

URL   URL is a required string that specifies the XML file to import. You can specify this using the UNC or URL format. Examples of UNC include `C:\myXMLfile.xml` or `\\DepartmentServer\ invoices\5050.xml`. The use of a URL allows you to retrieve data from a web server. An example of a URL is `http://www.dakotatechgroup.com/invoices.aspx?invoice=5050`.

FIGURE 17.12

A mapped worksheet ready to receive XML data

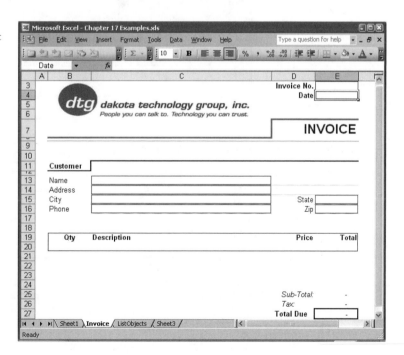

Overwrite   Overwrite is an optional Boolean parameter that specifies whether to overwrite existing data (overwrite = true) or append to existing data (overwrite=false). The default value is false.

The Import method returns an integer status code that can be conveniently captured using the XlXmlImportResult enumeration as demonstrated in the ImportXMLData procedure. Figure 17.13 shows the Invoice worksheet after running the ImportXMLData procedure.

Now all that is left is to learn how to export XML data. You can use two export-oriented methods for exporting XML data; both are methods of the XmlMap object.

Export (URL, Overwrite)   The Export method is used to write the contents of the cells mapped to the associated XmlMap object to the file specified by the URL parameter. The Overwrite parameter is a required Boolean. This method returns an xlXmlExportResult that is either xlXmlExportSuccess or xlXmlExportValidationFailed.

ExportXML (Data)   The ExportXML method is used to write the contents of the cells mapped to the associated XmlMap object to the string variable referred to by the Data parameter. This method also returns an xlXmlExportResult.

I think Listing 17.8 is the shortest listing in the book. Granted, it doesn't exhibit the robustness found in many examples, but exporting XML is a simple task.

FIGURE 17.13

An XML enabled invoice worksheet

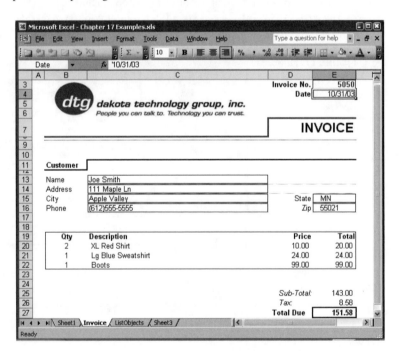

LISTING 17.8: EXPORTING XML

```
Sub ExportInvoiceXML()
    Dim xlMap As XmlMap

    Set xlMap = ThisWorkbook.XmlMaps("Invoice_Map")
    If xlMap.IsExportable Then
        xlMap.Export "C:\testxmljunk.xml"
    Else
        MsgBox "Sorry, this XML Map is not exportable", vbOKOnly
    End If

    Set xlMap = Nothing
End Sub
```

At a minimum, it is a good idea to make sure that the map is exportable before exporting it. You can do this easily using the IsExportable property of the map as shown in Listing 17.8.

A List Object Primer

Repeatable XML elements are displayed on a worksheet using list objects. Excel's list management capabilities in Excel 2003 took an evolutionary step forward compared to the capabilities of Excel 2002. In Excel 2003, lists exhibit the following characteristics by default.

◆ AutoFilter is enabled by default allowing you to easily perform sorting and filtering.

◆ The list is outlined by a thick blue border. The lower-right corner of the border contains a resizing handle that allows you to resize the list by dragging the handle.

◆ The last row in the list contains an asterisk in the first field. You can add data in this row to add a new record or item to the list.

Figure 17.14 shows an example of a simple list. Lists have a number of handy features—you can display a total row at the bottom of the list that automatically adjusts to the addition/removal of items or the application of filters. In Figure 17.14, I instructed the total to display an average score rather than a sum of all scores.

List functionality is exposed in VBA using ListObjects and ListObject. The main thing you'll use ListObjects for is either to get a reference to a specific ListObject or to add a new ListObject to a worksheet. I got a little confused the first time I used the Add method, so I'll spend a little time on that here. Other than the Add method, however, you use ListObjects much like any other collection object.

FIGURE 17.14

A simple list

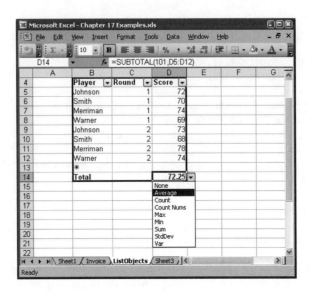

The syntax of the Add method of ListObjects is as follows:

```
Add([SourceType], [Source], [LinkSource], [HasHeaders], [Destination])
```

The parameters of the Add method are described in the following list.

SourceType SourceType is an optional parameter that indicates the kind of source for the list. You can use one of the following XlListObjectSourceType constants: xlSrcExternal or xlSr-cRange. The default is xlSrcRange.

Source Source is *optional* when the source type is a range. Source is a Range object representing the data source. Source is *required* when the source type is an external source. In this case, Source should be an array of string values that specify a connection to the source.

LinkSource LinkSource is optional and only applicable when SourceType is xlSrcExternal. LinkSource is a Boolean parameter that indicates whether an external data source is to be linked to the ListObject object. By default LinkSource is true. Do not use this parameter if SourceType is xlSrcRange as an error will occur.

HasHeaders HasHeaders is an optional variant that indicates whether the data the ListObject is being created from has column labels. You can use an XlYesNoGuess (xlGuess, xlNo, or xlYes) constant that indicates whether the data being imported has column labels. Excel automatically generates headers if the source doesn't have headers.

Destination Destination is a parameter that specifies a Range object representing a *single-cell* reference as the destination for the top-left corner of the new list object. Do not pass a range object that contains more than one cell or an error is generated. Destination *is required* when SourceType is set to xlSrcExternal. However, Destination *is ignored* if the SourceType is set to xlSrcRange.

The ListObject offers up quite a few properties and methods for your use. Table 17.3 lists some of the most useful.

TABLE 17.3: USEFUL LISTOBJECT PROPERTIES AND METHODS

PROPERTY/METHOD	DESCRIPTION
DataBodyRange property	A read-only Range representing the data area between the header row and the insert row
HeaderRowRange property	A read-only Range representing the header row of the list
InsertRowRange property	A read-only Range representing the insert row, if any, of the list
ListColumns property	A read-only collection of ListColumn objects that represent columns in the list
ListRows property	A read-only collection of ListRow objects that represent rows in the list
Range property	A read-only Range encompassing the entire list
ShowAutoFilter property	A read/write Boolean that indicates whether the list displays the AutoFilter feature
ShowTotals property	A read/write Boolean that indicates whether the list displays a total row
TotalsRowRange property	A read-only Range representing the Total row of the list
XmlMap property	A read-only XmlMap object that represents the schema map used for the list
Resize method	Allows you to resize a list over a new range
Unlist method	Removes the list functionality from the list thereby converting it to a standard range

Listing 17.9 demonstrates some of these properties as well as some various ListColumn properties by inspecting the list shown in Figure 17.14.

LISTING 17.9: INSPECTING A LISTOBJECT

```
' Example using various list properties
Sub ListInfo()
    Dim ws As Worksheet
    Dim lo As ListObject
    Dim lc As ListColumn
    Dim rg As Range

    Set ws = ThisWorkbook.Worksheets("ListObjects")
    Set lo = ws.ListObjects(1)

    ' Display column info
    Set rg = ws.Cells(17, 2)
    For Each lc In lo.ListColumns
```

```
            rg.Value = lc.Name
            rg.Offset(1, 0).Value = lc.Index
            rg.Offset(2, 0).Value = lc.Range.Address
            rg.Offset(4, 0).Value = _
                GetTotalsCalculation(lc.TotalsCalculation)
            Set rg = rg.Offset(0, 1)
        Next

        ' Display general list info
        Set rg = ws.Cells(25, 2)
        rg.Value = lo.HeaderRowRange.Address
        rg.Offset(1, 0).Value = lo.DataBodyRange.Address

        ' If the InsertRowRange is not currently displayed
        ' then InsertRowRange is nothing
        If Not lo.InsertRowRange Is Nothing Then
            rg.Offset(2, 0).Value = lo.InsertRowRange.Address
        Else
            rg.Offset(2, 0).Value = "N/A"
        End If

        ' If the TotalsRowRange is not being displayed
        ' then TotalsRowRange is nothing
        If lo.ShowTotals Then
            rg.Offset(3, 0).Value = lo.TotalsRowRange.Address
        Else
            rg.Offset(3, 0).Value = "N/A"
        End If

        ' Get some more information from the list object
        rg.Offset(4, 0).Value = lo.Range.Address
        rg.Offset(5, 0).Value = lo.ShowTotals
        rg.Offset(6, 0).Value = lo.ShowAutoFilter

        Set rg = Nothing
        Set lc = Nothing
        Set lo = Nothing
        Set ws = Nothing
End Sub

' Converts an XlTotalsCalculation enumeration value to
' a string
Function GetTotalsCalculation(xlCalc As XlTotalsCalculation) As String
    Select Case xlCalc
        Case Is = XlTotalsCalculation.xlTotalsCalculationAverage
            GetTotalsCalculation = "Average"
        Case Is = XlTotalsCalculation.xlTotalsCalculationCount
            GetTotalsCalculation = "Count"
```

```
        Case Is = XlTotalsCalculation.xlTotalsCalculationCountNums
            GetTotalsCalculation = "CountNums"
        Case Is = XlTotalsCalculation.xlTotalsCalculationMax
            GetTotalsCalculation = "Max"
        Case Is = XlTotalsCalculation.xlTotalsCalculationMin
            GetTotalsCalculation = "Min"
        Case Is = XlTotalsCalculation.xlTotalsCalculationNone
            GetTotalsCalculation = "None"
        Case Is = XlTotalsCalculation.xlTotalsCalculationStdDev
            GetTotalsCalculation = "StdDev"
        Case Is = XlTotalsCalculation.xlTotalsCalculationSum
            GetTotalsCalculation = "Sum"
        Case Is = XlTotalsCalculation.xlTotalsCalculationVar
            GetTotalsCalculation = "Var"
        Case Else
            GetTotalsCalculation = "Unknown"
    End Select
End Function
```

The output of ListInfo is shown in Figure 17.15. The one interesting thing to point out is that you can't use the InsertRowRange and TotalsRowRange without first checking to see if they are valid. The totals row can be turned on/off by the user, so it is not always present. The insert row is only valid when the active cell is within the boundaries of the list. You can validate these ranges by comparing them against the keyword Nothing.

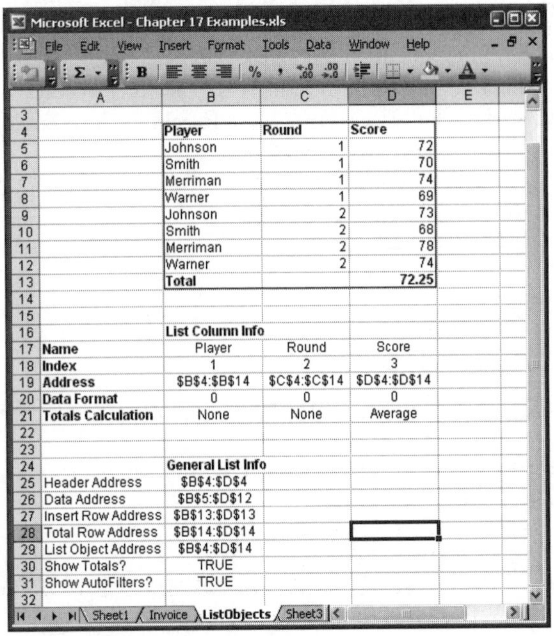

	A	B	C	D
4		Player	Round	Score
5		Johnson	1	72
6		Smith	1	70
7		Merriman	1	74
8		Warner	1	69
9		Johnson	2	73
10		Smith	2	68
11		Merriman	2	78
12		Warner	2	74
13		Total		72.25
16		List Column Info		
17	Name	Player	Round	Score
18	Index	1	2	3
19	Address	$B$4:$B$14	$C$4:$C$14	$D$4:$D$14
20	Data Format	0	0	0
21	Totals Calculation	None	None	Average
24		General List Info		
25	Header Address	$B$4:$D$4		
26	Data Address	$B$5:$D$12		
27	Insert Row Address	$B$13:$D$13		
28	Total Row Address	$B$14:$D$14		
29	List Object Address	$B$4:$D$14		
30	Show Totals?	TRUE		
31	Show AutoFilters?	TRUE		

FIGURE 17.15
The output of the ListInfo procedure

Summary

"XML, schmeXML. I don't need no XML."

Before you dismiss XML as another over-hyped technology, you should give it due consideration. Because XML is becoming more and more prevalent, chances are that it will increasingly be an option when you are dealing with data transfer and data collaboration between disparate applications. Because XML is self-describing, it offers a much richer way to move data instead of text files. Additionally, it is the preferred way to interact with web applications or services. In short, basic knowledge of XML is a useful tool for your development efforts.

With the XML functionality added to Excel 2003, you now have the ability to read and *write* XML data using schemas other than XMLSS—Excel's native spreadsheet schema. This is a monumental step forward in terms of incorporating Excel into business processes that are using XML. Prior to Excel's new XML functionality, you had to write lots of code to use XML data in Excel in a useful manner.

Whether you use Excel's interface or you do it programmatically, there are three types of tasks to perform to integrate XML data with Excel. First, you create an XML map by associating a schema with a workbook. If you don't have a schema (XSD file), you can show Excel an XML file and it will infer a schema based on that file. Second, you map elements in the schema to specific locations in the workbook. Finally, you can either import data from or export data to an XML file.

When working with XML programmatically, it is important to understand how to identify specific elements in an XML file. To do so, you use XPath. To map elements to a workbook, you set an object's (either a Range object or a ListColumn object) XPath property using the SetValue method.

Another object that you might want to invest a little time in becoming familiar with is the ListObject. ListObject is a new object in the Excel 2003 object model that is your programmatic gateway to manipulating worksheet lists. Excel uses such lists to display repeating XML elements.

The conclusion of this chapter also wraps up the section of this book that covers external data source interaction. The next section deals with user interface design and development. I'll kick this new section off with a chapter covering basic Excel user interfaces.

Part 5

Enhancing the End User Experience

Chapter 18

Basic User Interfaces

NEARLY EVERY APPLICATION YOU develop except for the most elementary utilities requires some sort of user interface. Without a user interface, most general Excel users will be hard-pressed to use your application effectively. They may be able to view some of your procedures in the Macros dialog box, but how will they know which one to execute or when to execute it?

One of the arguments I put forward early on in the book is that one of the benefits of using Excel as a development platform is that you can save a lot of time by building on top of its rich functionality. One area where this is particularly true is when you're developing a user interface. Excel offers quite a bit of functionality in terms of formatting, user interaction, and worksheet protection. Often you can creatively apply standard Excel functionality along with a few worksheet-based controls to get by. In this chapter, I'll present the information you'll need to build what I refer to as a *worksheet-based user interface*. A worksheet-based user interface is an Excel user interface that doesn't use command bars (which are covered in Chapter 19) or user forms (covered in Chapter 20).

User Interfaces in Excel

For the purposes of this chapter, when I refer to the term *user interface*, I'm referring to the user interface specific to your Excel-based solution. A user interface enables end users to direct the flow of an application. Some of the tasks that a user interface must facilitate include these:

◆ Collecting user input

◆ Managing application settings and configuration

◆ Displaying output

◆ Providing application navigation facilities

As the developer of an Excel application, you have many tools at your disposal regarding interface construction. Your application may include a number of different user interface elements. The following list displays some of the more common user interface elements found in Excel-based applications.

Worksheet Form controls Worksheet Form controls are controls created using the Forms toolbar (View ➢ Toolbars ➢ Forms). Form controls were introduced with Excel 5.0 before

ActiveX controls were available. Form controls are similar to ActiveX controls, but they differ in that they can be used on chart sheets and don't have event procedures associated with them. Form controls are great as simple worksheet-based controls because you can use them without having to write any code.

Worksheet ActiveX controls   ActiveX controls are controls created using the Control Toolbox toolbar (View ➤ Toolbars ➤ Control Toolbox). ActiveX controls offer richer functionality when compared to their Form control counterparts, and they can be used on worksheets and user forms, as you will see in Chapter 20. To use ActiveX controls, you attach VBA code to various event procedures associated with the control. You can modify the behavior and appearance of an ActiveX control by changing the properties associated with it.

Built-in dialog boxes   This category includes user interface elements found in the Excel object model or in VBA that allow you to interact with the user. Examples from this category include GetSaveAsFilename, GetOpenFilename, InputBox, and MsgBox. These kinds of elements can only be displayed using VBA.

Custom user forms   User forms are dialog boxes you design and build in the VBE. User forms offer the most flexibility. One negative aspect of user forms is that they can significantly increase the size of your workbook, so be sure to use them judiciously. User forms are covered in Chapter 20.

Command bars   Command bars include menus and toolbars. Using VBA, you can alter all of Excel's existing menus and toolbars as well as display your own custom menu. Command bars are covered in Chapter 19.

Native Excel functionality   Last but not least, you can create a user interface that consists of the creative application of standard Excel worksheet functionality. Some of the features you might employ to do this include data validation, worksheet protection, cell locking, hyperlinks, shapes (items drawn using the Drawing toolbar), and cell formatting.

So how do you choose from among the various elements when constructing an interface? Command bars and custom user forms offer the most flexibility and look the most professional, but they require a lot of development effort. Worksheet-based components such as Form and ActiveX controls provide a fair amount of functionality with minimal effort. On the downside, they are specific to a worksheet and have limited visual appeal. ActiveX controls require some VBA programming; Form controls do not. All Excel applications use some native Excel functionality as part of the interface. I mean, it is an Excel application, isn't it? In fact, you may get by with the creative application of native Excel functionality to provide a user interface.

Paleozoic Controls

315 million seconds ago (1993 AD), Microsoft released Excel 5.0. This version of Excel quickly rose up to dominate the spreadsheet world due to a conglomeration of factors. One such factor was the ~sion of a way to embed user interface controls on a worksheet. These controls are referred to as trols. Developers and power users alike soon embraced the controls as a way to enhance the ᴊerience when they're working with a complex Excel workbook.

FIGURE 18.1

The Forms toolbar

FIGURE 18.2

Control properties
determine what
happens to a control
when worksheet cells
are moved or resized.

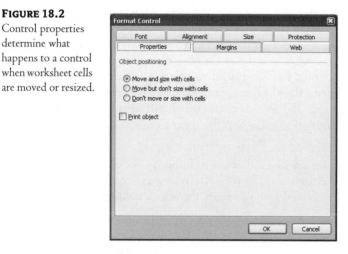

Even today, form controls still occupy a niche in the Excel ecosystem. For one thing, they are necessary for backward compatibility. Additionally, form controls are the only kind of control that can be used on a chart sheet. Finally, for simple control needs, form controls are a little easier to work with than their ActiveX counterparts. Form controls live on a remote toolbar named Forms. You can visit them by selecting View ➤ Toolbars ➤ Forms. The Forms toolbar is shown in Figure 18.1.

The Ubiquitous Button

Buttons are probably the most common control. Even if you don't need any of the other controls, you may elect to put a button somewhere in your workbook to allow users to launch a macro without having to select it from the Macros dialog box (Alt + F8). In fact, using a button to execute a macro is such a common action associated with buttons that when you add a button to a worksheet, Excel automatically displays a dialog box to assign a macro to the button.

TIP   *For precise control placement, select the control and use the directional arrows.*

A few formatting options associated with buttons (and other controls for that matter) are worth investigation—specifically, the items on the Properties tab of the Format control dialog box (Figure 18.2). The Format control dialog box can be displayed by right-clicking the control and selecting Format Control.

The object positioning choices on this tab are described in the following list. To understand how these choices work, it helps to think in terms of positions. You'll get a lot of exposure to this concept when you start constructing user forms in Chapter 20. For now, understand that an object's position on the worksheet can be described by measuring the distance from the top of the worksheet to the top of the object and the distance from the left of the worksheet to the left edge of the object. One unit of distance is called a *point*. So the position (50,100) means that the object is 50 points from the top of the worksheet and 100 points from the left edge of the worksheet. To fully describe an object's location on a worksheet, you also need to know the height and width of the object.

Move and size with cells   An object with this type of object positioning maintains a constant distance from the top left of the cell with which it is associated. It also maintains a constant distance between the object's lower-right corner and the top-left corner of the cell that contains the object's lower-right corner. The cell that the object is associated with is the cell containing the object's top-left corner. For example, if an object is associated with cell C5 and you insert a row above the fifth row thereby forcing cell C5 down to a new address of C6, the object will move down with the cell. The main behavior that is different with this option versus the other two options is that this option will also resize controls as you resize rows or columns associated with the cell.

Move but don't size with cells   An object with this type of object positioning maintains a constant distance from the top left of the *cell* with which the object is associated. The object's size remains constant regardless of how you resize the row or column.

Don't move or size with cells   An object with this type of object positioning maintains a constant distance from the top left of the *worksheet* no matter what happens to the rows and columns. If an object's position was originally 50,100 and you add 5 rows and resize all of the columns, the object will still be at 50,100. Likewise, the object's width and height remain constant as you resize the row and column that the object is on top of.

As you can see in Figure 18.2, you can also use this dialog box to specify whether the control should be output or not when printing. Figures 18.3 and 18.4 demonstrate the object positioning choices by showing a before and after shot of three buttons.

FIGURE 18.3

These three buttons look alike...

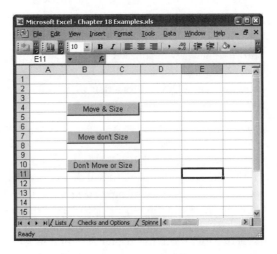

FIGURE 18.4

But they sure don't act alike.

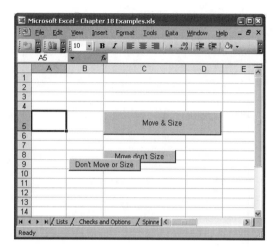

Free to Choose

For those occasions in which you want to allow your user to choose between a handful of options, you may want to present the choices using check boxes or option buttons. There is a distinct difference between check boxes and option buttons—the value or state of a check box is not dependent on any other check boxes, whereas option buttons operate in groups. An option button's state is dependent on other option buttons in the same group. Only one option button in a particular group may be selected at a given time.

Checkboxes are good candidates for situations in which you have a number of independent, two-state choices that you need to present to the user. These could be true/false, on/off, or yes/no choices.

To link a check box control to a cell, right-click the check box and select Format Control. Then, set the cell link option on the Control tab (Figure 18.5) to the desired cell. You can change the text displayed by the check box by right-clicking the control and selecting Edit Text. Alternatively, hold down the Ctrl key while selecting the control and then select and edit the control's text directly. When linking a control to a cell, occasionally it's convenient to place the control directly on top of the cell to which you're linking. If you change the fill of the control to automatic (on the Colors and Lines tab of the Format Control dialog box), the control will cover up the cell so that you can't see the value underneath. For example, in Figure 18.6, notice that I have cell B5 selected. The value shown in the formula bar is true, but you can't see the value on the worksheet because the control is covering it up.

Check boxes can have a value state called Mixed. This state can't be achieved by normal user interaction with the control, it can only be achieved by checking the Mixed value in the Format dialog box or placing the error value #N/A in the cell to which the check box is linked.

One potential use of check boxes is to allow users to easily show/hide worksheets in a workbook. In order to do this, you need to employ some VBA. Although I could go about this by creating a separate procedure for each check box, because the process of showing/hiding worksheets happens so quickly, I opted for a single procedure (Listing 18.1) that sets the visibility of all of the worksheets every time a check box is clicked. The SetWorksheetVisibility procedure is the macro assigned to the View Worksheets check box group shown in Figure 18.6. As you click the various check boxes, the worksheet associated with the check box you click is displayed or hidden.

FIGURE 18.5
The Format Control
dialog box

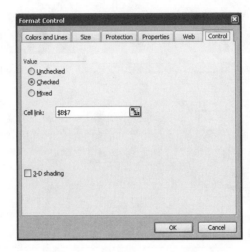

FIGURE 18.6
Check box controls
are useful for allowing
users to toggle settings
on/off.

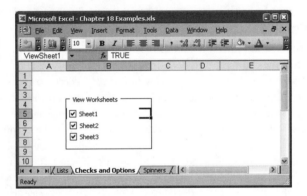

LISTING 18.1: CONTROLLING WORKSHEET VISIBILITY

```
Sub SetWorksheetVisibility()
    Dim ws As Worksheet

    On Error Resume Next

    Set ws = ThisWorkbook.Worksheets("Checks and Options")

    Application.ScreenUpdating = False
    ThisWorkbook.Worksheets("Sheet1").Visible = _
        CInt(ws.Range("ViewSheet1").Value)
    ThisWorkbook.Worksheets("Sheet2").Visible = _
        CInt(ws.Range("ViewSheet2").Value)
    ThisWorkbook.Worksheets("Sheet3").Visible = _
        CInt(ws.Range("ViewSheet3").Value)
```

```
    Application.ScreenUpdating = True

    Set ws = Nothing
End Sub
```

In order to understand how this procedure works, you should know that the check box labeled Sheet1 is linked to cell A5 and that cell A5 is named ViewSheet1. Likewise, the check box labeled Sheet2 is linked to cell A6 and cell A6 is named ViewSheet2. Finally, the check box labeled Sheet3 is linked to cell Z45 and cell Z45 is named CloseWorkbook. OK, just kidding on that last sentence. The Sheet3 check box follows the pattern established by the first two.

The SetWorksheetVisibility procedure does employ a little trick. Tricks are fun when you're aware of them, not as fun when you're the victim. Because I'm telling you about this trick, hopefully you'll find it useful. Throughout this book, I've used various Excel enumerations, such as xlSheetVisible and xlSheet-Hidden, without giving much consideration to the underlying value of the enumeration. An enumeration, you recall, is just a way to assign human-friendly words to a group of related choices. SetWorksheetVisibility takes advantage of the fact that xlSheetVisible (−1) = True (−1) and xlSheetHidden (0) = False (0). As you click a check box that is linked to a cell, the cell value toggles between true and false. Using the function CInt() you can convert the worksheet values true and false to integer values. By exploiting this fact, you save yourself the trouble of having to use multiple If…Then statements in this procedure.

SetWorksheetVisibility turns ScreenUpdating off near the beginning of the procedure and then turns it back on near the end to eliminate the flicker that would otherwise occur.

Option controls are useful for situations in which you need to provide a way for the user to select one and only one value from a group of possible choices. Normally related option buttons are grouped together inside a group box. Any option buttons outside a group box are considered part of the same group. Remember, only one option button in a grouping can be selected. To create groups of options, begin by placing a group box in the desired location and placing option controls in the group box rather than placing option controls on the worksheet and then enclosing them with a group box. Figure 18.7 shows an example of option controls used to indicate a report scaling preference. In order to demonstrate how I put this together, I didn't hide the control value behind the control as I did in the check box example.

FIGURE 18.7

Option controls are used to allow users to select one of several potential options.

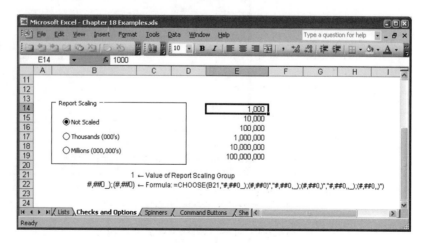

As you select the various options, cell B21 reflects the index number of the option button that is selected. In order to provide scaling, I created a formula using the Choose() worksheet function that returns various number format codes depending on the value of cell B21. The ScaleOption procedure in Listing 18.2 is responsible for updating the number format in the desired range.

LISTING 18.2: PROCEDURE TO SCALE A RANGE

```
Sub ScaleOption()
    Dim ws As Worksheet

    On Error Resume Next

    Set ws = ThisWorkbook.Worksheets("Checks and Options")

    ws.Range("ReportRange").NumberFormat = _
        ws.Range("ReportScale").Value

    Set ws = Nothing
End Sub
```

In order to make this whole thing work, I just assigned each option button the ScaleOption routine. Figure 18.8 demonstrates how the worksheet looks when another option is chosen.

The Control tab of the Format control dialog box for option controls looks just like the one for check box controls (Figure 18.5) with one exception: the Mixed value is disabled. Option controls can't be in a mixed state—they are either on or off. Also, once you link a cell value to one of the option controls in a group, you have effectively linked all of the group's options to the cell you specify.

FIGURE 18.8

Report scaling in action

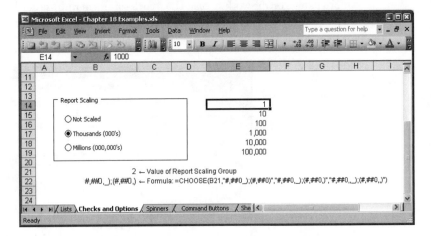

Makin' a List

The list box and combo box are useful for providing a way for users to choose among objects in a list. I've been told Santa uses something like the worksheet pictured in Figure 18.9 to keep track of how all the children have been behaving.

There are two distinct differences between a combo box and a list box. First, a list box uses more screen real estate whereas a combo box only displays its list choices when the user expands it. The second difference is that with the list box, you can allow multiple selections from the list whereas you can only make single selections with the combo box. Figure 18.10 shows the Control tab from a combo box's Format Control dialog box.

The worksheet shown in Figure 18.9 is functional. As you choose a child in the combo box, the worksheet updates itself to reflect the current verdict on the child. Likewise, if you change the verdict, the child's verdict is updated in the list. In order to provide this kind of functionality, I employed one worksheet formula and a couple VBA procedures. In order to make things a little easier, I assigned range names to a few key cells. Figure 18.10 shows how the combo box is linked to the worksheet. The ChildNumber range is cell D3. Cell C8 (named "Verdict") is linked to the option buttons. Finally, cell B14 is named "ChildList". Armed with this information, you shouldn't have much trouble comprehending Listing 18.3.

FIGURE 18.9

Combo boxes are used to present many choices to users.

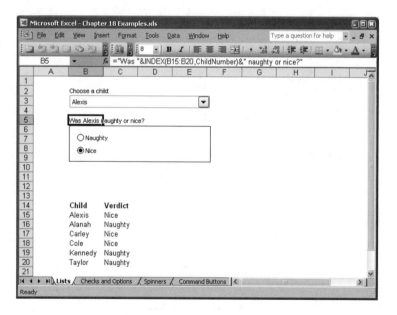

FIGURE 18.10
Using the Control tab, you can hook your combo box up to cells on a worksheet.

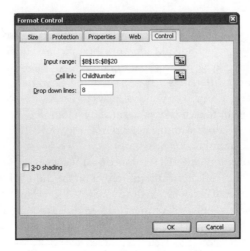

LISTING 18.3: COORDINATING LIST INFORMATION

```vba
Sub GetVerdict()
    Dim ws As Worksheet
    Dim nChildNumber As Integer
    Dim sVerdict As String

    On Error Resume Next

    Set ws = ThisWorkbook.Worksheets("Lists")

    nChildNumber = ws.Range("ChildNumber")

    ' Get the current verdict associated with the child
    sVerdict = ws.Range("ChildList").Offset(nChildNumber, 1)

    If sVerdict = "Naughty" Then
        ' Activate the Naughty option
        ws.Range("Verdict").Value = 1
    Else
        ' Activate the Nice option
        ws.Range("Verdict").Value = 2
    End If

    Set ws = Nothing
End Sub
```

```
Sub SetVerdict()
    Dim ws As Worksheet
    Dim nChildNumber As Integer

    On Error Resume Next

    Set ws = ThisWorkbook.Worksheets("Lists")
    nChildNumber = ws.Range("ChildNumber")

    If ws.Range("Verdict").Value = 1 Then
        ' Update the child's verdict to Naughty
        ws.Range("ChildList").Offset(nChildNumber, 1) _
            .Value = "Naughty"
    Else
        ' Update the child's verdict to Nice
        ws.Range("ChildList").Offset(nChildNumber, 1) _
            .Value = "Nice"
    End If

    Set ws = Nothing
End Sub
```

I assigned the GetVerdict procedure to the combo box so that every time you change the combo box, it will execute GetVerdict to activate the appropriate option button associated with the given child's verdict. On the other hand, I assigned the SetVerdict procedure to the option buttons so that if you change the verdict, the verdict shown in the list will get updated as well.

Oh yes—one more thing. Did you notice the nice touch in cell B5 (Figure 18.9)? As you choose different children, this cell updates itself to display the current child's name. The formula for this cell is shown in the following snippet:

```
="Was "&INDEX(B15:B20,ChildNumber)&" naughty or nice?"
```

The value of a combo box represents the item number of the selected item. To translate the item number to the item that it represents, you can use the Index() function. The first parameter of the function should be the address of the range used to provide values to the combo box. The second parameter is the address of the cell containing the value of the combo box.

Scrolling and Spinning

Two controls are useful for setting numeric values or setting a value relative to a range of values. For this type of activity, check out the scroll bar control or the spinner control. An example of both controls is shown in Figure 18.11.

FIGURE 18.11

The scroll bar and spinner controls are useful for selecting a value relative to a range of values.

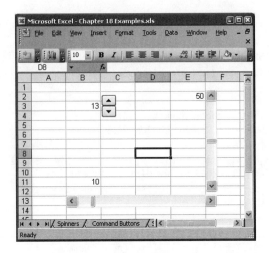

Figure 18.12 shows the Control tab from a spinner control's Format Control dialog box. The Control tab for a scroll bar looks exactly the same except the Page Change option is enabled.

FIGURE 18.12

Controlling the spinner control

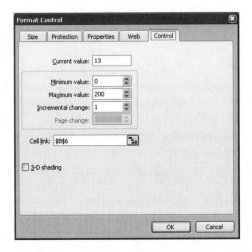

Spinner controls are helpful when you want to provide the user with a way to select a specific value from a wide range of values. A spinner control is helpful because you can set the range of values that the spinner will work against. For example, one project that I worked on required the worksheet and workbook to be tightly locked down so that users could make hardly any changes to them. I quickly discovered that some users needed to use the worksheet with such large values that the value couldn't be displayed properly using the default column widths. I needed a way to allow users to adjust column widths without allowing them to directly unprotect the worksheet to do it. In order to do this, I used a spinner control in conjunction with some VBA code.

Listing 18.4 presents the code necessary to implement such a feature. If you need to use this on a protected worksheet, you would need to add code to unlock and then relock the worksheet.

LISTING 18.4: ADJUSTING COLUMN WIDTHS

```
Sub AdjustColumns()
    Dim ws As Worksheet

    On Error Resume Next

    Set ws = ThisWorkbook.Worksheets("Spinners")
    ws.Columns.ColumnWidth = ws.Range("ColumnWidth").Value
    Set ws = Nothing
End Sub
```

Figure 18.12 showed how the spinner control was hooked up to the worksheet. The cell that the control is linked to (B6) is named ColumnWidth. Figure 18.13 shows a picture of the Spinners worksheet.

Like a Kid in a Candy Store

Whereas the form controls are convenient for some purposes, the ActiveX controls found in the Control Toolbox toolbar offer a lot more flexibility. In addition to having a much richer programming interface than form controls, you can use any of the numerous ActiveX controls present on your computer. Figure 18.14 shows a picture of the Control Toolbox toolbar. In this figure, I have clicked the More Controls tool button and am browsing through the controls available on my computer.

FIGURE 18.13
Using the spinner control

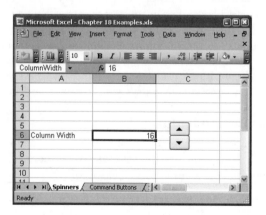

FIGURE 18.14

There are many more controls to choose from besides those already on the toolbar.

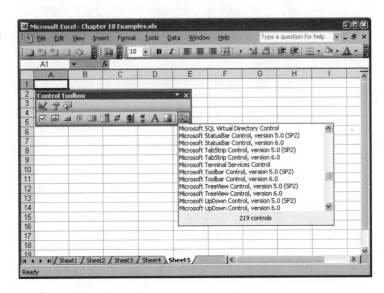

WARNING *Before you go hog wild using some of the obscure controls that may be present on your computer, consider what controls may be present on your users' computers. They may not have all of the same controls that you do.*

In addition to the plethora of controls available that are relative to the forms controls, ActiveX controls allow you to respond to various events associated with the controls—click, double-click, and change events, for instance.

Oh, and did I mention all of the properties that you can set? Well, the number of properties varies by control, but you have a lot more control over the appearance and behavior of ActiveX controls, especially compared to their form control counterparts. A good way to demonstrate all of these advantages is by taking a look at the common command button control.

NOTE *Although you can use ActiveX controls on worksheets, they are much more common on user forms. Consequently, you'll find more coverage of ActiveX controls when I cover user forms in Chapter 20.*

The Ubiquitous Button Redux

The command button is a perfect example for demonstrating all of the advantages offered by the ActiveX controls. Here is a little exercise that walks you through how to work with an ActiveX control. It will help illustrate the richness these controls offer.

1. If the Control Toolbox toolbar isn't visible, show it by selecting View ➤ Toolbars ➤ Control Toolbox.

2. Click the Command Button toolbar button.

3. Click the location on the worksheet where you would like the top-left corner of the command button to be located. If you click and release, a command button with a default size will appear. If you click and drag, you can control how big the button will be.

FIGURE 18.15

The Properties window associated with a command button

4. Right-click the button and choose Properties. A Properties window appears (Figure 18.15). Take a minute to browse the properties associated with a command button. I'll cover some of the more common properties later in this section.

5. Right-click the button and choose View Code. You'll see that Excel places you in the VBE. By default you are placed in the click event procedure of the button.

6. Click the drop-down arrow of the Procedures combo box in the upper-right part of the code window. You'll see all of the events to which you can respond.

As you saw in this exercise, the command button is rich in terms of the properties with which you can interact and the number of events to which the button knows how to respond. Table 18.1 lists some of the most commonly modified properties.

TABLE 18.1: COMMAND BUTTON PROPERTIES

PROPERTY	DESCRIPTION
Name	The name of the control. You use the value of this property to refer to the control programmatically.
Accelerator	Use this property to provide a keyboard shortcut. For example, if the caption of the button is Stop and the accelerator is S, then the button will be displayed with a line under the S indicating that you can use Alt+S to click it.
BackColor	This is the color used by the background of the button.
Caption	The text displayed by the button.

TABLE 18.1: COMMAND BUTTON PROPERTIES *(continued)*

PROPERTY	DESCRIPTION
Enabled	This property indicates whether the button is on (responds to events) or off.
ForeColor	This is the color of the foreground of the button. The foreground contains the font.
Height	The height of the button in points. A point is $1/72^{nd}$ of an inch.
Left	The distance between the left edge of the control and the object that contains it.
TakeFocusOnClick	This property specifies whether the button takes the focus when you click it. When a button is placed on a worksheet, you'll probably want to set this to false.
Top	The distance between the top edge of the control and the object that contains it.
Width	The width of the button in points.

When you compare the process of creating and using a command button with the process of creating and using a button from the Forms toolbar, you'll find them different in a number of ways. The most obvious difference is that you create a command button using the Control toolbox toolbar rather than the Forms toolbar used to create a button. Another key difference is that rather than assigning a macro to the control, you write code that responds to one or more of the control's events. Regarding the command button, generally you respond to the click event. Finally, once you create the command button, in order to modify it, you need to put Excel in design mode by clicking Design Mode on the Control toolbox toolbar. The following exercise demonstrates these differences by creating a new command button that just displays a short message when clicked.

1. Display the Controls toolbox by selecting View ➢ Toolbars ➢ Control Toolbox.

2. Click the Command Button toolbar button once.

3. Click the location on the worksheet where you would like to place the command button.

4. Right-click the button and choose Properties. Set the properties as shown in the following table. Figure 18.15 shows an example.

TABLE 18.2: EXAMPLE COMMAND BUTTON PROPERTY VALUES

PROPERTY VALUE	VALUE
Name	cmdExample
Accelerator	E
BackColor	&H00FFFFFF&
Caption	Example
TakeFocusOnClick	False

5. Right-click the button and select View Code.

6. In the default click event procedure called cmdExample_Click, enter this statement:

```
MsgBox "You clicked me."
```

7. Switch back to Excel and click the Exit Design Mode button on the Control toolbox.

8. Close the Properties window and the Control toolbox.

9. Test the Example button. Figure 18.16 shows the result of my test.

In order to understand the behavior of the TakeFocusOnClick property, it would be a good idea to set the TakeFocusOnClick property to true and then observe the behavior. By default, Take-FocusOnClick is true when you add a command button to the worksheet. I find this behavior annoying because, as a user, I have to click off of the button to move the focus back to the worksheet. As a result, I have to make two mouse clicks to perform what should be a one-click operation.

Did you notice that once you closed the command button's Properties window and the Control toolbox, you can't modify the control without displaying the Control toolbox and clicking the design mode command bar button? With the Form controls, unless you protect the worksheet, it is easier for a user to modify the control. Just by right-clicking a Form control you can assign it to a different macro or change how it is linked to the worksheet. This sort of casual modification of the control is less likely when you're using ActiveX controls.

Combo Box Capabilities

Before I leave the section on ActiveX controls, I'd like to show you the capabilities of an ActiveX combo box including how to link this control to a worksheet. Figure 18.17 shows the Properties window associated with a combo box.

FIGURE 18.16

Testing a command button

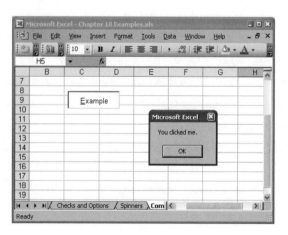

FIGURE 18.17
The combo box has no shortage of properties.

Just browsing over the partial list of properties in Figure 18.17 should give you an idea of how much more power the ActiveX combo box has compared to the Forms combo box. Table 18.3 lists some of the more interesting combo box properties.

TABLE 18.3: INTERESTING COMBO BOX PROPERTIES

PROPERTY	DESCRIPTION
BoundColumn	Identifies the source of data in a multicolumn combo box
ColumnCount	Specifies the number of columns used in a combo box
ColumnHeads	Specifies whether the combo box displays a header row or not
ColumnWidths	Dictates the width of each column in a multicolumn column box
LinkedCell	Denotes the address of the cell to which the combo box is linked
ListFillRange	Specifies the address of the range containing the data to populate the list
MatchRequired	Indicates whether a user can enter a value that doesn't match an item in the list

As you can see, you can create combo boxes whose list is composed of multiple columns. As an example, take a look at Figure 18.18. The combo box shown has two columns of data and is linked to cells on a worksheet.

FIGURE 18.18

You can have combo boxes with multiple columns of data.

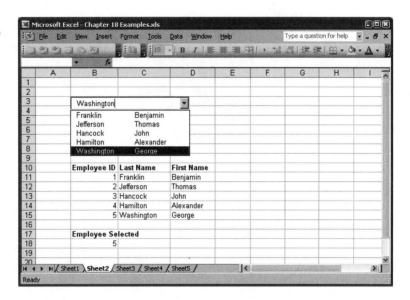

It is not as obvious how to link an ActiveX combo box to cells on a worksheet. You can't just select a range of cells like you can when you're using the Form combo box. Instead, you have to enter the range address directly in the Properties window. You can see this in the Properties window pictured in Figure 18.17. This is the Properties window for the combo box shown in Figure 18.18. Notice that the ListFillRange is Sheet2!B9:D13. Did you notice that the ColumnCount property is 3 yet only two columns show up in Figure 18.18? To achieve this effect, I used the ColumnWidths property. To control each column width, you need to enter each columns' width separated by a semicolon. You can specify a column width in points, centimeters, or inches, but points is the default unit of measurement. For the combo box pictured in Figure 18.18, I specified a width of zero for the first column. This is a handy technique when you are working with data from a database. Generally databases identify items using a numeric value. Of course, users prefer a less cryptic way to refer to items. By using a combo box with multiple columns, you can retrieve the database ID of the selected item rather than have to look up the ID when given a user friendly value.

Judge a Book by Its Cover

You've undoubtedly heard the saying "Don't judge a book by its cover" many times. When it comes to a professional looking Excel workbook, toss that advice out the window. One way to intimidate users is to create a workbook with many worksheets without some sort of mechanism to make sense of it all. No table of contents, no navigation system, or no documentation that explains the main point the workbook is trying to convey. One good way to demonstrate the basic user interface elements is to show you an example of a menu worksheet and talk about some of the techniques I used to build it. Check out the example menu worksheet in Figure 18.19.

FIGURE 18.19

A menu worksheet

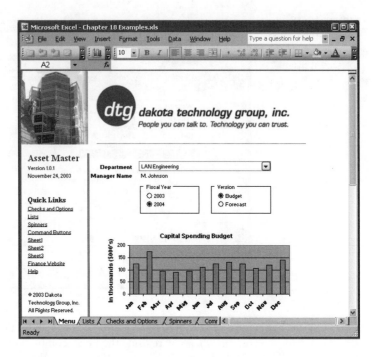

A menu worksheet can serve many purposes. For example, a menu worksheet may serve one or more of the following purposes:

♦ Provide a starting point or point of reference in a workbook.

♦ Provide simple navigation to other worksheets or areas of interest. This could include named ranges, other workbooks, documentation, or relevant websites.

♦ Display workbook version information such as version number and date.

♦ Show key performance indicators or a graph that provides a high-level synopsis of the analysis the workbook was designed to perform.

♦ Allow the user to enter general high-level inputs

The menu worksheet shown in Figure 18.19 incorporates many of these ideas using a variety of user interface elements. Part of the battle in designing an effective menu sheet is formatting. I like to frame the menu by hiding all of the unused columns and attempting to create a menu that will fit in a monitor with at least 1024×768 resolution without scrolling. If possible, I'll limit the menu worksheet's used width so that it will also fit horizontally in an 800×600 resolution. This means that a user with 800×600 resolution will not need to use the horizontal scrollbar but may still need to use the vertical scrollbar.

Additionally, because a menu should be visually appealing, I generally turn the grid lines and row and column headers off. These worksheet-specific options are found on the View tab of the Options dialog box (Tools ➢ Options).

Another technique the example menu uses involves employing hyperlinks as a navigation aid. This is a nice touch, especially when the workbook is just one component of a system. For example, you could have links that refer to other workbooks, Word documents, web pages, or to locations within the workbook. If you adopt this practice, you may find the following listing rather handy. Listing 18.5 creates hyperlinks to each worksheet in the workbook.

LISTING 18.5: CREATING A HYPERLINK MENU

```
' Creates a hyperlink to each worksheet in the
' workbook excluding the worksheet containing
' rgLinks.
Sub CreateLinks(rgLinks As Range)
    Dim ws As Worksheet

    For Each ws In ThisWorkbook.Worksheets
        If ws.Name <> rgLinks.Parent.Name Then
            rgLinks.Hyperlinks.Add rgLinks, ThisWorkbook.Name, _
                "'" & ws.Name & "'!A1", ws.Name, ws.Name
            Set rgLinks = rgLinks.Offset(1, 0)
        End If
    Next

    Set ws = Nothing
End Sub

' Example of how to use the CreateLinks procedure
' to create hyperlinks on the Menu worksheet.
' Assumes a range name "TOC" is present that
' represents where the links should go.
Sub CreateMenuLinks()
    CreateLinks ThisWorkbook.Worksheets("Menu"). _
        Range("TOC").Offset(1, 0)
End Sub
```

The CreateLinks procedure uses a method that I haven't presented yet: the Add method of the Hyperlinks object. The syntax of Add is as follows:

```
Hyperlinks.Add Anchor, Address, [SubAddress], _
    [ScreenTip], [TextToDisplay]
```

The parameters of the Add method are discussed in the following list.

Anchor Anchor is a required parameter that specifies where the hyperlink should be displayed. The anchor can be either a Range or a Shape object.

Address Address is a required parameter that specifies the file location and filename of the document to which the link refers.

SubAddress   SubAddress is an optional parameter that specifies a specific location within the document referred to by the Address parameter.

ScreenTip   ScreenTip is an optional parameter that specifies the text to display when the mouse is hovered over the hyperlink.

TextToDisplay   TextToDisplay is an optional parameter that specifies the text displayed by the hyperlink.

Another helpful technique for menu worksheets involves unlocking only the cells that a user should interact with (select the cell and press CTRL+1, then switch to the Protection tab) and then protecting the worksheet. When you protect the worksheet, uncheck the option that allows users to select locked cells as shown in the following screenshot.

The benefit of protecting the menu worksheet in this manner is that it makes it more clear to the user which cells they can interact with. Also, it prevents casual modification of the layout of the worksheet such as changing the location of pictures or controls. Without protecting the worksheet, it is easy to accidentally change the location of these objects when clicking them.

NOTE   Cells containing hyperlinks need to be unlocked in order for the hyperlinks to work.

Summary

A user interface serves many purposes in an application. It collects user input, displays output, and allows users to direct the execution of a program. By building on top of Excel, you, as a developer, don't need to do nearly as much work as you would if you had to start from scratch. You'll get an idea of how much work this entails in Chapter 20 when you see what is involved in building your own user form.

For many Excel applications, your user interface needs can be met using worksheet-based user interface elements. A worksheet-based user interface is an interface that does not use command bars or user forms. This type of interface is developed using the creative application of standard Excel formatting combined with a few form or ActiveX controls. Two benefits of a worksheet-based interface are that they are much easier to develop and they don't lead to file-size bloat.

To spice up a worksheet-based user interface, you can use either form controls or ActiveX controls. Form controls are created using the Forms toolbar whereas ActiveX controls come from the Control toolbox. There are a few key differences between these two types of controls. Form controls are a little easier to use but are not as flexible as ActiveX controls. Form controls don't have event procedures; ActiveX controls do. To hook code up to a form control, you "assign" a macro to it; to hook code up to an ActiveX control, you place code in the event procedure that you want to trigger your code. Finally, form controls can be used on a chart sheet but not on a user form. On the other hand, ActiveX controls can be used on a user form but not on a chart sheet.

Although you'd be surprised how sophisticated you can get using a worksheet-based interface, you will encounter situations in which you need more horsepower. In the next chapter, I'll cover the details involved in working with command bars. Command bars encompass all of the functionality associated with menus and toolbars. After covering command bars, I'll cover user form development in Chapter 20.

Chapter 19

Taking Control of Command Bars

IN THE LAST CHAPTER, you learned how to create a worksheet-based user interface. Although a worksheet-based user interface offers many advantages, one of the biggest disadvantages is that this type of user interface is worksheet specific. What do you do when you want to offer the user functionality regardless of the active worksheet? You basically have two choices: duplicate the necessary user interface elements on every worksheet, or create your own menu item or toolbar that allows the user to access the functionality regardless of the active worksheet. One of the problems with duplicating is that it ignores the fact that users may add new worksheets. Because of this possibility, creating your own menu item or toolbar is often the best choice.

In order to manipulate existing menus or toolbars or create new ones, you need to learn how to use the CommandBar object and various related objects, particularly the CommandBarControl object. This chapter aims to present the information you need to know to have success with command bars.

Taking Inventory with CommandBars

One way to get familiar with command bars is to take inventory of all the command bars in Excel. You can achieve this by looping through all of the CommandBar objects in the CommandBars collection.

Listing 19.1 presents a procedure that loops through all of the CommandBar objects in Excel. It loops through each of the CommandBar objects and outputs various CommandBar properties to a worksheet named Inventory along the way. This listing doesn't use any named ranges, so all you need to do is be sure to name one of the worksheets in your workbook "Inventory" or modify the Inventory procedure to use a worksheet of your choice. Also, I manually added the column headings to the output shown in Figure 19.1, though you could do this programmatically of course.

LISTING 19.1: LISTING APPLICATION COMMANDBARS

```
' Lists all of the command bars on a worksheet named Inventory
Sub Inventory()
    Dim cb As CommandBar
    Dim rg As Range
```

```vba
    Set rg = ThisWorkbook.Worksheets("Inventory").Cells(2, 1)

    ' Loop through all the command bars in Excel
    For Each cb In Application.CommandBars
        rg.Value = cb.Name
        rg.Offset(0, 1).Value = cb.Index
        rg.Offset(0, 2).Value = cb.BuiltIn
        rg.Offset(0, 3).Value = cb.Enabled
        rg.Offset(0, 4).Value = cb.Visible
        rg.Offset(0, 5).Value = _
            TranslateCommandBarType(cb.Type)
        rg.Offset(0, 6).Value = _
            TranslateCommandBarPosition(cb.Position)
        rg.Offset(0, 7).Value = cb.Controls.Count
        ' Move down to the next row
        Set rg = rg.Offset(1, 0)
    Next

    Set rg = Nothing
    Set cb = Nothing
End Sub

' Translates a MsoBarType enumeration into a text description
' of the bar type.
Function TranslateCommandBarType(vType As MsoBarType) As String
    Dim sType As String

    Select Case vType
        Case Is = MsoBarType.msoBarTypeMenuBar
            sType = "Menu Bar"
        Case Is = MsoBarType.msoBarTypeNormal
            sType = "Normal"
        Case Is = MsoBarType.msoBarTypePopup
            sType = "Popup"
        Case Else
            sType = "Unknown type"
    End Select
    TranslateCommandBarType = sType
End Function

' Translates a MsoBarPosition enumeration into a text description
' of the bar position.
Function TranslateCommandBarPosition(vType As MsoBarPosition) _
    As String

    Dim sPosition As String
```

```
    Select Case vType
        Case Is = MsoBarPosition.msoBarBottom
            sPosition = "Bottom"
        Case Is = MsoBarPosition.msoBarFloating
            sPosition = "Floating"
        Case Is = MsoBarPosition.msoBarLeft
            sPosition = "Left"
        Case Is = MsoBarPosition.msoBarMenuBar
                sPosition = "Menu Bar"
        Case Is = MsoBarPosition.msoBarPopup
            sPosition = "Popup"
        Case Is = MsoBarPosition.msoBarRight
            sPosition = "Right"
        Case Is = MsoBarPosition.msoBarTop
            sPosition = "Top"
        Case Else
            sPosition = "Unknown position"
    End Select

    TranslateCommandBarPosition = sPosition
End Function
```

Figure 19.1 shows a partial output of the Inventory procedure. Your results may vary, but on my PC, the Inventory procedure documented 128 command bars. Listing 19.1 consists of three procedures: Inventory, TranslateCommandBarType, and TranslateCommandBarPosition. The Inventory procedure is the main procedure in this listing. The two Translate procedures convert enumeration values into to a user-friendly description.

The Inventory procedure loops through each command bar found in the collection of command bars associated with the Application object. For each command bar, the process outputs various properties of the current CommandBar object before moving down a row on the Inventory worksheet and moving on to the next CommandBar object.

NOTE *As with any collection object, you can return a specific CommandBar using the CommandBars object by referring to either the CommandBar's name or its index.*

Before I move on to the CommandBar object, it might be helpful to present a couple useful command bar procedures. First off, you need to have a routine that validates the existence of a command bar name before using it to set a reference to a CommandBar object. The function in Listing 19.2 named CommandBarExists can be used for just this purpose. Second, it is helpful to have a simple routine to show/hide a specific command bar. The procedure named ShowCommandBar in Listing 19.2 is useful because it allows you to show/hide specific command bars without first having to validate the existence of the command bar. Listing 19.2 also contains a test procedure that demonstrates how to use these two procedures.

FIGURE 19.1

A listing of command bars generated by the Inventory procedure

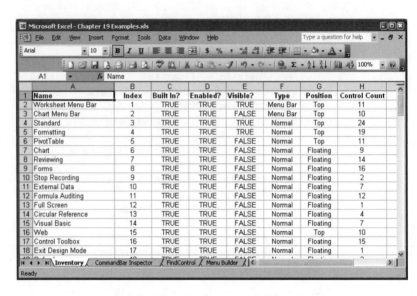

LISTING 19.2: VALIDATING A COMMANDBAR

```
' Tests CommandBarExists and ShowCommandBar
Sub TestCommandBarUtilities()
    Debug.Print CommandBarExists("Worksheet Menu Bar")
    Debug.Print CommandBarExists("Formatting")
    Debug.Print CommandBarExists("Not a command bar")
    ShowCommandBar "Borders", True
End Sub

' Determines if a given command bar name exists
Function CommandBarExists(sName As String) As Boolean
    Dim s As String

    On Error GoTo bWorksheetExistsErr

    s = Application.CommandBars(sName).Name
    CommandBarExists = True
    Exit Function

bWorksheetExistsErr:
    CommandBarExists = False
End Function
```

```
' Shows or hides a command bar. You do not need
' to validate sName before using this procedure.
' Depends on CommandBarExists function.
Sub ShowCommandBar(sName As String, bShow As Boolean)
    If CommandBarExists(sName) Then
        Application.CommandBars(sName).Visible = bShow
    End If
End Sub
```

Here is the output of TestCommandBarUtilities:

```
True
True
False
```

The CommandBarExists function uses an algorithm you've seen a few times already. Command-BarExists attempts to set a reference to a CommandBar object using the name passed to it. Two potential outcomes of setting a reference in this manner exist: either a reference will be set or an error will occur. By enabling error handling in a manner that instructs the execution point to go to a special error handling location in the event of an error, you can determine the result of the function. If an error occurs, the command bar name does not exist. If an error does not occur, the command bar name exists.

ShowCommandBar is useful because it performs the necessary command bar validation and either shows or hides the command bar in one convenient procedure. ShowCommandBar uses the CommandBarExists function to validate the name passed in. If a valid command bar name was passed, ShowCommandBar sets the Visible property of the CommandBar as indicated by the bShow parameter.

Reflecting on a CommandBar

Now that you have a list of command bars to play with and a way to validate, show, and hide them, how about inspecting specific command bars in more depth? In fact, how about building a worksheet that you can use to inspect individual command bars merely by selecting the desired command bar from a combo box? Figure 19.2 shows an example of the desired end product.

I developed the desired functionality in two phases. Originally, I developed the code to generate the report shown in Figure 19.2 as a separate stand-alone report. From there, it was easy to add a combo box to the worksheet and hook it up to my prebuilt functionality. Listing 19.3 presents the hardest part of the Command Bar Inspector—the code to generate the report. As you'll see, it's not all that hard; it's just the lengthiest aspect of this utility.

NOTE *Listing 19.3 uses the TranslateCommandBarType and TranslateCommandBarPosition procedures from Listing 19.1.*

FIGURE 19.2

The Command Bar Inspector utility

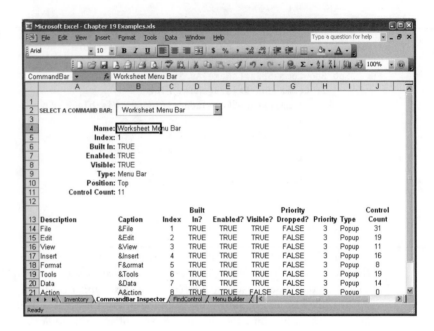

LISTING 19.3: INSPECTING A COMMANDBAR

```vba
Sub InspectCommandBar(cb As CommandBar, rgOutput As Range)
    DisplayGeneralInfo cb, rgOutput
    Set rgOutput = rgOutput.End(xlDown).Offset(2, 0)
    DisplayControlDetail cb, rgOutput
End Sub

Private Sub DisplayGeneralInfo(cb As CommandBar, rgOutput As Range)
    rgOutput.Value = "Name:"
    rgOutput.Offset(0, 1).Value = cb.Name

    rgOutput.Offset(1, 0).Value = "Index:"
    rgOutput.Offset(1, 1).Value = cb.Index

    rgOutput.Offset(2, 0).Value = "Built In:"
    rgOutput.Offset(2, 1).Value = cb.BuiltIn

    rgOutput.Offset(3, 0).Value = "Enabled:"
    rgOutput.Offset(3, 1).Value = cb.Enabled

    rgOutput.Offset(4, 0).Value = "Visible:"
    rgOutput.Offset(4, 1).Value = cb.Visible
```

```
    rgOutput.Offset(5, 0).Value = "Type:"
    rgOutput.Offset(5, 1).Value = _
        TranslateCommandBarType(cb.Type)

    rgOutput.Offset(6, 0).Value = "Position:"
    rgOutput.Offset(6, 1).Value = _
        TranslateCommandBarPosition(cb.Position)

    rgOutput.Offset(7, 0).Value = "Control Count:"
    rgOutput.Offset(7, 1).Value = cb.Controls.Count

    With rgOutput.Resize(8, 1)
        .Font.Bold = True
        .HorizontalAlignment = xlRight
    End With
End Sub

Private Sub DisplayControlDetail(cb As CommandBar, rgOutput As Range)
    Dim cbc As CommandBarControl

    On Error Resume Next

    ' Make column header
    rgOutput.Value = "Description"
    rgOutput.Offset(0, 1).Value = "Caption"
    rgOutput.Offset(0, 2).Value = "Index"
    rgOutput.Offset(0, 3).Value = "Built In?"
    rgOutput.Offset(0, 4).Value = "Enabled?"
    rgOutput.Offset(0, 5).Value = "Visible?"
    rgOutput.Offset(0, 6).Value = "Priority Dropped?"
    rgOutput.Offset(0, 7).Value = "Priority"
    rgOutput.Offset(0, 8).Value = "Type"
    rgOutput.Offset(0, 9).Value = "Control Count"
    rgOutput.Resize(1, 10).Font.Bold = True
    Set rgOutput = rgOutput.Offset(1, 0)

    ' Get control detail
    For Each cbc In cb.Controls

        rgOutput.Value = Replace(cbc.Caption, "&", "")
        rgOutput.Offset(0, 1).Value = cbc.Caption
        rgOutput.Offset(0, 2).Value = cbc.Index
        rgOutput.Offset(0, 3).Value = cbc.BuiltIn
        rgOutput.Offset(0, 4).Value = cbc.Enabled
        rgOutput.Offset(0, 5).Value = cbc.Visible
        rgOutput.Offset(0, 6).Value = cbc.IsPriorityDropped
        rgOutput.Offset(0, 7).Value = cbc.Priority
        rgOutput.Offset(0, 8).Value = TranslateControlType(cbc.Type)
```

```
        rgOutput.Offset(0, 9).Value = cbc.Controls.Count

    Set rgOutput = rgOutput.Offset(1, 0)
Next

'Clean up.
Set cbc = Nothing

End Sub

' Translates a MsoControlType enumeration into a text description
' of the control type.
Function TranslateControlType(vType As MsoControlType) As String
    Dim sType As String

    Select Case vType
        Case Is = MsoControlType.msoControlActiveX
            sType = "ActiveX"
        Case Is = MsoControlType.msoControlAutoCompleteCombo
            sType = "Auto Complete Combo"
        Case Is = MsoControlType.msoControlButton
            sType = "Button"
        Case Is = MsoControlType.msoControlButtonDropdown
            sType = "Button Dropdown"
        Case Is = MsoControlType.msoControlButtonPopup
            sType = "Button Popup"
        Case Is = MsoControlType.msoControlComboBox
            sType = "Combo Box"
        Case Is = MsoControlType.msoControlCustom
            sType = "Custom"
        Case Is = MsoControlType.msoControlDropdown
            sType = "Dropdown"
        Case Is = MsoControlType.msoControlEdit
            sType = "Edit"
        Case Is = MsoControlType.msoControlExpandingGrid
            sType = "Expanding Grid"
        Case Is = MsoControlType.msoControlGauge
            sType = "Gauge"
        Case Is = MsoControlType.msoControlGenericDropdown
            sType = "Generic Dropdown"
        Case Is = MsoControlType.msoControlGraphicCombo
            sType = "Graphic Combo"
        Case Is = MsoControlType.msoControlGraphicDropdown
            sType = "Graphic Dropdown"
        Case Is = MsoControlType.msoControlGraphicPopup
            sType = "Graphic Popup"
        Case Is = MsoControlType.msoControlGrid
            sType = "Grid"
```

```
        Case Is = MsoControlType.msoControlLabel
            sType = "Label"
        Case Is = MsoControlType.msoControlLabelEx
            sType = "Label Ex"
        Case Is = MsoControlType.msoControlOCXDropdown
            sType = "OCX Dropdown"
        Case Is = MsoControlType.msoControlPane
            sType = "Pane"
        Case Is = MsoControlType.msoControlPopup
            sType = "Popup"
        Case Is = MsoControlType.msoControlSpinner
            sType = "Spinner"
        Case Is = MsoControlType.msoControlSplitButtonMRUPopup
            sType = "Split Button MRU Popup"
        Case Is = MsoControlType.msoControlSplitButtonPopup
            sType = "Split Button Popup"
        Case Is = MsoControlType.msoControlSplitDropdown
            sType = "Split Dropdown"
        Case Is = MsoControlType.msoControlSplitExpandingGrid
            sType = "Split Expanding Grid"
        Case Is = MsoControlType.msoControlWorkPane
            sType = "Work Pane"
        Case Else
            sType = "Unknown control type"
    End Select

    TranslateControlType = sType
End Function
```

Table 19.1 lists the four procedures in Listing 19.3 along with the two procedures from Listing 19.1 that are utilized.

TABLE 19.1: PROCEDURES USED TO INSPECT A COMMAND BAR

PROCEDURE	LOCATION	DESCRIPTION
InspectCommandBar	Listing 19.3	The primary procedure used to inspect a command bar. This is the procedure that should be hooked up to the combo box.
DisplayGeneralInfo	Listing 19.3	Responsible for listing general command bar information. In Figure 19.2, the range A4:B11 was built by DisplayGeneralInfo.
DisplayControlInfo	Listing 19.3	Loops through all of the controls on the command bar and displays information about each control. In Figure 19.2, everything from row 13 down is output from DisplayControlInfo.

TABLE 19.1: PROCEDURES USED TO INSPECT A COMMAND BAR *(continued)*

PROCEDURE	LOCATION	DESCRIPTION
TranslateCommandBarPosition	Listing 19.1	Called by DisplayGeneralInfo to translate a command bar position enumeration into user-friendly text.
TranslateCommandBarType	Listing 19.1	Called by DisplayGeneralInfo to translate a command bar type enumeration into user-friendly text.
TranslateControlType	Listing 19.3	Called by DisplayControlDetail to translate a control type enumeration into user-friendly text.

Because these command bar inspection procedures were constructed in a manner that would allow you to output the result of the inspection in a location of your choosing, you see that many lines of code in the DisplayGeneralInfo and DisplayControlInfo procedures are dedicated to constructing row and column labels. Also, translating a type enumeration is a simple but lengthy process. If it weren't for displaying row and column labels and translating type enumerations, this would be a much more compact listing.

All of the interesting stuff in Listing 19.3 occurs in the DisplayControlInfo procedure. Right off the bat, you may have noticed the declaration of a CommandBarControl variable. A CommandBarControl object is a built-in or custom control on a menu bar, toolbar, menu, submenu, or shortcut menu. This is interesting because it is an object you haven't seen yet. DisplayControlInfo works by looping through all of the CommandBarControl objects in the Controls collection of the given CommandBar object.

The other comment I have regarding Listing 19.3 is related to the On Error Resume Next statement. This statement is necessary due to the statement

```
rgOutput.Offset(0, 9).Value = cbc.Controls.Count
```

near the end of the procedure. Not all types of CommandBarControl objects have the capability to serve as a container for more controls. Consequently, this statement isn't always valid—hence the need for On Error Resume Next.

Now that you have the capability to display detailed command bar information, its time to hook this up to a combo box. This is a relatively easy process. The first thing I did was name the list of command bars generated by the Inventory procedure in Listing 19.1. As you can see in Figure 19.3, I named the data in the first column CommandBars.

Next, I named cell B4 on the Command Bar Inspector worksheet CommandBar. This cell is a little more important than other cells on the Command Bar Inspector worksheet because it will be linked directly to the combo box. Additionally, it will need to be referenced by a statement in your code.

The next thing to do is place the combo box on the worksheet. I used the ActiveX combo box found on the Control Toolbox toolbar. Table 19.2 details the properties that I modified for this example.

FIGURE 19.3

A list of command bars for the Command Bar Inspector utility

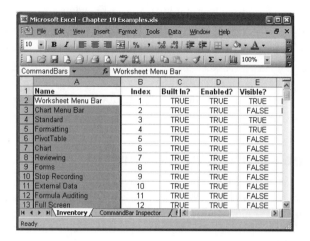

TABLE 19.2: COMBO BOX PROPERTIES REQUIRING MODIFICATION

PROPERTY	VALUE
Name	cboCommandBars
ListRows	16
LinkedCell	'Chapter 19 Examples.xls'!CommandBar
ListFillRange	'Chapter 19 Examples.xls'!CommandBars

NOTE   *For the LinkedCell and ListFillRange properties, you will need to substitute the name of your workbook in place of Chapter 19 Examples.xls.*

The final thing to do is place some code in the Change event of the combo box. Listing 19.4 shows the code that is necessary. To enter this code, right-click the combo box and select View Code.

LISTING 19.4: TYING THE COMBO BOX TO THE INSPECTCOMMANDBAR PROCEDURE

```
Private Sub cboCommandBars_Change()
    ' Make sure the correct worksheet is active. Changing
    ' the name of other worksheets can trigger
    ' this event unexpectedly.
    If ActiveSheet.Name = Me.Name Then
        ' Clear the details associated with the
        ' previous command bar
        Me.Range("A14:J65536").ClearContents
        ' Inspect the command bar
```

```
        InspectCommandBar Application.CommandBars _
            (Me.Range("CommandBar").Value), Me.Range("A4")
    End If
End Sub
```

All right! Now test it out while learning about the various command bars. Figure 19.4 shows the Command Bar Inspector in action.

The Bendy CommandBarControl Object

An understanding of the CommandBarControl object and its variants is key to understanding how to manipulate command bars. The CommandBarControl object is somewhat generic, and therefore, quite flexible. I was going to title this section the Flexible CommandBarControl object, but bendy seems like a little more fun. I don't recall ever using the word bendy in conversation, but my brother-in-law uses it all the time so it must be all right (just ask my wife). Hopefully she doesn't read this section; otherwise I'm in trouble.

The CommandBarControl object represents a control on a command bar. In addition to the standard CommandBarControl object, three variations of this object exist: CommandBarButton, CommandBarComboBox, and CommandBarPopup. The properties and methods of the CommandBarControl are shared by its three variations. Usually you use the CommandBarControl object when you are working with any of the built-in controls and one of the three variants when you are working with custom command bar controls.

FIGURE 19.4

Success! Instant command bar information at your fingertips.

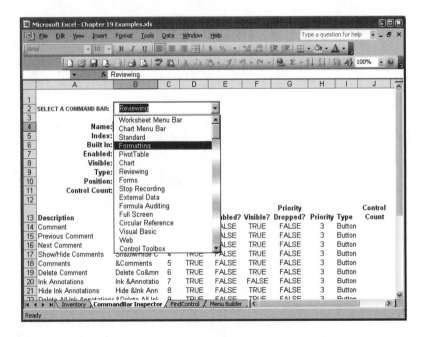

In Listing 19.3, you saw an example of using a CommandBarControl to retrieve various properties associated with controls related to a specific command bar. Table 19.3 lists some of the key properties associated with a CommandBarControl object.

TABLE 19.3: KEY COMMANDBARCONTROL PROPERTIES

PROPERTY	DESCRIPTION
BeginGroup	A read/write Boolean property that specifies whether the control appears at the beginning of a group of command bar controls.
Caption	A read/write string that returns or sets the caption of the control.
DescriptionText	A read/write string that can be used for documenting the behavior of a control from a developer perspective. This property is never displayed to the end user.
Enabled	A read/write Boolean property that determines whether the user can interact with the control.
IsPriorityDropped	A read only Boolean property that indicates whether the control has been dropped from the command bar based on usage statistics and layout space.
OnAction	A read/write string that contains the name of the VBA procedure that will be executed when the user clicks or changes the value of the control.
Parameter	A read/write string that can be used to execute a command. This property can be used sort of like a second Tag property.
Priority	Returns or sets the priority of a control. Excel determines which controls to display on a command bar by examining the Priority property of each control.
Tag	A read/write string that serves as a container to store information about the control.
TooltipText	A read/write string that indicates the control's screen tip that is displayed when you hover over the control.
Type	A read only property that returns the control type using the MsoControlType enumeration.
Visible	A read/write Boolean property that indicates whether the control is visible.

The Caption property is one property that requires a little more explanation. You may think that Caption would return the exact text displayed by the CommandBarControl. The problem with this thought is that it doesn't account for a way to indicate which character is serving as the accelerator (the accelerator is the character that allows you to access the item using a combination of the Alt key and the accelerator). If the CommandBarControl had an accelerator property like the Command-Button does, this wouldn't be a problem. Because it doesn't have an accelerator property and you can't have underlined values in a string, the accelerator character is indicated by placing an ampersand (&)

just before the accelerator character. You can see an example of this in Listing 19.3 and repeated in the following snippet.

```
rgOutput.Value = Replace(cbc.Caption, "&", "")
rgOutput.Offset(0, 1).Value = cbc.Caption
```

The DisplayControlDetail procedure uses the Caption property twice: once as a parameter to the Replace function and once to retrieve the caption. As another example, consider the File item on the Worksheet Menu Bar. The Caption property would refer to the caption of this item as &File.

You use the OnAction property when you add your own controls to a command bar. Specifically, you use the OnAction property to assign a procedure to a command bar control. The procedure specified by the OnAction property will run any time the user clicks or interacts with the control.

Visualization, Prioritization, and CommandBarControls

Have you ever wondered how Excel determines which menu items or toolbar buttons to show or hide? This behavior is exposed to you through the Priority and IsPriorityDropped properties of the CommandBarControl object. It can be kind of confusing to determine why a particular control isn't showing up on a given command bar. A control might not show up because its Visible property has been set to false. A control with Visible set to true, however, may not be immediately visible on a Personalized Menu or Toolbar if IsPriorityDropped is true.

Excel is in charge of determining the priority dropped state of command bar controls. For Personalized Menus, it does this by keeping track of the number of times you use the control and the number of application sessions in which you use the menu the control belongs to without using the control itself. When this value reaches certain threshold values, the count is decremented. When the count reaches zero, IsPriorityDropped is set to true. As a developer, you cannot set the session value, the threshold value, or the IsPriorityDropped property. You can, however, use the AdaptiveMenus property to disable adaptive (or personalized) menus for specific menus in an application.

Toolbars are treated a bit differently. Toolbars always display as many controls as they have space to show. To determine when to set IsPriorityDropped to true for a specific toolbar control, Excel maintains a list of the order in which all the controls on that toolbar were last executed and rank orders them from most frequently used to least frequently used. The exception to this process concerns controls with Priority set to 1, which will always be shown even if the toolbar needs to wrap rows to show them. You can use the Priority property to ensure that specific toolbar controls are always shown, or to reposition toolbars so that they have enough space to display all of their controls.

Finding Controls

When working with built-in command bars, a common task is the need to locate a specific menu. For finding controls, consider using either the FindControl or FindControls methods of the CommandBarControl object.

The syntax of FindControl is as follows.

```
Application.CommandBars.FindControl([Type], _
    [Id], [Tag], [Visible], [Recursive])
```

The parameters of FindControl are detailed in the following list.

Type   This is an optional parameter that should be an MsoControlType enumeration value.

ID   ID is an optional variant parameter that specifies the control ID to look for.

Tag   Tag is an optional variant parameter that specifies the control tag to search for.

Visible   An optional variant parameter. Set Visible to true to include only visible command bar controls in the search. By default, Visible is false. Visible command bars include all visible toolbars and any menus that are open at the time the FindControl method is executed.

Recursive   Recursive is an optional Boolean parameter that specifies how deep to search for the control. If you set recursive to true, Find includes all of the pop-up submenus and the toolbar. By default Recursive is false.

WARNING   If FindControl locates two or more controls that match the criteria, it returns the first match only. If you need to find all of the controls associated with a particular control, use FindControls. FindControls takes the same parameters as FindControl but returns a collection of CommandBarControls rather than a single CommandBarControl.

Listing 19.5 presents an example of using the FindControls method to list all of the visible controls. The FindVisibleControls listing finds all of the visible controls and begins listing details associated with each found control at the range provided to the function. The ShowVisibleControls procedure tests the FindVisibleControls function by having FindVisibleControls output its information to a range named FoundControls on a worksheet named FindControl. You can either name a worksheet and range using the same names or modify the ShowVisibleControls procedure to use a worksheet and range of your choosing.

NOTE   Listing 19.5 uses the TranslateControlType procedure from Listing 19.3.

LISTING 19.5: FINDING VISIBLE CONTROLS WITH FINDCONTROLS

```
Sub ShowVisibleControls()
    FindVisibleControls ThisWorkbook.Worksheets("FindControl"). _
        Range("FoundControls").Offset(1, 0)
End Sub

' Displays information on all visible controls
Sub FindVisibleControls(rg As Range)
    Dim ctrls As CommandBarControls
    Dim ctrl As CommandBarControl

    Set ctrls = Application.CommandBars.FindControls(, , , True)

    For Each ctrl In ctrls
        rg.Value = ctrl.Parent.Name
        rg.Offset(0, 1).Value = ctrl.Caption
        rg.Offset(0, 2).Value = ctrl.Index
        rg.Offset(0, 3).Value = ctrl.ID
        rg.Offset(0, 4).Value = ctrl.Enabled
        rg.Offset(0, 5).Value = ctrl.Visible
```

```
        rg.Offset(0, 6).Value = ctrl.IsPriorityDropped
        rg.Offset(0, 7).Value = TranslateControlType(ctrl.Type)
        Set rg = rg.Offset(1, 0)
    Next

    Set ctrl = Nothing
    Set ctrls = Nothing
End Sub
```

This is a simple example that shows how to use FindControls, but it doesn't really help you envision how you might use this method in practice. For example, one way that this could come in handy is if you created your own menu item. You could set the Tag property of each command bar control and then use FindControl to find a control that has a specific tag. You'll see an example of this in Listing 19.6. Using FindControl to look for controls with a specific tag is much easier than the alternative way, which is to loop through all of the controls associated with a command bar and check the Caption property. Figure 19.5 shows the results of running the ShowVisibleControls procedure.

FIGURE 19.5

A listing of visible controls

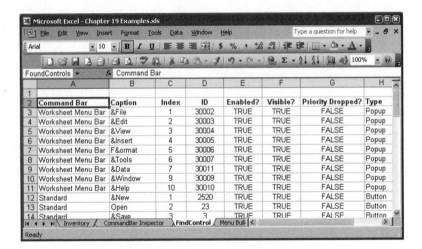

Crafting Custom Command Bars

Let me move on to the good stuff—modifying existing command bars and creating new ones. I'll start with modifying existing command bars. One of the most common command bar–oriented tasks Excel developers will do is modify the Worksheet Menu Bar. The Worksheet Menu Bar is the main Excel menu. A common user request is to be able to access custom functionality that you have developed using the Excel menu. In other words, they want to see custom menu items alongside built-in menu items. In order to satisfy this request, you need to learn how to use the Add method of the CommandBarControls object. The syntax of Add is as shown next.

```
CommandBarControls.Add([Type], [ID], [Parameter], _
[Before], [Temporary])
```

The parameters of Add are discussed in the following list.

Type   Type is an optional parameter that specifies the kind of control to add. Use one of the following MsoControlType constants: msoControlButton, msoControlEdit, msoControlDropdown, msoControlComboBox, or msoControlPopup.

ID   ID is an optional variant (integer) parameter that specifies the ID of a built-in control. If the value of this argument is 1, or if this argument is omitted, a blank custom control of the specified type will be added to the command bar.

Parameter   Parameter is an optional parameter. For built-in controls, the parameter argument is used by the container application to run the command. For custom controls, you can use Parameter to send information to a VBA procedure, or you can use it to store information about the control.

Before   Before is an optional variant (integer) parameter that specifies the position of the new control on the command bar. The new control will be inserted before the control at this position. By default the control is added at the end of the specified command bar.

Temporary   Temporary is an optional variant (Boolean) parameter that indicates whether to make the new control temporary. Temporary controls are automatically deleted when the container application is closed. The default value is false.

WARNING   *I prefer to mark controls as temporary (Temporary = True) unless I have a good reason not to, otherwise I may occasionally find phantom controls—controls that I thought were deleted but really weren't. This phenomenon has the potential to cause hard-to-detect bugs.*

As a simple example of adding a new menu item to Excel's menu and then adding menu choices underneath the menu item, take a look at Listing 19.6. This example adds a menu item named MyMenu to Excel's main menu (the Worksheet Menu Bar) and six individual menu items underneath MyMenu. For this example, I set the OnAction property of each menu item to refer to a tiny procedure named Say-Hello that just displays a message box.

LISTING 19.6: CREATING A MENU BAR

```
Public Sub AddMenuItemExample()
    Dim cbWSMenuBar As CommandBar
    Dim cbc As CommandBarControl

    Set cbWSMenuBar = Application.CommandBars("Worksheet Menu Bar")

    ' Add a menu item
    Set cbc = cbWSMenuBar.Controls.Add(Type:=msoControlPopup, Temporary:=True)
```

```vba
    ' Set its tag so it can be easily found and referred to in VBA
    cbc.Tag = "MyMenu"

    With cbc
        .Caption = "&My Menu"
        With .Controls.Add(Type:=msoControlButton, Temporary:=True)
            .Caption = "Item &1"
            .OnAction = "ThisWorkbook.SayHello"
            .Tag = "Item1"
        End With
        With .Controls.Add(Type:=msoControlButton, Temporary:=True)
            .Caption = "Item &2"
            .OnAction = "ThisWorkbook.SayHello"
            .Tag = "Item2"
        End With
        With .Controls.Add(Type:=msoControlButton, Temporary:=True)
            .Caption = "Item &3"
            .OnAction = "ThisWorkbook.SayHello"
            .Tag = "Item 3"
        End With
        With .Controls.Add(Type:=msoControlButton, Temporary:=True)
            .Caption = "Item &4"
            .OnAction = "ThisWorkbook.SayHello"
            .BeginGroup = True
            .Tag = "Item4"
        End With
        With .Controls.Add(Type:=msoControlButton, Temporary:=True)
            .Caption = "Item &5"
            .OnAction = "ThisWorkbook.SayHello"
            .Tag = "Item5"
            .BeginGroup = True
        End With
        With .Controls.Add(Type:=msoControlButton, Temporary:=True)
            .Caption = "Item &6"
            .OnAction = "ThisWorkbook.SayHello"
            .Tag = "Item6"
        End With
    End With
End Sub

Private Sub SayHello()
    MsgBox "Hello", vbOKOnly
End Sub

' Restores the Worksheet Menu Bar to its native state
Private Sub ResetCommandBar()
    Application.CommandBars("Worksheet Menu Bar").Reset
End Sub
```

FIGURE 19.6

A custom menu on the worksheet menu bar

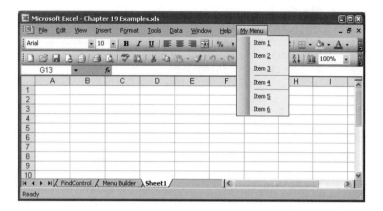

Figure 19.6 shows an example of the menu created by running the AddMenuItemExample procedure. You can run ResetCommandBar to restore the command bar to its original state.

When adding a new menu item to the Excel menu, you initially add an msoCommandPopup command bar control. The items underneath the menu can be any of the other types, though Listing 19.6 stuck with the generic type msoControlButton.

TIP   When tagging menu items with an accelerator using the ampersand, double-check that you do not assign the same accelerator to more than one item on the menu.

For menu items number four and five, I used the BeginGroup property to display separator bars in the menu. BeginGroup is a read/write Boolean property that is false by default.

Notice that I tagged each item I added using the Tag property. This makes it easy to quickly find my controls at a later time using the FindControl method. As an example, take a look at Listing 19.7. This listing provides a procedure named SetControlVisibility, which hides or shows a command bar control, and an example, which uses the procedure to show or hide the MyMenu item that I added in Listing 19.6.

LISTING 19.7: CONTROLING A COMMANDBARCONTROL'S VISIBILITY

```
Sub SetVisibilityExample()
    Dim vResponse As Variant

    vResponse = MsgBox("Do you want to show MyMenu item?", vbYesNo)
    If vResponse = vbYes Then
        SetControlVisibility "MyMenu", True
    Else
        SetControlVisibility "MyMenu", False
    End If
End Sub


Sub SetControlVisibility(sTag As String, IsVisible As Boolean)
```

```
        Dim cbc As CommandBarControl

        Set cbc = Application.CommandBars.FindControl(, , sTag)

        If Not cbc Is Nothing Then
            cbc.Visible = IsVisible
        End If

        Set cbc = Nothing
    End Sub
```

SetControlVisibility works by using the FindControl method to search for a control that is tagged with the string represented by the sTag parameter. If it finds a control, it sets the control's Visible property as indicated by the IsVisible parameter. The SetVisibilityExample procedure demonstrates how to put SetControlVisibility to good use by displaying a Yes/No message box, which asks whether to show the MyMenu item created in Listing 19.6, and then calling SetControlVisibility appropriately.

Do you know what would really be cool? A way to add items to Excel's menu simply by entering the appropriate settings on a worksheet. Figure19.7 shows a picture of a simple worksheet used to build menu items.

The goal is to build some procedures to interpret the Menu Builder worksheet and build the appropriate menu items. Other than the ParentTag column (column A), all of the other columns can be directly mapped to various CommandBarControl properties. The ParentTag column is used to indicate whether the control is a new top-level menu item (if N/A), a regular menu item, or a submenu item. Figure 19.8 shows an example of the menus created based on the data shown in Figure 19.7.

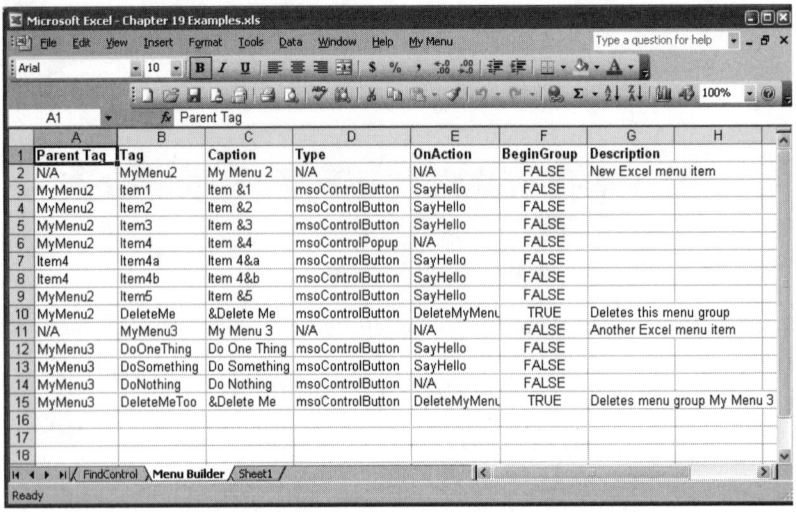

Parent Tag	Tag	Caption	Type	OnAction	BeginGroup	Description
N/A	MyMenu2	My Menu 2	N/A	N/A	FALSE	New Excel menu item
MyMenu2	Item1	Item &1	msoControlButton	SayHello	FALSE	
MyMenu2	Item2	Item &2	msoControlButton	SayHello	FALSE	
MyMenu2	Item3	Item &3	msoControlButton	SayHello	FALSE	
MyMenu2	Item4	Item &4	msoControlPopup	N/A	FALSE	
Item4	Item4a	Item 4&a	msoControlButton	SayHello	FALSE	
Item4	Item4b	Item 4&b	msoControlButton	SayHello	FALSE	
MyMenu2	Item5	Item &5	msoControlButton	SayHello	FALSE	
MyMenu2	DeleteMe	&Delete Me	msoControlButton	DeleteMyMenu	TRUE	Deletes this menu group
N/A	MyMenu3	My Menu 3	N/A	N/A	FALSE	Another Excel menu item
MyMenu3	DoOneThing	Do One Thing	msoControlButton	SayHello	FALSE	
MyMenu3	DoSomething	Do Something	msoControlButton	SayHello	FALSE	
MyMenu3	DoNothing	Do Nothing	msoControlButton	N/A	FALSE	
MyMenu3	DeleteMeToo	&Delete Me	msoControlButton	DeleteMyMenu	TRUE	Deletes menu group My Menu 3

FIGURE 19.7
The Menu Builder worksheet

FIGURE 19.8

Menus created using data shown in Figure 19.7

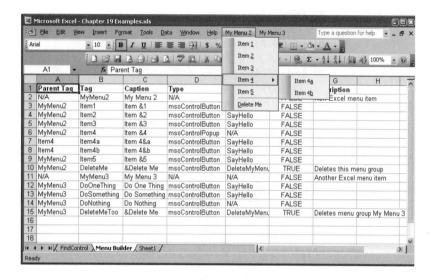

In order to keep this listing from getting too lengthy, I made a few simplifying assumptions. If this functionality appeals to you, you may want to modify the listing to make it a little more robust and feature rich. For example, you may want to add columns that dictate each control's Visible and Enabled properties.

The most critical assumption in this listing is that the values in the tag column are unique. In order to find controls, this listing uses the FindControl method and looks for control tags. As you may recall, the FindControl method returns the first match it finds. If you have two or more controls that have the same tag, this listing will not work as expected.

In order to use this listing, all you need to do is name a worksheet Menu Builder or modify the line in the BuildMenu procedure that references this worksheet to use a worksheet name of your choice.

LISTING 19.8: A WORKSHEET-BASED MENU CONSTRUCTION PROCESS

```
Option Explicit

Const NA = "N/A"

' COLUMN OFFSETS
Const TAG_OFFSET = 1
Const CAPTION_OFFSET = 2
Const TYPE_OFFSET = 3
Const ONACTION_OFFSET = 4
Const BEGINGROUP_OFFSET = 5
Const DESCRIPTION_OFFSET = 6
```

```vb
Sub BuildMenu()
    Dim ws As Worksheet
    Dim rg As Range

    On Error GoTo ErrHandler

    Set ws = ThisWorkbook.Worksheets("Menu Builder")

    ' Start on second row because the first row
    ' contains column headers
    Set rg = ws.Cells(2, 1)

    Do Until IsEmpty(rg)
        If rg.Value = NA Then
            ' New top level menu item
            AddTopLevelItem rg
        Else
            ' Sub-item of existing control
            AddSubItem rg
        End If

        ' Move down to the next row
        Set rg = rg.Offset(1, 0)
    Loop

ExitPoint:
    Set rg = Nothing
    Set ws = Nothing
    Exit Sub
ErrHandler:
    Debug.Print Err.Description
    Resume ExitPoint
End Sub

' Adds a new menu item to the Worksheet Menu Bar
Private Function AddTopLevelItem(rg As Range) As CommandBarControl
    Dim cbWSMenuBar As CommandBar
    Dim cbc As CommandBarControl

    On Error GoTo ErrHandler

    Set cbWSMenuBar = Application.CommandBars("Worksheet Menu Bar")

    ' Add a menu item
    Set cbc = cbWSMenuBar.Controls.Add(msoControlPopup, , , , True)
    cbc.Tag = rg.Offset(0, TAG_OFFSET).Value
    cbc.DescriptionText = rg.Offset(0, DESCRIPTION_OFFSET).Value
    cbc.Caption = rg.Offset(0, CAPTION_OFFSET).Value
```

```vba
    ' Return the newly added menu item
    Set AddTopLevelItem = cbc
ExitPoint:
    Set cbc = Nothing
    Set cbWSMenuBar = Nothing
    Exit Function
ErrHandler:
    Set AddTopLevelItem = Nothing
    Resume ExitPoint
End Function

' Adds a new menu item to the Worksheet Menu Bar
Private Function AddSubItem(rg As Range) As CommandBarControl
    Dim cbcParent As CommandBarControl
    Dim cbc As CommandBarControl

    On Error GoTo ErrHandler

    ' Locate parent based on parent tag
    Set cbcParent = Application.CommandBars.FindControl(, , rg.Value)

    If Not cbcParent Is Nothing Then
        ' Add a menu item
        Set cbc = cbcParent.Controls.Add(GetType(rg))

        ' Make sure the item has an OnAction value
        ' other than N/A.
        If rg.Offset(0, ONACTION_OFFSET).Value <> NA Then
            cbc.OnAction = rg.Offset(0, ONACTION_OFFSET).Value
        End If

        cbc.Tag = rg.Offset(0, TAG_OFFSET).Value
        cbc.DescriptionText = rg.Offset(0, DESCRIPTION_OFFSET).Value
        cbc.Caption = rg.Offset(0, CAPTION_OFFSET).Value
        cbc.BeginGroup = rg.Offset(0, BEGINGROUP_OFFSET).Value

        ' Return the newly added control
        Set AddSubItem = cbc
    Else
        ' Can't find parent control - return nothing
        Set AddSubItem = Nothing
    End If

ExitPoint:
    Set cbc = Nothing
    Set cbcParent = Nothing
    Exit Function
ErrHandler:
```

```
        Debug.Print Err.Description
        Set AddSubItem = Nothing
        Resume ExitPoint
End Function


' Converts selected msoControlType enumerations to values
Private Function GetType(rg As Range) As Long
    Dim sType As String

    sType = rg.Offset(0, TYPE_OFFSET).Value

    Select Case sType
        Case Is = "msoControlPopup"
            GetType = msoControlPopup
        Case Is = "msoControlButton"
            GetType = msoControlButton
        Case Is = "msoControlDropDown"
            GetType = msoControlDropdown
        Case Else ' including N/A
            ' Default to msoControlPopup
            GetType = msoControlPopup
    End Select
End Function


' Deletes a control tagged "MyMenu2"
Sub DeleteMyMenu2()
    DeleteMenu "MyMenu2"
End Sub


Sub DeleteMyMenu3()
    DeleteMenu "MyMenu3"
End Sub


Private Sub DeleteMenu(sTag As String)
    Dim cbc As CommandBarControl

    Set cbc = Application.CommandBars.FindControl(Tag:=sTag)

    If Not cbc Is Nothing Then
        cbc.Delete
    End If

    Set cbc = Nothing
End Sub
```

The main procedure in this listing is the BuildMenu procedure. BuildMenu loops through the cells in column A of the Menu Builder worksheet starting at row 2 and ending as soon as it finds an empty cell. For each cell, BuildMenu checks to see whether the value is equal to N/A (the NA constant) or not. If a cell value is N/A, then BuildMenu calls the AddTopLevelItem process, which creates a new menu item on the worksheet menu bar. If a cell value is not N/A, then BuildMenu calls the AddSubItem procedure, which adds a new control to the control whose tag is equal to the tag found in the Parent Tag column.

In order to keep things a little easier here, AddTopLevelItem ignores the Type and OnAction columns and automatically adds a control of type msoControlPopup. The AddSubItem procedure, however, uses the values found in every column with the exception of the OnAction column. For the OnAction property, AddSubItem needs to check the value of the OnAction column to be sure that it doesn't contain the N/A value. If it does contain N/A, AddSubItem does not set the OnAction property.

The GetType function is used by the AddSubItem procedure to translate the msoControlType enumeration found in the Type column to the numeric value that the enumerated value represents. You could extend this listing by modifying the GetType function to recognize the other valid control types.

I used the final three procedures in this listing to provide a convenient way to delete the menu items created if you use the data shown in Figure 19.7. The DeleteMenu procedure could be reused for other purposes. DeleteMenu deletes the first control it finds that is tagged with the value given by the sTag parameter. Again, this assumes that you are careful to assign unique values to each control's Tag property.

Building a New Command Bar

New command bars are built directly in Excel (no code necessary). Once you build a command bar, you can "attach" it to a workbook so that as you distribute the workbook, the command bar is distributed with it. The following steps lead you through the process of creating a new command bar from scratch.

1. Select View ➤ Toolbars ➤ Customize to display the Customize dialog box as shown in Figure 19.9.

FIGURE 19.9

You can create new toolbars using the Customize dialog box.

2. Click New on the Toolbars menu.

3. Name the new toolbar as shown in the following screenshot and click OK.

4. Select the Commands tab of the Customize dialog box.

5. For toolbar buttons, you can add built-in buttons to the command bar or add a custom button and then add an image to it. To use a built-in button, locate the button you want in the Commands list and drag it onto your toolbar.

6. Add a custom button by selecting the Macros category and dragging the Custom Button onto your toolbar. Figure 19.10 shows an example of the toolbar and the Customize dialog box after adding these two buttons to the Example Bar toolbar.

FIGURE 19.10

Drag and drop buttons from the Customize dialog box onto your toolbar to build a custom toolbar.

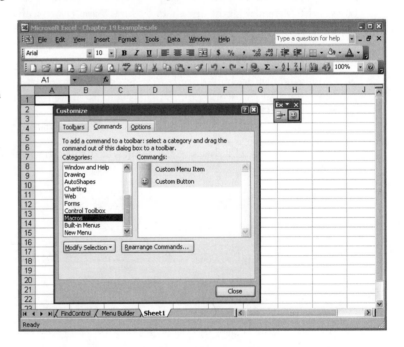

7. Select the first button on the toolbar and then click Modify Selection on the Customize dialog box. Figure 19.11 shows the button formatting options this action uncovers.

FIGURE 19.11

Button formatting options abound when you click Modify Selection.

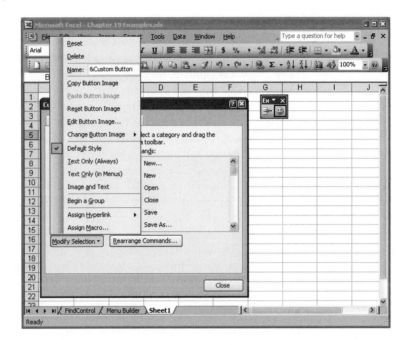

FIGURE 19.12

Attaching a toolbar to a workbook

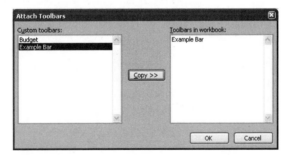

At this point, you could make the appropriate formatting changes and assign a macro to the button. When you are all finished, you can attach the toolbar to the workbook by choosing View ➤ Toolbars ➤ Customize and then clicking Attach on the Toolbars tab. Select the custom toolbar you want to attach in the Attach Toolbars dialog box and then click Copy. Figure 19.12 shows an example of this.

Summary

Customizing menus or creating your own toolbars is a common user interface development task you'll need to perform. In order to complete this type of task, you need to become familiar with the use of the CommandBar and CommandBarControl objects.

The CommandBars object provides you access to all of the built-in command bars and provides a method to add new command bars. You can set a reference to a CommandBar by name or index. The most commonly used built-in command bars are the Worksheet Menu Bar (the main Excel menu), the Formatting toolbar, and the Standard toolbar. After modifying a built-in CommandBar, you can reset it back to its original state using the Reset method.

Individual items on a CommandBar are represented using the CommandBarControl object. One confusing aspect of the CommandBarControl for users and developers is the relationship between visibility and two CommandBarControl properties: Visible and IsPriorityDropped. Depending on how often an item is used and the available space to display command bar objects, Excel may hide the control. In this scenario, the Visible property of the CommandBarControl object will be true whereas the IsPriorityDropped property will be false.

In the next chapter, you'll learn how to develop user forms. Developing user forms can be challenging and exciting. User forms can be challenging to develop because you need to handle many event procedures, and often the process of handling one event causes another event to occur. You need to code appropriately to handle the cascade of events. User forms are often exciting to develop because they often add a bit of "WOW!" factor to your application.

Chapter 20

User Form Construction

WHEN I FIRST STARTED learning how to program, I remember thinking that after I learned how to develop user forms or dialog boxes, I had really arrived. My experience may have been unique, but looking back, I definitely put too much emphasis on learning how to develop user forms at the expense of learning more important programming concepts such as developing classes and learning how to interact with databases. Why did I place so much emphasis on learning how to develop user forms? Because users forms are exciting, tangible (as tangible as software can be anyway) proof that you know how to program.

User forms serve a useful role in many Excel applications and can add a sense of professionalism to your application. User forms offer many opportunities to enhance the user experience. As you may have gathered from the opening paragraph, however, you need to be careful not to overemphasize your user form development skills because there is a lot more to programming than developing user forms.

User Form Development Features

Before I get to the actual mechanics of developing user forms, I need to point out the Visual Basic Editor (VBE) features aimed at user form development. In order to see these features, you need to insert an empty user form into a project (Insert ➤ UserForm). Figure 20.1 shows an example of the VBE after an empty user form has been inserted.

If the Properties window is not visible, you will definitely want to show it by pressing F4 (or View ➤ Properties Window). The Properties window assumes a much greater level of importance when developing user forms.

When you have a user form open in the VBE and the form window has the focus (i.e., the form window is the active window), the VBE will also display the Toolbox. The Toolbox is similar to the Control Toolbox toolbar you saw in Chapter 18 when you were developing worksheet-based user interfaces. You can add additional controls to this toolbox by right-clicking it and selecting Additional Controls. Performing this action will display an Additional Controls dialog box similar to the one shown in Figure 20.2. Check or uncheck the desired control to add or remove controls from the Toolbox.

FIGURE 20.1

An empty user form in the VBE

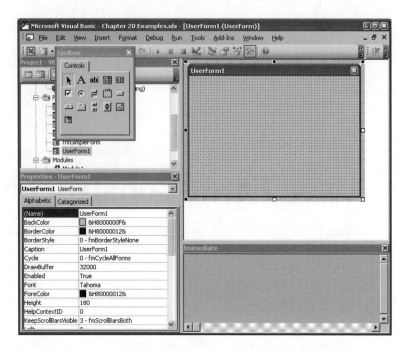

FIGURE 20.2

You can add additional controls to the Toolbox.

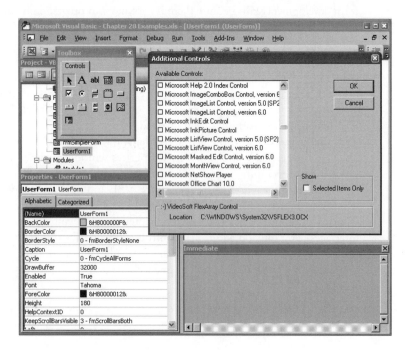

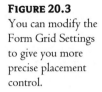

FIGURE 20.3
You can modify the Form Grid Settings to give you more precise placement control.

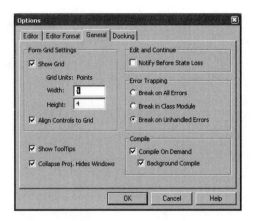

WARNING   *Your users may not have the same controls available on their computers. Some controls may require a setup program to properly install the necessary files required to use a control.*

Another VBE feature you may want to enable when working with user forms is the UserForm toolbar. The UserForm toolbar provides quick access to the functionality found under the Format menu item. In particular, this toolbar is handy when you have a number of controls on a form that you need to position precisely. This can be a huge help when your mouse isn't cooperating or you're developing a form on a laptop with a pointing stick or touch pad.

The General tab of the Options dialog box (Tools ➢ Options) contains a few settings related to user forms. An example of this tab is shown in Figure 20.3.

I like to set the width and height grid units from the default of 6 points to 4 points for more precise control placement. Additionally, I find it helpful to align controls to the grid.

NOTE   *If you are working in a team environment, it is helpful to standardize on the grid settings.*

A Simple Form Walkthrough

In order to get a feel for everything involved with developing and then using a user form, it may help to start by developing a simple form. In this section, I will walk you through the steps necessary to develop a simple form that displays the name of the active worksheet and allows you to change the name. Figure 20.4 shows an example of the desired form.

The first thing to do is insert an empty form into the desired project by selecting Insert ➢ UserForm. Using the Properties window, set the initial properties for the user form as shown in Table 20.1.

FIGURE 20.4

A simple form to re-name the active sheet

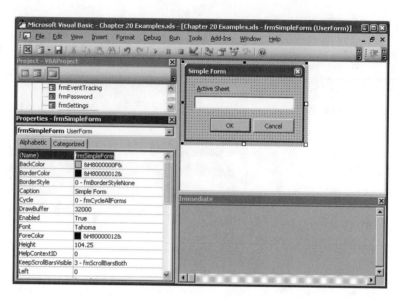

NOTE *I will not bother specifying control positional data in this chapter (top, left, height, width). These properties, through aesthetically important, do not have any affect on the functionality of the examples. For learning purposes, I wouldn't get too hung up on precise control positioning and sizing. Positioning and sizing controls to create a visually pleasing form is a subjective activity that you can spend a lot of time on. At this point, your time would be better spent learning how to use the various controls or practicing how to respond to events.*

The Name property is the name that you'll use to refer to the form programmatically, so it is helpful to name it appropriately. User forms are conventionally named using a prefix of frm. The Caption property is the text that appears in the title bar of the form when it is displayed to the user.

Next, add a label and a text box to the form. Controls are added to the form by clicking the control you'd like to add and then clicking the spot on the form that should be used as the top-left corner of the control. When you add a control in this manner, the control is placed on the form with default settings for the height and width. You can also add a control to the form by clicking the control you'd like to add and then clicking the spot on the form that should be used as the one of the control's corners. While holding the left-mouse button down, you can indicate the desired size of the control by moving the mouse to the opposite corner and then releasing the left-mouse button.

TABLE 20.1: USERFORM PROPERTIES

PROPERTY	VALUE
(Name)	frmSimpleForm
Caption	Simple Form

Set the label and text box properties as indicated in Table 20.2. You can direct which control's properties show up in the Properties window either by selecting the control on the form or by choosing it from the drop-down list at the top of the Properties window.

TABLE 20.2: Label and TextBox Properties for the Simple Form

CONTROL	PROPERTY	VALUE
Label	(Name)	lblActiveSheet
Label	Accelerator	A
Label	Caption	Active Sheet
TextBox	(Name)	txtActiveSheet

You'll need two command buttons for this form: one command button to close the form while saving any changes, and another to close the form without saving any changes. Go ahead and add two command buttons to the form. Set the properties of the command buttons as shown in Table 20.3.

TABLE 20.3: Command Button Properties

CONTROL	PROPERTY	VALUE
CommandButton1	(Name)	cmdOK
CommandButton1	Caption	OK
CommandButton1	Default	True
CommandButton2	(Name)	cmdCancel
CommandButton2	Cancel	True
CommandButton2	Caption	Cancel

At this point, the form's visual structure is complete and you are almost ready to move on to the "wiring." That is, write some VBA to make it work—to give it power.

Before you begin writing the code for the form, however, it is a good idea to take your form on a little test ride to make sure everything works correctly from a visual and accessibility standpoint. To test-drive a form, press F5 or select Run ➢ Run Sub/UserForm while viewing the form in the VBE.

TIP *When test driving a form, you can close it by clicking the Close button in the top-right corner (the X in the title bar).*

Other than the visual aesthetics of the form, you should ensure that every control on the form can be accessed using the keyboard, that the tab order is logical, and that the form follows basic Windows conventions.

For example, most native Excel dialog boxes have two buttons: one labeled OK and another labeled Cancel. When you click OK, any change that you made using the dialog box is applied or saved. OK is normally the default button and responds to the Enter key. OK does not have an accelerator on the O (i.e., the O is not underlined)—instead, the Enter key is the accelerator.

When you click Cancel, the dialog box closes without making any changes. Cancel does not have an accelerator on the C—instead, Cancel is accessed from the keyboard by the Esc key.

Where applicable, your forms should use the OK and Cancel conventions exactly as they are applied in Excel. Although your users will not notice when you use this convention, I almost guarantee you'll hear about it if you do not use it or if you misapply it.

During the test drive, you should also cycle through all of the controls by pressing the Tab key. If the focus (the active control is said to have the focus) jumps around from control to control in an illogical order, be sure to go back in and set the TabIndex property of each control appropriately. The control with TabIndex = 0 will have the focus when the form is displayed. The control with Tab-Index = 1 will have the focus if you press Tab once, the control with TabIndex = 2 will get the focus if you press Tab again, and so on. Set a control's TabStop property to false if the control should not receive the focus when cycling through the controls using Tab.

Once you're satisfied that the control looks right and exhibits normal keyboard behavior, it's time to start writing the code that will bring it to life. Listing 20.1 presents all of the code necessary to implement the desired functionality. To view the code associated with a form, press F7 or select View ➢ Code while viewing the form in the VBE.

Rather than entering Listing 20.1 directly into the form's code module, you may want to experiment with generating the event procedure stubs yourself. For example, when you're viewing the form in the VBE, if you double-click the cmdOK button, you'll automatically be transported to the cmdOK click event procedure. If a click event procedure stub hasn't been generated for the button yet, the VBE will generate the stub for you.

LISTING 20.1: SIMPLE FORM, SIMPLE CODE

```vba
Option Explicit

Private Sub cmdCancel_Click()
    Unload Me
End Sub

Private Sub cmdOK_Click()
    SaveSheetName
    Unload Me
End Sub

Private Sub SaveSheetName()
    On Error Resume Next
    ActiveSheet.Name = txtActiveSheet.Text
End Sub

Private Sub UserForm_Initialize()
    txtActiveSheet.Text = ActiveSheet.Name
    ' Pre-select all of the text in the text box
    txtActiveSheet.SelStart = 0
    txtActiveSheet.SelLength = Len(txtActiveSheet.Text)
End Sub
```

There isn't much to this one, is there? Granted, this is a simple form, but usually the code in the event procedures associated with the various controls on a form is fairly compact. Every form you create will use either the Activate or Initialize event to populate its controls before the form actually gets displayed to the user. The Initialize event only occurs once in a form's lifetime; it is the first thing to happen when a form gets created. The Activate event can occur multiple times in a form's lifetime. An Activate event typically, though not necessarily, occurs just after the Initialize event. You'll see the difference between these two events later in the chapter in the section titled "The Form Lifecycle." For now, you can see that I've used the Initialize event to populate the text box with the name of the active sheet and then preselected the text in the text box. If I didn't preselect the text, the cursor would appear at the end of the text, which is not very convenient from a user's perspective.

The only other comment I have regarding this listing is that the SaveSheetName procedure is called by the cmdOK click event procedure. In order to keep it simple, I'm not bothering to check if the user actually changes the sheet name or not. I mean, what's the point? Does it make a difference if the sheet name is set to the exact same value? I think not. Also, rather than worry about validating the name entered, it is much easier to let Excel do the validating for me and just continue on my business if an error occurs. If this were a production type application, I would probably want to inspect any error that does occur so that I can notify the user why the name couldn't be changed.

Forms Are Meant to Be Shown

Of course, you can't expect your users to open the VBE, select the form they want to run, and then press F5 to run it. You need some way to allow them to see the form or show it when certain events happen. Depending on your needs, you have a few ways to go about displaying a form to a user: using the Show method, using the Load statement, or instantiating a form as an object.

Show First, Ask Questions Later

The easiest and perhaps most frequently used method is the form's Show method. The syntax of Show is

```
frm.Show [modal]
```

The modal parameter controls a key behavior of a form. A form can be modal (vbModal) or modeless (vbModeless). When a form is modal, the user must complete her interaction with the form before she can use any other aspect of Excel. Additionally, any subsequent code is not executed until the form is hidden or unloaded. When a form is modeless, any subsequent code is executed as it's encountered.

Listing 20.2 presents an example that displays the Simple form developed previously in the chapter. The SimpleFormExample shows the form twice—once as a modal form and once as a modeless form.

LISTING 20.2: USING THE SHOW METHOD TO DISPLAY A FORM

```
Sub SimpleFormExample()
    ' Show form modally
    ShowSimpleForm True

    MsgBox "OK - Same form now, but modeless.", vbOKOnly
```

```
    ' Show form modeless
    ShowSimpleForm False

    MsgBox "Exiting the SimpleFormExample procedure.", vbOKOnly
End Sub

' Display the simple form
Private Sub ShowSimpleForm(bModal As Boolean)
    If bModal Then
        frmSimpleForm.Show vbModal
    Else
        frmSimpleForm.Show vbModeless
    End If
End Sub
```

When you run the SimpleFormExample, notice that you don't get the first message box until after you dismiss the form the first time. The second message box, however, is displayed immediately after the form is displayed the second time—before you even get a chance to dismiss the form. As you run this example, it would also be beneficial to try and interact with Excel as each form is displayed so that you can experience the full difference between these two behaviors.

Switching from modal to modeless or vice versa often causes trouble because it affects how your code executes and thus will violate the implicit assumptions you made regarding the execution of your code when you originally coded it. Therefore, you should choose wisely the first time. In fact, the Simple form demonstrates the impact of this. Simple form was developed in a manner that assumed the form would be modal. Consequently, Simple form works by modifying the name of the active sheet. When you run Simple form as a modeless form, it is possible to change worksheets while the form is still open. If you change the name of the sheet and then change worksheets before clicking OK, Simple form changes the name of the currently active sheet rather than the sheet that was active when Simple form was originally displayed.

Load and Show

Although most of the time you will simply use the Show method to display forms, occasionally you'll need a way to manipulate the form prior to displaying it to the user. In order to achieve this, you need to use the Load statement to load the form into memory. Once the form is loaded into memory (but not displayed to the user), you can interact with the form programmatically prior to displaying the form using the Show method as before. Load gives you a lot more flexibility than just using Show alone. In fact, when you use Show without using Load, Show calls Load internally for you. Listing 20.3 presents an example that demonstrates this method.

LISTING 20.3: LOADING A FORM INTO MEMORY PRIOR TO DISPLAYING IT

```
' Modify the simple form before showing it
Sub ModifySimpleForm()
    Dim sNewCaption As String

    ' Load the form into memory
```

```
    Load frmSimpleForm

    ' Prompt for a new caption
    sNewCaption = InputBox("Enter a caption for the form.")

    ' Set the new caption
    frmSimpleForm.Caption = sNewCaption

    ' Show the form
    frmSimpleForm.Show

    ' Show another instance of the form
    MsgBox "OK - same form again except with default caption", vbOKOnly
    frmSimpleForm.Show
End Sub
```

In addition to demonstrating how to use the Load then Show method of displaying a form, this listing also helps illuminate another facet of using forms. As you'll see in the following section, a form is really a fancy class module that knows how to display user interface controls. Because of this, when you modify the Caption property for one instance of the form, you do not affect any other form instances. This fact is illustrated in this listing when the last statement shows a (second) instance of the Simple form by displaying a new form using the Show method.

Classy Forms

So far, you have seen that using the Load then Show method for displaying a form offers more flexibility than using Show alone. You can wring even more flexibility out of your forms by designing them and using them in the same manner that you would design and use any other class module. As I mentioned earlier, a form module is really a special kind of class module. You can use your forms exactly as you would any other class. In order to take advantage of this fact, you should design your forms appropriately.

The Simple form you developed earlier suffers from one flaw that limits its flexibility. In Listing 20.1, you can see that both the cmdOK_Click and cmdCancel_Click procedures contain one fatal (literally) statement—Unload Me. Unload is a VBA statement that unloads an object from memory, whereas Me is a way to get an object to refer to itself. In order to have the ultimate amount of flexibility, you should place the responsibility of destroying a form with the code that instantiates it.

NOTE *Although it is good practice to explicitly dereference objects when you're done using them, VBA automatically dereferences objects that fall out of scope. For example, an object that is declared local to a procedure is automatically dereferenced sometime after the procedure finishes executing.*

Though traditionally the former two methods for displaying a form are taught, this method isn't that radical of an idea. With any other object that you use, either objects that you develop or native objects from the Excel object model, if you instantiate an object, then it's yours to use until you dereference it by setting it to Nothing. Objects rarely decide to unload themselves (though VBA may unload them once it deems that they are no longer being used).

FIGURE 20.5

The Classy form

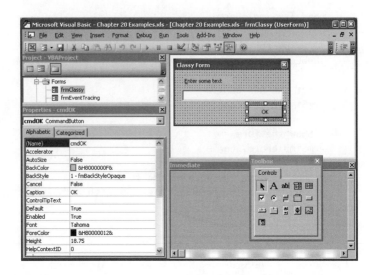

That being said, you could argue that the two methods for displaying forms that I've already presented are unorthodox; I wouldn't disagree. Anyway, perhaps a quick example would clear all of this up for you. In order to demonstrate this concept, I developed the Classy form shown in Figure 20.5.

All Classy does is allow you to enter some text in a text box and click OK. Pretty boring, eh? Table 20.4 provides the control properties that I modified when creating Classy.

TABLE 20.4: CLASSY CONTROL PROPERTY VALUES

CONTROL	PROPERTY	VALUE
Lable1	(Name)	lblStuff
Label1	Accelerator	E
TextBox1	(Name)	txtStuff
CommandButton1	(Name)	cmdOK
CommandButton1	Caption	OK
CommandButton1	Default	True

In order to make this form work, I only needed to code one event procedure, as shown in Listing 20.4.

LISTING 20.4: CLASSY'S CODE

```
Option Explicit

Private Sub cmdOK_Click()
    Me.Hide
End Sub
```

With those few lines of code, I have finished a form that is fundamentally different from the previous form. In the previous form, the Simple form unloaded itself when you clicked OK. Classy, on the other hand, just hides itself. As a result, the form is still accessible in memory even though the user can't see it. Listing 20.5 provides an example of how to use such a form.

LISTING 20.5: A CLASSY EXAMPLE

```
Sub ClassyFormExample()
    Dim frm As frmClassy
    Dim vResponse As Variant

    ' Instantiate frmClassy
    ' This has the same effect as: Load frmClassy
    Set frm = New frmClassy

    ' Prefill the edit box with a value (just for fun)
    frm.txtStuff = "Good Stuff"
    frm.Show

    ' Form is now hidden, but you can still manipulate it
    vResponse = MsgBox("The Classy form text box says: " & _
        frm.txtStuff & ". View again?", vbYesNo)

    If vResponse = vbYes Then
        ' The form is still alive - show it
        ' See - txtStuff has the same value as before
        frm.Show
    End If

    ' RIP o Classy one
    Set frm = Nothing
End Sub
```

Doesn't this kind of coding style look familiar? This is the same way you'd go about using an object. In the first declaration statement, I declare a variable named frm that is typed as an frmClassy object. Two statements later, I create a new instance of an frmClassy. This statement performs the exact same process you'd get if you used the Load statement. As you saw in the Load and Show example (Listing 20.3), once you create a new instance of the form, you can set various form property values programmatically. Once you click OK after displaying Classy, Classy is hidden by the cmdClick event procedure. If you click Yes in response to the message box, Classy is seemingly revived from the dead—complete with all of its values as you left them before you clicked OK. Finally, the next to last statement unloads Classy from memory by setting the variable used to point to the form to Nothing.

As another example, consider Listing 20.6. This listing creates two separate instances of Classy.

LISTING 20.6: MULTIPLE INSTANCES OF THE CLASSY FORM

```
Sub ClassyFormExample2()
    Dim frm1 As frmClassy
    Dim frm2 As frmClassy

    Set frm1 = New frmClassy
    Set frm2 = New frmClassy

    frm1.Caption = "I am Classy"
    frm1.Show
    frm2.Caption = "I am Classy too."
    frm2.txtStuff = "I am Classy said '" & frm1.txtStuff & "'"
    frm2.Show

    Set frm1 = Nothing
    Set frm2 = Nothing
End Sub
```

This listing helps drive home the point that forms are classes and can be used as such, particularly when you don't destroy the form from within by embedding the Unload statement in one of the form's event procedures. Listing 20.6 creates two instances of frmClassy. After you close the first instance, the second instance reads what you entered in the first instance and tells you what you said.

The Form Lifecycle

As I mentioned earlier, you use one of two form event procedures to perform form initialization chores: either Activate or Initialize. The Initialize event occurs in response to the form being loaded into memory, whereas the Activate event occurs in response to the form being shown. That is why Initialize always runs once and only once for a given form instance whereas Activate may occur multiple times. Depending on which of the methods you use to display the form, the implications of choosing Activate and Initialize can yield drastically different results.

Choosing the proper event to respond to doesn't stop with the choice between using Activate or Initialize. Nearly every control you add to a form requires you to handle one or more of its events in order to provide any useful functionality. Many times you will identify more than one event for a particular control that may serve as a trigger to run code that implements some sort of behavior. In order to make an informed decision as to which event procedure to use, I often find it helpful to trace the events that occur in a form during the development process. You can trace events by including a simple statement in each event procedure of interest that either displays a message box, writes a message to the Immediate window using Debug.Print, or records each event on a worksheet in your workbook. Figure 20.6 shows an example of a form that traces events by writing events of interest to a worksheet.

FIGURE 20.6
The Event Tracing form in action

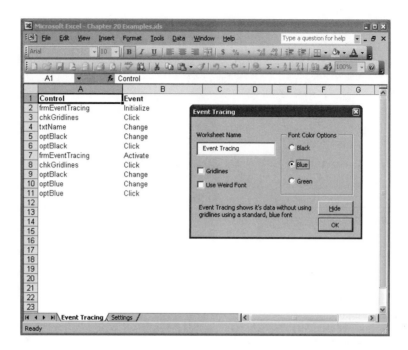

In order to have plenty of events to play with, the form has controls on it that implement random functionality that changes the appearance of a worksheet with a *code* name of wsEventTracing. You can set the code name of a worksheet in the VBE by selecting the worksheet that you want to rename under the Microsoft Excel Objects item in the Project Explorer window and changing the Name property in the Properties window. As you can see in Figure 20.6, I placed the text "Control" and "Event" in cells A1 and B1 respectively. Table 20.5 lists the properties I modified as I added controls to the Event Tracing form.

TABLE 20.5: EVENT TRACING CONTROL PROPERTIES

CONTROL	PROPERTY	VALUE
UserForm	(Name)	frmEventTracing
frmEventTracing	Caption	Event Tracing
Label	(Name)	lblWorksheetName
lblWorksheetName	Caption	Worksheet Name
TextBox	(Name)	txtName
CheckBox	(Name)	chkGridlines
chkGridlines	Caption	Gridlines
CheckBox	(Name)	chkWeirdFont

TABLE 20.5: EVENT TRACING CONTROL PROPERTIES *(continued)*

CONTROL	PROPERTY	VALUE
chkWeirdFont	Caption	Use Weird Font
Frame	(Name)	frmOptions
frmOptions	Caption	Font Color Options
OptionButton	(Name)	optBlack
optBlack	Caption	Black
OptionButton	(Name)	optBlue
optBlue	Caption	Blue
OptionButton	(Name)	optGreen
optGreen	Caption	Green
CommandButton	(Name)	cmdHide
cmdHide	Accelerator	H
cmdHide	Caption	Hide
CommandButton	(Name)	cmdOK
cmdOK	Caption	OK
cmdOK	Default	True
Label	(Name)	lblSummary

Listing 20.7 contains the code necessary to implement the functionality of the Event Tracing form.

LISTING 20.7: TRACING FORM EVENTS

```
Option Explicit

Dim mws As Worksheet
Dim msColor As String

Private Sub chkGridlines_Click()
    RecordEvent chkGridlines.Name, "Click"
    ActiveWindow.DisplayGridlines = chkGridlines.Value
    SetSummary
End Sub

Private Sub chkWeirdFont_Click()

    ' It is possible that the font "Bradley Hand ITC"
```

```vb
    ' may not be present on every PC
    On Error Resume Next

    RecordEvent chkWeirdFont.Name, "Click"

    If chkWeirdFont.Value Then
        mws.Cells.Font.Name = "Bradley Hand ITC"
    Else
        mws.Cells.Font.Name = "Arial"
    End If
    SetSummary
End Sub

Private Sub cmdHide_Click()
    RecordEvent cmdHide.Name, "Click"
    Me.Hide
    ' Pause for a brief period and
    ' then reshow the form
    Application.Wait Now + 0.00003
    Me.Show
End Sub

Private Sub cmdOK_Click()
    RecordEvent cmdOK.Name, "Click"
    Unload Me
End Sub

Private Function RecordEvent(sControl As String, sEvent As String)
    Dim rg As Range

    Set rg = mws.Cells(65536, 1).End(xlUp).Offset(1, 0)
    rg.Value = sControl
    rg.Offset(0, 1).Value = sEvent
    Set rg = Nothing
End Function

Private Sub frmOptions_Click()
    RecordEvent frmOptions.Name, "Click"
End Sub

Private Sub optBlack_Change()
    RecordEvent optBlack.Name, "Change"
End Sub

Private Sub optBlack_Click()
    RecordEvent optBlack.Name, "Click"
    msColor = "black"
    mws.Cells.Font.Color = vbBlack
```

```vba
        SetSummary
End Sub

Private Sub optBlue_Change()
    RecordEvent optBlue.Name, "Change"
End Sub

Private Sub optBlue_Click()
    RecordEvent optBlue.Name, "Click"
    msColor = "blue"
    mws.Cells.Font.Color = vbBlue
    SetSummary
End Sub

Private Sub optGreen_Change()
    RecordEvent optGreen.Name, "Change"
End Sub

Private Sub optGreen_Click()
    RecordEvent optGreen.Name, "Click"
    msColor = "green"
    mws.Cells.Font.Color = vbGreen
    SetSummary
End Sub

Private Sub txtName_AfterUpdate()
    RecordEvent txtName.Name, "AfterUpdate"
    mws.Name = txtName.Value
    SetSummary
End Sub

Private Sub txtName_Change()
    On Error Resume Next
    RecordEvent txtName.Name, "Change"
End Sub

Private Sub UserForm_Activate()
    RecordEvent Me.Name, "Activate"
End Sub

Private Sub UserForm_Deactivate()
    RecordEvent Me.Name, "Deactivate"
End Sub

Private Sub UserForm_Initialize()
    On Error GoTo ErrHandler

    ' Refer via worksheet code name
```

```vba
    ' since this form can change the display name
    Set mws = wsEventTracing

    RecordEvent Me.Name, "Initialize"
    ' Activate the worksheet so you
    ' can watch the events occur
    mws.Activate

    ' Initialize controls on the form
    chkGridlines.Value = ActiveWindow.DisplayGridlines
    txtName.Text = mws.Name
    If mws.Cells.Font.Name <> "Bradley Hand ITC" Then
        chkWeirdFont.Value = False
    Else
        chkWeirdFont.Value = True
    End If
    InitializeBackgroundOptions
    SetSummary

    Exit Sub
ErrHandler:
    Debug.Print "UserForm_Initialize: " & Err.Description
    Unload Me
End Sub

Private Sub UserForm_Terminate()
    RecordEvent Me.Name, "Terminate"
End Sub

Private Sub InitializeBackgroundOptions()
    Select Case mws.Cells.Font.Color
        Case Is = vbBlack
            optBlack.Value = True
            msColor = "black"
        Case Is = vbBlue
            optBlue.Value = True
            msColor = "blue"
        Case Is = vbGreen
            optGreen.Value = True
            msColor = "green"
        Case Else
            mws.Cells.Interior.Color = vbBlack
            optBlack.Value = True
    End Select
End Sub

Private Sub SetSummary()
    Dim sGridlines As String
```

```
        Dim sColor As String
        Dim sFont As String

        If chkWeirdFont.Value Then
            sFont = "weird"
        Else
            sFont = "standard"
        End If

        If chkGridlines.Value Then
            sGridlines = "using gridlines"
        Else
            sGridlines = "without using gridlines"
        End If

        lblSummary.Caption = mws.Name & " shows its data " & _
            sGridlines & " using a " & sFont & ", " & _
            msColor & " font "
    End Sub
```

Don't let the length of Listing 20.7 intimidate you, it's really a simple form. Most of the code consists of many small event procedures containing a handful of statements at most. The UserForm_Initialize procedure has three main tasks as it prepares the form to be displayed: set a module-level reference to the worksheet of interest, record the event, and set the controls on the form with appropriate values.

Because the Event Tracing form has functionality to record events and change the appearance of the worksheet it is logging events to, I declared a module-level variable named mws to hold a reference to the worksheet. Because one of the things the Event Tracing form can do is rename the worksheet it operates on, it is easier to refer to the worksheet using its code name, which is presumably a rather static value. You can use a worksheet's code name directly in your code without having to access through the Worksheets collection associated with a workbook. Rather than performing validation on the worksheet code name prior to using it, I simply enabled error handling for this procedure.

Every event procedure in the listing includes a call to the RecordEvent procedure, and UserForm_Initialize is no different. The RecordEvent procedure just writes the control name and event name associated with an event procedure to the worksheet used to trace events.

The final task that the UserForm_Initialize procedure must perform is initializing the controls on the form with default values. The process of initializing controls in this manner is a task common to nearly every form you'll develop.

Notice the cmdHide_Click event procedure. This event just hides the form briefly before redisplaying it. I included this functionality in order to help demonstrate the difference between the Initialize event and the Activate event. As you experiment with this form, notice that the Activate event, but not the Initialize event, is triggered after the form is hidden and then redisplayed. Also, notice that when you first run the form, a number of events occur between the Initialize event and the Activate event. Figure 20.7 shows an example of the events that occur after clicking Hide.

FIGURE 20.7

Event Tracing example after clicking Hide

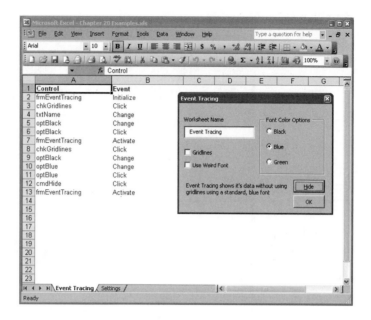

Before moving on to the next section, I would encourage you to play with the Event Tracing form for awhile, including calling the RecordEvent procedure from other event procedures that I haven't shown here. This is beneficial practice because it helps illustrate the flow of events that occurs as a user interacts with a form.

User Friendly Settings

In Chapter 12, I presented two classes useful for storing useful bits of information on a worksheet: the Setting and Settings classes. As I have used these classes and their predecessors over the past few years, I have frequently needed to provide an easy way for users to modify certain settings. In order to provide this functionality, I developed the user form shown in Figure 20.8. Let me now explain how this works.

Because this form is for managing settings, before you begin, you might want to make sure you have all the required pieces in place. In particular, you need the Setting (Listing 12.1) and Settings (Listing 12.2) classes I presented in Chapter 12. These classes also require the Settings worksheet (Figure 12.2). All of these pieces need to be in the same project or workbook.

Once you have finished all the prerequisites, go ahead and insert a UserForm into the project. Table 20.6 lists the pertinent properties you'll need to set for each control on the form. Because so many more controls exist on this form than the previous forms in this chapter, I listed them a little differently in Table 20.6. The first time a control is referenced in the table, I list the name given to the control. All following references to the control use the control's name. Also, because a screen shot doesn't provide you with much perspective regarding the size of the form, I listed the form's height and width. As before, however, I'll leave the positional properties on all of the form's controls to your own visual preferences.

FIGURE 20.8

A user-friendly form for managing settings

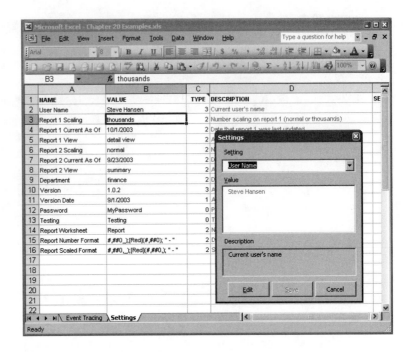

TABLE 20.6: SETTINGS FORM CONTROL PROPERTIES

CONTROL	PROPERTY	VALUE
UserForm	(Name)	frmSettings
frmSettings	Caption	Settings
frmSettings	Height	232.5
frmSettings	Width	204
Label	(Name)	lblSetting
lblSetting	Accelerator	t
lblSetting	Caption	Setting
ComboBox	(Name)	cboSetting
cboSetting	TabIndex	0
Label	(Name)	lblValue
lblValue	Accelerator	V
lblValue	Caption	Value

TABLE 20.6: SETTINGS FORM CONTROL PROPERTIES *(continued)*

CONTROL	PROPERTY	VALUE
TextBox	(Name)	txtValue
txtValue	TabIndex	2
Label	(Name)	lblDescription
lblDescription	Caption	Description
TextBox	(Name)	txtDescription
txtDescription	BackColor	&H8000000F&
CommandButton	(Name)	cmdEdit
cmdEdit	Accelerator	E
cmdEdit	Caption	Edit
cmdEdit	TabIndex	1
cmdEdit	TakeFocusOnClick	False
CommandButton	(Name)	cmdSave
cmdSave	Accelerator	S
cmdSave	Caption	Save
cmdSave	TabIndex	3
cmdSave	TakeFocusOnClick	False
CommandButton	(Name)	cmdCancel
cmdCancel	Cancel	True
cmdCancel	Caption	Cancel
cmdCancel	TabIndex	4
cmdCancel	TakeFocusOnClick	False

Once you have the visual aspect of the form complete, it's time to add the code (Listing 20.8) to implement the desired functionality. There is a lot to discuss regarding this listing. As you browse over the listing for the first time, you may notice a reference to another form named frmPassword. frmPassword is a simple form I'll present after this listing (see the section titled "Primitive Password Collection") that collects a password from the user when required. If you recall, the Setting class implements a SettingType property. One type of setting allows users to modify the setting's value only if they provide a valid password. This is why you need a way to allow the user to enter a password.

LISTING 20.8: MANAGING THE SETTINGS FORM

```
Option Explicit

Dim moSetting As Setting
Dim moSettings As Settings

Private Sub cboSetting_Change()
    ' Get indicated setting and update
    ' controls appropriately
    RefreshControls
End Sub

Private Sub cmdCancel_Click()
    Unload Me
End Sub

Private Sub cmdEdit_Click()
    Dim sPassword As String

    If Not moSetting Is Nothing Then

        ' For setReadProtectedWrite, you need to call
        ' ChangeEditMode using the Password parameter
        If moSetting.SettingType = setReadProtectedWrite Then

            ' Have the user fill in their password
            frmPassword.Show
            sPassword = frmPassword.Password
            Unload frmPassword

            ' Make sure they entered a password
            If frmPassword.Tag = cStr(vbCancel) Then Exit Sub

            ' Try and change the edit mode
            If moSetting.ChangeEditMode(True, sPassword) Then
                txtValue.Enabled = True
            Else
                txtValue.Enabled = False
                MsgBox "Invalid password", vbOKOnly
            End If

        Else

            ' Don't need a password for unrestricted
            ' read/write settings.
            moSetting.ChangeEditMode True
```

```vb
            txtValue.Enabled = True
        End If

    End If
End Sub

Private Sub cmdSave_Click()
    If Not moSetting Is Nothing Then
        moSetting.Value = txtValue.Text

        ' Turn off editing ability
        moSetting.ChangeEditMode False
        cmdSave.Enabled = False
        txtValue.Enabled = False
    End If
End Sub

Private Sub txtValue_Change()
    cmdSave.Enabled = True
End Sub

Private Sub UserForm_Initialize()
    Set moSettings = New Settings
    cmdSave.Enabled = False

    ' Load cboSetting with settings
    LoadSettings

    ' Default to first setting in list
    If cboSetting.ListCount > 0 Then
        cboSetting.ListIndex = 0
    End If
End Sub

Private Sub LoadSettings()
    Dim lRow As Long
    Dim oSetting As Setting
    Dim nSettingCount As Integer
    Dim nSetting As Integer

    nSettingCount = moSettings.Count

    ' Exit if there aren't any settings
    If nSettingCount = 0 Then Exit Sub

    For nSetting = 1 To nSettingCount
        ' Get setting
        Set oSetting = moSettings.Item(nSetting)
```

```
                    ' Add all settings EXCEPT private settings
                    If oSetting.SettingType <> setPrivate Then
                        cboSetting.AddItem oSetting.Name
                    End If
            Next

            Set oSetting = Nothing
        End Sub

        Private Sub RefreshControls()
            Dim sSetting As String
            Dim sValue As String
            Dim sComment As String

            Set moSetting = moSettings.Item(cboSetting.Value)

            If Not moSetting Is Nothing Then
                ' Disable edit ability for read-only settings
                If moSetting.SettingType = setReadOnly Then
                    cmdEdit.Enabled = False
                Else
                    ' Enable edit ability for other settings
                    cmdEdit.Enabled = True
                End If

                txtValue.Text = moSetting.Value
                txtDescription.Text = moSetting.Description
            End If

            txtValue.Enabled = False
            cmdSave.Enabled = False
        End Sub
```

Maybe a good way to kick off the discussion of this listing is to present a table (Table 20.7) that lists all of the procedures in this listing along with a short description of what each does.

TABLE 20.7: PROCEDURES REQUIRED BY THE SETTINGS FORM

PROCEDURE	DESCRIPTION
cboSetting_Change	An event procedure that calls the RefeshControls procedure
cmdCancel_Click	An event procedure that closes the form and unloads it from memory
cmdEdit_Click	An event procedure that puts the current setting in Edit mode
cmdSave_Click	An event procedure that updates the current setting with the value found in txtValue

TABLE 20.7: PROCEDURES REQUIRED BY THE SETTINGS FORM *(continued)*

PROCEDURE	DESCRIPTION
LoadSettings	Loads cboSetting with settings retrieved from a Settings object
RefreshControls	Updates txtDescription and txtValue with the appropriate values as different settings are selected in cboSetting
txtValue_Change	An event procedure that enables cmdSave so that the user can save the change
UserForm_Initialize	A form event procedure that initializes the form by calling LoadSettings

Notice that the Settings form uses two module level variables: moSettings and moSetting. moSettings is a Settings object used to load the combo box and to provide quick and easy access to individual Setting objects. moSettings is set by the UserForm_Initialize procedure. Once moSettings is initialized, it is held in memory and not changed until the form is unloaded. moSetting is a Setting object representing the current setting being displayed by the form. moSetting is set by the Refresh-Controls procedure. Because RefreshControls is executed any time a new selection is made in the combo box, moSetting is frequently reset to a new setting.

The LoadSettings procedure is in charge of populating the combo box (cboSetting) with a list of settings. In order to do this, LoadSettings obtains a count of the settings contained in moSettings and then loops through the individual settings, retrieving each item by index number. In order to deal with one of the clunkiest (programmer slang for unorthodox) features of the Setting class, LoadSettings observes the SettingType property to see if it is a private setting or not. Private settings are settings that should never be displayed to the user. This feature is clunky because ideally the Setting class should implement its features in a way that either simplifies or eliminates the need for consumers of the class to perform this check.

After the UserForm_Initialize procedure executes LoadSettings, it then makes sure at least one setting exists before instructing cboSetting to display the first item in its list using the ListIndex property of the combo box. Changing a combo box's ListIndex programmatically triggers a Change event on the combo box—in this case it triggers the cboSetting_Change procedure, which in turn calls the RefreshControls procedure.

The first thing RefreshControls needs to do is retrieve the Setting object specified by cboSetting. After retrieving the Setting into the module-level variable moSetting, I added a check to validate that the setting was retrieved. If the Settings class has any problems retrieving a particular setting it will return Nothing.

The next order of business is to decide whether to enable the Edit button or not. Because the Load-Settings procedure eliminated the possibility of listing any private settings, the only kind of setting that can never be edited is a read-only setting. Therefore, if the current setting is read-only, the Edit button should be disabled. Any other type of setting can be edited. After making this determination, it is simple to make sure the appropriate text is displayed in the Value and Description text boxes. The final task in this procedure is to make sure that the Value text box and Save button controls are disabled.

At this point, you could add an Unload Me statement to the Close button click event and have a useful form for displaying setting information. The rest of the functionality is all related to enabling the ability to edit the values associated with individual settings. I chose to embed an Unload Me statement into this form rather than use Me.Hide as I did in the Classy Forms section. The reason is that

I couldn't think of any reason why I would ever have a need for this form to hang around in memory after the user dismisses it. This form is displayed, performs a useful purpose, and once dismissed, has no residual value. Further, it can be displayed instantly, so there is no performance benefit for just hiding it in case the user wants to display it later. In some instances, if it takes awhile to display a form, it may be advantageous to hide the form after its first use and then redisplay it (rather than recreate it) if it's needed later.

If you recall, the Setting object requires you to put the Setting in edit mode prior to making any changes to the Value property. The Setting object has a ChangeEditMode method that has a Boolean parameter that indicates whether edit mode should be on (AllowEditing = True) or off, and it has an optional Password parameter that is applicable if the SettingType is setReadProtectedWrite. Inside the cmdEdit_Click event procedure, you need to check the SettingType to see if you need to collect a password or not. You can use the Password form presented in the next section to collect a password if one is required. If a password is not required, then all you need to do is call ChangeEditMode and set the Enabled property of txtValue to true.

Once the form is in edit mode, it isn't really necessary to enable the Save button unless a change is made to the value. In order to determine when a change is made, I use the Change event of txtValue. Once the Save button is enabled, if the user clicks it, all you need to do is set the current setting's (represented by moSetting) Value property equal to the Value property of txtValue.

Figure 20.9 shows another picture of the Settings form. In this screenshot, I have already clicked the Edit button and have changed the setting value shown in Figure 20.8.

FIGURE 20.9

Editing a setting value with the Settings form

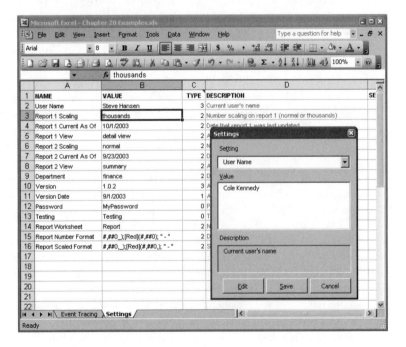

Primitive Password Collection

As discussed in the previous section, the Settings form needs a way to allow a user to enter a password in order to modify the value associated with a Setting object of type setReadProtectedWrite. In order to do this, you need to develop a simple form that the Settings form can display when it determines that a password is required. A picture of the Password form is shown in the following picture.

Table 20.8 lists the various control properties that I modified in the process of creating the Password form.

TABLE 20.8: PASSWORD FORM CONTROL PROPERTIES

CONTROL	PROPERTY	VALUE
UserForm	(Name)	frmPassword
frmPassword	Caption	Enter Password
Label	(Name)	lblPassword
lblPassword	Accelerator	P
lblPassword	Caption	Password:
TextBox	(Name)	txtPassword
txtPassword	PasswordChar	*
CommandButton	(Name)	cmdOK
cmdOK	Caption	OK
cmdOK	Default	True
CommandButton	(Name)	cmdCancel
cmdCancel	Cancel	True
cmdCancel	Caption	Cancel

The Password form is a good example of a form that needs to be hidden when the user clicks OK or Cancel rather than unloaded. If you unload this form from within rather than hide it, you won't have a convenient way to tell the procedure that calls the form what password the user enters. Listing 20.9 presents the code required by the Password form.

LISTING 20.9: EVENT PROCEDURES FOR THE PASSWORD FORM

```
Option Explicit

Dim msPassword As String

Public Property Get Password() As Variant
    Password = msPassword
End Property

Private Sub cmdCancel_Click()
    msPassword = CStr(vbCancel)
    ' Tag form to indicate how the form was dispatched
    Me.Tag = vbCancel
    Me.Hide
End Sub

Private Sub cmdOK_Click()
    msPassword = txtPassword.Text
    ' Tag form to indicate how the form was dispatched
    Me.Tag = vbOK
    Me.Hide
End Sub

Private Sub UserForm_Initialize()
    txtPassword.SetFocus
End Sub
```

As another example of how you can approach a form module exactly as you would a class module, notice how I added a Property Get procedure to implement the Password as a property of the form. This makes retrieving the password a more natural process than it is when the Password is retrieved directly from txtPassword. In Listing 20.10, I've highlighted this difference by showing two alternative ways to retrieve the password.

LISTING 20.10:RETRIEVING THE PASSWORD FROM THE PASSWORD FORM

```
Sub DemonstratePassword()
    ' Example 1: Retrieve password by inspecting txtPassword.Value
    frmPassword.Show
    If frmPassword.Tag <> vbCancel Then
        MsgBox "You entered: " & _
            frmPassword.txtPassword.Value, vbOKOnly
    Else
        MsgBox "You clicked Cancel.", vbOKOnly
    End If
```

```
    ' Unload form from memory
    Unload frmPassword

    ' Example 2: Retrieve password as a property of the form
    frmPassword.Show
    If frmPassword.Tag <> vbCancel Then
        MsgBox "You entered: " & _
            frmPassword.Password, vbOKOnly
    Else
        MsgBox "You clicked Cancel.", vbOKOnly
    End If
    ' Unload form from memory
    Unload frmPassword
End Sub
```

Listing 20.10 presents a subtle difference because this example only interacts with the value associated with one control. Because you need to programmatically interact with more controls on a form, this difference becomes even more noticeable. Listing 20.10 also helps illustrate the use of the Tag property. Many controls that you use on a form as well as UserForms themselves implement a Tag property. One common use of the Tag property is to indicate how the user dispatches a form. In this example, if the user dispatched the form by clicking the Cancel button, the password (or lack thereof) is irrelevant. Therefore, it is important that the procedure that displays the Password form has a way of knowing how the user closed the form so that it can act accordingly.

Summary

For those instances in which you need to provide custom functionality that cannot be presented using Excel's normal user interface, you need to develop a user form. To develop a user form, you add a UserForm module to your project. A UserForm module is a special kind of module in the VBE that allows you to visually develop a user form or dialog box. To develop the visual aspects of a form, you drag and drop controls found on the Toolbox (View ➤ Toolbox) on to your user form. From there, you can select each control on the form and modify its Properties using the Properties window (F4 or View ➤ Properties Window).

Once you have laid out the visual components of the form, you proceed to write code that implements the functionality of the form. In particular, you decide which events your form must respond to and code the appropriate event procedures. For example, when you add a command button to a form, you must write code that executes when the user clicks the button.

After you've developed a form, there are three methods by which you can use the form in other procedures. The easiest way is to use the Show method of the form. The next easiest way is to use the Load statement along with the name of the form you want to load, manipulate the form in some way before it is displayed to the user, and then use the Show method to display the form to the user. The final method is to use the form as you would any other object. That is, declare a variable that is typed as the form you want to display, use the New keyword to create a new instance of the form, and then use the Show method to display the form to the user. To unload a form in response to a user's actions, either you can use the Unload statement along with the name of the form (or the Me keyword when used within the form itself), or you can use the Hide method followed up by the Unload statement.

The trickiest aspect of form development (other than trivial forms) is handling all of the events appropriately and dealing with the, sometimes complex, interaction that occurs as your event procedures trigger other events, which trigger other events, and so on. One thing that can help is for you to develop a better understanding of event interaction. During the development process, you can understand the sequence of events in your form by incorporating Debug.Print statements or message boxes in your event procedures that allow you to follow what is happening. Once you determine the sequence of events, you can add logic in your event procedures that determines why the event procedure occurred and selectively runs chunks of code based on how the event was triggered.

In the next chapter, you'll learn about some of the newest user interface elements that you can utilize in your project—the so-called "smart" user-interface technologies—smart tags and smart documents.

Chapter 21

One Smart Cookie: Smart Documents with Excel 2003

THE MOST CUTTING EDGE user interface concept in Microsoft Office 2003 is the concept of a smart document. Smart documents are documents that respond to a user's actions in order to provide relevant assistance to the user as he works.

I feel compelled to tell you that some readers are going to be disappointed with the information I'm about to deliver. You cannot develop smart documents using VBA. That's right—they are one of the best new features of Excel 2003 and you cannot develop solutions incorporating them with VBA alone. As a VBA developer, this disappoints me immensely. Look on the bright side, though; you can use one of VBA's relatives—either Visual Basic 6.0 or Visual Basic .NET.

Another thing that may disappoint some readers is that you'll need to be fairly proficient with XML. If you haven't had a compelling reason to do anything with XML yet and therefore haven't spent much time learning XML, this may be a good excuse to start—smart documents are that compelling.

Although much of what you've learned so far can be applied to this kind of development, it's a stretch to assume that you'll comprehend everything that I'm about to present unless you've had prior experience with VB (or VB .NET) and XML. It would take another book to present all of the necessary background. My goal, then, is to provide a general overview and example of a smart document in order to get you started in the right direction.

Smart Document Basics

A smart document is a document that is programmed to "sense" what users are doing and provide relevant help and functionality to assist the user. Smart documents can help users complete a process such as creating a budget, filling out an expense report, or using a complex financial model. Before I get into the details of actually creating a smart document, it is important that you understand just what a smart document is and how a document comes to acquire intelligence.

Being Smart Has Benefits

A smart document delivers its "smarts" via the task pane. The task pane is the multitalented window fragment that appears when you initially start Excel. To display the task pane, press Ctrl + F1 (or View ➤ Task Pane). I call the task pane multitalented because, as you can see in Figure 21.1, it can perform many functions. The task pane refers to the functionality related to smart documents as Document Actions.

Let's start with an example of what a smart document can do. Say you like the loan amortization template provided with Excel but would like to have it provide more guidance to a user as she fills it out. An instance of the original loan template is shown in Figure 21.2.

NOTE   You can create a loan amortization worksheet by using the Loan Amortization template located on the Spreadsheet Solutions tab of the templates dialog box. Select File ➤ New and then click On My Computer underneath the Templates section on the task pane.

Now, the original loan amortization worksheet isn't that difficult to figure out. After a few moments, it is apparent that in order to use the worksheet you need to enter the values in the range D6:D11. By adding smart document functionality, however, you can provide useful information to the user when she opens up the document and as she moves from item to item. You can even allow the user to enter values directly in the task pane and then transfer them to the appropriate section of the worksheet. Figure 21.3 shows and example of a smarter loan amortization worksheet.

FIGURE 21.1

The Task Pane performs many functions besides hosting smart document functionality.

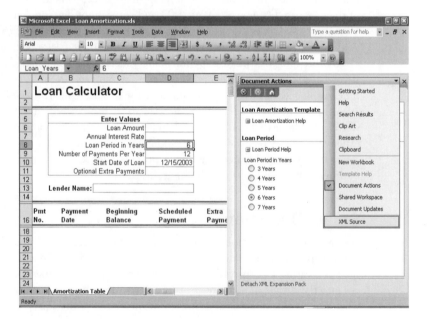

FIGURE 21.2

A basic loan amortization worksheet.

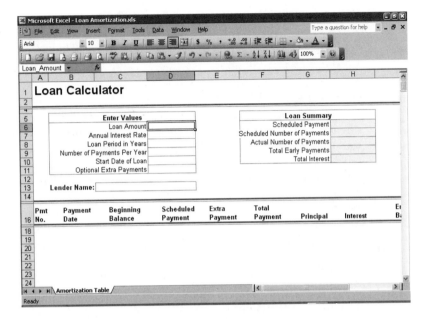

FIGURE 21.3

A smarter loan amortization worksheet

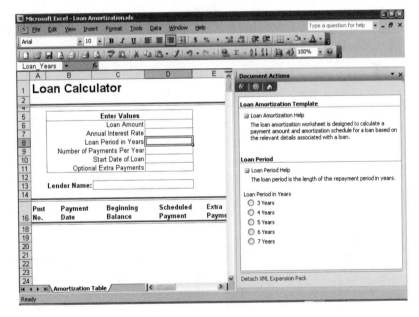

By providing task-specific guidance and functionality from a single location on the document (or screen), a smart document can tame a complex process so that a user can complete the process without any, or as much training, and without having an in-depth knowledge of the structure or layout of the underlying workbook.

A Smart Prerequisite

Not just any document can become a smart document—only documents associated with an XML schema can become enlightened. In Chapter 17, you learned how to associate an XML Map with a workbook and map individual XML elements from the map to specific locations on a worksheet. This process assumes a new level of importance as you attempt to build smart documents. The reason is that smart documents work by noticing when the user selects a cell that is mapped to an XML element.

Simplistically, when you develop the functionality to implement a smart document, you basically map functionality to the same XML elements. For example, in order to give the loan amortization worksheet smarts, you have to associate a loan schema with the workbook. Assuming the schema specifies an element named LoanAmount, when the user selects a cell that is mapped to the LoanAmount element (cell D6 in Figure 21.2), the smart document looks to see what functionality, if any, has been mapped to the LoanAmount element and instructs the task pane to configure itself accordingly.

Key Components of Smart Document

Once you've met the first prerequisite, that is, once you've mapped XML elements from an XML Map to cells on your worksheet, a document still doesn't acquire its smarts until you attach an XML expansion pack to it. An expansion pack provides Excel with a roadmap to all of the other components of the smart document. A smart document may consist of numerous files including, but not limited to, XML files and schemas, image files, HTML files, and dynamic link libraries (DLLs).

An XML expansion pack is in charge of loading all of the other components that provide smart document functionality. An XML expansion pack is implemented as an XML file that conforms to the XML Expansion Pack Manifest Schema. In technical references, the expansion pack is referred to as a manifest file or simply as the manifest.

The manifest file specifies all the components and files that are part of a smart document including the location and names of the components that Excel needs to install in order to make a smart document functional. As most smart documents are constructed using DLLs, the manifest may also provide setup-related information such as CLSIDs (a CLSID is a globally unique identifier used to identify a particular class) and whether to register COM components.

Though there can be other components of a smart document, the only other key component of a smart document is a DLL that implements the smart document functionality. You can develop this DLL using numerous programming languages such as Visual Basic (6.0 and .NET), Visual C++ (6.0 and .NET), or any of the other .NET programming languages. A smart document DLL can't be any old DLL; it must implement the ISmartDocument interface.

An interface is sort of like a class specification in that it specifies all of the properties and methods that a class must implement in order to be considered an implementation of the interface. Interfaces allow developers to specify ways in which other programmers can interact with the classes they create. For example, Microsoft developed the smart document technology in Excel and Word. The code that

Microsoft wrote to display the Document Actions task pane must make certain assumptions about the properties and methods it can call to figure out how it is supposed to display the task pane. By wrapping up these assumed properties and methods in an interface and writing their code to work only with objects that implement the interface, Microsoft has done two things. First, they have formally specified what a smart document class must look like so that we, as smart document developers, know what our class must look like. Second, by requiring smart document classes that you develop to implement an interface the code that display's the task pane can be certain of the properties and methods that your class implements.

Smart Document Security

Microsoft has been working very hard to improve the security of its products. The smart document security model reflects this effort. Smart document security occurs at two levels. First of all, Office 2003 makes sure that an XML expansion pack has been digitally signed by the developer before it is installed. Only expansion packs signed by a source you have designated as "trusted" can be loaded. Second, the individual code components that implement the smart document are also subject to security checks.

Excel will not prompt users to enable or disable the functionality of an unsigned smart document as it would an unsigned macro (assuming you have set macro security to medium). When Excel encounters an unsigned manifest file, it simply won't install and load the components necessary to make the smart document function. Excel will still load the workbook—it just won't be smart. As a consolation to losing the smarts, Excel will display the following message. Of course, if the expansion pack did indeed contain functionality of a malicious nature, this would be a good thing.

When Excel encounters signed expansion packs, one of two things happens. If the expansion pack is signed by someone that you have designated as a trusted publisher, the expansion pack installs itself. If the expansion pack is signed, but not by someone you have designated as a trusted publisher, Excel notifies you and asks you if you want to enable the macros or not.

In order to facilitate development and testing, it is possible to temporarily bypass expansion pack security by making a change to the Windows Registry.

1. Open a text editor (Notepad will work) and enter the following text in a file.

```
Windows Registry Editor Version 5.00
[HKEY_LOCAL_MACHINE\Software\Microsoft\Office\Common\Smart Tag]
"DisableManifestSecurityCheck"=dword:00000001
```

2. Save the file as DisableManifestSecurityCheck.reg.

3. Execute the file by double-clicking it in Windows Explorer.

After you disable expansion pack security in this manner, you will be presented with the following dialog box when you attempt to add an expansion pack.

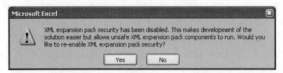

In addition to the security checks applied to the manifest file, the individual code components listed by the manifest file are also subjected to security checks. The details of the actual security check performed depend on whether the code that provides the smart functionality was developed using COM (VB 6.0 or VC++ 6.0) or using .NET. The checks on a COM-based solution are the same as Office would normally perform when installing an add-in or when a user opens a document containing a macro. For a .NET solution, the security implications become a little more complex—more complex than I plan on getting into. Therefore, if you choose to implement a .NET smart document solution, you'll want to dig into the security details outlined in the Microsoft Office 2003 Smart Document Software Development Kit (SDK). See the section titled "Smart Document Resources" near the end of this chapter for information about the Smart Document SDK.

A Smart Document Walkthrough

Because I realize that a lot of what I'm about to present requires more background than I can possibly provide, I am going to use this section to provide you with all of the steps required to make a smart loan amortization worksheet. This example uses Visual Basic 6.0. Unless you have more experience using one of the .NET programming languages or Visual C++ 6.0, I'd suggest you use VB 6.0 as your development environment because it will allow you to apply many of the skills you have learned in this book. Using VB 6.0 also simplifies things technically because it avoids the hoops you have to jump through when you are trying to integrate a COM-based architecture (Microsoft Office) with a .NET-based architecture (managed code developed using a .NET language).

This example is fairly lengthy when compared to other listings in the book. Consequently, I'm going to break it up into multiple listings so that when I point things out, you don't have to flip back so many pages to look at the code in question. Also, I'm going to present the example in multiple subsections that correspond to each component in the smart document solution. This example has four components: the loan amortization workbook, a loan amortization XML schema, a DLL containing the smart document functionality, and an XML manifest file that is used to attach the solution to the workbook.

A Not So Smart Document (with Lots of Potential)

The first place to start when developing a smart document is with the document itself. You have enough to do in this example in addition to creating a document from scratch, so I created a loan amortization workbook based on the Loan Amortization template included with Excel. To set up this workbook, follow these steps.

1. Choose File ➢ New in Excel.

2. Select the On My Computer item under the Templates section in the task pane.

3. Choose the Loan Amortization template on the Spreadsheet Solutions tab.

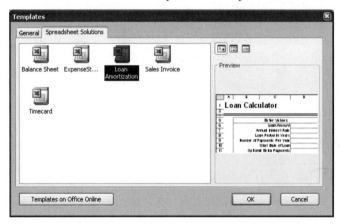

4. Click Tools ➤ Protection ➤ Unprotect Sheet.

5. Click in cell D11 and observe the note that appears. Because your smart document will be displaying this same information, you don't need a note to appear on the worksheet in such an obtrusive manner.

6. Copy cell D9 (select it and press CTRL+C) and paste it on cell D11 (select D11 and press CTRL+V).

7. Save the workbook as Loan Amortization.xls.

At this point, you have a basic Loan Amortization worksheet that works like any other worksheet. Refer back to Figure 21.2 to see an example of what the worksheet looks like.

XML Helps Make You Smart

In Chapter 17, you learned how to associate an XML schema with a workbook and then map elements from the schema to specific locations on a worksheet. This process is an essential part of developing a smart document as only worksheet cells that have been mapped to an XML element can exhibit smart functionality. As a result, you need to develop a loan amortization schema that contains elements that correspond to items of interest on the loan amortization worksheet.

Listing 21.1 presents the loan amortization schema needed for this example. You can create this schema using a text editor such as Notepad.

LISTING 21.1: A LOAN AMORTIZATION SCHEMA (LOANAMORTIZATION.XSD)

```
<xsd:schema xmlns:xsd="http://www.w3.org/2001/XMLSchema"
    xmlns="LoanAmortization"
    targetNamespace="LoanAmortization"
```

```
        elementFormDefault="qualified">

    <xsd:complexType name="LoanVariables">
       <xsd:all>
          <xsd:element name="LoanAmount" type="xsd:string" />
          <xsd:element name="AnnualInterestRate" type="xsd:string" />
          <xsd:element name="LoanPeriod" type="xsd:string" />
          <xsd:element name="PaymentsPerYear" type="xsd:string" />
          <xsd:element name="StartDate" type="xsd:string" />
          <xsd:element name="OptionalExtraPayments" type="xsd:string" />
          <xsd:element name="LenderName" type="xsd:string" />
       </xsd:all>
    </xsd:complexType>

    <xsd:element name="Loan" type="LoanVariables" />
 </xsd:schema>
```

The Loan Amortization schema is fairly simple. As you can see, all I've done is specify a complex type named LoanVariables that contains individual elements representing the various inputs to the loan amortization worksheet. Then, in the next to last line, I've specified one instance of a LoanVariables type named Loan. Pay attention to the names used in this schema because you'll need to refer to them from within the smart document code. Also, keep in mind that XML is case sensitive as you refer to the elements from various components of the smart document.

After you create the loan amortization schema, save it into the same directory that you saved the loan amortization worksheet and name the file LoanAmortization.xsd.

With the schema complete, you can go back and add this schema as an XML Map to the loan amortization workbook and then map the elements to items on the worksheet. This process is outlined in the following steps:

1. Open the Loan Amortization workbook you created earlier.

2. Select Data ➢ XML ➢ XML Source.

3. Click XML Maps on the XML Source task pane.

4. Click Add on the XML Maps dialog box.

5. Locate and open the LoanAmortization.xsd file from Listing 21.1.

6. Click OK to close the XML Maps dialog box.

7. On the XML task pane, drag and drop each element onto the appropriate cell on the worksheet. For example, drag the element ns1:LoanAmount from the XML task pane and drop it onto cell D6. You may get a dialog that states, "The data that you are attempting to map contains formatting that is incompatible with the format specified in the worksheet." Go ahead and click "Match element data type."

Figure 21.4 shows an example of the loan amortization worksheet after mapping all of the elements from the loan amortization schema.

FIGURE 21.4

The XML mapped
loan amortization
worksheet

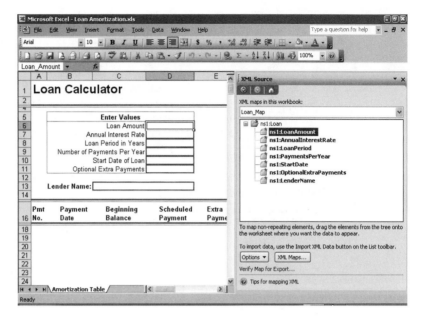

Implementing ISmartDocument Makes You Smarter

Now comes the hard part, creating a DLL that contains the functionality the smart document should exhibit as the user selects cells of interest (cells that you have mapped to an XML schema). In order to complete this section, you need to fire up Microsoft Visual Basic 6.0. The following steps show how to create an empty LoanSmartDocument project workspace.

1. Create a new ActiveX DLL project.

2. Rename the project LoanSmartDocument by selecting the project in the Project Explorer window and changing its name using the Properties window.

3. Rename the default class LoanSmarts by selecting the default class in the Project Explorer window and changing its name using the Properties window.

4. Set a reference (Project ➢ References) to the Microsoft Smart Tags 2.0 Type Library.

WARNING *Bug Alert: The Microsoft Smart Tags 2.0 Type Library might not be listed in your list of references. If you don't see it but do see the Microsoft Smart Tags 1.0 Type Library, go ahead and select the 1.0 library. After you select this library it will "magically" rename itself the 2.0 library. You will see the new name if you close and then reopen the References dialog box.*

5. While you're at it, set a reference to the Microsoft Excel 11.0 Object Library.

6. You'll also require a reference to the calendar control. Click the Browse button on the References dialog box.

7. Change the Files of Type drop-down to ActiveX Controls (*.ocx).

8. Locate and open the MSCAL.OCX file. This file is installed by default to the C:\Program Files\Microsoft Office\Office 11 folder.

WARNING *Bug Alert: The MSCAL.OCX file will not appear in the References dialog box even after you add a reference to it. Even though the control will not appear, you will still have a reference to it.*

9. Go ahead and save your work so far accepting the default names proposed by Visual Basic (assuming you completed steps 2 and 3).

Figure 21.5 shows an example of what your workspace may look like at this point, assuming you have all of the same windows displayed.

If Mark Twain were writing this book using Huck Finn's spelling, he'd write something like "it's time to git a codin" (and his editor wouldn't strike it). I think I'd enjoy computer books by Mark Twain. How about *Huckleberry Finn Bytes Back: A Proactive Approach to Network Security* or *Daze Lost: Tom Sawyer's Adventures with Primary Interop Assemblies*.

For the LoanSmarts class, the declarations section seems like a good place to begin—it's nice and short and doesn't require too many brain cells, so it'll give your brain a chance to warm up. Listing 21.2 contains the declarations section of the LoanSmarts class.

FIGURE 21.5

An empty Loan-
SmartDocument
project

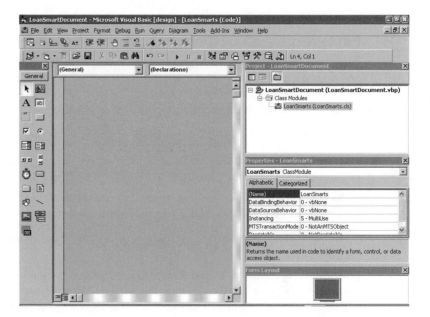

```
Option Explicit

' A smart document must implement the ISmartDocument interface
Implements ISmartDocument

' Namespace constant
Const NAMESPACE As String = "LoanAmortization"

'XML Element constants
Const LOAN As String = NAMESPACE & "#Loan"
Const LOAN_AMOUNT As String = NAMESPACE & "#LoanAmount"
Const ANNUAL_INTEREST_RATE As String = _
    NAMESPACE & "#AnnualInterestRate"
Const LOAN_PERIOD As String = NAMESPACE & "#LoanPeriod"
Const PAYMENTS_PER_YEAR As String = _
    NAMESPACE & "#PaymentsPerYear"
Const START_DATE As String = NAMESPACE & "#StartDate"
Const OPTIONAL_EXTRA_PAYMENTS As String = _
    NAMESPACE & "#OptionalExtraPayments"
Const LENDER_NAME As String = NAMESPACE & "#LenderName"

' Number of element constants
Const TYPE_COUNT = 8

' Class level variable to hold reference to the calendar
Private WithEvents moCal As Calendar
Private msAppName As String
```

Throughout the LoanSmarts class, you'll need to refer to elements using the form *namespace#element*. The namespace and element constants provide a convenient way to refer to elements specified in the loan amortization schema you created earlier. The TYPE_COUNT constant represents the number of elements in the schema that have one or more smart document actions associated with them.

The declarations section declares two class-level variables. For the start date associated with a loan, you will have the task pane display a calendar that will allow the user to select a start date by clicking a date on the calendar. The moCal variable is necessary to hold a reference to the calendar control you'll use to provide this functionality. Meanwhile, the msAppName variable will store the name of the application that is hosting the smart document. In this example, it will be Excel.

Listing 21.2 contains an extremely important statement, perhaps the most important statement in this class—Implements ISmartDocument. This statement indicates that the LoanSmarts class will implement the ISmartDocument interface.

An interface is sort of like a specification and sort of like a contract. An interface specifies the properties and methods that a class is required to implement in order to be considered an implementation of the type specified by the interface. In order to be a smart document, a class must implement the properties and methods specified by the ISmartDocument interface. And not just some of the properties and methods, all of them—even if it means including empty procedures or stubs.

Because I must implement everything that is required by an interface once I use the Implements statement, I prefer to code all of the procedure stubs required by the interface immediately after declaring that I'll implement the interface using the Implements statement. In this case, one benefit of this practice is that it'll save me a lot of typing. If you browse all of the remaining listings for this example, I think that you'll appreciate this time-savings benefit. Many of the procedures in the ISmartDocument interface have lengthy parameter lists.

To insert stubs for all of the required ISmartDocument procedures, select the ISmartDocument item from the Objects drop-down list and then go through and select each item that appears in the Procedures drop-down list. Procedures listed in bold have stubs present in the class. If a procedure is listed in normal font, it does not have a stub in the class yet. Figure 21.6 shows an example of this as I work through putting all of the interface stubs in the class.

Because there are so many procedures in this class compared to other listings in this book, and because I've split the class into multiple listings, I thought it might be beneficial to present a roadmap to this class before diving into the code for the procedures. Table 21.1 shows a list of the procedures along with the object with which the procedure is associated, the listing in which it can be found, and its purpose.

FIGURE 21.6

Stubbing the ISmart-Document interface

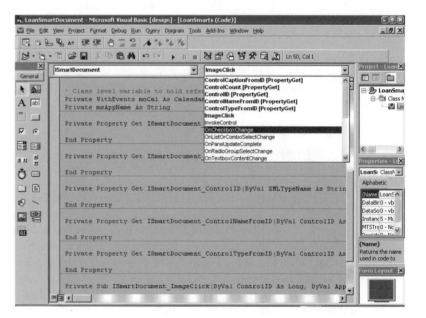

TABLE 21.1: A LOANSMARTS PROCEDURE ROADMAP

OBJECT	PROCEDURE	LISTING	PURPOSE
(General)	GetComboSelection	21.5	Determines the number of payments per year currently displayed on the worksheet
(General)	GetInitialLoanPeriod	21.5	Determines the loan period currently displayed on the worksheet
(General)	XLSmartTagActionExists	21.6	Determines if a particular smart tag action is defined on the worksheet
ISmartDocument	ControlCaptionFromID	21.4	Specifies smart document control captions
ISmartDocument	ControlCount	21.4	Specifies the number of controls for a given XML element
ISmartDocument	ControlID	21.4	Specifies a control number for a control
ISmartDocument	ControlNameFromID	21.4	Specifies a string that can be used to access the control from VBA
ISmartDocument	ControlTypeFromID	21.4	Specifies the type of a control
ISmartDocument	ImageClick	21.6	Specifies actions to perform when a user clicks an image
ISmartDocument	InvokeControl	21.6	Specifies actions to perform when a user clicks a hyperlink, button, or document fragment
ISmartDocument	OnCheckboxChange	21.6	Specifies actions to perform when a user clicks a check box
ISmartDocument	OnListOrComboSelectChange	21.6	Specifies actions to perform when a user clicks an item in a list box or combo box
ISmartDocument	OnPaneUpdateComplete	21.6	Specifies what happens when the Document Actions task pane is updated
ISmartDocument	OnRadioGroupSelectChange	21.6	Specifies actions to perform when a user clicks a radio group item
ISmartDocument	OnTextboxContentChange	21.6	Specifies actions to perform when a user changes the value of a text box

TABLE 21.1: A LOANSMARTS PROCEDURE ROADMAP *(continued)*

OBJECT	PROCEDURE	LISTING	PURPOSE
ISmartDocument	PopulateActiveXProps	21.5	Used to access and set the properties associated with an ActiveX control
ISmartDocument	PopulateCheckbox	21.5	Sets the appearance of a check box
ISmartDocument	PopulateDocumentFragment	21.5	Loads the contents of a document fragment
ISmartDocument	PopulateHelpContent	21.5	Loads the contents of a help control
ISmartDocument	PopulateImage	21.5	Loads an image control with content
ISmartDocument	PopulateListOrComboContent	21.5	Specifies the contents of a list or combo box
ISmartDocument	PopulateOther	21.5	Specifies the appearance of label, separator, button and hyperlink controls
ISmartDocument	PopulateRadioGroup	21.5	Loads the contents of a radio group
ISmartDocument	PopulateTextboxContent	21.5	Specifies the appearance of text box controls
ISmartDocument	SmartDocInitialize	21.3	Specifies the tasks to perform when initializing a smart document
ISmartDocument	SmartDocXMLTypeCaption	21.3	Specifies the caption for a group of controls associated with a particular XML element
ISmartDocument	SmartDocXMLTypeCount	21.3	Specifies the number of XML elements that have smart document actions associated with them
ISmartDocument	SmartDocXMLTypeName	21.3	Specifies the name of an element that has controls associated with it
moCal	Click	21.6	Specifies the tasks to perform when a user clicks the calendar

Basically I broke the listings down by high-level task orientation. Listing 21.3 contains code that deals with the details associated with XML elements that have smart document functionality associated with them. The procedures in Listing 21.4 go a little deeper in that they deal with the details associated with the individual controls that are mapped to the XML elements. Listing 21.5 contains the procedures that populate the various controls with content. Finally, Listing 21.6 contains the event procedures associated with the controls. Without further ado, here is Listing 21.3.

LISTING 21.3: PUTTING THE SMARTS IN LOANSMARTS (1 OF 4)

```
Private Sub ISmartDocument_SmartDocInitialize _
    (ByVal ApplicationName As String, ByVal Document As Object, _
    ByVal SolutionPath As String, _
    ByVal SolutionRegKeyRoot As String)

    On Error GoTo ErrHandler

    msAppName = Document.Application.Name

    Exit Sub
ErrHandler:
    MsgBox "SmartDocInitialize - Error: " & Err.Description
End Sub

' Gets the caption displayed by a particular XMLTypeID
Private Property Get ISmartDocument_SmartDocXmlTypeCaption _
    (ByVal XMLTypeID As Long, ByVal LocaleID As Long) As String

    On Error GoTo ErrHandler

    Select Case XMLTypeID
        Case 1
            ISmartDocument_SmartDocXmlTypeCaption = _
                "Loan Amortization Template"
        Case 2
            ISmartDocument_SmartDocXmlTypeCaption = _
                "Loan Amount"
        Case 3
            ISmartDocument_SmartDocXmlTypeCaption = _
                "Annual Interest Rate"
        Case 4
            ISmartDocument_SmartDocXmlTypeCaption = _
                "Loan Period"
        Case 5
            ISmartDocument_SmartDocXmlTypeCaption = _
                "Payments Per Year"
        Case 6
            ISmartDocument_SmartDocXmlTypeCaption = _
                "Start Date"
        Case 7
            ISmartDocument_SmartDocXmlTypeCaption = _
```

```
                    "Optional Extra Payments"
            Case 8
                ISmartDocument_SmartDocXmlTypeCaption = _
                    "Lender Name"
            Case Else
                MsgBox "SmartDocXmlTypeCaption - " & _
                    "Unknown XMLTypeID: " & XMLTypeID
        End Select

        Exit Sub
    ErrHandler:
        MsgBox "SmartDocXmlTypeCaption - Error: " & Err.Description
    End Property

    ' Returns the number of XML elements that have smart document
    ' funtionality mapped to them
    Private Property Get ISmartDocument_SmartDocXmlTypeCount() As Long
        ISmartDocument_SmartDocXmlTypeCount = TYPE_COUNT
    End Property

    ' Returns the element that the XMLTypeID is mapped to.
    Private Property Get ISmartDocument_SmartDocXmlTypeName _
        (ByVal XMLTypeID As Long) As String

        On Error GoTo ErrHandler

        Select Case XMLTypeID
            Case 1
                ISmartDocument_SmartDocXmlTypeName = LOAN
            Case 2
                ISmartDocument_SmartDocXmlTypeName = LOAN_AMOUNT
            Case 3
                ISmartDocument_SmartDocXmlTypeName = _
                    ANNUAL_INTEREST_RATE
            Case 4
                ISmartDocument_SmartDocXmlTypeName = LOAN_PERIOD
            Case 5
                ISmartDocument_SmartDocXmlTypeName = PAYMENTS_PER_YEAR
            Case 6
                ISmartDocument_SmartDocXmlTypeName = START_DATE
            Case 7
                ISmartDocument_SmartDocXmlTypeName = _
                    OPTIONAL_EXTRA_PAYMENTS
            Case 8
                ISmartDocument_SmartDocXmlTypeName = LENDER_NAME
            Case Else
                MsgBox "SmartDocXmlTypeName - Unknown XMLTypeID: " & _
                    XMLTypeID
```

```
        End Select

        Exit Sub
ErrHandler:
        MsgBox "SmartDocXmlTypeName - Error: " & Err.Description
End Property
```

The procedures in Listing 21.3 are fairly easy to understand. The first procedure in the listing, ISmartDocument_SmartDocInitialize, is actually an event procedure that occurs when the smart document is instantiated. The only thing you need to do during initialization for this procedure is store the name of the application that is hosting the smart document. Truth be told, because this smart document functionality is aimed at Excel and assumes Excel is the host in other locations, you really don't even need to do this. The only procedure that uses the msAppName variable is moCal_Click, an event procedure associated with a Calendar object. If you modified the moCal_Click procedure slightly (so that it assumed the host was Excel), you could do away with using msAppName.

The procedure named ISmartDocument_SmartDocXmlTypeCaption is responsible for assigning the captions that are displayed in response to moving to a range that is mapped to an XML element. For example, if you select cell D8 on the loan amortization worksheet, you'll see two sections appear in the document actions task pane. One section has the caption Loan Amortization Template: the other Loan Period. Why do two sections appear? It is obvious why the Loan Period caption appears—cell D8 is mapped directly to the XML element LoanPeriod. The Loan Amortization Template caption appears because this is the caption associated with the XML element named Loan. If you look at the schema in Listing 21.1, you see that the Loan element is actually an instance of the complex type LoanVariables. The LoanPeriod element is a subelement of LoanVariables. This means that no matter which of the cells mapped to the loan amortization schema you click, you will always see the caption associated with the Loan element because everything you've mapped is a subelement of the complex type LoanVariables.

The procedure named ISmartDocument_SmartDocXmlTypeName maps an XMLTypeID to an XML element name. The XMLTypeID is automatically generated by the host application (Excel) based on the value reported to it by the ISmartDocument_SmartDocXmlTypeCount procedure (which simply reports the value associated with the TYPE_COUNT constant you created in the declarations section). You may have noticed that the ISmartDocument_SmartDocXmlTypeCaption procedure also used the XMLTypeID parameter.

You need not be concerned with the actual value you use for a particular element when creating the Select...Case statement in these procedures, only that you are consistent in your usage between both procedures. For example, for the SmartDocXmlTypeName procedure (I'll omit the ISmartDocument_ prefix for the remainder of this section for brevity's sake), I've associated the value of 1 (one) with the XML element specified by the LOAN constant. In order to have the smart document display the caption "Loan Amortization Template," any time a cell associated with the loan element is selected, I need to place this caption within the case statement where XMLTypeID equals 1 (one) in the SmartDocXmlTypeCaption procedure.

In Listing 21.4, the main theme is defining the details associated with each control that you'll use. You need to define each control's caption, name, type, and ID, as well as define how many controls are associated with each XML element.

LISTING 21.4: PUTTING THE SMARTS IN LOANSMARTS (2 OF 4)

```vb
' Returns the caption associated with a particular control
Private Property Get ISmartDocument_ControlCaptionFromID( _
    ByVal ControlID As Long, ByVal ApplicationName As String, _
    ByVal LocaleID As Long, ByVal Text As String, _
    ByVal Xml As String, ByVal Target As Object) As String

    On Error GoTo ErrHandler

    Select Case ControlID
        Case 1
            ISmartDocument_ControlCaptionFromID = _
                "Loan Amortization Help"
        Case 101
            ISmartDocument_ControlCaptionFromID = _
                "Loan Amount Help"
        Case 201
            ISmartDocument_ControlCaptionFromID = _
                "Annual Interest Rate Help"
        Case 301
            ISmartDocument_ControlCaptionFromID = _
                "Loan Period Help"
        Case 302
            ISmartDocument_ControlCaptionFromID = _
                "Loan Period in Years"
        Case 401
            ISmartDocument_ControlCaptionFromID = _
                "Payments Per Year Help"
        Case 402
            ISmartDocument_ControlCaptionFromID = _
                "Number of payments per year"
        Case 502
            ISmartDocument_ControlCaptionFromID = _
                "Start Date Help"
        Case 501
            ISmartDocument_ControlCaptionFromID = _
                "{8E27C92B-1264-101C-8A2F-040224009C02}"
        Case 601
            ISmartDocument_ControlCaptionFromID = _
                "Optional Extra Payments Help"
        Case 701
            ISmartDocument_ControlCaptionFromID = _
                "Lender Name Help"
        Case Else
            MsgBox "ControlCaptionFromID - " & _
                "Unknown ControlID: " & ControlID
```

```vb
        End Select

    Exit Property
ErrHandler:
    MsgBox "ControlCaptionFromID - Error: " & Err.Description
End Property

' Returns the number of controls associated with an XML element
Private Property Get ISmartDocument_ControlCount _
    (ByVal XMLTypeName As String) As Long

    On Error GoTo ErrHandler

    Select Case XMLTypeName
        Case LOAN
            ISmartDocument_ControlCount = 1
        Case LOAN_AMOUNT
            ISmartDocument_ControlCount = 1
        Case ANNUAL_INTEREST_RATE
            ISmartDocument_ControlCount = 1
        Case LOAN_PERIOD
            ISmartDocument_ControlCount = 2
        Case PAYMENTS_PER_YEAR
            ISmartDocument_ControlCount = 2
        Case START_DATE
            ISmartDocument_ControlCount = 2
        Case OPTIONAL_EXTRA_PAYMENTS
            ISmartDocument_ControlCount = 1
        Case LENDER_NAME
            ISmartDocument_ControlCount = 1
        Case Else
            MsgBox "ControlCount - Unknown XMLTypeName: " & _
                XMLTypeName
    End Select

    Exit Sub
ErrHandler:
    MsgBox "ControlCount - Error: " & Err.Description
End Property

' Returns the control ID associated with an XML element _
' and control index
Private Property Get ISmartDocument_ControlID _
    (ByVal XMLTypeName As String, _
    ByVal ControlIndex As Long) As Long

    On Error GoTo ErrHandler
```

```
    Select Case XMLTypeName
        Case LOAN
            ISmartDocument_ControlID = ControlIndex
        Case LOAN_AMOUNT
            ISmartDocument_ControlID = ControlIndex + 100
        Case ANNUAL_INTEREST_RATE
            ISmartDocument_ControlID = ControlIndex + 200
        Case LOAN_PERIOD
            ISmartDocument_ControlID = ControlIndex + 300
        Case PAYMENTS_PER_YEAR
            ISmartDocument_ControlID = ControlIndex + 400
        Case START_DATE
            ISmartDocument_ControlID = ControlIndex + 500
        Case OPTIONAL_EXTRA_PAYMENTS
            ISmartDocument_ControlID = ControlIndex + 600
        Case LENDER_NAME
            ISmartDocument_ControlID = ControlIndex + 700
        Case Else
            MsgBox "ControlID - Unknown XMLTypeName: " & _
                XMLTypeName
    End Select

    Exit Property
ErrHandler:
    MsgBox "ControlID - Error: " & Err.Description
End Property


' Returns a control name
Private Property Get ISmartDocument_ControlNameFromID _
    (ByVal ControlID As Long) As String

    Select Case ControlID
        Case 501
            ISmartDocument_ControlNameFromID = "Calendar"
        Case Else
            ISmartDocument_ControlNameFromID = NAMESPACE & _
                ControlID
    End Select

End Property


' Gets the control type associated with a  particular control
Private Property Get ISmartDocument_ControlTypeFromID _
    (ByVal ControlID As Long, ByVal ApplicationName As String, _
    ByVal LocaleID As Long) As SmartTagLib.C_TYPE

    On Error GoTo ErrHandler
```

```
    Select Case ControlID
        Case 1
            ISmartDocument_ControlTypeFromID = C_TYPE_HELP
        Case 101
            ISmartDocument_ControlTypeFromID = C_TYPE_HELP
        Case 201
            ISmartDocument_ControlTypeFromID = C_TYPE_HELP
        Case 301
            ISmartDocument_ControlTypeFromID = C_TYPE_HELP
        Case 302
            ISmartDocument_ControlTypeFromID = C_TYPE_RADIOGROUP
        Case 401
            ISmartDocument_ControlTypeFromID = C_TYPE_HELP
        Case 402
            ISmartDocument_ControlTypeFromID = C_TYPE_COMBO
        Case 502
            ISmartDocument_ControlTypeFromID = C_TYPE_HELP
        Case 501
            ISmartDocument_ControlTypeFromID = C_TYPE_ACTIVEX
        Case 601
            ISmartDocument_ControlTypeFromID = C_TYPE_HELP
        Case 701
            ISmartDocument_ControlTypeFromID = C_TYPE_HELP
        Case Else
            MsgBox "ControlTypeFromID - Unknown ControlID: " & _
                ControlID
    End Select

    Exit Sub
ErrHandler:
    MsgBox "ControlTypeFromID - Error: " & Err.Description
End Property
```

The first procedure in Listing 21.4, ControlCaptionFromID, is easy enough as long as you understand what the numbers mean (I'll get to this in the next paragraph). ControlCaptionFromID is responsible for setting the caption for each control used in the smart document. The only odd caption is the caption for the calendar, which is an ActiveX control. For any ActiveX controls you use, the ControlCaptionFromID property should return the globally unique identifier (GUID). You can find the GUID associated with an ActiveX control by using the Registry Editor (Start ➤ Run, enter **regedit**, and click OK) and searching for the name of the control you're using until you find the CLSID for the control. You may need to use Find Next a few times to get to the CLSID.

OK, back to the number issue. As you look over many of the remaining procedures, you'll see many references to these numbers (1, 101, 201, 301, 302). If this were a production type application, I would probably define constants for these numbers to give them meaning. Even if I had used constant names, however, you would still need to know why you need to use numbers as I did. The basic problem is that you need a way to refer to and identify individual controls from within the DLL. In order for each control to be identifiable, each control must have a ControlID. You can see the ControlID property in Listing 21.4 as well. In order to set a ControlID, you use the ControlIndex parameter passed to the ControlID property. The problem with just using ControlIndex alone is that ControlIndex is the index applicable to a specific XML element. So if element X has two controls, the first control will be ControlIndex=1 and the second control will be ControlIndex=2. Element Y, meanwhile, may also have two controls. Guess what the ControlIndex would be for the first control? You got it—ControlIndex=1. This means that in order to generate unique IDs, you need to use some sort of mechanism that differentiates between the controls associated with different XML elements. The method I've used here segments each element by 100.

The ControlNameFromID property provides a way for you to assign names to each control that can be used in place of an ID to refer to a control. The only control I gave a useful name to was the calendar control; otherwise I concatenated the namespace constant with the ControlID.

The ControlTypeFromID property sets the type of each control using type constants defined by C_TYPE, which is defined in the Smart Tag Library.

Listing 21.5 contains the procedures used to populate and display the various controls you've defined in Listing 21.4. Listing 21.5 contains a few stub procedures that you need to implement ISmartDocument but are otherwise dead weight because the loan amortization example doesn't include any controls of the given type. As long as you stubbed the interface as described earlier, you shouldn't have nearly as much to enter for this listing as you might otherwise think.

LISTING 21.5: PUTTING THE SMARTS IN LOANSMARTS (3 OF 4)

```
Private Sub ISmartDocument_PopulateActiveXProps( _
    ByVal ControlID As Long, ByVal ApplicationName As String, _
    ByVal LocaleID As Long, ByVal Text As String, _
    ByVal Xml As String, ByVal Target As Object, _
    ByVal Props As SmartTagLib.ISmartDocProperties, _
    ByVal ActiveXPropBag As SmartTagLib.ISmartDocProperties)

    Select Case ControlID
        Case 501
            Props.Write Key:="W", Value:="250"
            Props.Write Key:="H", Value:="200"
        Case Else
    End Select

End Sub

Private Sub ISmartDocument_PopulateCheckbox( _
    ByVal ControlID As Long, ByVal ApplicationName As String, _
    ByVal LocaleID As Long, ByVal Text As String, _
    ByVal Xml As String, ByVal Target As Object, _
    ByVal Props As SmartTagLib.ISmartDocProperties, _
    Checked As Boolean)
    ' INTENTIONALLY EMPTY: This stub is needed to
```

```vb
    ' implement ISmartDocument
End Sub

Private Sub ISmartDocument_PopulateDocumentFragment _
    (ByVal ControlID As Long, ByVal ApplicationName As String, _
    ByVal LocaleID As Long, ByVal Text As String, _
    ByVal Xml As String, ByVal Target As Object, _
    ByVal Props As SmartTagLib.ISmartDocProperties, _
    DocumentFragment As String)
    ' INTENTIONALLY EMPTY: This stub is needed to
    ' implement ISmartDocument
End Sub

' Places help content on the task pane
Private Sub ISmartDocument_PopulateHelpContent( _
    ByVal ControlID As Long, ByVal ApplicationName As String, _
    ByVal LocaleID As Long, ByVal Text As String, _
    ByVal Xml As String, ByVal Target As Object, _
    ByVal Props As SmartTagLib.ISmartDocProperties, _
    Content As String)

    Dim sPreHTML As String
    Dim sPostHTML As String

    On Error GoTo ErrHandler

    sPreHTML = "<html><body><p>"
    sPostHTML = "</p></body></html>"

    Select Case ControlID
        Case 1
            Content = sPreHTML & "The loan amortization " & _
                "worksheet is designed to calculate a payment " & _
                "amount and amortization schedule for a loan " & _
                "based on the relevant details associated " & _
                "with a loan." & sPostHTML
        Case 101
            Content = sPreHTML & "Enter the amount of money you " & _
                "would like to borrow." & sPostHTML
        Case 201
            Content = sPreHTML & "Enter the annual interest " & _
                "rate quoted by the lender." & sPostHTML
        Case 301
            Content = sPreHTML & "The loan period is the " & _
                "length of the repayment period in years." & _
                sPostHTML
        Case 401
            Content = sPreHTML & "Generally payments are made " & _
```

```
                        "monthly (12 payments per year). If you've " & _
                        "made special arrangements with the lender " & _
                        "for a different payment frequency, enter " & _
                        "the number of annual payments here." & _
                        sPostHTML
                Case 502
                    Content = sPreHTML & "The start date is the date " & _
                        "that the loan funds are distributed to you." & _
                        sPostHTML
                Case 601
                    Content = sPreHTML & "If you'll be making a set " & _
                        "additional payment amount each month enter " & _
                        "it here. Otherwise you can adjust the Extra " & _
                        "Payment column appropriately." & sPostHTML
                Case 701
                    Content = sPreHTML & "The lender name is the name " & _
                        "of the bank that you will be borrowing money " & _
                        "from." & sPostHTML
                Case Else
                    MsgBox "PopulateHelpContent - Unknown ControlID: " & _
                        ControlID
            End Select


            ' Show collapsed initially
            Props.Write "ExpandHelp", "False"


            Exit Sub
        ErrHandler:
            MsgBox "PopulateHelpContent - Error: " & Err.Description
        End Sub


        Private Sub ISmartDocument_PopulateImage(ByVal ControlID As Long, _
            ByVal ApplicationName As String, ByVal LocaleID As Long, _
            ByVal Text As String, ByVal Xml As String, _
            ByVal Target As Object, _
            ByVal Props As SmartTagLib.ISmartDocProperties, _
            ImageSrc As String)
            ' INTENTIONALLY EMPTY: This stub is needed to
            ' implement ISmartDocument
        End Sub


        ' Populates a particular list or combo control with values
        Private Sub ISmartDocument_PopulateListOrComboContent _
            (ByVal ControlID As Long, ByVal ApplicationName As String, _
            ByVal LocaleID As Long, ByVal Text As String, _
            ByVal Xml As String, ByVal Target As Object, _
            ByVal Props As SmartTagLib.ISmartDocProperties, _
            List() As String, Count As Long, InitialSelected As Long)
```

```vba
    Select Case ControlID
        Case 402
            Count = 5
            ReDim List(1 To 5) As String
            List(1) = "12"
            List(2) = "6"
            List(3) = "4"
            List(4) = "2"
            List(5) = "1"
            InitialSelected = GetComboSelection(Target.Value)
        Case Else
    End Select

End Sub


' Private function to pre-select a combo box with the value
' currently used in the workbook (as passed in through the Payments
' parameter
Private Function GetComboSelection(Payments As Variant) As Integer

    If IsNumeric(Payments) Then
        Select Case Payments
            Case Is = 12
                GetComboSelection = 1
            Case Is = 6
                GetComboSelection = 2
            Case Is = 4
                GetComboSelection = 3
            Case Is = 2
                GetComboSelection = 4
            Case Is = 1
                GetComboSelection = 5
            Case Else
                GetComboSelection = -1
        End Select
    Else
        GetComboSelection = -1
    End If

End Function



Private Sub ISmartDocument_PopulateOther(ByVal ControlID As Long, _
    ByVal ApplicationName As String, ByVal LocaleID As Long, _
    ByVal Text As String, ByVal Xml As String, _
    ByVal Target As Object, _
    ByVal Props As SmartTagLib.ISmartDocProperties)
```

```vb
    ' INTENTIONALLY EMPTY: This stub is needed to
    ' implement ISmartDocument
End Sub


' Adds options to a radio group
Private Sub ISmartDocument_PopulateRadioGroup( _
    ByVal ControlID As Long, ByVal ApplicationName As String, _
    ByVal LocaleID As Long, ByVal Text As String, _
    ByVal Xml As String, ByVal Target As Object, _
    ByVal Props As SmartTagLib.ISmartDocProperties, _
    List() As String, Count As Long, InitialSelected As Long)

    Select Case ControlID
        Case Is = 302
            Count = 5
            ReDim List(1 To Count) As String
            List(1) = "3 Years"
            List(2) = "4 Years"
            List(3) = "5 Years"
            List(4) = "6 Years"
            List(5) = "7 Years"
            InitialSelected = GetInitialLoanPeriod(Target.Value)
        Case Else
    End Select

End Sub

' Private function to pre-select a radio grouping with the value
' currently used in the workbook (as passed in through the Period
' parameter
Private Function GetInitialLoanPeriod(Period As Variant) As Integer

    If IsNumeric(Period) Then
        Select Case Period
            Case Is = 3
                GetInitialLoanPeriod = 1
            Case Is = 4
                GetInitialLoanPeriod = 2
            Case Is = 5
                GetInitialLoanPeriod = 3
            Case Is = 6
                GetInitialLoanPeriod = 4
            Case Is = 7
                GetInitialLoanPeriod = 5
            Case Else
                GetInitialLoanPeriod = -1
        End Select
```

```
        Else
            GetInitialLoanPeriod = -1
        End If

    End Function

    Private Sub ISmartDocument_PopulateTextboxContent( _
        ByVal ControlID As Long, ByVal ApplicationName As String, _
        ByVal LocaleID As Long, ByVal Text As String, _
        ByVal Xml As String, ByVal Target As Object, _
        ByVal Props As SmartTagLib.ISmartDocProperties, _
        Value As String)
        ' INTENTIONALLY EMPTY: This stub is needed to
        ' implement ISmartDocument
    End Sub
```

The hardest part of Listing 21.5 is all of the typing associated with PopulateHelpContent. Though I put all of the help content directly in the DLL, you can also load help content by referring to external HTML files. This is preferable for most cases because it gives you the ability to modify help content without recompiling and redistributing the DLL.

PopulateListOrComboContent is a somewhat interesting procedure. Like all of the other populate methods, PopulateListOrComboContent uses a Select Case statement to define actions associated with a specific control. Because this example only uses one combo control, you could theoretically get by with an If...Then statement. However, I chose to use a Select...Case from the get-go in case I decided to add another combo box or list box later on.

In order to populate the combo box, you need to ReDim the List array that is passed to the procedure as a parameter. Notice that the array is one-based rather than a traditional zero-based array. Another interesting thing to notice is that you need to set the Count parameter to indicate how many items you're putting in the array. Although you may not use the Count parameter within the procedure, the process that calls this method may depend on having the Count parameter set to the appropriate number.

All of the populate methods include a parameter named Target in their parameter list. Target represents the Excel Range object that is mapped to the XML element for which the control is defined. You can use this parameter to see what the current value is for the number of payments per year element on the loan amortization worksheet. I created the GetComboSelection function to return the number of payments per year. If GetComboSelection can't translate the number of payments per year as indicated by the Payments parameter, GetComboSelection returns −1, which, when passed to the InitialSelected property in PopulateListOrComboContent, instructs the combo box not to preselect an item in the list.

PopulateRadioGroup is similar to PopulateListOrComboContent in that you need to ReDim the list to the number of elements required and then add items by changing the value associated with each list array element. GetInitialLoanPeriod determines which radio option should be selected based on the value that currently appears on the loan amortization worksheet.

In Listing 21.6, you'll hook up all of the event procedures associated with any controls that you added.

LISTING 21.6: PUTTING THE SMARTS IN LOANSMARTS (4 OF 4)

```
Private Sub ISmartDocument_ImageClick(ByVal ControlID As Long, _
    ByVal ApplicationName As String, ByVal Target As Object, _
    ByVal Text As String, ByVal Xml As String, _
    ByVal LocaleID As Long, ByVal XCoordinate As Long, _
    ByVal YCoordinate As Long)
    ' INTENTIONALLY EMPTY: This stub is needed to
    ' implement ISmartDocument
End Sub

Private Sub ISmartDocument_InvokeControl(ByVal ControlID As Long, _
    ByVal ApplicationName As String, ByVal Target As Object, _
    ByVal Text As String, ByVal Xml As String, _
    ByVal LocaleID As Long)
    ' INTENTIONALLY EMPTY: This stub is needed to
    ' implement ISmartDocument
End Sub

Private Sub ISmartDocument_OnCheckboxChange( _
    ByVal ControlID As Long, ByVal Target As Object, _
    ByVal Checked As Boolean)
    ' INTENTIONALLY EMPTY: This stub is needed to
    ' implement ISmartDocument
End Sub

Private Sub ISmartDocument_OnListOrComboSelectChange _
    (ByVal ControlID As Long, ByVal Target As Object, _
    ByVal Selected As Long, ByVal Value As String)

    Select Case ControlID
        Case Is = 402
            Target.Value = CInt(Value)
        Case Else
    End Select

End Sub

Private Sub ISmartDocument_OnPaneUpdateComplete( _
    ByVal Document As Object)

    Dim objXlCal As Excel.SmartTagAction

    On Error GoTo ErrHandler

    If XLSmartTagActionExists(Document, START_DATE, _
        "Calendar") Then
```

```
        Set objXlCal = Document.ActiveSheet. _
            SmartTags(START_DATE).SmartTagActions("Calendar")

        If objXlCal.PresentInPane Then
            Set moCal = objXlCal.ActiveXControl
        End If

    End If

    Exit Sub
ErrHandler:
    MsgBox "OnPaneUpdateComplete - Error: " & Err.Description
End Sub

Private Function XLSmartTagActionExists(Document As Object, _
    sSmartTag As String, sSmartTagAction As String) As Boolean

    Dim objXLSmartTagAction As Excel.SmartTagAction

    On Error GoTo ErrHandler

    Set objXLSmartTagAction = Document.ActiveSheet. _
        SmartTags(sSmartTag).SmartTagActions(sSmartTagAction)

    XLSmartTagActionExists = True
    Set objXLSmartTagAction = Nothing

    Exit Function
ErrHandler:
    XLSmartTagActionExists = False
End Function

Private Sub ISmartDocument_OnRadioGroupSelectChange( _
    ByVal ControlID As Long, ByVal Target As Object, _
    ByVal Selected As Long, ByVal Value As String)

    Select Case ControlID
        Case Is = 302
            Target.Value = Selected + 2
        Case Else
    End Select

End Sub

Private Sub ISmartDocument_OnTextboxContentChange( _
    ByVal ControlID As Long, ByVal Target As Object, _
    ByVal Value As String)
```

```
      ' INTENTIONALLY EMPTY: This stub is needed to
      ' implement ISmartDocument
End Sub

Private Sub moCal_Click()
    Dim oXl As Excel.Application

    On Error GoTo ErrHandler

    If InStr(1, msAppName, "Excel") > 0 Then
        Set oXl = GetObject(Class:="Excel.Application")
        oXl.ActiveSheet.Range("Loan_Start").Value = moCal.Value
        Set oXl = Nothing
    End If

    Exit Sub
ErrHandler:
    Set oXl = Nothing
    MsgBox "moCal_Click - Error: " & Err.Description
End Sub
```

There are three controls that have events you need to handle for this example. The combo box contains choices for the number of payments per year, the radio group of loan period choices, and the calendar. Whenever the user makes a change to one of these controls, you can use the event associated with the change to update the loan amortization worksheet. In addition to handling these three events, you need two other procedures in this listing in order for the calendar control to function properly: OnPaneUpdateComplete and XLSmartTagActionExists.

OnListOrComboSelectChange and OnRadioGroupSelectChange work very similarly to one another. Both of these event procedures receive a Target parameter that represents the range on the worksheet associated with the XML element that is associated with the control. All you need to do is set the Value property of the Target parameter (a Range object) to the value desired and voilà—you've got an interactive smart document.

Hooking up to the events associated with an ActiveX control is a little more involved. Did you catch the WithEvents keyword in the declaration of the calendar variable named moCal in Listing 21.2? WithEvents notifies the LoanSmarts class that the calendar object represented by moCal is capable of triggering events and that you would like write event procedures that can respond to those events. In the LoanSmarts class, you'll respond to the calendar click event.

The problem with using an ActiveX control is that you don't get the convenience of having a Target parameter passed into your event procedures. Instead, you have to acquire your own reference to Excel and then come up with a way to get a reference to the appropriate range in Excel. As a result, you see the use of the GetObject function to retrieve a reference to Excel. Once you have Excel, you should be able to use the active sheet to get a reference to the worksheet associated with the smart document. This is true because your smart document code can only receive events if the worksheet the smart document was associated with was active. To get a reference to the appropriate cell, I used the range name associated with the loan's start date.

Another problem with using an ActiveX control is that you don't have a native reference to the ActiveX control. Once you add the control, you need to use the OnPaneUpdateComplete event procedure to see if there is a smart tag action defined for the control, figure out if the control is currently displayed in the task pane, and if so, get a reference to it and store the reference in a class level variable (moCal in this case). You need the XLSmartTagActionExists function to make sure that a smart tag action has been defined on the loan amortization worksheet prior to blindly setting a reference to it. You can't just set a reference to it because smart tag actions aren't defined on a worksheet unless the XML element associated with a smart tag action actually has a value associated with it.

After entering Listing 21.6, go ahead and make the DLL by selecting File ➤ Make LoanSmart-Document.dll and saving the DLL to the same directory that you placed the Loan Amortization workbook (Loan Amortization.xls) and loan amortization schema (LoanAmortization.xsd).

Connect the Dots with a Manifest

The last step in developing a smart document is creating a manifest file. A manifest is an XML file that instructs Excel where to locate all of the components of the smart document. Listing 21.7 shows the manifest I created for the loan amortization example. If you are following along, you can create the manifest by entering this listing in a text editor such as Notepad. Save the file manifest.xml in the same directory as the LoanSmartDocument.dll and LoanAmortization.xsd files.

LISTING 21.7: A MANIFEST FOR THE LOAN AMORTIZATION SMART DOCUMENT

```xml
<?xml version="1.0" encoding="UTF-8" standalone="no"?>
<manifest
    xmlns="http://schemas.microsoft.com/office/xmlexpansionpacks/2003">
    <version>1.0</version>
    <updateFrequency>20160</updateFrequency>
    <uri>LoanAmortization</uri>
    <solution>
        <solutionID>{314F6E98-30D5-493b-BE6C-5B9C18F7E1C3}</solutionID>
        <type>smartDocument</type>
        <alias lcid="*">Loan Amortization Smart Document</alias>
        <file>
            <type>solutionActionHandler</type>
            <version>1.0</version>
            <filePath>LoanSmartDocument.dll</filePath>
            <CLSID>{0CB2A65A-8078-42E8-A616-C70424090CC5}</CLSID>
            <regsvr32/>
        </file>
    </solution>
    <solution>
        <solutionID>schema</solutionID>
        <type>schema</type>
        <alias lcid="*">Loan Amortization</alias>
        <file>
            <type>schema</type>
            <version>1.0</version>
```

```
        <filePath>LoanAmortization.xsd</filePath>
      </file>
    </solution>
  </manifest>
```

The loan amortization smart document contains two components: the DLL that provides the smart functionality and the loan amortization schema. For the purposes of creating a manifest, the document that you'll turn into a smart document (the loan amortization workbook) doesn't count as a component and does not need to be in the manifest file. For more comprehensive solutions, the manifest may include many more components such as HTML files, images files, or other XML files.

For each component listed in the manifest there is a file element that is a file path subelement. In this example, I placed all of the files in the same directory and thus didn't explicitly specify a full file path. If you place the files in separate directories from the manifest, you'll need to update the file path with either an absolute or relative reference to the file location.

Finally, it is important to update the CLSID element inside the file element that is associated with the LoanSmartDocument.dll. In order to find the CLSID associated with the DLL, you need to search in the Windows Registry using RegEdit. Run RegEdit and search for the LoanSmartDocument.LoanSmarts until you find the CLSID. I found mine in the Registry at My Computer\HKEY_CLASSES_ROOT\LoanSmartDocument.LoanSmarts\Clsid.

WARNING *If you don't update the CLSID in the manifest file when you try this example, you'll get an Invalid Expansion Pack error when you try to add it as an XML expansion pack in Excel.*

See How Smart It Is

At this point, you're ready to test the fruits of your labor and attach the smart document functionality to the loan amortization workbook. If all goes well, this is a simple process as detailed in the following steps.

NOTE *These instructions assume that you have disabled smart document security for testing and development purposes as discussed previously in the section titled "Smart Document Security."*

1. Open the loan amortization workbook.

2. Select Data ➢ XML ➢ XML Expansion Packs to display the XML Expansion Packs dialog box shown in the following screen shot.

3. Click Add.

4. Locate and select the manifest.xml file you created and then click Open.

5. When prompted about reenabling XML expansion pack security, click No.

6. As you can see in the following screen shot, you've now made the XML expansion pack available but haven't attached it to the current document.

7. Select the Loan Amortization Smart Document expansion pack and click Attach.

8. Click OK to close the XML Expansion Packs dialog box.

TIP   *To turn off the borders around the cells that are mapped to XML elements, choose Data ➤ List ➤ Hide Border of Inactive Lists.*

Hopefully you didn't make any mistakes and you are enjoying success while envisioning the possibilities offered via developing smart documents. If you are not enjoying success, the next section is for you.

Troubleshooting Smart Documents

If things don't work out as planned, the first thing to do is isolate which component is causing problems. For the loan amortization example, three components could be the culprits. First, you might have an issue with the loan amortization schema (LoanAmortization.xsd). However, if you were able to map this schema to the loan amortization workbook, it is doubtful that this is the source of your problems.

Second, the DLL (LoanSmartDocument.dll) may not be behaving as it should. This can be frustrating because you cannot debug a DLL as easily as you can debug a procedure written in VBA. One technique that I've found useful in this situation is using some kind of tracing mechanism. I used the MsgBox function for this in the loan amortization example, but you may want to use a less intrusive method such as logging data to a log file. In order for a log file to be helpful, you want to be sure to trap errors that occur in any procedure and list the name of the procedure that generated the error.

Finally, you could have a problem with the manifest itself. If you're not sure which component is causing problems when you get an Invalid Expansion Pack error, you can zero in on the source of the problem by eliminating the solution element that specifies the DLL and then trying to add the expansion pack. If you are successful adding the expansion pack after eliminating the DLL solution element, then you know that the problem has to do with the DLL itself or one of the values that you assigned to the various solution subelements associated with the DLL solution element.

In the next section, I've listed some resources for further information. The Smart Document SDK includes a section on testing and troubleshooting in its help files, which may be of further assistance.

Smart Document Resources

Because smart document development involves many skills outside the scope of this book, I thought you might appreciate it if I directed you to a couple of resources that should provide you with some useful information regarding smart document development.

Your first task should be to obtain the Microsoft Office 2003 Smart Document SDK. The Smart Document SDK contains smart document samples, tools, XML schemas and documentation (including some tutorials) that are intended to present developers with the information they need to begin developing smart documents. For information about this SDK, visit `http://msdn.microsoft.com/library/default.asp?url=/library/en-us/sdsdk/html/sdconGettingStartedAbout.asp`.

While you're checking out the Smart Document SDK, I'd recommend exploring Microsoft's Microsoft Developer Network (MSDN) site for a while. The MSDN site contains all sorts of useful developer content. In fact, after the SDK, I'd say the next thing you should do is go to `http://msdn.microsoft.com` and do a search for **Smart Documents**. This search will return numerous articles that will be of assistance to you.

Summary

Smart document technology is an exciting new way to create documents that deliver context-sensitive assistance to users as they work with a document. Smart documents have the potential to create value by allowing you to develop solutions that guide users through complex business processes.

Like many new technologies, however, developing smart document functionality isn't quite as easy as you might expect. One reason that this is so is that you can't develop smart documents using VBA. In order to develop smart documents, you need to be comfortable with XML and XML Schemas and one of the Visual Studio programming languages. Additionally, you need to study the Smart Document SDK to gain a clear understanding of how smart documents work and what you need to do in order to develop them.

Suffice it to say, if you are a beginning or intermediate programmer and do not have experience with the items just mentioned, you may have your work cut out for you. If this is the case, I strongly suggest using VB 6.0 as your development environment because it will allow you to apply many of the skills you have learned in this book. Using VB 6.0 also simplifies things technically because it avoids the hoops you have to jump through when you are trying to integrate a COM-based architecture (Microsoft Office) with a .NET-based architecture (managed code developed using a .NET language).

Smart document development involves the following high-level tasks. First, you must prepare the document you want to provide with smarts. Next, if you do not have an XML schema containing elements that you can map to the document, you'll need to develop a schema that you can map to the document. Once you've prepared a document and mapped an XML schema to it, you're ready to develop the functionality that you'd like the smart document to exhibit. This process is completed using Visual Basic (6.0 or .NET), Visual C++ (6.0 or .NET), or one of the other .NET languages. A smart document must implement the ISmartDocument interface. Finally, you can create an XML expansion pack by creating an XML manifest file that instructs Excel where to find all of the components associated with the smart document. If everything goes as planned, you can give the original document smarts by adding the expansion pack (the manifest file) and then attaching it to the original document.

You've now learned many useful skills and techniques for creating valuable Excel-based applications. In many cases, you can send your creation on to your colleagues and they can instantly benefit from your talent. On other occasions, you'll need to consider other methods for deploying your creation. In the next chapter, I'll cover some of the various methods you can use for deploying Excel applications so that you can choose wisely.

Chapter 22

Application Deployment Strategies

ONE THING THAT WILL become evident to you shortly after you release your first Excel application is that even though you've finished developing, your work is far from complete. You have users to support, bugs to fix (though many strive for it, nobody's perfect), and new features to add. You know the saying "If you fail to plan, you plan to fail"? After just a couple of releases, if you don't plan your application releases and upgrades, you may find your state of affairs bordering on chaos—especially if you've got lots of users (dozens to hundreds).

In order to manage the product distribution and release cycle, you can employ numerous strategies, from rudimentary to comprehensive fail-proof release management systems. This chapter introduces you to a few strategies you can use to manage application distribution.

Another issue related to application deployment is determining what form your application will be in when you distribute it. You can choose from distributing your application as a standard workbook, a template, or an add-in. I'll present the pros and cons of each form so that you can make an informed choice. The choice of an application deployment strategy is a decision that is best made near the beginning of the development process because the decisions you make during the development process can be impacted depending on the distribution form of your application.

Choose the Form

Do you remember the movie *Ghostbusters* (1984)? The Ghostbusters are fighting the evil demon Gozer (aka Gozer the Gozerian, Gozer the Destructor, Voguss Zildrohar, The Traveller). Just prior to assuming a physical presence, Gozer asks the Ghostbusters to choose the form of their destroyer. As they all stop to ponder their decision, Gozer appears as a giant Stay Puft marshmallow man. Sure enough, Stantz (played by Dan Akroyd) made the mental decision without the input of his colleagues. His reasoning? "I tried to think of the most harmless thing... something that could never destroy us... something I loved from my childhood." As it turned out, the Ghostbusters eventually destroyed Gozer before Gozer could bring about worldwide destruction.

When it comes to choosing the form of distribution for your application, it's safe to say that your choice won't have worldwide life and death consequences. There are consequences however.

I Like Vanilla

The most common form an Excel application takes is as a plain vanilla workbook. This next sentence is very important so pay attention. In order to create an application that assumes this form, you must save your workbook (File ➤ Save). OK, I'm playing a little bit. Telling you how to save a workbook is kind of like telling you how to breathe.

The biggest benefit of using a standard Excel workbook is that you don't need to worry about installing it before using it. You can e-mail the workbook, place it in a shared network folder, or save it to portable media. As long as your users can open the workbook, they can use the functionality it supplies, provided it passes the Microsoft Office security checks.

That said, it is not uncommon for a handful of your users to experience issues related to either a faulty Office or Excel installation. Well, it's not necessarily that the original Excel installation was faulty—rather something probably happened to the computer after the fact that caused an incompatibility or removed critical system files. If your application works for the vast majority of your users and doesn't work at all for a tiny minority, your leading suspect should be the details associated with these individual computers. If you quiz these users, usually you'll find out that they recently had software package X (substitute any number of software programs here) installed or removed, and that ever since, Excel has exhibited unpredictable behavior. If my application doesn't work after I verify that all of the software requirements it needs have been met, I'll devise a trivial procedure that should work on every computer to test the offending computers. If the trivial procedure fails as well, I'll have the users or their IT support department reinstall Microsoft Office and all applicable service packs. Most of the time this solves the problem.

Repeat Your Success with Templates

Another form your solution can assume is a template. Templates are useful for applications that provide functionality that is used to help automate repeated processes or procedures.

For example, maybe your firm has a standard capital spending approval process that requires financial justification as part of the approval process. You could develop a template that facilitates this process by assisting users with the data input process, producing reports, and submitting workbook data for approval.

Though you could add functionality to a normal workbook solution to make it act like a template, why not just save the original as a template and get all of the template functionality for free? (A counterpoint is provided in two paragraphs.) When your users need to create a new capital spending approval request, all they need to do is select File ➤ New, choose the On My Computer link underneath Templates in the task pane, and then select the capital spending template.

Templates also allow you to develop worksheet-based solutions. That is, you can develop a worksheet that performs some specific task and then save it as a worksheet template. Then you can insert the worksheet template as a new worksheet in any workbook that requires the functionality provided by the worksheet.

The minor disadvantage of a template is that it requires a little more knowledge to use than a standard workbook. Occasionally I find it difficult to remember that some people don't know how to add two cells together in Excel (probably a larger percentage of users than you think). The fact is, if your solution is being distributed to a large number of users, you'll need to create a utility to install the template to the proper template directory (or provide documentation on how to do this manually). Additionally, you will also need to train people on how to create a workbook based on a template. How you deliver this training (proactive documentation, proactive communication/training, or reactive communication) is up to you, but you will end up delivering it.

The alternative to using a template is to distribute a standard workbook that contains a user interface element that says something like "Create New <your solution>". When you click the Create New button, or whatever, all your code needs to do is provide a way for the user to name the new workbook and select a location to save it (you can use the GetSaveAsFilename method) and then save the solution workbook using the new name and location. Whenever the user needs to create a new document, they open up the original file you distributed and click the Create New button.

Perhaps an example of the different alternatives for delivering template functionality is in order at this point. I'd like to demonstrate three things: how to create a template, how to create a workbook that acts like a template, and how to create a worksheet template.

As an example of how to create a template and how to create a workbook that acts like a template, I've taken the Setting and Settings classes along with the Settings worksheet from Chapter 12 and placed them into a workbook with two empty worksheets. Because I use the settings functionality in nearly every Excel project, my goal is to create a template that I can use to kick off each Excel application I build. Though this example just adds the settings functionality to this workbook, you may want to add other components that you find yourself using in nearly every project. Figure 22.1 shows an example of the Excel Project workbook that I'll turn into a template.

Creating a template given an existing workbook is easy as the following steps illustrate:

1. Select File ➤ Save As.

2. Change Save As Type to Template (*.xlt).

3. In order to have the template appear in the list of templates displayed by the Templates dialog box, you should save the file to the Templates folder, which is located by default at C:\Documents and Settings*username*\Application Data\Microsoft\Templates. I saved mine with the name Excel Project.

FIGURE 22.1

This otherwise empty workbook contains the components necessary to implement settings as covered in Chapter 12.

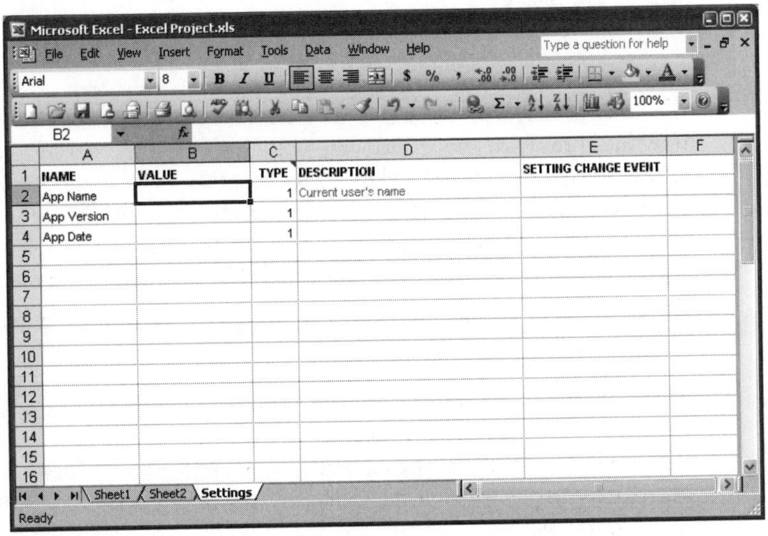

TIP   *You can determine the path to the Templates folder programmatically using Application.TemplatesPath.*

Piece of cake! To use the template, follow these steps:

1. Select File ➢ New

2. Choose the On My Computer option underneath the Templates section in the task pane.

3. Double-click the Excel Project template.

WARNING   *The most common error made by users trying to use a template is that they open the template itself (by opening a template workbook directly) rather than creating a new workbook based on a copy of the template.*

As you might infer from the warning about opening templates directly being the most common error, in order to modify a template, you need to open the template up directly by selecting File ➢ Open and then selecting the template file.

In order to create a pseudo-template (a workbook that imitates Template functionality) you need to use some VBA. Listing 22.1 presents an example of code you can use to implement pseudo-template functionality. If some of the procedures in this listing look familiar, it's because you saw a few of them in Chapter 6 when you learned about the Workbook object.

LISTING 22.1: IMPLEMENTING PSEUDO-TEMPLATE FUNCTIONALITY

```
Option Explicit

' Create new workbook based on this workbook
Sub SimplePsuedoTemplate()
    Dim wb As Workbook
    Dim sName As String
    Dim sDefault As String
    Dim sFilter As String

    ' Default file name
    sDefault = GetDefaultName
    ' Filter for GetSaveAsFilename method
    sFilter = "Microsoft Office Excel Workbook (*.xls), *.xls"
    ' Ask user where to save new file
    sName = Application.GetSaveAsFilename(sDefault, sFilter)

    ' False means user clicked cancel or dismissed dialog box
    ' without making a choice
    If sName <> "False" Then
        ' See if a file already exists at the selected location
        If FileExists(sName) Then
            ' There IS an existing file - see if the user
            ' wants to overwrite it.
```

```vba
            If OkToOverwrite(sName) Then
                ' Turn off alerts so Excel doesn't bug
                ' the user about the existing file
                Application.DisplayAlerts = False
                ThisWorkbook.SaveAs sName
                ' Turn alerts back on
                Application.DisplayAlerts = True
            End If
        Else
            ' There IS NOT an existing file so
            ' go ahead and save thisworkbook as sName
            ThisWorkbook.SaveAs sName
        End If
    End If
    Set wb = Nothing
End Sub

' Generates a default file name
Function GetDefaultName() As String
    Dim bGotName As Boolean
    Dim sName As String
    Dim nIndex As Integer

    nIndex = 1
    bGotName = False

    Do
        sName = Left(ThisWorkbook.Name, Len(ThisWorkbook.Name) - 4) & _
            CStr(nIndex)
        If IsWorkbookOpen(sName & ".xls") Then
            nIndex = nIndex + 1
        Else
            bGotName = True
        End If
    Loop Until bGotName

    GetDefaultName = sName & ".xls"
End Function

' See if a given workbook is open or not
Function IsWorkbookOpen(sWorkbookName As String) As Boolean
    Dim wb As Workbook

    IsWorkbookOpen = False
    For Each wb In Workbooks
        If StrComp(sWorkbookName, wb.Name, vbTextCompare) = 0 Then
            IsWorkbookOpen = True
            Exit For
```

```
            End If
        Next

        Set wb = Nothing
    End Function

    ' Ask if it's ok to overwrite a file
    Function OkToOverwrite(sFullName As String) As Boolean
        Dim sMsg As String
        Dim nButtons As Long
        Dim nResponse As Long
        Dim bOverwrite As Boolean

        bOverwrite = False

        sMsg = sFullName & " already exists.  Do you want to overwrite it?"
        nButtons = vbYesNoCancel + vbExclamation + vbDefaultButton2

        nResponse = MsgBox(sMsg, nButtons, "Overwrite File?")

        If nResponse = vbYes Then
            bOverwrite = True
        End If

        OkToOverwrite = bOverwrite
    End Function

    ' See if a file exists or not
    Function FileExists(sFullName As String) As Boolean
        Dim bExists As Boolean
        Dim nLength As Integer

        nLength = Len(Dir(sFullName))

        If nLength > 0 Then
            bExists = True
        Else
            bExists = False
        End If

        FileExists = bExists
    End Function
```

Basically all this listing does is save the workbook using a different name. In order to be a little more convenient, the listing does things like generate a default filename, prompt the user for a file-name and storage location, check to see if a file with the same name already exists, and if so, ask if it's

OK to overwrite the existing file. Of course, to make things even more user friendly, if this were a production application, you would want to add a user interface element (menu item, command button, etc.) that calls the SimplePsuedoTemplate procedure for the user.

One of the advantages of using a pseudo-template in place of a real template is that you can build initialization code into the process that creates the new workbook. For example, it would be easy to modify Listing 21.1 to prompt for the initial settings for the project such as the App Name, App Version, and App Date.

USING WORKSHEET TEMPLATES

Though many people are not aware of it or don't take advantage of it, you can also create a worksheet template. Worksheet templates allow you to insert worksheets exhibiting predefined formatting or functionality into a workbook. Using the Settings functionality as an example, let me explain one way that you could put a worksheet template to good use—by creating a Settings worksheet template. Then, if you wanted to add Settings functionality to a particular workbook, you could add a new Settings worksheet (based on the Settings template you'll create shortly) and import the two classes that provide setting functionality (the Settings and Setting classes).

Creating a worksheet template is very similar to creating a workbook template. The main difference is that you need to be sure to limit the worksheets in the workbook to just those that you want to appear when you insert them into a workbook based on the template. To create a worksheet template based on the Settings worksheet, follow these steps:

1. Create a workbook that contains just one worksheet (the Settings worksheet).

2. Select File ➢ Save As.

3. Change Save As Type to Template (*.xlt).

4. In order to have the template appear in the list of templates displayed by the Templates dialog box, you should save the file to the Templates folder, which is located by default at C:\Documents and Settings*username*\Application Data\Microsoft\Templates. I saved mine with the name Settings.

Using a worksheet template is easy enough if you know where to look. The only way I know to insert a worksheet template is to right-click the worksheet tab that I want to insert a worksheet in front of and select Insert. This displays the Insert dialog box shown in Figure 22.2. Then all I need to do is select the desired template and click OK.

NOTE *If you select a template containing more than one worksheet, Excel will insert a worksheet for every worksheet found in the template.*

Blend in with Add-Ins

Add-ins are useful when you have functionality that is not workbook specific—for example, you could develop a bunch of user-defined functions and distribute them as an add-in. This works wonderfully, because generally you'll want to use the functions from within many different workbooks.

FIGURE 22.2
Inserting a work-
sheet based on a
template is as easy
as double-clicking
the appropriate
template.

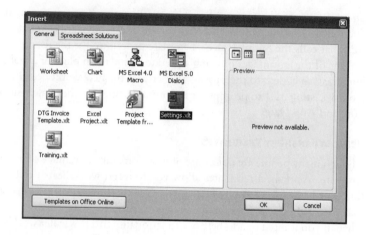

Another benefit of an add-in is that its structure is not visible to the user. A workbook (and there-fore a template) must have at least one visible worksheet. This rule does not apply to an add-in. Though you can protect a workbook so that it is difficult, at best, to modify, add-ins cannot be modified in anyway by a user. The only way to modify an add-in is to modify the workbook with which the add-in was created.

As an example, I've created a simple add-in that contains two user-defined functions: one function that prints out the connection details of the query table associated with a given range and another that lists all of the very hidden worksheets in the active workbook. To test this out, create a new workbook and enter the code from Listing 22.2.

LISTING 22.2:USEFUL ADD-IN FUNCTIONS

```
Option Explicit

' Lists the connection details of the query table that
' intersects with the QueryTableCell parameter
Function ViewQueryTableConnection(QueryTableCell As Range) As String
    Dim sResult As String

    On Error Resume Next

    sResult = ""

    If QueryTableCell.QueryTable Is Nothing Then
        sResult = "No query table."
    Else
        sResult = QueryTableCell.QueryTable.Connection
    End If
```

```
        ViewQueryTableConnection = sResult
End Function


' Lists any worksheets in the active workbook
' that are very hidden
Function ListVeryHiddenSheets(AnyCell As Range) As String
    Dim ws As Worksheet
    Dim sResult As String

    On Error Resume Next

    sResult = ""

    For Each ws In AnyCell.Parent.Parent.Worksheets
        If ws.Visible = xlSheetVeryHidden Then
            sResult = sResult & ws.Name & ", "
        End If
    Next

    ' Strip off trailing ", " if needed
    If Len(sResult) > 2 Then
        sResult = Left(sResult, Len(sResult) - 2)
    Else
        sResult = "There are no very hidden worksheets."
    End If

    Set ws = Nothing
    ListVeryHiddenSheets = sResult
End Function
```

The ViewQueryTableConnection function is useful to view the connection details associated with a query table. When you use Microsoft Query to bring data from a database into a worksheet, the data is displayed in a range of cells called a query table. If you use Microsoft Query frequently, occasionally you will need to figure out what database a particular query table is associated with. You can use ViewQueryTableConnection to display this information. To use ViewQueryTableConnection, all you need to do is pass it a reference to a cell that is part of the query table. Figure 22.3 shows an example that uses ViewQueryTableConnection.

I added the ListVeryHiddenSheets function as another example in case you wanted to test an add-in without creating a query table. Pass this function as a reference to any cell in the workbook you want to inspect and it will return a comma-delimited list of the names of any very hidden worksheets in the workbook.

To make an add-in, all you need to do is save a workbook as one. Prior to saving the workbook, you may want to lock the VBA project so that people can't view the code that implements your add-in. For this example, perform the following actions:

FIGURE 22.3

Viewing the details associated with a query table

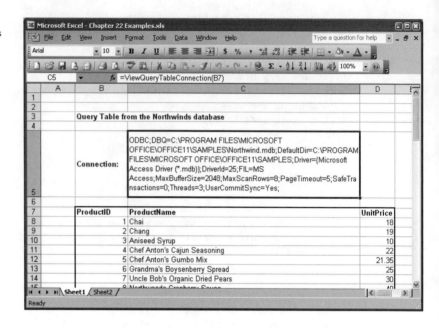

1. Select the VBA project associated with Listing 22.2 in the Project Explorer window.

2. Right-click and select VBAProject Properties.

3. Click the Protection tab.

4. Check Lock project for viewing and provide a password (I used "password").

5. Save the workbook as Simple Add-in.xls.

6. Now you're ready to make the add-in. Save the workbook as Simple Add-in.xla. You can do this by changing the file type to Microsoft Office Excel Add-in (*.xla). When you do this, Excel will automatically select the AddIns folder associated with your user ID. On my computer, the default AddIn folder is C:\Documents and Settings\shansen\Application Data\Microsoft\AddIns.

To test the add-in, you need to load it into memory. In addition, the first time you use an add-in, you need to instruct Excel where to find it. To test the Simple Add-in, follow these steps.

1. Select Tools ➢ Add-Ins from the Excel menu.

2. The first time you use an Add-In you need to add it to the list of Add-Ins by clicking Browse.

3. Locate the Add-In file you created in step 6 of the previous set of instructions. Select the Add-In and click OK to add the add-in to the list of Add-Ins.

4. Once an add-in appears in the list, you can load/unload it by checking/unchecking it in the Add-Ins dialog box. In the following screenshot I've loaded the Simple Add-In add-in.

Managing Change

Now that you understand the various ways that you can deliver your solution, let's move on. It has now been six months since you released your application to dozens or possibly hundreds of happy users. You've got minor issues to correct and a list of enhancements to implement. One of your biggest considerations is going to be how to go about releasing another version. Addressing that consideration is the topic of this section.

One way you can reduce the impact of version management is to deploy "master" copies to shared network locations and then create shortcut links on users computers that point to the master copies.

In case of emergency, you can take measures to upgrade or fix existing applications by creating your own "service pack" that you distribute to your users. A service pack contains all of the code necessary to fix an existing application.

The best way to go about version management, however, is to plan for it from the beginning. Expect that you will need to release future versions from day one in the development cycle. By incorporating this expectation into the decisions you make as you develop an application, you can take advantage of the opportunity to make design decisions that will facilitate version management. You will learn more about this topic later on in the section titled "Implementing Version Awareness."

Employing Centralized Template Deployment

One problem that is associated with releasing new versions is that it complicates support because not all of your users may be using the same version. Depending on the extent of your changes, the versions may not be compatible. Dealing with multiple versions and slow adoption of the latest version are most often problems when you are distributing your application using a plain old workbook (not as a template or add-in) and are using a loosely defined distribution mechanism such as e-mail.

One way that you can reduce the impact of this issue for template-based applications is to use shortcuts in the Template folder that point to a centralized master copy. The shortcut could point to a template on a shared server, the intranet, or the Internet. That way, every time a user creates a new workbook based on the template, they'll be assured they've used the most recent version of the template available. Of course, this tip does not address any deficiencies in workbooks created using older versions of the template.

As an example, let's assume that you placed the Excel Project template that you saved earlier in the chapter on your company's intranet and the URL to the template is `http://intranet/templates/Excel%20Project.xlt`. Rather than have your users constantly refer to the site to check for updates, it is much more efficient to instruct them to put a shortcut to this URL in their templates folder as the following exercise demonstrates.

1. Right click the Windows Start button and select Explore. Using Windows XP Professional, this action places you in Windows Explorer at the Start folder associated with your user ID.

2. Locate and expand the Templates folder associated with your user ID. By default, the relative path to this starting with the documents folder associated with your login (i.e. C:\Documents and Settings\shansen) is Application Data\Microsoft\Templates. Figure 22.4 shows an example of this.

3. With the Templates folder selected, choose File ➢ New ➢ Shortcut.

FIGURE 22.4

Create a shortcut to master copies of a template in the Templates folder.

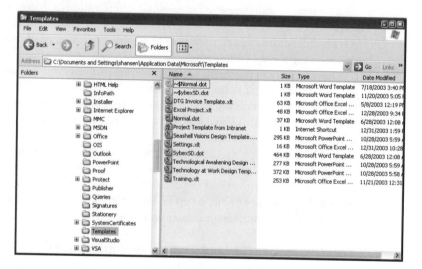

4. In the Create dialog box, browse for or enter the URL to the desired template, such as `http:/`
`/intranet/templates/Excel%20Project.xlt`, and then click OK. (Substitute the actual URL
to your template). The following screenshot shows an example of this.

5. Enter the name of the shortcut and click OK. The text you enter here will appear in the Templates dialog box when you create a new workbook based on a template.

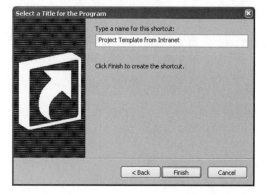

Once you've created the shortcut, from the user's perspective, it works just like any other template.
Go ahead, give it a try!

Implementing Version Awareness

For the ultimate amount of control regarding version management, you can build version awareness
into your solution. Version awareness is functionality that allows the application to know which version it is and check to see if it is up to date or not, this functionality also communicates any versioning
issues to the user, and has some ability for self-healing and updating. How much or how little of this
functionality you develop depends on your needs. The most basic solution just checks to see if the
version being used is the most current and displays a message to the user. Ultimately the amount of
functionality you build is only limited by your time and imagination.

Version awareness solutions aren't for all types of applications. For one thing, it can take a great deal of effort to implement version awareness depending on how much functionality you build into it. Also, any version awareness solution is going to need access to version data (typically stored in a database) located on another computer. Because not everyone is connected to a network all of the time (especially those users using laptops), the version awareness functionality must not assume constant network availability. Finally, you want to be very careful with the version awareness functionality that you implement. Nothing's worse than bugs in the functionality that's supposed to help fix bugs.

In order to stimulate your thoughts, I'll walk you through a basic version awareness implementation. As I mentioned earlier, typically a database is used as a centralized store of the version information needed to facilitate the required functionality. Though I'm using Access for this example, you could easily modify the example to work with other database products.

STEP 1: BUILD THE DATABASE

To begin, create a new database in Access. I named my database versions.mdb. You can get by with one table for the basic version awareness implemented in this exercise. Create a new table and add the fields shown in Table 22.1. Name this table VersionInfo and make the VersionID field the primary key.

TABLE 22.1: FIELDS NEEDED IN THE VERSIONINFO TABLE

FIELD NAME	DATA TYPE	FIELD SIZE	DESCRIPTION
VersionID	AutoNumber	Long Integer	Version ID of the version
MinimumVersionID	Number	Long Integer	Version ID of the earliest version that is still compatible with this version
CurrentMessage	Text	255	Message displayed if the user's version is equal to this version
NonCurrentMessage	Text	255	Message displayed if the user's version is not current, but is still compatible
NonCompatibleMessage	Text	255	Message displayed if the user's version is not current and is not compatible with this version
IsCurrent	Yes/No	Yes/No	Flag to indicate whether the version is current or not
Version	Text	10	Version number in major.minor.revision format (ex: 1.3.13)
VersionComment	Text	255	Description of comment about the version
VersionLocation	Text	255	Instructions on how to obtain the version
ReleaseDate	Date/Time	Short Date	Date the version was released

This table will work fine, though it is not optimal. More astute database readers may want to tweak this to either use more tables or take advantage of features available in their database product of choice. For example, the MinimumVersionID field is related to the VersionID field. The only valid values in the MinimumVersionID field should be those values that are already found in VersionID. It would be a good idea to enforce this relationship.

Another minor flaw in using a simple table structure like this can be found in the IsCurrent field. Theoretically, only one record should be in the table that has the value YES; this is because only one version can be current. Nothing is preventing you from having multiple records with the value YES in this table. This isn't much of a problem as long as you know about it in advance and write queries that have a way to determine the "real" current version in case more than one version is marked as current. Later in the implementation, you'll see that I also sorted the results of my query that checks for the latest version so that they descend by VersionID. If more than one record is marked as current, the implementation will use the one that was added most recently. A better way to do this may be to have a separate table with just one record and one field that contains the VersionID of the current version. Anyway, I digress, for this is a book about Excel VBA, not about database design.

While you still have the database open, you could go ahead and enter a few test versions into the VersionInfo table. Table 22.2 lists some example data you could use. For the fields that aren't shown in Table 22.2, go ahead and make up an appropriate message for the CurrentMessage, NonCurrent-Message, and NonCompatibleMessage fields.

TABLE 22.2: SAMPLE DATA FOR THE VERSIONINFO TABLE

VERSIONID	MINIMUMVERSIONID	ISCURRENT	VERSION
1	1	No	0.3.3
2	2	No	1.0.0
3	2	Yes	1.0.1

STEP 2: PREPARE AN EXCEL PROJECT

The next thing to do is to put the handy Excel Project template you created earlier in the chapter to good use and create an empty Excel Project workbook. If you recall, the Excel Project template creates a workbook that contains the Setting and Settings classes along with a Settings worksheet. You still have a few details to take care of before you start writing any code.

1. On the Settings worksheet, provide a value for the App Version setting. Choose a version number that can be found in the Version field of the VersionInfo table.

2. You could provide values for the App Name and App Date settings but these settings are not needed for this exercise.

3. Add a setting named Version Connection. This setting will hold the connection string used to connect to the versions database. The value of this setting should be Provider= Microsoft.Jet.OLEDB.4.0;Data Source=C:\versions.mdb. If you placed the versions database somewhere else, modify the data source aspect of the connection string appropriately.

4. Switch over to the VBE and add a reference (Tools ➤ References) to Microsoft ActiveX Data Objects 2.7 Library.

NOTE *Not all of your users may have the latest version of ADO. It is a good idea to sample some of your users' computers before choosing which version of ADO to use. Choose the latest version that is available on each user's computer. Alternatively, you can have your users update their computers with the latest available version. For more information see http://msdn.microsoft.com/data/.*

5. Save the workbook. I saved mine as Version Example.xls.

STEP 3: IMPLEMENT VERSION AWARENESS

Now you're ready to write some code. Insert a module into the project and add the code shown in Listing 22.3. Listing 22.3 contains six procedures as shown in Table 22.3.

TABLE 22.3: PROCEDURES NEEDED TO IMPLEMENT VERSION AWARENESS

PROCEDURE	DESCRIPTION
PerformVersionCheck	This is the main procedure and the only one that should be called by a user or user interface element.
CheckVersion	CheckVersion compares the version indicated in the workbook against the current version indicated in the database and displays a message indicating the results.
GetVersionID	Retrieves the VersionID in the database that is associated with the version given by the App Version setting.
QueryDB	A generic procedure that executes a query against the database and returns a recordset containing the results.
GetConnection	Retrieves the connection string stored in the Version Connection setting.
IsConnectionAvailable	Determines whether a connection to the database can be made or not.

LISTING 22.3: IMPLEMENTING BASIC VERSION AWARENESS

```
Option Explicit

Sub PerformVersionCheck()
    ' see if you can make a connection
    ' to the database before checking
    If IsConnectionAvailable Then
        CheckVersion
    Else
        MsgBox "Sorry, can't check version at this time."
```

```
        End If
End Sub

Private Sub CheckVersion()
    Dim rst As ADODB.Recordset
    Dim nWBVersion As Integer
    Dim sSQL As String

    On Error GoTo ErrHandler

    ' SQL statement to retrieve list of employees
    sSQL = "SELECT VersionID, MinimumVersionID, " & _
        "CurrentMessage, NonCurrentMessage, " & _
        "NonCompatibleMessage, IsCurrent, Version " & _
        "FROM VersionInfo " & _
        "WHERE IsCurrent=YES " & _
        "ORDER BY VersionID DESC"

    ' Open the recordset
    Set rst = QueryDB(sSQL)

    ' Make sure we got a recordset. If QueryDB runs into problems
    ' it returns nothing
    If rst Is Nothing Then Exit Sub

    If Not rst.EOF Then

        ' Get the version ID associated with the version indicated
        ' on the settings worksheet
        nWBVersion = GetVersionID

        ' Compare the version ID against various possibilities
        Select Case nWBVersion
            Case Is = -1
                MsgBox "Unknown version status. Could not find " & _
                    "version information in the database related " & _
                    "to the version indicated in this workbook."
            Case Is = rst.Fields("VersionID").Value
                If Not IsNull(rst.Fields("CurrentMessage").Value) Then
                    MsgBox rst.Fields("CurrentMessage").Value
                Else
                    MsgBox "Your version is current.", vbOKOnly
                End If
            Case Is >= rst.Fields("MinimumVersionID").Value
                If Not IsNull( _
                    rst.Fields("NonCurrentMessage").Value) Then
                    MsgBox rst.Fields("NonCurrentMessage").Value & _
                        " The current version is: " & _
```

```
                            rst.Fields("Version").Value
                    Else
                        MsgBox "Your version is out of date but still " & _
                            "compatible.", vbOKOnly
                    End If
                Case Is < rst.Fields("MinimumVersionID").Value
                    If Not IsNull( _
                        rst.Fields("NonCompatibleMessage").Value) Then
                        MsgBox rst.Fields("NonCompatibleMessage").Value & _
                            " The current version is: " & _
                            rst.Fields("Version").Value
                    Else
                        MsgBox "Your version is out of date and no " & _
                            "longer compatible.", vbOKOnly + vbCritical
                    End If
                Case Else
                    ' greater than current version in database
                    ' database not updated
                    ' or incorrect version number in workbook
                    MsgBox "You are using a version newer " & _
                        "than the current version."
            End Select

    Else
        MsgBox "Unable to determine the current version."
    End If

ExitPoint:
    Set rst = Nothing
    Exit Sub
ErrHandler:
    MsgBox "Error checking version: " & Err.Description, vbOKOnly
    Resume ExitPoint
End Sub


' Retrieves the version ID associated with the version
' indicated in this workbook
Private Function GetVersionID() As Integer
    Dim rst As ADODB.Recordset
    Dim oSettings As New Settings
    Dim sVersion As String
    Dim sSQL As String

    On Error GoTo ErrHandler

    sVersion = oSettings.Item("App Version").Value

    ' SQL statement to retrieve list of employees
```

```
        sSQL = "SELECT VersionID FROM VersionInfo " & _
            "WHERE Version='" & sVersion & "';"

        ' Open the recordset
        Set rst = QueryDB(sSQL)

        If Not rst.EOF Then
            GetVersionID = rst.Fields(0).Value
        Else
            GetVersionID = -1
        End If

        If rst.State = adStateOpen Then rst.Close

ExitPoint:
        Set oSettings = Nothing
        Set rst = Nothing
        Exit Function
ErrHandler:
        GetVersionID = -1
        Resume ExitPoint
End Function

' Generic function to retrieve a query into a recordset
Private Function QueryDB(sSQL As String) As ADODB.Recordset
        Dim sConn As String
        Dim rst As ADODB.Recordset

        On Error GoTo ErrHandler

        ' Create a new recordset object
        Set rst = New ADODB.Recordset

        ' Get connection details
        sConn = GetConnection

        ' Open the recordset
        rst.Open sSQL, sConn

        Set QueryDB = rst

ExitPoint:
        Set rst = Nothing
        Exit Function
ErrHandler:
        Debug.Print "QueryDB error: " & Err.Description
        Set QueryDB = Nothing
        Resume ExitPoint
```

```
End Function

' Retrieve the connection string stored on
' the settings worksheet
Private Function GetConnection() As String
    Dim oSettings As New Settings

    On Error GoTo ErrHandler

    ' Connection details - this is the kind of thing
    ' that you can use the Settings class for
    GetConnection = oSettings.Item("Version Connection").Value

ExitPoint:
    Set oSettings = Nothing
    Exit Function
ErrHandler:
    GetConnection = ""
    Resume ExitPoint
End Function

' Check to see if a connnection can be made to the database
Private Function IsConnectionAvailable() As Boolean
    Dim sConn As String
    Dim conn As New ADODB.Connection

    On Error GoTo ErrHandler

    sConn = GetConnection

    conn.Open sConn

    If conn.State = adStateOpen Then conn.Close

    IsConnectionAvailable = True
ExitPoint:
    Set conn = Nothing
    Exit Function
ErrHandler:
    IsConnectionAvailable = False
    Resume ExitPoint
End Function
```

I added the PerformVersionCheck procedure primarily so that I could make sure a database connection is available before I use CheckVersion. Validating that you can make a database connection is more important when you need to access a database that is located on another computer.

FIGURE 22.5

Basic version aware-
ness in action.

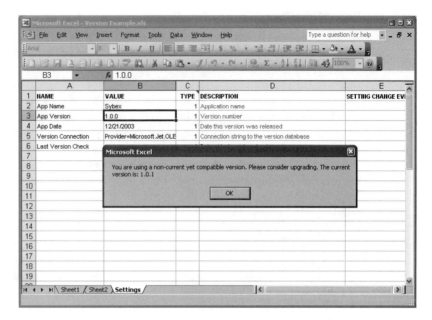

CheckVersion works by querying the VersionInfo database to retrieve the record marked as current (IsCurrent=YES). In order to account for the possibility that more than one record is marked as current, the query orders the records in descending order by VersionID, and only the first record is used. Because VersionID is an AutoNumber field in this example, it should represent the last record that was added (and is marked as current). Once you have the data associated with the current version from the database, you need to figure out what version is indicated in the workbook. To do this, I used the GetVersionID procedure to query the database for the VersionID associated with the version indicated in the workbook. GetVersionID returns −1 if it cannot find the VersionID associated with a given version. Anyway, CheckVersion compares (using a Select...Case statement) the VersionID associated with the workbook's version to the VersionID of the version that is flagged in the database as current to figure out which message to display to the user.

QueryDB is a fairly generic procedure used to query the database. QueryDB depends on the GetConnection procedure to retrieve the connection string stored on the Settings worksheet. Figure 22.5 demonstrates an example of basic version awareness.

So there you have a basic example of version awareness. You could call the PerformVersionCheck procedure from the Workbook Open event procedure and/or call the procedure when the user interacts with a given user interface element such as a command button or menu item. If you spend more than five minutes thinking about it, I bet you could come up with a decent list of enhancements that you could easily implement. For example, because you have to go to the database to check version info, why not use this database for more things such as news items or messages that are displayed somewhere in the workbook. You could also build in functionality for basic self-healing. For example, maybe you have a table that contains formula fixes that lists worksheet name, cell address, and new formula. You could build a process to look in this table and then "fix" a workbook with corrected formulas, values, or whatever. To learn more, read on....

Fear Not When Things Go Wrong

Mistakes happen—if you haven't learned that yet, if you build any applications that get distributed to other users, you will. Whether it is through programmer error, misinformation supplied to programmers, or misunderstanding. Depending on the severity of the consequences of the mistake, how widely the application is distributed, and other factors, the anxiety associated with the mistake will vary widely. Although it is often embarrassing and tempting to point fingers, don't blow your top. You have a lot of options available for rectifying the situation.

Of course, you can always fix the error and redistribute. Occasionally, however, this may be impractical and should be seen as a last-resort option. For example, if your users have already expended a lot of effort entering information into a financial model, they will loathe anything that requires them to throw away their work and start from scratch. Inconvenience notwithstanding, starting over may be expensive to boot. For example, if you've distributed an application to 500 users and each user has 2 hours of time invested in customizing, entering data into, or otherwise working with the application in a way that a new version will undo, that's 1000 hours of work that would be thrown out. All of a sudden, the extra work associated with a solution that fixes existing applications rather than replaces them seems worth it. Hmm, an extra 8 or 16 hours to figure out how to distribute a service pack or 1000 hours of collective user effort. I know which one I'd recommend.

In the previous section, I hinted at using a version database to provide self-healing functionality. Due to space concerns, I'm not going to show you how to do this. However, I will show you a solution using many of the procedures you've seen throughout this book. From there, it's not much of a stretch to make the modifications necessary to make this work from the database.

You've already seen the framework that can enable this functionality. From a high level you need to

1. Provide a way for the user to indicate which workbook(s) need to be fixed.

2. Loop through the set of workbooks indicated by the user.

3. Open, fix, save, and close each workbook.

Keeping these three needs in mind, go back to Chapter 6 and skim over the ProcessFileBatch listing (Listing 6.1). This procedure, along with the procedures it depends on, handles maybe 90 percent of the work you need to do to provide service pack functionality. All you need to do is write a procedure to fix the workbook and then call this procedure from within ProcessFileBatch.

As an example, let's say you need to fix a bunch of formulas in a workbook that you released. You could use a procedure similar to Listing 22.4 to fix the workbook and call it from ProcessFileBatch.

NOTE   *I've included ProcessFileBatch and its dependencies in Listing 22.4 for your convenience. For discussion and analysis of these procedures please refer back to Chapters 5 and 6.*

LISTING 22.4: SIMPLE PROCEDURE TO FIX A WORKBOOK

```
Option Explicit

Private Sub FixWorkbook(wb As Workbook)
    Dim ws As Worksheet
```

```
        ' It'd be best to test the worksheet name for safety
        Set ws = wb.Worksheets("Sheet1")

        ws.Range("A1").Formula = "=b1+c1"
        ws.Range("A2").Formula = "=b2+c2"
        ws.Range("A3").Formula = "=b3+c3"

        Set ws = Nothing
    End Sub


    Sub ProcessFileBatch()
        Dim nIndex As Integer
        Dim vFiles As Variant
        Dim wb As Workbook
        Dim bAlreadyOpen As Boolean
        Dim sFile As String

        On Error GoTo ErrHandler

        ' Get a batch of Excel files
        vFiles = GetExcelFiles("Select Workbooks for Processing")

        ' Make sure dialog wasn't cancelled - in which case
        ' vFiles would equal FALSE and therefore is not an array.
        If Not IsArray(vFiles) Then
            Debug.Print "No files selected."
            Exit Sub
        End If

        Application.ScreenUpdating = False

        ' OK - loop through the file names
        For nIndex = 1 To UBound(vFiles)

            ' Get the workbook
            If IsWorkbookOpen(CStr(vFiles(nIndex))) Then
                Set wb = Workbooks(GetShortName(CStr(vFiles(nIndex))))
                Debug.Print "Workbook already open: " & wb.Name
                bAlreadyOpen = True
            Else
                Set wb = Workbooks.Open(CStr(vFiles(nIndex)), False)
                Debug.Print "Opened workbook: " & wb.Name
                bAlreadyOpen = False
            End If

            Application.StatusBar = "Processing workbook: " & wb.Name

            ' Code to process the file goes here
```

```vba
        FixWorkbook wb

        ' Close workbook unless it was already open
        If Not bAlreadyOpen Then
            Debug.Print "Closing workbook: " & wb.Name
            wb.Close True
        End If
    Next nIndex

ErrHandler:
    Application.StatusBar = False
    Application.ScreenUpdating = True
End Sub


' This function checks to see if a given workbook
' is open or not. This function can be used
' using a short name such as MyWorkbook.xls
' or a full name such as C:\Testing\MyWorkbook.xls
Function IsWorkbookOpen(sWorkbook As String) As Boolean
    Dim sname As String
    Dim sPath As String
    Dim sFullName As String

    On Error Resume Next
    IsWorkbookOpen = True

    ' See if we were given a short name or a long name
    If InStr(1, sWorkbook, "\", vbTextCompare) > 0 Then
        ' We have a long name
        ' Need to break it down
        sFullName = sWorkbook
        BreakdownName sFullName, sname, sPath
        If StrComp(Workbooks(sname).FullName, sWorkbook, 1) <> 0 Then
            IsWorkbookOpen = False
        End If
    Else
        ' We have a short name
        If StrComp(Workbooks(sWorkbook).Name, sWorkbook, 1) <> 0 Then
            IsWorkbookOpen = False
        End If
    End If
End Function


' Presents user with a GetOpenFileName dialog that allows
' multiple file selection.
' Returns an array of filenames.
Function GetExcelFiles(sTitle As String) As Variant
    Dim sFilter As String
```

```
    Dim bMultiSelect As Boolean

    sFilter = "Workbooks (*.xls), *.xls"
    bMultiSelect = True

    GetExcelFiles = Application.GetOpenFilename(FileFilter:=sFilter, _
        Title:=sTitle, MultiSelect:=bMultiSelect)
End Function

Function GetShortName(sLongName As String) As String
    Dim sPath As String
    Dim sShortName As String

    BreakdownName sLongName, sShortName, sPath

    GetShortName = sShortName
End Function


Sub BreakdownName(sFullName As String, _
                ByRef sname As String, _
                ByRef sPath As String)

    Dim nPos As Integer

    ' Find out where the file name begins
    nPos = FileNamePosition(sFullName)

    If nPos > 0 Then
        sname = Right(sFullName, Len(sFullName) - nPos)
        sPath = Left(sFullName, nPos - 1)
    Else
        'Invalid sFullName - don't change anything
    End If
End Sub

' Returns the position or index of the first
' character of the file name given a full name
' A full name consists of a path and a filename
' Ex. FileNamePosition("C:\Testing\Test.txt") = 11
Function FileNamePosition(sFullName As String) As Integer
    Dim bFound As Boolean
    Dim nPosition As Integer

    bFound = False
    nPosition = Len(sFullName)

    Do While bFound = False
```

```
            ' Make sure we were not dealt a
            ' zero-length string
            If nPosition = 0 Then Exit Do

            ' We are looking for the first "\"
            ' from the right.
            If Mid(sFullName, nPosition, 1) = "\" Then
                bFound = True
            Else
                ' Working right to left
                nPosition = nPosition - 1
            End If
        Loop

        If bFound = False Then
            FileNamePosition = 0
        Else
            FileNamePosition = nPosition
        End If
    End Function
```

Believe it or not, some service packs are as easy as the FixWorkbook procedure. Of course, other times you'll have to overcome many more issues. For example, you might have to consider whether worksheets have been renamed, added, or deleted. Also, rows and columns may shift as they are added or deleted. In situations such as this, you'll come to appreciate your foresight in incorporating multiple points of reference in your workbook and other decisions you made during the development process "just in case." Named ranges and worksheet code names come in very handy for this purpose.

Summary

Depending on the functionality delivered by your solution, you may choose to deliver your application in one of three forms: as a standard workbook, as a template, or as an add-in. The most common form for an application is as a standard workbook. Standard workbooks have the advantage of being easy to distribute as well as easy to use and develop.

Templates are useful for situations in which your application will be used repeatedly, but each use needs to remain distinct from others. Though templates aren't hard to use, you'll have to provide some basic instruction to some of your users on how to use a template and how to set it up (unless you write a utility to install it in the correct location). You can help minimize the ills associated with upgrading templates by putting a master template on your network and having users install shortcuts to the master copy in their template directories.

Add-ins are useful in situations in which you need to develop functionality that needs to be accessed from all workbooks. An add-in essentially extends the functionality of Excel. Though you construct an add-in using a normal Excel workbook, when a user installs an add-in, they do not see any of the underlying Excel structure (the worksheets) that makes up the add-in.

Regardless of which form you choose to use, once you release an application. invariably you'll need to release updated versions in the future that fix bugs or provide additional functionality. Consider the possibility of future updates from day one so that you can incorporate features into the application that will aid the update process.

For the ultimate amount of control, consider building version awareness into your applications. Version awareness functionality can range from the simple version-checking example presented in this chapter to elaborate self-updating/healing solutions. This type of functionality requires a central versioning database of some sort to store version information.

Finally, when things don't go right or you have an urgent need to fix a widely distributed application, don't fret. It is fairly easy to create your own "service pack" that you can distribute to your users with which they can fix their copy of the application.

Index

Note to the Reader: Throughout this index **boldfaced** page numbers indicate primary discussions of a topic. *Italicized* page numbers indicate illustrations.

S

JUL -- 2005

TELL US WHAT YOU THINK!

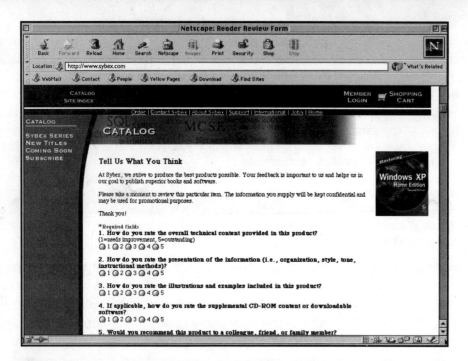

Your feedback is critical to our efforts to provide you with the best books and software on the market. Tell us what you think about the products you've purchased. It's simple:

1. Go to the Sybex website.
2. Find your book by typing the ISBN or title into the Search field.
3. Click on the book title when it appears.
4. Click **Submit a Review.**
5. Fill out the questionnaire and comments.
6. Click **Submit.**

With your feedback, we can continue to publish the highest quality computer books and software products that today's busy IT professionals deserve.

www.sybex.com

SYBEX Inc. • 1151 Marina Village Parkway, Alameda, CA 94501 • 510-523-8233